A Humanities Press Book

# THE CONCEPT OF EDUCATION

## Contributors

R. S. PETERS

D. W. HAMLYN

PAUL H. HIRST

G. VESEY

R. F. DEARDEN

MAX BLACK

GILBERT RYLE

ISRAEL SCHEFFLER

MICHAEL OAKESHOTT

J. P. WHITE

JOHN PASSMORE

# THE CONCEPT OF EDUCATION

*Edited by*
R. S. PETERS

NEW YORK
THE HUMANITIES PRESS

*First published
in the United States of America* 1967
*by Humanities Press Inc.
303 Park Avenue South
New York, N.Y.* 10010

© *Routledge and Kegan Paul, Ltd* 1967

*Library of Congress Catalog Card No.* 66–28682

*Printed in Great Britain*

# CONTENTS

1112-88

# PREFACE

This collection of articles originated in a series of Public Lectures given in the early part of 1965 at the University of London Institute of Education. This provided a nucleus (Chs. 1, 2, 7, and 10) around which the collection was gathered.

The objection to many collections of articles is often made that they are a rather haphazard agglomeration of heterogeneous items lacking any unifying theme. It was felt that merely providing a general title such as 'The Concept of Education' was insufficient to provide such a unifying theme; for the philosophy of education is in such an undeveloped state that being asked to write an article under a rubric as general as that would approximate to a Rorschach test. The editor therefore wrote the first article attempting to map the main contours of the concept, circulated it, and invited lecturers and contributors to sketch in one of the important areas in more detail. Inevitably some areas have been neglected. There is, for instance, nothing in any detail about the crucial processes of imitation and identification. But it is hoped that the collection will at least do something to indicate the main areas where work has to be done.

The authors of the articles are either 'pure' philosophers who are interested in education as an area in need of philosophical investigation, or people professionally employed as philosophers of education. Perhaps this difference is reflected in the degree of concreteness with which the discussion is related to educational issues. If there is such a difference in emphasis it is hoped that it will make the collection of interest to students both of philosophy and of education alike.

Thanks are due to the Harvard Educational Review for permission to print Professor Scheffler's article on 'Philosophical Models of Teaching' and to the University of London Institute of Education for permission to base this collection on their Public Lecture series.

R. S. PETERS

*January* 1966

vii

# NOTES ON CONTRIBUTORS

MAX BLACK, Professor of Philosophy, Cornell University. Author of *Language and Philosophy, Problems of Analysis*, etc., and editor of *Philosophy in America*.

ROBERT F. DEARDEN, Lecturer in the Philosophy of Education, University of London Institute of Education.

DAVID W. HAMLYN, Professor of Philosophy, Birkbeck College, University of London. Author of *Sensation and Perception; The Psychology of Perception*.

PAUL H. HIRST, Professor of Education, King's College, University of London.

MICHAEL OAKESHOTT, Professor of Politics, London School of Economics and Political Science. Author of *Experience and its Modes, Rationalism in Politics*.

JOHN PASSMORE, Professor of Philosophy, Australian National University. Author of *Hume's Intentions, A Hundred Years of Philosophy, Philosophical Reasoning*.

RICHARD S. PETERS, Professor of the Philosophy of Education, University of London Institute of Education. Author of *Hobbes, The Concept of Motivation, Ethics and Education*, etc.

GILBERT RYLE, Waynflete Professor of Metaphysical Philosophy, University of Oxford. Author of *The Concept of Mind, Dilemmas, Plato's Progress*.

ISRAEL SCHEFFLER, Victor S. Thomas Professor of Education and Philosophy, Harvard Graduate School of Education. Author of *The Language of Education, The Anatomy of Enquiry, Conditions of Knowledge*.

GEOFFREY VESEY, Reader in Philosophy, King's College, University of London. Author of *The Embodied Mind* and editor of *Body and Mind*.

JOHN P. WHITE, Lecturer in the Philosophy of Education, University of London Institute of Education.

# WHAT IS AN EDUCATIONAL PROCESS?

## R. S. Peters

### INTRODUCTION

In exploring the concept of education a territory is being entered where there are few signposts. To use Ryle's phrase, the 'logical geography' of concepts in the area of education has not yet been mapped. This feature of the field of education was vividly brought home to me in the autumn of 1963 when I was working on my Inaugural Lecture on *Education as Initiation*, and was unable to unearth any previous explicit attempt to demarcate the concept of 'education'. It is not surprising, therefore, that in presenting at the start what amounts to a bird's eye view of the contours of this territory, I have to rely mainly on my own previous attempt to map it.

### 1. THE TASK-ACHIEVEMENT ANALYSIS OF 'EDUCATION'

Any such survey must start with the observation that 'education' is a concept which is not very close to the ground. By this I mean that it is not a concept like 'red' which picks out a simple quality, like 'horse' which picks out an object, or like 'running' or 'smiling' which pick out observable occurrences. We do not ask 'Are you instructing him in algebra or are you educating him in algebra?' as if these were two alternative processes. But we might ask 'Are you educating him by instructing him in algebra?' 'Education', in other words, refers to no particular process; rather it encapsulates criteria to which any one of a family of processes must conform. In this respect it is rather like 'reform'. 'Reform' picks out no particular process. People can be reformed, perhaps, by preventive detention, by reading the Bible, or by the devotion of a loving wife. In a similar way people can be educated by reading books, by exploring their environment, by travel and conversation—even by talk and chalk in a classroom. The concepts of 'reform' and 'education' have proper application if these processes satisfy certain criteria. 'Education' and 'reform' are not part of the furniture of the earth or mind; they are more like stamps of approval issued by 'Good Housekeeping' proclaiming that furniture has come up to certain standards.

How then are we to conceive of processes by means of which such standards are to be achieved? In my Inaugural Lecture I attacked misleading models which provide pictures of what goes on in terms of shaping material according to a specification, or of allowing children to 'grow'. I mentioned in a footnote, which I did not have time to develop, that a much more adequate way of conceiving of what goes on, which provides a rationale for my notion of education as initiation, is to regard processes of education as tasks relative to achievements. This accounts for the feature of education, which I rather laboured, that its standards are intrinsic not extrinsic to it. This task-achievement analysis I now propose to explain.

Aristotle made the point long ago in relation to performances such as 'learning' and 'inferring', that the end is built into the concepts. Ryle has made it more recently in relation to activities such as 'looking' and 'running'. When a man finds something that he has lost or wins a race, he does not indulge in something different from looking or running, neither does he produce something or reach an end which is extrinsic to the activity in which he is engaged. He merely succeeds in it. He achieves the standard or attains the end which is internal to the activity and which gives it point. In a similar way a man who is educated is a man who has succeeded in relation to certain tasks on which he and his teacher have been engaged for a considerable period of time. Just as 'finding' is the achievement relative to 'looking', so 'being educated' is the achievement relative to a family of tasks which we call processes of education.

'Education' is, of course, different in certain respects from the examples of achievements that Ryle gives. To start with 'education' like 'teaching' can be used as both a task and an achievement verb.[1] Teachers can work away at teaching without success, and still be teaching; but there is a sense, also, in which teaching someone something implies success. 'I taught the boy the ablative absolute construction' implies that I was successful in my task. But I can also say 'I taught him Latin for years, but he learnt nothing.' Similarly I can work away at educating people, without the implication that I or they achieve success in the various tasks which are engaged in; but if I talk of them as 'educated' there is an implication of success.

But whose success are we talking about? That of the teacher or of the learner? This is tantamount to asking to whose tasks the achievements which constitute 'being educated' are relative, those of the teacher or those of the learner. Obviously both are usually involved, but it is important to realize that the tasks of the teacher could not be characterized unless we had a notion of the tasks of the learner. For whereas 'learning' could be characterized without introducing the notion of 'teaching', 'teaching' could not be characterized without the notion of 'learning'. The tasks of the teacher consist in the employment of various methods to get learning processes going. These processes of learning in their turn cannot be characterized without reference to the achievements in which they culminate. For to learn something *is* to come up to some standard, to succeed in some respect. So the achievement must be that of the learner in the end. The teacher's success, in other words, can only be defined in terms of that of the learner. This presumably is the logical truth dormant in the saying that all education is self-education. This is what makes the notion of 'initiation' an appropriate one to characterize an educational situation; for a learner is 'initiated' by another into something which he has to master, know, or remember. 'Education' picks out processes by means of which people get started on the road to such achievements.

## 2. THE MORAL REQUIREMENTS OF 'EDUCATION'

The second way in which 'education' is different from ordinary cases of tasks and achievements is that it is inseparable from judgements of value. It is, as I have pointed out, a logical truth that any method of education employed by a teacher must put the pupil in a situation where he is learning, where some sort of task is presented to him. But a teacher might try to condition children to 'pick up' certain things without their realizing that they were picking anything up. In saying that this is not a process of education we would be implying that this was morally bad, because conditions of wittingness and voluntariness on the part of the pupil were missing; for we regard it as morally unjustifiable to treat others in this way. To say that we are educating people commits us, in other words, to morally legitimate procedures. Often such minimal moral demands, which are connected with respect for persons, are further extended to exclude procedures such as giving children orders, which is thought by some to involve some sort of moral indignity. Discouragement of individual choice would be another procedure which many might condemn as being morally reprehensible. They might express their disapproval by saying that this was not 'education'.

The way in which moral considerations enter into the achievement aspects of education is clearer than the way in which they enter into the task aspect. For it is obvious enough that the achievements or states of mind that give content to the notion of an educated man must be regarded as valuable. Finding a thimble that has been hidden is a Rylean type of achievement: but it is a trivial one. The achievements involved in education cannot be of this type. For if something is to count as 'education', what is learnt must be regarded as worth-while just as the manner in which it is learnt must be regarded as morally unobjectionable; for not all learning is 'educational' in relation to the content of what is learnt. If it were we might have periods on the time-table devoted to astrology and to Bingo and homilies by headmasters on the art of torture.

In this respect, also, 'education' is like 'reform'; for it would be as much of a contradiction to say 'My son has been educated but has learnt nothing of value' as it would be to say 'My son has been reformed but has changed in no way for the better.' This, by the way, is a purely conceptual point. The connexion between 'education' and what is valuable can be made explicit without commitment to content. It is a *further question* what the particular standards are in virtue of which achievements are thought to be of value and what grounds there might be for claiming that these are the correct ones. It may well be that arguments can be produced to show why rational men should value some standards rather than others; but at the moment there is no such established harmony. So when people speak of 'education' it is essential to know what their standards of valuation are in order to ascertain the aspect under which some process or state of mind is being commended.

This connexion with commendation does not, of course, prevent us from speaking of 'poor' education when a worth-while job has been botched or of 'bad education' when we think that much of what people are working at is not worth-while, though it is a nice question to determine at what point we pass from saying that something is 'bad education' to saying that it is not education at all. Neither does it prevent us from using the word in a purely external descriptive way when we speak of an 'educational system' just as we can use the term 'moral' of someone else's code without committing ourselves to the judgements of value of those whose code it is. Anthropologists can talk of the moral system of a tribe; so also can we talk as sociologists or economists of the educational system of a community. In employing the concept in this derivative sense we need not think that what is going on is worth-while, but members of the society, whose system it is, must think it is.

Talk of 'education', then, from the inside of a form of life, is inseparable from talk of what is worth-while, but with the additional notion written into it that what is worth-while has been or is being transmitted in a morally unobjectionable manner. But under this general ægis of desirability 'education' picks out no one type of task or achievement. People differ in their estimates of desirability. They therefore differ in the emphasis which they place on achievement and states of mind that can be thought of as desirable. This diversity is what makes talk of 'aims of education' apposite; for people who talk in this way are not suggesting aims extrinsic to education: They are enunciating their priorities in giving content to the notion of an 'educated man'.

To take a parallel: it might be said that the aim of reform was to make men better. This is harmless enough provided that it is realized that 'making men better' is built into the concept of 'reform' But something more specific might be said such as the aim of reform is to encourage a sense of responsibility. This might be countered by saying that the aim of reform is to get people to have respect for persons. Such a dispute would be an attempt to give precise content to the general notion of 'making a man better'. Similarly discussions about the aims of education are attempts to give more precise content to the notion of the 'educated man' or of a man who has achieved some desirable state of mind. Is moral education more important, for instance, than the development of scientific understanding? This might have particular point when talking about some of the children referred to in the Newsom Report. Or perhaps we talk about 'wholeness' in order to emphasize all-round excellence and sensitivity. Or we may want to stress the importance of cutting the coat of what is worth-while according to the cloth of individual aptitude. Talk of developing the potentialities of the individual is then appropriate. Such 'aims' point out specific achievements and states of mind which give content to the formal notion of 'the educated man' which is a short-hand for summarizing our notion of a form of life which is worth-while enough to deserve being handed on from generation to generation.[2]

So much, then, for the moral aspect of 'education' as a family of tasks and achievements which make it rather different from the simpler cases used by Ryle to illustrate this way of conceiving of certain classes of intentional activities. I want now to consider other criteria of 'being educated' as an achievement which have to do with knowledge and understanding. I shall then deal with the tasks which lead up to achievements falling under these criteria.

### 3. THE ACHIEVEMENT ASPECT OF 'EDUCATION'

We do not call a person educated who has simply mastered a skill even though the skill may be very worth-while, like that of moulding clay. For a man to be educated it is insufficient that he should possess a 'know-how' or knack. He must also know that certain things are the case. He must have developed some sort of conceptual scheme at least in the area in which he is skilled and must have organized a fair amount of information by means of it.

But even this is not enough; for we would be disinclined to call a man who was merely well-informed an educated man. To be educated requires also some understanding of principles, of the 'reason why' of things. The Spartans, for instance, were military and morally trained. They knew how to fight; they knew what was right and wrong; they were possessed of a certain kind of lore, which stood them in good stead in stock situations. They were thus able to comb their hair with aplomb when the Persians were approaching at Thermopylæ. But we could not say that they had received a military or moral education; for they had never been encouraged to understand the principles underlying their code. They had mastered the content of forms of thought and behaviour without ever grasping or being able to operate with the principles that could enable them to manage on their own. They were notorious for falling victims to potentates, priests, and profligates on leaving their natural habitat where their code was part of the order of things. Failure to grasp underlying principles leads to unintelligent rule of thumb application of rules, to the inability to make exceptions on relevant grounds and to bewilderment when confronted with novel situations.

Given, then, that being educated implies the possession of knowledge, but rules out *mere* knowledge, in that it also requires understanding of principles, could a man be educated whose knowledge and understanding is confined to one sphere—mathematics, for instance? There is a strong inclination to deny that we could call a man 'educated' who had only developed his awareness and understanding in such a limited way; for our notion of an educated man suggests a more all-round type of development. When we say that people go to a university to become educated and not just to become scientists, from what does this antithesis derive? Does it derive from the concept of 'education' or from our underlying valuations about the constituents of the good life which ought to be passed on which includes e.g. aesthetic and moral awareness as well as scientific understanding? Certainly 'training' always suggests confinement. People are trained *for* jobs, *as* mechanics, and *in* science. No one can be trained in a general sort of way. But this lack of specificity is just what is suggested by 'education'. It is not clear to me whether this is due to the concept of 'education' itself or to our refusal to grant that what is worth-while could be confined to one form of awareness. To pose the problem succinctly : Is the saying 'Education is of the whole man' a conceptual truth in that 'education' rules out one-sided development? Or is it an expression of our moral valuations about what is worth-while?

There is no necessity, for the purposes of this article, to decide between these two alternatives, as it has no particular implications for what is to count as an educational process. There is, however, another aspect of the knowledge requirement built into 'education' which has implications. This is its attitudinal aspect. By this I mean that the knowledge which a man must possess to qualify as being educated must be built into his way of looking at things. It cannot be merely inert. It is possible for a man to know a lot of history, in the sense that he can give correct answers to questions in classrooms and in examinations, without ever developing a historical sense. For instance he might fail to connect his knowledge of the Industrial Revolution with what he sees when visiting Manchester or the Welsh Valleys. We might describe such a man as 'knowledgeable' but we would never describe him as 'educated'; for 'education' implies that a man's outlook is transformed by what he knows.

It is this requirement built into 'education' that makes the usual contrast between 'education' and 'life' rather ridiculous. Those who make it usually have in mind a contrast between the activities that go on in classrooms and studies and those that go on in industry, politics, agriculture, and rearing a family. The curriculum of schools and universities is then criticized because, as the knowledge passed on is not instrumental in any obvious sense to 'living', it is assumed that is is 'academic' or relevant only to the classroom, cloister, study, and library. What is forgotten is that activities like history, literary appreciation, and philosophy, unlike Bingo and billiards, involve forms of thought and awareness that can and should spill over into things that go on outside and transform them. For they are concerned with the explanation, evaluation and imaginative exploration of forms of life. As a result of them what is called 'life' develops different dimensions. In schools and universities there is concentration on the development of this determinant of our form of life. The problem of the educator is to pass on this knowledge and understanding in such a way that they develop a life of their own in the minds of others and transform how they see the world, and hence how they feel about it.

There is another element in what I have called the 'attitudinal aspect' of the sort of knowledge which is built into the concept of 'being educated' which was first stressed by Socrates and Plato in their doctrine that 'virtue is knowledge'. Such knowledge must not be 'inert' in another sense; it must involve the kind of commitment which comes through being on the inside of a form of thought and awareness. A man cannot really understand what it is to think scientifically unless he not only knows that evidence must be found for assumptions, but cares that it should be found; in forms of thought where proof is possible, cogency, simplicity, and elegance must be felt to matter. And what would historical or philosophical thought amount to if there was no concern about relevance or coherence? All forms of thought and awareness have their own internal standards of appraisal. To be on the inside of them is both to understand this and to care. Indeed the understanding is difficult to distinguish from the caring; for without such care the activities lose their point. I do not think that we would call a person 'educated' whose knowledge of such forms of thought and awareness was purely external and 'inert' in this way. There can be no End of the Affair where The Heart of the Matter is lacking. And, of course, there never *is* an End of the Affair. For to be educated is not to have arrived; it is to travel with a different view.

The achievement aspect of 'education' connected with knowledge has now been sketched. Before passing to the task aspect, under which educational processes have to be considered, it will be as well to pause and summarize the main criteria of 'education' under this aspect which are to be satisfied by an 'educated' man.

(i) An educated man is one whose form of life, as exhibited in his conduct, the activities to which he is committed, his judgements, and feelings, is thought to be desirable.

(ii) Whatever he is trained to do he must have knowledge, not just knack, and an understanding of principles. His form of life must also exhibit some mastery of forms of thought and awareness, which are not harnessed purely to utilitarian or vocational purposes or completely confined to one mode.

(iii) His knowledge and understanding must not be inert either in the sense that they make no difference to his general view of the world, his actions within it and reactions to it *or* in the sense that they involve no concern for the standards immanent in forms of thought and awareness, as well as the ability to attain them.

## 4. CRITERIA INVOLVED IN THE TASK ASPECT OF 'EDUCATION'

Educational processes are related to these various activities and modes of thought and conduct characterizing an 'educated man' as task is related to achievement. They are those in which people are initiated into or got going on activities and forms of thought and conduct which they eventually come to master. I have argued already that, apart from the requirement that processes belonging to this family be morally unobjectionable, they must also be considered from the point of view of the learner whose achievements give content to the concept of an 'educated man'. They must therefore approximate to tasks in which the learner knows what he is doing and gradually develops towards those standards of excellence which constitute the relevant achievement. In this family obviously are included processes such as training, instruction, learning by experience, teaching, and so on.

If we look at such processes from the teacher's point of view he is intentionally trying to get learning processes going by exhibiting, drawing attention to, emphasizing, or explicating some feature of what has to be learnt and putting the learner in a position where his experience is likely to become structured along desirable lines. From the learner's point of view such processes must be ones in which he

9

knows what he is doing. Things may happen to him while asleep or under hypnosis which bring about modifications of his conscious-ness; but we would not call them processes of education. The learner must know what he is doing, must be conscious of something that he is trying to master, understand, or remember. Such processes, there-fore, must involve attention on his part and some type of action, activity, or performance by means of which he begins to structure his movements and consciousness according to the public standards immanent in what has to be learnt.

It is necessary, however, to distinguish educational processes proper from other processes bordering on them which do not satisfy one or other of these criteria. There are first of all what I will call extrinsic aids and secondly what I will call rather loosely processes of 'picking things up'. Let us consider them briefly in this order.

*(a) Extrinsic aids*

There are all sorts of things done by teachers in classrooms which help children to learn things which are really aids to education rather than processes of education. I mean conditions such as praise and reward which help children to learn things. These are not processes of education; for their connexion with what is learnt is purely extrin-sic. They may facilitate the learning of anything; but what is involved in learning anything can be explicated without reference to them. To take a parallel; it is an empirical fact that children learn things better if they are nice and warm rather than shivering with cold. So a sensible teacher will make sure that the radiators in the classroom are turned on. It may also be the case that children learn things better if the teacher smiles approvingly when the child gets things right. This is, perhaps, another empirical fact which is rele-vant to education. But neither turning on the radiators nor smiling at children are educational processes, whatever their status as aids to education.

The appeal to children's interests occupies a more twilight sort of status because of ambiguities in the notion of 'interests'. Such in-terests can be intrinsic or extrinsic to what has to be learnt. Children are naturally curious at certain ages and have a desire to master things and get them right. They may also be interested in finding out about and mastering the specific things that have to be learnt. As an interest in such worth-while things is part of what is meant by 'an educated man' the job in this case is that of fostering such intrinsic interests and superimposing on them the precision and standards of achievement which are necessary. Having such intrinsic interests is not part of what is meant by an educational process; it is built into the achievement, and this aspect of the achievement can be present at the start.

Unfortunately few children are motivated in this way all the time and many children scarcely at all. Therefore extrinsic interests have to be used, as well as other forms of pressure. For children do not have to be interested in something in order to learn it; it is often sufficient that they attend to it, for whatever reason. If they attend long enough, and if the teacher is skilled and imaginative, they may become interested. The ability to *stimulate* interest is one of the greatest gifts of a teacher. The danger of too much reliance on extrinsic interests is that a child may pick up something that the teacher does not intend, namely to become a thorough instrumentalist, the prisoner of an attitude which always looks to what things lead to rather than what they are in themselves. A child may be interested in outstripping his fellows and may be willing to learn almost anything that is geared to this end. This may be educationally very bad if what is 'picked up' is the conviction that effort should only be made if gain results. Using these sorts of interests may not be in the interests of the child. So we pass to processes of 'picking things up'.

## (b) Picking things up

I used the word 'picked up' rather than 'learnt' advisedly to characterize a way of acquiring an attitude that borders on education, without being a process of education in a strict sense.[3] Obviously enough this attitude is implicit in the practice of the teacher who employs such a method and is passed on partly by identification. All sorts of things are picked up in this way—desirable things such as a passion for poetry, nuances of style and argument, objectivity towards facts, respect for persons; undesirable things such as partisan allegiances, contempt for people of different persuasions, bad manners, and class-consciousness; and trivial things such as mannerisms, a tone of voice, gestures.

My reluctance to call such goings-on processes of education is not just due to the fact that what is passed on may be trivial or undesirable, but to the difficulty of conceiving of them as tasks either on the part of the teacher or of the learner. From the teacher's point of view he is explicitly trying to get children on the inside of a form of thought or awareness; to do this he uses certain methods. Yet the fact is that so much is caught rather than explicitly taught. The best teachers are not necessarily those who are au fait with all the latest methods or very knowledgeable about their subject. They are those whose genuine concern for what they are passing on is manifest in the manner in which they do it. Education, like most meetings between human beings, is a very chancy business. The wind of the spirit bloweth where it listeth. Some catch on; others don't. It depends so much whether the learners are drawn to the teacher or not. And what is more chancy than human attractions? If the learners are so drawn, then identification, suggestion, and other such indeterminate transactions may occur. These are not 'learning' processes in a full sense; for they are different from explicit imitation or copying, where something is explicitly attended to for assimilation. They happen to people; they are not achievements. Nevertheless this kind of contagion only actually spreads if both teacher and learner are actively engaged on something. It does not happen if the teacher is just fiddling about or the children are staring out of the window. The attention of both has to be focussed on some task; then these subsidiary processes may get going. If the teacher gets too self-conscious about them, the business gets blurred. He has to have his mind on what Lawrence called 'the holy ground' between teacher and taught. His dedication to it may then become incorporated in the consciousness of his pupils, and many other nuances may be imparted.

### (c) Conditioning

Cases where children pick up things without being aware of them are not confined to processes such as identification and suggestion; there are also those falling under the concept of 'conditioning'. Classical conditioning is, of course, completely irrelevant as it was concerned only with involuntary behaviour such as salivation and eye-blinks which could never be thought of as achievements. In operant conditioning what has to be learnt is not grasped by the learner to start with, if ever, as being instrumentally related to what counts as a reinforcement. Some movement is made, often of a random sort, which brings about acute pain or something attractive like food or a mate. This is not like rewarding children or punishing them when we do at least explain to them what will happen if they do something, and when what has to be learnt is presented as a means to the reward and can come to be thought of as such. Nothing like this happens in strict conditioning. Secondly there is no consciousness in conditioning of what has to be learnt as a *task*. A movement or series of movements is made and miraculously something like a pellet of food appears. It is really something of an anthropomorphism to say that the animal learns to press the lever. All that has happened is that some movement has been stamped in which we regard as an achievement. But it is more an achievement on the part of the experimenter than on the part of the animal.

It is very questionable, as a matter of fact, how much of animal learning, outside the narrow confines of laboratories, takes place according to principles of conditioning. For how often are animals in a position where their random responses are systematically reinforced? How often, too, are the situations in which they learn things such that there is no discernible relationship between obtaining something like food and movements which have to be learnt as means to this? Looked at objectively animals are 'conditioned' to do such incredibly trivial and non-functional things—pressing bars, running mazes, leaping grids, begging for biscuits, and balancing balls on their noses. The situations in which they 'learn' things by 'conditioning' are those in which opportunities for the use of intelligence are cut down to a minimum. So even at the animal level a certain amount of scepticism is necessary about the applicability of 'conditioning', in any strict sense, to the learning of animals. This perhaps should be extended to some of the things allegedly learnt in this way in laboratories.

At the human level, a fortiori, the applicability of conditioning is even more questionable. Presumably certain positive and negative reactions are picked up in this way and simple sequences of movements are stamped in before the consciousness of a child has been sufficiently differentiated to pick out objects in a public world which he wants and means that can be taken to get them. But once he can distinguish himself from others and can copy others and understand instructions, once he begins to develop a grasp of causal and means-end connexions, it is very difficult to conceive of what could be learnt by strict conditioning. For how can we be sure that what is to be learnt presents itself in no way as an intelligible means to a desired end or as something to be mastered or copied? How do we know that it is not picked up by imitation or suggestion? Certainly it is difficult to call such forms of 'learning' educational processes on the account here given of 'education'. For, apart from the moral objections to treating other human beings in this way, which do not derive solely from what is learnt, these goings-on cannot possibly be regarded as tasks culminating in achievements. When things happen to us, which occasion the development of phobias or of stereotyped patterns of reaction, is seems odd to call such goings-on processes of 'education'. For 'education' does suggest some kind of intentionality on the part of the learner, however embryonic.

## 5. EDUCATIONAL PROCESSES

I have now, as it were, got out of the way what I called aids to education and processes of picking things up, both of which border on being processes of education. I want now to pass on to processes of education proper which can be viewed as a family of tasks leading up to the achievement of being educated. The achievement of being 'educated', as I have set it out, is complex. It involves mastery of some skills, knowledge, and understanding of principles. For such an ideal to be realized many different sorts of things have to be learnt. In view of this it is improbable that there can be just one educational process. Too many educational theories are extrapolations from one type of learning situation which is taken as a paradigm for all. I propose therefore to isolate the different aspects of 'being educated' and consider briefly which educational processes are of particular relevance to each of them.

### (a) Training

Consider, first of all, the learning of skills. This presents itself preeminently as a task to the learner. He is usually presented with a paradigm of a skilled performance and, by a mixture of constant practice and imitation, he may eventually come to master it. A skill is not by its very nature something that could be learnt for all time in a flash of insight. Neither can it be learnt by reading books or by instruction alone. This helps of course, but only because it provides a guide for practice. Constant practice is absolutely essential, especially under the eye of a skilled performer who both corrects and provides a paradigm of the performance. Skills are difficult to master; so extrinsic forms of motivation usually have to supplement the intrinsic motivation provided by the desire to achieve or get something right.

To a teacher 'skills' usually denote reading, writing, and computation which have to be mastered before education can proceed very far. Because of the difficulties they present to a child, all kinds of attempts are made to harness the learning of these skills to other things that the child wants to do. But this is merely an intelligent way of providing an incentive to learning; it is nothing to do with the type of learning process required to master the skill. A child may be brought to the task of reading by the incentive of advertisements or by the necessity of reading instructions if he wants to cook. But when the actual reading begins there is no escape from practice, instruction, correction and example.

The general name we have for this type of learning process is 'training'. The concept of 'training' has application when (i) there is some specifiable type of performance that has to be mastered, (ii) practice is required for the mastery of it, (iii) little emphasis is placed on the underlying rationale. Example and instruction by another are a great help in the realm of skill, but they are not absolutely essential. A person might learn to type, for instance, without either, though it would be a lengthy business. But he could never learn to do this without practice. 'Training' has application, however, in a wider realm than that of skill; for roughly speaking the concept of 'training' also has application whenever anything coming up to a clear-cut specification has to be learnt. Military training includes not only arms drill and training skills such as shooting; it also includes the inculcation of habits such as punctuality and tidiness. Such habits cannot be learnt by practice and imitations alone as might a skill like swimming or swinging a golf club, because of the lack of close connexion with bodily movements. It is conceivable that something like swimming could be just picked up or 'caught' by practice and imitation without a word being said. But a habit like that of honesty, which is not just a kind of 'know-how' or knack, could never be picked up just like this.

Consider, for instance, what a child has got to know before he can develop a habit like that of stealing. He must be able to distinguish between himself and others and must have developed the notion of property; he must also grasp that people have a right to things and that these things must not be appropriated without permission. A child, strictly speaking, cannot 'steal' who has not a range of concepts such as these. He cannot learn what 'stealing' is just by watching others. For he cannot tell what an action is just from the outside; he has also to know how the agent conceives what he is doing. To realize that something is a case of theft he must, therefore, have developed the conceptual scheme without which 'theft' is an unintelligible notion. The notion of theft cannot be tied down, either, to any specifiable range of bodily movements. For all sorts of things can count as property and there are infinite number of ways of appropriating them. A child cannot therefore learn to steal or not to steal without instruction and correction as well as practice and imitation. The notion of 'moral training' as distinct from that of 'moral education' suggests the learning of a moral code which is tied down to specifiable rules such as 'Thou shalt not steal'. Moral education suggests, in addition, the passing on of the underlying rationale, the understanding of principles. But even training in this sphere, as well as in many others, involves much more than the mere mastery of a 'know-how' or 'knack'. The child has also to know that certain classes of action are wrong. Such knowledge could never just be 'caught'. The learning of skills is thus only one particular case of 'training'.

## (*b*) *Instruction and learning by experience*

Knowing what things are and that certain things are the case is a matter of developing a conceptual scheme that has to be fitted to phenomena. This can only be learnt by a process which involves the meaningful use of language by a teacher to structure relevant experience by the learner. In acquiring a body of knowledge of this sort instruction and explanation are as essential as first-hand experience. There is prevalent at the moment a widespread horror of instruction because this is associated with sitting children down in rows and telling them things which may be beyond their ken and which they may not be interested in learning about anyway. It is argued in reaction to this that children have at certain ages spontaneous curiosity in what things are and why they happen; they also have a natural desire to master things, provided they are not too difficult. A wise teacher will therefore be thoroughly cognizant of the stage of conceptual development which each child has reached. She will often take the children out of the classroom where the children can be confronted with the relevant experiences and will fill the classroom itself with things which are carefully related to these stages of conceptual development. She will be at hand always when the child's natural curiosity impels him to ask questions which are almost inevitable, given the confrontation between intriguing objects and a conceptual scheme which is ripe for the next increment. In this way there can be no danger of knowledge being inert. For what is learnt is always what the child is ready to absorb and eager to discover. In this way information from adults and from books can be built firmly into the developing cognitive structure of the child in relation to first-hand experience.

This is admirable provided that the teachers attempting to practise such a method are intelligent enough to understand what they are meant to be doing and skilful enough to make provision for children to whom they cannot be attending,[4] and provided that classroom conditions and the teacher-pupil ratio do not make it a pipe-dream. But it should be realized that it is really just a more intelligent method of instruction. Rather a lot of nonsense is talked in this context about children 'discovering' things which is rather reminiscent of Socrates' demonstration in *The Meno* that even a slave can make a geometrical 'discovery' if he is given the chance. The point is that a child may find out what others know, but he does not, if he is not asked the right sort of questions at the appropriate time, and if his experience is not guided in certain directions. A certain amount of practice is required for the child to learn to use the necessary concepts; but nothing like the same amount as in the case of skills. For once the rule has been grasped governing the use of the concept further instances are easily recognized. Of course knowledge acquired in this or any other way must be used fairly often or else it may be forgotten. But the supposition is that if it is required spontaneously in relation to first-hand experience forgetting is less likely.

### (c) *Teaching and the learning of principles*
If the knowledge of the human race had ended with Aristotle this account of knowledge and of the methods necessary to acquire it might be sufficient. It is indeed significant that those who advocate educational methods which stress the importance of first-hand experience have in mind mainly children of 7–12 who are at what Piaget calls the stage of concrete operational thought when the world of things presented through the senses is being ordered and structured. What is required at this stage is plenty of experience together with classificatory schemes to structure it. The classroom thus becomes a Lyceum in miniature.

But what of the grasp of principles necessary for understanding rather than low-level knowledge? What of the 'rape of the senses' necessary for principles like the law of inertia to emerge? What of the reliance on one typical and crucial instance so central to the hypothetico-deductive method of Galileo which Piaget postulates as developing almost naturally from the previous stage? Of what importance at this stage is all this dashing around and first-hand experience? As Hobbes put it, under the spell of Galileo: 'For when we calculate the magnitude and motions of heaven or earth, we do not ascend into heaven that we may divide it into parts, or measure the motions thereof, but we do it sitting still in our closets, or in the dark.'[5] Understanding of principles does not depend upon the accumulation of extra items of knowledge. Rather it requires reflection on what we already know, so that a principle can be found to illuminate the facts. This often involves the postulation of what is unobservable to explain what is observed. So it could never be lighted upon by 'experience'.

What then is there to be said about the learning of principles? The basic requisite is that people should first acquire in some way or other the low-level rules or assumptions which the principles illuminate. It is both logically absurd and educationally unsound to suppose that people could attain the necessary understanding of principles without first having acquired quite a lot of knowledge; for principles provide backing to rules or assumptions at a lower level of generality. In science, for instance, there could be no appeal to principles unless there were a mass of empirical generalizations which could be seen to fall under them; in morals there could be no appeal to principles without rules to justify by means of them. The grasp of principles, therefore, is inseparable from the acquisition of knowledge of a more mundane sort. This logical truth is often neglected by rationalistic educators who think that people can grasp scientific concepts, or pass them on to children, without knowing any science, or who believe that moral principles can be grasped by children who have not had a basic training in moral rules.

There is, of course, nothing absolute about what constitutes a principle. It is merely a higher-level assumption or rule that can be appealed to in order to substantiate and give unity to lower order ones. The one is thus immanent in the many. Evidence that the principles has been grasped is provided if a person knows how to go on and deal with new situations in the light of it. People are brought to a grasp of principles by a mixture of explanation and a selective survey of the many. Words like 'insight' are used in connexion with the grasp of principles. It is difficult to state precisely what is meant by such words, but once people have it very little in the way of further practice is necessary as in the case of skills. Neither are principles quickly forgotten like the lower-level information which they unify. The typical term for the educational process by means of which people are brought to understand principles is 'teaching'; for 'teach' unlike 'train' or 'instruct', suggests that a rationale is to be grasped behind the skill or body of knowledge.

*(d) The transmission of critical thought*
Societies can persist in which bodies of knowledge with principles immanent in them can be handed on without any systematic attempt to explain and justify them or to deal honestly with phenomena that do not fit. Fixed beliefs are thus perpetuated. When this is done we are presumably confronted with what is called indoctrination rather than teaching; for indoctrination is incompatible with the development of critical thought. Critical thought, however, is a rationalistic abstraction without a body of knowledge to be critical about. The problem of the teacher is to pass on a body of knowledge in such a way that a critical attitude towards it can also develop. If too much emphasis is placed on critical thought the danger is that all processes of education will be conceived too much in terms of what is necessary for a critical attitude to emerge. This is one of the dangers immanent in Dewey's system in which the concept of being 'educated' is more or less co-extensive with that of being critical.

There is no innate tendency to think critically, neither is it easy to acquire. Indeed as Bacon argued, it goes against the inveterate tendency of the human race which is to believe what we want to believe and to accept things that we are told on trust. The clue to how such an inveterate tendency can be overcome was provided by Plato when he described thought as the soul's dialogue with itself. It is a pity that this clue was not followed up. For the notion might not then have developed that reason is a sort of mental gadget that can be used by the individual if it is not too clogged up with passion or, as Hume described it, 'a wonderful and unintelligible instinct in our souls'. Given that critical thought about the assumptions in which we are nurtured rather goes against the grain, it will only develop if we keep critical company so that a critic is incorporated within our own consciousness. The dialogue within is a reflection of the dialogue without. This is a paradigm of an educational situation; for educational processes are those by means of which public modes of thought and awareness, which are mainly enshrined in language, take root in the consciousness of the individual and provide avenues of access to a public world.

The best way of making sure of such a living organic structure of thought is probably to employ the *ad hominem* method of question and answer used by Socrates. This brings the learner very quickly to probe into his presuppositions and to make explicit principles which were previously only dimly apprehended. If the learner is constantly prodded into doing this he gradually begins to think in a more clear, coherent, and structured way; for there is a sense in which we do not really know what we think about anything until we have had to state it explicitly and defend it. If this process continues for quite a time the learner gradually takes the questioner into his own mind and begins to develop the form of thought himself. He can come to formulate objections to his assumptions himself and keep on reformulating what he thinks or proposes to do until he hits on something to which he can find no objections.

It is important to realize that such a critical clarification of principles is a very different exercise from applying them in concrete circumstances. This seems to be the burden of Oakeshott's attack on rationalism and the starting point of his conception of political education.[6] He is not much interested in the discussion and justification of principles. What fascinates him is the judgement required to apply them in particular circumstances. He sees clearly that such judgement cannot be acquired in salons, studies, or seminars. It comes through practical experience in the presence of those who already have it.

It does not follow either that a person who has mastered a form of thought such as history, or one of the sciences, is skilled in testing the hypothesis that may emerge from reflection or discussion. He must, of course, be familiar from the inside with how experiments can be designed, or how records and manuscripts are interpreted. But many of the great theoretical scientists have been poor experimentalists just as some of the great historians have arranged the facts in a new pattern rather than discovered a lot of new ones by ingenious techniques of research. From the point of view of education what is essential is the grasp of a conceptual scheme for ordering facts rather than skill in research.[7] The various forms of thought—historical, moral, scientific, aesthetic—all have their own such schemes and thus provide different perspectives for the interpretation of experience. They can, however, only have such a transforming effect on a person's outlook if they are passed on in the right way at the right time and if they are informed by that passion for truth which lies at the heart of all of them. Without this critical discussion can degenerate into verbal leger-de-main and a parade of principles can be equivalent to name-dropping. Whether such a passion is due to fostering the natural curiosity of the child, whether it is caught from those who are already possessed by it, or whether it develops because an individual is confronted by conflicting opinions, is difficult to determine.

### (e) Conversation and 'the whole man'

What then of the processes which lead to the development of an educated man in the full sense of a man whose knowledge and understanding is not confined to one form of thought or awareness? Nowadays all sorts of educational experiments are being contrived to 'liberalize' vocational training and to ensure that premature specialization does not distort a man's view of the world. No doubt formalized correctives to specialization are necessary, though it is arguable that the proper place for them is at school rather than at university. But the question is whether explicit learning situations are sufficient to bring about this integrated outlook. The classical way of ensuring this, surely, has been not courses but conversation.

Conversation is not structured like a discussion group in terms of one form of thought, or towards the solution of a problem. In a conversation lecturing to others is bad form; so is using the remarks of others as springboards for self-display. The point is to create a common world to which all bring their distinctive contributions. By participating in such a shared experience much is learnt, though no one sets out to teach anyone anything. And one of the things that is learnt is to see the world from the viewpoint of another whose perspective is very different. To be able to take an active part in a real conversation is, of course, an achievement. It is not possible without knowledge, understanding, objectivity, and sensitivity to others. But it is also a learning situation of an informal sort. A vast amount of learning all through life takes place in such informal situations. Are we losing faith in the likelihood of anything emerging if it is not carefully contrived? Or are we just the victims of shortage of space, pressure of numbers, and the bureaucratization of our educational system?

This is the point of mentioning conversation at the culmination of a lecture on educational processes which has been concerned mainly with what goes on in formal situations. For just as educational processes are not confined to classrooms, so also for an educated man the distinction between formal and informal situations of learning is only one of degree. His experience is not only transformed by all that he has mastered, learnt, and understood, but is always exemplifying the processes by means of which such mastery, knowledge, and understanding has been acquired. The achievements constantly generate new tasks. Even in his middle age he can really listen to what people say irrespective of the use he can make of it or them. This is a considerable achievement. But then as Spinoza said of the state of human blessedness: 'all excellent things are as difficult as they are rare'.

## NOTES

1. See Scheffler, I., *The Language of Education* (Thomas, Springfield, 1960), Ch. IV.

2. It should be stressed that what has been said relates only to thinking of something as a form of *education*. It is only under this aspect that we are implying that there is something worth-while immanent in scientific activity, for instance, and that there is no discontinuity between the tasks and the achievements. But we can train people to do 'science' for purely utilitarian or vocational purposes if we wish. The same applies to carpentry or cooking. We *can* look at such activities in a purely instrumental way. Whether we should do so or not is a further question. In discussing this we are not engaged in a debate about the aims of education, but in a debate about whether we ought to educate people rather than train them, or whether something like science or carpentry has the intrinsic value which many would ascribe to it. It may well be too that there are many tasks and achievements engaged in at school, such as reading and computation, which, like boarding a bus or doing five-finger exercises, have a value which is almost entirely instrumental in relation to our educational aims. This may well be so. It does not contradict my thesis; rather it draws attention to the necessity of looking at what goes on in schools in a wider context. Schools are obviously concerned with things other than education—with health, for instance, with selection, and with vocational training.

3. The concept of education, could, perhaps, be extended to include such borderline processes. What exactly one calls 'education' in this

twilight area does not much matter provided that the similarities and differences are recognised.

4. See Sarason, S. B., Davidson, K. S., and Blatt, B., *The Preparation of Teachers* (John Wiley, N.Y., 1962).

5. Hobbes, T., *De Corpore* (Molesworth Ed., 1839), English Works 1, Ch. 7.

6. See Oakeshott, M., *Rationalism in Politics* (Methuen, London, 1962).

7. It is important to make this point at a time when there is a growing demand that universities should fulfil two functions which are not altogether compatible—develop research not so much for its own sake but in order to solve the practical problems of the nation, and provide a 'liberal' education for a larger percentage of the population than heretofore.

# 2

# THE LOGICAL AND PSYCHOLOGICAL
# ASPECTS OF LEARNING

## D. W. Hamlyn

It is, I suppose, obvious enough that some children learn better when there is a smile on the face of the teacher, just as it is conceivable that others may learn better when it is all done in time to music. Some learn better when they are happy, others perhaps when the conditions are austere or comfortable enough not to be distracting. The study of such individual differences is clearly a matter for psychology, since it will be a study of the psychological processes which bear on the facility with which individuals learn. It is even possible in principle to produce generalizations in this field, statements which may apply to people in general, although it may be doubted whether these will in fact amount to more than platitudes—that people learn better in general when encouraged or rewarded, when they are given opportunities for practice, when they are given material in digestible amounts, and so on. Nevertheless, these would certainly be *psychological* generalizations if not very exciting ones. But there are questions about learning which are not psychological questions—questions such as what learning is and what is implied when it is said that someone has learnt something. To answer such questions we have to clarify the concepts which we employ in this sphere, something that requires both reflection and some familiarity with the subject-matter to which those concepts apply. Investigations of this kind are not so much a matter for the psychologist as for the philosopher.

What, then, is it to learn something? In fact, this is a question which I shall, in effect, shelve for the time being, and it may be that I shall have nothing very illuminating to say about it directly. But I shelve it quite deliberately. One might of course say that to learn something is to acquire knowledge of it through experience; but this, although correct as far as it goes, is not likely to be enlightening because, apart from other vaguenesses in the formulation, much depends on the 'something' in question. To learn a list of words or a set of formulæ, to learn to play the piano or to ride a bicycle, to learn a language or a technique, and to learn a subject or a discipline are all very different things. Although they all involve the acquisition of knowledge, that knowledge is of quite different forms. To learn a list of words, simple rote-learning, as it is called, is nothing more than to memorize that list, and the knowledge involved is merely the knowledge of the words in their appropriate order. In skills such as that involved in riding a bicycle 'knowing how' comes to play a role, and the acquisition of such skills may involve practice as much as does rote-learning, even if in a different way. But here too other things begin to emerge; for few skills could be acquired by practice alone in the most rudimentary sense of that word, and few are in any way independent of some understanding of the issues involved. You could not play the piano without some such understanding, and practice in this case, if it deserves the name, must be intelligent practice. The existence of such understanding may indeed be implied whenever we speak of knowing how to do something, and this, among other things, distinguishes knowing how to do something from merely being able to do it. When we come to learning a language or a technique, and even more so with learning a subject, the appreciation and understanding of the subject and its principles comes to the fore. With the understanding of principles goes the ability to use certain concepts. If there is a distinction to be made between my two last categories, it is that learning a language or a technique is inevitably a practical matter in a way that learning a subject is not so obviously so. But this is a matter of emphasis only; technique and intellectual understanding, theory and practice cannot be completely divorced from each other.

What I have said so far is meant to show the complexities involved in any general discussion of learning. Fortunately, for educational purposes, it is surely unnecessary to go into all this. Rote-learning and simple practice may or may not be adequate tools for educational purposes, but they cannot in any way constitute anything in the way of the essence of education. This last, I suggest, is nothing unless it brings with it understanding and appreciation of principles, their relevance and their interconnections. Understanding, moreover, involves and presupposes the acquisition and use of concepts. One can understand nothing of a subject unless one has the concepts in which that understanding is to be expressed. Hence, the process of learning a subject goes hand in hand with the process of acquiring the relevant concepts, the concepts in terms of which the subject-matter and its principles are to be formulated. I shall try to say something by way of elucidation of this in the following. But my main concern will be with two points, both of which seem to me comparatively simple. They are as follows.

(1) The subjects into which knowledge is conveniently divided are not block-entities laid out, as it were, in a Platonic realm. There is an inclination, I believe, to think that there exists objectively something called, to take one example, mathematics, and that it is the aim of education to bring the learner to a confrontation with it. Subjects are, on this account, ideal entities available for contemplation. Given this, one can then argue about the best way of bringing about this contemplation, since the subjects are too complicated to grasp all at once. Is it better to concentrate on those parts of a subject which are somehow logically prior to others or on those which are psychologically easiest to grasp? The snag about this is that it is not immediately clear what the question means, what the distinctions amounts to. Certainly, I think, the question what is easy to grasp is not a matter for psychology. On the other hand, the notion of logical priority is perhaps obscure and it has different implications according to the ways in which it is interpreted. I shall enlarge on these points directly.

(2) No one could be said to have come to understand a subject, to have learned it, without some appreciation of general principles, some idea of what it is all about. But knowing and understanding general principles is not just a matter of being able to recite the relevant general propositions. Nothing is contributed by way of understanding when people are made to recite general propositions, even if these are fundamental to a subject. Thus, to present a very young child with, say, the general principles of number theory or algebra would be a futile business; for, he must be capable of cashing such general principles in terms which mean something to *him*, if understanding is to follow. There is in the growth of understanding of any subject an intimate connection between principles and their applications or instances. Principles must always be seen cashed in there instances, but instances must themselves be seen as cases to

which principles are relevant. Thus an appreciation of general principles implies in the full sense an appreciation of how they are to be applied. My point is analogous to one which could equally well be made about concepts; it may be expressed in Kant's famous or notorious slogan that 'thoughts without content are empty, intuitions without concepts are blind' (where by 'intuitions' Kant means something like the reference to instances). To present a child with little bits of information without reference to general principles at all is a sure way of preventing the development of understanding; such a child would be intellectually blind. But to go to the other extreme and concentrate on principles alone is another way of producing an equally unsatisfactory end-product; the child's thought, if this could be brought about, would be empty—without reference to any particular cases through which the general principles could mean something to him. There must always be a delicate balance between principles and cases; but since there are degrees of generality it is clear that the attainment of full understanding at one level of generality must presuppose something of a balance attained at a lower level of generality, a balance between an understanding of principles in general terms and an understanding of their relevance to particular cases. Otherwise, there is little hope of the relevance of the more general principles being seen. What is the point of presenting to children the principles of set-theory if they are not capable of understanding what it is for something to be a set? This has an obvious relevance to any discussion of Piaget's 'stages', especially to the distinction between concrete and abstract operations. Indeed, I suspect that Piaget is an essentially Kantian thinker in many respects.

I shall discuss my two points in turn. They are not of course unconnected. I have said that it is a superstition to think that subjects exist as block-entities, the contemplation of which should be the goal of the learner. I do not mean by this that there are no differences between, for example, history and physics. The historian may be distinguished from the physicist by, among other things, his interests, his methodology and the concepts which he brings to his subject-matter and in terms of which he thinks about it. There are also differences between the modes of explanation which the two employ—between historical and scientific theories. All these differences—and no doubt there are others—are important. But to suppose that the real difference is that there is one body of knowledge, expressible as a set of facts, called 'history' and another called 'physics', which the two are out to discover betrays a quite erroneous conception of learning. It is to suppose that learning consists merely in the acquisition of knowledge of a set of facts, the contemplation of a set of propositions. At its lowest, it reduces learning to simple rote-learning. But it cannot be anything like that in fact. Even at the simplest level the acquisition of knowledge of facts goes hand in hand with understanding. Even in rote-learning it is essential to understand what is going on, and in higher forms of learning understanding is much more important still. Thus words like 'history', 'physics' and 'mathematics' are not just the names of bodies of knowledge, in the sense of sets of true propositions; they are, if anything, the names of approaches to facts of generally different kinds. At a certain level, perhaps, we cannot even say that; distinctions between subjects tend to break down, they become an administrative matter only, or a question merely of the differences in the background of interests on the part of those who are concerned with them.

I may be thought to be labouring the obvious. Surely, it may be said, no one really thinks that subjects exist in *that* sense. Perhaps so, but I detect suggestions of this sort in certain discussions which imply that learning should start from what is logically prior in a subject, and even perhaps in those who deny this and insist that psychological priorities are everything. Let me explain what I mean —and the best way to do this is to indicate and explain one sense of the words 'logically prior', a sense which I shall directly come to repudiate in this context.

Explanatory theories, e.g. scientific theories, have a logical structure in the sense that the propositions of which the theory is constituted can be arranged in a certain order, so that certain propositions can be derived from others. It is indeed the fact that from general laws and statements of initial conditions it is possible to derive conclusions—the facts to be explained—that provides the basis of scientific, and no doubt other kinds of, explanation. We thus expect that with the help of reference to the general we shall be able to deduce the particular. It is because of logical relationships of this kind—relationships of entailment—that we can speak of the theory having a structure, and we may say, as Aristotle said, that the general is logically prior to the particular. The same sort of thing applies in mathematics. Insofar as it is true to say that set-theory provides the basis of arithmetic it is because arithmetic can be explained in terms of set-theory. Set-theory furnishes the more general point of view under which arithmetic can be subsumed. Hence, we might say that the notion of a set is logically prior to that of, say, a number, because the latter can be explained in terms of the former, but not vice versa. The direction in which explanation must proceed, and the logical relationships which go with it, thus determine what is logically prior within a discipline.

This, however, only applies where the discipline in question constitutes a theory—to parts of science, the foundations of mathematics and so on. Where questions of explanation do not arise and do not have a place, then this sort of consideration has no place either. It is difficult to see how large parts of history or literature could be said to have a structure in this sense. But even where it could be said that this is so—where a subject admits of the formulation of a theory of it—this could have few implications for education. Even if there is *a* sense in which someone could not be said *fully* to understand arithmetic without understanding set-theory, this is only in the sense in which it might be said that someone could not fully understand, say, the movements of billiard balls without understanding the principles of sub-atomic physics. And no one, I take it, would suggest that children should be introduced to physics *by that route*. The most fundamental concepts of a subject, from the point of view of explanation, are not likely to be the most familiar. To concentrate on such concepts may hinder the understanding of how the more familiar concepts are to be applied—a matter which is just as important for complete understanding. But, to repeat the remark which I made earlier, there are subjects for which none of this makes sense, since questions of explanation do not arise within them, or do so only to a minor extent.

If this is accepted, it may be suggested that the only remaining position is that, as far as learning is concerned, the only priorities are psychological priorities. For, from the point of view of learning, the priorities that the structure of explanation provides are not relevant. That is to say that the only possible procedure for an educationalist is to find out empirically what parts of a subject are the easiest to learn and to insist that learning should start from there. For there is now no question, it might be thought, of having to start from those elements which are logically necessary if anything else in the subject-matter is to be seen as it is. There is no question of having to see the subject arranged in its proper logical order. There are no logical conditions for a proper understanding of a subject; there are only psychological conditions, e.g. that no one could grasp the difficult parts before grasping the easy ones. So it might be said. To come to this conclusion would, I think, be far too quick a deduction from what has already been established, but there is in any case something very odd about the suggestion that the easiness or difficulty of a subject or a part of a subject is a matter for psychology. It is clearly enough a matter for psychology that something is easier for one person to learn than another; for, the question why this is so could be answered only by an investigation into the people concerned. The conditions under which individuals learn something more easily is also clearly enough a matter for psychology, as I indicated at the beginning of this lecture. It is not so clear that the same thing holds good of the question why one subject or part of a subject is easier than others.

In what ways might one subject be more difficult than another? It might demand knowledge of more facts (so I have heard it said about psychology in comparison with philosophy). It might be more abstract (so I have heard it said about philosophy in comparison with psychology). It might demand knowledge of skills, procedures or ways of thinking not demanded by the other, and it might even presuppose the other in one way or another. Factors like abstractness and complexity loom large here, although these factors may arise in many more ways than one, and I would not claim that these are the only factors at stake. However, abstractness and complexity are obviously very important and I shall concentrate on them in what follows. It may be thought that these factors are relevant because of the truth of psychological generalizations such as that people generally find the abstract and the complicated more difficult to understand or grasp than the specific and the simple. But is this just a psychological generalization? *Could* a man find the abstract easier to grasp than the specific, and the complicated easier to grasp than the simple? Would this indeed make any sense? If not, then we are confronted here, not just with empirical psychological generalizations, but with some sort of *a priori* or necessary truth. That is to say that in that event abstractness and complexity will be *criteria* of difficulty; if one subject is more abstract and complex than another then it will follow necessarily that the one is more difficult than the other. I do not claim that it is always obvious whether some branch of a subject *is* more abstract or complicated than another, and to discover the truth on the matter may require investigation of a kind. The way in which this might be done is by turning what I have said on its head. Given that people *normally* find X more difficult than Y, this will be a reason for saying that X may be more complicated or abstract than Y (depending on the exact nature of the difficulties reported). The idea of what is normal is very important here, and I shall return to it later in an analogous context. The point is that if a subject is difficult people may be expected normally to find it so—just as, if something is red it is to be expected that people will normally see it so. When I say 'normally', I do not mean 'generally'; I mean 'in normal conditions'. It is this notion of what is normal which provides the link between what something is and how it appears to people or how they find it. Thus, if abstractness and complexity are criteria of difficulty we may expect that people will normally find the abstract and complicated difficult; and conversely, if people normally find something difficult, this will be an indication of its abstractness or complexity.

We need, however, to look further at the idea that there is some kind of necessary connection between the notion of difficulty and those of complexity and abstractness. Can we even conceive of a man finding the complicated or abstract easier than the simple or specific? There are of course people who feel more at home with the complicated than the simple—people of whom we say that they cannot see the wood for the trees; and there may be people who are similarly more at home with the abstract than the specific, people who fail to bring issues down to earth. But this indicates something about their habits or qualities of mind; it indicates nothing directly about the comparative easiness of the subject-matter. The man who cannot see the wood for the trees may indeed find the simple too easy for his taste. It may come to be that the simplicity of a thing constitutes an obstacle to his understanding, just because of his cast of mind; we might perhaps say that for some reason he shuts his eyes to the simple. But his case provides no grounds for denying that the complicated is normally more difficult for people than the simple. Indeed, the special explanation that is required indicates that the case is not normal. The indications, then, are that we should expect people normally to find the complex difficult. Indeed, the connection between complexity and difficulty seems to turn on certain things about the concept of understanding. The complicated may, in fact, be described as that which puts a certain kind of demand on the understanding. To grasp a complicated whole is to grasp the simpler components in their relationship with each other; hence this kind of understanding presupposes the understanding of the simpler; and where a man appears not to find it easy to take in the simple by itself, we need a special explanation of the fact. The same is true of the relation between the abstract and the concrete or specific, although this raises considerations to which I have already referred under my second heading and to which I shall return later. I conclude, however, that factors like complexity and abstractness are in fact criteria of difficulty, and that it is thus not just a psychological truth that people find the complicated and abstract difficult.

These considerations, however, open up once again the question whether there are any priorities in a learner's approach to a subject which are more than psychological. (And that there *are* psychological considerations I have no wish to deny, since, for example, personality differences between people may make one way of putting over a subject more rewarding in one man's case than in another's. Factors relative to the learning of something on specific occasions and by specific individuals are always psychologically relevant.) Now, I think that there *are* priorities in learning which are more than psychological, and they might be described as epistemological, or logical in another sense from the one already discussed. In the growth of knowledge, certain things must be done before others. Not only is it the case that certain facts must sometimes be known if one is going on to make sense of others, but it is also the case that sometimes certain things must be understood, certain concepts grasped, before progress can be made at all. For example, in arithmetic it is essential that one should understand the notion of an ordinary integer if one is to understand that of a fraction. This is quite apart from such general considerations as the priority of the simple to the complicated, to which reference has already been made. The appreciation of certain subjects demands a certain order for knowledge. That this must be so is indicated by the existence of general principles for the establishment of curricula, and if it were not so any suggestion that programmes could be laid down for teaching machines would be impossible. What I am now saying is that such programmes, such principles of order, could be established only by decisions on what is the appropriate order for the development of the knowledge and understanding of a subject. To reach such decisions demands that very knowledge and understanding of the subject itself, plus an ability and willingness to reflect upon the exact relationships between the concepts presupposed within it. This is not a matter for psychology. I would emphasize this point.

Let us consider in some detail an example which brings out the kind of consideration which I have in mind. As is perhaps well enough known, Piaget and his associates have carried out a number of studies, which have become known as 'conservation studies', concerned with the child's appreciation of such general principles as the conservation of matter, size and weight. It has been brought out that children at a certain age do not always appreciate such principles and even appear to apply them inconsistently. Moreover, they do not come to accept them all at the same time. There appears to be a general assumption in Piaget's approach that they perhaps *should* do so, and that it is surprising that they do not. There is also perhaps a sense of surprise that children should fail at all to accept the principles, despite the fact that in the actual history of thought some of these principles were not formally established until comparatively recently, at any rate during the last three or four hundred years. These studies might be represented as concerned with the understanding of concepts which fall within the general field of physics, and may thus be described as studies in the child's understanding of elementary physics. The question that arises is what could be discovered about the situations under investigation merely by reflecting about them. Let us take a specific and simple case of a Piagetian type: we have, let us suppose, a definite quantity of liquid of a specific colour, which can be poured from a wide transparent container into a similar narrow one. When the liquid is poured from the wide container into the narrow one, a child at a certain stage of intellectual development might well say, because of the comparative depth of the liquid in the containers, that there is more liquid in the narrow one. This may be so even though he sees the liquid being poured from the one container into the other. What are we to suppose has gone on here—what concepts employed and how?

Many sorts of consideration are relevant. We, who know the right answers, know that change of place and container does not affect the identity of the liquid or its volume, and that volume is not a simple function of depth. But these are not factors which we can take for granted in a child, and it does not take a great deal of reflection to see that we cannot. Moreover, the notion of the identity of a liquid (or of any other object) is not necessarily an obvious one. After all, we allow some changes in things without thereby denying that they retain their identity. Liquids expand when heated without becoming thereby different liquids. If we were to maintain that the identity of a liquid has something to do with its mass, this is obviously by no means a simple notion, and is not one that could at all be taken for granted in a child. What *does* identity depend on for a child? I am anxious here only to raise such questions for consideration, and to bring out the complicated relationships that may exist between the concepts which we use even in situations which may seem obvious to us. *We* tend to take notions like that of identity for granted (even when we cannot give an account of them); but there is no saying that a child does. Nor should we expect insight into these relationships to emerge all at one time; for, some of them are more complicated than others. The notion of volume, for example, is a more complicated notion than that of depth—it introduces another dimension. The volume of a liquid is therefore necessarily more difficult to estimate than its depth. Hence, the apparent relationship between the identity of an object and its depth or height may well seem more obvious than that between the identity of an object and its volume. All this should be evident to one who is prepared merely to reflect about the situation, provided that he has the requisite concepts.

Furthermore, it is not surprising that at a certain stage of development a child may be pulled in different directions: it is the same object for him to the extent that nothing has apparently been done to it which could cause it to change its volume or indeed change at all; yet it is different because its apparent depth and therefore apparent volume have changed. In the development of the 'right' view of things social influences obviously play a large part—a point very much under-emphasized by Piaget. Similar considerations apply to the part played by the acquisition of linguistic tools. In other words, the facility with which a child may come to see the proper relationships between such factors as volume, depth and the identity of the object will depend on the extent to which he is subject to social influences of a certain sort and on his ability to formulate the relationships in words.

I have no wish to draw any other general moral than the one which I have already mentioned, i.e. the need for reflection on such situations. I certainly do not believe that it is possible to lay down any general law of development which the child must follow in acquiring concepts and coming to see the relationships between them. I would, however, point to the fact that concepts vary in complexity and abstractness, and that this determines certain general priorities. In considering how education should proceed one has to start from a knowledge of the concepts which a child possesses and the goal to be attained, and work out the intervening steps in the light of such general considerations as I have mentioned. This, I would emphasize again, can be done only by one who knows the subject and is prepared to reflect about it. There is no short cut, but that certain things must come before others in any process of this sort is a matter of logical necessity of a kind. How exactly, how precisely the priorities could be worked out is a matter for speculation, and the steps to be followed in the teaching of any given child will obviously depend on where that child is already, on what concepts he already has and on what relationships he already appreciates. For this reason, any generalized programme for teaching children of roughly the same stage of development must inevitably be a matter for compromise; but that *some* general principles can be laid down for the development of knowledge within any given sphere is of course a presupposition of any educational programme. In some disciplines the steps to be taken by the learner are comparatively easy to establish; hence their amenability to instruction by teaching machines. In other disciplines, any programme of teaching must inevitably be a hit and miss affair. It is all a question of the complexity of the relationships which exist between the concepts in terms of which the subject-matter is to be understood. An assessment of these relationships can come only from one who knows the subject. It is not a matter for one who has specialist psychological knowledge alone.

I may have given the impression that while subjects are not block entities, in the sense explained earlier, they nevertheless have a fixed order of development, and that learning consists in finding out what this is and following it up. I do not think that this would be the correct account of the situation. This is not just because it is unrealistic, not just because finding one's way may involve going down many blind alleys. Wittgenstein once described coming to understand the nature of mathematics as trying to find one's way round a strange town, and this is not a bad description of any attempt to learn a subject. Moreover, it may be that in the end one of the best ways of coming to understand the geography of a town is to get thoroughly lost and have to find one's way home despite this. The apparently blind alleys may turn out not to be blind after all. Sometimes too the best first step may be to acquire a habit of going in a certain direction; habits can always be adapted later, as long as they do not become ossified. All this is true, but it does not get to the root of the problem. The analogy may or may not work even at the most abstract level of a subject, although the idea of a settled geography to be discovered may be one to be retained at any rate as an ideal. But the child in a school is not so much learning the geography of an area as acquiring the tools and techniques by which he may eventually come to make a map of it. A tool is of little use until it is decided what purposes it may be used for. Maps also may be constructed for different purposes and with different projections.

The point of this analogy is that concepts too can be thought of as tools of this kind. In making a map one has to know not only the features of the terrain to be represented on it, but also what counts as a feature of a specific kind. Similarly, concepts may be thought of as instruments for the task of attaining a familiarity in thought with some range of facts and also for attaining an understanding of what counts as a fact of a given kind. And just as the map has a purpose, so too concepts may be regarded as devices for thinking of the facts in a way which may be useful for some further end. That is why I said earlier that in considering how education should proceed one should start not only from a knowledge of the concepts which a child already has but also from a knowledge of the goal to be attained. What is the goal to be attained in teaching a young child elementary arithmetic, the salient facts of an historical period or the rudiments of English grammar? Until questions of this sort are answered it is impossible to say how we should proceed or in what order concepts should be invoked. It has, in sum, to be decided what is the goal of any given inquiry. The problem is a well-known one in connection with the learning of Classics. Until the goal to be attained in studying Classics has been decided it is pointless to argue about how to go about studying it—whether, for example, the doing of Latin proses or the study of Ciceronian cadences has any utility. Concepts are, to change the analogy, like keys too; they open doors, but if they are to be of any use one must know what door each opens, whether the door leads anywhere and whether there is any point in opening it.

I have spoken of concepts long enough without really explaining the term. I must now say something of what it is to have and acquire

36

a concept, and this will bring me to my second main topic, about which I have in effect said something already. It must now be made explicit. The connection is this: I said earlier, in presenting my second main point, that it turned on what was involved in understanding principles. The notions of a concept and a principle are interconnected; to have a concept of something is to know the principle in accordance with which things are said to be of the relevant kind. To have a concept of, say, man is to know the principle whereby certain things may be collected together—those things, namely, which we call men. It is thus to know what it is to be a man. This entails not only being able to give an account of what sorts of things men are, but also thereby to recognise men as such. To acquire a concept thus involves acquiring this knowledge and this ability. Of course, someone may have a *certain* understanding of a concept without being able to recognise the things which fall under it. There is a sense in which a blind man may be said to have some understanding of the concept of redness. He may be able to tell you that it is a colour, and he may be able to give a formal account of what a colour is, e.g. that it is a property of the surfaces of objects that is accessible only to vision. He may indeed be able to give some account of the structure of colours and of the relation of red to the other colours. All this is possible without sight, and therefore without the experience necessary to a full understanding of what it is for an object to be red. Such a full understanding requires both the ability to give a formal account of redness and the ability to recognize instances. A concept thus gives one a principle of organization for a subject matter. If one has a given concept one has knowledge of that principle. That is why I have already talked of the understanding of a subject as a matter of appreciating certain concepts and their interrelationships.

It is a dogma of empiricism that one acquires a concept by reviewing a number of particular things and seeing what is common to them. This cannot be the correct view of the situation if only because in order to do this one must be in the position to regard those particular things *as instances*. It is necessary to know what things it is relevant to collect together for this purpose. Thus it might seem more pertinent to speak of applying concepts to things rather than abstracting them from things. The truth is what I have already said—that we have the concept in question only when we are both able to see a range of things as falling under the concept and also in the position to know what it is for them so to fall, what it is that makes them instances. For this reason, there is inevitably in the process of acquiring concepts a delicate balance between a kind of abstract understanding of what it is to be an X and a knowledge of what things conform to this criterion. In learning—that is to say, in the growth of knowledge and understanding of a subject-matter— there must at every stage be achieved a balance of this sort if progress is to be maintained. Habits of mind, habitual ways of thinking, however useful when considered merely as stages in a transition to greater understanding, become intellectually dangerous if allowed to ossify. But there are other dangers also, those which I referred to earlier. There is the danger of becoming too concerned with particular things to the extent that it becomes just one damned fact after another. There is also at the other extreme the danger of spinning out connections between concepts without stopping to ask for their cash value.[1]

These points which I have made are, as I indicated earlier, essentially Kantian. They are to be found also in a sense in Piaget, although in his case they receive a strange biological dress. A strictly philosophical point is tricked out under the guise of a rather vague and certainly misleading psychological or biological theory. I refer here to Piaget's notions of accommodation and assimilation and the balance to be achieved between these processes. What Piaget has in mind is the idea that our knowledge of objects is partly determined by what these objects are in themselves, partly by how we regard them. This comes down to the point which I have already set out, concerning the relationship between concepts and instances. But to use the notions of accommodation and assimilation to express the point is harmful in two ways at least.

(1) The idea that perception and the acquisition of knowledge generally involve accommodation and assimilation amounts to the idea that in this context there is a mutual modification of subject and object. (A parallel for this idea can again be found in Aristotle, in his view that perception consists in an actualization of the corresponding potentialities of sense-organ and sense-object.) But this sort of view depends on analogies which are supposed to exist between perception and other situations in which there is a reciprocal causal relationship. Such reciprocal causal relationships exist often enough in biological situations, where the attainment of a balance is the

function of an organism. Thus the proper working of the body depends on the existence of physiological balances of one kind or another. The stimuli which affect certain bodily organs are themselves affected and modified by a process of feed-back when the balance is disturbed. But the relationship which comes to exist between concept and object in perception is not a causal relationship at all. A concept is not the sort of thing which can have a causal relation with an object; it makes no sense to suppose so. For, concepts are not things of this kind, as should be clear when it is remembered that, as I have already said, to have a concept of X is to know what it is for something to be an X. Correspondingly, the growth of knowledge is not itself a causal matter (however much it may depend on causal factors of a physiological kind, i.e. on bodily conditions).

(2) If the employment of a biological model is misleading in giving us an incorrect understanding of what the acquisition of knowledge consists in, it also has misleading implications of a more directly philosophical kind. It suggests that the balance to be attained is one between something about the individual which is essentially subjective, i.e. the concept, and something about the world around us which is clearly objective, i.e. the object. Knowledge is thus a blend of the subjective and the objective. But the relationship to which I have pointed as existing between concept and instance is not one between the subjective and the objective. It is not up to an individual to organize in thought what he is confronted with in any way he pleases—or if anyone shows signs of so doing we think of him as mad. I have already said more than once that to have a concept of X is to know what it is for something to be an X; hence, to see something as an instance of X is to see it as something to which this knowledge is appropriate. There is nothing subjective about this. In fitting something to a concept we are not imposing on it a subjective point of view; for, given what I have said, to have a concept can be as much an objective matter as anything else. The objectivity of a concept is bound up with the idea that it must be inter-subjective, interpersonal, just as knowledge is. Hence, it is impossible to look on the growth of knowledge as some kind of transaction between an individual and his environment, as if social, inter-personal, factors had no part to play. I have commented already on the serious under-estimation of the social in Piaget's thought. This is borne out by his adoption of this curious biological model, which effectively rules out the social

factor, and thereby undermines the objectivity of knowledge. It is most important to note the extent to which notions like that of knowledge and concepts are social ideas, and the extent to which objectivity depends on this point. For the same reason it is impossible to think of education and learning at all except from a social point of view.

An important truth nevertheless remains in all this—that a balance must be attained between the formal understanding of the principles of a subject and an appreciation of what counts as instances to which those principles are to be applied. Unless this balance is attained, one cannot be said to have a proper understanding of the concepts involved. Hence, being aware of the general principles of a subject, which itself presupposes having the concepts, the particular forms of knowledge, in which the subject-matter is to be formulated, implies also attention to instances. Of course, this is of itself to take an over-simple view of the situation, since concepts do not come by themselves, and any subject will involve connections between concepts of one degree or another of abstractness. To be made to learn these connections without any prior understanding of their relevance to instances would be to be given knowledge which was formal only, and therefore empty; the lack of understanding would make the learning equivalent to rote-learning. It would be the learning by rote of empty phrases. It is perhaps arguable that in certain spheres of knowledge progress might be better made by instilling the formal knowledge and then cashing it in instances than by building up from instances in the first place. But this is merely to make the point which I have laboured all along—that at every stage in the development of knowledge a balance is required between formal knowledge of principles and appreciation of what counts as instances, and that it is of less importance which one invokes first than that a balance should be attained. Nevertheless, it is clearly futile to expect a child to move from one extreme to the other, and the concrete and particular is clearly more obvious than the abstract and general. Is it, therefore, any surprise that what Piaget calls the stage of concrete operations must in general precede that of abstract operations? As Aristotle said, while in knowledge the general is prior in itself, the particular is prior relative to us. This is what Piaget's point comes down to.

What do I mean when I say that the concrete and particular is more obvious than the abstract and general? I do not present this as a mere fact of human psychology. It seems to me a consequence of the situation in which human-beings find themselves, of the nature of human experience. The possibility of creatures who come to knowledge of, say, the principles of physics before knowledge of their immediate surroundings is a science-fiction conception, but it corresponds to nothing human. In so far as our concept of knowledge is really a concept of *human* knowledge, it is doubtful whether the possibility which I have mentioned is even one which is intelligible to us. The development of human knowledge may be represented as an enlargement of experience, an enlargement of the individual's intellectual environment. (The part played in this by social factors is obvious.) The things which are the individual's immediate and original concern are particular and concrete. As experience is widened and enlarged, as too it becomes more inter-personal, so it must inevitably become more general and abstract.

Given all this, what seems at first sight to be merely a natural transition from the concrete to the abstract in the development of human thinking emerges as some sort of necessary principle. It is necessary because this transition is just what, as we conceive it, the development of human experience must consist in. That development can of course fail to take place, but it can have no other order; otherwise it would not be *development*. But, it may be said, has not Piaget shown by empirical investigations that the concrete comes before the abstract as a matter of fact? How can something which is supposed to be a necessary truth be discovered by empirical investigations? We must be careful here. Let us consider what Piaget's response might be to hypothetical counter-examples to his thesis. Presumably, if children did not develop from the concrete to the abstract at all, he would have to say that they were not normal children—and we would agree. If the development occurred in the reverse order, would he not have to say, as I have already indicated, that they were not human? The presumption in his investigations is that he is concerned with normal human children. One thing that he may be said to have discovered is that the subjects who at one stage employ concrete operations and only later abstract operations are indeed normal human children. What else should we expect to happen in such circumstances? The situation is similar to the one which I mentioned earlier in stressing the connection between abstractness and complexity on the one hand and difficulty on the other. If there is a way of establishing the abstractness and complexity of a subject, this is *eo ipso* a way of establishing that people normally find it difficult, and vice versa. Similarly, if there is a way of establishing that children are normal human children, that their experience is what is normal, then this will *eo ipso* establish that their intellectual development will be along certain general lines, and vice versa.

It seems to me that Piaget's discoveries here are like discovering that circles when presented to people in a frontal plane look round to them. To insist that they generally do would be to labour the obvious. The point is that this is the normal case, and it is by reference to it that the application of concepts like 'roundness' is established; it is the norm for what counts as round. If circles presented in a frontal plane did not normally look round our understanding of notions like that of a circle and roundness would be completely different; indeed, we should not know what to think. Hence, given that the people and the situation are normal, it could not be otherwise. It needs no empirical investigation to discover that circles seen in the frontal plane look round in normal conditions. Analogously, I do not claim that the stages found in Piaget's subjects are not there as a matter of fact; I do claim that *if his subjects are normal human children*, we could not conceive it otherwise. Hence, the priority of the concrete to the abstract is something that all normal human-beings could discover by reflection on what they know about the nature of human development, of human learning; it needs no further empirical investigation. On the other hand, of course, it does need empirical investigation to discover *when* John or Mary pass from one general stage of development to another, and whether they do so at roughly the same age. But such findings of course presuppose our present educational and cultural set-up; there is no reason to suppose that the norms are unalterable. Hence, what needs even further investigation is whether what is true of John and Mary is also true of Fritz, Ali and Kwame, i.e. we need to know the effects of different cultural and perhaps genetic backgrounds on the general development of children.

Finally, let me say again that if it is thought desirable that the process of intellectual development be accelerated (something that is perhaps arguable, considering that *intellectual* development is not the only thing), then the best people to provide the answers how this is to be done are those who have reflected most deeply on what is involved conceptually in their own subject, what is best understood first, and so on. That is to say that the best person to say how the teaching of, say, mathematics should proceed is the mathematician who has reflected adequately, and perhaps philosophically, on what is involved in his own subject (especially, in the first place, in its application to experience). Of course, here again the difficulties in the way of coming up with any firm answers may be insurmountable; in which case, the only hope is to find out empirically what courses of learning children do as a matter of fact normally find most easy. For, as I have said, easiness goes with concreteness and simplicity of subject-matter, and this provides a clue to what should come first and what second in learning.

My intention in what I have had to say has been above all perhaps to delimit the roles to be performed by philosophy and psychology in this field, and to emphasize the differences between empirical and conceptual inquiries here. Psychology has much to tell us about learning—about, for example, particular cases and individual differences. It can also tell us about the effect on learning of all those factors in people which we can call psychological—personality traits, intelligence, and so on. What I have been urging is, amongst other things, that there is also required proper reflection on what learning and education are, and what they involve in consequence. For, only in this way can we be rid of misleading models which may inhibit our understanding of intellectual development and education.

## NOTES

1. I ignore here the possibility of *a priori* concepts, but these would be intelligible only in some sort of connection with concepts which do have the application discussed above.

# 3

# THE LOGICAL AND PSYCHOLOGICAL
# ASPECTS OF TEACHING A SUBJECT

Paul H. Hirst

Most teachers of a form of knowledge or understanding at some time ask themselves the fundamental questions : In what ways and to what extent is the effective teaching of a subject determined by the nature of the subject itself and in what ways and to what extent is the teaching dependent on factors studied in the psychology of learning and teaching? Or putting these questions another way, how are syllabuses and methods determined by the characteristics of what is to be taught and how are they to be determined by our empirical knowledge of teaching methods? Indeed, what sort of questions are questions about how best to teach a subject? This paper is an attempt to make clear something of what is involved in answering these questions. It will, however, be concerned almost entirely with the teaching of those subjects which are indisputably logically cohesive disciplines. I have argued elsewhere[1] that although the domain of human knowledge can be regarded as composed of a number of logically distinct forms of knowledge, we do in fact for many purposes, deliberately and self-consciously organize knowledge into a large variety of fields which often form the units employed in teaching. The problems that arise in teaching such complex fields as, say, geography and educational theory, are much more difficult to analyse than those arising in such forms as, say, mathematics, physics and history. And if the teaching of such fields necessarily involves the teaching of certain areas of more fundamental forms of knowledge, then it is only when questions about the latter have been settled that we can hope to answer questions about the former.

What sort of questions then, are questions about how best to teach a subject? Manifestly these are not questions that belong to the subject itself. How to teach history is not itself a historical question, nor is how to teach chemistry a chemical question. Maybe these questions will never be satisfactorily answered without a knowledge of history or chemistry, but such knowledge is at best a necessary condition for answering the questions, certainly it is not sufficient. Questions about the teaching of history are surely quite different logically from the questions of historical scholarship and where is the evidence that there is any correlation of abilities in these two domains?

If questions about teaching are manifestly not questions within the subject domain itself, are they then simply empirical questions? If so we could hope to discover directly by experiment and observation which activities do in fact lead to pupils learning history or chemistry, and thus which activities are successful as teaching methods. Certainly unless it is the case that activities result in pupils learning history or chemistry, they are useless as teaching methods, whatever the intentions of the teacher may be, and whether or not pupils learn successfully is a matter for empirical test. This answer is, however, too simple. For before any empirical investigation of teaching methods, that has any value, can be carried out, we have to decide what will count as pupils having learnt history. And once we start looking closely at what the learning of history involves, important logical features appear which must necessarily characterize what goes on if the activities we are interested in are even to count as the teaching of history. Here then will be features which on logical grounds must determine the teaching of the subject.

What then are we after in teaching a subject? What does learning it involve? In all subjects surely, we do not just want the learning of a string of propositions. If that were all, we could quickly set out what has to be learnt and find by empirical investigation how best to teach it. But even when handing on information, we want pupils not to become like parrots but to *understand* the information, and, as soon as we say that, difficulties arise as to what exactly we mean by this term and how we would know pupils had understood what was presented to them. Generally speaking we want yet more from our teaching than this, however. What we want is that pupils shall begin, however embryonically, to think historically, scientifically or mathematically; to think in the way distinctive of the particular subject involved and even to achieve some style and imagination in doing so. Thus before we can carry out any empirical investigation of teaching methods we are faced with the difficult task of getting clear what is involved in, say, thinking historically, and thus in learning to think in this way.

At first sight it might be thought that to discover what historical thinking is, we must somehow carry out psychological investigations of the thought processes of historians when doing their job. Certainly these thought sequences could be investigated, but to do that means that we must be able to pick out from all their thinking when they are thinking historically and not just say day-dreaming, plotting a family holiday or perhaps thinking mathematically. In fact we are back again on the same kind of question, how can you empirically investigate until you know the criteria of what you are looking for? And it follows from this that the criteria of what constitutes historical thinking must be found independently of such investigation. The only way in which we can successfully distinguish different forms of thought is in fact by reference to the particular set of terms and relations which each of the distinct forms of thought employs. These terms and relations are fully public, and if, therefore, we wish to characterize, say, scientific or historical thought, we must do this in the first place by examining the distinctive features of scientific theories and laws or historical explanations. In science, such an analysis will at the most general level make plain, for example, the particular use of terms in expressing empirical truths, the importance of general laws and the criteria for verifying these. In history, it will involve making plain the features of historical explanation of particular events by colligation, the use of general laws and evidence from sources. Granted an analysis of these public characteristics, it is not impossible to investigate empirically the thought sequences of particular historians. But just what such investigations of historical thought could provide by way of general psychological truths cannot be laid down a priori, nor can we know beforehand what bearing they might have on problems of teaching and learning. In general, however, it is surely true to say that when as teachers we seek to develop historical thought, say, we are not aiming at any particular pattern or sequence of thought episodes. Indeed many would wish to rule out of 'coming to think historically' any suggestions that thought sequences are being stereotyped, even if this were practically possible. It would be argued that thinking historically is thinking which, irrespective of the private thought sequence involved, results in propositions which constitute valid historical accounts and explanations. Historical thought necessarily involves the recognition of the rules that govern the meaningful use of concepts and the validity of propositions, but this involves no necessary temporal order to thought. Just as playing chess involves making moves in accordance with the rules of chess, though it involves no one particular order of moves, so thinking historically involves thinking in accordance with historical criteria, though it involves no particular sequences of thought.

Certainly, on this view of historical thinking, what we want pupils to acquire, both in structure and content, can be totally characterized without recourse to any psychological investigation of thought sequences. This does not, however, preclude the possibility that such investigation would enable us to find more effective means of teaching historical thinking, and it might ultimately lead to a reformulation of what we wish to achieve in history teaching. An empirical investigation, not only of the private thought sequences of historians, but also of their more public methods of procedure, for instance in marshalling sources, working from analogy and so on, might be of great value here. Yet whatever possibilities such empirical investigation might open up, it remains true that there must first be clear logical analysis of what criteria distinguish historical thought. This is in fact to say that the effective teaching of a subject necessarily depends on knowing certain features which characterize it, which can be disclosed only by logical analysis of the meaning of 'historical thinking', though once the criteria for this are plain, empirical evidence about thinking based on the use of these criteria becomes important too.

But granted this very rough indication of the boundaries between the logical and the psychological or empirical characterization of 'historical thinking', we now wish to know further how far the logical analysis of historical thinking determines the teaching of historical thinking. For having got to this point it might be argued that, given a grasp of the criteria of historical thinking, a philosophically self-conscious historian can in fact set out clearly all that is to be aimed at, and that it is then a matter of empirical investigation how far various teaching methods are successful in achieving these aims. Certainly such a historian could set out in detail what had to be mastered, the concepts, the forms of explanation and their criteria, the content, the methods of investigation and so on. But to make all other factors in determining teaching methods an empirical matter, is to take too simple a view of the contribution of logical analysis to determining the teaching of a subject. For though it is quite possible, granted a clear statement of what is to be taught, to

47

investigate different teaching methods, yet a great deal of investigation approached in this way might well turn out to be quite unnecessary. The reason is simply that experiment and observation cannot but confirm matters of logical truth, and all that is necessarily implied by learning to think historically has not yet been made clear. Maybe there are truths about teaching and learning which are rather like that hoary truth beloved of philosophers that all bachelors are unmarried. To prevent irrelevant complications let us take the proposition that all bachelors resident in the London postal area are unmarried. Faced with the question of the truth of this proposition someone might wish to answer the matter by conducting an empirical survey. This would, however, be impossible without clear criteria by which to distinguish bachelors and unmarried people. In the same way it has been maintained that empirical investigation into the teaching of historical thinking is impossible without criteria for distinguishing historical thinking. But granted such criteria, it is a further question whether or not the truth of the proposition depends on empirical investigation. In fact it is immediately clear that empirical investigation cannot but confirm the truth of the proposition as it happens to be logically true. Granted an understanding of the meaning of the terms, it is necessarily the case that the bachelors must be discovered to be unmarried and the empirical investigation is therefore redundant—it cannot but confirm what is logically true. In a similar way there might well be truths about the teaching and learning of historical thinking for which empirical evidence is quite beside the point. We must therefore take a closer look at what is implied logically, not simply in, say, historical thinking, but in coming to think historically.

In the first place such learning involves coming to understand historical propositions, and this in turn involves learning the use of a network of related concepts. It is necessarily the case that any area of knowledge can only be mastered in so far as the use of concepts according to the complex rules that relate them to each other is acquired. Granted this, even the briefest examination of these rules then seems to indicate that it is logically impossible to acquire certain concepts without previously acquiring others; for until the rule-governed use of some terms is achieved, the rule-governed use of others is beyond achievement. In this way the concept of being a bachelor presupposes the concept of marriage, the concept of acceleration presupposes the concept of velocity, the concept of revolution presupposes that of authority. Because of these relations it would seem to be a logical truth that one cannot learn, for instance, about acceleration without first learning about velocity and that therefore any teaching of this area of knowledge must recognize this order of priority in the concepts.

Further it would seem to be a necessary truth about any form of knowledge that there is some ordered sequence to the truths concerned, for the validity of some propositions presupposes the validity of others. If, therefore, the grounds of validity for propositions are to be understood by pupils, the teaching of the area of knowledge must reflect these logical priorities in the order of justification.

But what precisely can we say along these lines about teaching and learning? In the past extravagant claims have often been made to the effect that the problems of teaching a subject are simply problems of logical ordering and that for this, common-sense is all that is necessary beyond a knowledge of the subject itself. Recently there has been a tendency to swing to the opposite extreme with far too much ill-considered appeal to empirical investigation. What is needed is a much more careful examination of what the logically necessary features of areas of knowledge are and, in particular, the extent to which learning a subject involves adherence to what can loosely be called rules of logical order. Once these questions are answered, we can hope to see more useful empirical investigation in this area.

Although there is a strict limit to what can be said in general terms about the logical characteristics of knowledge, it is important to pursue further what is meant by such phrases as logical order, logical method and logical organization, as these play an important part in the now rapidly growing literature on these questions. John Dewey was the first philosopher to use such terms in an educational context. In a celebrated chapter in *Democracy and Education* he distinguishes two methods of teaching. In one, which is referred to as the logical method :

> Pupils began their study of science with texts in which the subject is organized into topics according to the order of the specialist. Technical concepts, with their definitions, are introduced at the outset. Laws are introduced at a very early stage, with at best a few indications of the way in which they were arrived at. The pupils learn a 'science' instead of learning the scientific way of treating the familiar material of ordinary experience.[2]

Of the logical order which such teaching follows he writes:

> Logical order is not a form imposed on what is known; it is the proper form of knowledge as perfected. For it means that the statement of subject matter is of a nature to exhibit to one who understands it the premisses from which it follows and the conclusions to which it points. . . . To the non-expert however this perfected form is a stumbling block. . . . From the standpoint of the learner scientific form is an ideal to be achieved, not a starting point from which to set out.[3]

The other method of teaching which is contrasted with the logical, Dewey refers to as the 'psychological' or chronological method. In this the pupil

> by following in connection with problems selected from the material of ordinary acquaintance, the methods by which scientific men have reached their perfected knowledge, (he) gains independent power to deal with material within his range and avoids the mental confusion and intellectual dictates attendant upon studying matter whose meaning is only symbolic.[4]

Dewey of course made no sharp distinctions between different forms of knowledge, regarding all knowledge as ultimately scientific in character. What he said about the two methods of teaching he therefore thought of very wide application, but so as to avoid complications arising from possible differences between science and other forms of knowledge, I shall here consider these remarks solely in relation to undisputably scientific content. Granted this, there is certainly no doubt which of the two methods of teaching Dewey thought more desirable, and these passages are in fact part of a sustained attack on traditional teaching methods. There have been more extreme attacks which question the existence of a logical order to knowledge at all, but the argument here certainly accepts a logical order of some kind in science. It denies, however, that this is of any significance for the temporal order of events in teaching. Logical order is the end product in scientific understanding. It is a pattern which in teaching is pieced together as one puts together the pattern of a jig-saw. The logical order does not prescribe a series of steps which must be taken. There is a great variety of ways in which the jig-saw can be made up and the same is true in teaching science. The logical order emerges as you go along. The order is not an order of learning or of teaching—it is strictly a logical order not a temporal one. From this it would seem at first sight that the temporal order in teaching, in piecing together the pattern of relations, is for Dewey a matter of the empirical investigation of ways for achieving the pattern. Just what non-logical determination of methods he advocated we will return to later.

The question to be asked first, however, is whether or not the logical features of some form of understanding can simply be regarded as an end product. Is logical order the ideal that Dewey implies? For was it not being suggested earlier that without adherence to the logical characteristics of some form of knowledge even the concepts which that subject uses cannot be grasped? Must not every element of historical knowledge that is taught, necessarily be true to the conceptual structure of that domain? Is it not false therefore to suggest that in developing understanding one can start *anywhere*? And even if logical order is an ideal in some sense, does it not exercise a perpetual control over the method by which it is approached? In a jig-saw the pieces will only fit together one way so as to make up the picture, and the picture has one and only one pattern in the end. Is not knowledge like that?

Obviously if we are to get any further with the problem we must get clearer what is meant by logical order. In doing this, it would seem to be important to recognize that, within any form of knowledge, in, say, a science like physics or in history, at least two separable levels of logical relations can be distinguished, at both of which elements of logical order can arise. There is first the network of relations between particular concepts, relationships by virtue of which meaningful propositions can be formed. In physics the term electron has a certain use. It is only meaningful to say certain things of it, it has to conform to a pattern of relations, and the rules for its use do not permit us to speak of its temperature, its aesthetic qualities or moral value. In religious discourse you cannot use the term God in any old way. He is not an object or being in space and time, he has no extension or colour. He does not act as a human being acts. We must, therefore, stick strictly to the rules for the use of the terms or we do not have meaning. At this level, a domain of knowledge can be said to have a logical grammar, which consists of the rules for the meaningful use of the terms it employs.

Secondly, there is the network of relations between propositions in terms of which valid historical or scientific explanations are formed. The logical analysis of historical or scientific explanations seeks to make plain the criteria for valid explanations in this area. But using these formal criteria in any given case does, of course, presuppose the validity of the propositions in terms of which the explanations are given. Thus the valid explanations in any subject area would seem to depend on the progressive establishment of what I shall call a logical sequence of validated propositions. Any explanation of the repeal of the corn laws in 1846, for instance, must rest on valid propositions about the economic effects of the laws, the famine in Ireland, the political policy of Peel and so on. Similarly, the explanation of the truth that the lengths of the sides of a right-angled triangle satisfy the equation $a^2 = b^2 + c^2$ rests on the truth of a sequence of earlier propositions which, in turn, depends on the axioms of Euclidean geometry.

If then there are two levels at which elements of logical order within a subject can occur, what are the implications of this for teaching? According to the first, any statement to be meaningful must necessarily be true to the logical grammar of the forms of knowledge. Thus the teaching of this form of understanding must always, in all respects, conform to the logical grammar if it is to be intelligible. This logical grammar is therefore no ideal, that might not be attained in some area of understanding. It is implicit in any meaningful statement that belongs to the domain at all, though no one statement will involve more than a very limited number of the rules of such a grammar. Coming to have a new concept involves mastering its often complex logical grammar, and this may involve a long period in which its relation with other concepts and its precise application are being learnt. The concept of a dog is relatively easy to acquire compared with, say, the concept of a matrix or the Christian concept of God. What elements of the logical grammar of a term a person comes to appreciate first may not be important, and many of our very hazy concepts become more refined in time as we acquire the appropriate grammar more thoroughly. In this process of acquiring new concepts a person is heavily dependent on the concepts he has already, but as extremely complex networks of relationships have to be built up in any area of knowledge, it is surely a mistake to think that there is only one order in which all our concepts can be acquired. Certain concepts do undoubtedly depend for their meaning on their relation to certain logically prior concepts. How can one know what a bachelor is unless one can distinguish between men and women, between the married and the unmarried? But how many of our concepts are so clearly and precisely related to others in logical order? In mathematics and the sciences there is frequently such an order, and new concepts are often explicitly composed in this tight way by defining them from other concepts. In many other areas of discourse, in moral and historical matters for instance, such conceptual relations are far from common, the relations are not hierarchical in this way. But in so far as there are elements of conceptual order in any subject the teaching of it must of course fully respect these.

Yet three things must be noted. First, in so far as a child has begun to make the distinctions between men and women and the married and the unmarried, he is, to that extent, able to begin to form the concept of a bachelor. In one sense, learning a concept is not an all or nothing business; for one can know some of the criteria for a concept without knowing them all, and one can begin to build other higher order concepts on this partial knowledge. Secondly, even if this order of conceptual development cannot be intelligibly ignored, yet the teacher does not have to approach the concept of a bachelor by verbal definition. Even if the order of acquisition is logically determined, the means or manner of acquisition is not. Thirdly developments in those subjects which do involve detailed conceptual order, can at times result in conceptual re-organization. New mathematical relations or physical properties can lead to a restructuring of a theory, or system, in which the order in which certain concepts enter is changed.

What emerges from this discussion is that it is necessary in teaching a subject that the logical grammar of its key concepts be understood by the teacher; for otherwise vital elements in what he is teaching are not fully clear to him and not adequately under his control. The logical grammar is something given for him; it is not something he can dispense with and yet continue to teach the subject. In so far as the logical grammar reveals elements of logical order, then the teaching must equally respect these too. What they are in any given subject is a matter for the detailed analysis of the concepts of that subject.

When Dewey objected to teaching methods that conformed to a logical order, if he was referring to order in the logical grammar of the subject, he was surely misdirecting his attack. All teaching must be true to this, if it is to be the teaching of the subject. In part he was certainly objecting to the presentation of science as an ordered body of statements developed from definitions, complaining that the

53

pupils then failed to understand. In this case his criticisms were no doubt warranted, but they must be construed as criticisms of the means and manner in which pupils were expected to acquire new concepts, not of the need for adherence to logical order in the learning of new concepts. To learn a new concept is to learn how to use the concept in relation to others and how to apply it. It is not to learn a series of truths about its relations with other concepts. Learning a concept is like learning to play tennis, not like learning to state the rules and principles that govern play. Equally learning to think scientifically is not learning the formal definitions of terms and a series of true propositions. Indeed such formal learning would seem to be not even a necessary, let alone a sufficient, condition for learning to think scientifically. As far as logical grammar is concerned then, Dewey's criticisms, to be valid, must be regarded as an attack on the manner of adherence to it rather than the necessity for such adherence.

But what of the question of the logical sequence of a subject? If, to be meaningful, the teaching must be true to the logical grammar, must it not, if the validity of the explanations and theories is to be communicated, follow a logical sequence in establishing the appropriate propositions? In so far as it is a body of knowledge one is teaching, and not just a body of beliefs, is there not an order in which its true propositions must be presented?

That there is *one* such logical sequence of the truths in any domain of knowledge must surely be rejected immediately. Even in mathematics the existence of alternative sets of axioms for any given system is now common knowledge. In the sciences equally, alternative ways of demonstrating scientific laws are a common phenomenon, and the discovery of whole new orders of demonstration is not unheard of. There is, therefore, no one logical sequence in which the truths of a subject must be communicated, even in those subjects which seem most strictly sequential. Maybe a great deal of the trouble here has sprung from a confusion between the two forms of logical order that are being distinguished, those elements of order in the logical grammar and those in what is here being called logical sequence. Once a strict distinction is drawn between them it can be seen that, though adherence to any elements of order within the logical grammar is necessary for intelligibility in teaching, no such adherence to any one logical sequence is demanded in the same way.

But if the idea of a domain of knowledge having *one* implicit logical sequence of truths must be rejected, this is not to say that a subject can be taught without attention to *some* appropriate logical sequence. In any teaching of a form of knowledge the question of the justification of the propositions, explanations and theories is vital, and pupils need to appreciate, not only why these particular elements are true, but the kind of justification there is in general within this form of knowledge. Without this one cannot be said to have taught this subject in any significant sense. The teaching must therefore involve the development of some logical sequence appropriate to the subject, that is it must involve the development of an ordered body of truths according to the criteria for validating historical explanations or mathematical theorems.

From this it is tempting to conclude that the subject must be taught so as to build up the truths in strict order, following in temporal sequence some particular logical sequence. In reply to this, it must first be remembered that logical sequence is not an order necessary to the intelligibility of the propositions, as elements of order within logical grammar are. It is only when one is concerned with questions of validity and justification that this matter of logical sequence ever arises. Further, it is surely a mistake to think that explanations are seen to be valid only when the elements are pieced together by a temporal following of a logical sequence. To grasp a valid proof or explanation is to recognize, in the end, an overall pattern of logical relations between propositions that satisfy certain criteria. To insist that this sequence of truths can only be grasped as truths, by temporally building on previously adequately established truths, is to take the characteristics of what is to be achieved as an end for the characteristics of the process by which the end is achieved. Maybe the analogy with a jig-saw puzzle is valuable here. In a valid explanation the elements must fit together as if to establish the pattern of the puzzle; but there is no one temporal order in which the pieces must be fitted together to produce the pattern.

A perpetual problem in teaching formal geometry illustrates this point; for pupils often find it difficult to grasp that the temporal sequence of the steps by which a geometrical problem is solved is rarely the logical sequence of steps laid out in the formal proof. To solve the problem one must somehow complete the vital logical sequence; the proof simply sets out the established sequence for all to see. To do a jig-saw puzzle is to somehow complete the picture which is then clear for all to see; but one does not have to start piecing together from the bottom left-hand corner or even the edges. Thus though the significant teaching of a subject must establish at least some logical sequence distinctive of that subject, this is not a demand that the order of teaching temporally follow along logically prescribed lines. The question of temporal sequence is a matter to be decided on empirical grounds, once the logical sequence to be established is clearly determined by the teacher.

Having said this, however, it must not be forgotten that because questions of logical grammar and intelligibility can to some extent be separated from questions of logical sequence and justification, a great deal of so called teaching can, of course, be conducted without much concern for any logical sequence. It is possible to have a great deal of scientific information and little idea of even the kind of justification on which it rests. How far teaching of this kind is defensible is a debatable and a non-philosophical question. To many, such teaching is not in any sense describable as teaching the subject; for the distinctive forms of justification and the criteria for truth in the domain are elements that are necessarily part of the form of knowledge, even if these prescribe no one logical sequence and no one teaching order. But that a great deal of such instruction goes on at present in schools cannot be denied.

In so far, then, as Dewey was objecting to teaching methods conforming to a logical sequence his criticisms are valid; for logical sequence must not be confused with a temporal learning sequence. His comments are, however, misleading in so far as they imply that there is in science, or any other form of knowledge, any one logical sequence. There are, in fact, many such sequences, similar in kind and exemplifying the distinctive logical characteristics of valid explanations in the domain. Further, in so far as his comments suggest that science can be taught without necessarily aiming at any logical sequence, and his views have sometimes been interpreted as implying that the logical 'ideal' of science is only important for would-be professional scientists, they would seem to be dangerously mistaken. Both the method he advocates and the method he rejects must, to be the teaching of science, be true to all the logical features of science, and thus involve the development of some logical sequence.

Some of Dewey's disciples certainly took him to be saying that the outcome of learning can be a personal or 'psychological' organization of knowledge rather than a logical organization appropriate for research specialists. Why cannot knowledge be organized round an interest in some practical activity for instance, rather than as a theoretical pursuit? Bode took this distinction between logical and psychological organizations to be worth the argument that the latter are of more limited value than the former.[5] But what is this a distinction between exactly? If what has been argued earlier is correct there is no non-logical organization of knowledge; the logical features are those which necessarily characterize knowledge. The contrast cannot, therefore, be between logical organization and non-logical organization. What is more, if someone acquires knowledge of any kind, this is necessarily a personal psychological matter. A person cannot have non-psychologically organized knowledge. The contrast can, therefore, only be one between the different organizations of knowledge which we present to children, organizations respecting both the logical features of the knowledge concerned and the necessity for the pupils to individually come to acquire this knowledge. In the end the distinction would seem to come down to whether or not we should teach as school subjects such distinct, logically cohesive disciplines as mathematics, physics and history, or rather teach second-order organizations of knowledge which we compose of elements from these primary divisions, such units as 'the neighbourhood', 'power' or 'the seventeenth-century mind'. Maybe the interest of pupils is more easily aroused when we organize what we teach in such second-order fields and they therefore learn more effectively. But there is here no different *logical* organization of knowledge as such. The pupils' grasp of the meaning and validity of all the elements in such a second-order organization depends on their appreciating these elements as logically related to other elements within the primary divisions of knowledge.[6] The distinction here then is a concern about what is taught but not one that turns on logical questions. Whether or not we should teach according to the primary divisions of knowledge or according to second-order units is a matter that cannot be settled on philosophical grounds.

It might be expected that Dewey's rejection of what he calls the logical teaching method would be complemented by his advocating the empirical investigation of teaching and that his 'psychological' approach would be based squarely on the results of this. In fact this is not what he does; for the method he advocates, though justified to some extent by practical experience with children, rests primarily on assumptions as theoretical and doctrinaire as those behind the method he rejects. Instead of following some logical sequence Dewey suggests that teaching methods should follow the method that lies behind scientific investigation and discovery. This method he elaborates in a series of stages in which from a 'genuine situation of experience', a problem develops 'as a stimulus to thought' about which information and observations are collected, a solution is formulated and tests for validity are carried out.[7]

Dewey advocated this method for reasons connected with his own distinctive views of logic and his pragmatic theory of truth. He considered the methods of enquiry found in science to be the foundation of all knowledge and thus wanted above all that pupils should master, not a subject, but the fundamentals of scientific method as he saw these. This meant that they must learn what is involved in enquiry by conducting enquiries themselves. Certainly *if* we want to teach skill in a methodology, we shall wish pupils to practise such methods; for a skill is necessarily something learnt in this way. This is but to say that the teaching methods employed must be activities designed to produce the relevant learning. But if we take a wider view of what is to be learnt, even within science, we may well question whether the methodology of scientific discovery, assuming there is such a thing, should provide the basis of a general teaching method. Certainly discovery is one way of learning, but it is not the only way, and whether or not it is in general the best way, is an open question that Dewey never seems to consider. Whether or not there is a methodology of scientific discovery and, if there is, whether Dewey is right in his characterizations of it, are also large questions on which there is room for a great divergence of opinion. If, however, we consider other areas of knowledge than science, there would seem little reason to think that scientific methodology can solve our problems of teaching method. And to take in each area the methodology of the subject as a paradigm for the methodology of teaching the subject, is either to confuse methods which are in many ways concerned with achieving different ends, or to prejudge matters which can only be determined on the basis of much empirical evidence. It is, to say the least, ironical that Dewey, in his desire that pupils should acquire a problem-solving outlook, was himself as guilty of pre-judging some of the very empirical questions of teaching method as the advocators of the logical method he so condemned.

In this paper I have tried to maintain that :

(*a*) A subject like physics or history has a logical grammar which governs the meaningful use of the terms of the subject. All teaching of the subject must necessarily conform to the rules of this grammar or it will not be the teaching of the subject at all.

(*b*) In some cases this logical grammar involves an order of terms such that the meaning of certain terms presupposes the meaning of others. In this case the teaching of the subject must of course respect these elements of logical order.

(*c*) An understanding of the meaning of terms is not to be thought of as necessarily built up in strict order as a wall is built with bricks. Concepts are acquired by learning the complex use of terms in relation to other terms and their application in particular cases. A subject's logical grammar and the order within it must be respected in all teaching methods, but this leaves a vast area in which experimental investigations about the effectiveness of different methods can and must be carried out.

(*d*) Any subject like history or physics or mathematics is based on the use of certain logical principles in terms of which the explanation and theories distinctive of the subject are validated. I refer here to the logic of historical explanations, of scientific explanations, mathematical proofs and so on. These principles, however, do not determine any *one* particular logical sequence for the propositions. Any teaching method for the subject must therefore respect the fundamental logical principles without which no understanding of the distinctive form of validity peculiar to this subject is possible. This means that *some* logical sequence of propositions using these logical principles must emerge in the teaching of the subject. There are alternative logical sequences which may be taken and advances in knowledge often suggest new sequences.

(*e*) To say that some logical sequence must emerge in the teaching of the subject is not to say that the teaching must follow that sequence in temporal order. It is an order that is understood to hold together in the end. It does not have to be built up in any one way.

(*f*) The logical grammar involved and the various possibilities for the logical sequence to be used, are matters for determination by an analysis of the subject to be taught, not for empirical investigation. How far these logical features do determine the teaching of a subject, and areas within the subject, can be worked out in detail only in terms of the specific content that is to be taught.

(g) It is only when the fullest logical analysis of what is involved in teaching a subject has been carried out, that the profitable empirical investigation of methods can be conducted. How much further we can get by general philosophical discussion of the kind in this paper is not clear. What is clear, however, is that, if our teaching methods are not to remain the hit and miss business they are at the moment, the careful, detailed analysis of the logical features of exactly what we wish to teach must be pursued far more thoroughly than it has been thus far. More philosophical clarity can, of its own, certainly help us to produce more effective and more rationally defensible teaching methods.

## NOTES

1. Hirst, P. H., 'Liberal Education and the Nature of Knowledge', in Archambault, R. D. (ed.), *Philosophical Analysis and Education* (Routledge and Kegan Paul, 1965).
2. Dewey, J., *Democracy and Education* (Macmillan, N.Y., 1916), p. 257.
3. Dewey, J., pp. 256–7.
4. Dewey, J., p. 258.
5. Bode, B. H., *Modern Educational Theories* (Vintage Books), Ch. 3.
6. See Hirst, P. H., op. cit.
7. Dewey, J., p. 192.

# CONDITIONING AND LEARNING

## Godfrey Vesey

(I) Is being conditioned to do something learning to do it? (II) If not, could we have been conditioned to do the sort of things we have in fact learnt to do?

## [I]

The first of these questions must be answered affirmatively if the criterion of learning having taken place is that someone has acquired, otherwise than simply by maturation, an ability to respond to a situation in a new way. Most modern psychologists do, in fact, accept this as the criterion of learning having taken place. They may talk, not of 'response', but of 'behaviour', but they mean by this neither what is ordinarily meant ('behave' being opposed to 'misbehave'), nor even what one might reasonably suppose them to mean ('behaviour' referring to a person's actions, like kicking a football, as opposed to mere responses, like the knee-jerk reflex). If there is any opposition at all implied in psychologists' use of the term 'behaviour' it would seem to depend on views about the proper manner of psychological investigation (not by introspection) and the proper level of psychological explanation (not the level of physiological explanation). Thus, behaviour is publicly observable, and is 'molar'.

I shall not beg the first question by adopting the psychologists' use of the word 'learn'. Instead I shall try to answer both questions in terms of what we ordinarily mean by 'learning' and by 'doing things'. Furthermore I shall not, in my answer, go beyond what can be said on the basis of these ordinary meanings. I shall consider only whether it makes sense to talk of our abilities being acquired by a process of being conditioned, not whether they could in fact be so acquired. In other words, my investigation is a purely conceptual one, as befits a philosopher.

What, then, do we ordinarily mean when we say that someone has learnt to do something?

We are less likely to fall into dogmatism if we develop our conceptual distinctions against the background of some fairly life-like situations. Let us consider three such situations. One of them might occur in a primary school, another in a technical school, and the third in a University psychological laboratory.

A. A little girl acquires the ability to skip with a skipping rope to music. At first she sees the teacher doing it, and tries to do the same, but with no success; she cannot even skip, never mind skip in time with the music. The teacher holds her by the hands, facing her, and does the jump and rebound movements in time with the music. The little girl picks it up and can soon do the jump and rebound movements by herself. Then come the arm and wrist movements. Perhaps it takes a little time for these to become co-ordinated with the jump and rebound movements. Finally, the skipping rope. The teacher holds her breath : has the little girl acquired the knack or not? Yes, she has, thanks to her natural muscular sense and the right sort of coaching. With some children, even though they may be brighter than the others when it comes to the theory of movement, it is always an uphill battle. But to this little girl it came fairly easily. She was naturally rhythmical, naturally well co-ordinated.

B. A boy is being taught about the internal combustion engine, with the aid of diagrams and an actual motor car engine. He learns how one can start the engine using a handle, and also how one can start it using a starting-motor powered by a battery. He thus acquires the ability to start suitably equipped engines in either of these two ways.

C. In a psychological laboratory a student is enabled 'to obtain voluntary control of what is for most persons an involuntary reflex'.[1]

> In one experiment of this nature, the pupil of a man's eye was trained to contract at command. In the first stage of training, a bell was rung immediately before a light was shone in his eyes. After some trials, the sound of the bell alone would cause his pupil to contract. Then the man was instructed to close and open the circuit for both bell and light by closing and opening his hand at the verbal command of the experimenter. In this way verbal command became connected through the hand movement and the sound of the bell to the pupilary reflex. The next step in the experiment was to eliminate both the hand movement and the bell. This left only the vocal instruction of the experimenter as the conditioned stimulus, and the man's pupil now contracted to it alone. The last stage of the experiment consisted in having

the subject himself repeat the verbal instructions, first aloud, then in a whisper and finally subvocally. Each of these forms of stimulation, it was found, could become the condition for the contraction of the pupil. So the man could, at the end of the experiment, effectively command his own pupilary reflex, and this ability was still present fifteen days later, without practice in the meantime.

Let us begin with the question : Is learning *how* to do something always a matter of learning *that* doing so-and-so brings about such-and-such an effect? Consider case B—the boy who learns how to start engines. Clearly the boy could pass on what he had learnt by word of mouth. Engines can be started either by turning the handle, or by using a starter-motor. But what about case A? Suppose the little girl is asked how she skips in time with the music. She can say 'Like this', and demonstrate her ability. But this is *showing,* not *saying,* how she does it. Indeed, it is not very clear what, other than a demonstration, can be meant by 'how she does it' in this situation. It is not as if she has to do something else to make herself skip as the boy has to turn the handle to make the engine start. We may give a meaning to 'how she does it' in terms of what goes on in her body : the impulses in the afferent and efferent nerves, the muscle-contractions and expansions, their timing in relation to one another, and so on. But we would be regarding the little girl in rather an odd light if we said that these 'goings-on' were things she *does.* It would be like saying that digesting her breakfast is something she does. In a sense it is, but it is not the sense in which eating her breakfast is something she does.

But cannot something be said on the following lines? For the little girl's feet to be off the ground when the skipping rope is in the 'down' position she has to be beginning her jump when it is in the horizontal position. To skip successfully she has to learn *that* beginning her jump when the skipping rope is horizontal has the effect that the rope passes under her feet.

I do not find this very convincing. For one thing, she could have learnt this and still not be able to time her jump. But I am not convinced that learning this is even a necessary, never mind a sufficient, condition of being able to skip. Perhaps I can make my point— which is that knowing *how* is not reducible to knowing *that*—more convincingly with examples of unlearnt abilities. Suppose I am asked how I clench my fist, or suck. A schoolboy may be told that what he is doing when he sucks milk up a straw is creating a lower pressure at one end of the straw than there is at the other. This is the scientific explanation of the milk going up the straw. Similarly I may be told that what I am doing when I clench my fist is contracting certain muscles. But people can suck, and clench their fists, without knowing anything about pressures or muscles.

It might be said that acquiring the ability to do something, if it does not involve learning *that* (e.g. learning that doing so-and-so brings about such-and-such an effect), is not *learning* how to do it. The idea would be that learning is essentially an intellectual process. This idea does not seem to me to be in accord with our ordinary concept of learning. For better or worse we are not pure intellects. It seems to me desirable to retain a concept of learning which reflects this fact. There is what might be called 'purely bodily learning'. It plays a large part in the gymnast's skill, a smaller part in the surgeon's skill, but is essential to both.

Before going on to other questions about learning how to do something, let us notice some respects in which case C is like, and unlike, cases A and B.

(*i*) In case C—the pupil-contracting case—a stimulus (the subvocal command) produces a response (the contraction of the pupil). Case B—the engine-starting one—can also be described in stimulus-response terminology : a stimulus (turning the handle) produces a response (the engine starts). But the cases are not quite analogous. If the subvocal command is to bring about the pupil-contracting response a connection between the two has first to be induced. It was, in fact, induced by the stimulus-substitution procedure known as 'conditioning' (or, to be more precise, 'Pavlovian' or 'classical' conditioning). But it is conceivable that it should have been induced in other ways—perhaps simply by implanting a nerve between the speech muscles and the pupil-contracting muscles. This would be comparable to implanting a starter-motor and a starting button in the car, so that the engine responded to a stimulus other than manual cranking.

(*ii*) In case B the boy turns the handle, or presses the starting button, to make the engine start. It is the engine, not he, who starts. The pupil-contracting case seems different. The pupil which contracts is the pupil of the person who gives the subvocal command : it is part of him in a way in which the car, though the boy may own it, is not part of him. And yet the situation is not like that in case A. The person has to do something else (giving the subvocal command) to make his pupil contract. The little girl does not have to do something else to make her skipping occur. She simply skips.

Now let us ask ourselves: Does the man in case C learn to contract the pupils of his eyes? If we gave a negative answer to this question it would, I think, be for one, or both, of two reasons.

(*a*) In the sense in which skipping is something the little girl does, contracting the pupils of his eyes is not something the man does. He *makes* the pupils of his eyes contract. The fact that he can make them contract by a subvocal command, instead of by shining a light in them, does not mean that he contracts them *at will*. He no more contracts them at will than the boy starts the car at will (i.e. without turning the handle, or pushing the starting button). Strictly speaking, a person can be said to have learnt to do only what he does at will. Otherwise, what he has learnt is what to do to bring about a desired result. When we loosely speak of someone having learnt to start a car what we mean is that he has learnt what to do to get it to start.

(*b*) Whatever one does, in learning to do something, must itself really be something one *does,* something in which one is actively engaged. It cannot be simply something which happens to one. But 'being conditioned' is precisely not something one does. It is something which is done to one—either by oneself or, as is usually the case, by someone else.

Are these good reasons for denying that the man in case C learns to contract the pupils of his eyes?

I feel less sure about the second of them, so perhaps it would be as well to begin with that one.

There would seem to be two distinct things we may have in mind when we say of someone that he is learning, or has learnt, to do something. One is his acquiring the ability in question; the other is his having done something to acquire it. Are both these things necessary? Can a person be said to be learning to do something (for instance, to do a backward somersault) if whatever he is doing does not result in his acquiring the desired ability? Can a person be said to have learnt to do X if there is nothing he did previously which was 'learning to do X'?

I am inclined to give an affirmative answer to the last but one of these questions, and a negative answer to the last. But I do not think the precedent for these answers, in our everyday use of 'learn', is very strong. What we mean by 'learn' depends so much on the context, and even on the tense. In most contexts 'Has he learnt?' means 'Has he acquired the ability yet?'; but in some it means 'Did he acquire the ability by learning?'. In most contexts 'Is he learning?' means 'Is he engaged in the activity of learning?'; but in some it means 'Is he in fact acquiring the ability?'. It is because the word 'learn' may be used in these different but related ways that I do not feel confident about saying that an ability acquired by being conditioned is not an ability acquired by learning. It all depends on which of the features of the use of 'learn' one has in mind. I do not propose to legislate that we should always have both in mind.

This leaves us with the first supposed reason for denying that the man in case C learns to contract the pupils of his eyes—namely, that contracting the pupils of his eyes is not something he does, and hence not something he learns to do.

Is the implied distinction valid? If the pupils of someone's eyes contract through something he does how can it reasonably be denied that he contracts them? The experiment is described as one in which a man is enabled 'to obtain voluntary control of what is for most persons an involuntary reflex'. It can reasonably be denied, it was suggested, because contracting them is not something he does 'at will'. What does this mean?

One answer which, it might be thought, could hardly be wrong, is that it means that the immediate cause of their contraction is not his *willing* them to contract. This either gets us nowhere (willing them to contract = contracting them at will) or invites our acceptance of a new concept which has some of the features of the ordinary concept of action but lacks others (for instance, one cannot learn to 'will', or learn which 'acts of will' cause which movements). I reject this invitation, and accordingly say that to say that a person can do something 'at will' is not to say anything positive but is to *deny* that to do it he must do something else. To say that a person can do X at will is to deny that there is something else, Y, he must do if he is to do X, his doing Y being instrumental in his doing X. Thus, if a person can make his hair stand on end, but only by, say, brushing it upwards, he cannot stand it on end at will. And if a person can make the pupils of his eyes contract, but only by shining a light in them, or giving himself a subvocal command, he cannot contract them at will.

But has the man who has been conditioned learnt nothing? He may, indeed, have learnt nothing; for it is conceivable that he may not know that giving himself the subvocal command now has the effect that his pupils contract. On the other hand, he may know this, in which case we can say that he has learnt that he can now make his pupils contract in this new way. But he has not learnt to contract them, in the sense of now being able to contract them at will.

To sum up, the process of being conditioned, as it is exemplified in case C, is not itself an instance of someone learning something, either learning to do something, or learning that doing so-and-so brings about such-and-such an effect.

[II]

In the first half of this chapter I have taken conditioning to be a process of stimulus-substitution, whereby a reflex becomes associated with a new stimulus. This led to my giving a negative answer to the question 'Is being conditioned to do something learning to do it?' It would also lead to my giving a negative answer to the question, 'Could we have been conditioned to do the sort of things we have in fact learnt to do?'. But the term 'conditioning' may be used for less restricted processes, such as that sometimes called 'operant' conditioning to distinguish it from 'Pavlovian' or 'classical' conditioning. In this half of the chapter I propose to consider such processes. I shall begin with a very general question. For the question 'Could we have been conditioned, in any sense, to do the sort of things we have in fact learnt to do?' to have an affirmative answer, this very general question must have an affirmative answer. The question is 'Could we have been *caused* to do the sort of things we have in fact learnt to do?'

I want, in particular, to consider an argument for a negative answer to this question, which is based on what philosophers have recently been saying on such related topics as 'intention', 'motivation' and 'free action'. I shall call it the 'Action/Happening' argument, and formulate my own version of it.

Observing a small child occupied with clay and paper and scissors and matchsticks, I may ask 'What is he doing?' This may meet with the reply, 'Can't you see?' The answer to this is that there is a perfectly good sense in which 'what he is doing' may be in doubt when what is to be seen is not in doubt. If we ask him, he might have said 'I'm making a giraffe', but that this was what he was doing may not be obvious even when he has completed his task.

On the other hand, it might be said, I can see what he is doing in that I can see that he is cutting paper with scissors, pushing matchsticks into a lump of clay, etc. (These are things he does which are instrumental to his achieving his aim.)

In the light of what can be seen, it would, of course, be ridiculous to deny that the child was cutting paper with scissors. But it is not difficult to imagine cases in which even a description (in terms of what a person is doing) which seems not to go any way beyond what can be seen, can be false. He may not be doing anything; what we mistakenly interpret as an action may be convulsive, involuntary movements (as in Parkinson's disease), which he may even not know are taking place.

To the question 'What is he doing?' we have so far distinguished three replies. The first is in terms of his aim. He is making a giraffe. The second is in terms of what he is doing to achieve his aim. He is cutting paper with scissors, etc. The third is a denial that he is doing anything. It's Parkinson's disease. A fourth possible reply is in terms of a result of what he is doing in either of the first two senses, but a result to produce which was not his aim. For instance, he is making a mess (unwanted paper on the floor, etc.). Now although it was not his aim to make a mess he may have known that he could not make a giraffe without making a mess. In that case he will be 'morally' as well as causally responsible for the mess. If he did not know he would make a mess we say he made it unintentionally. If he did know he would make a mess we say neither that he made it intentionally nor that he made it unintentionally, but that although he knew he was bound to make a mess that was not his aim.

When animals, and particularly when human beings, are involved, it is natural for us to describe what we see in terms of what they are doing in the first two senses distinguished. In certain circumstances—for instance, when we are giving evidence in a court of law—we may be asked to report only on what we saw happen. It is then that the distinction is brought home to us between what is objectively there to be seen and our interpretation of it in terms of people's aims and what they do to achieve them. The importance of this distinction, in this context, is that two different interpretations may be possible of the same happening, one meaning that the accused person is guilty of an offence, the other that he is not guilty. It is up to the jury, not the people called to give evidence, to decide which interpretation is correct.

The first main point in the 'Action/Happening' argument is that a description of what is to be seen, *qua* happening, may be compatible with either of two incompatible descriptions of what is to be seen, *qua* what a person is doing. Another way of putting this would be to say that the concept of what a person is doing is not a concept of what is publicly observable: the person concerned is the final authority on what he is doing in a way in which no one is the final authority when it comes to what is happening or what is the result of what he is doing. The significance of this for causal explanation is that we know what it is to explain, causally, what happens, but it is not so clear what can be meant by causal explanation of what a person is doing.

One line that might be taken is to say that the causal explanation of someone's making a giraffe is his having the aim of making a giraffe. If this seems to be merely a linguistic device to retain the applicability of the concept of causation, we can talk, not of 'aims', but of 'intentions' or, better still, of 'desires'. He would not have made a giraffe unless he had felt a desire to make one. The point of talking of 'desires' instead of 'aims' is that desires may seem separated from (and therefore possible causes of) actions, in a way aims do not. Desires may even be locatable bodily feelings, as in the case of hunger, the desire for food.

The question is: If we spoke of desires, intentions, or aims as causes of actions, would we be explaining actions as we can explain happenings? This leads to the second main point in the 'Action/Happening' argument. It is that whereas we can individuate the cause of a happening independently of its effects we cannot do this for the alleged causes of actions. Aims, intentions, and desires are essentially directed to some end, and cannot be individuated independently of that end. Therefore, whatever else they may be, they are not what might be called 'Humean' causes. (Hume held that if $C$ is the cause of $E$ then one cannot say, prior to experience of their conjunction, anything about $E$ from a consideration of $C$ alone.)

Another line that might be taken is to assimilate the question 'What is he doing?' (in the sense in which he is the final authority) to the question 'To what end or goal are the observed changes directed?' (in the sense in which, say, a psychologist with knowledge of psychological 'defence mechanisms' may be better placed than the person in whom the changes are taking place, to answer the question). Once this step is taken, as it has been by those psychologists who speak of 'purposive behaviour', 'goal-directed behaviour', 'means-end-readiness', etc. the report of the person concerned, as to what he is doing, loses its unique significance. An honest report will still be valuable, but it will no longer be regarded as settling the question. The person can be mistaken about what he is 'doing', about what his 'desires' are, and so on.

The advantage of this assimilation is, of course, that broadly the same kinds of explanation can be used for humans as are used for animals. The difference becomes an inconsequential one : to some extent humans know, and can say, to what goals their 'behaviour' is directed. There is an 'epiphenomenon' of consciousness. The disadvantage of the assimilation arises from its being our own actions which are reduced to 'behaviour'. We, as agents, are deposed, deprived of our freedom, made subservient to alien, blind, behaviouristic men, with wants replaced by needs, and private aims by publicly-ascertained goals.

All this having been said we must now return to the question : Is the 'Action/Happening' argument for a negative answer to the question 'Could we have been caused to do the sort of things we have in fact learnt to do?' valid? Attractive though the argument may be, I do not think it is valid. Its seeming validity arises from the equation, in the formulation of the question, of the ability to do something, with doing it. What is acquired by learning is an ability to do something. This is what is meant by talk of someone having learnt to do something. The question is, really, 'Could there be a causal explanation of our having acquired the sort of abilities we have in fact acquired by learning?' Once the question is reformulated in this way, the answer becomes obvious : the fact that an ability is acquired by learning is as compatible with an account being given of the conditions under which it is acquired as would be its being acquired by maturation or in any other way.

Now, to the question 'Could we have been conditioned to do the sort of things we have in fact learnt to do?' we earlier gave the answer 'No, if conditioning is taken to be a process of stimulus-substitution, whereby a reflex becomes associated with a new stimulus, for reflexes are not action.' The answer we have just given to the question 'Could there be a causal explanation of our having acquired the sort of abilities we have in fact acquired by learning?', however,

raises the possibility of a different answer. It is: 'Yes, if by our having been conditioned is meant no more than that we acquire the
abilities in question under certain conditions, and not under others.'
The term 'conditioning' is not used by psychologists in this very
wide sense. It is, however, sometimes used in a sense which is less
restricted than that in which conditioning is a process of stimulus-
substitution. This is the 'operant conditioning' to which I referred
earlier. It is called 'conditioning' because of certain features it shares
with classical conditioning. In both, responses are 'stamped in' by
providing the subjects with things thought of by the experimenter
as rewards. Such responses are said to be 'reinforced'. They differ in
that in operant conditioning the response is not a reflex, but is a
movement initiated by the subject. An example may make this clear.
Suppose a hungry animal is in a box which contains no food but
does contain three levers which it can press with its feet. On its tour
of the box it discovers that these levers can be pressed. When it
presses the right-hand one a pellet of food drops from a hole in the
roof. When it presses the other two it is given a mild electric shock.
After this has happened a number of times the animal goes straight
to the right-hand lever (if food has more reinforcing effect than
electric shocks).

Operant conditioning is sometimes called 'instrumental' conditioning, but this is a misnomer if it is taken to mean that the subject
recognizes either that, or how, its response is instrumental in its
obtaining the 'reward'. In so far as the subject does recognize these
things, more is involved than simply its being conditioned.

The conclusion to be drawn from this is that if by 'conditioning'
is meant *no more than* the 'stamping in' of a response then at least
those abilities which do involve 'knowledge that' cannot be acquired
by anyone simply by a process of being conditioned. Whether what
I earlier called 'purely bodily learning' can be explained in terms of
conditioning is another matter. In the example I used to introduce
the notion of 'purely bodily learning'—the little girl learning to
skip in time with music—there were certain features present (not
least of which is that she saw what had to be done, and somebody
doing it) which play no part in strict conditioning. How important
such features are is a matter to be settled by the scientist, not by the
philosopher.

## NOTES

1. This phrase, and the account which follows, are taken from E. G. Boring, H. S. Langfeld, and H. P. Weld (Eds.) *Foundations of Psychology* (1948), pp. 44–5.

5

# THE CONCEPT OF PLAY
R. F. Dearden

## I. INTRODUCTION

'Play', educationalists often assert, 'is a serious business,' though at least on the face of it this is precisely what play is not. Is this perhaps just a deliberately paradoxical way of drawing our attention to the psychological, or even to the metaphysical, significance of play? Certainly there is a mass of psychological theorizing and observation available on this subject, while if we view play as does Froebel, through the spectacles of German Idealist philosophy, then it will be seen to have a metaphysical significance too. And if play can be viewed as having a significance as unexpected as that, then perhaps the assertion of its seriousness is not so much an interesting new fact about it as a moral demand that adults be less casual in the notice which they give to it.

But more puzzlement than this is occasioned in education by play. Parents and even children may be perplexed about it. Having learned from their parents to frame their expectations of school under the aspect of 'work', children are often surprised and some-times disappointed to find that on going to school at five nothing very different may be expected of them from what they are accus-tomed elsewhere to regard as 'play'. How could that be appro-priate in a school, a place to which one goes in order to be taught? No such perplexity arises where the pre-infant, nursery stage is con-cerned, since there never was a tradition of 'work' at that stage the memory of which could be the cause of reactionary discontent, and in fact the whole period is regarded by the more traditionally-minded as an educational write-off. Even if the appropriateness of play at the nursery stage is not disputed, the value of it may be. It may be questioned how play could possibly be an *educational process*, and the claim of nursery school mistresses to be 'teachers' may be seriously disputed.

73

It is plain, therefore, that in thinking about play in relation to education quite a number of puzzling questions raise themselves. For example, in what sense, if any, *could* play properly be called 'serious'? How do the various psychological theories of play relate to our ordinary concept of it? Could it be claimed at all defensibly to have a place in schooling once the nursery stage has been passed? And could the supervision of play possibly be regarded as 'teaching'? But logically prior to all these questions is the conceptual question : What is 'play'? Perhaps if we could get a little clearer about that, then the answer to some of the other questions just raised would be rather more obvious. The first task then must be to try to demarcate and characterize those among our activities that we have in mind when we talk about 'play'.

At first glance, it might seem a simple enough task to say what play is, but anyone who thinks so ought to try it. The Concise Oxford Dictionary gives twenty-four separately numbered sets of entries for the verb alone, and a multitude of idioms has developed round the word. A detailed linguistic inquiry might reveal all sorts of interesting analogies and affinities of one such idiom to another, but that sort of inquiry is no task for the philosopher. What he has to do is to try to pick out as best he can what seems to be the central concept round which these varied shifting meanings circle, and then count himself fortunate if he can set up criteria for the application of this concept which are at least sufficiently precise for his purpose.

## 2. FACT AND IDEAL

If the concept of play is to be demarcated at all clearly, then we must, to begin with, avoid the tendency which exists in some educational writing to restrict the concept just to those activities which fit into a certain *ideal* of child development. In this respect, 'play' shares with 'growth' a persistent ambiguity in such writing which leaves it always uncertain whether it is children as they are or children as they ought to be who are being described. Hitler grew, and play can be spiteful and destructive, yet clearly when play or growth are eulogized it is neither dictatorship nor nastiness that we are being encouraged to foster. This ambiguity between fact and ideal in the theory of child development has existed there ever since Rousseau launched it with a word which is the very paradigm of ambiguity : the word 'nature'. From Rousseau to the present day, many writers on child development have viewed themselves as describing something called 'education according to nature', or some variant on this such as 'natural learning'.[1] But there are at least three senses of 'nature' being run together when it is said that play is 'natural'.

The first sense is that of being spontaneous: the child bubbles into play activity, it does not have to be prompted in him, and this spontaneous activity is regarded as being naturally good, at least until the child has been corrupted by adults or by his environment. The second sense, especially dear to Rousseau, is that of being opposed to the artificialities of social convention and stems from the view that the simple life of the countryside is the best life for man. Dressing children in hussars' uniforms and regarding them as manikins are far from 'natural' in this sense. The third sense of 'nature' is that of the 'essence' of something. This notion is dominant in Froebel's view of play, where it is part of a metaphysical scheme which has its origins ultimately in Aristotle.[2] It implies a perfection of form towards which something is developing. On this view, living things, including children, are seen as having in themselves the seeds, as it were, of a potential unfolding and perfect flowering. Thus Froebel requires a kindergarten, or 'child-garden', where the essential nature of the child can be unfolded without stunting or distortion, whereas Rousseau describes Emile, at twelve years of age, as seeming (to the non-metaphysician that is) to be just a rough, vulgar little boy, whereas in fact he has unfolded 'the perfection of childhood'.

As a matter of history, children have benefited enormously from this confusion between fact and ideal. Through the reforms thus initiated children's play has come to be seen with fresh eyes, and educational psychology, which cannot get started without there being a prior conception of what is of educational value,[3] has been switched onto the investigation of children's play. But if we are ever to achieve clarity in discussions about play, the confusion between fact and ideal, between children as they actually are and children as we would have them be, must be dispelled. To some extent, the very research inspired by the reformers has itself served to dispel this confusion, especially the study of children's activities which starts from the less optimistic premises of psychoanalytic theory, so that a less value-loaded use of 'natural' is now more common. But to say that play is 'natural', in the sense just of something which can be counted on to appear, does nothing to explicate what is meant by 'play', though it may help to explain the forms which it takes. The upshot of this, therefore, is that the concept of 'play' is not to be equated with an ideal activity ambiguously described as 'natural'. Rough, quarrelsome, destructive, uncreative and unseemly play are all still 'play', and an adequate analysis of the concept must cover such cases quite as readily as others which may evoke in us smiles of approval.

### 3. CHILDREN'S ACTIVITIES

A useful next step will be to cite some examples of children's play, and to add some examples of activities of other sorts as a reminder that a 'child's interest' is *not* 'all in play', as Caldwell Cook once asserted it to be.[4] For a first example of children's play, we can take make-believe, in which the roles of adults and others are assumed and acted out. Thus children play at schools, mothers and fathers, nurses and patients, and so on. We might call this 'playing at' something or other. A second kind of play, 'playing with', centres round the manipulation of objects rather than acting out people's roles, as in play with sand, water, clay, bricks, soldiers, jig-saws and construction kits. As with role play, so with object play, representation can be as loose or precise as the child wishes. He may be a perfect mimic, or get no further than a crude identification in belief; he may labour to represent in clay with complete fidelity, or be content with a fingered blob. A third kind of play is predominantly physical, as in skipping, climbing, chasing, playing ball-games, skating and scooting. Play such as this may be freely made up or quite extensively rule-governed. Piaget's classic discussion of marbles, and the changing attitudes of children to the rules of the game as they pass through the primary school, illustrates this.[5] These three kinds of play, then, role play, object play and physical play, should provide sufficient examples against which to check any criteria of play which may later be suggested.

But children even of pre-infant school age engage in activities other than play. Increasingly, children like to do some 'work', in the form of helping adults in doing real tasks such as washing up, dusting, shopping and tidying up. Going to school is usually regarded, at least in part, also as 'work'. Work and play, however, do not, contrary to what we might too hastily assume, provide an exhaustive classification of children's activities. Routine activities such as washing, eating, dressing and getting ready for bed are neither work nor play, and neither are involvements in adult social activities, as in visiting, conversing, or 'going out'. Whatever the distinction might turn out to be, therefore, it is clear that there *is* a distinction between play and activities of other sorts, a distinction which, to avoid entanglements over what 'work' is and to avoid the misleading contrast of work with play, we can simply call for the moment that between play and non-play. That, at least, seems a safe distinction.

## 4. SOME SUGGESTED CRITERIA OF PLAY

In seeking to pick out the criteria implicit in applying the concept of 'play' one is not at a loss for want of precedents, but to review all of the suggestions that have been made would consume far too much time, so that only a few of the more representative and more widely canvassed of them will be considered here. A temptation that can often be found among these suggestions is that of pitching on one particular *sort* of play, or of allowing oneself to be steered by an ideal picture of 'the child' into noticing only those sorts of play that fit into that picture, but two questions need always to be asked of any such suggested criteria. First, are there any other sorts of play in which this feature must clearly be admitted to be absent? If there are, then it cannot be a condition necessary for applying the concept. An example of this mistake would be to suggest that 'play' implies some kind of make-believe, since plainly such forms of play as ball-games do not involve this. Secondly, are there any examples of non-play in which the suggested feature is present? If there are, then it cannot be sufficient for demarcating the concept. An example of this might be the suggestion that 'play' means being overtly active, since cooking and shopping involve overt activity but they are not play.

If we now turn to some actual suggestions that have been put forward, a massive sweeping away of possibilities can be effected right at the start by dismissing all suggestions which look to what children include in their play. It would be useless to wonder whether toys are always involved, for example, because the concept of a 'toy' cannot be explicated in terms of any perceptible properties possessed by an object, but is internally related to the concept of 'play' as being the concept of an object given a play use, whether special or temporary. A hammer may be father's 'tool' at one moment and his son's 'toy' at the next, but the hammer has not changed. Again, if we bracket together all the things that children play at, such as mothers and fathers, tea-parties, schools and so on, and look for some observable feature of behaviour which distinguishes them from the 'real' activities which they represent, we shall not find it, because whether this *is* representation or not is a question of the child's intention, of what he sees himself as doing, and not of the form which the activity takes.

Much more plausible as suggestions, however, are the various 'psychological' criteria of play, one of the most often canvassed of which is 'spontaneity'. A 'spontaneous' activity, in the sense required, seems to be one the origin or shape of which lies in the child's own unsolicited impulse. Such activity 'bubbles' out of children in a manner which is often unpredictable. This criterion, however, certainly could not be sufficient, since non-play activities may also be the objects of such spontaneous attraction. Parents often have to dampen spontaneous willingness to help in the performance of some task, such as painting or weeding, on account of the likelihood of a mess or an accident, while in other cases such spontaneous offers of help may be welcome. But neither is spontaneity a necessary condition, since the origin of play often lies in the suggestion of other children, while in some cases bored children may plead with adults to suggest what they might do. Moreover, the 'shape' of play, far from being spontaneously determined, is often stringently rule-governed, as we have seen. While 'spontaneity' doubtless picks out something which is often present in play, it therefore fails as a criterion for the application of the concept.

Another common 'psychological' approach to characterizing play is in terms of 'absorbed interest'. As Caldwell Cook once asserted: 'To do anything with interest, to get at the heart of the matter and live there active—that is Play.'[6] And it is true that children often do show a concentration and absorption in their play which resents interruption or interference. Such absorbed interest, however, may as readily be shown in non-play, as perhaps in writing a letter or in doing some kinds of school work, so that is cannot be sufficient, while on the other hand not all play is like this, so that it cannot be necessary either. Playing cricket, for example, can be quite boring, and children often play with something just because there seems nothing better to do. Again, the attractive feature in some sorts of play seems to be not so much absorbed interest as the containment of some such emotion as fear or excitement.

'Emotional satisfaction' is another common suggestion. Piaget[7] is in this area when he includes play under 'assimilation', as he calls it, by which he means here an activity orientated towards personal satisfaction rather than towards 'accommodation'. But although such satisfaction often is derived from much play, it is also derived from much else, so that it cannot be sufficient. And furthermore, there are intellectual forms of play, such as word and board games, which involve an exercise of wits rather than any obvious emotion, so that emotional satisfaction does not seem to be necessary either. However, this suggestion is one to which we shall later return.

We now seem to have been driven into the kind of impasse into which Wittgenstein was led in enquiring what it was that all games had in common : board-games, card-games, ball-games, Olympic games, solitary games like patience, ring-a-ring-a-roses and spontaneously made up games like throwing a ball against a wall. It does not seem to be amusement, or contest, or skill, or luck.

> What is common to them all?—Don't say : 'There *must* be something common, or they would not be called "games" '—but *look and see* whether there is anything common to all—For if you look at them you will not see something that is common to *all,* but similarities, relationships, and a whole series of them at that. To repeat : don't think, but look ![8]

To describe this state of affairs, in which there are many overlapping similarities but none overall, Wittgenstein coined the phrase 'family resemblances'. We might say, therefore, that the various activities we call 'play' do show a network of family resemblances, but no *overall* features or similarities. We may be even more strongly tempted to settle for this solution if we recall that not only children but also adults can properly be said to 'play', though adults' games are obviously more formalized and structured than are those of children. What is hopscotch likely to have in common with chess, for example, or bowls with playing at mothers and fathers? Yet we call them all 'play'. Wittgenstein says : 'don't think, but look'. But *looking* at play activities is just what we have been doing, though without much success; so that the suspicion must surely now arise that 'play' is not to be demarcated by looking for some feature present always in play activities, whether something open to immediate view or some felt quality of experience, but by making a move quite different from these usual ones.

### 5. PLAY AND SOCIAL LIFE

We can start by noticing that children do not have to be taught to play, in the way that they do have to be taught to keep themselves clean. The impulse to engage in activities we should call 'play' is there already, and in that sense is natural. But what children do have to be taught is *which* among their various activities count as 'play' and which do not, and they have to be taught the concept by adults who make the same distinction amongst their own activities. For example, the impulse to dabble with water, to pretend, and to chase need little or no encouragement, but the grouping together of such activities under a single concept labelled 'play', and the implied contrast with activities of other sorts, is an expression of how adults conceive some among the various activities which make up a form of social life. A promising move to make, therefore, would seem to be not to look at play by itself, as we have been doing, but to think of it in relation to social life generally. This is the move that I now want to make and to develop as a positive suggestion.

If we consider the activities which make up by far the largest part of adult life, the typical activities of adults that is to say, then a word which aptly characterizes them is 'serious'. They are serious in the sense that they are engaged in to further some purpose the omission of which would constitute neglect. Such purposes may be dictated by common prudence as being in our own interests, or they may be dictated by obligations and duties deriving perhaps from law, morality, religion or what is customarily regarded as proper to a particular social role. To say that the typical activities of adults are serious in this sense has got nothing to do with laughter or sobriety, or any expression on people's faces, but is an objective *evaluation* of certain activities. Whether particular individuals do or do not treat them as serious, they are serious, and a man who failed to regard them as such would be neglecting either his own interests or those of others. He would be neglecting the ordinary business of living, responsible attention to which is a condition of viability both for individuals and for society as a whole. In many cases a man who trifled here would be said to be 'playing at' whatever it was. In this way we condemn a man for 'playing at politics', or a woman ignores a man's attentions because he is 'only playing', or someone who ought to be getting on with a job is said to be 'playing around' or 'playing about'. A child's socialization largely consists in his being taught to recog-

nize, respect and by degrees to involve himself in these seriously purposeful activities which make up the main business of ordinary
living.

Of course, to say that the judgment of seriousness here is an objective evaluation is not to say that reappraisal is impossible, and a
person who disregarded the ordinary view might not be a trifler but
a person who genuinely disagreed with the usual judgment. Behind
the conception of what is serious in a form of life lies an understanding of ourselves and of our situation, a picture of the nature of reality which may in fact be mistaken in some respects : in thinking that
we have to propitiate the sea before sailing on it safely, or in thinking
that a communal dance is necessary to bring on rain, for example.
Though such activities might be thought to be part of the serious,
they would nevertheless rest on a mistake about people and their
situation. Behind our view as to what is serious, then, lies a picture
of reality which is the background against which our various purposes are pursued, though in a particular society this background is
likely to be so much taken for granted as to escape much remark.

Now the first thing that we can say about play is that the person
who plays does not *regard* his activity as being serious in this objectively evaluative sense. Play is neither the pursuit of purposes dictated by common prudence, nor is it the fulfilling of an obligation to
anybody. We could, therefore, scarcely neglect to play, but, being
free from the demands of the serious, we can do as we please. A
child at the sink, for example, may or may not be playing, depending
on how he regards his activity. If he does just as he pleases, then he
is playing; if he sees what he does as a task, so that not to remove
some egg from a spoon or not to finish would be neglect by the
norms of the task, then he is not playing. The same would be true of
an adult, except that since washing up would normally be a matter
of obligation for him, not taking it seriously would be 'playing' at it
in a condemnatory sense. We may move even further from the
serious, as in make-believe, and free ourselves from what we know
our real situation to be. Of course, even in pretending the real and
the serious are not completely lost sight of,[9] since that would be a
form of madness, but they are temporarily bracketed off and deliberately held in abeyance. A baby who had not yet learned to conceive
of his real situation could not properly be said to play, nor could a
completely autistic child who had no notion of the background
reality against which his activities took place.[10] Play is to be

contrasted with, and presupposes, the serious and the real, so that a child can properly be said to play only in proportion as he becomes aware of these.

Cannot play be serious then? Is it just false to say that 'play is a serious business'? For the moment, let us be content with the following. A boy may take the operation of his model railway or a man may take his golf very seriously indeed. Both may attach great importance to making the correct moves and in the correct order, be in earnest in the attention that he gives, be annoyed if things are not done properly, and so on. Consider the game of chess, for example, and one can clearly see the truth of saying that play may be serious. But the point to be noticed here is that this 'taking it seriously' is itself part of the game, while the game as a whole, considered not from the inside but in its relation to ordinary life, remains non-serious. The seriousness exhibited in play is not that dictated by prudence or obligation. We do not recognize our responsibilities by taking seriously our trains or our golf, or neglect to play at these things. However serious our attitude may be *within* play, objectively the activity remains non-serious in the sense that I have described. We may place ourselves under the spell of the serious as part of the game, but we remain free to break it without neglect either to our interests or to our obligations. If it ceased to be so, and we confused the pretend seriousness of play with the objectively serious, we should have to be reminded or reassured of the true nature of our activity. 'It's only play, you know,' we sometimes have to say to children, or 'It's only a game' to an adult, and the evaluative 'only' here stresses the contrast with the objectively serious. Rather differently, when we hear of Drake continuing with his bowls while the Armada approached, we may well be so perplexed as not to know quite what to think.

There is another way in which the non-seriousness of play can be brought out which derives from the fact that what is serious is not the same from society to society. Of course, if we visited another culture very different from our own we might still be able to recognize some play activities reliably enough, partly because of their overtness and partly because it is unimaginable that they could be serious. But many play activities represent the serious activities of a society, while others derive their content from a particular social tradition of child activity,[11] and these we might well not to be able reliably to recognize until we knew what was regarded as serious in that society. What looked like finger-play or a playful dance might be a religious ritual and therefore serious, while what looked like the purposeful use of an implement might be play with a toy. Such culture-relative play activities could not reliably be identified till we knew which of the forms of the social life concerned were regarded as serious.

Again, we might notice that in the frequent characterization of the activities of young animals as 'play' there seems once more to be implied the contrast between the serious and the non-serious. The serious business for animals includes hunting, feeding, grooming, escape, defence of a territory and so on, whereas young animals are conspicuously free from involvement in such serious activities. Of course, it is only analogies with human social life which are involved here, but the contrast I have been insisting on as distinctive of play does seem to be very clear in the very much simpler lives of animals.

A concept similar in some respects to that of 'play' is the concept of 'dreaming', though of course dreaming is not an activity. What is a dream? Immediately, we recollect particular dreams and try to identify features common to them all, just as we look for something common in all play. But just as there is nothing that could not be played at, so there is nothing that we could not dream.[12] The similarity to the 'serious' or to the 'real' in each case can be conceived of as being as exact as one pleases, so that 'content' will not serve as a criterion of demarcation. We might then shift to 'psychological qualities' and notice that there are indeed, just as in play, similarities often to be found among dreams in their felt qualities, qualities which may even lead the dreamer into the incoherent judgment 'this is a dream'. In the end, however, one is driven to the conclusion that dreams, like play, must be demarcated negatively, perhaps in some such way as that dreams are the experiences which we have while we are not awake, just as play is the activity which we engage in when we are free from the demands of the serious. Play, like dreaming in these respects, might be said to form a separate world.

A further feature of play which now comes into view, as an implication of its non-seriousness, is that it must be self-contained. No constraint is placed on play by a means-end relationship linked with the serious, as there would be in making something useful, or in movement with a purpose beyond the activity itself, and make-believe is still more obviously cut off. Even the rule-structures of games, elaborate as they may be, stand in disconnection from the serious and form no part of the legal system or our moral duty, quite unlike the bye-laws of the building or recreation ground in which the game might be played, or the moral rule of non-injury which would still have to be observed while playing. The only point which the rules of the game have is to make a game.[13] This self-contained character of play is further confirmed by noticing, with Huizinga,[14] that play typically has its special places, times and objects. It has its nurseries, play spaces and play grounds, its play periods with a clear start and finish, its toys and other apparatus. Play stands apart from the web of purposes which make up the serious, and in this sense is self-contained.

But now, if play is cut off from the serious in this way, so that its primary function cannot be to further people's interests, what reason have we to play? People often go to great trouble and expense to provide for themselves or others an opportunity to play, so what could be the reason for that? Whereas in stressing the non-serious and self-contained character of play it is made to seem something negative, as indeed it is in these respects, we now have to notice that the motive for engaging in it is the positive one that it is worthwhile in itself. We play, not thereby to achieve some further purpose or to fulfil some obligation, but just for what is involved in the activity itself. We do it 'for fun' as we say, which at one and the same time suggests both its non-seriousness and its intrinsic satisfactions. This, of course, is the feature of play being concentrated on by people who consider play by itself and suggest spontaneity, absorbed interest or emotional satisfaction as criteria of it. But these features cannot by themselves be sufficient and fall better into place once play has been located on the social map as non-serious and self-contained, for then it follows that its motivation could not be other than intrinsic to the activity itself. We play necessarily for what there is in the activity itself, whether it is the satisfaction of going down a slide, the absorbing interest of chess, the excitement of chasing, the fun of a party, the contained fear of being hunted by a 'lion', the amusement of mimicry, the struggle and possible victory of contest, or the engagement of our intellectual wits as in word games.

Play, then, is a non-serious and self-contained activity which we engage in just for the satisfaction involved in it, and this analysis is confirmed, I think, if one considers each of the three types of children's activities earlier distinguished, role play, object play and physical play, or indeed if one considers the various games which adults play. They are all of them non-serious, in that they have no purpose dictated by prudence, nor do they fulfil any kind of obligation. They are therefore all self-contained, both in having a clear start and finish and in having a point and structure purely internal to them, and as a further implication of their non-seriousness they are all engaged in for the intrinsic satisfactions which they give. Of course, this account of play could be complicated in all sorts of ways, for example by considering what to say of those people who have a professional interest in games, or those who play for the purpose of maintaining health or getting business contacts, but to chase such cases would be merely tedious. When one is trying to get somewhere, one does not pause to explore every lane and sidetrack.

Before leaving the question of what play is, however, something ought to be said about an important class of activities which on the face of it do satisfy the criteria suggested, yet which we should not call 'play'. These activities are the various arts and sciences when they are pursued quite apart from any obvious applications which they may have to the serious business of living. On the face of it, therefore, they could well be non-serious, but a closer look shows this not to be so. Though they often do give satisfaction to those who pursue them, the reason for pursuing them as worthwhile in themselves is rather that they seek to establish or to create something of objective value, whether this is some mathematical proof, scientific law or object of aesthetic merit. They are to be assessed not primarily by the satisfactions which they give, but by impersonal criteria of truth and of merit. Furthermore, though not themselves dictated either by prudence or by obligation, and hence not in that sense serious, they do have a very intimate connection with the serious in that they explore aspects of the conception of ourselves and of our situation which is the background against which our objective evaluations of seriousness are made.[15] They are concerned with the various sorts of 'reality' which are presupposed in asserting the validity of all such judgements.[16] The similarity of these activities to play, therefore, is no more than apparent.[17]

## 6. 'THEORIES' OF PLAY

The question which we can now go on to ask is where psychological theorizing and observation fit into this, especially in relation to children's play. Such theories have at various times been put forward as that play is a way of preparing for 'life' (the serious), or that it is a way of resolving difficulties and releasing emotions, while the analysts of dreams have seen also in play the sometimes bizarre comments of one mode of experience upon another. Observation of play directed to seeing what kinds of learning take place in it has discovered progress in speech, in co-operation with others, in gaining awareness of one's strengths and capabilities, in gaining familiarity with the physical properties of things, and so on. These, then, are just some of the ways in which psychology bears upon play.

Now commentaries such as these tell us nothing about the *concept* of play; indeed, a knowledge of the 'meaning' of play, in this conceptual sense of 'meaning', is a presupposition and not the outcome of these inquiries. It is not the concept of play which is observed, theorized about and reported upon, but the particular things done by children at play. If it were otherwise, then the vast majority of language-users, who know nothing of theories of play, would be uttering a senseless noise in using the word at all, and furthermore it is hard to see how the theorist himself would have as his initial datum a *class* of activities to theorize about. Since our inquiry so far has been concerned with the *concept* of play, it is therefore not to be upset by any findings of psychology about the particular things done by children at play.

A second point about these observations and theorizings is that they tell us nothing of what children 'do', in the sense of 'do' in which a person knows what he is doing. For example, if we asked a child with a doll what she was 'doing', an appropriate reply might be 'feeding her', 'changing her clothes', 'telling her she has been naughty', and so on. If, however, she replied that she was 'preparing for motherhood', 'learning the role of mother' or 'effecting a therapeutic release of aggression', we should not only be staggered at the precocity of her language but forced to conclude that this was not play at all, since consciously preparing for life and deliberately sought therapy both fall under the aspect of the serious. The theorist, then, not only tells us nothing of what is meant by 'play', but he tells us nothing of what children are aware of doing in playing. What he does tell us something about is the *function* of play in growing up, and this distinction between what is meant by 'play' and what children see themselves as doing on the one hand, and what an intelligent observer perceives to be the function of their play on the other, is crucially important in trying to clear up some of the confusions which were mentioned at the outset. Something more must therefore be said about an observer's description of the function of play.

When we consider the 'function' of something, we are considering what is effected or brought about by it, but this may be viewed in at least three ways. We may be considering what *ought* to be brought about, or what people *think* is brought about, or what is *in fact* brought about, and these three do not always coincide. For example, perhaps the function of a particular priest ought to be to minister to his flock, whereas he thinks of his job in terms of providing himself with a comfortable living, while a Marxist observer sees it as in fact diverting social discontents from their proper object. Where play is concerned, the psychologist is like the Marxist in this example. He does not regard play as the child himself or the ordinary adult does, but detects in it various kinds of unsuspected and non-obvious functional significance, such as its therapeutic function and its learning function. What has to be especially noticed here is that the effect of this is partially to undercut the non-seriousness implied by the concept. Play, it was suggested, is an activity engaged in when our attention is released from the serious, and this must remain true if theorists are to be left with a distinguishable activity to theorize about. But the functional significance of play revealed by the theorist puts it in a quite different light as being, from *his* point of view, indeed 'a serious business'. Whether play is viewed therapeutically, or in terms of learning, or even as the first act in Froebel's metaphysical drama of unfolding,[18] it is then seen by the *observer* as serious.

It is this new dimension of seriousness revealed by the theorist which produces such paradoxes as that 'play is a serious business', or that 'play is the child's work'. Such a result is not uncommon when a concept antedates psychological discoveries relevant to its application. For example, 'responsibility' and 'punishment' are other concepts which have been made uncertain in their application in this way. While theorists tell us nothing of what 'play' means, therefore, or of what children are conscious of doing, what they do reveal is something about the unsuspected functions of play, functions which link it with the serious in such a way as to place adult observers of it under an obligation in regard to it, for neglect suitably to provide for it could have results which must, on already existing assumptions, be regarded as harmful. This, of course, is to take it for granted that the theories and observations concerned are true, a question on which a philosopher may not be competent to decide. But taking this for granted, I want now to turn to consider, in the light of its functional significance, play as a possible educational process.

If a parent thinking of sending a child to a nursery school knows only that children 'play' there, then the activities of the nursery school are smartly marshalled under the non-serious. Why should anyone go to the trouble or expense, it might be thought, of arranging for children just to 'play', when they can do that perfectly well elsewhere, in the garden, street, or park for example? Various answers could be given to this, such as that in a well-run nursery children are safe and their health is looked after, that there are many opportunities to work out personal difficulties and to achieve some sort of balanced emotional development, that children learn to talk to each other freely, to share, co-operate, help others and so on. Above all, it might be said, a child who goes to a nursery has a greater chance of being secure and happy. But while each of these things that have just been mentioned is very important, and nothing that I shall say will minimize its importance, it is not education. The concept of 'education' does indeed imply, as Professor Peters has shown,[19] some kind of improvement, but not any kind of improvement. Certainly seeing that children develop safely, in good health, without unsolved emotional difficulties and in happy interaction with other children is a commendable function for anyone to perform, and certainly many kinds of improvements may take place under such a regime, but there is nothing specifically educational here. There is nothing here which is even aimed at later achieving the kind of cognitive perspective, or building up of a differentiated understanding, which is one criterion for picking out a process as being educational.[20] And indeed where a good many nurseries are concerned, such as those run by health authorities or by private individuals, there is no claim to be doing anything specifically of educational value, unless perhaps it is that a good basis for later making a start at educating children is being laid.

In some nurseries, however, play is regarded in such a way as to lay claim to being thought of as an educational process; the staff regard themselves as teachers and the institution itself is regarded as a school. Not all nurseries are or claim to be nursery schools, but these do. An objection that might immediately be made to this is that there is little or no set instruction given in such institutions, so how can the staff be regarded as teachers? The answer to this is that the concept of 'teaching' is much wider than that of 'instructing', which implies an imparting or telling of what is to be learned. 'Teaching' leaves it open how learning will be brought about, the only restrictions placed on possible forms of teaching being derivative from what it is to learn some particular thing. For the staff of a nursery school to claim to be 'teachers', therefore, it is by no means necessary that they should give set instruction in anything: many other forms of teaching remain open to them, such as arranging carefully selected activities, asking leading questions, commenting on things being done and making suggestions about them, and so on.[21] It is really very easy to show that the staffs of such schools could be said to 'teach', therefore. But once again, not all teaching by any means is educational, so that to show that nursery school teachers are indeed teachers does not imply that they educate, or that play is an educational process. Teaching someone to tie his shoe-laces, for example, is useful, but hardly scores as an educational success.

For the play activities which are arranged in a nursery, or indeed in an infant school, to be regarded as specifically educational, and not just useful, therapeutic, or happiness-producing, it would have to be shown that they are continuous with the development of the kind of differentiated understanding which has been referred to as giving 'cognitive perspective' to one's experience. And since it is no accident that such a development is what is to be sought during the more formal schooling which follows the nursery stage, we can say that if the activities of the nursery are to be regarded as educational, then they must be continuous with what is to be sought in later schooling, and not just arranged with an eye to health and safe amusement. Guided in that way by a directional framework of values formed with an eye on what is to follow in later schooling, and guided by a theoretical knowledge of how play can be so arranged as to have this learning function, the adults who supervise such play would indeed be teachers and would also have arranged an educational situation. The learning which it is the function of such play to develop may be more chancy than in the more familiar instructional setting common in formal schooling, but it is much less chancy and unselected than is what is learned in unsupervised play, or play supervised by adults who lack the requisite theoretical knowledge to be aware of the possible educational functions of it. But of course, I have only described how things would have to be for the play activities of a nursery to be regarded as educational; whether any particular institution satisfies this description is a further question which only knowledge of that institution would enable one to answer.

In conclusion, however, it must be said that it is doubtful whether much of *substantial* educational value could be learned by a process of unconscious 'picking up' during play activities. So much of school learning must be more deliberate than that, in requiring practice, for example. This is not to say that all activity which could *properly* be called play ought quite suddenly to cease in school at, say, six years of age, but that by then it should be gradually giving way to activities which children themselves regard as serious, and therefore not as play. Such activities may well be interesting and enjoyable, but to call them 'play' is to fail to take children as seriously as they are then coming to take themselves, and it is unnecessarily to invite the hostility of adults to what are in fact enlightened methods of setting about the serious business of education.

## NOTES

1. Other variants are discussed in Hardie, C. D., *Truth and Fallacy in Educational Theory* (1942), Ch. 1.
2. Popper, K. R., *The Open Society and its Enemies* (1945), Vol. 2, Ch. 11.
3. Best, E., 'Common Confusions in Educational Theory' in *Philosophical Analysis and Education* (1965), ed. Archambault, R. D.
4. Caldwell Cook, H., *The Play Way* (1917), p. 3.
5. Piaget, J., *The Moral Judgement of the Child* (English Edn. 1932).
6. Caldwell Cook, H., op. cit., p. 9.
7. Piaget, J., *Play, Dreams and Imitation in Childhood* (Eng. trans. 1951).
8. Wittgenstein, L., *Philosophical Investigations* (1953), Sect. 66.
9. Austin, J. L., 'Pretending' in *Proceedings of the Aristotelian Society* (1956–7).
10. Cf. Kenny, A., *Action, Emotion and Will* (1963), pp. 42–3 on the possible impropriety of attributing to babies emotions such as fear or love.
11. Opie, I. and Opie, P., *Lore and Language of Schoolchildren* (1959).
12. Descartes, *Meditations*, Ch. 1.
13. Toulmin, S. E., *The Place of Reason in Ethics* (1950), Ch. 6, Sect. 6.
14. Huizinga, J., *Homo Ludens* (English edn. 1949).
15. Peters, R. S., *Ethics and Education* (1966), Ch. 5.
16. On this use of 'reality' see Toulmin, S. E., op. cit., Ch. 8.

17. Cf. Oakeshott, M., 'The Voice of Poetry in the Conversation of Mankind' in *Rationalism in Politics* (1962), pp. 197–202.

18. Froebel, F., *The Education of Man* (1826).

19. Peters, R. S., op. cit., Ch. 1.

20. Peters, R. S., ibid.

21. On the ways in which a teacher can give this kind of informal guidance see for example, Gardner, D. E. M. and Cass, J. E., *The Role of the Teacher in the Infant and Nursery School* (1965).

# RULES AND ROUTINES
## Max Black

I take it for granted that education consists in large part of a sustained effort to generate capacities for skilful performance. Even 'theoretical knowledge' of facts and principles, if it is to be of any value, must be manifested in certain modes of activity. All education aims, in the first instance, at 'know-how'.

Two distinct ideals of intelligent and skilful performance have an immediate appeal. The first is of graceful, free-flowing, action unimpeded by self-conscious reference to instructions. One thinks immediately of the natural movements of animals—but also of certain exercises of high skill: Menuhin's playing the violin as if it were as easy as breathing. Action of this kind gives an impression of freedom from conscious effort or calculation: the musician 'loses himself in the music', though with intense control and awareness. A contrasting ideal is of deliberate calculating action according to an articulated program. An example might be a mathematician expounding a formal proof in public, with each step explicitly defended by cited reasons. Absence of ease and grace in such a performance is compensated by a high degree of 'rationality'. 'Free-flowing' activity, at its best, looks like a dance: 'rational' activity, at its worst, like drill.[1]

The antithesis between 'dance' and 'drill', between free-flowing and calculated action is too vague to have much value as a guide to education. Instead of pursuing it, I shall try to take a hard look at a particular type of 'calculated action', characterized by the presence of governing *rules*. My object is to become somewhat clearer than I now am about the nature and the educational significance of such 'rule-governed action'.

I

Consider the differences between two familiar activities: doodling (D) and completing an income tax form (F). Both may be intentional and voluntary, but seem to have almost nothing else in common. About F, we can say the following things, none of which are true of D:

(1) It makes sense to say of one of the steps taken in $F$ that it was a *mistake*, or that it was *wrong*.

(2) Nobody can be regarded as doing $F$ unless he would treat certain entries as mistakes, and would try to *correct* them.

(3) Each step in $F$ has an *intrinsic reason,*[2] which can be offered as an explanation, clarification, or defence of what he is doing.

(4) Nobody can count as doing $F$ unless he treats as obvious reasons that justify what he is doing.

(5) It makes sense of a particular instance of $F$ to say that it is *unfinished* or incomplete.

(6) In order to be doing $F$, the agent must have the completion of the task as an end in view.

(7) Anybody doing $F$ must know *how to do it*, which implies that he could do $F$ on other occasions and could show another person how to do it.

(8) To do $F$ is to make repeated reference to the *instructions* for doing F, each of them being treated as an injunction to be followed, 'obeyed'.

Now it would be absurd to say of a doodler, that he had made a wrong stroke, was trying to correct it, had a good or bad reason for doing it that way, had left the doodle unfinished, knew how to teach doodling, or was following instructions for doodling.[3] To doodle is to do as one pleases, in the spirit of the Abbey of Thelème, under the sole sway of pleasure; but to follow instructions, as in $F$, is to enter the realm of right-and-wrong, justification by reasons, standards of completeness, and built-in generality of procedure—in short to behave rationally.

Completing an income tax form is a perspicuous instance of *rule-invoking* (or explicitly rule-governed) action. In the only sense that needs consideration here,[4] a rule is a *general instruction*, expressed in a formula that states *what is to be done* in order to achieve some stated or understood end in view. A standard formula for such a rule is: 'In order to arrive at $E$, do $A1$ $A2$ . . . . , in such-and-such a sequence and in such-and-such combinations.' A rule is a recipe for a designated achievement.

Of the eight features of rule-invoking action listed above, the last encompasses all the others. For instance, following the rule in question is necessarily being ready and able to treat some acts as mistaken (point 2): the rule defines classes of actions that are correct *according to the rule* and there is no logical gap between obeying the rule and obeying the rule correctly.[5] On the other hand, none of the first seven points separately, nor all of them together, suffice to define rule-invoking action. A man may do something wrong because he fails to respond correctly to a specific command (*not* a rule!); my reason for drinking may be that I am thirsty, but it would be perverse to insist that I am following a rule, and so on. Even a man whose actions conform to all seven of the points, need not be regarded as rule-governed in his behaviour.

What, then, is it to *obey* a rule explicitly invoked?

## 2

Of course, the rule must be understood and the agent must try to do as the rule prescribes. Is there anything more? Must we suppose some distinctive act of 'obedience' intervening between understanding and acting? In general, not. Cases where an agent reads a recipe, hesitates, says aloud 'I'll use it,' and then proceeds to do so might plausibly be regarded as including distinctive acts of 'obedience'. But this is unusual. Very likely, the cook reads the recipe and at once starts arranging the ingredients for a Dundee cake without any intervening act of recipe-adoption. *Obedience to the rule is shown by trying to do as instructed.* If this were not so, somebody could read the instructions, do exactly as he was told (with repeated reference to the explicit instructions) and still be able to claim that he 'simply chose to do what the recipe required' without really obeying it. The claim would be absurd : here actions really do speak louder than words and their force cannot be cancelled by a protest or a mental reservation.

Knowing how to respond to a rule *as a rule* is something that has to be learned : it is not a natural aptitude like breathing, but a distinctively human mode of behaviour. The practice of giving and receiving rules involves a complex pattern of demands, objections, claims, and defences, that we overlook only because we were initiated into it so long ago. It is no more 'natural' than the practice of playing games according to fixed rules. (We can easily imagine human beings unable to understand what it is to play conventional games; a human society lacking the 'practice' of rule-giving admittedly strains the imagination.) This prior initiation and training, itself not induced by rule-invocation, makes it possible for an agent to *obey* a rule.[6]

It is this earlier training, not some distinctive act of 'obedience', that is essential for *following* a rule.[7]

This view of the matter has an important consequence. Participation in the rule-giving-and-receiving practice depends, as in all human institutions, upon a general presumption of *justifiable trust*. Unless rule-givers were usually trustworthy and rules for the most part 'worked', there could be no viable institution of rule-using. (For the same reasons, if adults lied to their children, irresponsibly and unsystematically, most of the time, the children could never learn to talk.)

The general presumption of trust generates more specific presumptions concerning presented rules. It is impossible (logically impossible, I think) for anybody to follow an instruction, *qua* rule of action, while thinking it detrimental to the end in view. If, so thinking, he performs the acts prescribed, he is transforming the rule into a rule for another purpose—or into something other than a rule. Sceptical as I am about the accuracy of cook books, I can still *follow* a recipe for haggis for want of a better alternative. But if I think the printed recipe will produce only a nasty inedible mess, I cannot *accept* it as a rule for making haggis. (If I 'go through the motions', my motive may be curiosity, the desire not to offend a Scotch friend, or something else; I am then 'obeying' the rule only in some Pickwickian sense.) Obedience to a rule demands *some* confidence in the rule-giver.

No teacher needs to be told that the requisite confidence—the *consent of the taught*, as we might say—is often lacking: the child, acting under duress, does not really think that Teacher is usually right, or that the instructions thrust upon him really 'work' (too often they don't!). The intended instructions are then responded to as *orders* or commands, to be obeyed (in another sense of that word). The task changes into that of 'passing the test'—or, more generally, 'satisfying Teacher'. This, too, is education of a sort—education in how to coexist with arbitrary authority.

3

Rules, general instructions, purport to specify *good* ways to approach stated or assumed objectives (ends in view). A given rule may be defective in two distinct ways: by leading away from the end in view or by being unsuitable for use—roughly speaking, by being misdirected or by being inefficient. Similarly for other instruments: a hammer may be a poor one because it is too flimsy to drive nails home, or else because it is too heavy to be handled. The apocryphal rule for counting sheep by adding the number of feet and dividing by four is not misdirected, but is plainly inefficient. Let us call a rule that is not misdirected, that does prescribe actions conducive to the end in view, *right*; and a rule that is both right and efficient a *good* one. The goodness of rules is plainly a matter of degree.

Overlooking the vagueness in the notions of rules being 'right' or 'efficient', we can say that a question about the goodness of a given rule is determinable, in principle, by appeal to logic or to matters of fact. We can *prove* that hugging the wall of a maze will eventually lead to an exit; but it is a matter of experience that bread stays fresh in a refrigerator. Whether a rule is good is a cognitive issue, demanding knowledge, not decision or commitment. That is why rules can be freely adopted, when taken to be right and efficient, with no ultimate reliance upon authority. Given a chosen end in view and determinate skill, the rule's credentials are, in the end, rooted in the nature of the external world. Hence the step from a rule ('something to be done') to a corresponding principle ('the way things are') may need only a change of grammatical mood.

There is, to be sure, a certain duplicity in rules. The imperative mood in which they are naturally formulated suggests some external source whose special knowledge or expertise lends weight to the rule, giving it something of the force of recommendation, piece of advice, or even an order. ('Do such-and-such, because *I* say so, with proper authority.') Indeed, the practical point of obeying rules issuing from another is to relinquish initiative and responsibility for the time being. While I follow the recipe, my role as agent shrinks to the simpler and more passive one of *doing as I am told*—as if an experienced chef stood at my elbow. My interest shifts from the primary task of baking a cake to the secondary one of correctly following instructions, which is so much easier.[8] I act upon authority—and wish to. But such submission is, in the long run, wholesome only if eventually subjected to criticism. Sooner or later, provisional submission to the authority of rules must be tested by logic and against the facts. As justice must not only be done, but must be *seen* to be done, so also the goodness of rules (in any educational programme aspiring to be rational) must in the end be *shown*—and not indefinitely assumed by an act of trust.

4

A man who deliberately obeys, 'invokes', a rule can cite that rule as a *reason* for his action; one who blindly follows a routine, behaves regularly, cannot offer a reason of that kind—and may be able to offer no reasons at all. ('Why are you taking the walking stick?' 'Because I want to!' That tells us nothing : we know that he was not taking it inadvertently.)

Reasons for actions are typically offered in order to defend or to justify the actions; to render them intelligible; or to amplify their descriptions, by reference to intention, motive or purpose. In performing such meta-activities (as they might be called), the rule-invoking agent has intellectual resources unavailable to somebody performing superficially similar actions, routinely, blindly, 'out of mere habit' or even 'unaware'. Let us say, for short, that rule-invoking-action is potentially and distinctively *self-critical*. (By 'self-criticism' I mean the processes of justification, explanation and verbal elaboration already alluded to.) Paradoxically, the constraints imposed by adherence to a rule are balanced by greater scope and freedom to act at the 'meta'-level. (This is why metamathematics demands *formalized* object-languages; and also why a sonnet in traditional form is easier to criticize than a piece of free verse.)

Reasons can render actions intelligible. When we say, of another's action, 'We don't know what he is doing' or, sometimes, more explicitly, 'We don't *understand* what he is doing', we can sometimes be enlightened by a statement of the agent's reasons and their supposed connection with his end in view. Given the rule invoked— if there is such a rule—we can make immediate sense of what is being done, whatever our ultimate reservations about the goodness of the rule employed. Conversely, where rule-connected reasons cannot be given, because the behaviour in question is a blind routine, *this* mode of understanding is excluded—although causal explanation may still be available.[9]

Now apply this to a man's view of his own action. If invoking a rule, he understands up to a point precisely what he is doing—that is, treating the given rule as defining a good procedure for achieving an accepted end in view. But when a man's behaviour is blind routine, there is an important sense in which he does not know *what* he is doing, or *why* he is doing it. This need not be discreditable if there is nothing to explain, nothing to understand; but is generally taken to be so, in moderation, where reasons might be given, by reference to an appropriate rule. A man unable to supply reasons when appropriate reasons are available falls short of acting with full rationality. The tie between rule-governed behaviour and rationality goes far to explain and to justify educational emphasis upon such behaviour.

5

I have been using the expression 'rule-invoking action' to apply, in the first instance, to episodes in which attention is paid to printed or written instructions. It is natural to include under the same rubric the analogous cases in which the agent *recites* the rule to himself, aloud or 'in his head'. A rule thus recited may be remembered as issuing from some authority—or may simply have been discovered by the agent himself. These new cases are clearly 'rule-governed'.

Less clear, but in some ways more interesting, are actions satisfying most of the criteria for rule-invocation listed in Section 2 above, but in which there is no discernible explicit reference *to* any rule. A man who can still remember how to solve quadratic equations, as he was taught to do in school, does not perform the task with an open Algebra book at his elbow, nor is he heard to mutter 'Must do this; then do that . . . ' Indeed either of these would indicate imperfect mastery of the relevant rule of procedure, would be a sure sign that the rule had not fully entered into *his own possession*.

The well-taught solver of quadratic equations should have little trouble in formulating the controlling rule of procedure upon demand. But if he has trouble in describing his procedure, we may be able to do it for him. In either case, if all goes well, he will immediately *accept* the verbal formulation : he will say perhaps, 'Yes—that is what I was doing all along!' Solving the equation is a very clear case of what I propose to call *rule-accepting* action. For paradigm instances of rule-acceptance, it is essential that the correct formulation of the rule seem obvious (and hence easy to find) and that once formulated it will be accepted unhesitatingly by the agent himself. The harder it is to formulate the rule, and the more reluctant the agent is to receive it, the less inclined we ought to be to treat the episode as a clear case of rule-acceptance.

There is a deliberate ambiguity in the label 'rule-accepting', between 'accepting the rule *all along*' and 'accepting the rule *retroactively*'. I think there is no harm in it. Some writers would speak of 'implicitly rule-governed action' and of 'subconscious' or even 'unconscious' awareness of the rule. The accompanying imagery of the rule concealed in the wings, waiting to be brought before the footlights of consciousness—out of sight, but not out of mind, as it were—is admissible if not taken too seriously.[10] However we choose to think about this, we shall need to grant the following points : (1) rule-accepting action, prior to its verbal articulation, already possesses most of the interesting features of rule-invoking action (correction of 'mistakes', etc.); (2) it can readily be transformed[11] into potentially rule-invoking behaviour by supplying the rule; (3) once this is done, the full resources of the self-critical 'meta-activities' become available to the agent himself.

6

What shall we say, now, about actions manifesting many of the distinctive features of 'rule-governed behaviour' in which, however, the agent *cannot* formulate the rule and cannot or will not accept the verbal formula supplied by another? Take the case of a man riding a bicycle, without conscious effort or more than peripheral awareness of what he is doing. Professor Michael Polanyi has provided what he calls 'the rule observed by the cyclist',[12] but his formulation occupies ten lines and contains reference to such technical notions as 'angle of unbalance', 'square of the speed' and 'inverse proportionality'. Obviously, the ordinary cyclist could not even understand the rule—and, if he did, would be unable to follow it (as Polanyi himself points out).

This type of case needs to be sharply distinguished from those already discussed. If we call such action *rule-covered,* as I would propose, we ought to take that to mean only that an outside analyst can give a certain kind of description of it—can view it *sub specie regulae*, as it were. This kind of verbal articulation is of no value, by way of 'self-criticism', to the agent himself, although it may have considerable importance elsewhere. (If we want to simulate rule-covered action by machines, we need to formulate the rule, in order to supply the machine with a programme. In general, many logically equivalent programmes could be contrived. If we thought of the human agent as '*really* following *one* of these programmes', we would have the embarrassment of choosing among equivalent rules, none of which the agent himself would accept.)

Rule-covered behaviour, as defined above, is easily confused with cases in which the agent's justified refusal to adopt a proposed 'articulation' is due to inadequacy of the language of description.

Consider the following illustration. A beginner's book on chess might contain the rule : 'A Knight moves from one corner of a rectangle composed of three squares by two to the diagonally opposite corner, if that square is unoccupied, without regard for any other pieces in that rectangle.' In moving a Knight, a very slow-witted learner might perhaps be heard reciting this clumsy formula; a somewhat brisker chap might be observed using a finger to trace out a 3 by 2 rectangle and checking that the diagonally opposite square is empty before moving. (In our terminology, the first action would be 'rule-invoking', the second 'rule-accepting'.) But anybody who *had* to do either of these things would never make much of a chess player. If all goes well, a kind of *phenomenological compression* of the original formula occurs: a reduction to essentials, as it were. The player comes to *see* the target square as available for the Knight —and, indeed, at the same time, to see the other available squares, arranged in a constellation of related positions. (The 'assimilation' of the original formula demanded may require hard work and much practice, with varying degress of success. Even with experienced players, 'blindness' to possibilities is not uncommon.) The phenomenological prominence of the target-square now functions as a criterion, and the criteria embodied in the original formula may be so effectively suppressed that 'verbal articulation' may be disconcertingly difficult. (Consider how easy it may be to tie a reef knot—and how hard to say *what* one does.)

In such cases, the agent's resistance to a proposed articulation (which usually looks absurdly complex) may arise from his use of a private symbolism of visual cues, that has ousted the public and official terminology of the original instructions. Such symbolism is not 'private' in the philosopher's technical sense of unintelligibility in principle to another. The structuring of a chess player's visual field, at which I have hinted, might be shown in a 'public' diagram —for instance, in a film of a lone Knight on a chessboard, upon which the 'target squares' are suddenly made 'prominent' (by being brought into relief by being outlined, changing colour, etc). If such a non-verbal diagram were correctly understood, it would serve the function of the 'verbal articulation' in rule-accepting behaviour. I shall speak in such cases of *rule-guided action*.

Rule-guided action, that is appropriately articulated by non-verbal symbolism, and the intuitive transformation or 'condensation' that makes it possible, seems to me of fundamental importance to educational method. (In spite of the efforts of Gestalt psychologists, it is still an unjustly neglected field of research.) It is connected in the most intimate way with the learner's necessary effort to impose a memorable order upon what looks initially like a chaos of unrelated items.[13] Whatever the topic—a mathematical proof, the conjugation of a verb, the salient features of the Industrial Revolution—the data must be 'rendered down', simplified, structured, if they are to be assimilated, remembered and properly used. Only in this way does '*the* rule' for achieving something become '*my* rule'.

## 8

Much of my discussion has turned, one way or another, upon the possibility of a verbal formulation of a rule. It may be as well, therefore, to consider certain fundamental limitations upon such 'articulation'. (I shall neglect some obvious practical limitations arising from lack of skill on the part of teacher or learner.)

The first limitation may be introduced by as trivial an example as that of somebody knitting a scarf. Whether or not the knitter resorts to printed instructions, *we* can certainly articulate a governing rule : say 'Knit plain and purl for a hundred stitches, then turn and continue' (call this formula *A*). Now the correct application of formula *A* is itself a rule-governed activity which might be articulated by another formula, *B* say, explaining how to make 'plain' and 'purl' stitches, and so on. (Cf. the 'Instructions' sometimes appended to official forms, telling one how to do what one has been told to do!) Could one then not envisage a further formula, *C,* articulating the mode of application of *B*, and so on without end?

The infinite regress that threatens here is factitious. The chain of rules will quickly terminate, for want of an adequate vocabulary. The nearer we come to what is readily *seen* by an apt learner, the harder it becomes to articulate the governing rule and a point is soon reached at which the effort of attending to the verbal formula positively interferes with the primary performance. (Try saying *what* you are doing while knitting—or while running downstairs.)

Of course, sensible men soon abandon *saying* in favour of *showing* : however hard it may be to teach knitting by example, it is incomparably harder to do so by talking about it.

This point can be generalized : successful use of articulated rules presupposes mastery of skills (rule-governed performances) not controlled by *explicit* rules. Hence, 'practice' must precede the critical activity of rule formulation. Only in this way can the intellectual and educational values of rule-formulation be realized : without the prior foundation of more or less 'blind' practice and experience, the rules degenerate into sterile verbalism.

9

I have tried to perform a preliminary survey—rough, but serviceable—of the complex notion of 'rule-governed behaviour'. One moral I would like to draw is that the learner and the teacher are never faced with a stark choice between blind, unconscious, mastery ('rule-covered behaviour' or the even more primitive outcome of 'conditioning') and self-conscious adherence to explicitly formulated principles ('rule-invoking behaviour'). Between these extremes, we have been able to discern types of intelligent and skilful performance ('rule-accepting' and 'rule-guided' behaviour), which combine the virtues of 'free-flowing' and 'prescribed' behaviour. Here, ideally, there is no longer any conflict between the two ideals I invoked at the outset, and submission to the discipline of rules, freely adopted, becomes indistinguishable from the freedom of self-realization.

In working for this ideal harmony, a good teacher will be sensitively alert to the supreme importance of timing—the rhythm of alternation between the different modes of action. He will not shrink from brute conditioning, to lay a necessary foundation of primitive habits of response. But unless he wants his pupils to be no better than trained circus animals, he will try, at the right time, to change blind response into self-directed control by justified rules. He will be willing to break down primitive habits by analysis and criticism, if only for the sake of ultimately inducing higher levels of performance. (The ideal cycle, indefinitely repeated, will be from 'rule-covering behaviour' to 'rule-invoking behaviour' and then to 'rule-accepting behaviour' and 'rule-guided' behaviour.)

There are, alas, no firm rules for what is 'the right time'. Rules are defeasible, hedged about with *ceteribus paribus* clauses to be applied at the discretion of their users. But there are no useful rules for the application of discretion, tact or judgment. A sub-title for this essay might have been 'In Defence of Rules and Principles'. I have hoped it might be read by those who will know that there is a time for throwing rule-books away.

## NOTES

1. But consider the following description : 'A moment before they had been swaying drunk. The touch of arms sobered them : they went through the manual from A to Z before us perfectly. More than mechanically perfect it was : a living, intelligent pattern and poem of movement' (T. E. Lawrence, *The Mint,* Jonathan Cape, 1955, p. 186). Drill *can* have the aesthetic grace of a 'dance'.

2. I shall not try to define this. If asked why I am entering my age on the form, I should be giving an intrinsic reason if I said 'Because the instruction asks for it.' An extrinsic reason would be : 'Because I am afraid of the penalty for omission.'

3. This must not be taken too literally, of course. One can, more or less playfully, treat even doodling as a kind of task. But the artificiality is patent.

4. Further discussion of the concept of a rule is to be found in Chapter 6 of my *Models and Metaphors* (Ithaca, N.Y., 1962).

5. This is an important reason why imputation of rule-governed behaviour involves the presence of more than mere irregularity of behaviour. Sometimes I push at a door marked 'push', sometimes not; I may or may not take my walking stick when I go for a stroll. Both types of deviation from simple regularity might be predictable by some causal theory. What distinguishes the first from the second as 'rule-governed' is the way in which the agent *treats* the deviation. If I curse when I realize I have left the stick behind, insist on going back for it, etc. that is *some* evidence that I am conforming to a rule.

6. If the reader thinks that reference to prior initiation into the 'practice' shifts the burden of conceptual clarification without disposing of it, I would agree. Much more needs to be done by way of clarifying the nature of the practice.

7. I have no space to discuss *disobedience* to rules (a mode of behaviour of some interest to teachers). It may be enough to make the obvious point that disobedience or violation implies a kind of weak recognition of the rule : you cannot break a rule (in the primary sense of 'break') without knowing what the rule is and understanding its pretensions to validity. The innocent can misbehave, but cannot break rules. It is tempting, but mistaken, to say that the violator stands the rule on its head, replacing it by an opposed rule, on the principle of 'Your right

shall be my wrong'. But rule-breaking need not be done to rule (wrong-doing need not be principled): the rule can simply be ignored (suppressed, forgotten.) Active and principled disobedience is a backhanded kind of tribute paid to the rule by the rule-breaker.

8. The consequent division and deflection of attention may have something to do with the jerky, angular or monotonous rhythm of *prescribed* behaviour, that is so much despised by admirers of the free-flowing and spontaneous. Deflected attention has obvious dangers: it is all too easy to get too interested in the recipe and to forget about the cake. Any schoolroom can provide examples.

9. Reasons may be given, sometimes, for intentional or purposive action that is not rule-governed. This is too large a topic to be pursued here.

10. If the reader is strongly inclined to think that the conception of implicit or sub-conscious obedience *must* be right, let him consider the following. My regular practice of washing in the morning is *as if* I were obeying a command. Am I to be taken as obeying an implicit *command*?

11. Verbal articulation will *change* the performance, in subtle or massive ways. Indeed its main point will often be to correct and to improve the performance.

12. Michael Polanyi, *Personal Knowledge* (London, 1958), p. 49.

13. See, for instance, Polanyi's discussion of 'the kind of topographic knowledge which an experienced surgeon possesses of the regions on which he operates' (op. cit., p. 89). It seems to me unduly pessimistic to call such knowledge 'ineffable'.

# 7

# TEACHING AND TRAINING

## Gilbert Ryle

I have no teaching tricks or pedagogic maxims to impart to you, and I should not impart them to you if I had any. What I want to do is to sort out and locate a notion which is cardinal to the notions of teaching, training, education, etc. about which too little is ordinarily said. This notion is that of *teaching oneself* which goes hand in glove with the notion of *thinking for oneself*. You will all agree, I think, that teaching fails, that is, either the teacher is a failure or the pupil is a failure, if the pupil does not sooner or later become able and apt to arrive at his own solutions to problems. But how, in logic, can anyone be taught to do untaught things? I repeat, how, in logic, can anyone be taught to do untaught things?

To clear the air, let me begin by quickly putting on one side an unimportant but familiar notion, that of the self-taught man. Normally when we describe someone as a self-taught man we think of a man who having been deprived of tuition from other teachers tries to make himself an historian, say, or a linguist or an astronomer, without criticism, advice or stimulation from anyone else, save from the authors of such textbooks, encyclopaedia articles and linguaphone records as he may happen to hit on. He hits on these, of course, randomly, without having anyone or anything to tell him whether they are good ones, silly ones, old-fashioned ones or cranky ones. We admire the devotion with which he studies, but, save for the rare exception, we pity him for having been the devoted pupil only of that solitary and untrained teacher, himself. However, I am not interested in him.

What I am interested in is this. Take the case of an ordinary unbrilliant, unstupid boy who is learning to read. He has learned to spell and read monosyllables like 'bat', 'bad', 'at', 'ring', 'sing' etc. and some two-syllable words like 'running', 'dagger' and a few others. We have never taught him, say, the word 'batting'. Yet we find him quite soon reading and spelling unhesitantly the word 'batting'. We ask him who taught him this word and, if he remembers, he says that he had found it out for himself. He has learned from himself how the word 'batting' looks in print, how to write it down on paper and how to spell it out aloud, so in a sense he has taught himself this word—taught it to himself without yet knowing it. How can this be? How can a boy who does not know what 'b-a-t-t-i-n-g' spells teach himself what it spells?

In real life we are not a bit puzzled. It is just what we expect of a not totally stupid child. Yet there is the semblance of a conceptual paradox here, for we seem to be describing him as at a certain stage being able to teach himself something new, which *ipso facto* was not yet in his repertoire to teach. Here his teacher was as ignorant as the pupil, for they were the same boy. So how can the one learn something from the other?

What should we say? Well, clearly we want to say that the prior things that we *had* taught him, namely words like 'bat', 'bad', 'rat' and longer words like 'butter', 'running' etc. enabled him and perhaps encouraged him to make a new bit of independent, uncoached progress on his own. We had taught him *how* to read some monosyllables, *how* to run some of them together in dissyllables, and so on. We had taught him a way or some ways of coping with combinations of printed letters, though not in their particular application to this new word 'batting'. He had made this particular application himself. So to speak, we had previously from the deck shown him the ropes and now he climbs one of them with his own hands and feet; that is to say, not being totally stupid, he was able and ready to employ this slightly general knowledge that we had given to him on a new concrete and particular problem that we had not solved for him. We had given him the wherewithal with which to think it out for himself—and this thinking out was his doing and not ours. I could just as well have taken an example from the much more sophisticated stratum where a brilliant undergraduate makes a good philosophical move that no one else has ever taught him, and maybe no one else has ever made.

Naturally, most often the boy or the undergraduate, if asked Who taught you that? would reply not that he had taught it to himself or that he had learned it from himself, but rather that he had found it out or thought it out or worked it out for himself. Just this brings out a big part of what interests me, namely, that though in one way it is obviously impossible for one person's own discovery, whether trivial or important, to be simply what someone else had previously taught him—since it would then not be his discovery—, yet in another way it is and ought to be one main business of a teacher precisely to get his pupils to advance beyond their instructions and to discover new things for themselves, that is, to get them to think things out for themselves. I teach Tommy to read a few words like 'bat', 'run' and 'running' in order that he may then, of his own motion, find out how to read lots and lots of other words, like 'batting', that we have not taught to him. Indeed we do not deem him really able to spell or read until he can spell and read things that he has not been introduced to. Nor, to leave the schoolroom for the moment, do I think that Tommy has learned to bicycle until he can do things on his bicycle far more elaborate, speedy, tricky and delicate than the things I drilled him in on the first morning. I taught him the few elements on the first morning just in order that he might then find out for himself how to cope with hosts of non-elementary tasks. I gave him a few stereotyped exercises, and, as I had hoped and expected, in a couple of days he had developed for himself on this basis a fair wealth of boyish skills and dexterities, though he acquired these while I was away in London.

However, there remains a slight feeling of a puzzle or paradox here, and it comes, I think, from this source. A familiar and indispensable part or sort of teaching consists in teaching by rote lists of truths or facts, for example the proposition that $7 \times 7$ is 49, etc., the proposition that Waterloo was fought in 1815, etc., and the proposition that Madrid is the capital of Spain, etc. That the pupil has learned a lesson of this propositional sort is shown, in the first instance, by his being able and reasonably ready to reproduce word-perfectly these pieces of information. He gets them by heart, and he can come out with them on demand. Now every teacher knows that only a vanishingly small fraction of his teaching-day really consists in simply reciting lists of such snippets of information to pupils, but very unfortunately, it happens to be the solitary part which un-schooled parents, Sergeant Majors, some silly publicists and some educationalists always think of when they think of teaching and learning. They think or half-think that the request 'Recite what you have learned in school today, Tommy' is a natural and proper one, as if all that Tommy could or should have learned is a number of memorizable propositions; or as if to have learned anything consisted simply in being able to echo it, like a gramophone. As you all know, most teaching has nothing whatsoever in common with this crude, semi-surgical picture of teaching as the forcible insertion into the pupil's memory of strings of officially approved propositions; and I hope to show before long that even that small and of course indispensable part of instruction which is the imparting of factual information is grossly mis-pictured when pictured as literal cramming. Yet, bad as the picture is, it has a powerful hold over people's general theorizings about teaching and learning. Even Tommy's father, after spending the morning in teaching Tommy to swim, to dribble the football or to diagnose and repair what is wrong with the kitchen clock, in the afternoon cheerfully writes to the newspapers letters which take it for granted that all lessons are strings of memorizable propositions. His practice is perfectly sensible, yet still his theory is as silly as it could be.

Perhaps the prevalence of this very thin and partial notion of teaching and learning inherits something from the teaching and learning that are done in the nursery, where things such as 'Hickory Dickory Dock' and simple tunes are learned by heart from that mere vocal repetition which enables the parrot to pick them up too.

Well, in opposition to this shibboleth, I want to switch the centre of gravity of the whole topic on to the notions of Teaching-to so and so, and Learning-to so and so, that is, on to the notion of the development of abilities and competences. Let us forget for a while the memorization of truths, and, of course, of rhymes and tunes, and attend, instead, to the acquisition of skills, knacks and efficiencies. Consider, for example, lessons in drawing, arithmetic and cricket—and, if you like, in philosophy. These lessons cannot consist of and cannot even contain much of dictated propositions. However many true propositions the child has got by heart, he has not begun to learn to draw or play cricket until he has been given a pencil or a bat and a ball and has practised doing things with them; and even if he progresses magnificently in these arts, he will have little or nothing to reply to his parents if they ask him in the evening to recite to them the propositions that he has learned. He can *exhibit* what he has begun to master, but he cannot *quote* it. To avoid the ambiguity between 'teach' in the sense of 'teach that' and 'teach' in the sense of 'teach to' or 'teach how to', I shall now sometimes use the word 'train'. The drawing-master, the language-teacher or the cricket-coach *trains* his pupils in drawing or in French pronunciation or in batting or bowling, and this training incorporates only a few items of quotable information. The same is true of philosophy.

Part, but only part of this notion of training is the notion of drilling, i.e. putting the pupil through stereotyped exercises which he masters by sheer repetition. Thus the recruit learns to slope arms just by going through the same sequence of motions time after time, until he can, so to speak, perform them in his sleep. Circus-dogs and circus-seals are trained in the same way. At the start piano-playing, counting and gear-changing are also taught by simple habituation. But disciplines do not reduce to such sheer drills. Sheer drill, though it is the indispensable beginning of training, is, for most abilities, only their very beginning. Having become able to do certain low-level things automatically and without thinking, the pupil is expected to advance beyond this point and to employ his inculcated automatisms in higher level tasks which are not automatic, and cannot be done without thinking. Skills, tastes and scruples are more than mere habits, and the disciplines and the self-disciplines which develop them are more than mere rote-exercises.

His translators and commentators have been very unjust to Aristotle on this matter. Though he was the first thinker and is still the best, systematically to study the notions of ability, skill, training, character, learning, discipline, self-discipline, etc. the translators of his works nearly always render his key-ideas by such terms as 'habit' and 'habituation'—as if, for example, a person who has been trained and self-trained to play the violin, or to behave scrupulously in his dealings with other people acts from sheer habit, in the way in which I do tie up my shoelaces quite automatically and without thinking what I am doing or how to do it. Of course Aristotle knew better than this, and the Greek words that he used are quite grossly mistranslated when rendered merely by such words as 'habit' and 'habituation'. The well-disciplined soldier, who does indeed slope arms automatically, does not also shoot automatically or scout by blind habit or read maps like a marionette.

Nor is Tommy's control of his bicycle merely a rote-performance, though he cannot begin to control his bicycle until he has got some movements by rote. Having learned through sheer habit-formation to keep his balance on his bicycle with both hands on the handlebars, Tommy can now try to ride with one hand off, and later still with both hands in his pockets and his feet off the pedals. He now progresses by experimentation. Or, having got by heart the run of the alphabet from ABC through to XYZ, he can now, but not without thinking, tell you what three letters run *backwards* from RQP, though he has never learned by heart this reversed sequence.

I suggest that our initial seeming paradox, that a learner can sometimes of himself, after a bit of instruction, better his instructions, is beginning to seem less formidable. The possibility of it is of the same pattern as the familiar fact that the toddler who has this morning taken a few aided steps, tries this afternoon with or without success to take some unaided steps. The swimmer who can now keep himself up in salt water, comes by himself, at first with a bit of extra splashing, to keep himself up in fresh water. How do any formerly difficult things change into now easy things? Or any once untried things into now feasible ones? The answer is just in terms of the familiar notions of the development of abilities by practice, that is trying and failing and then trying again and not failing so often or so badly, and so on.

Notoriously a very few pupils are, over some tasks, so stupid, idle, scared, hostile, bored or defective, that they make no efforts of their own beyond those imposed on them as drill by their trainer. But to be non-stupid, vigorous and interested *is* to be inclined to make, if only as a game, moves beyond the drilled moves, and to practise of oneself, e.g. to multiply beyond 12 × 12, to run through the alphabet backwards, to bicycle with one hand off the handlebar, or to slope arms in the dark with a walking-stick when no drill-sergeant is there. As Aristotle says 'the things that we have got to do when we have learned to do them, we learn to do by doing them.' What I can do today I could not do easily or well or successfully yesterday; and the day before I could not even try to do them; and if I had not tried unsuccessfully yesterday, I should not be succeeding today.

Before returning to go further into some of these key notions of ability, practice, trying, learning to, teaching to, and so on, I want to look back for a moment to the two over-influential notions of teaching *that* so and so, i.e. telling or informing, and of learning *that* so and so, i.e. the old notion of propositional cramming. In a number of nursery, school and university subjects, there are necessarily some or many true propositions to be accumulated by the student. He must, for example, learn that Oslo is the capital of Norway, Stockholm is the capital of Sweden and Copenhagen is the capital of Denmark. Or he must learn that the Battle of Trafalgar was fought in 1805 and that of Waterloo in 1815. Or that $7 + 5 = 12$, $7 + 6 = 13$, $7 + 7 = 14$, etc.

At the very start, maybe, the child just memorizes these strings of propositions as he memorizes 'Hickory Dickory Dock', the alphabet or 'Thirty days hath September'. But so long as parroting is all he can do, he does not yet know the geographical fact, say, that Stockholm is the capital of Sweden, since if you ask him what Stockholm is the capital of, or whether Madrid is the capital of Sweden, he has no idea how to move. He can repeat, but he cannot yet use the memorized dictum. All he can do is to go through the memorized sequence of European capitals from start through to the required one. He does not qualify as knowing that Stockholm is the capital of Sweden until he can detach this proposition from the memorized rigmarole; and can, for example, answer new-type questions like 'of which country out of the three, Italy, Spain and Sweden is Stockholm the capital?' or 'Here is Stockholm on the globe—whereabouts is Sweden?' and so on. To know the geographical fact requires having taken it in, i.e. being able and ready to operate with it, from it, around it and upon it. To possess a piece of information is to be able to mobilize it apart from its rote-neighbours and out of its rote-formulation in unhackneyed and *ad hoc* tasks. Nor does the pupil know that $7 + 7 = 14$ while this is for him only a still undetachable bit of a memorized sing-song, but only when, for example, he can find fault with someone's assertion that $7 + 8 = 14$, or can answer the new-type question. How many 7s are there in 14?, or the new-type question 'If there are seven boys and seven girls in a room, how many children are in the room?' etc. Only then has he taken it in.

In other words, even to have learned the piece of information *that something is so* is more than merely to be able to parrot the original telling of it—somewhat as to have digested a biscuit is more than merely to have had it popped into one's mouth. Can he or can he not infer from the information that Madrid is the capital of Spain that Madrid is not in Sweden? Can he or can he not tell us what sea-battle occurred ten years before Waterloo?

Notice that I am not in the least deprecating the inculcation of rotes like the alphabet, the figures of the syllogism, 'Hickory Dickory Dock', the dates of the Kings of England, or sloping arms. A person who has not acquired such rotes cannot progress from and beyond them. All that I am arguing is that he does not qualify as knowing even that Waterloo was fought in 1815 if all that he can do is to sing out this sentence inside the sing-song of a memorized string of such sentences. If he can only echo the syllables that he has heard, he has not yet taken in the information meant to be conveyed by them. He has not grasped it if he cannot handle it. But if he could not even echo things told to him, *a fortiori* he could not operate with, from or upon their informative content. One cannot digest a biscuit unless it is first popped into one's mouth. So we see that even to have learned a true proposition is to have learned *to do* things other than repeating the words in which the truth had been dictated. To have learned even a simple geographical fact is to have become able to cope with some unhabitual geographical tasks, however elementary.

We must now come back to our central question : How is it possible that a person should learn from himself something which he previously did not know, and had not, e.g., been taught by someone else ? This question is or embodies the apparently perplexing question : How can one person teach another person to think things out for himself, since if he gives him, say, the new arithmetical thoughts, then they are not the pupil's own thoughts; or if they are his own thoughts, then he did not get them from his teacher ? Having led the horse to the water, how can we make him drink ? But I have, I hope, shifted the centre of gravity of this seeming puzzle, by making the notions of *learning-to* and *teaching-to* the primary notions. In its new form the question is : How, on the basis of some tuition, can a person today get himself to do something which he had not been able to do yesterday or last year ? How can competences, abilities and skills develop ? How can trying ever succeed ? We are so familiar, in practice, with the fact that abilities do develop, and that tryings can succeed that we find little to puzzle us in the idea that they do.

Looked at from the end of the teacher the question is : How can the teacher get his pupil to make independent moves of his own ? If this question is tortured into the shape : How can the teacher make or force his pupil to do things which he is not made or forced to do ? i.e. How can the teacher be the initiator of the pupil's initiatives ? the answer is obvious. He cannot. I cannot compel the horse to drink thirstily. I cannot coerce Tommy into doing spontaneous things. Either he is not coerced, or they are not spontaneous.

As every teacher, like every drill-sergeant or animal trainer knows in his practice, teaching and training have virtually not yet begun, so long as the pupil is too young, too stupid, too scared or too sulky to respond—and to respond is not just to yield. Where there is a modicum of alacrity, interest or anyhow docility in the pupil, where he tries, however faintheartedly, to get things right rather than wrong, fast rather than slow, neat rather than awkward, where, even, he registers even a slight contempt for the poor performances of others or chagrin at his own, pleasure at his own successes and envy of those of others, then he is, in however slight a degree, co-operating and so self-moving. He is doing something, though very likely not much, and is not merely having things done to him. He is, however unambitiously and however desultorily, attempting the still difficult. He has at least a little impetus of his own. A corner, however small a corner of his heart is now in the task. The eager pupil is, of course, the one who, when taught, say, to read or spell a few words like 'at', 'bat' and 'mat' travels home on the bus trying out, just for fun, all the other monosyllables that rhyme with 'at', to see which of them are words. When taught to read and spell a dissyllable or two, he tries his hand, just for fun and often but not always unsuccessfully, on the polysyllables on the advertisement-hoardings; and just for fun he challenges his father to spell long words when he gets home. He does this for fun; but like much play it is spontaneous self-practising. When he returns to school after the holidays, although his spelling and reading are now far in advance of their peak of last term, he will stoutly deny that he has done any work during the holidays. It has not been work, it has been absorption in a new hobby, like exercising a new limb.

His over-modest teacher may say that he has taught this boy next to nothing—nor has he, save for the very beginnings of everything.

However, we should remember that although a total absence of eagerness or even willingness spells total unteachability, the presence of energy, adventurousness and self-motion is not by itself enough. The wild guesser and the haphazard plunger have freedom of movement of a sort, but not of the best sort. Learning how to do new and therefore more or less difficult things does indeed require trying things out for oneself, but if this trying-out is not controlled by any testing or making sure, then its adventurousness is recklessness and not enterprise. He is like the gambler, not like the investor. The moves made, though spontaneous, are irresponsible and they yield no dividends. Nothing can be learned by him from their unsuccesses or from their occasional fortuitous successes. He shoots away, but learns nothing from his misses—or from his fluke hits.

It is just here, with the notion of taking care when taking risks, that there enters on the scenes the cardinal notion of *method*, i.e. of techniques, *modi operandi*, rules, canons, procedures, knacks, and even tricks of the trade. In doing a thing that he has never done before, a person may, but need not, operate according to a method, sometimes, even according to a sheer drill that he has adhered to before. If he does, then his action is still an innovation, although the pattern of his action is a familiar and inculcated one. The poet composes a sonnet, taking care to adhere to the regulation 14 lines, to the regulation rhyming scheme, to the regulation metrical pattern, or else perhaps to one of the several permitted patterns—yet, nonetheless, his sonnet is a new one. No one has ever composed *it* before. His teacher who taught him how to compose sonnets had not and could not have made him compose this sonnet, else it would be the teacher's and not the pupil's sonnet. Teaching people how to do things just *is* teaching them methods or *modi operandi;* and it is just because it is one thing to have learned a method and another thing to essay a new application of it that we can say without paradox that the learner's new move is his own move and yet that he may have learned the *how* of making it from someone else. The cook's pudding is a new one and piping hot, but its recipe was known to Mrs. Beeton in the days of Queen Victoria.

Well, then, what sort of a thing is a method? First for what it is not. Despite what many folk would say, a method is not a stereotyped sequence-pattern or routine of actions, inculcatable by pure rote, like sloping arms or going through the alphabet. The parrot that can run through 'Hickory Dickory Dock' has not learned how to do anything or therefore how not to do it. There is nothing that he takes care not to do.

A method is a learnable way of doing something, where the word 'way' connotes more than mere rote or routine. A way of doing something, or a *modus operandi*, is something general, and general in at least two dimensions. First, the way in which you do a thing, say mount your bicycle, can be the way or a way in which some other people or perhaps most other people mount or try to mount their bicycles. Even if you happen to be the only person who yet does something in a certain way, it is possible that others should in future learn from you or find out for themselves the very same way of doing it. *Modi operandi* are, in principle, public property, though a particular action performed in this way is my action and not yours, or else it is your action and not mine. We mount our bicycles in the same way, but my bicycle-mounting is my action and not yours. You do not make my mincepies, even though we both follow the same Victorian recipe.

The second way in which a method is something general is the obvious one, that there is no limit to the number of actions that may be done in that way. The method is, roughly, applicable anywhere and anywhen, as well as by anyone. For however many people are known by me to have mounted their bicycles in a certain way, I know that there could have been and there could be going to be any number of other bicycle-mountings performed by myself and others in the same way.

Next, methods can be helpfully, if apparently cynically, thought of as systems of avoidances or as patterns of 'don'ts'. The rules, say, of English grammar do not tell us positively what to say or write; they tell us negatively not to say or write such things as 'A dog *are* . . . ' and 'Those dogs *is* . . . ', and learning the art of rock-climbing or tree-climbing is, among hundreds of other things, learning never, or hardly ever, to trust one's whole weight to an untried projection or to a branch that is leafless in summer time.

People sometimes grumble at the Ten Commandments on the score that most of them are prohibitions, and not positive injunctions. They have not realized that the notice 'Keep off the grass' licenses us to walk anywhere else we choose; where the notice 'Keep to the gravel' leaves us with almost no freedom of movement. Similarly to have learned a method is to have learned to take care against certain specified kinds of risk, muddle, blind alley, waste, etc. But carefully keeping away from this cliff and from that morass leaves the rest of the countryside open for us to walk lightheartedly in. If I teach you even twenty kinds of things that would make your sonnet a bad sonnet or your argument a bad argument, I have still left you an indefinite amount of elbow-room within which you can construct your own sonnet or argument, and this sonnet or argument of yours, whether brilliant or ordinary or weak, will at least be free of faults of those twenty kinds.

There exists in some quarters the sentimental idea that the teacher who teaches his pupils how to do things is hindering them, as if his apron-strings coerced their leg-movements. We should think of the

inculcation of methods rather as training the pupils to avoid specified muddles, blockages, sidetracks and thin ice by training them to
recognize these for what they are. Enabling them to avoid troubles,
disasters, nuisances and wasted efforts is helping them to move where
they want to move. Road signs are not, for the most part, impediments to the flow of traffic. They are preventives of impediments to
the flow of traffic.

Of course we can easily think of silly ways of doing things which
continue to be taught by grown-ups to children and adhered to by
the grown-ups themselves. Not all methods are good methods, or all
recipes good recipes. For example, the traditional ban on splitting the
infinitive was a silly rule. But the gratuitous though trivial bother
of conforming to this particular veto was negligible compared with
the handicap that would be suffered by the child who had never
been taught or picked up for himself any of the procedures for composing or construing sentences. He would have been kept back at
the level of total infancy. He could not say or follow anything at all
if, for example, he had not mastered conjunctions, or even verbs,
and mastering them involves learning how *not* to make hashes of
them.

How does one teach methods or ways of doing things? Well,
there is no simple answer to this. Different arts and crafts require
different kinds of disciplines; and in some one particular field, say
drawing, one teacher works very differently from another. Sometimes a little, sometimes a lot can be told; there is much that cannot
be told, but can be shown by example, by caricature and so on. But
one thing is indispensable. The pupil himself must, whether under
pressure or from interest or ambition or conscientiousness, practise
doing what he is learning how to do. Whether in his exercises in the
art he religiously models his strokes after Bradman, or whether he
tries to win the praise or avoid the strictures or sarcasms of a feared,
respected or loved coach, he learns by performing and improves by
trying to better his own and his fellows' previous performances by
eradicating their faults. The methods of operating taught to him
become his personal methods of operating by his own criticized and
self-criticized practice. Whether in spelling, in Latin grammar,
fencing, arithmetic or philosophy, he learns the ropes, not much by
gazing at them or hearing about them, but by trying to climb them—
and by trying to climb them less awkwardly, slowly and riskily
today than he did yesterday.

So far I have been, for simplicity, dividing the contributions of the teacher and the pupil by saying that the teacher in teaching how to so and so is teaching a method or way of operating, while the pupil keeps his initiative by making his own at the start somewhat arduous, because new applications of that method. The teacher introduces the pupil to the ropes, but it is for the pupil to try to climb them.

But now we should pay some attention to the fact that pretty soon the pupil has become familiar with the quite general fact that for lots and lots of widely different kinds of operations—spelling, say, skating and bowling at cricket—there exist different *modi operandi.* There are spelling-mistakes and there are bowling-faults, and neither spelling nor bowling can go right unless these faults are systematically avoided. So now, when he undertakes an altogether new kind of operation, canoeing, say, he from the start expects there to be *modi operandi* here too. This too will be a thing that he will have to learn how to do, partly by learning how not to do it. But this time, it may be, there is no one to teach him, and not even any other canoeist to imitate. He has got to find out for himself the way, or anyhow a way, of balancing, propelling and steering his canoe. Well, at first he tries a lot of random things, and nearly all of them end in immersion or collision; but he does after a time find out some ways of managing his craft. He may not achieve elegance or speed, but he does find out how not to topple over and how not to run into obstacles. He is trained, this time purely self-trained, regularly to avoid some kinds of faulty watermanship. But it is because he had previously learned by practice, coaching and imitation the 'hows' of lots of other things such as tree-climbing, spelling and skating, that he now takes it for granted that canoeing has its 'hows' as well, which similarly can be learned by practice, trial and error, and looking for ways of avoiding the repetition of errors. Here, as elsewhere, he has to study in order to improve; but this time he has nothing to study save his own unsuccesses and successes.

His more reckless and impatient brother, though full of go, just makes a dash at it, and then another quite different dash at it, and learns nothing or almost nothing from the failures which generally result, or even from the successes which sometimes just happen to result. He is not a self-trainer.

The third brother is uninterested, slow in the uptake, scared or idle. He never chances his arm. He tries nothing, and so initiates nothing either successfully or unsuccessfully. So he never learns to canoe; never, perhaps, even regrets not having learned it or envies those who have. There is no question of his training himself in this particular art, or even, if he is a very bad case, of his being trained by anyone else; just as there was fifty years ago no real question of me training myself or of my being trained by anyone else in the arts of cricket or music.

The supreme reward of the teacher is to turn out from time to time the student who comes to be not merely abreast of his teacher but ahead of him, the student, namely, who advances his subject or his craft not just by adding to it further applications of the established ways of operating, but by discovering new methods or procedures of types which no one could have taught to him. He has given to his subject or his craft a new idea or a battery of new ideas. He is original. He himself, if of a grateful nature, will say that his original idea just grew of itself out of what he had learned from his teachers, his competitors and his colleagues; while they, if of a grateful nature, will say that the new idea was his discovery. Both will be right. His new idea is the fruit of a tree that others had planted and pruned. It is really his own fruit and he is really their tree.

We started off with the apparent paradox that though the teacher in teaching is doing something to his pupil, yet the pupil has learned virtually nothing unless he becomes able and ready to do things of his own motion other than what the teacher exported to him. We asked; How in logic can the teacher dragoon his pupil into thinking for himself, impose initiative upon him, drive him into self-motion, conscript him into volunteering, enforce originality upon him, or make him operate spontaneously? The answer is that he cannot—and the reason why we half felt that he must do so was that we were unwittingly enslaved by the crude, semi-hydraulic idea that in essence to teach is to pump propositions, like 'Waterloo, 1815' into the pupils' ears, until they regurgitate them automatically.

When we switched from the notion of 'hydraulic injection' to the notion of 'teaching to' or 'teaching how to', the paradox began to disappear. I can introduce you to a way or the way of doing something, and still your actual essays in the exercise of this craft or competence are yours and not mine. I do not literally make you do them, but I do enable you to do them. I give you the *modus operandi*, but your operatings or tryings to operate according to this *modus* are your own doings and not my inflictings and the practising by which you master the method is your exertion and not mine. I have given you some equipment against failing, *if* you try. But that you try is not something that I can coerce. Teaching is not gate-shutting but gate-opening, yet still the dull or the scared or the lame calf does not walk out into the open field. All this does not imply the popular sentimental corollary that teachers should never be strict, demanding, peremptory or uncondoning. It is often the hard task-master who alone succeeds in instilling mistrust of primrose paths. The father may enlarge the child's freedom of movement by refusing to hold his hand, and the boxing-instructor or the philosophy-tutor may enlarge his pupil's powers of defence and attack by hitting him hard and often. It is not the chocolates and the sponge-cakes that strengthen the child's jaw-muscles. They have other virtues, but not this one.

# 8

## PHILOSOPHICAL MODELS OF TEACHING
Israel Scheffler

### I. INTRODUCTION

Teaching may be characterized as an activity aimed at the achievement of learning, and practised in such manner as to respect the student's intellectual integrity and capacity for independent judgment. Such a characterization is important for at least two reasons : First, it brings out the intentional nature of teaching, the fact that teaching is a distinctive goal-oriented activity, rather than a distinctively patterned sequence of behavioural steps executed by the teacher. Secondly, it differentiates the activity of teaching from such other activities as propaganda, conditioning, suggestion, and indoctrination, which are aimed at modifying the person but strive at all costs to avoid a genuine engagement of his judgment on underlying issues.

This characterization of teaching, which I believe to be correct, fails, nevertheless, to answer certain critical questions of the teacher : What sort of learning shall I aim to achieve? In what does such learning consist? How shall I strive to achieve it? Such questions are, respectively, normative, epistemological, and empirical in import, and the answers that are provided for them give point and substance to the educational enterprise. Rather than trying to separate these questions, however, and deal with each abstractly and explicitly, I should like, on the present occasion, to approach them indirectly and as a group, through a consideration of three influential models of teaching, which provide, or at any rate suggest, certain relevant answers. These models do not so much aim to *describe* teaching as to *orient* it, by weaving a coherent picture out of epistemological, psychological, and normative elements. Like all models, they simplify, but such simplification is a legitimate way of highlighting what are thought to be important features of the subject. The primary issue, in each case, is whether these features are indeed critically important, whether we should allow our educational thinking to be guided by a model which fastens upon them, or whether we should rather reject or revise the model in question. Although I shall mention some historical affiliations of each model, I make no pretence to historical accuracy. My main purpose is, rather, systematic or dialectical, that is, to outline and examine the three models and to see what, if anything, each has to offer us in our own quest for a satisfactory conception of teaching. I turn, then, first to what may be called the 'impression model'.

## 2. THE IMPRESSION MODEL

The impression model is perhaps the simplest and most widespread of the three, picturing the mind essentially as sifting and storing the external impressions to which it is receptive. The desired end result of teaching is an accumulation in the learner of basic elements fed in from without, organized and processed in standard ways, but, in any event, not generated by the learner himself. In the empiricist variant of this model generally associated with John Locke, learning involves the input by experience of simple ideas of sensation and reflection, which are clustered, related, generalized, and retained by the mind. Blank at birth, the mind is thus formed by its particular experiences, which it keeps available for its future use. In Locke's words (Bk. II, Ch. I, Sect. 2 of the *Essay Concerning Human Understanding*) :

> Let us then suppose the mind to be, as we say, white paper, void of all characters, without any ideas; how comes it to be furnished? Whence comes it by that vast store, which the busy and boundless fancy of man has painted on it with an almost endless variety? Whence has it all the materials of reason and knowledge? To this I answer, in one word, From experience; in that all our knowledge is founded, and from that it ultimately derives itself. Our observation, employed either about external sensible objects, or about the internal operations of our minds, perceived and reflected on by ourselves, is that which supplies our understandings with all the materials of thinking. These two are the fountains of knowledge, from whence all the ideas we have, or can naturally have, do spring.

Teaching, by implication, should concern itself with exercising the mental powers engaged in receiving and processing incoming

ideas, more particularly powers of perception, discrimination, retention, combination, abstraction, and representation. But, more important, teaching needs to strive for the optimum selection and organization of this experiential input. For potentially, the teacher has
enormous power; by controlling the input of sensory units, he can,
to a large degree, shape the mind. As Dewey remarked,[1]

> Locke's statements...seemed to do justice to both mind and matter....
> One of the two supplied the matter of knowledge and the object upon
> which the mind should work. The other supplied definite mental
> powers, which were few in number and which might be trained by
> specific exercises.

The process of learning in the child was taken as paralleling the
growth of knowledge generally, for all knowledge is constructed
out of elementary units of experience, which are grouped, related,
and generalized. The teacher's object should thus be to provide data
not only useful in themselves, but collectively rich enough to support the progressive growth of adult knowledge in the learner's
mind.

The impression model, as I have sketched it, has certain obvious
strong points. It sets forth the appeal to experience as a general tool
of criticism to be employed in the examination of all claims and
doctrines, and it demands that they square with it. Surely such a
demand is legitimate, for knowledge does rest upon experience in
some way or other. Further, the mind is, in a clear sense, as the
impression model suggests, a function of its particular experiences,
and it is capable of increased growth with experience. The richness
and variety of the child's experiences are thus important considerations in the process of educational planning.

The impression model nevertheless suffers from fatal difficulties.
The notions of absolutely simple ideas and of abstract mental powers
improvable through exercise have been often and rightly criticized
as mythological:[2] Simplicity is a relative, not an absolute, concept
and reflects a particular way of analysing experience; it is, in short,
not given but made. And mental powers or faculties invariant with
subject matter have, as everyone knows, been expunged from psychology on empirical as well as theoretical grounds. A more fundamental criticism, perhaps, is that the implicit conception of the
growth of knowledge is false. Knowledge is not achieved through
any standard set of operations for the processing of sensory parti-

culars, however conceived. Knowledge is, first and foremost, embodied in language, and involves a conceptual apparatus not derivable from the sensory data but imposed upon them. Nor is such apparatus built into the human mind; it is, at least in good part a product of guesswork and invention, borne along by culture and by custom. Knowledge further involves *theory*, and theory is surely not simply a matter of generalizing the data, even assuming such data organized by a given conceptual apparatus. Theory is a creative and individualistic enterprise that goes beyond the data in distinctive ways, involving not only generalization, but postulation of entities, deployment of analogies, evaluation of relative simplicity, and, indeed, invention of new languages. Experience is relevant to knowledge through providing tests of our theories; it does not automatically generate these theories, even when processed by the human mind. That we have the theories we do is, therefore, a fact, not simply about the human mind, but about our history and our intellectual heritage.

In the process of learning, the child gets not only sense experiences but the language and theory of his heritage in complicated linkages with discriminable contexts. He is heir to the complex culture of belief built up out of innumerable creative acts of intellect of the past, and comprising a patterned view of the world. To give the child even the richest selection of sense data or particular facts alone would in no way guarantee his building up anything resembling what we think of as knowledge, much less his developing the ability to retrieve and apply such knowledge in new circumstances.

A *verbal* variant of the impression model of teaching naturally suggests itself, then, as having certain advantages over the *sensory* version we have just considered: What is to be impressed on the mind is not only sense experience but language and, moreover, accepted theory. We need to feed in not only sense data but the correlated verbal patterning of such data, that is, the *statements* about such data which we ourselves accept. The student's knowledge consists in his stored accumulation of these statements, which have application to new cases in the future. He is no longer, as before, assumed capable of generating our conceptual heritage by operating in certain standard ways on his sense data, for part of what *we* are required to feed into his mind is this very heritage itself.

This verbal variant, which has close affinities to contemporary behaviourism, does have certain advantages over its predecessor, but retains grave inadequacies still, as a model of teaching. To *store* all accepted theories is not the same as being able to *use* them properly in context. Nor, even if some practical correlation with sense data is achieved, does it imply an understanding of what is thus stored, nor an appreciation of the theoretical motivation and experimental evidence upon which it rests.

All versions of the impression model, finally, have this defect: They fail to make adequate room for radical *innovation* by the learner. We do not, after all, feed into the learner's mind all that we hope he will have as an end result of our teaching. Nor can we construe the critical surplus as generated in standard ways out of materials we do supply. We do not, indeed cannot, so construe insight, understanding, new applications of our theories, new theories, new achievements in scholarship, history, poetry, philosophy. There is a fundamental gap which teaching cannot bridge simply by expansion or reorganization of the curriculum input. This gap sets *theoretical* limits to the power and control of the teacher; moreover, it is where his control ends that his fondest hopes for education begin.

### 3. THE INSIGHT MODEL

The next model I shall consider, the 'insight model', represents a radically different approach. Where the impression model supposes the teacher to be conveying ideas or bits of knowledge into the student's mental treasury, the insight model denies the very possibility of such conveyance. Knowledge, it insists, is a matter of vision, and vision cannot be dissected into elementary sensory or verbal units that can be conveyed from one person to another. It can, at most, be stimulated or prompted by what the teacher does, and if it indeed occurs, it goes beyond what is thus done. Vision defines and organizes particular experiences, and points up their significance. It is vision, or insight into meaning, which makes the crucial difference between simply storing and reproducing learned sentences, on the one hand, and understanding their basis and application, on the other.

The insight model is due to Plato, but I shall here consider the version of St. Augustine, in his dialogue, 'The Teacher',[3] for it bears precisely on the points we have dealt with. Augustine argues roughly as follows: The teacher is commonly thought to convey knowledge by his use of language. But knowledge, or rather *new* knowledge, is not conveyed simply by words sounding in the ear. Words are mere noises unless they signify realities present in some way to the mind. Hence a paradox: If the student already knows the realities to which the teacher's words refer, the teacher teaches him nothing new. Whereas, if the student does not know these realities, the teacher's words can have no meaning for him, and must be mere noises. Augustine concludes that language must have a function wholly distinct from that of the signification of realities; it is used to *prompt* people in certain ways. The teacher's words, in particular, prompt the student to search for realities not already known by him. Finding these realities, which are illuminated for him by internal vision, he acquires new knowledge for himself, though indirectly as a result of the teacher's prompting activity. To *believe* something simply on the basis of authority or hearsay is indeed possible, on Augustine's view; to *know* it is not. Mere beliefs may, in his opinion, of course, be useful; they are not therefore knowledge. For knowledge, in short, requires the individual himself to have a grasp of the realities lying behind the words.

The insight model is strong where the impression model is weakest. While the latter, in its concern with the conservation of knowledge, fails to do justice to innovation, the former addresses itself from the start to the problem of *new* knowledge resulting from teaching. Where the latter stresses atomic manipulable bits at the expense of understanding, the former stresses primarily the acquisition of insight. Where the latter gives inordinate place to the feeding in of materials from the outside, the former stresses the importance of firsthand inspection of realities by the student, the necessity for the student to earn his knowledge by his own efforts.

I should argue, nevertheless, that the case offered by Augustine for the prompting theory is not, as it stands, satisfactory. If the student does not know the realities behind the teacher's words, these words are, presumably, mere noises and can serve only to prompt the student to inquire for himself. Yet if they *are* mere noises, how can they even serve to prompt? If they are not understood in any way by the student, how can they lead him to search for the appropriate realities which underlie them? Augustine, furthermore, allows that a person may believe, though not know, what he accepts on mere authority, without having confronted the relevant realities. Such a person might, presumably, pass from the state of belief to that of knowledge, as a result of prompting, under certain conditions. But what, we may ask, could have been the content of his initial belief if the formulation of it had been literally unintelligible to him? The prompting theory, it seems, will not do as a way of escaping Augustine's original paradox.

There is, however, an easier escape. For the paradox itself rests on a confusion of the meaning of *words* with that of *sentences*. Let me explain. Augustine holds that words acquire intelligibility only through acquaintance with reality. Now it may perhaps be initially objected that understanding a word does not always require acquaintance with its signified reality, for words may also acquire intelligibility through definition, lacking such direct acquaintance. But let us waive this objection and grant, for the sake of argument, that understanding a word *always* does require such acquaintance; it still does not follow that understanding a true sentence similarly requires acquaintance with the state of affairs which it represents. We understand new sentences all the time, on the basis of an understanding of their constituent words and of the grammar by which they are concatenated. Thus, given a sentence signifying some fact, it is simply not true that, unless the student already knows this fact, the sentence must be mere noise to him. For he can understand its meaning indirectly, by a synthesis of its parts, and be led thereafter to inquire whether it is, in reality, true or false.

If my argument is correct, then Augustine's paradox of teaching can be simply rejected, on the ground that we *can* understand statements before becoming acquainted with their signified realities. It follows that the teacher can indeed *inform* the student of new facts by means of language. And it further seems to follow that the basis for Augustine's prompting theory of teaching wholly collapses. We are back to the impression model, with the teacher using language not to prompt the student to inner vision, but simply to inform him of new facts.

The latter conclusion seems to me, however, mistaken. For it does *not* follow that the student will *know* these new facts simply because he has been *informed*; on this point Augustine seems to me perfectly right. It is knowing, after all, that Augustine is interested in, and knowing requires something more than the receipt and acceptance of true information. It requires that the student earn the right to his assurance of the truth of the information in question. New *information*, in short, can be intelligibly conveyed by statements; new *knowledge* cannot. Augustine, I suggest, confuses the two cases, arguing in effect for the impossibility of conveying new knowledge by words, on the basis of an alleged similar impossibility for information. I have been urging the falsity of the latter premise. But if Augustine's premise is indeed false, his conclusion as regards knowledge seems to me perfectly true : To *know* the proposition expressed by a sentence is more than just to have been told it, to have grasped its meaning, and to have accepted it. It is to have earned the right, through one's own effort or position, to an assurance of its truth.

Augustine puts the matter in terms of an insightful searching of reality, an inquiry carried out by oneself, and resting in no way on authority. Indeed, he is perhaps too austerely individualistic in this regard, rejecting even legitimate arguments from authority as a basis for knowledge. But his main thesis seems to me correct : One cannot convey new knowledge by words alone. For knowledge is not simply a storage of information by the learner.

The teacher does, of course, employ *language*, according to the insight model, but its primary function is not to impress his statements on the student's mind for later reproduction. The teacher's statements are, rather, instrumental to the student's own search of reality and vision thereof; teaching is consummated in the student's own insight. The reference to such insight seems to explain, at least partially, how the student can be expected to apply his learning to new situations in the future. For, having acquired this learning not merely by external suggestion but through a personal engagement with reality, the student can appreciate the particular fit which his theories have with real circumstances, and, hence, the proper occasions for them to be brought into play.

There is, furthermore, no reason to construe adoption of the insight model as eliminating the impression model altogether. For the impression model, it may be admitted, does reflect something genuine and important, but mislocates it. It reflects the increase of the culture's written lore, the growth of knowledge as a public and recorded possession. Furthermore, it reflects the primary importance of conserving such knowledge, as a collective heritage. But knowledge in this public sense has nothing to do with the process of learning and the activity of teaching, that is, with the growth of knowledge in the individual learner. The public treasury of knowledge constitutes a basic source of materials for the teacher, but he cannot hope to transfer it bit by bit in growing accumulation within the student's mind. In conducting his teaching, he must rather give up the hope of such simple transfer, and strive instead to encourage individual insight into the meaning and use of public knowledge.

Despite the important emphases of the insight model which we have been considering, there are, however, two respects in which it falls short. One concerns the simplicity of its constituent notion of insight, or vision, as a condition of knowing; the other relates to its specifically cognitive bias, which it shares with the impression model earlier considered. First, the notion that what is crucial in knowledge is a vision of underlying realities, a consulting of what is found within the mind, is far too simple. Certainly, as we have seen, the knower must satisfy *some* condition beyond simply being informed, in order to have the right to his assurance on the matter in question. But to construe this condition in terms of an intellectual inspection of reality is not at all satisfactory. It is plausible only if we restrict ourselves to very simple cases of truths accessible to observation or introspection. As soon as we attempt to characterize the knowing of propositions normally encountered in practical affairs, in the sciences, in politics, history, or the law, we realize that the concept of a *vision of reality* is impossibly simple. Vision is just the wrong metaphor. What seems indubitably more appropriate in all these cases of knowing is an emphasis on the processes of deliberation, argument, judgment, appraisal of reasons *pro* and *con,* weighing of evidence, appeal to principles, and decision-making, none of which fits at all well with the insight model. This model, in short, does not make adequate room for principled deliberation in the characterization of knowing. It is in terms of such principled deliberation, or the potentiality for it, rather than in terms of simple vision, that the distinctiveness of knowing is primarily to be understood.

Secondly, the insight model is specifically cognitive in emphasis, and cannot readily be stretched so as to cover important aspects of teaching. We noted above, for example, that the application of truths to new situations is somewhat better off in the insight than in the impression model, since the appropriateness of a truth for new situations is better judged with awareness of underlying realities than without. But a judgment of appropriateness is not all there is to application; habits of proper execution are also required, and insight itself does not necessitate such habits. Insight also fails to cover the concept of character and the related notions of attitude and disposition. Character, it is clear, goes beyond insight as well as beyond the impression of information. For it involves general principles of conduct logically independent of both insight and the accumulation of information. Moreover, what has been said of character can be applied also to the various institutions of civilization, including those which channel cognition itself. Science, for example, is not just a collection of true insights; it is embodied in a living tradition composed of demanding principles of judgment and conduct. Beyond the cognitive insight, lies the fundamental commitment to principles by which insights are to be criticized and assessed, in the light of publicly available evidence or reasons. In sum, then, the shortcoming of the insight model may be said to lie in the fact that it provides no role for the concept of *principles,* and the associated concept of *reasons.* This omission is very serious indeed, for the concept of principles and the concept of reasons together underlie not only the notions of rational deliberation and critical judgment, but also the notions of rational and moral conduct.

## 4. THE RULE MODEL

The shortcoming of the insight model just discussed is remedied in the 'rule model', which I associate with Kant. For Kant, the primary philosophical emphasis is on reason, and reason is always a matter of abiding by general rules or principles. Reason stands always in contrast with inconsistency and with expediency, in the judgment of particular issues. In the cognitive realm, reason is a kind of justice to the evidence, a fair treatment of the merits of the case, in the interests of truth. In the moral realm, reason is action on principle, action which therefore does not bend with the wind, nor lean to the side of advantage or power out of weakness or self-interest. Whether in the cognitive or the moral realm, reason is always a matter of treating equal reasons equally, and of judging the issues in the light of general principles to which one has bound oneself.

In thus binding myself to a set of principles, I act freely; this is my dignity as a being with the power of choice. But my own free commitment obligates me to obey the principles I have adopted, when they rule against me. This is what fairness or consistency in conduct means : if I could judge reasons differently when they bear on my interests, or disregard my principles when they conflict with my own advantage, I should have no principles at all. The concepts of *principles*, *reasons*, and *consistency* thus go together and they apply both in the cognitive judgment of beliefs and the moral assessment of conduct. In fact, they define a general concept of rationality. A rational man is one who is consistent in thought and in action, abiding by impartial and generalizable principles freely chosen as binding upon himself. Rationality is an essential aspect of human dignity and the rational goal of humanity is to construct a society in which such dignity shall flower, a society so ordered as to adjudicate rationally the affairs of free rational agents, an international and democratic republic. The job of education is to develop character in the broadest sense, that is, principled thought and action, in which the dignity of man is manifest.

In contrast to the insight model, the rule model clearly emphasizes the role of principles in the exercise of cognitive judgment. The strong point of the insight model can thus be preserved : The knower must indeed satisfy a further condition beyond the mere receiving and storing of a bit of information. But this condition need not, as in the insight model, be taken to involve simply the vision of an underlying reality; rather, it generally involves the capacity for a principled assessment of reasons bearing on justification of the belief in question. The knower, in short, must typically earn the right to confidence in his belief by acquiring the capacity to make a reasonable case for the belief in question. Nor is it sufficient for this case to have been explicitly taught. What is generally expected of the knower is that his autonomy be evidenced in the ability to construct and evaluate fresh and alternative arguments, the power to innovate, rather than just the capacity to reproduce stale arguments earlier stored. The emphasis on innovation, which we found to be an advantage of the insight model, is thus capable of being preserved by the rule model as well.

Nor does the rule model in any way deny the psychological phenomenon of insight. It merely stresses that insight itself, wherever it is relevant to decision or judgment, is filtered through a network of background principles. It brings out thereby that insight is not an isolated, momentary, or personal matter, that the growth of knowledge is not to be construed as a personal interaction between teacher and student, but rather as mediated by general principles definitive of rationality.

Furthermore, while the previous models, as we have seen, are peculiarly and narrowly *cognitive* in relevance, the rule model embraces *conduct* as well as cognition, itself broadly conceived as includ-

130

ing processes of judgment and deliberation. Teaching, it suggests, should be geared not simply to the transfer of information nor even to the development of insight, but to the inculcation of principled judgment and conduct, the building of autonomous and rational character which underlies the enterprises of science, morality and culture. Such inculcation should not, of course, be construed mechanically. Rational character and critical judgment grow only through increased participation in adult experience and criticism, through treatment which respects the dignity of learner as well as teacher. We have here, again, a radical gap which cannot be closed by the teacher's efforts alone. He must rely on the spirit of rational dialogue and critical reflection for the development of character, acknowledging that this implies the freedom to reject as well as to accept what is taught. Kant himself holds, however, that rational principles are somehow embedded in the structure of the human mind, so that education builds on a solid foundation. In any event, the stakes are high, for on such building by education depends the prospect of humanity as an ideal quality of life.

There is much of value in the rule model, as I have sketched it. Certainly, rationality is a fundamental cognitive and moral virtue and as such should, I believe, form a basic objective of teaching. Nor should the many historical connotations of the term 'rationality' here mislead us. There is no intent to suggest a faculty of reason, nor to oppose reason to experience or to the emotions. Nor is rationality being construed as the process of making logical deductions. What is in point here is simply the autonomy of the student's judgment, his right to seek reasons in support of claims upon his credibilities and loyalties, and his correlative obligation to deal with such reasons in a principled manner.

Moreover, adoption of the rule model does not necessarily exclude what is important in the other two models; in fact, it can be construed quite plausibly as supplementing their legitimate emphases. For, intermediate between the public treasury of accumulated lore mirrored by the impression model, and the personal and intuitive grasp of the student mirrored by the insight model, it places general principles of rational judgment capable of linking them.

Yet, there is something too formal and abstract in the rule model, as I have thus far presented it. For the operative principles of rational judgment at any given time are, after all, much more detailed and specific than a mere requirement of formal consistency. Such con-

sistency is certainly fundamental, but the way its demands are con-
cretely interpreted, elaborated, and supplemented in any field of
inquiry or practice, varies with the field, the state of knowledge, and
the advance of relevant methodological sophistication. The concrete
rules governing inference and procedure in the special sciences, for
example, are surely not all embedded in the human mind, even if
the demands of formal consistency, as such, *are* universally compelling. These concrete rules and standards, techniques and methodological criteria evolve and grow with the advance of knowledge
itself; they form a live tradition of rationality in the realm of science.

Indeed, the notion of tradition is a better guide here, it seems to
me, than appeal to the innate structure of the human mind. Rationality in natural inquiry is embodied in the relatively young tradition
of science, which defines and redefines those principles by means of
which evidence is to be interpreted and meshed with theory.
Rational judgment in the realm of science is, consequently, judgment which accords with such principles, as crystallized at the time
in question. To teach rationality in science is to interiorize these
principles in the student, but furthermore, to introduce him to the
live and evolving *tradition* of natural science, which forms their
significant context of development and purpose.

Scholarship in history is subject to an analogous interpretation,
for beyond the formal demands of reason, in the sense of consistency, there is a concrete tradition of technique and methodology
defining the historian's procedure and his assessment of reasons for
or against particular historical accounts. To teach rationality in history is, in effect, here also to introduce the student to a live tradition
of historical scholarship. Similar remarks might be made also with
respect to other areas, e.g. law, philosophy and the politics of democratic society. The fundamental point is that rationality cannot be
taken simply as an abstract and general ideal. It is embodied in
*multiple evolving traditions*, in which the basic condition holds that
issues are resolved by reference to *reasons*, themselves defined by
*principles* purporting to be impartial and universal. These traditions
should, I believe, provide an important focus for teaching.

### 5. CONCLUSION

I have intimated that I find something important in each of the
models we have considered. The impression model reflects, as I

have said, the cumulative growth of knowledge in its *public* sense. Our aim in teaching should surely be to preserve and extend this growth. But we cannot do this by storing it piecemeal within the learner. We preserve it, as the insight model stresses, only if we succeed in transmitting the live spark that keeps it growing, the insight which is a product of each learner's efforts to make sense of public knowledge in his own terms, and to confront it with reality. Finally, as the rule model suggests, such confrontation involves deliberation and judgment, and hence presupposes general and impartial principles governing the assessment of reasons bearing on the issues. Without such guiding principles, the very conception of rational deliberation collapses, and the concepts of rational and moral conduct, moreover, lose their meaning. Our teaching needs thus to introduce students to those principles we ourselves acknowledge as fundamental, general, and impartial, in the various departments of thought and action.

We need not pretend that these principles of ours are immutable or innate. It is enough that they are what we ourselves acknowledge, that they are the best we know, and that we are prepared to improve them should the need and occasion arise. Such improvement is possible, however, only if we succeed in passing on, too, the multiple live traditions in which they are embodied, and in which a sense of their history, spirit, and direction may be discerned. Teaching, from this point of view, is clearly not, as the behaviourists would have it, a matter of the teacher's shaping the student's behaviour or of controlling his mind. It is a matter of passing on those traditions of principled thought and action which define the rational life for teacher as well as student.

As Professor Richard Peters has recently written,[4]

The critical procedures by means of which established content is assessed, revised, and adapted to new discoveries have public criteria written into them that stand as impersonal standards to which both teacher and learner must give their allegiance. . . . To liken education to therapy, to conceive of it as imposing a pattern on another person or as fixing the environment so that he 'grows', fails to do justice to the shared impersonality both of the content that is handed on and of the criteria by reference to which it is criticized and revised. The teacher is not a detached operator who is bringing about some kind of result in another person which is external to him. His task is to try to get others on the inside of a public form of life that he shares and considers to be worthwhile.

In teaching, we do not impose our wills on the student, but introduce him to the many mansions of the heritage in which we ourselves strive to live, and to the improvement of which we are ourselves dedicated.

## NOTES

1. Dewey, J., *Democracy and Education* (New York, The Macmillan Company, 1916), p. 62.

2. Dewey, J., ibid., 'The supposed original faculties of observation, recollection, willing, thinking, etc. are purely mythological. There are no such ready-made powers waiting to be exercised and thereby trained.'

3. *Ancient Christian Writers*, No. 9, St. Augustine, 'The Teacher', edited by Quasten, J. and Plumpe, J. C., translated and annotated by Colleran, J. M., Newman Press, Westminster, Md.: 1950; relevant passages may also be found in Price, Kingsley, *Education and Philosophical Thought* (Boston, Allyn and Bacon, Inc., 1962), pp. 145–59.

4. *Education as Initiation*, an inaugural lecture delivered at the University of London Institute of Education, 9 December 1963; published for the University of London Institute of Education by Evans Brothers, Ltd, London.

# 9

# INSTRUCTION AND LEARNING BY DISCOVERY
## R. F. Dearden

### I. INTRODUCTION: 'TEACHING'

The purpose of this article is to examine and compare two conceptions of teaching which have often been set in sharp contrast to each other. The contrast which I have in mind is that between the teacher as an instructor and the teacher as a facilitator of the children's own creations and discoveries. This contrast has been much more prominent in discussions of primary education than of education at any other stage and is representative of two distinct traditions of teaching which are present at that stage. These might be called, as Blyth calls them in his recent book,[1] the elementary school tradition and the developmental tradition, which latter is especially associated with Froebel and those theories often referred to as 'child-centred'. There are, of course, many aspects to the contrast between these two traditions. One could discuss it in terms of personal relationships, pupil motivation, creativity, classroom climate and so on, but the aspect which I want quite specifically to focus attention on is that of knowledge and the passing on of that knowledge. It is for that reason that the title 'Instruction and Learning by Discovery', which has a strong cognitive flavour to it, seemed most apt.

Now it might well seem to some that a misleading twist or bias is already being imported into the discussion at the start by insisting that instruction and learning by discovery pick out two conceptions of *teaching*. For the point about learning by discovery, it might be objected, is precisely that the teacher does not teach: the children find out everything for themselves. The answer to this is immediately to grant the point of the objection, namely that being told something is quite different from finding it out for oneself, but to deny that it is only in the case of instruction that we can properly speak of 'teaching'. This 'finding out for oneself' which is contrasted with being instructed is of a peculiar kind. No sane person really supposes that children are going to rediscover the whole of what they need to know quite apart from the teacher's agency; if that were possible we should not need schools at all. In other words, it is not by chance that these discoveries are made but as a result of the teacher's deliberate contrivance, in 'structuring the environment' for example, or in practising discovery 'methods'. Both in the case of instruction and in the case of learning by discovery, then, the teacher's agency and influence are present, though admittedly they are present in very different ways.

Behind the objection to allowing that learning by discovery involves 'teaching' there lies a confusion over what sort of concept 'teaching' is. It may seem that for a variety of operations all to be called 'teaching' there must be some one nuclear operation common to them all on account of which the concept is applied. In that case instruction might readily suggest itself as the most promising candidate for this nuclear role, and then there would be some justice in denying that learning by discovery involved teaching. But the assumption at work here is mistaken, and the way in which it is mistaken merits attention. It can be brought out by some examples which I have adapted from Ryle's *Concept of Mind*.

If we were to consider 'farming' as an activity, we might note that ploughing was one farming job and tree-spraying another, while applying fertilizer is a third job and milking is a fourth, yet there is no one common nuclear operation by virtue of doing which alone a man is to be called a farmer. Similarly with solicitoring, drafting wills is one job and arranging for the transfer of property another, while defending a client in court is a third and explaining some point of law is a fourth, but again there is no one common nuclear operation present in all. So with teaching, I suggest, there is a whole range of operations any of which may, under suitable conditions, be examples of it, such as writing on a blackboard, correcting exercises, punishing, answering questions, demonstrating a procedure, setting material for reading, supervising practical work and so on. Teaching is what Ryle has called a 'polymorphous' concept : it can take many forms, and instructing is only one of them.

What, then, is characteristic of teaching as an activity, if it is not some nuclear operation such as instructing? This question is not to be answered by a review, even a very extensive review, of the particular things which a teacher might do, but by considering the central *intention* which lies behind his efforts. That intention is to bring it about that someone learns something. Teaching is not just placing things before people for their consideration, or informing, or telling, or conversing, or narrating, but taking such measures as will bring it about that something envisaged by the teacher is learned, by which I mean that it is both understood and remembered. What we teach is intended not just to be registered, but to be kept in mind : teaching involves the deliberate equipping of a person in some way, whether in respect of knowledge, skill or settled habit.

The next question to ask is whether there are any restrictions to be placed on this process vaguely called 'bringing it about'. Since it is necessarily the aim of the teacher to get someone to understand and remember something, such measures as he adopts must be consistent with achieving that aim. But nothing more specific than that is implied. What *method* to adopt in teaching, or what kind of *approach* to use, is not further indicated by the concept, but depends on the specific sorts of thing we wish to teach and the various psychological and other conditions which bear upon being effective in teaching. If we know that a person has been teaching, and we have no other clues supplied by the context as to what in particular he has been teaching, or how, then we know very little indeed of the form which his activities took. Such images as come to mind will reflect the idiosyncrasies, experience or prejudices of the particular individuals whose images they are and will be in no way warranted by the information here given. But what people customarily think of when they hear a word is of no philosophical interest; it is what they are entitled to think that matters, and that is a question of what is implied by a concept. Knowing that a person has been teaching entitles us to think only that he has been active in such ways as are consistent with the intention to bring it about that someone will learn something. That way may have been to instruct, or to have staged the making of discoveries by someone—discoveries relative to the learner and not to the teacher, that is—so that we return once again to the point that it is two conceptions of teaching that are being compared here.

## 2. INSTRUCTION

If we turn now to consider instruction, we shall have to be on our guard against the very same mistake that was pointed out in connection with the concept of teaching. On hearing the word 'instruction', we may form a picture of a browbeating, hectoring, offensive teacher of a sort admittedly sufficiently common in the past to have formed a public stereotype, and in rejecting this *picture* we may think that we have validly rejected all instruction. But that would be so only if it could first be shown that all instruction must necessarily be of this bullying and insensitive kind. A further feature of this picture which is no necessary accompaniment of instruction is that of baldly telling someone something, for example who followed whom on the throne of England, or what the exports of South Wales are, so that things are learned by rote. Instruction *need* not be confined to such a bald exposition of various items of information, but may include a reasoned explanation of something or an experimental demonstration of it. The principle of 'learning by experience' may be interpreted here as requiring *sense*-experience and be satisfied by a reference to what can be seen in some visual aid, or by an excursion to some instructive museum, gallery or historical site. Again, instruction *need* not be given by word of mouth, but may be given by referring the learner to a lesson in a textbook or to the appropriate programme in a machine. Far from being tied to some particular form which the accident of tradition has given to it, instruction may take many forms and be given in more than one manner. Furthermore, an important distinction often unmade in discussing instruction is that between formal instruction and incidental instruction, the former implying a set time when the teacher or teacher-substitute delivers some planned lesson, while the latter may be present in a much more loosely structured classroom regime. The one may be defensible where the other is not.

If we ask what is distinctive of instruction as a way of passing on knowledge, the answer would seem to be that in instruction this knowledge is directly imparted. Instruction does not hint at, or seek to elicit, or guide one in finding out for oneself, but directly imparts, and hence in this respect stands in sharp contrast as a way of teaching to contriving that children learn by discovery. Instruction stands in contrast also, though this is very often overlooked, to other forms of verbal teaching. The fact that instruction, as the imparting of knowledge, requires the use of language, does not entail the converse that all use of language by the teacher must be instruction. In Plato's dialogue the *Meno*, Socrates teaches a slave that a square double the area of a given square is to be constructed on the diagonal of the given square, and not by doubling the length of its sides, but he does not actually impart this information : he elicits it. At one point he comments to Meno as follows :

> Now notice what, starting from this state of perplexity, he will discover by seeking the truth in company with me . . . . Be ready to catch me if I give him any instruction or explanation instead of simply interrogating him on his own opinions.[2]

Though all instruction may require the use of language, then, not all teaching by the use of language is instruction, and though this may seem obvious enough when once it has been pointed out, it has nevertheless escaped the notice of the more extreme reactionaries against the teacher as instructor who dominates the elementary school tradition. To argue that a teacher ought not to teach by instructing does not mean that he must be silent, which would make him about as effective as a boxer with his hands tied behind his back, or an Alpine guide forbidden to use his feet, but leaves a great range of linguistic uses open to him, such as eliciting by questioning, hinting, commenting and even professing ignorance.

If teaching by instructing implies the imparting of knowledge, or more briefly if it is teaching by telling, what are we to think of it? No doubt there are many things to be said here about pupil motivation and so on, but I shall confine comment to an appraisal of the adequacy of instruction as a way of passing on *knowledge*. From this point of view it would seem sensible enough, if teachers have to pass on in a few years what has taken the labour of centuries and often the insight of genius to arrive at, to set up special institutions called schools and to make them places of instruction, though instruction doubtless enlightened by psychology and less harsh in manner than in the traditional picture. How better than by instruction could you teach French, handwriting, how to read, swimming, technical drawing or metalwork, assuming that you wanted to teach these things? Especially where *skill* is concerned, whether physical skills like swimming, or practical skills like carpentry, intelligent instruction, whether formal or incidental, together with practice, would seem to be quite the best way of teaching, and we may notice that wherever a teaching job is specifically that of passing on such a skill we do talk of 'instructors', such as driving, gunnery and flying instructors, or instructors in the various crafts.

There are, however, kinds of knowledge not normally referred to as 'skills' which require the acquisition and operational mastery of concepts, principles and criteria of critical appraisal, as for example in mathematics, science and history. To teach subjects such as these solely by instruction would be to treat them as collections of information, an error which was in fact conspicuously perpetrated in the elementary school tradition. Learning science or history, for example, was a stocking up with a mass of information imparted by the teacher, a conception of teaching which the Hadow Report of 1931 (Section 75) made famous in the phrase 'knowledge to be acquired and facts to be stored'. What are we to think of instruction, then, not in relation to French, handwriting, swimming, metalwork and so on, but in relation to such subjects as mathematics and science?

From the point of view of knowledge still, and not that of motivation, it might seem that instruction was to be criticized because the knowledge passed on was 'knowledge' only as being based on the authority of the teacher and not as being seen by the learner to be appropriately justified by proofs, evidences, arguments and so on. But this will not do, because there is no reason at all why proofs, evidences and arguments could not be made the content of instruction quite as much as what they are the reasons for. Nor is it the case that instruction must be limited to material of a fairly low level of generality. In primary school mathematics, for example, the laws of arithmetic and the concepts of place-value and of a base *could* all be made the objects of instruction. So long as there is something definite to be imparted, then it can be made the content of instruction. If instruction is to be found inadequate, therefore, it cannot be from the point of view of the instructor, but from the point of view of the learner's mastery of the instruction.

If not just memorization of the content of instruction is desirable, but an intelligent mastery of it, involving judgment in its application, then instruction cannot be wholly adequate. But the implication of this is that instruction needs to be supplemented, not supplanted. It needs to be supplemented by opportunities for trying out for oneself how the knowledge which is being imparted is to be applied. Just as instruction in a skill needs to be supplemented by practice if performance is to be raised to the level of being 'good at' whatever skill it is, so with instruction in the various academic subjects opportunities need to be given for exercising judgment in applying the concepts, principles and criteria in a suitable variety of cases. And when that is done, then instruction would seem to be at its most intelligent, and from the point of view of knowledge and passing on that knowledge, would seem not to be open to any important objection. We might next consider, then, the much canvassed alternative to it of learning by discovery, in which what is to be learnt is not imparted and then mastered but is found out by oneself in the first place.

## 3. 'DISCOVERY'

In discussing discovery methods, or 'finding out' as opposed to being told, not a great deal turns on analysis of the meanings of these words. It is the particular conception of *how* one is supposed to discover, or find out, that is crucial. But there are one or two points perhaps worth making about discovery in general before proceeding to a more particularized discussion. In the first place, the frequently rhapsodic description of making a discovery in terms of thrills and glows is apt to suggest that discovery is essentially an exciting psychological experience, perhaps the sort of experience that we have on finding a cherished object we thought we had lost, or on finishing a difficult piece of work with a sigh of deep satisfaction. But such a connection between making a discovery and glows of satisfaction is purely contingent, since one could have all of these feelings in the *false* belief that one had discovered something, and on the other hand one really could have discovered something yet without feeling anything in particular about it.

'Discovery' and 'finding out' are what Ryle has called 'achievement words' like winning, seeing and hearing, which are to be contrasted with 'task words', such as running, travelling, looking and listening. In using an achievement word we are asserting there to be some state of affairs over and above the person's activity or state of mind, and a biographical account of a person's efforts and feelings does not by itself tell us whether he has brought about that state of affairs or not. We may try in vain, or try and rashly claim success, but whether what we do is to count as an achievement depends on how things are in the end, not on how we feel or the effort we exerted. Faced with finding the area of a parallelogram for the first time, I may have the most thrilling and deeply satisfying experience you can imagine of seeing how it is to be done, but unless I have got it *right* this cannot count as a discovery, or a finding out, or an insight, in spite of all the thrills and glows, because 'discovery' carries an implication of the *truth* of what is put forward. A false or mistaken discovery is a contradiction. The achievement implied by discovery, then, is that of getting at the truth in some sought for respect, and this is a matter independent of our pleasures or pains.

The consequence of ignoring this point is that 'discovery methods' of teaching may be made to sound more reliable than they really are, but the illusion of guaranteed success engendered by the proleptic use of 'discovery' here is like talking of 'creative writing' before anyone has yet had a chance to have a look at it. The upshot of a lot of bustling activity might be confusion, muddle, uncritical acceptance of first ideas, or failure to have any ideas at all, as well as possibly having the result of making a discovery. Evidently this teaching method must involve considerable art if the chances of success are in fact to be high. But having noticed that the epithet 'discovery' could easily falsely prejudge the issue, I shall pass on to consider some particular conceptions of *how* success is to be reasonably assured, since it is here that the really important issues are likely to lie. One of the main points of what follows will be to try to show that the blanket term 'discovery methods' conceals and confuses certain crucial distinctions, distinctions of which we ought to be sharply aware if muddled practice is to be avoided.

### 4. LEARNING BY DISCOVERY

#### (1) *The pre-school model*

A convenient point at which to begin is with what is frequently held up as the very paradigm of how children should learn, namely the learning of the pre-school child as he trots round the garden, plays with his friends or explores the neighbourhood. He discovers in this way a bird's nest in a hedge, that worms wriggle, that table tops are slippy, where the milkman goes, and so on. School learning, it is said, should be just like that, or as near like it as possible : a discovering for oneself under the pressure of real interest and in the course of a spontaneous activity. Finding out about mathematics and science should be an eager lighting on one fascinating fact after another, just like exploring a wood or seeing what is in a pond; for mathematics and science, it is pointed out, are not confined to the study or laboratory, but are 'all around us'.

Now what needs to be questioned here is not the validity which this conception may have for the learning of various miscellaneous facts about the world. There would seem to be no reason to deny that a child would, in normal circumstances, almost inevitably learn many facts about himself and his situation simply as a condition of forming and carrying out purposes. It is the validity of this as a conception of how we could learn such subjects as mathematics or science which is questionable. To take the case of science first, if all that is meant is a pottering about in which one may or may not notice that reflections in a spoon are distorted, what things look like when seen through coloured glass, that some objects float while others sink and so on, then no doubt this account is unexceptionable. With very young children especially there is an important place for this kind of learning, but such limited and undirected curiosity does not amount to science. All of this could and did and does go on where science has never been heard of. Such finding out does not even begin to resemble science until problems start to present themselves which cannot be solved without putting forward, and then testing experimentally, suggested solutions of a non-obvious kind.[3] Even the perception of a scientific problem requires more than naïve curiosity, and the concept of an experiment implies more than pushing and poking at things. This point tends to be obscured by the belief that scientific discoveries are accidents which could happen to anybody. Certainly a scientific discovery might be made by accident, but the point to notice is that these accidents only happen to people with a certain kind of training and with certain things preoccupying them. 'Discovery, like surprise, favors the well prepared mind.'[4]

If elementary scientific investigation was as natural as this account likes to make out, it would require explaining how it is that this tradition of inquiry is historically so late to get started and geographically still so limited in extent. Even to try to classify what floats and what sinks, quite apart from trying to arrive at the general conditions for flotation, marks a sophistication which would still be strange to many. Far from being like trotting round a garden, learning science and what is characteristic of a scientific inquiry involves initiation into a particular social tradition of inquiry and is therefore something which, one way or another, has to be taught. In case this should now seem so obvious as not to be worth pointing out, it must be added that not only is it thought by some that science somehow just arises out of pottering about with things, but it may also be thought not even necessary that the teacher should know any science for this to happen. According to a recent article in *Educational Research*,[5] 'such is the interest among our young children that even the non-scientist can do a great deal by merely providing opportunities and encouragement'. How it is that a person himself ignorant of science is nevertheless able to 'provide opportunities' and reliably to ascertain that scientific 'discoveries' are in fact being made by his class is left unexplained in this article. But there cannot be many practising teachers who suppose that ignorance of anything is a qualification for teaching it. To teach something in ignorance of it is not just difficult : it is logically impossible.

With mathematics, the pre-school model is even less adequate, since the concepts and truths of mathematics are not even empirical, and hence can even less plausibly be represented as wide open to the curious gaze of tireless young investigators. Indeed, there have been and are societies which have never progressed beyond such primitive forms of counting as the tally-stick, though they probably all noticed that worms wriggle, what floats and a similar mixed assortment of empirical facts. But although a spontaneous generation theory of mathematical knowledge might seem to be implicit in the doctrines of the more extreme reactionaries against instruction, if these theorists were faced with the implications of their view, they would probably disown it, at least verbally. Much more usual, and at least apparently less extreme, is a conception of learning by discovery in terms of 'planned experience'. That is to say, the teacher is to contrive situations or to present materials which are so 'structured' that appropriate experiences must be provided for the children. What we do, on this theory, is to embed a conceptual structure in some materials, or in a 'concept kindergarten', from which it can then be 'abstracted' in the course of play. The child is to 'notice' the common features which certain things have, or the relationships which they have one to another, and 'abstract' them, this 'abstraction' being regarded as a *process*.

## (2) *Abstractionism*

A clear example of abstractionism as a theory of concept formation is provided by the writings of Dr. Z. P. Dienes, whose wooden blocks for forming concepts of place-value and of a base are now quite well known. Dienes writes of the child as 'extracting' the requisite features and as 'discarding' irrelevances, almost as if a mental prising off of what the designer had embedded in the blocks were going on. The process, he writes, 'should probably run as follows : an abstraction process, followed by a symbolization process, followed again by the learning of the use of the symbols'.[6] The 'abstraction process', it should be added, is allotted by Dienes to a period of a few weeks of free play with the materials. Again, the recent publication *Mathematics in Primary Schools* similarly speaks of 'abstractive teaching methods',[7] the 'abstraction of an idea'[8] and of what happens 'once a child has abstracted the concept'.[9] And just as Dienes writes of following up the abstraction process with 'symbolization', so here there is a process of 'making explicit' what has already been learned in the 'planned' experience provided.

This theory is, of course, at least quite as old as John Locke, whose *Essay Concerning Human Understanding,* published in the seventeenth century, based a whole theory of knowledge on abstraction. It lies behind the view that science is 'inductive', in the sense that the scientist is supposed to proceed by gathering instances and then moving to cautious generalizations based on them, rather than by boldly setting up hypotheses and then testing them experimentally. It was implicit also in the didactic apparatus of Montessori and the idea of 'sense training', so that it is not some brand new theory that we are here invited to espouse. A convincing refutation of abstractionism as a theory of concept formation, however, was recently given by Geach, so that only a few points specifically tailored to this as a theoretical basis for discovery methods of teaching need to be made here.[10]

To begin with, we may agree that any situation or state of affairs can always be conceived of in a great variety of ways, depending for example on the present interests and past learning of those who come to it. Assuming that a certain moving object in a field has been discriminated, we may conceive of it as an animal, a quadruped, a horned creature, a ruminant, the mother of a calf, a menace to our safe passage, a milk production unit, or indeed just as a cow. In fact, the potential variety of the ways in which something may be conceived is now being exploited in the so-called 'creativity tests' in which the person tested is called on to conceive of some object, such as a brick, in as many different ways as possible. Suppose we take as a further example a child's toy, say a set of bricks. What conceptions of the bricks will he develop in the course of playing with them? Here again we may agree that the potential variety is enormous. He may conceive of a tower, a ship, a train, a pattern of colours, a sorting of the bricks into various kinds, their use as missiles, and so on, depending on the concepts which he has acquired and his present interests.

Now the point I want to make is this. When a teacher presents a child with some apparatus or materials, such as Cuisenaire rods, Dienes blocks or an assortment of objects on an investigation table, he typically has in mind some one particular conception of what he presents in this way. But then the incredible assumption seems to be made that the teacher's conception of the situation somehow confers a special uniqueness upon it such that the children must also quite inevitably conceive of it in this way too, even though they may not even possess the concepts involved. In some mysterious way, a special potency is thought to inhere in teaching apparatus such that if children play with it or manipulate it, significant experiences must be had, and important concepts must be abstracted. For example, if we let children play with Cuisenaire rods, then in building houses with them and so on it is reasonable to suppose that they will find out that two sticks placed end to end give the same length whichever way round the sticks go. But because the *teacher* sees this fact as a concrete illustration of the commutative law that a + b = b + a, the *child* is credited with having had an important mathematical experience. Far from having just played with sticks, he is seen as being poised on the brink of, or even as having made, a major mathematical discovery. Again, a child given a block of Plasticine to play with naturally breaks it up for modelling purposes and later puts it together again. But he has not just fingered Plasticine it is thought. The sage onlooking of the hovering teacher has conferred a special significance on his manipulations such that important steps have been taken in this episode towards abstracting the concept of the conservation of volume. To put the point quite generally, an unconscious assumption behind the advocacy of *this* notion of discovery methods is that in spite of the variety of ways in which any situation may be conceived, the teacher's conceiving of it in one particular way is somehow thought to confer a special uniqueness on it such that children must come to conceive of it in that way too.

The explanation of this strange belief seems to be twofold. In the first place it is reasoned, quite correctly, that instead of just *telling* children about various things they ought to know, it would be valuable to provide concrete examples or models of those things. We can provide a set of sticks which supply a model of the natural numbers from 1 to 10, or a set of blocks which model the relative values of different places in number notation. This is correct and important. But then it is falsely assumed that a person who does not possess the knowledge that we possess must still see these materials as *examples* or *models,* and hence will be able to 'get back' to the way in which we conceive them. Yet without possession of our concepts in the first place, it makes no sense to talk of examples or models, because an example, or a model, or an instance, or a feature, is always an example, model, instance or feature *of* something, and unless you know what follows this 'of' you logically cannot perceive the thing *as* an example, model, and so on. This is not to say that there can be no value in a short initial period of play with new materials, for example to satisfy curiosity, but that such value as there may be is quite different from what it is here being claimed to be.

Suppose I wish to teach someone syllogistic logic, and to do this I require to make clear to him the logical powers of expressions such as 'all S is P', 'some S is not P', 'no S is P' and so on, where S and P stand for classes of things. I might do this by drawing various circles, some overlapping and some wholly outside or inside others. This would be a model of the various class relationships involved. But instead I issue compasses to a class and instruct them freely to draw circles. Can I say that important experiences in syllogistic logic are being provided here? Can I say that during four weeks or so of play with circles, important abstractings have been going on and now need merely to be symbolized, or just to be made explicit, as logical relationships? Surely this is no more likely, short of Divine intervention, than that advances have been made in the design of spectacle frames, or that the symbol of the Olympic Games has been arrived at, or that a value for pi has been discovered? While freely drawing circles may look to *me,* with my preconceptions, to be an important logical or pre-logical experience, and I may write books on the abstraction of formal logic from play with circles, the fact remains that from the child's point of view the truest description of what occurred is probably that fun was had just drawing circles. To return to the real case, we may well ask why it is that although children have played with blocks and bricks for years, it is only now, when they are provided in schools, that important mathematical concept-abstractings are supposed to accompany play with them. Perhaps it is the sign of a new state of mathematical grace which has now descended upon children.

A second explanation of the belief in abstractionism may lie in the experiments which psychologists have carried out on concept-formation. Bruner, for example, has done a famous series of experiments[11] in which sets of cards, each set patterned in such a way as to have some one feature which makes it a set, are presented to subjects who are then asked to find the feature which the cards have in common. In this way, Bruner has produced interesting results about the strategies adopted by different people in setting about this task. Now it might be said that in giving children apparatus which illustrates or exemplifies some concept or relationship, we are doing nothing very different from what Bruner did, so why is abstractionism so plainly erroneous? The answer is that there is all the difference in the world between experiments such as Bruner's and free play with concept-forming blocks of wood. In Bruner's case it is a requirement of the experimental set-up that the subjects shall have clear instructions as to what they must try to do. They do not just play, while Bruner hovers in the background weaving stories round their play, but at the very start of the experiment, when they are instructed what to do, they already have a vague concept of what they are looking for; they know the *sort* of thing it is, and their task is to specify that vague concept more precisely. There is no abstractionism here, but the usual guess-and-test of purposeful enquiry. But a child who is presented with apparatus which *we* call structured, and who is then left to 'have experiences', is not in this position at all. He is not searching for anything of which he has been given a rough idea already, but is just playing as he pleases, and only the belief in innate ideas and a natural tendency towards mathematical understanding could lead us to suppose that he will do more than learn a few very obvious empirical facts about the materials with which he is playing.

Even if a child has some mathematical knowledge, however, all sorts of unconscious assumptions on our part may blind us to the possible variety of conceptions open to him. For example, if we take this arrangement of Cuisenaire rods

it is by no means obvious that this is a structured representation of anything mathematical. It may be just a pattern of colours, the start of a model wall, a test to see whether the two layers are exactly the same in length, and so on. Even if we give the rods their usual values in the Cuisenaire system of 2, 4 and 6, and say that this arrangement represents $2 + 4 = 6$, all sorts of conventions of representation are being presupposed here. For example, we could as well regard this as a representation of $2 + 4 + 6 = 12$, so bringing out the assumed convention of what represents 'equality'. We could regard it as $\frac{1}{3} + \frac{2}{3} = 1$, or as $40 + 80 = 120$, so bringing out the assumed convention of what represents a unit. In short, the situation is 'structured', not in some sense 'by itself', but only in the eyes of the person who has been specifically taught how to conceive of it, though how he conceives of it may come to seem so natural and obvious to *him* that he may assume anyone must conceive of it in this way too. In just the same way it is often assumed that if we put pictures over the sentences in a reading primer, it must be just *obvious* to the child what the sentence 'says' from looking at the picture, whereas it may be doubted how many adults would respond in the way required if someone presented them with a picture and just said 'What sentence does this depict?'[12]

'Mathematics is all around us' the advocates of this sort of discovery say. And of course mathematics is all around us; so too are atomic physics, gravitation, molecular biology and organic chemistry. They are all, in a sense, though not all in the same sense, 'there': but the point is that you need more than eyes to see them, and if children are to conceive of their environment in mathematical or in scientific ways, they will have to be more than placed in contact with it. They will have to be taught *how* to conceive it, though the fact that other influences besides that of the school are always at work may blur the issue by making it really seem that some child has just spun it all out of his head, or 'abstracted' it from apparatus. Children are not, as seems often to be assumed, like a teacher on a refresher course who enjoys finding all sorts of new and interesting ways of applying his already *existing* knowledge to the latest apparatus, but are more like such a teacher faced with set theory, if he has never met that before. Even this, however, is an unfair analogy, since such a teacher has at least a notion of the sort of thing that a mathematical relation or structure is, whereas in all of this young children are complete beginners.

## (3) *Problem solving*

The two conceptions of learning by discovery which have been considered so far, and strongly criticized, do not exhaust the possibilities however. 'Learning by discovery' can be given another, and much more plausible, interpretation besides the interpretations based on the model of pre-school learning or on abstractionism. What this alternative is we can begin to see by returning to the point, made earlier in discussing instruction, that not all use of language by the teacher need be instruction. For example, in questioning Meno's slave, Socrates drew attention to what the boy was discovering. This alternative conception, in which the teacher much more actively participates, is often present alongside the conceptions that have already been criticized, but is rarely distinguished from them. Yet the resemblance is in fact slight. *Mathematics in Primary Schools,* for example, vacillates throughout between 'providing experience' and something like the Socratic method. In that recent publication of the new Schools Council, the Socratic method is in fact in one place explicitly endorsed,[13] and *discussion* is stressed in several places. For instance, after citing an example of the discovery of the commutative law of addition, that a + b = b + a, the text continues: 'It was quite clear that if the teacher had not discussed the number patterns with the boy, and questioned him, he would not have made the discovery at all.'[14] But the writer seems to be quite unconscious of the fact that this is a very different sort of 'discovery method' from the 'planned experiences' of abstractionism.

In this third conception of discovery methods, the teacher is much more than the hovering provider of materials, or the structurer of an environment from which new concepts are supposed to be abstracted in the course of undirected activity. In this third conception, the teacher questions, discusses, hints, suggests and instructs what to do to find out. But this way of teaching is not, or not predominantly, a way of instruction, because what has actually to be learned is not imparted. The stress is on the individual's mastery of knowledge, so that throughout all this teacher activity what the teacher says is specific enough to focus attention and effort in the desired direction, but at the same time open enough to leave genuine discoveries still to be made, discoveries which the teacher can be reasonably confident will be made on the basis of what he knows has already been learned in the past and the deliberate guidance he is now giving. For example, he may instruct that squares of numbers be drawn and that the answers to some multiplication tables be shaded on them, but leave open the discovery of the patterns so revealed. He may instruct in the conventions governing the representation of cardinal numbers and the four processes of arithmetic with certain materials, but leave open the discovery of a multitude of particular number relationships which can then be made. Posing the problem of how to find the area of an irregular shape, he may alternately prompt, tell, question, encourage and then watch, in a subtle interplay of minds which follows no set pattern. Where elementary science is concerned, he may suggest, orally or on a card, a certain problem and indicate or discuss how the solution might be found, but leave open the finding of the answer. For example, he may suggest an enquiry into how a bean extends itself in growth, and suggest marking it at intervals as a way of finding out; but he does not say what will be found out, whether the bean extends at its tip, emerges from the ground or stretches like elastic, for example. Similarly, it may be suggested in discussion that electric bulbs could be wired in series or in parallel, but without actually saying how this affects brightness, or how the failure of one of the bulbs affects the others : that can be left to be found out. He may give instructions for the use of a hydrometer in fresh and salt water and in paraffin, but leave it to be discovered how flotation is affected in each case. And once the concept of an experiment has been taught, there is no reason to doubt that a few children at least will be able sometimes to devise simple experimental tests for themselves to answer questions that have come up.

This interpretation of 'learning by discovery' has to be set in the strongest possible contrast to the interpretations based on pre-school learning or on abstractionism which have already been discussed. This kind of discovery is not a romantic sailing forth into the unknown on a journey which will bring who-knows-what ecstatic joys and thrills, nor is it the illumination of the soul by an intellectual grace which somehow proceeds from apparatus. The teacher does not 'provide experiences' but *guides* experience, by the subtle use of language, towards learning something that is regarded as educationally valuable. In its recognition of the crucial role of language this conception is more like instruction than it is like abstractionism, though the centre of attention is the individual's mastery of what is to be learned rather than the instructional imparting of it. Again like instruction, this conception of teaching involves the planning of work, both to ensure steady progression and to allow for practice or revision, though the planning is more flexible than with a course of instruction since the sequence of learning is deliberately less closely controlled, and can be adapted to any useful side-interests that may arise. The only resemblance of this conception to abstractionism lies in its recognition of the importance of instances or examples of what is learned.

What are the merits of teaching by this kind of 'discovery method' as against teaching by instruction? Plainly it would be far too time-consuming for *everything* to have to be found out in this way.[15] Before trying to answer this question any further however, it needs to be pointed out that we do not have to make an exclusive choice between these two and presumably the intelligent teacher, as opposed to the doctrinaire who fervently adheres to the dogmas of a particular ideology, will make his own judgment as to what a particular occasion requires in the light of all its special circumstances. To vary what one does according to the situation is part of what it means to be intelligent. But the merits of the alternatives have to be appreciated to do this, so that the virtues of the discovery method have to be known.

Much is often said on the merits of learning by discovery from the point of view of improved motivation and the better retention of what is learned, though to discuss these points would fall outside the restricted scope of the present discussion. We might note, however, that in the midst of the acclaim for a new golden road to knowledge there are cautious and informed voices that doubt the factual basis of some of the claims which are being made.[16] What has to be considered here, however, is the possible merit of learning by discovery from the point of view of the *knowledge* gained by it. Is it superior in any important way to knowledge gained by formal or incidental instruction, for example?

One way in which learning by discovery is often thought to have merit is that in this way children do not just learn, but they 'learn how to learn'. The source of this popular, if somewhat obscure, phrase can be traced back to some experiments performed on monkeys by Harlow.[17] Harlow set a long and varied series of discrimination problems to his monkeys and found that their ability to solve them improved very considerably as the experiment proceeded. They were somehow using past experience to cope more easily with new problems. In short, they had done something, called by Harlow 'forming a learning set', which made the solution of new but similar problems much more efficient. The notion would therefore seem to be a variant on our old friend, transfer of training, the special point of this new experiment having been to refute the reduction of all learning to the formation of stimulus-response bonds by trial and error. Where school learning is concerned, what we would seem to have to suppose is that in learning by discovery children form certain general heuristic principles which enable them to get onto the right track with new problems much more rapidly and efficiently than would have been the case if the knowledge had been imparted by instruction. Two points need to be made about that.

First, whether there could be such general principles is not an empirical matter for psychologists to settle, though contentment with showing a correlation without seeking its explanation may make it seem otherwise. It is not obvious, for example, how discovering the area of a parallelogram would later facilitate discovering which numbers are prime, or how discovering which materials are electrical conductors would later facilitate finding out the conditions governing the period of a pendulum. A person might do better through greater confidence or interest gained from the previous success, but that is not 'learning how to learn' in any conceivable sense. The second point is that in so far as there could be general principles which would facilitate later learning, there does not seem to be any reason why they should not be made part of the content of instruction, as is done by people who lecture and write books on how to study, for example. The fact that instruction has in the past often been uninformed by the psychology of learning, and has been of a narrow and mentally limiting kind, is no argument at all against all possible forms of instruction, as was stressed earlier.

Another alternative, however, is that learning by discovery may have an advantage over instruction in respect of the mastery of what has to be learned, and for the kind of reason that Dewey gave. A pupil being instructed is in a receptive role which requires that the pace at which he goes and the sequence of what he attends to are determined by someone else, whereas a pupil working to find something out for himself can proceed at a pace individually suited to him and by a sequence of acts intelligently ordered in view of the end towards which he sees himself as moving. In short, learning by discovery allows more room for individual differences and permits a more intelligent appreciation of what one is doing. But to offset this gain a little is the greater chanciness which then necessarily enters into learning, since a teaching method which genuinely leaves things open for discovery also necessarily leaves open the opportunity for not discovering them. It would seem, however, that there really is the possibility here of a superiority over instruction in learning by discovery.

What I have tried to distinguish, then, is a conception of teaching by discovery which draws in the active verbal participation of the teacher in framing problems, suggesting, discussing, or instructing what initially to do, but which leaves the result of the learner's activity open in some important respect, so that what is to be learned has indeed to be found out, and is not imparted. The only resemblance between this conception of learning by discovery and the conception based on abstractionism is in the stress on first-hand experience wherever possible, but apart from that it is analogous more to instruction. The possible superiority of this third conception of learning by discovery over learning from intelligent instruction would need to be shown empirically, though one can see that on some occasions at least it might well be superior on account of its greater adaptation to individual differences and greater scope for intelligence. But whether this possibility is in fact realized is something that a philosopher ought to realize is not possible for him to say. In fact, with some idea of what we are looking for in mind, it is precisely the sort of thing that we could usefully set out to discover.

## NOTES

1. Blyth, W. A. L., *English Primary Education* (1965), Vol. 2, Ch. 2.
2. Plato, *Meno*, 84 c.d. (W. K. C. Guthrie's translation).
3. Toulmin, S. E., *The Philosophy of Science* (1953), Ch. 2.
4. Bruner, J. S., 'The Act of Discovery' in *Readings in the Psychology of Cognition* (1965), ed. Anderson, R. C. and Ausubel, D. P., p. 607.
5. Barker, D., 'Primary School Science' in *Educational Research*, Vol. VII, No. 2 (Feb. 1965), p. 157.
6. Dienes, Z. P., 'Research in Progress' in *New Approaches to Mathematics Teaching* (1963), ed. Land, F. W.
7. H.M.S.O., *Mathematics in Primary Schools* (Curriculum Bulletin No. 1. of the Schools Council, 1965), p. 8.
8. Op. cit., p. 53.
9. Op. cit., p. 92.
10. Geach, P., *Mental Acts* (1957), sects. 4–11. Geach criticizes abstractionism as giving an impossible account of how we could *learn* new concepts, i.e. by supposedly noticing and abstracting common features of things. For : (i) How could *logical* concepts such as 'not' and 'or' be abstracted in this way? Where are the features of 'nottishness' or 'alternativeness' to abstract from? (ii) With *arithmetical* concepts we must first conceive of things as being of a certain kind, e.g. people or molecules,

before it is even intelligible to talk of their number. Moreover, the concept of number is much wider than just of how many in a visible group. (iii) With *relations* abstractionism fails, for where is that feature, e.g. of bigness, possessed by big fleas and big elephants, but not by little elephants, which we are to abstract? (iv) Even with *colour* concepts the theory fails, for where are the three separable features in an object which might truly be described as its being yellow, lemon and coloured? Geach stresses that such distinctions and classifications as our concepts mark do not just hit us when we open our eyes but are *made* by the mind. Language, of course, is crucially important in leading us to make such distinctions. Far from 'symbolization' being a trivial capping of concepts already formed, it would be truer to say that forming a concept *is* learning the use of a symbol. Cf. also Wittgenstein, L., *Philosophical Investigations* (1953), Pt. I, sects. 1–43.

11. Described in Thomson R., *The Psychology of Thinking* (Pelican, 1959), pp. 67–70.

12. Cf. Daitz, E., 'The Picture Theory of Meaning' in *Essays in Conceptual Analysis* (1956), ed. Flew, A. G. N. Of course, pictures may be a considerable aid to someone already able to read *part* of the sentence, since then the picture particularizes something of which he already has a rough idea.

13. Op. cit., p. 86.

14. Op. cit., p. 12 (see also pp. 7 and 92).

15. Cf. Ausubel, D. F., 'In Defence of Verbal Learning' in *Educational Theory* (1961), p. 15.

16. E.g. Friedlander, B. Z., 'A Psychologist's Second Thoughts on Concepts, Curiosity and Discovery in Teaching and Learning' in *Harvard Ed. Review* (Winter 1965).

17. Harlow, H., 'The Formation of Learning Sets' in *Psychological Review* (1949), p. 51.

# 10

# LEARNING AND TEACHING
## Michael Oakeshott

Even an amateur, like myself, when he fishes around in his head for some bright ideas, hopes to catch something. But nowadays fish don't come so easily; and I wish that what I have found to say on this topic did not look to me so shamefully dull. Let me, however, detain you a while with some clumsy thoughts on learning and teaching.

### 1

Learning is the comprehensive activity in which we come to know ourselves and the world around us. It is a paradoxical activity : it is doing and submitting at the same time. And its achievements range from merely being aware, to what may be called understanding and being able to explain.

In each of us, it begins at birth; it takes place not in some ideal abstract world, but in the local world we inhabit; for the individual it terminates only in death, for a civilization it ends in the collapse of the characteristic manner of life, and for the race it is, in principle, interminable.

The activity of learning may, however, be suspended from time to time while we enjoy what we have learned. The distinction between a driver and a learner-driver is not insignificant; a master-tailor making a suit of clothes is doing something other than learning to make a suit of clothes. But the suspension is, perhaps, never either decisive or complete : learning itself often entails practising what we have in some sense learned already, and there is probably a component of learning in every notable performance. Moreover, some activities, like intellectual enquiries, remain always activities of learning.

By learning I mean an activity possible only to an intelligence capable of choice and self-direction in relation to his own impulses and to the world around him. These, of course, are pre-eminently human characteristics, and, as I understand it, only human beings are capable of learning. A learner is not a passive recipient of impressions, or one whose accomplishments spring from mere reactions to circumstances, or one who attempts nothing he does not know how to accomplish. He is a creature of wants rather than of needs, of recollection as well as memory; he wants to know what to think and what to believe and not merely what to do. Learning concerns conduct, not behaviour. In short, these analogies of clay and wax, of receptacles to be filled and empty rooms to be furnished, have nothing to do with learning and learners.

I do not mean that the attention of a learner is focussed always upon understanding and being able to explain, or that nothing can be learned which is not understood; nor do I mean that human beings are uniquely predestined learners whatever their circumstances. I mean only that an activity which may include understanding and being able to explain within its range is different, not only at this point, but at all points in the scale of its achievements, from one to which this possibility is denied.

Teaching is a practical activity in which a 'learned' person (to use an archaism) 'learns' his pupils. No doubt one may properly be said to learn from books, from gazing at the sky or from listening to the waves (so long as one's disposition is that mixture of activity and submission we call curiosity), but to say that the book, the sky or the sea has taught us anything, or that we have taught ourselves, is to speak in the language of unfortunate metaphor. The counterpart of the teacher is not the learner in general, but the pupil. And I am concerned with the learner as pupil, one who learns from a teacher, one who learns by being taught. This does not mean that I subscribe to the prejudice which attributes all learning to teaching, it means only that I am concerned here with learning when it is the counterpart of teaching.

The activity of the teacher is, then, specified in the first place by the character of his partner. The ruler is partnered by the citizen, the physician by his patient, the master by his servant, the duenna by her charge, the commander by his subordinates, the lawyer by his client, the prophet by his disciple, the clown by his audience, the hypnotist by his subject, and both the tamer and trainer by creatures whose aptitudes are of being tamed or trained. Each of these is engaged in a practical activity, but it is not teaching; each has a partner, but he is not a pupil. Teaching is not taming or ruling or restoring to health, or conditioning, or commanding, because none of these activities is possible in relation to a pupil. Like the ruler, or the hypnotist, the teacher communicates something to his partner; his peculiarity is that what he communicates is appropriate to a partner who is a pupil—it is something which may be received only by being learned. And there can, I think, be no doubt about what this is.

Every human being is born an heir to an inheritance to which he can succeed only in a process of learning. If this inheritance were an estate composed of woods and meadows, a villa in Venice, a portion of Pimlico and a chain of village stores, the heir would expect to succeed to it automatically, on the death of his father or on coming of age. It would be conveyed to him by lawyers, and the most that would be expected of him would be legal acknowledgement.

But the inheritance I speak of is not exactly like this; and, indeed, this is not exactly like what I have made it out to be. What every man is born an heir to is an inheritance of human achievements; an inheritance of feelings, emotions, images, visions, thoughts, beliefs, ideas, understandings, intellectual and practical enterprises, languages, relationships, organizations, canons and maxims of conduct, procedures, rituals, skills, works of art, books, musical compositions, tools, artefacts and utensils—in short, what Dilthey called a *geistige Welt*.

The components of this world are not abstractions ('physical objects') but beliefs. It is a world of facts, not 'things'; of 'expressions' which have meanings and require to be understood because they are the 'expressions' of human minds. The landed estate itself belongs to this world; indeed, this is the only world known to human beings. The starry heavens above us and the moral law within, are alike human achievements. And it is a world, not because it has itself any meaning (it has none), but because it is a whole of interlocking meanings which establish and interpret one another.

Now, this world can be entered, possessed and enjoyed only in a process of learning. A 'picture' may be purchased, but one cannot purchase an understanding of it. And I have called this world our common inheritance because to enter it is the only way of becoming a human being, and to inhabit it is to be a human being. It is into this *geistige Welt* that the child, even in its earliest adventures in awareness, initiates itself; and to initiate his pupils into it is the business of the teacher. Not only may it be entered only by learning, but there is nothing else for a pupil to learn. If, from one point of view, the analogies of wax and clay are inappropriate to learning, from

158

another point of view the analogies of sagacious apes and accomplished horses are no less inappropriate. These admirable creatures have no such inheritance; they may only be trained to react to a stimulus and to perform tricks.[1]

There is an ancient oriental image of human life which recognizes this account of our circumstances. In it the child is understood to owe its physical life to its father, a debt to be acknowledged with appropriate respect. But initiation into the *geistige Welt* of human achievement is owed to the Sage, the teacher : and this debt is to be acknowledged with the profoundest reverence—for to whom can a man be more deeply indebted than to the one to whom he owes, not his mere existence, but his participation in human life? It is the Sage, the teacher, who is the agent of civilization. And, as Dr. Johnson said, not to name the school and the masters of illustrious men is a kind of historical fraud.

## 2

Now, most of what I have to say about learning and teaching relates to the character of what is taught and learned, and to the bearing of this upon the activities concerned; but there are two general considerations, one about the teacher and the other about the pupil, which I must notice first.

It is difficult to think of any circumstances where learning may be said to be impossible. Of course, in some conditions it will take place more rapidly and more successfully than in others; but, in principle, it does not depend upon any specifiable degree of attention, and it is not uncommon to find oneself to have learned without knowing how or when it happened. Thus, the random utterances of anyone, however foolish or ignorant, may serve to enlighten a learner, who receives from them as much or as little as he happens to be ready to receive, and receives often what the speaker did not himself know or did not know he was conveying.

But such casual utterances are not teaching; and he who scatters them is not, properly speaking, a teacher. Teaching is the deliberate and intentional initiation of a pupil into the world of human achievement, or into some part of it. The teacher is one whose utterances (or silences) are designed to promote this initiation in respect of a pupil—that is, in respect of a learner whom he recognizes to be ready to receive what he has resolved to communicate. In short, a pupil is a learner known to a teacher; and teaching, properly speaking, is impossible in his absence.

This, of course, does not mean that 'readiness to receive' is an easily discernible condition, or that it should be identified as the condition in which reception will come most easily. Jean Paul Richter's maxim that in teaching a two-year-old one should speak to him as if he were six, may be a profound observation. Nor does it mean that the relationship of teacher and pupil is emancipated from the latitudes and imprecisions common to all human relationships. Indeed, it is probably more subject to these imprecisions than any other relationship. What it means is that a teacher is one who studies his pupil, that the initiation *he* undertakes is one which has a deliberated order and arrangement, and that, as well as knowing what he designs to transmit, he has considered the manner of transmission. I once knew a wise man who, wishing to learn the art of the farrier, looked, not only for a man practised in the art, but for one accustomed to teaching, and he was gratified when he found a farrier who was also a teacher of boxing.

With regard to the pupil, there is a famous dilemma which has haunted reflection on education for long enough. Is learning to be understood as acquiring knowledge, or is it to be regarded as the development of the personality of the learner? Is teaching concerned with initiating a pupil into an inheritance of human achievement, or is it enabling the pupil to make the most or the best of himself? Like many such cruxes, this one points to what I believe to be a genuine discrepancy, but misinterprets it.

To escape from it we may recognize learning, not merely as the acquisition of knowledge, but also as the extension of the ability to learn, as the education and not merely the furnishing of a mind, as an inheritance coming to be possessed in such a manner that it loses its second-hand or antique character; and we may recognize teaching, not as passing on something to be received, nor as merely planting a seed, but as setting on foot the cultivation of a mind so that what is planted may grow. But the escape from the dilemma this affords us is imperfect; and, in any case, it is not an escape but a resolution we should be seeking.

What, I think, we must understand is that there is no discrepancy between a pupil succeeding to his inheritance of human achievement and his making the most of himself. 'Self-realization' for human beings is not, of course, the realization of an exactly predetermined end which requires only circumstances favourable to this end in order that it should be achieved; but nor is this self an infinite, unknown potentiality which an inheritance of human achievement is as likely to thwart as to promote. Selves are not rational abstractions, they are historic personalities, they are among the components of this world of human achievements; and there is no other way for a human being to make the most of himself than by learning to recognize himself in the mirror of this inheritance.

A discrepancy, however, remains; but it is a discrepancy, not between the self and its world, but between learning and teaching. It is a divergence of point of view. For the pupil, to learn is not to endeavour to make the most of himself, it is to acquire knowledge, to distinguish between truth and error, to understand and become possessor of what he was born heir to. But to the teacher things must appear differently. Obliquely and upon a consequence he is an agent of civilization. But his direct relationship is with his pupil. His engagement is, specifically, to get his pupil to make the most of himself by teaching him to recognize himself in the mirror of the human achievements which compose his inheritance. This is the somewhat complicated manner in which he performs his work of initiation, and this is what distinguishes him from others who hand on the fruits of civilization; namely, that he has a pupil.

Now, to make a 'civilization' available to a pupil is not to put him in touch with the dead, nor is it to rehearse before him the social history of mankind. Death belongs to nature, not *geist*; and it is only in nature that generation involves a process of recapitulating all earlier forms of life. To initiate a pupil into the world of human achievement is to make available to him much that does not lie upon the surface of his present world. An inheritance will contain much that may not be in current use, much that has come to be neglected and something even that for the time being is forgotten. And to know only the dominant is to become acquainted with only an attenuated version of this inheritance. To see oneself reflected in the mirror of the present modish world is to see a sadly distorted image of a human being; for there is nothing to encourage us to believe that what has captured current fancy is the most valuable part of our inheritance, or that the better survives more readily than the worse. And nothing survives in this world which is not cared for by human beings. The business of the teacher (indeed, this may be said to be his peculiar quality as an agent of civilization) is to release his pupils from servitude to the current dominant feelings, emotions, images, ideas, beliefs and even skills, not by inventing alternatives to them which seem to him more desirable, but by making available to him something which approximates more closely to the whole of his inheritance.

But this inheritance is an historic achievement; it is 'positive', not 'necessary'; it is contingent upon circumstances, it is miscellaneous and incoherent; it is what human beings have achieved, not by the impulsion of a final cause, but by exploiting the opportunities of fortune and by means of their own efforts. It comprises the standards of conduct to which from time to time they have given their pre- ferences, the pro- and con- feelings to which they have given their approval and disapproval, the intellectual enterprises they have hap- pened upon and pursued, the duties they have imposed upon them- selves, the activities they have delighted in, the hopes they have entertained and the disappointments they have suffered. The notions of 'finished' and 'unfinished' are equally inapplicable to it. It does deliver to us a clear and unambiguous message; it speaks often in riddles; it offers us advice and suggestion, recommendations, aids to reflection, rather than directives. It has been put together, not by designers but by men who knew only dimly what they did. It has no meaning as a whole; it cannot be learnt or taught in principle, only in detail.

A teacher, then, engaged in initiating his pupils into so contingent an inheritance, might be excused for thinking that he needed some assurance of its worth. For, like many of us, he may be expected to have a superstitious prejudice against the human race and to be satisfied only when he can feel himself anchored to something for which human beings are not responsible. But he must be urged to have the courage of his circumstances. This man-made inheritance contains everything to which value may be attributed; it is the ground and context of every judgment of better and worse. If there were a mirror of perfection which he could hold up to his pupils, he might be expected to prefer it to this home-made article. But there is no such mirror. He may be excused if he finds the present dominant image of civilized life too disagreeable to impart with any enthusiasm to his pupils. But if he has no confidence in any of the standards of worth written into this inheritance of human achieve- ment, he had better not be a teacher; he would have nothing to teach.

But teachers are modest people, and we are likely to disclaim so large an engagement as initiating our pupils into the civilized inheritance of mankind. We do not pretend to hand on anything but scraps of that inheritance; and it does not escape us that the civilization we are directly concerned with is not alone in the world and that this is a further limitation of our activities. And all this constitutes a renewed recognition of the contingency of what we have to teach. But the important point here is that whether we are concerned with a relatively simple or (like ours) an exceedingly complex civilization, whether we are concerned with a small or a large part of it, and whether we are concerned with practical skills, with moral conduct or with large intellectual enterprises (like philosophy or science), teaching and learning always relate to an historic inheritance of human achievement and that what is to be handed on and learned, known and understood, are thoughts and various 'expressions' of thoughts.

### 3

Now, from one important point of view, all we can be said to know constitutes a manifold of different 'abilities', different amounts of knowledge being represented in different degress of ability, and every complex ability being a manifold of simpler abilities.

When an ability is recognized as an ability to do or to make something, and it is recognized to be significantly composed of physical movements, we usually call it a skill. Playing billiards and ploughing a field are skills; each may be enjoyed in different degrees and each may be seen to be a manifold of simpler skills. Thus the ability to plough entails the ability to manage the horse as well as the plough; and the ability to manage the horse entails the ability to manage the leads and the ability to make the appropriate noises.

Further, we are apt to extend this notion of skill to abilities not so significantly composed of physical movements. A navigator, a chairman or a painter may be said to be 'skilful'. But when we say this we usually mean that the abilities concerned in these activities are large and complex and that in this case they are enjoyed to only a limited extent: we mean that his ability runs to a *merely* skilful performance. And this draws attention to abilities which we do not normally call skills.

These are usually more complicated, less obviously concerned with doing and making and more obviously concerned with the performance of mental operations—like speaking, diagnosing, understanding, describing, explaining, etc. And the complex 'abilities' denoted in the expressions engineer, latin scholar, explorer, actor, surgeon, lawyer, army commander, physicist, teacher, painter, farmer, etc. are each manifolds in which simpler abilities are grouped and given a specific focus.

This conjunction, in a concept of 'abilities', of what we know and the use we make of it, is not designed to prove anything, but merely to indicate the way in which we carry about with us what we may be said to know. What we are aware of is not a number of items of knowledge available for use, but having powers of specific kinds—the power of being able to solve a legal problem, or to understand a Latin inscription or to perform a surgical operation. What we know constitutes an equipment which we possess in terms of what it enables us to do or to understand. And the 'pragmatism' which this way of thinking might seem to commit us to may be avoided if it is recognized that abilities are of different kinds and cannot be assimilated to one another—that (for example) the ability to understand and to explain cannot be assimilated to the ability to do or to make.

Now, these abilities of various kinds and dimensions which constitute what we may be said to know will be found to be conjunctions of what is called 'information' and what I shall call 'judgment'.

The component of 'information' is easily recognized. It is the explicit ingredient of knowledge, where what we know may be itemized. Information consists of facts, specific intellectual artefacts (often arranged in sets or bunches). It is impersonal (not a matter of opinion). Most of it is accepted on authority, and it is to be found in dictionaries, manuals, textbooks and encyclopaedias. It is the appropriate answer to questions which ask : who? what? where? which? how long? how much? etc. Typical pieces of information are : the date of Shakespeare's death or St. Paul's conversion; the average annual rainfall in Bournemouth, the ingredients of welsh rarebit; the specific gravity of alcohol; the age of consent; the atomic structure of nitrogen; the reasons given by Milton for favouring polygamy; the seating capacity of the Albert Hall.

Except in quizzes, where it is notoriously inert, information is a component of knowledge, and (unlike knowledge itself) it may be useful or useless. Useful information is composed of facts related to a particular skill or ability. There is no inherently useless information; there are only facts irrelevant to the matter in hand.

Some facts seem to convey detached pieces of information—'Mummy, Mrs. Smith wears a wig', 'we cook on gas', 'that is a bicycle', 'this is a bassoon'—and they lose their inertness merely by reason of their place in a conversation. But the importance of information lies in its provision of rules or rule-like propositions relating to abilities. Every ability has its rules, and they are contained in that component of knowledge we call information. This is clearly the case with mathematical or chemical formulae, or with information like, 'glass is brittle', or 'hemlock is poisonous'; but it is also the case with other items of information. A recipe tells me what ingredients I should use in making a dish, and one of the uses of knowing the seating capacity of the Albert Hall is that it tells me how many tickets I may sell.

But rules or rule-like propositions such as are supplied in pieces of information may be related to knowledge (that is, to a specific ability or skill) in either of two different ways. They may be items of information which must be known as a condition of being able to perform; or they may constitute the criterion by means of which a performance may be known to be incorrect, though here they are never the only means by which mistakes may be detected.

First, nobody could read or receive a message in morse unless he were correctly informed about the morse-code equivalents of the letters of the alphabet. This is information in the exact sense. It is a set of facts (specific intellectual artefacts), not opinions; it is stated in propositions; it is received on authority; it is capable of being forgotten and it needs to be recollected; and it appears in rules to be followed—rules which must be known and recollected as a condition of being able to perform.

Secondly, the grammar of a language may be said to constitute the criterion by which a performance may be known to be incorrect. It consists of facts, stated in propositions, and it appears as rules. But, while this information may obliquely promote a laudable performance, it is not necessary to it. A laudable performance is possible to somebody who never possessed this information, or to somebody who once had it but has now forgotten it. There are a number of things directly related to a performance which a person ignorant of these facts could not do; but among them is neither the ability of speak intelligently and to understand what is said in the language, nor the ability to detect mistakes. The rules, here, are observed in the performance and they are capable of being known. They are the criterion for determining an incorrect performance, but a knowledge of them is not a condition of a laudable performance.

There is, indeed, a third sort of rule-like proposition which, in order to distinguish it from other sorts, is often called a 'principle'. These are propositions which are advanced in order to explain what is going in in any performance; they supply what may be called its 'underlying *rationale*'. And, consequently, as I understand them, they are never components of the knowledge which constitutes the performance. They belong to a separate performance of their own—the performance of explaining a performance. Let me offer two examples of what I mean.

First, riding a bicycle is a skill which consists wholly of making the appropriate physical movements. In order to enjoy this skill certain information must have been acquired, and there may also be what could be called the 'grammar' of the skill. But beyond all this, the skill may be said to be an exemplification of certain principles of mechanics. But these principles are utterly unknown to even the most successful cyclist, and being able to recite them would not help him to be more proficient. They do not constitute a criterion. Their sole value is the contribution they may make to our understanding of what is going on. In short, they are unrelated either to learning or to practising the skill. They belong to a separate performance, the performance of explaining.

Secondly, moral conduct may be said to be the ability to behave well. Here, again, certain information must be known; and there may also be what could be called the 'grammar' of moral conduct—the rules and rule-like propositions which constitute the criterion by means of which a performance may be known to be 'incorrect'. But, again, beyond all this there are, or may be, 'principles' in terms of which what is going on in moral conduct may be understood and explained. Aristotle, for example, in the 'principle of the Mean', formulated what he believed to be the 'underlying *rationale*' of all good conduct. But a knowledge of this, or of any other such 'principle', is not a condition of being able to behave well, nor does this principle constitute a criterion by means of which a performance may be known to be 'incorrect'. It is unrelated either to learning good conduct or to a good performance.

There is, then, as I understand it, a sort of information which is designed to explain a performance (and also to explain the rules of a performance), but which is never a component of the knowledge which constitutes the performance. And this, of course, is so even when the performance is itself a performance of understanding and explanation, as, for example, in history or in science.

But, to return from this not unnecessary digression; there is in all knowledge an ingredient of information. It consists of facts which may range from the recognitions and identifications in which knowledge of any sort emerges from indeterminate awareness, to rules or rule-like propositions which inform the skills and abilities in which we carry about what we may be said to know, and which are sometimes, but not always, expressly known and followed. This ingredient of information, however, never constitutes the whole of what we know. Before any concrete skill or ability can appear, information must be partnered by 'judgment', 'knowing *how*' must be added to the 'knowing *what*' of information.

By 'judgment' I mean the tacit or implicit component of knowledge, the ingredient which is not merely unspecified in propositions but is unspecifiable in propositions. It is the component of knowledge which does not appear in the form of rules and which, therefore, cannot be resolved into information or itemized in the manner characteristic of information.

That we enjoy such knowledge has seemed to some writers undeniable. They direct our attention, in the first place, to skills—that is, to abilities which are significantly composed of physical movements. We may know how to do something without being able to state explicitly the manner of acting involved. This, for example, appears to be the case in swimming, riding a horse, playing a fish, using a chisel and in turning a bowl on a potter's wheel. And these writers point out, further, that we may recognize an action as being of a known kind without being able to specify how we recognized it; that we are able to discover similarities in things without being able to say what they consist of, or patterns without being aware of the elements they are composed of or the rules they exemplify; and that we may speak a language without knowing the rules we are following and even without those rules ever having been formulated.

All this, I think, is true. But what it suggests to me is that there are skills and abilities where what is known may lack certain sorts of informatory content (particularly the sort of information we call 'the rules'), rather than that there is a 'knowing *how*' which can be divorced from any 'knowing *what*'. And I have used 'judgment' to distinguish 'knowing *how*' from information because I think 'knowing *how*' is an ingredient of all genuine knowledge, and not a separate kind of knowing specified by an ignorance of rules.

Facts, rules, all that may come to us as information, itemized and explicit, never themselves endow us with an ability to do, or to make, or to understand and explain anything. Information has to be used, and it does not itself indicate how, on any occasion, it should be used. What is required in addition to information is knowledge which enables us to interpret it, to decide upon its relevance, to recognize what rule to apply and to discover what action permitted by the rule should, in the circumstances, be performed, knowledge (in short) capable of carrying us across those wide open spaces, to be found in every ability, where no rule runs. For rules are always disjunctive. They specify only an act or a conclusion of a certain general kind and they never relieve us of the necessity of choice. And they never yield more than partial explanations : to understand anything as an example of the operation of a rule is to understand it very imperfectly.

'Judgment', then, is not to be recognized as merely information of another sort; its deliverances cannot be itemized, they cannot be specified in propositions, and they are neither remembered not forgotten. It is, for example, all that is contained in what has been called 'the unspecifiable art of scientific enquiry' without which 'the articulate contents of scientific knowledge' remains unintelligible.

And if we are obliged to retreat a little from the notion of an entirely independent 'knowing *how*' (because every ability has an ingredient of fact, recognized as fact and specifiable in propositions), I do not think we can avoid recognizing what I have called 'judgment' as a partner, not only in those abilities we call skills, but in all abilities whatever, and, indeed, more particularly in those abilities which are almost exclusively concerned with mental operations.

The connoisseurship we recognize to belong to the knowledge entailed in riding a horse, for example, or in transmitting or receiving a message in the morse code, has its counterpart elsewhere. Indeed, the further we go from manual and sensual skills the larger becomes the place occupied by this component of knowledge. Whatever its place in tea-tasting and in the diagnosis of disease, its place in art and literature, in historical, philosophical or scientific understanding is almost immeasurably greater.

It is represented, for example, in the so-called *divinatio* of the textual critic in which a corrupt reading is detected and an emendation suggested. It is what comes into play where the information to be got from the collation of MSS and recension stops. It is all that goes beyond the point where critical rules and methods leave off, and all that is required to drag appropriate precepts from these rules. It is what escapes even the most meticulous list of the qualities required for practising the craft of the textual critic.

A similar ingredient appears in the practical relationships of human beings. The moral and legal rules which set out in propositional form the recognized rights and duties, and the prudential maxims which give some flexibility to those rules, constitute only a small part of the knowledge comprised in the ability to live a civilized life. The precepts themselves require interpretation in respect of persons and circumstances; where there is a conflict between precepts, it cannot be resolved by the application of other rules. 'Casuistry', as it has been said, 'is the grave of moral judgment.'

In short, in every 'ability' there is an ingredient of knowledge which cannot be resolved into information, and in some skills this may be the greater part of the knowledge required for their practice. Moreover, 'abilities' do not exist in the abstract but in individual examples: the norms by which they are recognized are afterthoughts, not categorical imperatives. And each individual example has what may be called a style or idiom of its own which cannot be specified in propositions. Not to detect a man's style is to have missed three-quarters of the meaning of his actions and utterances; and not to have acquired a style is to have shut oneself off from the ability to convey any but the crudest meanings.

What, then, is significant is not the observation that one may know how to speak a language without knowing the rules one is following, but the observation that until one can speak the language in a manner not expressly provided for in the rules, one can make no significant utterance in it. And, of course, by a 'language' I do not mean merely Latin and Spanish, I mean also the languages of history, philosophy, science and practical life. The rules of art are there, but they do not determine the practice of the art; the rules of understanding are there, but they do not themselves endow us with understanding. They set limits—often telling us only what *not* to do if we wish to speak any of the languages of our civilization; but they provide no prescription for all that must go on in the interval between these limits.

4

The inheritance of human achievements into which the teacher is to initiate his pupil is knowledge; and (on this reading of it) knowledge is to be recognized as manifolds of abilities, in each of which there is a synthesis of 'information' and 'judgment'. What bearing has this view of things upon the activities of learning and teaching— learning which is succeeding to the inheritance, and teaching which is deliberately initiating a pupil into it? I doubt very much whether there are any practical conclusions to be drawn from it for either learners or teachers; but I think it may have some virtue as part of an attempt to understand what is going on in learning and teaching.

It suggests, first, that what I have called the two components of knowledge ('information' and 'judgment') can both be communicated and acquired, but cannot be communicated or acquired separately—at least, not on separate occasions or in separate 'lessons'. This, I think, is certainly true in respect of all the more important abilities and passages in the inheritance, and it is not seriously qualified by the observations that it is possible to communicate and acquire inert information, and that there are some skills in which the component of information is minimal.

But, secondly, it suggests that these two components of knowledge cannot be communicated in the same manner. Indeed, as I understand it, the distinction between 'information' and 'judgment' is a distinction between different manners of communication rather than a dichotomy in what is known; and for me it springs from reflecting upon teaching and learning rather than from reflecting upon the nature of knowledge. Thus teaching may be said to be a twofold activity of communicating 'information' (which I shall call 'instructing') and communicating 'judgment' (which I shall call 'imparting'); and learning may be said to be a twofold activity of acquiring 'information' and coming to possess 'judgment'.

And the rest of what I have to say concerns this distinction and the understanding it may give of what is going on in learning and teaching.

All teaching has a component of instruction, because all knowledge has a component of information. The teacher as instructor is the deliberate conveyor of information to his pupil.

The facts which compose information are specific, impersonal and mostly to be taken on trust; they are also apt to be hard, isolated, arbitrary and inert. They may be stored in encyclopaedias and dictionaries. Their immediate appeal is not to the pupil's desire to understand, but to his curiosity, his desire not to be ignorant—that is, perhaps, to his vanity. And this desire not to be ignorant is, for the most part, satisfied by knowing things in terms of their names and by knowing the signification of words and expressions. From his earliest years the pupil has been used to making such discoveries for himself; he has become accustomed to distinguishing in an elementary way between fact and not-fact—without, of course, knowing the rules he is observing in doing so. And, for the most part, he is used to doing all this as part of the process of coming to be at home in the world he inhabits. Thus, when he falls into the hands of an instructor, he is already familiar with the activity of acquiring information, particularly information of immediate use.

Now the task of the teacher as instructor is to introduce his pupil to facts which have no immediate practical significance. (If there were no such facts, or if they composed an unimportant part of our inheritance, he would be a luxury rather than a necessity.) And, therefore, his first business is to consider and decide what information to convey to his pupil. This may be decided by circumstances : the Sergeant-Instructor does not have to consider whether or not he shall inform his class about the names and uses of the parts of the Bren-gun. But, if it is not decided by such circumstances as these, it is something which falls to the teacher as instructor to consider. What part or parts of our inheritance of information shall be transmitted to his pupil?

His second task is to make the information he has to convey more readily learnable by giving it an organisation in which the inertness of its component facts is modified.

The organization provided by an immediate application to the practical life of his pupil is spurious; much of the information he has to convey has no such application and would be corrupted by being turned in this direction. The organization provided by a dictionary or an encyclopaedia is not designed for learning but for the rapid discovery of items of information in reponse to a recognition of specific ignorance. And the organization of information in terms of the modes of thought, or languages, which are the greatest achievements of civilization, is much too sophisticated for the beginner. In these circumstances, what we have settled for, and what the instructor may be expected to settle for, is the organization of information in terms of the more or less arbitrarily distinguished 'subjects' of a school or university curriculum: geography, Latin, chemistry, arithmetic, 'current affairs' or what-not. Each of these is an organization of information and not a mode of thought; but each permits facts to begin to reveal their rule-like character (that is, their character as tools to be used in doing, making or understanding) and thus to throw off some of their inertness. Moreover, there is, I think, some positive advantage in devising, for pedagogical purposes, special organizations of information which differ from the significant modes of thought of our civilization. For these modes of thought are not themselves organizations of information; and when one of them appears as a school 'subject'—as, for example, 'philosophy' in the curriculum of a *lycée*—its character is apt to be misrepresented. No great harm may be thought to come from representing 'geography' or even 'Latin' as information to be acquired, but there is something odd about 'philosophy' when it appears as the ability (for example) to remember and rehearse the second proof for the existence of God or what Descartes said about dreams.

There are, I think, two other tasks which obviously fall to the teacher as instructor. First, he has to consider the order in which the information contained in each of these somewhat arbitrary organizations of facts shall be transmitted to his pupil. It is this sort of consideration which goes into devising a syllabus, writing a textbook, or composing the programme of an instructing machine. And second, he has to exercise his pupil in this information so that what has been acquired may be recognized in forms other than those in which it was first acquired, and may be recollected on all the occasions when it is relevant. That is, the instructor has not only to hear his pupils recite the Catechism, the Highway Code, the Capes and Bays, the eight-times multiplication table and the Kings of England, but he has also to see that they can answer questions in which this information is properly used. For the importance of information is the accuracy with which it is learned and the readiness with which it can be recollected and used.

Nevertheless, our inheritance of information is so great that, whatever devices the instructor may use to modify its inertness, much of it must be acquired with only the dimmest notion of how it might be used. No doubt it would be a good thing (as Lichtenberg said) if we could be educated in such a way that everything unclear to us was totally incomprehensible; but this is not possible. Learning begins not in ignorance, but in error. Besides, in acquiring information we may learn something else, other and more valuable than either the information itself or perceiving that it is something to be used. And to understand what this is we must turn from 'information' to 'judgment', from the activity of 'instructing' to the activity of 'imparting'.

Now, something of what I mean by 'judgment' has begun to appear whenever the pupil perceives that information must be used, and perceives the possibility of irrelevance. And something of this is imparted in the organization of information itself; although these organizations are apt to give a restrictive impression of relevance. It is clear that this is not itself information; it cannot be taught in the way in which information may be conveyed, and it cannot be learned, recollected or forgotten in the way in which information may be learned, recollected and forgotten. But it is clear, also, that this is only an intimation of 'judgment', for there is much more to be noticed which no mere organization of information can impart. To perceive that facts are rules or tools, to perceive that rules are always disjunctive and never categorical, is one thing, to have acquired the ability to use them is another.

'Judgment', then, is that which, when united with information, generates knowledge or 'ability' to do, to make, or to understand and explain. It is being able to think—not to think in no manner in particular, but to think with an appreciation of the considerations which belong to different modes of thought. This, of course, is something which must be *learned*; it does not belong to the pupil by the light of nature, and it is as much a part of our civilized inheritance as the information which is its counterpart. But since learning to think is not acquiring additional information it cannot be pursued in the same way as we add to our stock of information.

Further, 'judgment' may be *taught*; and it belongs to the deliberate enterprise of the teacher to teach it. But, although a pupil cannot be explicitly instructed in how to think (there being, here, no rules), 'judgment' can be taught only in conjunction with the transmission of information. That is to say, it cannot be taught in a separate lesson which is not (for example) a geography, a Latin or an algebra lesson. Thus, from the pupil's point of view, the ability to think is something learned as a by-product of acquiring information; and, from the teacher's point of view, it is something which, if it is taught, must be imparted obliquely in the course of instruction. How this is done is to be understood from considering the character of what has to be imparted.

'Judgment', the ability to think, appears first, not in merely being aware that information is to be used, that it is a capital and not a stock, but in the ability to use it—the ability to invest it in answering questions. The rules may have been mastered, the maxims may be familiar, the facts may be available to recollection; but what do they look like in a concrete situation, and how may a concrete situation (an artefact or an understanding) be generated from this information? How does Latin grammar appear in a page from Cicero (whence, indeed, it was abstracted) and how can it be made to generate a page of genuine Latin prose? What do the copybook maxims look like in moral conduct observed, and how can they be made to generate conduct? These are the facts, but what conclusions do they authorize or forbid? This is the literature—the articulate contents, for example, of current knowledge about magnetic effects—but how does a pupil learn to speak the language in which it is written down : the language of science? How does he acquire the connoisseurship which enables him to determine relevance, which allows him to distinguish between different sorts of questions and the different sorts of answers they call for, which emancipates him from crude absolutes and suffers him to give his assent or dissent in graduate terms?

But learning to think is not merely learning how to judge, to interpret and to use information, it is learning to recognize and enjoy the intellectual virtues. How does a pupil learn disinterested curiosity, patience, intellectual honesty, exactness, industry, concentration and doubt? How does he acquire a sensibility to small differences and the ability to recognize intellectual elegance? How does he come to inherit the disposition to submit to refutation? How does he, not merely learn the love of truth and justice, but learn it in such a way as to escape the reproach of fanaticism?

And beyond all this there is something more difficult to acquire, but more important than any of it; namely, the ability to detect the individual intelligence which is at work in every utterance, even in those which convey impersonal information. For every significant act or utterance has a style of its own, a personal idiom, an individual manner of thinking of which it is a reflection. This, what I have called style, is the choice made, not according to the rules, but within the area of freedom left by the negative operation of rules. We may listen to what a man has to say, but unless we overhear in it a mind at work and can detect the idiom of thought, we have understood nothing. Art and conduct, science, philosophy and history, these are not modes of thought *defined* by rules; they exist only in personal explorations of territories only the boundaries of which are subject to definition. To have command over the languages of our civilization is, not to know the rules of their grammar, but to have the opportunity of a syntax and a vocabulary, rich in fine distinctions, in which to think for oneself. Learning, then, is acquiring the ability to feel and to think, and the pupil will never acquire these abilities unless he has learned to listen for them and to recognize them in the conduct and utterances of others.

Besides information, then, this is what has to be learned; for this (and not the dead weight of its products) is the real substance of our inheritance—and nothing can be inherited without learning. And this is what the teacher has to 'impart' to his pupil, together with whatever information he chooses to convey.

It cannot be *learned* separately; it is never explicitly learned and it is known only in practice; but it may be learned in everything that is learned, in the carpentry shop as well as in the Latin or chemistry lesson. If it is learned, it can never be forgotten, and it does not need to be recollected in order to be enjoyed. It is, indeed, often enough, the residue which remains when all else is forgotten; the shadow of lost knowledge.

It cannot be *taught* separately; it can have no place of its own in a timetable of a curriculum. It cannot be taught overtly, by precept, because it comprises what is required to animate precept; but it may be taught in everything that is taught. It is implanted unobstrusively in the manner in which information is conveyed, in a tone of voice, in the gesture which accompanies instruction, in asides and oblique utterances, and by example. For 'teaching by example', which is sometimes dismissed as an inferior sort of teaching, generating inflexible knowledge because the rules of what is known remain concealed, is emancipating the pupil from the half-utterances of rules by making him aware of a concrete situation. And in imitating the example he acquires, not merely a model for the particular occasion, but the disposition to recognize everything as an occasion. It is a habit of listening for an individual intelligence at work in every utterance that may be acquired by imitating a teacher who has this habit. And the intellectual virtues may be imparted only by a teacher who really cares about them for their own sake and never stoops to the priggishness of mentioning them. Not the cry, but the rising of the wild duck impels the flock to follow him in flight.

When I consider, as in private duty bound, how I first became dimly aware that there was something else in learning than the acquisition of information, that the way a man thought was more important than what he said, it was, I think, on the occasion when we had before us concrete situations. It was when we had, not an array of historical 'facts', but (for a moment) the facts suspended in an historian's argument. It was on those occasions when we were made to learn by heart, not the declension of *bonus* (which, of course, had to be learned), but a passage of literature, the reflection of a mind at work in a language. It was on those occasions when one was not being talked to but had the opportunity of overhearing an intelligent conversation.

And if you were to ask me the circumstances in which patience, accuracy, economy, elegance and style first dawned upon me, I would have to say that I did not come to recognize them in literature, in argument or in geometrical proof until I had first recognized them elsewhere; and that I owed this recognition to a Sergeant gymnastics instructor who lived long before the days of 'physical education' and for whom gymnastics was an intellectual art—and I owed it to him, not on account of anything he ever said, but because he was a man of patience, accuracy, economy, elegance and style.


NOTES

1. The horses I refer to are, of course, those of Elberfield. But it is, perhaps, worth recalling that the ancient Athenians delighted in the horse above all other animals because they recognized in it an affinity to man, and an animal uniquely capable of education. The horse had no *geistige* inheritance of its own, but (while other animals might be set to work) the horse was capable of sharing an inheritance imparted to it by man. And, in partnership with a rider (so Xenophon observed), it could acquire talents, accomplishments and even a grace of movement unknown to it in its 'natural' condition.

# 11

# INDOCTRINATION
## J. P. White

### I. INTRODUCTION

When I used to teach 'Liberal Studies' to Technical College students, I used to find myself in a dilemma. I had given up history teaching in a Grammar School because I did not want to teach about May Day in Shakespeare's England to the younger boys or the causes of the Hundred Years' War to sixth-formers. I began to teach, among other things, about the rise of the Labour Party and the origin of the Welfare State. But, at the same time, I felt that I was treading on dangerous ground. How far was I getting my students consciously or unconsciously to share my own political beliefs, however carefully I stuck to the 'facts'? And if they did come to share them was I not indoctrinating them, not educating them? In my very selection of topics to include these political issues was I not doing with different content what a planner of a history syllabus in Soviet Russia does— and wasn't this indoctrination? I thought back to what my head master had told me after a disastrous lesson on sex I had given to a class of fourteen-year-old boys in a Secondary Modern School when I first taught: 'I've always said so, and I'll say it again, lad: you can teach anything you like in school, as long as you keep off just three things: religion, sex and politics.'

History teaching in schools is one area where the question 'Is this indoctrination?' is notoriously apt to arise; another is religious education. But there are two further contexts in which it appears, in one of which the question is likely to be aired by certain moral philosophers, and in the other by certain educational theorists. The first of these is the moral education of the very young child. Children are brought up to obey moral rules. They cannot be given reasons for following these rules, for any reason that might be provided would be incomprehensible to them. So they have to be made to follow the rules by non-rational means, e.g. by fear of the withdrawal of their mother's love if they are disobedient. The question is: is this non-rationally based moral 'education' indoctrination? Green[1] argues that it is. Indoctrination is marked, for Green, by a person coming to hold a belief unintelligently, that is, without evidence. 'Indoctrination', he says, 'may be useful as the prelude to teaching (i.e. teaching which is rationally based)[2] . . . we need not offer reasons for every belief we think important for children and adults to hold.' Atkinson,[3] on the other hand, holds that one must distinguish between two sorts of 'non-rational teaching procedures that we may be obliged to use . . . . because of the immaturity and/or incapacity of the taught'. We are instructing, not indoctrinating, if the non-rational beliefs which the child learns, *can* be justified, and if they are inculcated in such a way as not to impair, or impair as little as possible the recipient's capacity for subsequent instruction and training. But if the beliefs are unjustifiable we must be indoctrinating. So, for Atkinson, the crucial issue in early moral education is the objectivity or otherwise of moral judgments. 'There can be moral teaching, instruction in, as opposed to instruction about morality, only if there are criteria of truth, cogency, correctness, in the field. Are there such criteria?' Hare[4] differs, yet again, in giving a negative answer to the last question (there are no objective moral judgments; the latter depends on 'decisions of principle' which each must freely make for himself) while claiming that early moral education is not indoctrination, as long as the teacher's aim is not to 'stop the growth in our children of the capacity to think for themselves about moral questions' (p. 52). Briefly, then, Green holds all early moral education to be indoctrination, independently of the question whether moral judgments can be known to be true or false; Atkinson holds that it is indoctrination only if they cannot be known to be true or false; and Hare holds that it is not necessarily indoctrination even though they cannot be known to be true or false. I do not want to examine these positions here, although I shall do so later; I merely want to indicate the philosophical controversy that can arise over questions of indoctrination in the moral sphere.

The other area of interest in indoctrination comes from the controversy between 'child centred' and 'traditional' theories of education. One of the charges of the former way of thinking against the latter is that the traditional teacher merely tries to implant items of information into some pupils' minds, without letting them discover this information for themselves. For some child-centred theorists, any attempt the teacher makes to get children to learn things, is

by crop failures. The effectiveness of precipitation depends not only on the amount but also on a number of other factors, including seasonal distribution, intensity of rainfall and runoff, evaporation, temperatures, humidity, and wind velocity.

Generally speaking, the distribution of rainfall between the seasons in the Northern Plains is good on the average. Most of it occurs during the growing season, April through September (Figure 8). Unfortunately, this desirable pattern cannot be counted on in any given year; the variation in seasonal distribution from one year to the next is substantial, as is illustrated by the data on rainfall at Loup City, Nebraska, over a twenty-nine–year period (Figure 7).

Furthermore, precipitation data for any given month fail to reveal the effectiveness of the rainfall. At times, precipitation occurs in the form of short, hard rains with a high percentage of runoff. An even larger proportion of the rain comes in the form

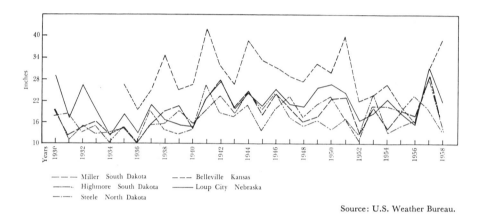

Source: U.S. Weather Bureau.

FIG. 6.   ANNUAL RAINFALL AT FIVE LOCATIONS, 1930–58

of light showers—less than half an inch. As indicated in Table 1, 35 percent of the April-through-August rainfall at Belleville, Kansas (north-central Kansas), occurred in rains of half an inch or less. Precipitation of this kind is of questionable value because of shallow penetration (6 inches or less) and surface evaporation, especially if farmers make a practice of working the ground as soon afterwards as possible.

Moreover, monthly totals do not indicate the timing of rainfall in relation to the critical need-stages of plant development. It is not uncommon in this region to have one-half to two-thirds of the rainfall for an entire month fall in a matter of a few hours on one or two days during the month. The amount of rainfall is reflected in the monthly totals, of course, but such rains may be poorly timed in relation to plant needs. If such rains are followed by several weeks of hot, windy, dry weather, as is frequently the case, the crop may still be without moisture just at the time it is most needed. Water needs of crops are high when the crop is growing rapidly, in July and August. ˙A combination of high temperatures, low humidity, wind, and fairly long periods without rain may be disastrous to a corn crop, particularly at the time of silking or tasseling. Transpiration may take place faster than the roots can absorb the needed moisture.

What little precipitation falls in the form of snow during the winter is often of

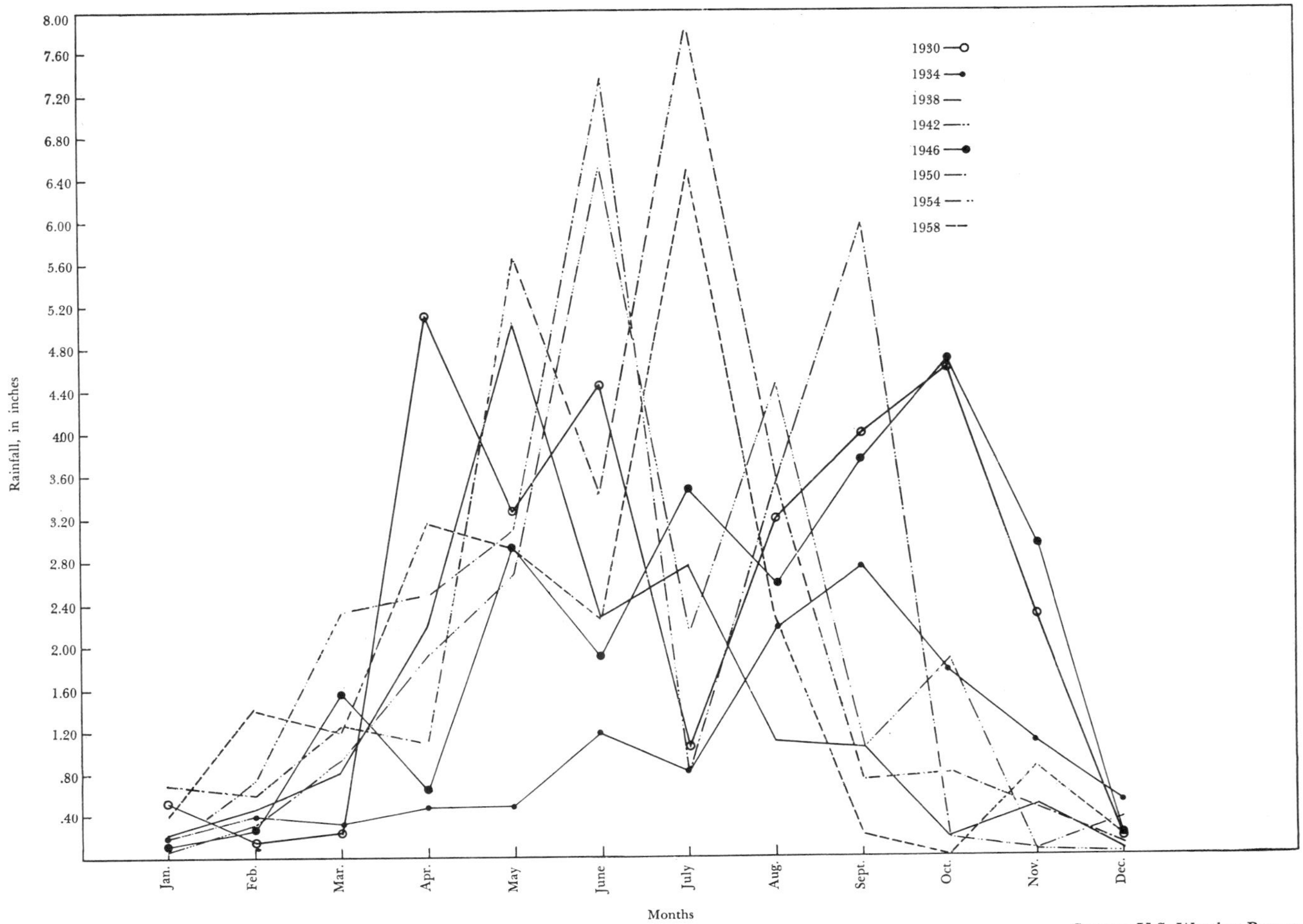

Source: U.S. Weather Bureau.

Fig. 7. Variation in Seasonal Distribution of Rainfall at Loup City, Nebraska

questionable value. The ground is frequently frozen when the snow falls, so that moisture penetration from the melting snow is greatly decreased. Snows are often accompanied by driving winds. Consequently, unless fields have a good cover of stubble, weeds, or cornstalks, much of the snow accumulates in drifts along a fence or road. (Obviously, it is rather ineffective there, as far as use by crops is concerned. Its chief accomplishment may be blocked highways, more work for road maintenance men, and headaches for those who have to travel the road before the snowplow gets there.)

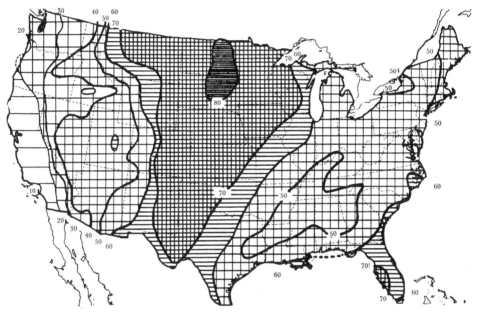

Source: Stephen S. Visher, *Climatic Atlas of the United States* (Cambridge: Harvard University Press, 1954), map 502, p. 200.

Fig. 8.    Percentage of Annual Precipitation Occurring During April through September

One of the hazards of the area is the "blizzard," characterized by rather heavy snowfall, driving winds, and low temperatures. During such storms, visibility is sometimes limited to as little as a few hundred feet (or less). Blizzards have been particularly hazardous for the livestock farmer in the Northern Plains. In seeking to avoid the blinding snow and piercing cold, cattle drift with the wind until they come to a fence, a body of water, ice, some other barrier, or to shelter. In particularly bad storms of this kind, large numbers of cattle have been lost. Weaker and smaller animals may be trampled as the cattle crowd and mill together in an effort to keep warm. People become confused and lost—sometimes within short distances of shelter.

Part of the treachery of the prairie blizzard lies in its tendency to come quickly and unexpectedly. Winds may shift 180 degrees within a few minutes; their velocity may change from a near calm to 50 or 60 miles an hour, almost as quickly. Temperatures sometimes drop by as much as 50 or 60 degrees within a few hours. Such changes,

TABLE 1. DISTRIBUTION OF RAINFALL IN NORTH-CENTRAL SECTION OF KANSAS, 1896–1935

| *Inches of Precipitation* | Jan. | Feb. | Mar. | Apr. | May | June | July | Aug. | Sept. | Oct. | Nov. | Dec. | Total |
|---|---|---|---|---|---|---|---|---|---|---|---|---|---|
| | | | | | | NUMBER OF RAINS | | | | | | | |
| .01– .25 . . . . . . . | 97 | 116 | 140 | 175 | 209 | 211 | 163 | 163 | 152 | 120 | 103 | 104 | 1753 |
| .26– .50 . . . . . . . | 16 | 28 | 32 | 57 | 72 | 69 | 50 | 52 | 43 | 44 | 28 | 18 | 509 |
| .51– .75 . . . . . . . | 7 | 8 | 13 | 28 | 36 | 44 | 27 | 32 | 22 | 13 | 12 | 7 | 249 |
| .76–1.00 . . . . . . . | 1 | 5 | 4 | 16 | 26 | 21 | 14 | 18 | 14 | 11 | 5 | 5 | 140 |
| 1.01–1.50 . . . . . . . | 0 | 1 | 4 | 12 | 18 | 24 | 17 | 20 | 12 | 11 | 5 | 2 | 126 |
| 1.51–2.00 . . . . . . . | 0 | 1 | 1 | 3 | 8 | 10 | 11 | 9 | 9 | 6 | 3 | 1 | 62 |
| 2.01–3.00 . . . . . . . | 0 | — | — | 2 | 3 | 4 | 7 | 6 | 4 | 3 | 1 | 0 | 30 |
| 3.01 and over . . . . . | 0 | 0 | 0 | 1 | 2 | 1 | 1 | 2 | 2 | 1 | — | 0 | 10 |
| Total . . . . . | 121 | 159 | 194 | 294 | 374 | 384 | 290 | 302 | 258 | 209 | 157 | 137 | 2879 |

Source: Andrew D. Robb, "Rains in Kansas," *Monthly Weather Review* (September, 1938), pp. 277–79.

when accompanied by snow, have proved disastrous both to people and animals. In the absence of radio and television, severe storms of this kind sometimes strike with little, if any, warning. Youngsters at school have had to spend the night in the schoolhouse or stop at a neighbor's, being unable to reach home.

*Evaporation as an Important Factor*

Evaporation tends to be relatively high in the Plains. The area has been described by Trewartha as one in which "annual precipitation exceeds potential evaporation but usually not by a very great margin."[10] Thornthwaite shows a division between an area which he describes as having little or no deficit in any season and one which has little or no surplus in any season. This line of demarcation coincides rather closely with the eastern boundary of the Northern Plains transition area.[11] Visher shows a similar division.[12] Evaporation tends to increase as average summer temperatures increase. Consequently, evaporation tends to be somewhat higher in the southern states. Factors contributing to high rates of evaporation include low atmospheric humidity, high temperatures, and high wind velocity.

*Temperature and Humidity*

Average January temperatures range from near zero in North Dakota to 30 degrees in central Kansas. There is less difference between temperatures near the Canadian border and those in central Kansas in the summertime than there is in January. Humidity tends to run five to ten points lower in the Plains transition area than in the eastern part of the corn-belt.

With temperatures as with rainfall, averages may be misleading. The average summer temperatures of 75–80 degrees are about the same as in many other parts of the United States, but it is the exception to the average which is significant to crop

[10] *Op. cit.*, p. 168.

[11] "An Approach toward a Rational Classification of Climate," *Geographical Review*, 38, No. 1 (1948), 20.

[12] Stephen Sargent Visher, *Climatic Atlas of the United States* (Cambridge: Harvard University Press, 1954), p. 195.

production. Not infrequently, temperatures of 100 degrees or more are experienced in the Plains. When these high temperatures coincide with lack of rainfall and comparatively high wind velocities, moisture supplies of plants are severely strained. Prolonged periods of such a combination of weather characteristics cut yields of crops, particularly if the crop is at a critical stage in its development.

The margin between the average set of circumstances and one which is intolerable for successful crop production is relatively small. Deviations of one or more of these climatic factors from the average toward the less favorable may spell disaster for the Plains farmer.

Temperature extremes in winter, like those in summer, are most disastrous when combined with other weather characteristics. Cattle, for example, can tolerate still, dry cold comparatively well; but when cold is accompanied by snow or freezing rain and wind, younger and weaker animals may succumb.

*Hail and Tornadoes*

Crop losses due to hail, frequent in the Northern Plains, are most common in western Nebraska, southeastern Wyoming, and southwestern South Dakota. They are not as heavy in the transition area. On the other hand, tornadoes are most frequent in eastern South Dakota, Nebraska, and Kansas, which lie in the "tornado alley" of the central part of the country.

# CHAPTER 3

# Area History to 1900

ALTHOUGH this is not intended as a book of history, a survey of the past is helpful. To fully understand the conditions, problems, and institutions under which today's Plains people find themselves we must start at the beginning.[1]

### THE FIRST INHABITANTS—THE INDIANS

Within the Great Plains there were thirty-one Indian tribes, eleven of which were typical of the Plains heartland—the High Plains—and which depended largely on the buffalo as a source of livelihood. In the eastern part of the Plains were fourteen other tribes, which represented a transition between the nomadic Plains Indians and those of areas to the east who were more dependent upon agriculture, particularly the raising of maize. The eastern transition tribes were the Arikara, Hidatsa, Mandan, Santee-Dakota, and Yanton of the present Dakota area; the Ponca, Omaha, Pawnee, and Otoe in Nebraska; the Kansas, Wichita, and Osage of Kansas and Oklahoma— plus the Iowa and the Missouri, located in the states that now bear their names.

Most of these tribes lived in close proximity to the 100th meridian. The transition tribes hunted buffalo, but raised maize and other plants, and had more permanent homes—typically along streams—than the Indians of the High Plains.[2] However, they retained a considerable degree of mobility, the trait which characterized the Indians of the High Plains, particularly after they acquired the horse from the early Spaniards.

There has been insufficient appreciation of the degree of adaptation to their environment accomplished by the Indians of the Plains area. They were not the simple, uncultured barbarians pictured by the early whites; in fact, their social organization

[1] There are a number of excellent historical sources to which the reader is referred if he would like more complete accounts of various phases of Plains settlement than space permits here. These include: Walter Webb, *The Great Plains* (Boston: Ginn & Company, 1931); Wallace Stegner, *Beyond the Hundredth Meridian* (Boston: Houghton Mifflin Company, 1954); Benjamin Horace Hibbard, *A History of the Public Land Policies* (New York: The Macmillan Company, 1924); James C. Olson, *History of Nebraska* (Lincoln: University of Nebraska Press, 1955); Carl Frederick Kraenzel, *The Great Plains in Transition* (Norman: University of Oklahoma Press, 1955); Harold E. Briggs, *Frontiers of the Northwest* (New York: Appleton-Century, 1940); and Mary Wilma M. Hargreaves, *Dry Farming in the Northern Great Plains, 1900–1925* (Cambridge: Harvard University Press, 1957).

[2] Clark Wissler, *The American Indian* (Gloucester, Mass.: Peter Smith, 1950), pp. 220–22.

and mores—as well as their concepts of property and religion—were understood by very few whites during the settlement period. Lack of understanding, the pressure of settlement, and the violation of arrangements made with them all contributed to a record in which the white man can take little pride. Only recently has there begun to appear literature that strips away the veneers of romance or barbarianism with which the Indians have been painted to uncover the real human beings beneath.[3]

## EARLY EXPLORATION

The first white men to visit the Northern Plains were the Spaniards, beginning with Coronado, who traveled up from the Rio Grande—in 1541—as far north and east as north-central Kansas. They were followed by the French in the early 1700's, led first by Bourgmond, who explored the Missouri up to the Platte, and later by the Mallet brothers, who in 1739 traversed the area now occupied by South Dakota, Nebraska, Kansas, Colorado, and New Mexico. Finally, the British penetrated into the area from the north, with the coming of the Hudson's Bay Company's traders. However, none of these early efforts resulted in actual settlement of the Northern Plains area. For two and a half centuries the interests of white men in the Plains centered around gold, adventure, and fur.

The event that led to physical investment in the Northern Plains was the Louisiana Purchase of 1803 (see Figure 9). In a single transaction negotiated with France, the United States acquired title to over 500 million acres of land, or one-fourth of its present continental area, at a total cost of $27 million—including the initial payment, settlement of claims, and interest paid. This was no small undertaking, especially at a time when the annual federal budget amounted only to eight or ten million dollars. It would be equivalent today to the purchase of an area larger than the continental United States for $200 billion, a proposal that would give any president pause, yet Jefferson did not even have prior Congressional approval.

The Louisiana Purchase called for more exploration. Lewis and Clark in 1804–6, Pike in 1806–7, and Long in 1819–20 (the Yellowstone Expedition) led expeditions that acquainted the American public with the new lands between the Missouri River and the Rocky Mountains. Some drought conditions were encountered since parts of the routes lay in arid or semiarid regions. These explorers "confirmed" the previously held notion of the Plains region as the Great American Desert—the term applied to it on the maps between 1820 and 1860. Dr. James, of Long's expedition, indicated that a dividing line between the timbered country and the Plains lay at the 96th meridian. He further observed that the change was not abrupt, as a line marked by distinctly identifiable features, but was a gradual one.[4] His was the first mention of a transition area.

Simultaneously with the official explorations came the fur traders and trappers who crossed the Plains from east to west and from north to south between 1804 and 1846. They accumulated a large stock of common knowledge about the region, and

[3] Good examples are: Mari Sandoz's, *Cheyenne Autumn* (New York: McGraw-Hill Book Company, 1953), and *Crazy Horse, The Strange Man of the Oglalas* (Lincoln: University of Nebraska Press, 1961).
[4] Webb, *op. cit.*, p. 157.

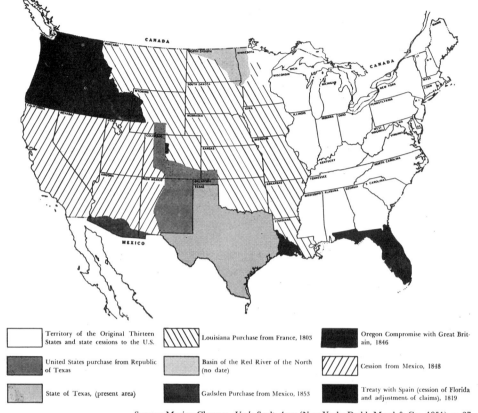

| | Territory of the Original Thirteen States and state cessions to the U.S. | | Louisiana Purchase from France, 1803 | | Oregon Compromise with Great Britain, 1846 |
|---|---|---|---|---|---|
| | United States purchase from Republic of Texas | | Basin of the Red River of the North (no date) | | Cession from Mexico, 1848 |
| | State of Texas, (present area) | | Gadsden Purchase from Mexico, 1853 | | Treaty with Spain (cession of Florida and adjustment of claims), 1819 |

Source: Marion Clawson, *Uncle Sam's Acres* (New York: Dodd, Mead & Co., 1951), p. 27.

FIG. 9.    CONTINENTAL EXPANSION OF THE UNITED STATES (TO 1853)

therefore were used as guides by later expeditions—such as Fremont's—by settlers on their way to California or Oregon, and by the Army.

## A LAND TO CROSS

The first mass movements of people into the Northern Plains did not arise out of an interest in the area itself. The area served merely as a national highway to the lands farther west. In 1841, what was to become known as the Oregon Trail saw the first settlers following the Platte River on their way to the new lands in the northwest. Next, the Mormons, starting in 1847, sought the "promised land"; their bands also beat their tedious and sometimes painful way along the Platte. Finally, in 1849, the discovery of gold in California unleashed further thousands of migrants along the Platte Valley–South Pass Trail. So heavy were these migrations that by 1851 California had been admitted to the Union, and Oregon, New Mexico, and Utah had been organized as territories.

Few of these migrants remained in the Plains. Except for the Indians, the only permanent residents were soldiers at the military posts and tradesmen and others who supplied goods and services to the migrants and the fur traders and trappers.

There were several reasons for this. The Oregonians were seeking the timbered and watered country of the northwest, the Californians sought gold, and the Mormons were interested in getting beyond the bounds of federal and state laws. Some of the conditions encountered in the Plains—dust storms, lack of water, and the shortage of grass along the trails—strengthened the Great American Desert concept in the minds of the travelers. Less effective, perhaps, were the restrictions on the entry of whites into territory reserved for the Indians which were written into federal legislation in 1830 and later, since legal restrictions tended to be eased along the western fringes of settlement.

The most important deterrent to settlement, however, was the availability of more accessible land in Illinois, Iowa, Minnesota, and Wisconsin; this was sufficient to satisfy the demand at the moment. But, with the advent of the 1850's and the exhaustion of this supply, the Northern Plains experienced the same types of population in-movement which had occurred east and west of them. Several factors affected the course of this settlement.

### Territorial Organization and the Opening of Indian Lands

The politics of the slavery controversy before the Civil War hastened the organization of the Northern Plains country. The Minnesota Territory, organized in 1849, included the portions of the Dakotas lying east of the Missouri, and the Kansas-Nebraska Act of 1854 organized this area as two territories. Kansas Territory included some of present-day Colorado, while Nebraska included the entire area between the Rocky Mountains and the Missouri River north of the Kansas boundary. These developments, plus negotiations between the Indians and the Commissioner of Indian Affairs, opened the country west of the 98th meridian to settlement.

Once the Indian titles to the land were relinquished, the vast territories of Kansas and Nebraska became part of the public domain, available for acquisition by settlers. In 1854, property in these territories could be acquired in one of three ways: (1) purchase under the Preemption Law of 1841, by which a person could file for 160 acres of public domain and acquire title by payment of $1.25 per acre after the land was put up for sale; (2) purchase with military bounty land warrants; or (3) direct purchase when the land was put up for public auction. As in most of the westward expansion of the United States, the settlers moved in before the land was surveyed, creating the basis for later litigation over conflicting land claims.

This was a time of drawing lines on a blank map. As soon as the lands were opened, they were surveyed. The survey was nearly complete by 1857 in the territory presently occupied by Kansas and Nebraska, and it was under way in eastern South Dakota by 1860. The surveyors were not soils specialists, geologists, land-use planners, or economists; they were engineers, charged with the single task of plotting the land into townships 6 miles square, containing 36-square-mile sections. It was simply a continuation of the practice of the General Land Office, in use since 1812, and one that had been instituted to improve the often confused surveys of colonial times.

Thus, in a very short time, a rigid pattern for settlement was set in the Plains. The square quarter of 160 acres was neat and orderly, and it was consistent with the popular agrarian policy which encouraged the settlement of the frontier in small farms. These square tracts took no account of the varying productivity of western soils, of water supplies, of topography, and of the level and variability of rainfall. They implied that central Nebraska was like central Illinois; 160 acres was large enough to keep a man and his animals busy, and, presumably, to provide him with the basis for a living. Ironically, these grid lines were drawn across land which had heretofore been termed the Great American Desert. However, the desert myth was fading, being rapidly replaced by a vision of the land at the 100th meridian as a garden, a veritable land of Canaan.

*First Settlement and the Boomers*

Land speculators and promoters came to the new country, along with the settlers. From Kansas to the Dakota Territory, "land boomers" feverishly began to stake out claims and sell town lots at exorbitant prices. Land companies were organized to establish towns; they would stake out the 120 acres allowed under the federal Townsites Act and then individually preempt adjacent quarter sections. This land was then subdivided into lots and sold on shares. The companies then petitioned the legislature for special acts of incorporation. Once the "city" (most of these townsites had the word *city* in their names) was incorporated, its promoters set about "booming" it. Newspapers advertising the beauties and natural advantages of each individual town were circulated in the eastern United States. Lithographs showing pictures of broad, shaded streets, of churches, fine residences, and wharves with puffing steamers deceived hundreds of gullible prospective settlers, who were bitterly disappointed—after they had purchased lots and arrived at the new town—to discover that it existed only on paper.

If towns developed only in the imaginations of the "boomers," the foundations of the banks were no more solid. Territorial financial transactions were fascinating but unorthodox—to say the least. It was easy to establish a bank and print and circulate banknotes. Some bankers didn't bother with a legislative charter, but set up shop anyway. The following is a verbatim account of how one "banker" got started.

> Well, I didn't have much else to do and so I rented an empty store building and painted "bank" on the window. The first day I was open for business a man came in and deposited one hundred dollars. The second day another deposited two-hundred fifty dollars, and so along about the third day I got confidence enough in the bank to put in a hundred myself.[5]

The financial bubble soon burst. By the autumn of 1857, word came of a general financial panic in the east, and the territorial banks folded like morning glories in a noonday sun. The worthlessness of most of them was soon apparent. One bank in De Soto, Nebraska, for example, was found to have nothing to show for itself except its name engraved upon the bills. This so-called bank had been operated by nonresidents, had held no charter, and had issued over $200,000 in notes.[6] The closing of the banks meant hard times for the territories. Town lots decreased in value, businesses failed, and money became so scarce it was practically nonexistent.

During the 1850's the settlers favored the free-homestead idea as the best solution

[5] Everett Dick, *The Sod-house Frontier, 1854–1890* (Lincoln: Johnsen Publishing Company, 1954), p. 90.
[6] *Ibid.*

for disposing of government lands. They were against putting the land up for sale because they believed it would place them in the clutches of speculators and money-lenders. This fear proved well-founded when the land was put up for sale at public auctions during the summer of 1859. Settlers, already hard pressed for funds, and still suffering from the panic of 1857, had to borrow money at high rates to salvage their claims. Speculators, who bought military land warrants from needy soldiers and widows for as little as 50 cents per acre, sold them to settlers at the full price plus interest. Many a settler's dream of owning his own farm and making a good living for himself was shattered when he found it impossible to meet the high interest payments on his land.

Despite the financial panic, the fifties was a period of rapid expansion and settlement. By 1858, Minnesota was admitted to the Union, and settlers pushed west beyond its borders. By 1860 the clamor for organized government in the Dakota country forced the creation of the Dakota Territory, which included the present states of North and South Dakota and Wyoming. The discovery of gold in Montana brought a rush of people to that area. The Territory of Montana was created in 1864, with a population of nearly 10,000 persons. In 1868 the western part of the Territory of Dakota was organized as the Territory of Wyoming.

The Civil War halted the influx of settlers and the economic development of the Northern Plains, but the pause was only temporary. In the meantime, new developments created the basis for a renewed surge of immigration following that struggle.

### The Homestead Act and Its Modifications

The passage of the Homestead Act—on May 1, 1862—settled a question that had haunted Congress for twenty years, and that had its roots in the previous century. It also completed a bargain the new Republican party had made to insure western support in 1860. The absence of southerners from Congress also was instrumental in its passage.

Under this act, any person twenty-one years or over, or the head of a family and a citizen, or an alien having filed his intention of becoming a citizen, could, upon payment of a $10.00 fee, file a claim on as much as 160 acres, i.e., a quarter section, of unappropriated public land. After he had resided upon it for a term of five years, and cultivated it, he could then receive his final patent for the land from the government. One additional provision enabled the homesteader, after residence of six months, to acquire immediate title by paying $1.25 per acre for the land, a transaction called *commutation*. Commuting was relatively uncommon at first, but, by the first decade after 1900, more land had been commuted than had been obtained by final proof.

The Homestead Act was of great historical significance, and was hailed as such at the time of its passage. However, as previously noted, it was remarkably ill adapted to the area to which it was applied. By 1862, most of the land opened to homesteading lay west of the Missouri. It must be said that many of the present problems of the Plains had their origin in the system of doling out land in quarter sections. In the words of Bernard De Voto: "In the arid regions 160 acres were not a homestead. They were just a mathematical expression whose meanings in relation to agricultural settlement were disastrous." [7]

[7] Bernard De Voto, "Introduction" in W. Stegner's *Beyond the Hundredth Meridian*, p. xix.

The big trouble was that neither the American people nor their government realized that institutions and habits that had worked in the eastern half of the country were not adapted to the Plains. The quarter section had almost a mystical significance as the proper size for a homestead. Admittedly, 160 acres of farmland in Wisconsin or Illinois was plenty of land to assure a good farmer an adequate living. But west of the Missouri the situation was different. As people pushed farther west, into the more arid lands, the ideal of the 160-acre homestead as an adequate unit to support a family became increasingly difficult to maintain.

Carving the land up into sections, with no regard for water supply or land contour, increased the difficulties of farming in a land of erratic rainfall. One hundred-sixty acres of rangeland was insufficient to support enough animals to maintain a family. On the other hand, in irrigable areas 160 acres was too large a tract for the settlers to develop and operate under irrigation.

Finally, as land policies changed to allow settlement in larger units in the dryer areas, the dispersed location of farmsteads over the countryside meant that road maintenance, schools, and other community services became so expensive that minimum standards could not be maintained. Again, in the words of De Voto:

> What the western realities demanded was not the ranch pattern of the Dakotas but the village pattern of the Spanish-American Southwest and of Mormon Utah. And in the arid region the traditional political organization within the states, by counties, would be cumbersome, illogical, and intolerably expensive. Far better to avoid such irrational units and to organize politically in accord with the western realities, by river valley or watershed.[8]

Nevertheless, the act was extremely popular, and thousands of settlers hastened to take advantage of its provisions. In the state of Nebraska alone, about 131,561 entrymen filed on 18,393,541 acres of the public domain between 1864 and 1895. Of this number, only 68,862 had received final patents by 1900. The total acreage transferred to individual homesteaders was only 9,609,922 acres, about half of the original filings.[9] Conditions in the rest of the Great Plains were similar.

The disparity between the number of homesteaders filing for land and those receiving final patents is significant. Free land lured many settlers who had little or no farming experience, and no resources to fall back on in case of a crop failure. Even those who had farmed elsewhere had a difficult time because of climatic conditions. Crops and farm practices that had been successful back home were of little value in the new land.

> The Homestead Act encouraged failure by not requiring more than the mere minimum of a shack for a home, only ten acres under cultivation and a well. There were no mentions of personal qualifications and equipment, and no provisions for loans. Thousands were deceived into thinking that securing a piece of land was all that was necessary to make a competence for the owner.[10]

Around the turn of the century this disparity was intensified as thousands filed for land with no intention whatever of farming it but rather to commute the homestead and sell it.

[8] De Voto, *op. cit.*, p. xxi.
[9] Olson, *op. cit.*, p. 166.
[10] Dick, *op. cit.*, p. 131.

Once out on the Plains, it quickly became apparent that 160 acres was not sufficient. Whoever controlled the water supply in a particular area was master of the situation. Ways and means were found to get around the law. Land frauds and speculation were common. Wealthy cattlemen, for example, often hired persons to file homestead claims, and after six months would have the claims commuted by payment of the minimum price of $1.25 per acre—whereupon the title would pass to the employer who had put up the money. A class of persons who made "settling" a business came into being. Stegner suggests that

> In actual practice almost the only real benefit that the landless and moneyless man, the mechanic, or immigrant farm boy, could derive from the public and laws was the chance for a little graft.[11]

Often it was not necessary to get legal possession of all the land. If a person had control of the water supply, or if his land was so arranged that blocks of government land remained enclosed by it, he had the use of a much larger acreage. Dick tells of a man in Potter County, Dakota Territory, who filed on 480 acres by homesteading, preempted, and—using a tree claim (see below) within a square of 640 acres—left the center plot unclaimed. He was able to use the 640 acres for a long time before his neighbors realized what he had done.[12]

Farther west, examples of fraudulent filing and illegal use of government land were even more common. Since it was virtually impossible to grow trees, the Timber Culture Act was subject to even more fraud than the Homestead Act. Passed in 1873, it provided that homesteaders could acquire an additional quarter section by planting 40 acres to trees and tending them for ten years. This act, sponsored by Nebraska Senator Hitchcock, was designed to encourage tree planting in the Plains. The act was applied to all homestead areas, regardless of climatic conditions and the possibility of actually growing trees.

Most of the land disposed of under this act was in the four Northern Plains states. Clawson says that "probably no other statute was as generally evaded as the Timber Culture Act."[13] In his report for 1885 the Commissioner of the General Land Office wrote:

> I have traveled hundreds of miles of land in western Kansas, Nebraska, and central Dakota, nearly one-fourth of which has been taken under the "timber culture act," without seeing an artificial grove, even in incipience.[14]

The act did, however, enable many homesteaders in the Northern Plains to double their acreages, and thus was unintentionally beneficial from this standpoint.

The Desert Land Act of 1877 was a greater modification of the Homestead Act than the Timber Act, but it applied in the Northern Plains states only to the Dakotas. It provided for the sale of a section of land to a settler who would irrigate it within *three* years after filing; the total payment amounted to $1.25 per acre. In both conception and application, this act was doomed to failure. Although sizable acreages were entered under it, only a few thousand acres were finally patented. Stockmen took possession of rangeland under it by paying the entry fee of 25 cents per acre, holding

---

[11] Stegner, *op. cit.*, p. 222.

[12] Dick, *op. cit.*, pp. 122–23.

[13] Marion Clawson, *Uncle Sam's Acres* (New York: Dodd, Mead & Co., 1951), p. 67.

[14] Olson, *op. cit.*, p. 168.

it for three years, then selling it. Others held large quantities of desert land for sheer speculation. There are tales of how some land was developed for irrigation by the simple means of plowing a few furrows, and then introducing water by pouring it from a pail into these ditches!

Congress amended the act in 1891 to restrict to 320 acres the amount of desert land that could be entered by one person. Also, improvements of $3.00 per acre were now required during the first three years, and one-eighth of the land was to be put under cultivation.[15]

## The Railroads

The railroads played a multiple role in the settling of the Northern Great Plains. With the completion of the Union Pacific–Central Pacific line in 1869, railroads rapidly became the chief means of transportation across the Plains. They brought in hunters, who killed the buffalo, thus facilitating the creation of the range-cattle industry, which covered the Plains for two decades. Finally, they were important colonizing agents and disposers of land.

Under the Pacific Railroad Act of 1862, the above two roads received 10 sections of land per mile of mainline, plus a government loan of $16,000 per mile for construction across the Plains—and greater amounts in the rougher lands to the west. These terms proved insufficient to attract capital, and Congress, in 1864—under pressure from the railroads—doubled the land grant. Similarly, the Northern Pacific received 40 sections per mile of mainline in the territories, and 20 sections per mile in the states. The Santa Fe, Southern Pacific, and Burlington lines received similar grants. The magnitude of the government's largesse is shown by the fact that in Nebraska one out of six acres was awarded to the railroads. (See Figure 10.)

The railroad grants put the railroads into competition with the Homestead Act in the disposal of land. Of course, the railroad grants consisted of every other section of land on both sides of the line, extending out far enough to make up the total, and settlers were interested in staying near the line. Also, the railroads waited—in some cases—until the homestead land had been taken up before actively selling. They sold their lands for higher prices than the commutation price of homestead land. The Burlington got an average of $6.05 per acre for its land, while the Union Pacific received $4.27 per acre.

With the dual incentive to build up the freight and passenger business and to sell land, the railroads became assiduous in attracting settlers. They established land departments that put immigration agents in the chief cities of the eastern United States, and in European countries, to encourage immigrants to buy their land. They distributed literature describing its beauty and fertility; lecturers were sent out on tours throughout the country; and educational programs were promoted.

So powerful a force were the railroads that Harold Briggs, in his *Frontiers of the Northwest*, blames the lack of early settlers in the Dakotas on the influence of the Union Pacific, which, understandably, did everything in its power to induce settlers to take up residence farther south in Nebraska. The Union Pacific was too formidable an opponent for the Dakotas to combat.[16]

[15] Hibbard, *op. cit.*, p. 431.
[16] Briggs, *op. cit.*, p. 367.

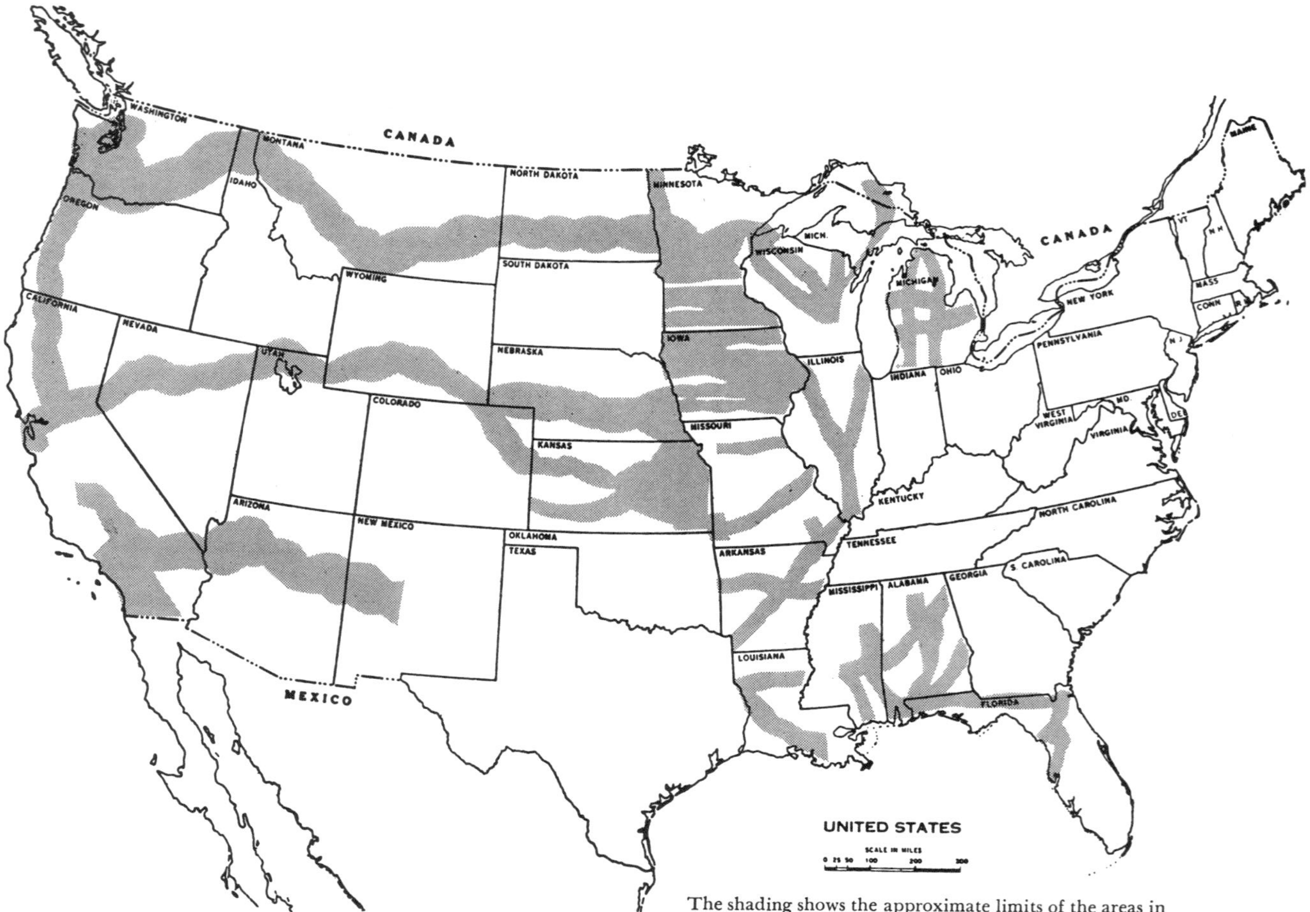

The shading shows the approximate limits of the areas in which the railroads received their land grants

Source: Marion Clawson, *Uncle Sam's Acres* (New York: Dodd, Mead & Co., 1951), p. 73.

Fig. 10. Federal Land Grants to the Railroads

*The State Land Grants*

The states also received grants of land from the federal government, for several purposes, and thus found themselves in the land market. Grants were made to states for railroad construction (Kansas), for common schools, for land-grant colleges, for institutions for the blind, and the like. Thus North Dakota received 3.2 million acres, South Dakota 3.4 million, Nebraska 3.5 million, and Kansas 7.8 million acres of land or these purposes.

State governments were not backward in promoting settlement within their boundaries. State immigration bureaus were created. Displays of agricultural products were exhibited throughout the country; state agents were located in various cities; and every advertising device known to the time was used to attract settlers.

*Progress of Settlement*

In spite of the Homestead Act and the other lands made available, settlement of the Northern Plains did not proceed steadily. The first rush was into Kansas and Nebraska, as can be seen in Table 2. These states were settled to the 98th meridian by 1870, with

TABLE 2. POPULATION IN NORTHERN GREAT PLAINS STATES, 1860–1900

| States | 1860 | 1870 | 1880 | 1890 | 1900 |
|---|---|---|---|---|---|
| Kansas . . . . . . . | 107,206 | 364,339 | 996,096 | 1,427,096 | 1,470,495 |
| Nebraska . . . . . . | 28,841 | 122,993 | 452,402 | 1,058,910 | 1,066,910 |
| South Dakota ⎫ . . . . | 4,837 | 11,776 | 98,268 | 328,808 | 401,570 |
| North Dakota ⎭ | | 2,405 | 36,909 | 182,719 | 319,146 |
| Total . . . . . . . | 140,884 | 501,573 | 1,583,675 | 2,997,533 | 3,258,121 |

Source: *Statistical Abstract of the United States.*

nearly half a million people. Small settlements also took place in the Dakota Territory along the lower segments of the Big Sioux, the Vermillion, and the James rivers, although they had been retarded by the Civil War, the Indian outbreaks, lack of transportation, and fear of grasshoppers and drought. After 1870 there was a pause. The stream of settlement lacked the drive generated earlier, though it was to be renewed later. As Kraenzel puts it, there was "hesitation along the ninety-eighth meridian." [17]

Several factors provided the basis for the renewed pace of population in-movement, which can be seen in the census data for 1880 and 1890 and in Figure 11. Additional railroad lines were completed in the Dakotas, opening up new lands to settlers. The invention of barbed wire enabled the homesteader to enclose his acres rapidly, and reduced his need for timber. Wire fences meant the end of the open range. The windmill made settlers and ranchers less dependent on streams and shallow water tables, and it enabled people to settle in areas previously untenable. The sod house, invented in the Plains, and cool in the summer and warm in the winter, further lessened the need for wood.

Other technologies were also important. The steel breaking-plow (the "sod-buster"), invented earlier, was essential in the conversion of native prairie for tillage.

[17] Kraenzel, *op. cit.*, p. 125.

The endgate seeder, the drill, the corn planter, the binder, the mower, the hay rake, the thresher, and the gang plow are examples of the mechanization of American agriculture that was taking place at this time. These machines enabled the Plains farmer to work the land more efficiently; they were labor-saving, and thus helped whet his appetite for more land.

Natural and general economic factors also influenced the course of settlement. After the boom period of 1868–73, the panic of 1873 struck, and the attendant depression—which lasted until 1878—slowed railroad expansion, immigration, and development of the Plains area in general. Drought also occurred during the first part of the decade, along with the famous grasshopper plagues of 1874, 1875, and 1877.

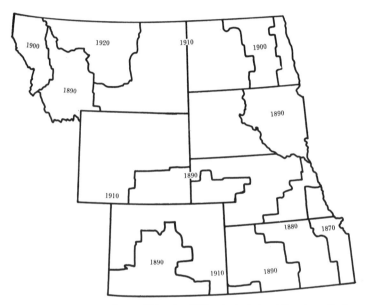

Source: University of Nebraska Agricultural Experiment Station.

FIG. 11.   YEARS IN WHICH POPULATION REACHED 50 PER CENT OF THE
1940 LEVEL IN THE NORTHERN PLAINS

Economic conditions improved in 1877, however, and eastern families bankrupted by depression saw in the free land in the west a chance to recoup. A series of wet years and heavy crops confirmed the promise of the Plains. The tide of immigration ran full again. It was the time of the "Great Dakota Boom." Claims on 1.4 million acres of land in the Dakotas were filed in 1878, and on nearly 1.7 million acres in the next year.[18] In Nebraska, claims on 827,000 acres were filed in 1880, a record for its day.[19]

The force of settlement now broke through the Plains–corn-belt transition area and was carried, by its own momentum, through the lands to the west. Settlement followed the river valleys—along the Republican, the Platte, and the Elkhorn in Nebraska, and the James, the Missouri, and the Cheyenne in Dakota. By 1878 several counties had

[18] Briggs, *op. cit.*, p. 392.
[19] Olson, *op. cit.*, p. 167.

been organized in the transition area of the Dakotas: Burleigh, Stutsman, La Moure, Barnes, Hughes, Hyde, Spink, Kingsbury, Miner, Hanson, and Hutchinson (some names and boundaries have since been changed). In Nebraska and Kansas, most of the present-day transition counties had been organized by 1875.

In this surge of optimism—supported, as it seemed to be, by the fortuitous combination of rain and favorable prices—the sober warnings of a few men, like Thomas and Powell, were disregarded and were often bitterly resented. In 1870, Cyrus Thomas had set the dividing line at the 99th meridian, east of which the rainfall was considered sufficient for crop production and west of which irrigation was necessary.[20] In 1879, Major J. W. Powell wrote his report, "Lands of the Arid Region," designating the 100th meridian as the western limit of agriculture, and that portion of the land receiving less than 28 inches of rainfall annually as marginal. He recommended 80 acres as the homestead unit for irrigated farms, and for pasture farms he visualized units of 2,500 acres—sixteen times the size of the 160-acre homestead. He also proposed land surveys based on topography, which would permit farms to be as irregular as necessary to give each a water frontage and a tract of irrigable soil.[21]

If these warnings and proposals had been taken seriously, the history of the region might have been much different. But since they represented such a complete break with tradition, and were contrary to the interests of promoters, they were largely ignored—or greeted with indignation and scorn. The thinking of Dr. Samuel Aughey, Professor of Natural Sciences at the University of Nebraska, was much more in keeping with the boom spirit of the times. He suggested that rain would follow the plow, and that, with the push of the settlers west, rainfall would increase. The years immediately following his statements happened to be unusually wet, thus apparently supporting Dr. Aughey and refuting Powell and Thomas. The main idea of the times was to push westward. In the words of Hargreaves:

> Regional opinion, as expressed in shaping of national land policy, state land programs, and the dealings of private operators, manifested general approbation of the effort to put settlers onto the land as quickly as possible.[22]

The eighties continued prosperous for most of the Northern Plains. People continued to pour into Dakota, where the population jumped from 135,000 in 1880 to about 511,000 in 1883.[23] Nebraska's population rose from 452,402 in 1880 to 1,058,910 in 1890. Towns and cities competed sharply to attract new residents, and there is evidence that city officials sometimes padded population figures. For example, according to the official census of 1890, Hastings, Nebraska, reported 13,584 persons, but a later estimate—based upon school census, numbers voting, city directory figures, and other records—indicates that the actual number was closer to 6,000.[24]

By 1885 the peak of the boom had passed. The general business depression in the following year affected the Plains states along with the rest of the country. To make

---

[20] James Malin, "Agricultural Regionalism of the Trans-Mississippi West, as Delineated by Cyrus Thomas," *Agricultural History*, 21 (October, 1947), 210.

[21] Stegner, *op. cit.*, p. 227.

[22] Hargreaves, *op. cit.*, p. 434.

[23] Briggs, *op. cit.*, p. 410.

[24] Edgar Z. Palmer, "The Correctness of the 1890 Census of Population for Nebraska Cities," *Nebraska History*, 32 (December, 1951), 261 and 266.

matters worse, several dry years ensued, beginning with 1886. These culminated in the drought of 1889, which was widespread throughout the central portion of the United States.

By 1890 almost all of Kansas and Nebraska, the eastern half of South Dakota, and large sections of North Dakota had been settled. In 1889 the Dakota territory was divided into North and South Dakota, which were admitted to the Union. The age of early settlement was over. Development of the region had been influenced by the whims of nature, by economic trends, and by national policy, as well as by individual and community initiative.

INSTITUTIONAL DEVELOPMENT

Along with the rapid growth of population in the Northern Plains came the development of social institutions: counties, schools, colleges. In most cases there were no formal laws guiding the formation of counties—they were established after enough settlers had arrived to warrant a formal organization. They were usually very small, owing to the rudimentary means of transportation and communication. Wyoming, farther west, enacted a law in 1890 requiring that counties include a minimum population of 1,500 persons and taxable property with an assessed valuation of $2 million.[25] Since it was sparsely populated range country, this provision ensured that the counties there would be much larger in area than in the Dakotas, Nebraska, and Kansas.

Competition between towns for the location of county seats was intense, and county histories are enlivened by tales of falsified election results, seizure of records by stealth, and issuance of injunctions to prevent a particular town from obtaining the precious records. It seemed logical, at the time, to limit the size of a county to accommodate farmers, who had to drive to the county seat with horses. Now the team and wagon are gone, and the population of many counties has decreased, but the small and outmoded county lives on.

Road building, road maintenance, and school organization were the main concerns of counties, if we can judge from early histories. Road building was a major project and consumed much of the county commissioners' time and energy. Because of the surveying and homesteading of the land in sections, with a dwelling on each quarter section, far more roads were built than would have been required if the land had been divided according to contour. Had farm families lived closer together, along main roads or in small hamlets, the cost of road construction and maintenance could have been greatly reduced.

In Sherman County, which is typical of central Nebraska, the roads were developed in several stages. First there were the Indian trails. Then came wagon trails, along the creeks, connecting the towns. Later, three county road districts were created and a fund of $16,000 in bonds was provided for bridges. State aid for road and bridge building was not provided until 1921. As late as 1952 there were thirty-seven road districts in Sherman County, with 31.7 miles of hard-surface road, 184 miles of gravel road, and 845 miles of dirt road.[26] In the early days each settler gave so many days' work per year on the roads in order to maintain them; later a road tax was levied.

[25] Briggs, *op. cit.*, pp. 475–76.
[26] Meroe J. Owens, "A Brief History of Sherman County, Nebraska," Norfolk *Daily News*, 1952, p. 38.

Public education was a matter of concern to the settlers right from the time of settlement. The federal government granted sections 16 and 36 of each township to the states for the support of the common schools. In Nebraska, more than 2.75 million acres was received from the government for this purpose, and in each county the lands were appraised and then offered at public sale to the highest bidder, no land being sold for less than $7.00—or its appraised value—per acre. Lands not disposed of by sale were leased to farmers by the county commissioners for twenty-five years, with rental established at 6 percent of the appraised valuation and paid annually in advance.[27]

School districts were formed as soon as they were needed. In Sherman County, district No. 1 (Loup City) was formed even before the county was created—in 1873. In order to finance the schools, bonds were issued and sold at sizable discounts. School bonds saddled the county with debt within a year after its organization. District organization proceeded rapidly, the high point in numbers coming in 1914, when there were eighty-one school districts in the county.[28] In Boone County the story is similar. By 1881 there were forty-two school districts, thirty-eight school houses valued at $6,045, and 1,422 children taught by forty-six teachers. School indebtedness totaled $14,562.89.[29]

Closely paralleling the settlement of the Plains was the formal chartering of state universities. The University of Kansas was chartered in 1864 and opened in 1866; and the University of Nebraska was chartered in 1869 and opened in 1871. The University of North Dakota was founded in 1883 and admitted its first students the next year. The University of South Dakota was chartered as early as 1862, but its doors were not open to students until 1882. It was then called the University of the Dakotas, and did not receive its present title until 1891.

Probably the greatest boost given to higher education, at least in the agricultural field, was the passage of the Morrill Act in 1862. This act provided that 30,000 acres of public land be granted each state for each of its representatives and senators, the proceeds of the sale or rental of the land to go toward the establishment of an agricultural college. Territories were allowed three years after achieving statehood to accept the offer. Kansas State College was opened in 1863, two years after Kansas became a state; North Dakota Agricultural College was founded in 1890. By 1870 much of the public land in Nebraska, particularly in the eastern section, which was thought the most desirable, was already taken up, and most of the 90,000 acres received by the state were located in Knox, Cedar, Pierce, and Wayne counties. The first sale of agricultural college lands in Nebraska was made in 1881, at the minimum legal price of $7.00 per acre, and by 1914 over 76,000 acres had been deeded to individuals. Nebraska received an average $8.37 per acre for its land, far more than many states realized. The total money-value derived from the act in Nebraska has been estimated at more than $750,000.[30]

While the money realized from the land grants was by no means sufficient to support

---

[27] Board of Educational Lands and Funds of the State of Nebraska, 39th Biennial Reports, 1952, p. 4.

[28] Owens, *op. cit.*, p. 64.

[29] *History of the State of Nebraska* (Chicago: The Western Historical Company, 1882), p. 387.

[30] Agnes Horton, "Nebraska's Agricultural College Land Grant," *Nebraska History*, 30 (March, 1949), 50–76.

the agricultural colleges, it gave an important impetus to their formation. For most of them it was a serious struggle in the beginning. One of the difficult problems was the shortage of personnel trained to teach agriculture. Entrance standards were low because most students were admitted directly from grade school. In time, teachers were trained, standards were raised, and research courses added. The land-grant colleges gradually became firmly established and influential in the life of the people.

Another significant event, in 1862, was the creation by Congress of the U.S. Department of Agriculture. This was established as an independent department, headed by a commissioner. It had several functions: to disseminate knowledge of agricultural improvements, collect and distribute valuable seeds and plants, encourage a spirit of inquiry among farmers, further scientific investigation, and organize an agricultural library. The Department of Agriculture has made notable contributions to the field of scientific agriculture. In 1862 the Chemistry Division was established, and the Entomology Division was created twenty years later. Gathering of crop statistics was begun in 1863; and the Bureau of Animal Industry was established in 1884. Finally, on February 9, 1889, the department was given cabinet status, and the Commissioner of Agriculture became the Secretary of Agriculture.[31]

It did not take the settlers long to discover that farming on the subsistence level, with relatively little need for cash, was impossible on the Plains. Getting started in farming took more than a mere pittance. Wood for buildings, fence wire, well drilling, and fuel all cost money. This was different from the east, where wood for dwellings, fencing, and fuel were available on the farm for the effort of cutting down trees, and where water was just as easily obtainable. More farm machinery was also necessary on the Plains. With the greater chance of crop failures and dry years, provident settlers tried to have enough cash reserves to tide them over. When all these things were taken into consideration, it has been estimated that a minimum of $1,000 was needed by the western homesteader to bring his land into production.[32]

Since many of the settlers arrived with practically no assets, the business of loaning money and mortgaging land flourished. Eastern investors found that western mortgages returned high rates of interest. In fact, the Populist press of the period painted the eastern bankers in the blackest colors. They were veritable Shylocks, lying in wait for each unfortunate settler's pound of flesh in the form of exorbitant interest payments, and, when the poor settler was unable to pay, eager to foreclose his property. But the investor's role was probably overdrawn. According to Bogue, while western mortgages were profitable, they were not devoid of risk.

As a general rule, loan companies preferred not to foreclose and take over the property; they were much more interested in getting their money. Interest rates varied from 12 percent in 1870 to 5 percent in 1900. Local banks loaned little of their own capital on the security of agricultural land; they acted mostly as agents for the eastern companies and used their own funds to make chattel and personal loans. But with the depression of the late 1880's and early 1890's, mortgage companies found themselves

[31] Everett Edwards, "American Agriculture the First 300 Years," *Farmers in the Changing World* (USDA Yearbook of Agriculture, 1941), pp. 247–251.

[32] Allan G. Bogue, *Money at Interest, the Farm Mortgage on the Middle Border* (Ithaca: Cornell University Press, 1955), p. 4.

in a hopeless position: between borrowers who either could not pay or had abandoned their farms, and investors who wanted their money.

LAND USE AFTER SETTLEMENT

During the settlement period before 1900, corn was the chief crop in Kansas and Nebraska, although other crops, mainly wheat, were also raised.[33] The first crop grown was sod corn, which yielded well on the fertile prairie soils and under the favorable weather conditions that prevailed during many of the early years.[34] Corn yields averaged 32 and 31 bushels in Kansas and Nebraska, respectively, in 1870–74; 41 and 38 bushels in 1875–79; and 33 bushels in both states in 1880–84.[35] The average yields were lower after that as land of lower productivity was brought into production. By 1890, Nebraska ranked fourth in corn production; in fact, the production of 278 million bushels in 1896 has not been equaled since. Kansas, with more acres but lower yields, was not far behind.

Kansas and Nebraska became leading corn states for several reasons, including the fact that the incoming settlers came from corn-producing states, like Iowa and Illinois, and found at least superficially similar conditions of soil and climate. The prairie could be broken easily and yields were higher than those for wheat. Corn machinery had been improved.

Wheat was at first thought to be unsuited to uplands. Spring wheat was most common, since competitive varieties of winter wheat had not yet been found. Spring wheat did not yield as well as corn. However, with the introduction of adapted Turkey Red hard red winter wheat and its derivatives, a very rapid shift was made from spring wheat to winter wheat between 1900 and 1909.[36] This shift was abetted by the experimental and educational work of the agricultural colleges.

The third most important crop in the developmental period in these two states was oats. It was used in rotation with corn, and was mostly fed to livestock rather than sold, owing to its bulky nature. Prior to 1900, the varieties grown were not adapted to the climate west of the Missouri, and yields were mediocre.

Smaller acreages of barley and rye were also raised. The tame hays—millet, clover, and timothy—occupied only a minor role in the agricultural economy of these states before 1890. Alfalfa was not included in the agricultural statistics until 1900.

In the eastern part of these states, most of the native grasses had been plowed up. In the western areas the range grasses were overstocked, and the range diminished in productivity during the dry years of the early 1890's.

Coming a little later, the Dakota experience was somewhat different. Although diversified agriculture was the general rule, wheat quickly became the cash crop, pushing rapidly westward to the 100th meridian with the initial settlement.[37] Corn, at first disregarded, was found to be adapted to the southeastern section, and soon

[33] Verne S. Sweedlun, "A History of the Evolution of Agriculture in Nebraska, 1870–1930" (University of Nebraska Ph.D. thesis, 1940).

[34] *Annual Report of the Nebraska State Board of Agriculture* (1871), p. 136.

[35] *Nebraska Agricultural Statistics, Historical Record, 1866–1954*, p. 12.

[36] Sweedlun, *op. cit.*, p. 115.

[37] Herbert S. Schell, "Adjustment Problems in South Dakota," *Agricultural History*, 14 (April, 1940), 69.

became dominant there. The superior milling quality of the hard spring wheat of the Dakotas contributed to its popularity during the settlement period.

## LIVESTOCK

Much of the history of the cattle industry in the Northern Plains has been tinged with romance, and has been told elsewhere at greater length than our space permits. Three phases in the early history of livestock on the Plains can be recognized: (1) the initial exploitation of the open range, which occurred rapidly after the demise of the buffalo and the enclosure of the Indians—both of which were accomplished by the late 1870's; (2) the end of the open range in the early 1890's and replacement of the large cattle companies by numerous smaller ranchers operating largely within fences; and (3) the coincidental development of livestock production by the homesteaders in conjunction with crop operations.

Beef cattle were first raised in the Plains to supply military posts, railroad crews, and Indian agencies with meat. Thus the nutritive qualities of range grasses were soon discovered. Beef herds were first trailed from Texas to railheads like Sedalia, Abilene, and Ogallala, but spilled over into the ranges of the Northern Plains of Wyoming, Nebraska, the Dakotas, and Montana after 1867. The initial supply of range cattle came from the large numbers built up in Texas during the Civil War, but soon the ranges of all the Plains area were contributing supplies of cattle for the booming market that held until 1873. After the depression that began in that year, the range-cattle industry recovered at an increasing rate as the decade came to a close.

The cattle boom of the early 1880's saw the movement of cattle outfits into even the most remote regions of the Plains area. Despite the voluminous reports on cowboy life of the time, it is not yet commonly known that the Plains had been blanketed by a fully developed cattle industry by 1886—and this in only a few years.

This industry, as originally established, was not destined to last. Yet it was not into a vacuum that homesteaders moved; they were more favored by the policies of the time and were in a position to push the rancher out of areas that seemed desirable for settlement. In the meantime, the lessons learned by the ranchers were presumably lost in their successors.

In Nebraska, the cattle population tripled from 1880 to 1884, and exceeded 1.5 million by 1885.[38] At first the cattle were brought there, as well as to Kansas, the Dakotas and other areas, by trail from Texas. They were held for wintering and fattening on the range. Starting in the vicinity of the Platte River, the industry in Nebraska spread to other parts, until the last region, the Sandhills, was appropriated by 1879.

Costs of production were reasonable: the range was free; taxes, wages, and building costs were very low. Favorable costs, favorable weather, and large amounts of outside capital combined to produce so strong a cattle boom in the early 80's that practically no range cattle were slaughtered between 1882 and 1884.[39] The boom was eventually dampened by the exhaustion of the free range; the ranges became overcrowded.

During this time, ranchers did what they could to maintain their position in the

[38] *Nebraska Agricultural Statistics Historical Record, 1866–1954*, p. 78.
[39] Sweedlun, *op. cit.*, p. 154.

face of advancing settlement. They used all available means, such as the new barbed wire, the purchase of large tracts of land on deferred payments, and share grazing. In addition to enclosing their own lands, the ranchers used barbed wire to fence thousands of acres of public lands, a practice frowned upon by the General Land Office in Washington. The ranchers countered by buying railroad sections and fencing them in such a way as to enclose federal land, without actually installing a fence on it. They also obtained land under the Homestead Act by having their cow-hand employees file claims as homesteaders, with title reverting to the boss when final entry was made.

But the pressure of the settlers was relentless, eventually forcing the ranchers to sell out or move farther west. Settlers used the rifle, wire cutters, and the law to prevent illegal occupancy and fencing by the rancher. Their own fences on small homestead tracts also hastened the cattleman's demise as they hampered the movement of cattle from the south and over the free range.

Finally, general economic developments resulted in the collapse of the cattle boom in the 1880's. Depressed price levels in the general economy eventually affected the prices of range cattle. The severe winter of 1886–87 took a heavy toll of cattle in Wyoming, Montana, and the Dakotas, and to a lesser extent in Nebraska. Between 1886 and 1888 the cattle population in Nebraska fell from 2,385,000 to 1,800,000.[40]

With the collapse of the cattle boom, and the pressure of settlers, the open-range era of the large cattle companies quickly came to an end. It was replaced by smaller ranches, completely under fence, as well as by farmer-stockmen in the tilled areas. By 1900 the range-cattle industry had shifted almost entirely to the new basis.

Livestock raising in homestead areas developed rather slowly; settlers tended to raise grain for quick, cash returns. However, during the 1880's farmers began to fatten cattle in areas where corn was an important crop. These cattle were obtained from the western range areas. At first, Texas cattle were used, but they were replaced by Shorthorn and Durham bulls, and later by Hereford bulls to improve the breeding of range cattle. With the growth of cattle feeding, the number of cattle increased. Thus, during the nine-year period ending in 1891, 2,538,793 cattle were received at the Omaha stockyards.[41]

Hog production also increased, in step with corn production, starting in 1870. By 1891 there were over 2.5 million hogs on farms in Nebraska. During this time corn acreage was replacing wheat, and the hog-corn ratio was favorable to hog production. Favorable prices continued until 1885, when a gradual decline set in.

ADJUSTMENTS IN FARMING BEGIN (1888–1900)

*Drought*

Almost as soon as the land of the Eastern Plains was settled, adjustments began to take place under the impact of drought and low farm prices. North Dakota suffered from below-average rainfall in 1888 and 1889, and again in 1894–95. Except for 1892, South Dakota experienced droughts from 1888 to 1895. Similarly in Kansas: in six

[40] Nebraska Agricultural Statistics, *Historical Record, 1866–1954*, p. 78.
[41] *Annual Report of the Nebraska State Board of Agriculture* (1891), p. 365.

of the ten years between 1887 and 1896, rainfall was greatly below average.[42] After eight years of unusually heavy rainfall in Nebraska, through 1886, there followed ten years of drought conditions, except for two seasons.[43] In western Nebraska the amount of harvested crops was small in five of those ten years. In 1894 the average yield of corn in the state was 7 bushels. Hot winds aggravated the effects of low rainfall. Chinch bugs attacked wheat and reduced its yields. The belief that rainfall followed plowing and tree planting was shaken.

The severity of human distress and hardship during these times is illustrated in the remarks of Charles H. Morrill, a prominent Nebraska pioneer.

> In the year of 1893 crops in Nebraska were almost totally destroyed by drouth and hot winds. Then came the panic and financial distress which paralyzed business. In 1894 Nebraska was doomed to have another crop failure. Farmers were obliged to ship in grain and even hay to feed their stock; many sacrificed their livestock by selling at very low prices. Some farmers shot their stock hogs to prevent their starving. Financial conditions grew worse and the entire state was almost in the grip of actual famine. Farmers could not pay interest on their mortgages; nor could land be sold at any price. One eastern loan company offered to sell forty quarter sections at $200 each.[44]

Relief, such as free seed grain, was made available by local and state governments, as well as by the federal government. Collection of taxes was not enforced.[45] Foreclosure proceedings on state lands were postponed until the turn of the century; and in 1890 Congress extended for one year the time required to complete payment on homestead and preemption entries. The same kind of action was taken in 1894.[46] Also extended during the 1890's were the payments on Indian lands, and in 1894 and 1904 Congress made it possible for all "who had lost their original homestead claims through sickness, drouth, or other unavoidable casualty to file again."[47]

Help was sought from professional rainmakers, and there was hope that rain might be induced by the use of gases and explosives. Congress appropriated $10,000 for rain experimentation in South Dakota in 1892. Interest in irrigation was high in many areas and "irrigate or emigrate" became a popular slogan. In response to requests from the Plains states, Congress appropriated funds in 1890 to investigate the proper location for artesian wells and their use in irrigation in the semiarid regions. Progress in developing irrigation from artesian wells was slow, however, and interest diminished as soon as the rains came again.

With the failure, during subsequent droughts, of the crops the settlers had brought with them—corn, oats, barley, rye, and soft wheat—much thought and discussion was given to alternatives. Diversification of crops was advocated.[48] Hard winter wheat became important as a cash crop, particularly in the western areas. Sorghum came to be raised for syrup, fodder, and seed, and the settlers learned that it almost never

---

[42] "Climate of the States," *Climate and Man* (USDA Yearbook of Agriculture, 1941), pp. 1048, 1113.

[43] Nebraska Agricultural Statistics, *Historical Record, 1866–1954*, p. 173.

[44] Olson, *op. cit.*, p. 243.

[45] Herbert S. Schell, "Drought and Agriculture in Eastern South Dakota during the Eighteen-nineties," *Agricultural History*, 5 (1931), 164.

[46] Hargreaves, *op. cit.*, p. 50.

[47] Hargreaves, *op. cit.*, p. 51.

[48] Harold E. Briggs, *Frontiers of the Northwest* (New York: Appleton-Century, 1940), pp. 487–88; H. S. Schell, "Drought and Agriculture in Eastern South Dakota during the Eighteen-nineties," p. 174.

failed.[49] There was much interest in kaffir corn in the Dakotas for a short time. Farmers began to list corn rather than check row it.

Early plowing for wheat in June and July was found to conserve moisture and increase the chances of successful fall seeding. The disc plow replaced the moldboard plow; it left the stubble on top, and enabled the farmer to plow after the ground was too hard and dry for the moldboard plow. Interest in silos developed. Settlers also discussed the merits of cash-crop farming as opposed to crop production for livestock feed. They saw in cooperatives the means of improving the marketing of their products.

Although one would expect cattle ranches to withstand the impact of drought more effectively than crop farms, it is apparent that even they had not learned to adapt to the Plains environment. A comment by a township census enumerator in Kansas in the spring of 1885 is revealing: " Most of the cattle died for want of food and not being acclimated and for want of shelter. Sheep ditto." [50]

The Kinsley *Graphic* reported, on January 25, 1886, that some stock raisers said the heavy losses meant a revision of the industry in western Kansas.[51] The raising of vast herds of low-grade animals would cease and more attention would be given to better breeding and shelter. At that time, few ranches provided feed reserves for their stock.

### Depression

The climatic difficulties of the late 1880's and early 1890's were compounded by a nationwide depression in agriculture that had begun in the previous decade. The wheat price received in Nebraska moved downward, from an average of 66 cents per bushel during the period 1871–75 to 50 cents per bushel in 1891–95. During the same period the price of corn averaged 30 cents or less during each of the five-year periods. This price was much lower, compared with wheat, than would be expected from their relative feeding values; but perhaps corn production forged ahead of livestock feeding and hog raising. Also, the opportunities for exporting corn to other areas were not comparable to those for wheat.

Of course, prices received are meaningless by themselves; one has to consider the cost of goods purchased. Using 1910–14 prices received and general wholesale prices at a base of 100, the "parity indices" for the important commodities at the beginning and at the end of the above period show that the relative purchasing power per unit had risen (Table 3). The drought conditions offset the somewhat more favorable prices,

TABLE 3.  PARITY INDICES FOR MAJOR NEBRASKA COMMODITIES, 1871–75 AND 1891–95 (1910–14 = 100)

|          | 1871–75 | 1891–95 |
|----------|---------|---------|
| Corn     | 42      | 83      |
| Wheat    | 62      | 84      |
| Hogs     | 37      | 71      |
| Cattle   | 61      | 76      |

Source: Verne S. Sweedlun, "A History of the Evolution of Agriculture in Nebraska, 1870–1930" (University of Nebraska unpublished Ph.D. dissertation, 1940).

[49] James C. Malin, "The Adaptation of the Agricultural System to Sub-humid Environment," *Agricultural History*, 10 (1936), 131.

[50] *Ibid.*, p. 123.

[51] *Ibid.*

however, and resulted in reduced farm incomes. The parity indices of the period 1891–95, although higher than before, indicate depressed prices in agriculture as compared with 1910–14. By the end of the period, in 1896 and 1897, corn was selling for 13 and 17 cents per bushel, respectively.

### Farmers Awaken to Politics

The period after the Civil War was one of a gradual awakening of farmers to the possibility of organizing for an attack on their common problems. They were concerned about farm prices, freight rates, and credit and monopolistic practices by the businesses that handled their products. And so there arose a succession of farm groups that were organized with the primary objective of applying political leverage: the Grangers in 1867, the Greenbackers in 1874, and the Farmers Alliances.

The Populist party had its roots in the prairies of the Dakotas, Nebraska, Kansas, and Iowa. Organized in Omaha in 1892, it demanded a safe national currency, free silver, a graduated income tax, postal savings banks, government ownership and control of railroads, and abolition of land monopolies. The party entered a candidate, General James Weaver of Iowa, in the presidential campaign of 1892, and it reached its height in the campaign of 1896—made famous by Bryan's "Cross of Gold" speech. After Bryan's defeat, the party declined to its eventual demise in 1912, which was hastened by the prosperity after the turn of the century. Yet its influence lives on, in the Northern Plains, in the Farmers Union organization and in the Nonpartisan League of North Dakota—as well as in such innovations as the state-owned flour mill and elevator of North Dakota and South Dakota's rural credit system.

### Adjustments in Land Use

The stringent effects of drought, depression, insects, hail, and blizzards combined to cause rapid adjustments in land use during the late 1880's and early 1890's in the Plains. And emigration from the region left some western areas virtually depopulated, except for cattlemen. For example, in 1891, it is said, 1,800 prairie schooners crossed the Missouri, going from Nebraska to Iowa. Most of these people had come from the western part of Nebraska. The decline in the central part of the state was moderate, while in the eastern counties the population increased, since this area had not been as much affected by drought.[52] The census of 1900 showed that from one-third to one-half of the counties in the state had fewer people than they had had in 1890. With the passing of the Kincaid Act in 1904, settlers again moved into the western part of the state, including the Sandhills, but once more they failed to adapt to the conditions they found.

The situation in South Dakota was much the same. Less than 5 percent of the lands of the Sioux reservation that had been opened to settlement had been occupied by 1900.[53] Dry-land farmers abandoned their operations in the western counties and the population there fell substantially between 1890 and 1900. While the adverse conditions had severe effects in the western areas, even more drastic adjustments were taking place farther east.

[52] Sweedlun, *op. cit.*, p. 34.
[53] Hargreaves, *op. cit.*, p. 49.

In an eighteen-county area in South Dakota, between the Missouri and the James rivers and north of a line between Woonsocket and Chamberlain, one out of every six persons there in 1890 had left by 1900.[54] This region is representative of the Northern Plains transition area. The number of farms decreased by 27 percent, as half of the farms increased their acreage. The average change in size was from 400 to 700 acres. There was a moderate increase in wheat acreage, but the number of beef cattle more than doubled, and the number of sheep more than tripled.

These terse facts are significant, and need elaboration. Despite the interest in better methods of wheat raising, the above increase in acreage was proportionately only a fifth of that occurring in the remaining counties to the east and south of this area. The main shift was to stock raising. The number of cattle increased from 179,888 to 433,504 during the ten-year period. The open range was free and unfenced; and attempts were made to modify the Herd Law to permit the cattle to range freely during the winter.

These conditions in central South Dakota were evidence of the hypothesis of John Wesley Powell about a "middle" transition area. Let us hear him as he speaks before the North Dakota legislature in Bismarck, in 1889.

> The state of North Dakota has a curious position geographically in relation to agriculture. . . . In the western portion all dependence on rains will ultimately bring disaster to the people. . . . They will soon learn in the western portion to depend upon irrigation and provide themselves with agencies for the artificial fructifying of the soil with water. In the eastern part they will depend on the rainfall, and in the middle portion they will have a series of years when they will have abundant crops; then for two or three years they will have less rainfall and there will be failure of crops and disaster will come on thousands of people, who will become discouraged and leave. . . . That is the history of all those who live on the border between humid and arid lands. Years will come of abundance and years will come of disaster, and between the two the people will be prosperous and unprosperous, and the thing to do is look the question squarely in the face. . . .[55]

Apparently, the eastern counties had already been developed more in keeping with their natural environment, and adjustments there were less drastic. A dairy industry came into being. Average farm size increased only slightly, and the population of these eastern counties rose during the decade. Their wheat acreage increased as they shifted from corn to wheat.

The decade beginning in the middle 1880's in a sense represents the type of retribution a region like the Plains can exact from those who dare to invade it without adequate knowledge and resources. Communities and individuals learned the hard way. This period, however, was one of adjustment by individuals, not so much by institutions. It was not characterized, to any significant extent, by the social innovations that were to appear in the 1930's. Many of the lessons learned during this rigorous period were forgotten during the heady times to follow.

The disasters of the 1890's were viewed as nonrecurring abnormalities. The first testing period came to a close by 1900, leaving it to the future again to try the settlers with the worst that weather and economics could offer.

[54] Schell, *op. cit.*, p. 179.

[55] Bruce Nelson, *Land of the Dacotahs* (Minneapolis: University of Minnesota Press, 1946), p. 139.

# CHAPTER 4

# New Settlement, the Golden Era, and World War I, 1900–1920

THE NEW CENTURY brought improved economic conditions for Plains farmers. A new era of prosperity and expansion in the general economy was reflected in the upward movement of farm prices, from an index of 69 in 1900 to 105 in 1910—an increase of 52 percent[1] (1909–13 = 100). Gross farm income rose by 55 per cent (in current prices) between 1900 and 1910, a rate of increase quite unusual in the history of U.S. agriculture.[2] Nor was agriculture merely sharing a general boom; its relative position is indicated by an increase of only 25 percent in the index of all wholesale prices during the same time. The period culminated in a series of five years of farm prosperity, 1910 to 1914, which has been termed the "golden age of agriculture." The cost–price relationships of this era became the norm against which farmers have measured their prosperity or lack of it ever since, expressed in the term *parity*. The cost–price relationships of this period were such that farmers experienced unusually favorable income levels.

Climate was also a factor in the improved economic conditions of the Eastern Plains after 1900. In central Nebraska, for example, annual rainfall was less than average only three years during the entire period 1900–20.[3] Similarly, below-average rainfall occurred in North Dakota only four times and in South Dakota and Kansas only six times during those twenty years.[4] Moreover, in most of these years of below-average rainfall the deficiencies were slight.

The first effect of these favorable economic conditions was to increase land prices in the settled areas. Between 1900 and 1910 land prices advanced by 189 percent in Kansas, 232 percent in Nebraska, 377 percent in South Dakota, and 321 percent in North Dakota.[5] This rise was due to the increase in prices of farm products, to the

---

[1] Frederick Strauss and Louis H. Bean, *Gross Farm Income and Indices of Farm Production and Prices in the United States, 1869–1937*, USDA Technical Bulletin 703, 1940, p. 4.

[2] Among the various causes to which these better economic conditions have been attributed, one of the most important was the increase in the supply of gold in the world and the shift of most countries to the gold standard. It was a period of inflation. As is commonly true during such periods, farm prices rose more rapidly than other prices.

[3] *Nebraska Agricultural Statistics Historical Record, 1866–1954*, p. 173.

[4] "Climates of the States," *Climate and Man*, USDA Yearbook of Agriculture, 1941, pp. 876, 971, 1048, 1112.

[5] John D. Hicks, "The Western Middle West, 1900–14," *Agricultural History* (April, 1946), p. 73.

improvements made on farms, and to speculative psychology. Credit was available in large quantities and at low interest rates.

During this period many farmers in the settled areas sold out and went westward to take up free land. There was also a movement of people from settled farming areas to the cities—where industrial activity was expanding, the demand for labor was increasing, and wages were rising. The situation was similar to that prevailing during and immediately following World War II. The decline in farm population in some of the settled areas was a source of concern to both their farm and city residents.[6] Others feared that agricultural production would be unable to keep pace with the demands of the expanding population in the nation as a whole. Both these concerns were the basis for the intensified interest in agricultural education which was shortly to bring into being some new educational methods and institutions.

### THE LAST STAGES OF SETTLEMENT

With better economic conditions after the turn of the century, a new homestead movement occurred in the Northern Plains. The population of North Dakota increased from 319,000 in 1900 to 577,000 in 1910.[7] The increases in population of South Dakota, Nebraska, and Kansas were smaller, but significant (Table 4).

TABLE 4.  POPULATION (IN THOUSANDS) OF THE NORTHERN PLAINS STATES, 1900–20

| States | 1900 | 1910 | 1920 |
|---|---|---|---|
| Kansas. . . . . . . | 1,470 | 1,691 | 1,769 |
| Nebraska . . . . . . | 1,066 | 1,192 | 1,296 |
| North Dakota . . . . | 319 | 577 | 647 |
| South Dakota . . . . | 402 | 584 | 637 |

Source: U.S. Census.

As might be expected, the settlement pattern was becoming more and more selective, depending upon the availability of land, either for homestead or purchase. In North Dakota the population of the western counties more than quadrupled from 1900 to 1910, while the western counties of South Dakota had an increase of 200 percent (Table 5).

TABLE 5.  FARM DEVELOPMENT IN THE WESTERN DAKOTAS, 1900–20

| | North Dakota | | | South Dakota | | |
|---|---|---|---|---|---|---|
| | 1900 | 1910 | 1920 | 1900 | 1910 | 1920 |
| | (Thousands) | | | | | |
| Rural population . . . . . . . . | 49 | 187 | 218 | 43 | 123 | 127 |
| Number of farms . . . . . . . . | 8 | 33 | 34 | 4 | 26 | 19 |
| Land in farms (acres) . . . . . . | 2,446 | 10,738 | 16,838 | 1,253 | 8,102 | 15,239 |
| Improved land (acres) . . . . . . | 782 | 6,308 | 8,908 | 318 | 1,924 | 3,357 |

Source: Hargreaves, *Dry Farming in the Northern Great Plains*, p. 441.

[6] Hicks, *op. cit.*, p. 75.

[7] *Historical Statistics of the United States, Colonial Times to 1957*, U.S. Government Printing Office, 1960, p. 12.

These census data conceal the dramatic details of settlement activity during this period. For example, an estimated 50,000 people entered North Dakota in 1902, settling mostly around Minot and toward the northwest along the Soo Railroad.[8] In 1906 large numbers of farmers were moving into the southwestern part of the state, attracted by the projected extension of the Milwaukee line.

In South Dakota, the settlement west of the Missouri was oriented more to the development of stock raising than to tillage, as is indicated by the small proportion of improved land shown in Table 5. However, intensive settlement activity took place in the northwestern part of the state—with the opening of the Milwaukee line in 1905, in Lyman and Stanley counties with the extension of the Chicago and Northwestern and Milwaukee railroads in 1906, and in Gregory and Tripp counties in the south with the opening of Indian lands in 1904 and 1908. The latter settlement has been called the greatest land lottery in history.[9]

The movement of people into Nebraska was particularly heavy in the central and northern transition areas and in the western part of the state. In Custer County, one of the transition-area counties, for example, the population increased from 2,200 people in 1880 to 21,800 in 1890; after a decline to 20,000 by 1900, it increased again by 33 percent during the next decade to nearly 26,000. The number of farms rose from 3,370 to 4,000 during the same time.[10] Between 1910 and 1920 the county population climbed to an all-time peak of 26,404. Similarly, Sherman County had 6,550 people in 1900 and almost 8,300 in 1910 and 1920. In Kansas, the heaviest immigration took place in the southwestern corner of the state.

By 1909 the boundary of settlement in the Northern Plains could be traced from Minot, North Dakota—at the 101st meridian—southeastward to the Missouri River, along the Missouri through South Dakota as far east as the 100th meridian, and then south to the Nebraska border (see Figure 11, Chapter 3). Nebraska had been settled, except for the southern panhandle, as had Kansas, except for its southwestern corner.

The in-movement of people was slowed considerably in the ten years between 1910 and 1920. In fact some counties, particularly in northern and eastern Kansas and southeastern Nebraska, had experienced population declines during the first decade of the century. These areas were similarly affected in the second decade, as were northern North Dakota and western and central South Dakota.[11] Thus, dry weather in South Dakota in 1910–11 caused many painful readjustments. Harding County, in the northwestern corner, was practically abandoned by the homesteaders. Some immigration continued, however, in the western Dakotas.

The role of the railroads in promoting settlement in the Northern Plains states after 1900 has not been fully recognized. Motivated by their desire to increase traffic, they engaged not only in educational programs for furthering agriculture but gave special rates to homesteaders and ran special settlers' trains. The Burlington, Great Northern, and Northern Pacific lines ran special agricultural display cars to eastern areas to

---

[8] M. W. M. Hargreaves, *Dry Farming in the Northern Great Plains, 1900–1925* (Cambridge: Harvard University Press, 1957), p. 444.

[9] Herbert S. Schell, "Adjustment Problems in South Dakota," *Agricultural History*, 14 (April, 1940), 66.

[10] *U.S. Census of Population, 1930*, 15th Census of the United States, p. 665; and *Eleventh Census, 1890*, p. 30.

[11] *U.S. Census of Population, 1930*, pp. 401, 665, 808, 1002.

arouse interest.[12] President Hill, of the Great Northern Railroad, believed that the Plains could support settlers on 160- or 320-acre farms; and he had a vision of "little green fields and little white houses and big red barns."[13]

### THE EXPANSION OF CULTIVATION

It has been commonly assumed that the expansion of cultivation in the Northern Plains states after the turn of the century was directly associated with and attributable to World War I. The analysis has repeatedly suggested that—with the wartime demand for farm products and the increases in prices, especially of cereals—new lands were plowed and farm production rose. The primary statistical basis for this analysis was a 1923 report of the Bureau of Agricultural Economics, which drew primarily on comparisons of census data for 1909 and 1919 for its conclusions.[14] Jorgenson finds, upon examination of annual data for the Northern Plains states, that an important part of the expansion actually took place between 1909 and 1914, before the start of the war. He concludes that the World War I expansion was actually an accelerated continuation of the one that developed during the post-1900 prosperity. Let us examine the data in more detail.

In Nebraska the total acreage in farms increased from 30 million in 1900 to nearly 39 million in 1910, while the number of farms rose from 121,500 to 129,700.[15] Land devoted to harvested crops increased by 1,430,000 acres during this period—a slower rate of expansion than previously. However, important shifts were taking place in land use. While corn acreage remained quite stable during the first two decades after 1900—at somewhat more than 7 million acres—the acreage of wheat harvested varied from 2.5 million to 3 million acres during the first decade, but it increased to 3.7 million acres in 1914 and to 4.4 million in 1919.

The data for the Northern Plains for the second decade, when divided into five-year segments, give further insight into this phenomenon (Table 6).

TABLE 6.  INCREASE OF CULTIVATED CROPLAND IN THE
NORTHERN PLAINS STATES, 1909–19

| State | 1909–14 | 1915–19 |
|---|---|---|
| | (Acres Increase) | |
| North Dakota . . . . . . | 2,764,000 | 2,653,000 |
| South Dakota . . . . . . | 894,000 | 1,423,000 |
| Nebraska . . . . . . . . | 1,036,000 | 2,867,000 |
| Kansas . . . . . . . . . | 689,000 | 3,077,000 |
| Total . . . . . . . . | 5,383,000 | 10,020,000 |

Source: Lloyd P. Jorgenson, "Agricultural Expansion into the Semi-arid Lands of the West North-central States during the First World War," *Agricultural History*, 23 (January, 1949), 33–40.

[12] Hargreaves, *op. cit.*, p. 231.

[13] C. F. Kraenzel, *The Great Plains in Transition*, p. 127. Copyright 1955 by the University of Oklahoma Press.

[14] Lloyd P. Jorgenson, "Agricultural Expansion into the Semi-arid Lands of the West North-central States during the First World War," *Agricultural History*, 23 (January, 1949), 30.

[15] *Statistical Abstract of the United States, 1924*, U.S. Government Printing Office, 1925, p. 566.

Several factors underlay this prewar expansion. In the first decade, settlement was continuing in what was later to become the wheat area. Turkey Red winter wheat was introduced in Nebraska and Kansas and substituted for spring wheat because of its superior yield and quality. Occupying only 29 percent of the harvested acreage in Nebraska in 1900, winter wheat comprised 86 percent of the harvested acreage by 1905. Also, the purchasing power of wheat (ratio of price received to prices paid) was relatively high, exceeding 100 in eight of the years from 1900 to 1914 (1910–14 = 100).[16] The parity index for corn was considerably lower during most of the period.

The relative prices for crops continued favorable after 1909, and general economic conditions were buoyant and optimistic. The development of cropland in the western areas was thought to be consistent with the general expansion of the country's economy, and "back to the land" was a popular theme of the times. The dry-farming movement emphasized the farm practices considered sufficient to cope with the climatic conditions of these areas, including fallowing, fall plowing in the spring wheat areas, subsoil packing, dust mulching, clean tillage, and drought-resistant crops. Many of these practices had been used before, but now were dramatized as the means by which crop farming would endure in even the semiarid areas. One of the best known protagonists of the movement was Hardy Webster Campbell, who published several editions of his *Soil Culture Manual*.[17]

Despite the somewhat muted reservations of some workers in state experiment stations and in the U.S. Department of Agriculture,[18] promotional agencies—such as the railroads, land dealers, bankers, merchants, the grain industry, and even state immigration bureaus and other state agencies—were infected with the optimism of the dry-farming propaganda and its oversimplification of the farming problems of the area. Land development proceeded with incomplete knowledge of climatic variation and in ignorance of the soils and their capabilities. Even modifications in the dry-farming doctrine—such as the emphasis on crop rotation and diversification that was embodied in the Better Farming Program—were actually imports from more humid regions rather than devices indigenous to these areas.

The coming of World War I reinforced and enhanced the economic incentives for the expansion of cultivation in the four states. The expansion took place both east and west of the 100th meridian, as is shown in Table 7.

It was during this period that wheat farming came into its own on a specialized basis. In Nebraska, wheat acreage in the southwest region more than doubled between 1915 and 1920; and this area became permanently committed to specialized wheat farming, as did the northwestern High Plains area. This specialization was encouraged by the introduction of large-scale machinery, more adequate transportation, and favorable prices. On the other hand, the potentialities of the Sandhills as a ranching region became clearer, and most of the Kinkaiders sold out to ranchers or became cattlemen themselves. Wheat production also increased in other parts of the state as this crop was substituted for corn and hogs because of the favorable price relations.

[16] V. S. Sweedlun, "A History of the Evolution of Agriculture in Nebraska, 1870–1930" (University of Nebraska, Ph.D. thesis, 1940) table 11, p. 25.

[17] Hargreaves, *op. cit.*, pp. 85, 87.

[18] For example, see E. C. Chilcott, "Some Misconceptions Concerning Dry Farming," *Yearbook of the U.S. Department of Agriculture*, 1911, p. 256.

TABLE 7.  ACREAGE INCREASES IN FIELD CROPS IN THE
NORTHERN PLAINS STATES, 1915–19

| State | East of 100th Meridian | West of 100th Meridian |
|---|---|---|
| North Dakota. . . . . . | 933,000 | 1,721,000 |
| South Dakota . . . . . . | 515,000 | 929,000 |
| Nebraska . . . . . . . . | 1,760,000 | 1,100,000 |
| Kansas . . . . . . . . . | 1,994,000 | 1,080,000 |
| Total  . . . . . . . | 5,202,000 | 4,830,000 |

Source: L. P. Jorgenson, "Agricultural Expansion . . . ," pp. 30–40.

At the same time, the steady increase in alfalfa acreage furnished the basis for expanded livestock production.

Specialized wheat production also developed in western Kansas, western South Dakota, and western North Dakota during this time. All told, more than half of the increased winter wheat production in the United States from 1914 to 1919 occurred in the Great Plains.

In view of more detailed attention to the Nebraska area in later sections, it is significant to note that from 1913 to 1919 the acreage of field crops increased there by 15 percent. The story in central South Dakota is similar; grassland was plowed and put into the cash crops of wheat and corn.[19]

As the second decade came to a close, portents of events to come clouded the aura of optimism which had accompanied the expansion of cultivation. Drought in 1917 drove crop production down to 65 percent of average in North Dakota, and to one-third to one-half of normal in western South Dakota. The severe winter of 1916–17 killed about 75 percent of the wheat crop in Nebraska, and this was followed by another poor year in 1918. The year 1919 was the worst on record in western North Dakota, while both 1919 and 1920 showed curtailed crop yields in western South Dakota. It is true that low production was somewhat offset by favorable prices, so the vagaries in weather were not taken as seriously as they were to be during later times.

INFLATED LAND PRICES AND INCREASED USE OF CREDIT

The increase in land values between 1900 and 1920 has been labeled unfortunate, as though somehow it need not and should not have occurred. As we shall see, it was not the rise in land values per se that had dire consequences but some of the phenomena associated with it—as well as the rapid shifts in the relation between farm incomes and farm costs at the end of the period, in the face of fixed commitments farmers had made.

After the initial settlement under homestead laws, the land market developed rapidly in the Northern Plains; many homesteaders took up land for speculative purposes, and then sold it when values had risen. Others borrowed money under mortgage, and abandoned their claims when they found they could not succeed financially. A survey indicated that about half of the entries under the Enlarged

[19] Schell, *op. cit.*, p. 70.

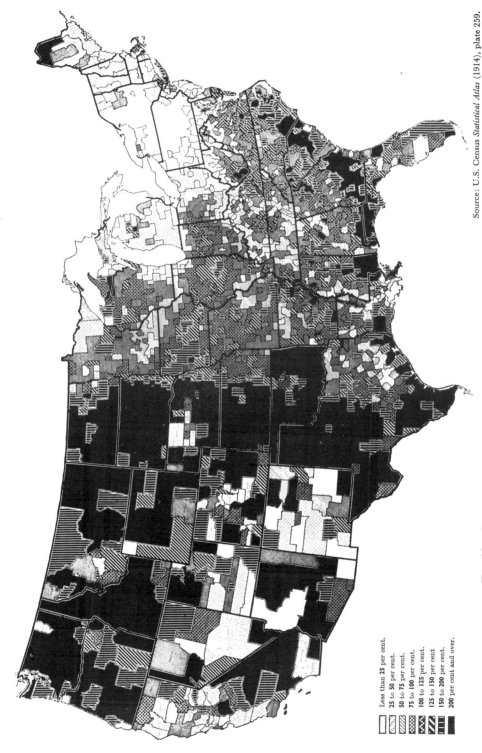

Less than **25** per cent.
**25** to **50** per cent.
**50** to **75** per cent.
**75** to **100** per cent.
**100** to **125** per cent.
**125** to **150** per cent.
**150** to **200** per cent
**200** per cent and over.

Fig. 12.   Percent of Increase in Average Farm Value per Acre, 1900–10

Source: U.S. Census *Statistical Atlas* (1914), plate 259.

Homestead and Stock-Raising Homestead Acts were relinquished or canceled.[20] The sale of relinquishments of claims on government land became a common feature of the land market, despite efforts to prevent it. More important was the emergence of the states and the railroads as sellers of the land that had been ceded to them by the federal government. The sale of land on a rising market was often a source of enormous profits to those who had acquired title to it during the settlement period.

The inflation in land prices after 1900 was spectacular. From 1900 to 1910 the increases in per acre value of farm real estate were lowest in the eastern parts of the Northern Plains states—amounting to less than 100 per cent. In central North Dakota, eastern South Dakota, and central Nebraska and Kansas the increases were slightly more than 100 percent. In some areas of southwestern North Dakota, central South Dakota, southwestern Nebraska, and western Kansas the increases ranged from 300 to 500 percent. (See Figure 12.) Further increases of from 100 to 200 percent occurred in central Nebraska and eastern South Dakota between 1910 and 1920.

A few examples will illustrate the increases. In the Diller community in southeastern Nebraska, land sold for $5.00 to $6.00 per acre in 1880, $25.00 per acre in 1890, $40.00 in 1900, $100 in 1910, and $150 to $175 in 1920.[21] The average value per acre of farm land in Nebraska was $19.00 in 1900, $47.00 in 1910, and $88.00 in 1920.[22] In Kingsbury County, South Dakota, land rose from $12.00 per acre in 1900 to four times that amount in 1910, and to $124 per acre in 1919.[23]

Actually, the increase in land values during the World War I period can be considered moderate; the real boom developed at the end of the war. In seven southeastern Nebraska counties, land sold by warranty deed brought $106 per acre in 1915, $106 in 1916, $109 in 1917, $128 in 1918, $152 in 1919, and $180 in 1920.[24] These increases in land values are not mysterious. They partly reflect the price-cost relations of the period—the widening margins between farm prices and farm costs, with profits increasing more than proportionately with prices received—and they stemmed from improvements farmers had made in land and buildings. They also reflected the basic optimism associated with the later stages of settlement, which originated from both the favorable economic conditions and the agrarianism characteristic of the times.

These increases were pleasant for the persons who had the money to invest in land for interest, which amounted to 5 to 10 percent of the value. The increases became self-generating as farmers found they could now pay off old mortgages easily, then invest free cash in more land, and as speculators shifted funds from stocks and bonds to land. All these factors, both on the supply side and the demand side, tended to inflate land values. The demand for good land was up and supply was down.

The shadow that gradually deepened over the land market was mortgage credit. Farm mortgage debt was increasing, and the pressure to repay loans was relaxed.

---

[20] Hargreaves, *op. cit.*, p. 381.

[21] Robert Diller, *Farm Ownership, Tenancy, and Land Use in a Nebraska Community* (Chicago: University of Chicago Press, 1941), p. 30.

[22] *Nebraska Agricultural Statistics, Historical Record, 1866–1954*, p. 5.

[23] W. F. Kumlien, "Kingsbury County through Sixty-seven Years," *Land Policy Review*, 4:14–20 (August, 1941), 15.

[24] J. C. Olson, *History of Nebraska*, p. 281.

There was a tendency to increase indebtedness and to use current income and the proceeds of new loans to improve farm buildings, herds, and equipment.

The upward trend was moderate at first. Farm mortgage debt in the United States rose from somewhat over $2 billion in 1900, to $3 billion in 1910, and $5 billion in 1915. Meanwhile, the value of land and buildings rose from about $16 billion in 1900 to $35 billion in 1910.[25] The asset position of farmers improved relative to their mortgage debt. Between 1915 and 1920, however, farmers' mortgage debt doubled to nearly $10 billion, and the value of land and buildings increased to $66 billion. Between 1910 and 1920, the ratio of farm debts to farm assets increased from 10.5 percent to 14.2 percent. In the Northern Plains states the increase was from 10.6 percent to 16.1 percent, being greatest in South Dakota and Nebraska. (See Table 8.)

TABLE 8.   FARM MORTGAGE DEBT IN THE PRAIRIE STATES, 1910 AND 1923

| State | 1910 | 1923 | Increase 1910–23 |
|-------|------|------|------------------|
|  | (Thousands of Dollars) | | % |
| North Dakota . . . . . | 97,830 | 312,870 | 220 |
| South Dakota . . . . . | 84,943 | 451,281 | 431 |
| Nebraska . . . . . . . | 148,366 | 691,732 | 366 |
| Kansas . . . . . . . . | 163,359 | 527,397 | 223 |
| United States . . . . . | 3,207,863 | 10,785,621 | 236 |

Based on data on pp. 219 and 220 in Donald C. Horton, Harald C. Larson, and Norman U. Wall, *Farm Mortgage Credit Facilities in the United States*, USDA Miscellaneous Publication No. 478, U.S. Government Printing Office, 1942.

We must recognize that had farm assets values not increased so much, the debt–asset ratio would be greater. Most of the increase in farm assets was attributable to price increases. With constant prices for farm assets, the ratio would have been 2.5 times larger in 1920 than in 1910 for the entire United States. It might be argued that the debts were also in inflated dollars. However, the dollar commitments still remained, and the incomes out of which the loans would be paid were to fall drastically a short time later.

Local data are even more revealing. In Nebraska, state and national banks increased their loans and discounts by 108 percent from 1915 to 1920.[26] In Custer County a farm sold for $108 per acre in 1918, being mortgaged to a life insurance company at the same time for $62.50 per acre. In 1919 the farm was sold for $110 per acre, with the purchaser assuming the mortgage. In 1920 it was sold again, for $170.50 per acre, still carrying the mortgage of $62.50 per acre. In addition, the purchaser gave the seller a second mortgage for $37.50 per acre. These mortgages were on a five-year basis, and were renewed as they expired. In 1929 the farm was sold again, the owner receiving one dollar for his equity; the two mortgages, still totaling $100 per acre, were assumed by the purchaser.[27]

[25] Alvin S. Tostlebee, *Capital in Agriculture: Its Formation and Financing since 1870* (Princeton: Princeton University Press, 1957), p. 54.

[26] Sweedlun, *op. cit.*, p. 282.

[27] W. M. Smith, "The Effects of World War I and the New Era on Custer County, Nebraska," (University of Nebraska, unpublished M.A. thesis, 1951), p. 66.

A growing uneasiness about farm credit was evident during this time. Farmers objected both to the high rates of interest and to the short terms of loans. Loans from banks and loan companies on real estate were for terms of five or three years, or even only one. The need for frequent renewal introduced an element of considerable risk for the borrower; and, the process of renewal represented an additional expense. Interest rates, which would be expected to be high because of risk, were commonly 12 percent on long-term loans in northwestern North Dakota.[28] Various closing costs plus advance deductions of interest from the face amounts of the loans brought the actual rates as high as 30 percent in Williams County, North Dakota, in 1908. In 1917, South Dakota set up a state rural credit agency; and North Dakota organized a state bank to lend money on farmland at rates of interest of from 6 to 7 percent.

After years of discussion of farm credit in Congress, action came also at the national level in 1916 with the passage of the Federal Farm Loan Act. Twelve federal land banks were established in 1917, under the control of a Federal Farm Loan Board. The funds used by these banks were obtained primarily by the sale of bonds. To borrow from the banks, farmers had to become members of local farm-loan associations.

Of most interest are the provisions of the land bank loans. They could run from five to forty years, and could be for amounts up to $10,000, with repayment under an amortization plan. This meant that payments included both interest and principal, combined so that the principal would be paid off at the end of the term of the loan. These practices represented an important break with the past in the mortgage loan field.

The volume of land bank loans was small until the mid-twenties. However, this new institution was the first of a series of measures to be taken by the federal government to alleviate farm finance problems.

## LAND POLICY DEVELOPMENTS

The first twenty years of the century saw a continuation of the arguments about what was desirable land policy. On one side were those, such as James J. Hill, who argued for the repeal of all homestead legislation (except the 1862 act) so that settlement of the remaining western public lands in small homestead tracts might be encouraged.[29] Those who were determined to keep this land out of the hands of large ranchers naturally supported him. On the other side were those who felt that the land would not support intensive cultivation and that it should be settled in mixed farming-grazing units, or in ranch units. They argued for a pause in settlement to allow time for classification of the land as to its ability to support homesteaders. The lack of sympathy for this view is illustrated in the words of Representative Taylor of Colorado:

> Clearly, agricultural land needs no classification. Let the homesteaders go on it, . . . and add billions of dollars of wealth to the West without waiting for some theoretical classification.[30]

[28] Hargreaves, *op. cit.*, pp. 521–22.

[29] Hargreaves, *op. cit.*, p. 338.

[30] Hargreaves, *op. cit.*, p. 332.

Apart from the Stock-raising Homestead Act of 1916, which authorized the designation of land as fit for grazing, no further classification of land was tried until the thirties.

President Roosevelt in 1903 appointed a Public Lands Commission to report on the condition, operation, and effect of land laws then in force. In a preliminary report early the next year, the commission stated that the land laws did not fit the condition of the remaining public land.

The next important event was the passage of the Kinkaid Act in 1904. This modification of the Homestead Act applied only to Nebraska and was intended to dispose of the lands of western Nebraska, hitherto rejected by preemptors and homesteaders. It permitted the acquisition of 640 acres of land and was directed particularly at the sandy lands of western Nebraska. Its author, Moses P. Kinkaid, who had originally written the bill to provide for 1,280-acre homesteads (changed to 640 acres by the House Committee on Public Lands, to which the bill had been referred), pointed out that for more than twenty-eight years after the final survey the land had been refused by settlers.[31] It was believed by the sponsoring committee that the act would encourage settlement by bona fide homesteaders and would prevent the passing of the lands into large holdings operated by ranchers. Even so, there was much fear in Congress that the bill was intended to assist the large cattle interests to obtain public domain.

Under the act, five years of residence on the homestead were required for title; and the homesteader also had to prove he had made improvements on his claim equivalent to $1.25 per acre. Cultivation was not required.

The Kinkaid Act resulted in a large increase in the population of the affected area. The General Land Office has no definite record of Kinkaid patents before 1910, although apparently about 1,600 patents were issued for 800,000 acres of land in the Kinkaid area. Between November, 1910, and July, 1917, a total of 18,919 patents was issued for 8,933,527 acres.

Large as was the change in policy represented by the Kinkaid Act, time has shown that even Mr. Kinkaid's original advocacy of 1,280 acres was not extreme; indeed, he did not go far enough. It would have been difficult to make a living on 1,280 acres in the Sandhills, where 15 to 20 acres are required for each cow. Pressed for funds as they were, many "Kinkaiders" plowed the sands and attempted to raise crops. This resulted in extensive blowing under even the best conditions. Many of them settled during the dry years of 1910–14 and saw their efforts result in failure. A large number left, either abandoning their farms or selling out at low prices to the ranchers. Thus in Holt County there were 377 farms in 1913, but only 144 in 1914.[32] Rusty machinery and weedy "go-back" fields still can be seen in the Sandhills as mementos of this period. The area rapidly changed from small-scale farming to large-scale ranching after 1920. In the high tablelands, however, the Kinkaiders' history was more successful; here the eventual shift was to extensive wheat farming.

The Enlarged Homestead Act of 1909 extended the larger acreage principle to other states, but with a limit of 320 acres. The law did not apply to the Northern Plains

[31] Verna Lee Tubbs, "The Settlement and Development of the Northeast Sandhills" (University of Nebraska, unpublished M.A. thesis, 1957), p. 120.

[32] Sweedlun, *op. cit.*, p. 192.

states, and the bill was not without opposition. In the words of Congressman Howland of Ohio:

> If the trouble is with the land, a greater quantity of that kind of land will not help the situation. If the trouble is with the homesteader, the amount of land he enters cuts very little figure.[33]

Again, many viewed this legislation as a means of assisting cattlemen to obtain more land. However, opposition to it gradually died down in the western states, and by 1915 North and South Dakota—as well as Idaho—had been included under the legislation. These states changed their position to one of support for the bill after realizing they could not attract more settlers without it.

A revised homestead law in 1912 reduced the residence requirement from five to three years, and authorized five months a year continuous leave of absence from claims. Webb says that this act

> ... seemed to grow out of the realization that on the remaining land the average family could not hold out for five years. The point of starvation was reached short of that, and consequently it would be humane to shorten the required time of residence to three years. The homesteader was furthermore permitted to absent himself five months out of each year, presumably with a view to making something to live on while enjoying his free homestead.[34]

Apparently the need felt by Congress to compete with more liberal Canadian land policies opened the way for the passage of the Stock-raising Homestead Act of 1916. Many settlers had been attracted to Canada, and the western states were aware of this loss of potential residents. Under this act, homesteading could take place on 640 acres of land designated as nonirrigable, chiefly for stock raising or for the raising of forage crops. Improvements amounting to $1.25 per acre could serve in place of cultivation. This was the first land legislation which directly recognized stock raising as a legitimate homesteading activity. The act aroused much discussion about the efficiencies of land classification, but it included no classification provision. Representative Martin of South Dakota states that "the area here, 640 acres, has been fixed as a result of experience."[35] Taylor of Colorado argued that

> Lands all over the west that were looked upon as utterly worthless ten, or even only five, years ago are today good homes .... No one now has the knowledge or the foresight to classify that land. The time may some time come when homesteading will practically cease, and there will undoubtedly ultimately be some large bodies of land that cannot be used for homes. But that time has not yet come. In fact it is a long way off.[36]

The new homestead policies were highly successful in moving public land into private hands. In North Dakota nearly 16 million acres were disposed of between 1900 and 1920 via the homestead mechanism. In South Dakota nearly 10 million acres were similarly settled.

As a collection of policies the Homestead legislation was an extremely important part of the setting in which the Northern Plains developed during the golden era. It

[33] Quoted in Hargreaves, *op. cit.*, p. 348.
[34] W. Webb, *The Great Plains* (1931), p. 423, reprinted through the courtesy of Blaisdell Publishing Co., a Division of Ginn & Company.
[35] Hargreaves, *op. cit.*, p. 362.
[36] Hargreaves, *op. cit.*, pp. 378–79.

is easy to see, from the vantage point of the present, how things might have been done differently. It is more difficult to appreciate the several factors that combined to cause settlement to take the course it took. At that time the land of the west was considered valueless unless put under cultivation; it seemed the national policy that these lands should be peopled and communities formed. The economic institutions that first came into being—railroads, states, counties—felt their continued existence and progress depended on bringing in more settlers. The American people as a whole kept shouting for more land, and the common citizen took comfort in the existence of a new area to which he could migrate if he wished to do so.

On the other hand, some things could have been improved. More knowledge was available even at that time about these lands than was utilized in forming national policy. People like Thomas and Powell had identified, with unusual sagacity, the problems created by overpopulating the land of the west. Had settlement been more deliberate and planned, and had it been based on more adequate knowledge of soil and climate, untold human miseries—not only of the nineties but also of the thirties— might have been largely avoided. And—ironically—this might better have achieved the ideal underlying the homestead legislation: the diffusion of wealth and the creation of family farms.

### Agricultural Education and Research

On May 8, 1914, the Smith-Lever Agricultural Extension Act was passed; this began the third phase of the work of the agricultural colleges. The act provided federal funds for each state, to be matched by state funds. Fifteen county agents were active in North Dakota, three in South Dakota, five in Nebraska, and ten in Kansas by the end of 1914.[37] The state extension services and the associated county extension programs became concerned with disease control, improved crop varieties, and other technical problems. However, until the entry of the United States into the war, the expansion of the program was slow because of the lack of local financial support. With the entry of the country into the war, county agents were also involved in other activities directly related to increasing food production. Emergency federal funds then financed the expansion of the system.

On February 23, 1917, Congress passed the Smith-Hughes Act, which provided for federal aid to schools offering vocational training in agriculture and home economics. This act created the second federal program, dedicated to the direct assistance of farm people via the training route.

These two programs were the first of a series which were to result not only in improving farming methods, but in reducing the isolation of farmers, making farming more attractive, and in some measure increasing farmers' mobility.

The agricultural experiment stations, created under the Hatch Act of 1887, also came into their own during this era. They were now attracting better-trained men, and they began to show results on such problems as hog cholera, tuberculosis in animals, brucellosis, and conservation of fertility elements in animal manures. A flow of scientific information was set in motion between the stations and the farmers. Great interest was shown in special varieties of domestic crops better adapted to the prairies'

---

[37] Hargreaves, *op. cit.*, p. 326.

subhumid areas; examples are the introduction of Turkestan alfalfa by Professor Hansen of the South Dakota Agricultural College and of durum wheat by Carleston of the U.S. Department of Agriculture.

The various activities of the U.S. Department of Agriculture became coordinated when the Bureau of Plant Industry was formed in 1901. Several dry-land agricultural experiment stations were established by the USDA and the states. E. C. Chilcott was appointed head of the Office of Dry Land Agriculture of the USDA in 1905. In 1910 he published his studies on cultivation methods and crop rotation for the Plains.

Experiment station workers may have given little firsthand assistance to dry-land settlers during this period. At least one analyst believes their influence was generally passive, or negative—especially when contrasted with the promotionalism that characterized the dry-farming movement led by such men as Campbell.[38] They lacked much basic knowledge, and were not equipped to suggest positive alternatives. In addition to their efforts in discovering and introducing new varieties, however, the workers of this period also laid the basis for practices that were eventually to become important: shallow tillage, stubble mulch, summer fallow, strip cropping, and other moisture conservation measures.

Mechanization

The golden era was a period of spectacular technological development in farming. In part this was abetted on the Plains by the pressure toward larger farm units; and the ability to buy new, more expensive equipment came with the higher incomes to farmers during the period. Gang plows replaced the sulky plow; headers, as well as wider grain drills and binders, were adopted. To pull these implements, hitches for larger teams of horses were devised.[39] Large threshing machines, powered by steam engines, were operated on a custom basis. Two row cultivators and listers replaced one row machines. Corn binders, shellers, and shredders came into common use. Hay loaders replaced pitchforks. Silage cutters were improved. Sod was broken by large breaker bottoms, powered by steam or gas tractors. Disc-style equipment for stubble plowing, harrowing, and seeding became common. Headers replaced binders in wheat harvesting on level land. Some combines began to be used late in the period.

The most radical innovation of the time was the farm tractor. The heavy steam and gasoline tractors of the late 1890's had been used mostly for threshing. However, by 1904 the Hart-Parr tractor had been adapted for plowing, and gas tractors were produced at increasing rates after 1910. In Nebraska there were 4,746 tractors by 1918, and 8,888 by 1920.[40] As these data suggest, however, tractors were mostly supplementary to horse power—except for a few very large-scale operations—until after 1920.

We can appreciate the impact of technological advance in the Northern Plains by looking at the aggregate data on machinery. From 1900 to 1920 the value of implements and machinery increased from $89 million to $302 million, (1910–14 prices) an increase of 240 percent. This compares with an increase of 135 percent for

[38] For a detailed and interesting discussion of this period, see Hargreaves, *op. cit.*, ch. VIII.

[39] M. L. Wilson, *Big Teams in Montana*, Montana State College Extension Publication No. 70, 1925, p. 68.

[40] Sweedlun, *op. cit.*, p. 396.

the United States as a whole.[41] Whereas machinery in the Northern Plains represented only 4 percent of non-land assets in 1900, it comprised 13 percent by 1920.

The process of mechanization was self-perpetuating. The need for larger farm units provided an incentive for farmers to invest in machinery by which they could cover more land; at the same time, the period of relative prosperity gave them the means for obtaining more machinery. Then the availability of machinery undergirded the pressure for more land for farm enlargement, as well as the pressure to plow up grassland. From 1910 to 1920, the acres per farm increased from 270 to 359 in the Northern Plains. Capital per worker in farming increased from $7,900 to $11,700, in 1910–14 dollars.[42] The growing use of machinery is reflected in the increase in implement and machinery investment per worker from $2,600 to $3,700 during the same time, again in constant dollars. By 1910 the value of machinery and implements per worker equaled that of horses and mules, and from that time on it surpassed it.

Another feature of mechanization that had far-reaching effects was the automobile. It reduced the isolation of the Plains farmer, in effect bringing shopping centers and marketing facilities closer to his farm. In time, it would weaken the social structure of neighborhoods and rural institutions, such as country stores, churches, and schools. The rapidity with which the automobile came into use is illustrated by data from Custer County.[43] In 1914 there were 651 cars registered in this county; by 1918 the number had increased to over 4,000, which represented one car for every six people in the county.

The coming of the automobile created a demand for better roads that has never since been satisfied. The first legislation in Nebraska in answer to "good roads" agitation was the State Aid Bridge Act of 1911. Under this legislation the state contributed 10 percent of the cost of roads and bridges in the counties; in addition, it paid half the cost of constructing bridges over 175 feet long. By 1914 the state had 1,204 miles of improved road, mostly sand-clay surfaced. In 1917 the legislature provided for the acceptance of federal aid, made available under the Federal Aid Road Act of 1916; but apparently construction under this new program did not begin in Custer County until 1920.

## RURAL COMMUNITIES AND INSTITUTIONS

From the standpoint of institutional development, this region was still young when World War I came. It had been only thirty years since the conversion of the Northern Plains from a frontier to a settled agricultural area. With the coming of the railroad, "communities" had begun to take shape. As families were distributed widely on their homesteads, rural villages began to dot the landscape. They had provided the basic supplies to a frontier population which depended upon horse transportation.

Rural commerce was generally small-scale and relatively unspecialized. "Business centers" grew up haphazardly, around trading posts, the railway depot, the elevator, and the post office. Local roads tended to follow the lines of the rectangular survey to provide access between the farm and the village. In the early 1900's, strategic

[41] Tostlebee, *op. cit.*, pp. 66, 68.

[42] Tostlebee, *op. cit.*, p. 88.

[43] Maurice C. Latta, "The Economic Development of Custer County through World War I, and the New Era: 1914–29," *Nebraska History*, 33 (1952), 139–53, plate II.

location resulted in rapid commercial growth of some of these places into central shopping and marketing points. The coming of the automobile greatly accelerated this differential growth. Some of the small villages began to fade away as inter-community competition increased. While the total employed labor force in Nebraska, for example, increased only 3.6 percent during the first decade of the century, significant shifts from farm to city reflected the emergence of a new pattern of differentiation in the economy.

Local government had also been conditioned by the frontier. While most villages and towns were incorporated places, with local government functions, many were never incorporated. County government had extended to all of Nebraska in the 1880's and the county seats had all been established by 1910. Good, economic county governments had become well entrenched by the end of World War I. Road development (grading) increased with the growth in automobile transportation, and county services were gradually improved.

The total population of Nebraska increased 9 percent between 1910 and 1920, and the trend to urbanization was accelerated. Urban places (population over 2,500) experienced a growth of 30 percent while farm population *declined* 7.5 percent during the decade. The rural town and village population rose about 13 percent. Though some of the smaller places lost population, it was a decade of growth for many strategic rural centers. County seat towns became increasingly significant as local government responded to an era of change.

Public education was affected by the emerging pattern of population shifts. School enrollment in Nebraska increased about 9 percent from 1910 to 1920, apparently owing to longer continuation in school and some increase in the 5–19 age group. Most county populations increased moderately during the decade, largely as a result of the growth of towns and cities. Exceptions were a few counties in the eastern half of the state, where a growing town in an adjoining county tended to dominate the area. The number of farms declined in many rural counties during the early 1900's, especially in the southwest and south-central parts of the state. This sometimes resulted in rural school enrollment losses. With the gain in the rural nonfarm population from 1910 to 1920, many centralized elementary schools increased their enrollments because of extension of districts by consolidation.

# CHAPTER 5

# The Agricultural Wringer
# 1920–1940

THE PERIOD we now consider was highly unstable from the economic standpoint, owing to national factors. Had World War I ended in 1917, the agricultural story of the following five years might have had quite a different plot. As it was, the inflation in the prices of farm products was both rapid and great.

The index of prices received for farm products rose until it was more than twice as high in 1919 as it had been three years before. The rise in grain prices was even more spectacular: in 1919 the price of wheat was 2.5 times its 1914 level. Corn prices moved in like fashion. Under the Food Control Act, the government guaranteed $2.00 for wheat in 1917 and $2.26 in 1918. The slogan was "Food will win the War!" So the plea of patriotism was added to the monetary incentive to increase wheat production. Wheat production surged forward in 1918 and 1919, after a short crop in 1917. Wheat was substituted for oats, corn, and alfalfa during those two years. Except for wheat, the increase in production of all agricultural products during the war period was moderate, amounting to about 1 percent per year up to 1919.

The movements of the general price level must be considered in evaluating the changes in farm prices. Prices paid by farmers, reflecting the movements of the general price level, had lagged behind farm prices during the war and did not catch up until 1920. Foreign demand for agricultural products fell off, and government price guarantees on wheat expired during that year. Farm prices had reached a peak in May.[1] By July, the index of prices received by farmers had declined 4 percent below that of May; by August, 7 percent more—and so on—until by December they were nearly 40 percent lower than they had been six months earlier.

In Nebraska, the price of wheat skidded from $2.46 in June to $1.35 in December; corn from $1.63 to 42 cents; cattle from $11.20 to $6.70; and hogs from $13.00 to $8.00.[2] The price weakness continued. By December, 1921, the index of prices received by Nebraska farmers had fallen to 100, as compared with 228 in June, 1920—a decline of 56 percent.

Although prices also dropped in other sectors of the economy, the declines were only about half as large. Thus the decline in purchasing power of farmers was no

[1] *Agricultural Prices and Parity*, USDA Agricultural Handbook 118, 1 (1957), 14.

[2] *Nebraska Agricultural Statistics: Historical Record, 1866–1954*, pp. 139, 141, 154, 156.

illusion. Net income to U.S. agriculture dropped 58 percent from 1920 to 1921. In real terms, the purchasing power of farmers declined more than 40 percent in one year.[3]

It is understandable that the depression was considered severe by farmers. "The truth is that we are passing through the most severe period of agricultural activities we have ever experienced."[4] The collapse was the more alarming because it was unexpected. Farmers had decided that a new and higher price level was here to stay. By the winter of 1921, some farmers in the Northern Plains were burning corn for fuel and trading wool for socks and shirts.[5]

Farmers had been caught in an extremely vulnerable position by the crash. Their 1920 crop had been produced with costs at record highs. Many farmers carrying large debts had contracted to buy land and machinery during the two previous years; it now took more than twice as much production to repay interest and principal on loans—and out of reduced incomes—as during the year before. Rural banks were loaded with farmers' notes. The tighter policies of the Federal Reserve system intensified the financial problems of agriculture.

To add to the burden, the prices of farmland began to go down. The value of farms in Nebraska declined by over $10,000, on the average, from 1920 to 1925. The total value of all farm property in the state declined by a third between 1920 and 1930, and the value of land and buildings by almost a half. Farmland now became a source of inventory loss, rather than gain. This did not affect people who paid for and kept their land, but it was of crucial concern to those who sold, either voluntarily or otherwise. In seven southeastern Nebraska counties there were 315 foreclosure sales between 1921 and 1930, in two east-central counties there were 156 sales, while in one Sandhills county there were 108. In other cases farmers simply deeded their farms to their creditors.[6]

The stress also affected banks. After only recently having urged farmers to borrow more, they now had to refuse additional loans and urge the repayment of existing ones. Their vulnerability is shown in the fact that nearly 100 Nebraska banks had to close in 1923, 28 in 1926, 19 in 1927, 44 in 1928, and 106 in 1929.[7] Five banks failed in Custer County alone during the same period. In Sherman County, two banks failed in 1929. However, seven other banks were in trouble at the time and were out of business by 1938, leaving only two in operation.[8]

The farm-mortgage debt in Nebraska increased by 37 percent from 1920 to 1925, and farmers turned to the Federal Land Bank for financing. Mortgage credit extended by the Omaha bank doubled between 1920 and 1925, with an equal increase in dollar terms in the next five years. By 1930 the Land Bank held over 10 percent of the mortgage indebtedness on farm real estate in Nebraska.

[3] *1955 Historical and Descriptive Supplement to Economic Indicators*, U.S. Government Printing Office, 1955, p. 13.

[4] V. S. Sweedlun, "A History of the Evolution of Agriculture in Nebraska, 1870–1930," (University of Nebraska, Ph.D. thesis, 1940) p. 288.

[5] Murray R. Benedict, *Farm Policies of the United States, 1790–1950* (New York: The Twentieth Century Fund, 1953), p. 172.

[6] H. Clyde Filley, *Effects of Inflation and Deflation upon Nebraska Agriculture, 1914 to 1932*, Nebraska Agricultural Experiment Station Research Bulletin 71 (1934), pp. 115, 116.

[7] Filley, *op. cit.*, pp. 99, 100.

[8] M. J. Owens, *A Brief History of Sherman County, Nebraska*, Norfolk Daily News, 1952, pp. 183–187.

Meanwhile, farm costs remained high. Fixed cash costs, such as taxes, were difficult to pay. At no time during the twenties did property tax levies in Nebraska fall below 122 percent of the 1913 levy. In 1927 the levy was 184 percent of the 1913 levy. Property taxes, which took 5 percent of average net farm incomes in 1914, took 20.4 percent in 1922, 13.5 percent in 1924, 10.6 percent in 1928, and 8.7 percent in 1929.

The situation in the other Northern Plains states during this period was much the same. Farm real estate values in South Dakota fell 58 percent from 1920 to 1930. Two thirds of the banks failed between 1920 and 1935,[9] and there were 115 failures in 1926 alone.[10] In one central county only one bank remained by 1940, where there had been 15 in 1925. There were 3,709 farm foreclosures, involving 836,000 acres of farmland, in South Dakota in 1924, the peak foreclosure year during the 1920's. This represented 2.3 percent of the farmland of the state.[11] In Kingsbury County land values dropped from $124.40 per acre in 1919 to $54.20 in 1929.

The effect of falling prices on banks can be seen in data on changes in the number of banks during this period, shown in Table 9. These states had been "overbanked"

TABLE 9.  CHANGES IN NUMBER OF BANKS IN THE NORTHERN PLAINS, 1920–40

| States | 1920 | 1940 |
|---|---|---|
| Kansas. . . . . . . . | 1,357 | 610 |
| Nebraska. . . . . . . | 1,276 | 418 |
| South Dakota . . . . . | 900 | 152 |
| North Dakota . . . . . | 693 | 170 |

From Robert F. Wallace, "Western Farm Areas in Two World Wars," *Journal of Farm Economics*, 32 (1950), 89.

prior to and during World War I because of state banking laws. The extent of this can be seen in the fact that New York state, with over three times the combined population of Kansas and Nebraska, had less than half as many banks in 1920. Massachusetts, with six times as many people as North Dakota, had half as many banks. Although a minor part of this difference can be attributed to the greater population density in the East, the evidence of excess numbers of banks in the Northern Plains is overwhelming.

### THE FARM BLOC AND THE BEGINNINGS OF GOVERNMENT INTERVENTION

A general financial crisis followed the farm price collapse in 1920. However, the recession in the business sector was short-lived; by 1922 recovery had set in and the business cycle was on its way up again. By 1923, industrial production exceeded that of 1920. Farmers were forced to carry the burden of postwar readjustments alone, although their only crime was their response to the need for food for the domestic populace during the war and of foreign populations at the war's close. Thus they had just cause for complaint. Their swelling protests blended into a powerful farm movement, which was to have a profound impact on farm policies.

[9] H. S. Schell, "Adjustment Problems in South Dakota," *Agricultural History*, 14 (April, 1940), 71.

[10] Bruce Nelson, *Land of the Dacotahs* (Minneapolis: University of Minnesota Press, 1946), p. 303.

[11] Gabriel Lundy and R. L. Berry, *The Economic Strength of South Dakota's Agriculture*, South Dakota Agricultural Experiment Station Circular 132 (1957), p. 60.

The Farmers Union and the Grange had been organized in the nineteenth century but had been only moderately active during the first part of the twentieth century. However, the Smith-Lever Act, with its provision for county farmer groups (called "farm bureaus"), laid the groundwork for a new national organization. The American Farm Bureau Federation officially came into existence in March, 1920, providing a national framework through which the local and state farm bureaus might act as a single body. In 1921, representatives of the Farm Bureau Federation, the National Grange, the National Board of Farm Organizations, the National Milk Producers Federation, the International Farm Congress, and the Farmers Union met in Washington, D.C. They spent ten days discussing farm legislation; a few days afterwards the bipartisan group of senators, which came to be known as the "farm bloc," was formed. These senators were later instrumental in passing several pieces of farm legislation.

Meanwhile, concern with the many farm problems that had developed was evident in the executive branch. Out of this concern came the increasingly active intervention by the federal government in farm problems during the 1920's, and the galaxy of agencies and programs of the 1930's.

Early in 1921, Congress created a Joint Commission of Agricultural Inquiry to investigate causal factors behind current financial conditions of farmers and to make recommendations for legislation to remedy these conditions. The commission subsequently recommended, among other measures, preferred legal status for marketing cooperatives, intermediate credit for agriculture, improved warehousing facilities, reduced freight rates, and better grading of farm products. At a national agricultural conference, called by President Harding in 1922, Secretary of Agriculture Wallace said that "the agriculture of the nation is in a bad state, and our entire business and industrial life is suffering in consequence." [12] Nevertheless, the President cautioned the conference that "It cannot be too strongly urged that the farmer must be ready to help himself . . . legislation can do little more than give the farmer the chance to organize and help himself." This conference set the stage for farm relief legislation.

At the same time, Peek and Johnson, of the Moline Plow Company of Moline, Illinois, had filed a brief, *Equality for Agriculture*, with the American Farm Bureau Federation in December, 1921. This document became the basis for the first extensive congressional farm-relief proposal, the McNary-Haugen Bill, which was considered in Congress five times between 1924 and 1928, and passed twice—only to be vetoed both times. The early versions provided for export-dumping of wheat through a government export corporation. The final draft provided for aid to farmers' cooperatives to expand their storage operations. Even though this legislation did not pass, the resulting discussion and associated pressures made the country more conscious of farm problems.

In the meantime, the agricultural industry began to recover. Some of the farmers' financial distress had been alleviated. The wheat acreage, which had fallen from 75 million acres in 1919 to 52 million acres in 1925, began to expand again in response to more favorable prices, reaching 59 million acres by 1929. Net income to agriculture

[12] Chester C. Davis, "The Development of Agricultural Policy since the End of the World War," *Farmers in a Changing World* (USDA Yearbook of Agriculture, 1940), p. 301.

rose from $3.3 billion in 1921 to $6.7 billion in 1925, and seemed to stabilize around $6 billion during the next four years.[13] However, the farm relief drive had attained such momentum that pressure for farm legislation continued; and the result was the passage of the Agricultural Marketing Act of 1929, which established the Federal Farm Board.

This act ended one of the most sustained struggles over a piece of agricultural legislation in the nation's history. The board received an initial appropriation of $500 million to help finance cooperative marketing associations that would perform storage functions and promote orderly marketing. In addition, it was supposed to promote education on cooperative principles, and help organize and develop effective farm cooperatives. Even under favorable conditions, it is unlikely that the Farm Board could have solved the income problem; it could not control supply, and its operations tended to stimulate production—resulting in more farm surpluses. It was soon overwhelmed by the magnitude of the economic collapse; nevertheless, it was a large first step toward the far-reaching types of federal intervention that shortly ensued.

## THE 1929 PANIC AND MORE FARM DEPRESSION

With almost the suddenness of a thunderstorm, the greatest stock-market crash in the country's history occurred in late 1929. Between October 24 and 29, the value of stocks on the New York Exchange shrank from $87 billion to $55 billion. More trouble for agriculture was close behind; in fact, wheat prices presaged the coming events, having weakened in September, 1929. In Nebraska they fell from $1.06 per bushel at that time to 67 cents a year later, to 51 cents by November, 1930, and to 28 cents by July, 1931.

Other farm products followed the same trend. The index of prices received by Nebraska farmers fell from 153 in 1929 to 128 in 1930, to 88 in 1931, and to 62 in 1932. Although prices of commodities purchased by farmers during this time also dropped, their decline was not as precipitous as that of farm prices; consequently the purchasing power (parity ratio) of Nebraska farm products (based on 1910–14 = 100) slid from 95 in 1929 to 85 in 1930, to 68 in 1931, and to 55 in 1932.

Farm incomes depend not only on prices but on production. In the Northern Plains states, and in the Plains in general, the effects of falling prices were compounded by climate. Rainfall in Nebraska was below average in 1931, 1932, 1933, and, in 1934—at 14.3 inches—the lowest since 1864. It was average in 1935, but again fell to 14.4 inches in 1936 and to 17.7 inches in 1937. The state's average corn yield was 2.5 bushels per acre in 1934 and 2.8 bushels in 1936. The wheat yield in 1934 was 5.2 bushels, but was not so adversely affected in the other years. The index of crop production, based on 1930 = 100, was 72 in 1931, 91 in 1932, 77 in 1933, 18 in 1934, 61 in 1935, and 32 in 1936. Similarly, the value of crop production in Nebraska, based on 1929 = 100, was 75 in 1930, 39 in 1931 and 1932, 50 in 1933, and 24 in 1934.

The effects of drought and low prices during the 1930's in the Northern Plains states have been described many times.[14] Dry weather brought dust storms, which

[13] *Economic Indicators*, p. 13.
[14] For a particularly lucid summary, see *The Future of the Great Plains*, chap. IV.

started in the Southern Plains in 1934; and these became more general during 1935–37. They were spectacular and terrifying; however, the underlying economic conditions were probably even more frightening.

TABLE 10. AVERAGE GROSS INCOME FROM FARM PRODUCTION—INCLUDING AAA SLAUGHTER PAYMENTS AND GOVERNMENT PURCHASES—PER FARM IN THE NORTHERN PLAINS

| State | 1929 | 1933 | 1934 | 1935 |
|-------|------|------|------|------|
| North Dakota . . . . . | $2,775 | $1,116 | $ 804 | $1,147 |
| South Dakota . . . . . | 2,850 | 905 | 839 | 1,210 |
| Nebraska . . . . . . . | 3,537 | 1,399 | 1,528 | 1,676 |
| Kansas . . . . . . . . | 2,632 | 988 | 1,166 | 1,398 |

Source: *The Future of the Great Plains*, report of the Great Plains Committee, U.S. Government Printing Office, 1936.

The most obvious problem was the pathetically low level of farmer incomes, shown in Table 10. Nebraska seems to have fared slightly better than the other Northern Plains states—though the incomes shown in the table indicate only differing degrees of poverty.

Mortgage indebtedness was another symptom of distress. Farmers in the Northern Plains entered the decade of the thirties with indebtedness equivalent to 20.8 percent of their assets, compared with 16.1 percent in 1920. The shrinkage in asset valuations accounted for much of this change; however, farmers had also been replacing and adding to their equipment. Then, in the early thirties, mortgage indebtedness declined (Table 11). This decrease between 1930 and 1935 was not due to the payment of debts, in the ordinary sense, but to wholesale liquidation of farms through foreclosures and voluntary deeding to creditors. The extent of such transactions is shown in Table 12 for the Northern Plains, as compared with the United States as a whole. Conditions were so serious that the Northern Plains states took the lead in passing laws to prohibit foreclosures, extend redemption periods, and eliminate deficiency judgments (Figure 13).

TABLE 11. ESTIMATED FARM MORTGAGE DEBT IN NORTHERN PLAINS
(THOUSANDS OF DOLLARS)

| State | 1920 | 1930 | 1935 |
|-------|------|------|------|
| North Dakota . . . . | 267,780 | 204,598 | 146,910 |
| South Dakota . . . . | 278,880 | 295,725 | 184,579 |
| Nebraska . . . . . . | 416,860 | 560,973 | 486,160 |
| Kansas . . . . . . . | 295,870 | 487,122 | 390,434 |

Source: *The Future of the Great Plains*.

In central and southern Nebraska, farms keeping farm accounts in cooperation with the College of Agriculture not only had low incomes, starting in 1930, but net losses—in 1931 and 1932. Their operating expenses did not decrease with income, and these were above-average farms.[15]

Depressed incomes quickly affected land values. In central Nebraska the price per

[15] W. L. Ruden and H. C. Filley, *Farm Size and Its Relation to Volume of Production, Operating Costs, and Net Returns: Central and Southern Nebraska, 1930–39*, Nebraska Agricultural Experiment Station Research Bulletin 349.

acre of farmland sold dropped from $56.00 in 1929 to $27.00 in 1934. By 1939, land values were only about half of what they had been a decade earlier. The decline during this ten-year period was 38 percent in southern Nebraska and in the state as a whole.[16] By 1931 the number of forced sales and defaults for Nebraska farms exceeded voluntary sales. Such involuntary transfers increased by 80 percent during 1932 and then doubled by 1933. In the latter year there were sixty-four forced transfers per 1,000 farms.[17] In one Custer County community, 35 percent of the land was transferred between 1930 and 1939, nearly half by foreclosure.[18]

TABLE 12.   NUMBER OF FORECLOSURE SALES AND RELATED DEFAULTS PER 1,000 FARMS IN THE
NORTHERN PLAINS, 1931–35

| State | 1931 | 1932 | 1933 | 1934 | 1935 |
|---|---|---|---|---|---|
| North Dakota. . . . . | 34.1 | 54.0 | 63.3 | 31.3 | 18.9 |
| South Dakota . . . . . | 33.2 | 49.2 | 78.0 | 64.2 | 62.4 |
| Nebraska. . . . . . . | 21.8 | 34.4 | 58.2 | 45.8 | 41.0 |
| Kansas. . . . . . . . | 20.1 | 26.3 | 23.2 | 24.0 | 23.4 |

Source: *The Future of the Great Plains.*

These transfers were not all made by farmers; a feature of the period was the distress sale of mortgages by insurance companies, banks, and loan companies to the federal loan agencies, notably to the Federal Land Bank.[19] Banks were going through strenuous times. In Custer County, Nebraska, three banks closed in 1930, seven in 1931, five in 1932, and one in 1934, cutting the number of banks in the county by half in five years.[20] They suffered from delinquent loans and from their inability to build up cash reserves. Drought combined with depression in dealing body blows. Rainfall records at Broken Bow show that for the ten years 1931 to 1940, the rainfall was below average, giving an accumulated deficit of nearly 45 inches, equivalent to two years of rainfall.[21]

As rainfall decreased, crop production was affected to an even greater extent, as can be seen in Figure 14. During the years 1930–33, Custer County farmers produced 25 million bushels of corn, valued at slightly more than $10 million; however, the next four years combined produced less than 5 million bushels, worth less than $4 million. From 1938 to 1941, production was up to 7 million bushels for the four years. Yet this did not even equal the single-year production of 1933. Stands of alfalfa were lost during the same bleak spell and could not be reestablished. Small grains were almost as poor as corn. Many acres were not even harvested.

[16] Eleanor H. Hinman, *Sales Value and Assessed Value of Nebraska Farm Land: 1921–1934.* Nebraska Agricultural Experiment Station Research Bulletin 77 (1935), p. 10. Also Louis Kaye Gauger, John Muehlbeier and Kris Kristjanson, *Land Values and Assessed Values in Nebraska* (1930–52), Nebraska Agricultural Experiment Station Miscellaneous Publication 3 (1954), p. 18.

[17] Frank Miller and H. C. Filley, *Land Prices,* Nebraska Experiment Station Bulletin 379 (1945), p. 16.

[18] Maurice C. Latta, "The Economic Effects of Drouth and Depression upon Custer County, 1929–42," *Nebraska History,* 35 (December, 1952), p. 233.

[19] Robert Diller, *Farm Ownership, Tenancy and Land Use in a Nebraska Community* (Chicago: University of Chicago Press, 1941), p. 32.

[20] Loyd Glover, Jr., "The Economic Effects of Drouth and Depression on Custer County" (unpublished M.A. thesis, University of Nebraska, 1950), p. 10.

[21] Latta, *op. cit.,* p. 223.

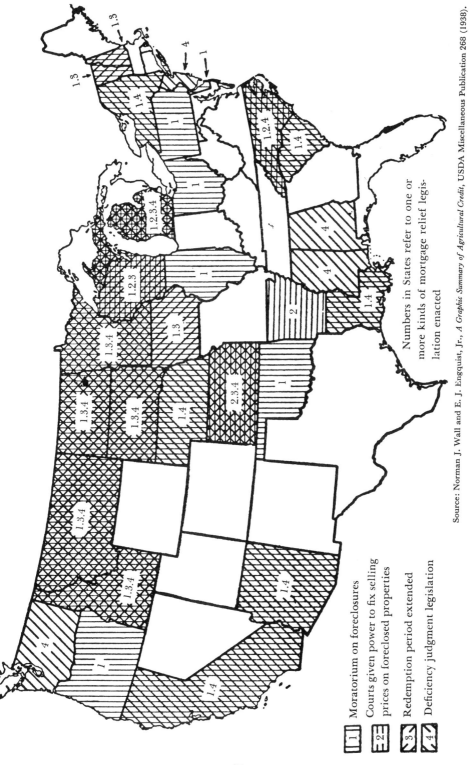

Numbers in States refer to one or more kinds of mortgage relief legislation enacted

Source: Norman J. Wall and E. J. Engquist, Jr., *A Graphic Summary of Agricultural Credit*, USDA Miscellaneous Publication 268 (1938).

Fig. 13. Summary of Mortgage Relief Legislation, by States (1930–63)

1 — Moratorium on foreclosures
2 — Courts given power to fix selling prices on foreclosed properties
3 — Redemption period extended
4 — Deficiency judgment legislation

71

1930=100%

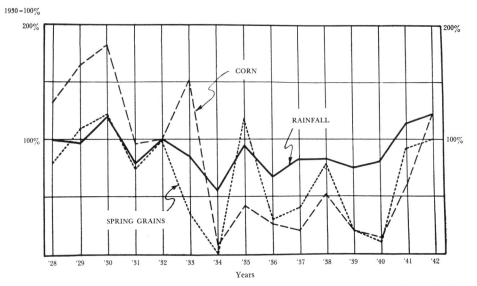

Source: Maurice Latta, "The Economic Effects of Drouth and Depression upon Custer County, 1929–42," *Nebraska History*, 35 (December, 1952), p. 227.

FIG. 14.   EFFECT OF RAINFALL ON CROP PRODUCTION, CUSTER COUNTY, NEBRASKA, 1928–42

The first year of drought in this county, 1934, found farmers with more cattle than they had held since 1920—146,000 head, in addition to 156,000 hogs. Crop failures caused rapid liquidation of livestock. By the next year, three-fourths of the hogs and nearly half of the cattle had disappeared. After 1935, cattle numbers stabilized at 100,000 and hog numbers never rose above 60,000, until the middle of World War II.

The drought had other impacts. Red Cross relief to needy people began in 1932. County commissioners provided $2.00 per week for food for them.[22] More than 5,000 people left Custer County in the decade 1930–40, four-fifths of whom had lived on farms, and three-fourths of these were youths of less than twenty-five years of age. Most of the migration took place in the latter half of the decade.

The decline in land values in Kansas was not as steep as in Nebraska; in the north-central area they dropped by a third from 1929 to 1933.[23] However, in central South Dakota, east of the Missouri, they fell by about a half between 1930 and 1935.[24] Between 1931 and 1940, mortgage foreclosures were initiated on about 40 percent of the farms in the ten-county North James area, and on about 30 percent of the farms in the South James area. The North James area and the land immediately to the east, comprising a sixteen-county region in north-central South Dakota east of the Missouri, had the highest foreclosure rate in the state during this period. In some of the counties, as much as 20 to 30 percent of the land was owned by creditors by 1938. This was not

[22] Glover, *op. cit.*, p. 10.

[23] Merton L. Otto, Hubert L. Collins and Wilfred H. Pine, *Trends in Land Values in Kansas*, Kansas Agricultural Experiment Station Circular 341 (1956), p. 8.

[24] Lundy and Berry, *op. cit.*, p. 11.

the whole story, however. Several counties also had as much as 15 to 20 percent of their land subject to tax deed at this time.

The vulnerability of the area between the 98th and 100th meridians was again evident. In Faulk County, only one bank remained by 1935, as compared with fourteen in 1920. Edmunds County, along the 99th meridian, lost 20 percent of its population between 1930 and 1935. Kingsbury County lost a quarter of its farm population. In South Dakota as a whole, 39 percent of the population was on relief— the highest figure for any state (North Dakota ranked second). This was three times the national average. Over half the farmers in the state were receiving relief, and 80 percent of the farmers in one central county were on relief in April, 1935. AAA payments kept the relief figures from being even higher.

The contribution of climate to these conditions is illustrated in Figures 15*A* and 15*B*. Rainfall was below average during the entire decade, 1930–40, in South Dakota. In 1934 it was only 13.3 inches, resulting in almost total crop failure in over two-thirds of the counties.

Land values for North Dakota as a whole fell by only 29 percent between 1930 and 1935, and another 16 percent by 1940.[25] However, the declines were much greater in the central counties. In Emmons County it was 65 percent for the decade; in Kidder County, 69 percent; in Burleigh County, 61 percent; in McHenry County, 52 percent; and in Montrail County, 48 percent. The percentage of real estate taxes that were delinquent was heavier in North Dakota in 1932–33 than in any other Plains state. Delinquency was particularly severe in the central and western areas, where it was commonly 45 percent or more.[26]

## GOVERNMENTAL INTERVENTION ON ALL FRONTS

The period 1929–33 was one in which confidence at the national level fell to a new low. There was a general lack of vigorous ideas as to how best to cope with the problems of the times. Governmental economy was the order of the day, and in 1930 tariffs were raised to all-time highs under the Smoot-Hawley Act. After 1930, the combination of a Republican administration and a Democratic House of Representatives further confused the deteriorating situation. Such programs as the Farm Board and the Reconstruction Finance Corporation had provided some measure of relief, but they did not go far enough.

Not since World War I had farm prices, employment, and industrial activity been so low. With the overwhelming victory of the Democrats in 1932, the stage was set for change. After groping along familiar paths, Congress and the American people were ready to support the new president in trying unorthodox remedies. There rapidly arose a host of "alphabetical organizations," many of which have survived even to the present time. Our purpose here is not to examine all of them in detail but to review those that were to have significant impact on the agricultural economies of the Northern Plains. The federal government now moved into jurisdictional areas

[25] Rainer Schickele and Reuben Engelking, *Land Values and the Land Market in North Dakota*, North Dakota Agricultural Experiment Station Bulletin 353 (1949), p. 16.
[26] *The Future of the Great Plains*, p. 61.

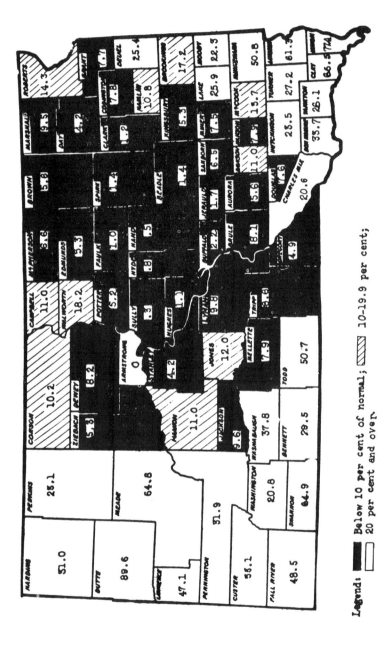

Legend: ■ Below 10 per cent of normal; ▨ 10–19.9 per cent;
□ 20 per cent and over.

Source: W. F. Kumlien, "A Graphic Summary of the Relief Situation in South Dakota (1930–35)," South Dakota Experiment Station Bulletin 310, p. 39.

FIG. 15A.  RATIO OF CROP VALUE TO NORMAL VALUE, 1933  (Base period is 1923–32, inclusive. Crops considered in arriving at the norm include corn, wheat, oats, barley, rye, flax, and potatoes.)

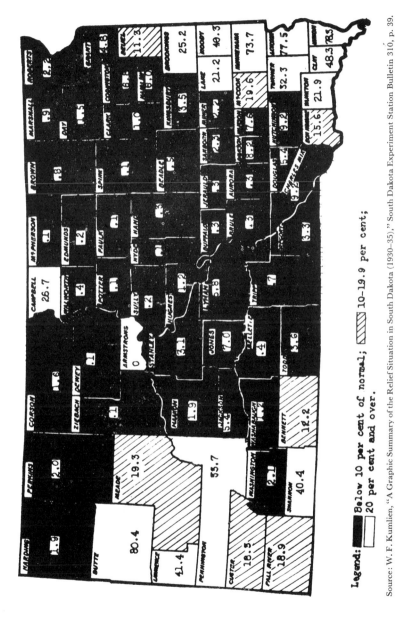

Source: W. F. Kumlien, "A Graphic Summary of the Relief Situation in South Dakota (1930–35)," South Dakota Experiment Station Bulletin 310, p. 39.

Fig. 15B. Ratio of Crop Value to Normal Value, 1934 (Base period is 1923–32, inclusive. Crops considered in arriving at the norm include corn, wheat, oats, barley, rye, flax, and potatoes.)

75

hitherto reserved for state and local government, especially where the latter had shown themselves unable to cope with the magnitude of the problems.

## THE BANK HOLIDAY

On March 5, one day after his inauguration, President Roosevelt closed every bank in the country. This was done to halt the withdrawal of funds, symptomatic of an incipient panic. The Emergency Banking Act, passed by Congress a few days later, empowered the President to call in all gold, to examine the financial condition of all banks, and to reopen all banks found to be sound. The rest were put under the supervision of "conservators," and were reopened if and when they regained solvency. The act creating the Federal Deposit Insurance Corporation was passed on June 16, providing for insurance on individual deposits in member banks.

Many of the banks in the Northern Plains that were closed at this time were never reopened; instead, they went through liquidation proceedings. These were generally the smaller, poorly financed banks.

## FARM CREDIT ADMINISTRATION (FCA)

The legislation that followed was designed to build upon the foundation created by the passage of the National Farm Loan Act of 1916, which established the federal land banks, and by the establishment of the federal intermediate banks in 1923. On March 27 the President, by executive order, abolished the Federal Farm Board and established the Farm Credit Administration—which was made permanent by Congress in June, 1933, with the passage of the Farm Credit Act. This act established twelve district banks for cooperatives and twelve production credit corporations to be administered by the Farm Credit Administration. The twelve land banks and the twelve intermediate credit banks were also transferred to this agency. The production credit corporations were to administer short-term credit, extended locally through cooperative production credit associations. Most of the money loaned by the land banks was through the cooperative national farm-loan associations.

Congress also passed the Emergency Farm Mortgage Act, on May 12, 1933. Among the more important provisions was that for the refinancing by the land banks of farm mortgages held by other lenders. The latter could exchange their mortgage for government-guaranteed bonds. The interest rate on land bank loans was lowered. Also provided were land bank commissioner "rescue" loans, which a farmer could obtain in addition to regular land bank loans.

Following the passage of this act, the lending activities of the land banks and the production credit corporations expanded rapidly. From May, 1933, to December, 1935, the land banks made almost $2.2 billion worth of loans, exceeding those made during the sixteen-year period before 1933. By 1936 they had almost doubled their farm-mortgage holdings. Thousands of farm mortgages being called by private lenders were refinanced by the land bank operations.

In the Northern Plains states the land bank held over 37 percent of the farm mortgages by 1933; during the following year this figure increased to 82 percent. Loans amounting to more than $600 million, largely for the refinancing of other debts, were made by land banks and the Land Bank Commissioner between May, 1933, and July, 1934, in the Northern Plains. This figure represents almost one-third of the lending operations of the entire land bank system in 1933–35. The intensity of lending activity by the land banks in the Northern Plains is shown in Figure 16. After 1935, more of the land bank loans were "new" loans, made for the purchase of farmland, rather than for refinancing existing obligations.

The funds appropriated by Congress in 1933 for land bank commissioner loans were soon exhausted, so in early 1934 the Federal Farm Mortgage Corporation was created. This corporation was granted the power to issue bonds, guaranteed by the U.S. government, to finance the operations of the land banks and the land bank commissioner. The security behind these bonds was land bank bonds and commissioner mortgages. Thus the system was provided with a dependable supply of loan funds, that could be expanded or contracted with credit needs, but was not subject to the caprice of the market—owing to its underlying federal support.

The land bank and commissioner operations in the Plains were not carried on without criticism. Farmers protested that while a borrower from a non-federal agency could refinance his loan through the land bank, with the possibility of reducing his debt, no such opportunity existed for land bank borrowers who had financed high-priced land before 1930 with land bank loans. Consequently, land banks—in 1935— were forced to foreclose on many farms: 1,300 in the Plains that year, and nearly 15,000 the following year.[27] Another irritant was the rigid policy of the Federal Farm Mortgage Corporation in foreclosing commissioner loans, many of which were shaky, particularly in view of the continuing drought. One-half of these foreclosures, 4,828 in number, were in the four Northern Plains states. As it happened, increasing farm incomes kept these problems from becoming severe, but they represented two serious defects in the program.

The reorganized land bank and the accompanying land bank commissioner loan programs were remarkably well timed to alleviate serious financial stress among Plains farmers. The land banks have been criticized for conservatism and lack of imagination in more recent years; nevertheless, the results illustrate what can be accomplished by a specific, well-organized program in a situation where a vacuum has been created by economic circumstances.

The production credit corporations and associations rapidly expanded their loan programs. By 1935 they had over $60 million in short-term loans outstanding, about 6 percent of the total. By 1937 they were extending $104 million in loans, or about 10 percent of the non-real-estate loans. In addition, the federal intermediate credit banks held discounted notes for other lenders, ranging in total value from $79 million in 1931 down to $32 million in 1940. While these figures are not large compared with the total amounts of non-real-estate credit used by farmers during this period, the influence of this source of credit should not be underestimated.

In the first place, these associations were cooperatively organized and operated, giving confidence to the farmers of an area, whether they became borrowers or not. Second, they introduced an element of competition to the commercial banks of an area from the standpoint of both interest charged and the adaptation of repayment terms to the peculiarities of farm production. Third, they were a source of emergency

[27] William G. Murray, *Agricultural Finance* (3d ed.; Ames: Iowa State College Press, 1953), p. 297.

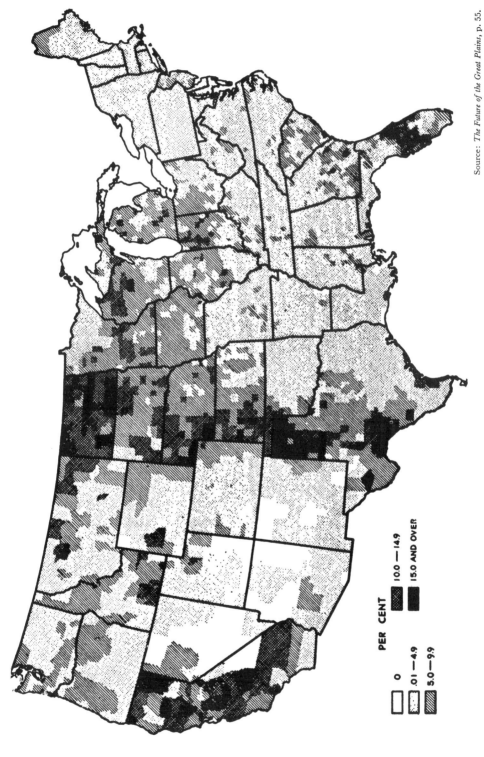

Fig. 16. Percentage of Farms Mortgaged to the Land Bank or Commissioner (May, 1933, to July, 1934)

PER CENT

0

.01 — 4.9

5.0 — 9.9

10.0 — 14.9

15.0 AND OVER

credit in areas where commercial facilities had broken down. The discounting of loans through the intermediate credit banks and the sale of debentures by the latter in the money markets served to expand the supply of credit in needy farm areas, where otherwise there might have been little or slow response to the demand.

## AGRICULTURAL ADJUSTMENT ACT AND THE COMMODITY CREDIT CORPORATION (AAA AND CCC)

The Agricultural Adjustment Act, passed on May 12, 1933, attracted more attention and controversy than the changes in farm-credit policy. Its objective was to control production and thus to raise farmer purchasing power to that of the years 1909–14. Under the act, the Secretary of Agriculture was empowered to make contracts with farmers by which they would reduce their acreage of the "basic" crops— wheat, cotton, rice, tobacco, and peanuts—in return for incentive payments. The cost of the operation was to be financed by a processing tax on the basic commodities. Measures were also included to deal with hogs, dairy products, beef, and other commodities. The program was to be administered by state and local committees, organized by the Secretary of Agriculture. This type of administration at the local level, as well as the explicit objective of supply control, were important departures from the philosophy behind the Farm Board. The program was to perform the function of an "ever-normal granary," in the words of the Secretary of Agriculture.[28]

As a corollary program, the Commodity Credit Corporation was established in October of the same year as an independent agency of the federal government. It was to lend money under non-recourse loans to farmers on storable commodities, such as wheat and corn, which it would place in storage. The farmers had a choice of selling the commodities and repaying the loans if prices rose above the loan levels, or surrendering the commodities to the government in repayment of the loan if prices remained below loan levels. The CCC had as its objectives both the raising of farm prices and the reduction of price fluctuations. It relied on the acreage control program to keep farmers from increasing their production in response to better prices, as they had done under the Farm Board.

A portion of the Agricultural Adjustment Act, the processing tax, was declared unconstitutional by the Supreme Court in January, 1936. Congress immediately replaced this act with the Soil Conservation and Domestic Allotment Act of 1936; in which the processing taxes were replaced by payments to farmers for the planting of soil-conserving crops. This legislation was later supplanted by the Agricultural Adjustment Act of 1938, which contained stronger supply-control measures. Specifically, it reestablished acreage allotments on basic crops, and payments to producers based on these allotments. It provided for marketing quotas if approved by two-thirds of the voting producers. It continued marketing agreements under which farmers could organize so as to control the supply of specific commodities. Soil Conservation payments for the subsidization of specific conservation practices were continued. This legislation, with periodic revisions, has been in effect down to the present time.

The impact of the new federal legislation was soon felt in the Northern Plains. About 470,000 cattle were purchased by the federal government in Nebraska for

---

[28] Geoffrey S. Shepherd, *Agricultural Price Policy* (2d ed.; Ames: Iowa State College Press, 1947), p. 40.

$6 million (in 1933) as a drought relief measure. In Custer County alone, a total of 45,168 head of cattle was sold to the federal government (by 2,231 farmers) after that county was declared an emergency area in 1934.[29] Likewise, "438,000 pigs and 36,000 piggy sows were purchased and slaughtered."[30] Approximately 35,000 wheat growers participated in the acreage allotment program in 1934–35. Similarly, about 41,000 farmers (about one-third of the total in the state) participated in the corn program, selling 53 million bushels of corn (41 percent of the production) and receiving loans amounting to $23 million. The governmental payments for corn, hogs, wheat, and cattle in Sherman County, Nebraska, had totaled over a half million dollars by December, 1935.[31]

The overall effects of the acreage adjustment programs of this period in reducing production and increasing prices were not large; drought, for example, was much more effective in reducing grain production than acreage restriction.[32] The "little pig" program was especially controversial—even though, from the moral standpoint, it did not differ from plowing up growing crops or from dumping surplus tanks and airplanes into the ocean after World War II. Despite the furor it raised, its effect on forthcoming production was slight.

Not to be overlooked, however, were the income effects of these programs, especially on farmers in the drought-stricken areas of the Northern Plains. For many, the opportunity to sell feed-short cattle to the government, even at low prices, probably spelled the difference between staying in business and bankruptcy. The size of government payments in Nebraska during the 1930's, compared with gross livestock and crop income, emphasizes their importance as a source of farm income.

| Year* | Crops and Livestock | Government Payments |
|-------|--------------------|--------------------|
| 1933 . . . . | $180,244,000 | $ 3,472,000 |
| 1934 . . . . | 211,202,000 | 29,916,000 |
| 1935 . . . . | 206,373,000 | 33,355,000 |
| 1936 . . . . | 278,106,000 | 17,293,000 |
| 1937 . . . . | 249,475,000 | 17,468,000 |
| 1938 . . . . | 203,568,000 | 15,371,000 |
| 1939 . . . . | 228,174,000 | 28,078,000 |
| 1940 . . . . | 224,289,000 | 46,296,000 |

* These statistics are from Olson, *op. cit.*, p. 311.

### FEDERAL EMERGENCY RELIEF ADMINISTRATION (FERA) AND WORKS PROGRESS ADMINISTRATION (WPA)

At the same time that the income effects of the AAA programs were being felt, other programs, more directly oriented to relief, were coming into being. In May, 1933, the Federal Emergency Relief Administration was created, placed in charge of Harry L. Hopkins—a professional social worker—and given an initial fund of $300 million. One of its branches was the Civil Works Administration, which was set up later in the year. Originally, the latter was established under a federal-state

[29] Glover, *op. cit.*, p. 48.
[30] James C. Olson, *History of Nebraska*, p. 310.
[31] Owens, *op. cit.*, p. 79.
[32] Benedict, *op. cit.*, p. 312.

matching arrangement. More and more federal funds were appropriated as time went on, and some of the states proved incapable of providing their share of financial support. (In January, 1935, FERA was contributing 87 percent of all public assistance in Nebraska.) FERA carried out its program primarily through direct relief to families that had lost their source of income, and thus was particularly helpful to families of farmers in drought areas.

The FERA was followed closely—in 1935—by the Works Progress Administration (WPA), under Harold L. Ickes. Congress provided this agency with an initial appropriation of nearly $5 billion so it could plan and execute various projects to provide work for the unemployed. The initial WPA still carries undesirable moral connotations for some, yet it must be recalled that this was an emergency program, created to tackle emergency problems. From the perspective of 1960, it is easy to criticize the slapdash way it was put together, its general lack of planning, and occasional slipshod administration. But to carp at its very existence is to betray our ignorance of the economic conditions of the time. It is hard to appreciate what the opportunities for constructive employment in building roads, courthouses, and other facilities meant to a people whose self-respect had been shaken by drought, loss of income, lack of alternative opportunities, and utter despair.

The relief programs assumed large proportions in the Northern Plains. This can be seen by the summary of the moneys spent by the federal government from 1933 to 1936.

| State* | FERA Expenditures April, 1933, through April, 1936 | WPA Expenditures April, 1935, through June, 1936 | Total |
|---|---|---|---|
| Kansas. . . . . . . . | $11,130,000 | $3,011,000 | $14,141,000 |
| Nebraska . . . . . . . | 6,541,000 | 2,084,000 | 8,625,000 |
| South Dakota . . . . . | 19,477,000 | 2,775,000 | 22,252,000 |
| North Dakota . . . . . | 19,981,000 | 3,598,000 | 23,579,000 |

* From *The Future of the Great Plains*, p. 56.

The intensity of the relief payments in the various counties can better be seen in Figure 17. It should be noted that the data in this chart include relief aid from AAA and Resettlement Administration sources as well as from FERA and WPA. Areas other than the transition portions of these states show up heavily. However, on a per capita basis, as well as on a per county basis, payments to some of the transition counties were large. In South Dakota, for example, 63.8 percent of the farmers in Aurora County, in the transition area, were on relief in March, 1935; in Brule County the proportion was 58.3 percent, while in Davison County it was 67.4 percent.[33] At that time the level for the state as a whole was somewhat less than 35 percent.[34] The percentage of farm families in these three counties receiving relief was generally higher than that in counties either to the east or to the west of them. Altogether, the Northern

[33] Elizabeth Eiselen, *A Geographic Traverse across South Dakota: A Study of the Subhumid Border* (University of Chicago published Ph.D. thesis, 1943), p. 103.

[34] W. F. Kumlien, *A Graphic Summary of the Relief Situation in South Dakota, 1930–35*, South Dakota Agricultural Experiment Station Bulletin 310 (1937), p. 23.

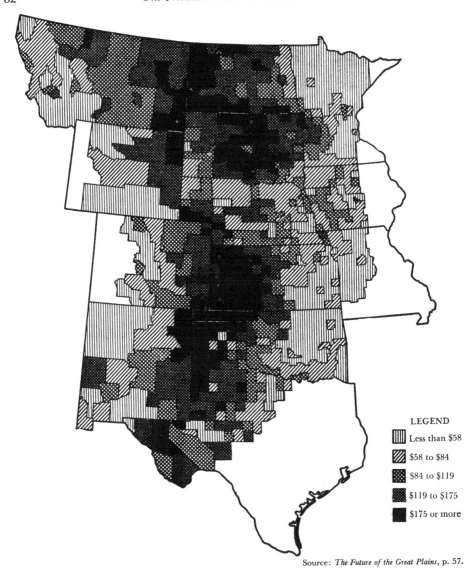

Source: *The Future of the Great Plains*, p. 57.

FIG. 17. INTENSITY OF FEDERAL AID PER CAPITA IN GREAT PLAINS DROUGHT AREA, 1933–36

Plains states accounted for 23.3 percent of the payments made under the FERA for drought relief and for the purchase and processing of cattle through 1935.

RESETTLEMENT ADMINISTRATION AND FARM SECURITY ADMINISTRATION (RA AND FSA)

One of the activities under the FERA was the program of the Rural Rehabilitation Division, established in April, 1934. It had several purposes. For established farmers on fertile land, it was to provide technical assistance, debt adjustment, and other aids. Farmers living on poor land were to be relocated on better, federally purchased land. After only a year of operation, the program was transferred to a new agency, created in 1935, the Resettlement Administration—under the direction of Rexford G. Tugwell. The new agency undertook programs similar to those of the parent agency: land purchase, rural rehabilitation, farm-debt adjustment, and subsistence homesteads.

The phase of the program that attracted most attention was that involving the purchase of "submarginal" lands, combining them into federally managed units, such as grazing districts, and resettling the displaced families on better land. This represented the first deliberate program of the federal government to "extensify" farming, to reverse the lines of development that had characterized the homestead legislation. Since this program meant a contraction of population in submarginal areas, there was much opposition in these areas, which was soon reflected in Congress. Consequently, this program tended to fade into the background after 1937, although a total of 12 million acres had been purchased under it by June 30, 1937.[35]

The rehabilitation program of the RA was an extension of feed-and-seed loans which the federal government had been making to farmers at various times since 1918. Loans and grants were made to farmers who lacked capital, resources, or knowledge to earn minimum adequate incomes, and who thus tended to be on relief. These farmers also received technical guidance in farming, and had to work out farm-and-home management plans in connection with their loans.

Under the subsistence homestead program, inexpensive homes were built on small plots of ground for "stranded" farm and industrial people. In many cases the size of these units was far too small; the program was oriented more toward providing immediate relief rather than long-run solutions, and was motivated by the strong "back to the land" philosophies of some of the administrators. The turnover of people was high; and all of these projects were eventually liquidated.

The Resettlement Administration aided in farm-debt adjustment by financing the meetings of voluntary farm-debt adjustment committees. These committees operated in connection with the new land bank and land bank commissioner loan programs.

The Farm Security Administration came into being in September, 1937, under the authority of the Bankhead-Jones Farm Tenant Act. Most of the activities of the Resettlement Administration were transferred to the new agency. It established county Farm Security offices whose staffs engaged in a variety of activities especially designed to help low-income farm families.

Title I of the act authorized the Secretary of Agriculture to make "tenant purchase loans" by which farm tenants and others could purchase land. The loans, to be repaid within forty years, provided for variable loan repayments and carried an interest charge of 3 percent. Title II authorized "rehabilitation loans" to farmers who could not obtain credit elsewhere for the purchase of livestock, equipment, and other farm-operating needs, and for family subsistence. Again, the repayment schedule was flexible, and the term was five to seven years. (The reader can recognize the modern versions of these two types of loans—farm-ownership loans and farm-operating loans —in the present Farmers Home Administration program.) Title III authorized the

---

[35] Benedict, *op. cit.*, p. 325.

submarginal land retirement program, which was transferred from the Resettlement Administration. The FSA also appointed local, voluntary debt-adjustment committees to mediate between creditors and farmers in getting debts of excessively burdened debtors scaled downward.

In Nebraska, rural rehabilitation loans totaling $12,695,000 had been made to 15,000 farm families by 1940. The typical loan amounted to $1,300.[36] Only seventy-five tenant purchase loans had been made by 1939. A total of over 5,000 farmers had been aided by debt-adjustment committees, having their debts scaled down by an average of 28.5 percent.

In South Dakota, the transition area counties of Aurora and Brule consistently ranked high in both the percent of farm families receiving subsistence grants from the FSA (as a relief measure or to put the family in position to carry a standard rehabilitation loan) and in the percent receiving standard loans—compared with counties to the east and west of them.[37] In January, 1940, 65 percent of the farm families in Aurora county and 37 percent of those in Brule were still receiving FSA grants; about 40 percent had standard loans.

In the Northern Plains states as a whole, the proportion of farm operators obtaining rehabilitation loans was relatively high. During the years 1935–43, the average percentages were: Kansas, 11.4; Nebraska, 15.6; South Dakota, 20.0; and North Dakota, 13.6.[38]

The Farm Security (later FHA) program has been the subject of much controversy since its initiation. It represented a new approach to the extension and use of credit. The relief and reform aspects of the program received heavy emphasis at the start, partly owing to the biases of early administrators. Some projects, such as subsistence homesteads, were economically unrealistic. On the other hand, many who criticized the program probably did not appreciate the severity of the human problems with which it dealt.

Out of the program have come some worthwhile innovations, including variable loan repayments geared to changing economic conditions, the extension of bona fide intermediate credit, and the management supervision given borrowers by the agency along with their loans. Geared to servicing farmers who cannot obtain credit elsewhere, the FHA has apparently come to be accepted by the commercial banks as an agency to which they can refer loan applicants whom they cannot service.

The FHA has sometimes been criticized for the small size of the farm on which borrowers are placed under farm-ownership loans. But the responsibility for this policy can often be traced to the restrictions Congress has occasionally written into the FHA appropriation acts.

Not all of the successful repayments of FHA loans can be attributed to the program. The rising price level also made an important contribution.

The basic dilemma faced by a program like FHA is its orientation toward the establishment in farming of people who might not be there without its help, as

[36] Ralph Waldemar Ordal, "History of the Federal Farm Program in Nebraska" (University of Nebraska, unpublished M.A. thesis, 1941), p. 26.

[37] Eiselen, *op. cit.*, p. 104.

[38] Rainer Schickele, *Agricultural Policy, Farm Programs and National Welfare* (New York: McGraw-Hill Book Company, 1954), p. 380.

opposed to the continuing labor surplus in agriculture and the need for a continuing population movement out of farming in some areas.

## SOIL CONSERVATION SERVICE (SCS)

Until the Soil Erosion Service was established, in 1933, there had been no federal program dealing with the problems of soil erosion. On March 25, 1935, this SES agency was converted, by act of Congress, into the Soil Conservation Service.

Interest in soil conservation had been growing in the United States since the turn of the century, led by such people as Gifford Pinchot and Theodore Roosevelt. Concern about resource conservation was diverted to other problems during World War I, and lay more or less dormant during the twenties. However, the appearance of drought and dust storms in the early thirties stimulated renewed interest in the nation's soil resources and its conservation.

The first conservation work was of the public works type, involving the use of Civilian Conservation Corps (CCC) personnel in the construction of check dams, tree planting, regrassing, and other measures—on both public and private land. Demonstration projects were created; for example, there were four in Nebraska—in Boone, Nance, Douglas, and Otoe counties—and there were sixteen CCC camps in operation in central and eastern parts of the state.

In 1936, as we have seen, the passage of the Soil Conservation and Domestic Allotment Act made soil conservation an official function of the Agricultural Adjustment Administration. Despite their different approaches and their truly different objectives, there has been considerable rivalry and friction between the Soil Conservation Service and the conservation program of the ASCS (formerly the AAA).

This year also marked the beginning of the Soil Conservation districts. These districts are organized by local farmers, frequently along county lines, and the SCS, since 1939, has made a policy of cooperating with farmers in soil conservation districts. In order to encourage their rapid organization, a model Soil Conservation District law was prepared by the Department of Agriculture, which was used by the states in setting up enabling legislation authorizing the creation of the districts. An interesting feature of these laws has been the authorization of the districts to use police power to enforce land-use and conservation regulations—although it has rarely been used.

Within the district, the SCS assists farmers in developing farm conservation plans; it provides technical assistance in laying out contours and designing other installations, and it helps the district in planning major projects and in securing heavy equipment for the construction of ponds, dams, and other large installations.

A newcomer in this period of the thirties, the SCS program was just getting started at the close of the decade. By 1940, eight soil conservation districts had been organized in Nebraska; and 2,205 farmers had signed five-year agreements with the SCS for effecting individual plans for soil erosion-control and land use.[39]

## LAND-USE PLANNING

In 1939 the U.S. Department of Agriculture introduced one of its most interesting and short-lived programs, the Agricultural Land-Use Planning Program. Under the "Mount Weather Agreement" of July, 1939, the Department of Agriculture and the land-grant colleges agreed to cooperate more closely at the local level and to give

[39] Ordal, *op. cit.*, p. 58.

farmers a larger voice in building land-use programs and agricultural policies. State and county land-use planning committees were to be established, the latter composed of representatives of the action agencies and at least ten farmers. The county committees were to evaluate the existing agricultural programs and make recommendations for their improvement.

The land-use planning committees also made inventories of the land resources in their respective counties, and they classified the land by use capability. They also made recommendations on conservation techniques, crop rotations, and other practices for specific soils.

By 1942 there were 1,891 counties and over 8,000 communities with planning committees. Serving on them were 125,000 farm people and 18,000 federal, state, and local government employees. Yet the program soon failed, for several reasons. First, the entrance of the country into war diverted the attention of people from land-use planning to other measures that were more immediately related to the war effort. In addition, there was a lack of active support—and even some opposition by certain USDA agencies, colleges, and farm groups, notably the Farm Bureau. The USDA withdrew from the program in 1942; however, in several states the extension services continued to work with the committees, and traces of the program still exist in some areas.[40]

Thus, after a brief life of three years, the project came to an end. It was the only program of its time that tried to coordinate the many farm policies and programs at the local level, and to develop local responsibility in their application.

### Rural Electrification Administration (REA)

A program that unobtrusively invaded the rural landscape of the Northern Plains was the Rural Electrification Administration. It was created by an act of Congress, in 1936, to make loans for rural electrification development; and private companies were expected to borrow these funds. When they did not develop sufficient interest, rural electric cooperatives, which were formed to fill the vacuum, applied for loans for construction. Since then, the REA has also supplied technical advice and supervision to the local REA system, which has expanded at a rapid rate. Just how pronounced this growth has been can be seen from the following figures. Between 1934 and 1937, the number of farmers reached by electricity had increased by 67 percent, despite the depression. Only 5.8 percent of the farmers in Nebraska had electricity in 1929, but, by 1951, 87 percent had been supplied. The role of electrification in the development of farm technology has not been fully appreciated.

### Federal Crop Insurance

Nebraska, North Dakota, and South Dakota each tried to provide hail insurance through state systems between 1911 and 1930. The programs were not successful, but during the drought years of the 1930's there were new demands for crop insurance protection. In 1938 Congress passed the Federal Crop Insurance Act, which established the Federal Crop Insurance Corporation (FCIC) to write all-risk crop insurance on low yields. The FCIC began to write insurance on wheat in 1939. Losses during the next few years were greater than the premiums that had been collected, in spite of

[40] Benedict, *op. cit.*, p. 395.

national yields well above average. In 1943 Congress appropriated enough money to liquidate the program, and no insurance was written in 1944 or 1945. This does not conclude the story, but further examination of the program will be resumed in Chapter 7.

### FARM ORGANIZATIONS DURING THE THIRTIES

Earlier we noted the attempts of the major farm organizations, after the farm price crash of 1920 to get more attention focused on the problems of agriculture. Now let us look at their actions during the 1930's.

Before 1932, all the farm organizations, including the Grange, the Farmers Union, and the Farm Bureau, had continued to support direct aid to agriculture through market- and price-oriented measures. They supported the Farm Board, higher tariffs, and stronger cooperative organizations. But they also changed with the times, being neither behind nor ahead of the general public as far as policy changes in agriculture were concerned. For example, the Grange favored parity prices and incomes for farmers, but opposed regimentation; it gave its blessing to soil conservation, but not to acreage allotments.[41] It still advocated high tariffs. It wanted the activities of the Farm Credit Administration decentralized, but it favored keeping the Farm Mortgage Credit Corporation and the Frazier-Lemke Amendment a while longer.

The Farm Bureau endorsed the AAA legislation, but wanted higher benefit payments from the U.S. treasury. It supported mandatory CCC loans at 85 percent of parity, and low interest rates on land bank loans. It favored reciprocal trade agreements, but didn't want farm prices affected by lower tariffs. It approved of the REA, but wanted it further decentralized. It traditionally advocated monetary management.

The Farmers Union also supported the soil conservation program and REA. It advocated crop insurance and favored the "ever-normal granary." It was a strong advocate of the Farm Security Program; and it also wanted 100 percent parity farm prices.

### THE GREAT PLAINS COUNCIL

In addition to the great amount of federal activity in the Plains, there also occurred at this time the beginnings of cooperation and coordination on a regional basis. In April, 1934, a meeting was called—by C. W. Warburton of the Federal Extension Service (at Amarillo, Texas)—of representatives of Southern Plains colleges—Kansas, Colorado, New Mexico, Oklahoma, and Texas—for the purpose of discussing wind erosion and methods of preventing soil blowing.[42] Following this, in 1935, Congress appropriated $2 million to this group, the Wind Erosion Committee, to finance the purchase of horse feed, equipment, power, and fuel to be used for wind erosion control.

This action was followed, in the same year, by an organizational step; the Resettlement Administration set up two committees concerned with drought conditions in the Plains. The first committee, of an interdepartmental nature, was composed of representatives of federal agencies in Washington which were interested in soil erosion work

[41] *Ibid.*, p. 386.

[42] Henry John Tomasek, "The Great Plains Agricultural Council" (University of Chicago, unpublished Ph.D. dissertation, 1959), pp. 19, 20.

in the Plains. The second committee was set up in the Plains, composed of representatives of the federal agencies and the land-grant colleges, to "coordinate the work of the various state agencies within each state in the region with that of the Washington group."[43]

In 1936 this committee changed its name to the Regional Advisory Committee on Land-Use Practices, and broadened its scope to include land-use problems. The members also became concerned with research coordination. They outlined the objectives of the committee under two headings: (1) The committee was to be advisory to the Washington interdepartmental committee; (2) It was to make recommendations to other state and federal agencies on land-use and related problems.

This committee almost disbanded in 1936 because of the formation of still another group, the President's Great Plains Drouth Area Committee, which had somewhat similar objectives. This committee was created on September 17, 1936, and was instructed to report not later than January 1 on "a long-term program for the efficient utilization of the resources of the Great Plains area."[44] The results of the efforts of this new group promptly became evident with the publication of the monumental report, *The Future of the Great Plains*, late in the same year.

The interdepartmental group slowly became inactive and disappeared. However, the Plains Advisory Committee fortunately did not disband, but reexamined its role. In 1937 it requested the appointment, by the U.S. Department of Agriculture, of a special assistant to the Secretary of Agriculture, to be headquartered in the Plains and to be responsible for the coordination of governmental programs in the dust bowl area. This request was granted. In 1939 the committee reorganized and called itself the Regional Agricultural Council of the Southern Great Plains States. (It was parallel in form to a similar group which had arisen in the Northern Plains states in March, 1938.) The southern group authorized the issuing of council reports and set up permanent committees on research and surveys, area planning, conservation districts, AAA, land retirement, and credit policies. The southern and northern councils held their first joint meetings in 1939 and 1940.

The southern council almost disbanded in 1942 because of disagreements between the USDA and the land-grant colleges over two issues.

First, the USDA had removed the AAA from the jurisdiction of the state extension directors. The Mount Weather Agreement (July, 1938) between the USDA and the land-grant colleges had established a broad basis for future relationships: the USDA would be responsible for action programs but would cooperate with the colleges in planning programs, and the state extension directors were to be chairmen of the state planning committees, with which the action agencies were to cooperate.[45] Land-use planning activities were carried on under this agreement between 1938 and 1941.

Second, the southern council was disturbed (in 1942) because the state extension directors had not been included on the newly created postwar planning committees. However, the northern council was a stabilizing influence at this point. In 1943 the two councils met jointly to formulate plans for the whole Plains area, and decided to meet jointly once a year and separately once a year.

Further consolidation of activities followed in 1946 with the formation of a Great

[43] *Ibid.*, p. 22.

[44] *The Future of the Great Plains*, p. 131.

[45] John M. Gaus and Leon O. Wolcott, *Public Administration in the United States Department of Agriculture* (Chicago: Public Administration Service, 1940), pp. 156–59.

Plains Agricultural Council, with southern and northern sections. The new arrangement provided for a secretary, to be employed by the USDA, and the council was to work with colleges and other agencies to effectuate its recommendations.

More definite action on membership was taken by the council in 1952; some revamping was necessary after the elections in that year and the consequent USDA reorganization. By 1964 the membership was very numerous; it included the agricultural college deans and the extension service and experiment station directors, representatives of the Agricultural Marketing Service, the Economic Research Service, the Agricultural Research Service, the Federal Extension Service, the Statistical Reporting Service, the Cooperative State Research Service, the Rural Electrification Administration, the state Agricultural Stabilization and Conservation Service chairmen, the state directors of the Farmers Home Administration and Federal Crop Insurance Corporation, the Regional Forester of the Forest Service, the director of the Rocky Mountain Forest and Range Experiment Station, and the ten-state SCS conservationists. The secretary continued to be employed by the USDA, but was furnished office facilities and staff by the land-grant colleges.

Thus, after a somewhat tenuous and uncertain beginning, the Great Plains Agricultural Council was firmly established as a permanent organization. Its contributions will be evaluated in more detail later; however, its most important contribution probably has been its provision of a regional board where ideas can be examined frankly and informally by people from the many agencies concerned with land use in the Plains. A second contribution lies in the fact that the secretary acts as a coordinator who brings the "combined impact of all the administrative services of a federal department to bear on the natural resource (and human) problems of a large interstate region. . . ."[46] The author of this statement might have included the various state agencies as well.

## WHERE HAD AGRICULTURE GONE BY 1940?

It had been a confusing twenty years. The second decade had been as replete with new programs and policies as the first had been barren of them. It was difficult to have even a nodding acquaintance with the new federal agencies that kept blossoming, without being called upon to evaluate them. Such objections as confusing, competing, overlapping, idealistic, and impractical could be aimed in their general direction, with a good chance of finding a mark somewhere. However, it was also a period of imagination, activity, and hope. Difficult problems were countered with prompt actions. The federal government had demonstrated that it could and would intervene in the affairs of people at a personal level. It has been said that the thirties cannot happen again, and there is reason to agree; the inference is that we will not *let* them happen again.

How was it with agriculture, particularly in the Northern Plains, as we paused on the threshold of another era? In the first place, the drought continued; only 16.3 inches of rain fell in Nebraska in 1939, and only 17.4 in 1940. After that, however, the long seige was broken by above-average rainfall for many years. The patterns were similar in the other Plains states. The index of prices received for farm commodities had been above 100 in 1935–37, but had slumped afterward. It started back up in

[46] Charles McKinley, *Uncle Sam in the Pacific Northwest* (Berkeley: University of California Press, 1952), p. 411.

1938, but did not reach 100 in the Northern Plains until 1940 or 1941. In the meantime, however, the index of prices paid had not fluctuated as much, and was at 124 in 1940 (1910–14 = 100). Consequently, the parity ratio in Nebraska was 74; in North Dakota, 71. Farm receipts were only slightly higher in 1940 than in previous years, and far below what they were to be even one year later. Government payments still accounted for 17 percent of these receipts in Nebraska and North Dakota. The depression was still felt in farm areas. Farm surpluses were stored in government and private facilities. However, they were shortly to be regarded as an integral part of the resources mobilized for war, a blessing rather than a curse.

The "export" of population from the Northern Plains characterized the period. The farm population of the country decreased moderately from 1920 to 1930, about 4.5 percent, but the proportion of total population represented by farmers declined from 30 percent to 25 percent. The farm population for the nation as a whole remained almost constant during the thirties; but the west north-central states—Minnesota, Iowa, Missouri, North Dakota, South Dakota, Nebraska, and Kansas—lost 7.3 percent of their farm population during the ten-year period, the highest rate of loss for any similar region in the country.

Actually, this loss was not steady. After a large drop in 1930, farm people stopped moving out, and some city people even went back to the farm during the next two years of depression in the cities. Then, however, the net out-migration started again, picking up speed rapidly until 1937, then falling off—but not stopping during the rest of the decade.

The effect of extreme economic conditions on the farms in the Northern Plains, and even more so in the transition area, is shown in Table 13. The rate of farm out-migration was two or three times as high in these four states as in the north-central region, and even higher in the transition area. Even though the Northern Plains showed slight increases in urban population during this time, and the transition area

TABLE 13.   CHANGES IN POPULATION IN THE NORTHERN PLAINS STATES AND IN THE TRANSITION AREA, 1930–40

| Area | 1930 Total Population | 1940 Total Population | Percent of change, 1930–40: Total | Percent of change, 1930–40: Farm |
|---|---|---|---|---|
| | (Thousands) | (Thousands) | | |
| North Dakota. . . . . . | 680.8 | 641.9 | − 5.7 | −17.5 |
| South Dakota . . . . . . | 692.8 | 643.0 | − 7.2 | −21.3 |
| Nebraska . . . . . . . . | 1,378.0 | 1,315.8 | − 4.5 | −15.0 |
| Kansas. . . . . . . . . | 1,881.0 | 1,801.0 | − 4.3 | −14.2 |
| North Dakota transition area . . . . | 386.1 | 353.4 | − 8.5 | −19.4 |
| Northern South Dakota transition area . . . . | 225.6 | 200.0 | −11.3 | −20.7 |
| South Dakota–Nebraska transition area . . . . | 456.3 | 408.9 | −10.4 | −18.5 |
| Nebraska–Northern Kansas transition area . . . . | 389.0 | 338.3 | −13.0 | −20.3 |
| Total . . . . . . | 1,457.0 | 1,300.6 | −10.8 | |

Source: U.S. Census data.

held its own, the heavy migration of farm population far outweighed them. Of course, individual counties show even more extreme trends: in the Nebraska transition area, Sherman County had a 25 percent loss in farm population between 1930–40 and Brule County, in the South Dakota transition area, had a farm population loss of 29.3 percent. Other counties had higher rates, but generally the numbers of people involved were smaller.

With the out-movement of farm people came adjustments in farm size as those who remained took control of the land. In Nebraska, the average size of farm increased from 345 to 391 acres (13 percent) between 1930 and 1940, mostly during the last five years. Surprisingly, some 2.5 million acres of land were added to production during this time. In South Dakota the increase in size of farm was 22 percent between 1935 and 1940; but it was very slight in North Dakota. For the Northern Plains as a whole, the change was 12 percent. The increases in the transition area were more dramatic.

TABLE 14.   CHANGES IN FARM ASSETS IN THE NORTHERN PLAINS STATES, 1930–40

| | 1930 | | 1935 | | 1940 | |
|---|---|---|---|---|---|---|
| | Current Dollars | 1910–14 Dollars | Current Dollars | 1910–14 Dollars | Current Dollars | 1910–14 Dollars |
| Total physical assets | 8,890 | 8,334 | 5,319 | 7,726 | 4,672 | 7,652 |
| Land . . . . . | 5,697 | 6,143 | 3,499 | 6,170 | 2,766 | 6,151 |
| Buildings . . . . | 1,316 | 691 | 942 | 597 | 789 | 477 |
| Machinery . . . | 545 | 368 | 355 | 239 | 350 | 220 |
| Livestock . . . . | 902 | 764 | 362 | 621 | 541 | 542 |
| Horses and mules | 166 | 315 | 147 | 250 | 99 | 177 |
| Other . . . . . | 736 | 449 | 215 | 371 | 442 | 365 |
| Crop inventories . . | 430 | 368 | 161 | 99 | 226 | 262 |

The financial structure of farming was different at the end of the period, as is shown in Table 14. Values of assets in both current and constant dollars are given. The current-dollar figures reflect deflation in values due to price changes, as well as changes in the assets themselves. However, by looking at the constant-dollar figures, one can see the real depreciation of buildings and the wearing out and obsolescence of machinery without the distracting influence of price movements. American farms as a whole did not show the same degree of disinvestment in assets as did those in the Northern Plains. In real terms, this disinvestment could be seen in the area in the form of vacant houses, unpainted buildings, and worn machinery. Actually, in these states, and for the average farmer, the loss of resources through deterioration offset the average increase in value gained by the addition of land to farm-units.

Our final comment is about technology. Despite the depression, and especially after 1937, the beginnings of the technological advance that was to characterize future times had become apparent. The most obvious evidence is the substitution of tractors for horse power. The number of tractors in the United States rose from 920,000 in 1930 to 1,445,000 in 1940, an increase of 59 percent. During the same years, the decline in horses and mules amounted to 28 percent nationally, and to 43 percent in the Northern Plains states. Meanwhile, the number of combines tripled and the number of cornpickers increased sixfold. These changes meant greater labor productivity. Between 1920 and 1939, the increase in output per worker in farming had been 37 percent in the United States, and 33 percent in the west north-central states. However, most of this occurred after 1934.

# CHAPTER 6

# War and Prosperity

HAD Pike and Long been able to see the Plains country in 1940, after nearly ten years of drought and depression, the view might well have justified their pessimistic forecasts. Abandoned farmsteads, the dilapidated condition of fences and occupied buildings, the still-visible signs of drifted soil, and the numerous dead trees were mute evidence of the lack of general prosperity within the area and the treachery of the climate.

The Northern Plains was struggling to get back on its feet. Recovery was particularly difficult in those areas where precipitation continued at below-average levels. There, crop production and incomes continued to be low. Abandonment of seeded winter wheat acreage was heavy at the turn of the decade, running as high as 80 or 90 percent in some counties in individual years. Meanwhile, farm costs were rising. At the same time, for the country as a whole, farm production was increasing more rapidly than demand. Although prices received by farmers had partially recovered by 1940, they were still below what they had been in 1930.

### REDUCED FARM LABOR SUPPLY AND MECHANIZATION

The out-migration of population in the 1930's left the Northern Plains with a greatly reduced supply of labor in farming communities, especially in the transition area. In contrast to the heavily populated industrial areas, where industrial workers sought to increase their incomes by working part-time at other jobs during off hours, there were few industries of any consequence in the Northern Plains—and hence no need of part-time help from those who were "fully" employed by industry on a 40-hour-week basis.

Farm labor supplies were depleted further by the military draft. Farm operators who were left were faced not only with the job of carrying on their own operations but also with the opportunity of taking over some of the land given up by those leaving farming. In order to accomplish all of this, some adjustments had to be made. With more land and fewer men, a shift to tractor mechanization became a must. The combination of improved financial conditions, the opportunity for increasing earnings through expanded operations, and the need for taking care of more land per man provided incentives for more mechanization.

The advantages of greater use of tractors and tractor equipment were fairly apparent, but there were disadvantages too. Recent experiences with drought, depression, and financial failure caused farmers to hesitate before committing themselves to the immediate capital outlay which further shifts to tractor operations would require. Moreover, cash operating expenses would be higher if the shift was made, and out-of-pocket losses would be greater in the case of severe crop failures.

Competition and the lure of potentially higher income was strong, however, and the changeover progressed at an increasingly rapid rate of speed. Capital outlays were held down by remodeling horse-drawn equipment to use behind newly acquired tractors. Conversion was virtually complete by the close of the decade, despite the delays caused by drought and depression during the late thirties and early forties, and by the rationing of farm machinery during the war years.

### Shift to Tractor Power Frees Cropland for New Uses

One of the important consequences of shifting from horses and mules to tractor power was the effect on the use made of cropland. Between 1920 and 1950 roughly 70 million acres of U.S. cropland was freed from the production of feed for horses and mules to other uses.[1] Thus, although the total amount of cropland had been relatively constant since 1920 (about the time that the numbers of horses and mules were at the peak), the equivalent of 17 percent more land was available to produce for other livestock, food grains, and fiber crops. This shift—along with decreased foreign shipments of agricultural commodities, improved weather conditions, improved soil management, increasing use of hybrid seed corn, and a moderate increase in acreage planted—resulted in growing carryovers of wheat, corn, and cotton, later recognized as important assets in the war effort.

### Impacts of War

In 1941 farm commodity prices in the United States began to reflect the war in Europe, which had been under way for more than a year. The 1941 index of all prices received by farmers averaged 24 percent higher than in 1940, and the parity ratio jumped from 81 to 93.

Economic conditions changed rapidly during the next five or six years. In fashion typical of war periods, prices received by farmers went up more rapidly than prices paid, resulting in a more favorable relationship between prices received and prices paid than at any time since 1919. Almost simultaneously, weather conditions in the Northern Plains states improved; and the overriding importance of prices and weather, both outside the control of the individual farmer, was vividly illustrated by their effect on the financial position of farmers in the transition area during the early 1940's. Foreclosures dropped off, debts were paid, and earnings went up sharply.

In some instances, families which had lost their farms through foreclosure were able to buy them back from the credit institutions which had taken them over. In general, lending institutions were anxious to get rid of the farms they had in their possession, and frequently they offered favorable terms to reputable farm families who were interested in buying. As the war continued and farm incomes remained at

---

[1] "Land Utilization: A Graphic Summary, 1960," Cooperative Report, Vol. V, Part 4, U.S. Department of Commerce (Bureau of the Census), and U.S. Department of Agriculture (Bureau of Agricultural Economics) (December, 1952), p. 16.

relatively high levels, the number of farms operated by tenants decreased as more and more tenants accumulated enough savings to buy land of their own. Land formerly operated as independent units by tenants was absorbed and became a part of larger units operated by part owners or owners.[2]

The good weather and unusually favorable price-cost relationships made it easy to make money at farming. The important thing was to be in business. Nevertheless, good management contributed to the rate of financial progress made by farm families. Alert and capable operators shifted rapidly to tractor equipment. They adopted hybrid seed corn early in the 1940's and realized substantial increases in yields as a result. Those who were livestock-minded took advantage of rising cattle prices and made good money at cattle feeding, largely as a result of unusually favorable price margins. The more optimistic risked what they had, or could borrow, to buy more land—contrary to warnings by some economists and college administrators who recalled the experiences following World War I. Those who bought land in the early forties either paid for it within a few years or greatly increased their equity.

*Inflation Sets In*

As incomes of farm and non-farm people rose, consumer buying power increased. At the same time, production of consumer goods was reduced as resources were diverted to the production of needed war materials. The stage was set for inflation.

It was apparent that some kind of controls would be needed if rapidly rising prices, due to inflation, were to be prevented. Many of the spokesmen for agriculture felt that agricultural commodities should be exempted from any price ceilings since prices received by farmers had shown little improvement prior to 1941; the parity ratio was still near 80 in 1941, about where it had been during most of the thirties. If ceilings on agricultural prices had to be imposed, they argued, they should not be set at any level lower than 110 percent of parity.

In 1941 the Office of Price Administration (OPA) was established by executive order. Its purposes included the stabilization of prices; the prevention of profiteering, hoarding, or speculation; and the determination of policies, plans, and programs for the equitable distribution of materials and commodities among competing civilian demands.[3] The Emergency Price Control Act of 1942 followed, with the same purposes.

For the most part, agriculture's viewpoint prevailed. The effectiveness of control efforts was weakened by black-market operations and by lowering of quality and/or quantity while prices were held constant. Hence indices of "legal" prices are not a fully accurate measurement of the extent of inflation. There is little question, however, that efforts of the OPA succeeded in holding prices of consumer goods down to a very marked extent, although one can only speculate on the level of prices had we not had such programs.[4] We know that prices moved up sharply when price ceilings were discontinued, and it seems logical that they might have reached even higher levels during the actual war period had there been no controls of any kind.

[2] "Farm Tenure: A Graphic Summary, 1950," Cooperative Report, Vol. V, Part 4, U.S. Department of Commerce (Bureau of the Census), and U.S. Department of Agriculture (Bureau of Agricultural Economics) (December, 1952), p. 16.

[3] "Price Control—OPA," Commerce Clearing House, pp. 47–48.

[4] For more detailed discussion of wartime policies and agencies, see Murray R. Benedict: *Farm Policies in the United States, 1790–1950* (New York: The Twentieth Century Fund, 1953).

*Black Market in Farm Machinery Thrives*

As a result of improved weather conditions and improvement in price-cost relationships, Northern Plains farmers found themselves rather suddenly in possession of greatly increased purchasing power. This, together with the fact that they had some catching up to do in the changeover to tractor equipment—and the opportunity to increase farm earnings if needed machinery could be obtained—resulted in a big demand for tractor machinery. The sharp upturn in the demand for machinery coincided with the beginning of rationing of farm machinery. It was ironical that needed machinery should become unavailable at the time these farmers were able to buy for the first time in many years. It is not surprising that black-market operators found farmers in this area ready customers for new or used machines.

*Farm Real Estate Prices Move Upward*

The prolonged drought in the Northern Plains, rising costs, and the recurring drop in prices during the late thirties caused land prices in the Northern Plains states to continue their downward trend into 1940 and 1941. The situation changed almost overnight, however, as precipitation increased and as the United States became directly involved in war.

With good crops and favorable price-cost relationships, farmers—as well as others—became interested in buying land. Owner-operators wanted to enlarge their existing units in order to increase yearly incomes, and in anticipation of the return of their sons from the service. Farmers and non-farmers looked at investments in land as a possible hedge against inflation and as a source of speculative profit. It was inevitable that land prices should rise in view of increased demand on all sides.

During the forties, farm real estate prices more than doubled in the Northern Plains states, as they did in most other parts of the United States. Prices of dry-land farms in the transition area did not go as high following World War II—in relation to World War I prices—as did land prices in general. The limiting effect of sparse rainfall, the threat of drought, and the rising costs of operation caused would-be buyers to be more conservative in the prices they offered than after World War I.

The end of the war and the removal of price ceilings heralded another upward surge in prices and farm incomes. Prices received by farmers increased by one-third from 1945 to 1947, bringing the parity ratio to 115—the highest level since 1918—and net farm earnings to an all-time high. Although prices received moved higher in 1948, prices paid by farmers moved up even more, and the parity ratio dropped to 110. The peak of prosperity for the farmer was over, although the next several years were still comparatively good. The first servicemen to return to civilian life and farming enjoyed several years of favorable price relationships, and, for the most part, a number of reasonably good crop years.

## CAPITAL REQUIREMENTS HIGHER

The returning servicemen found capital requirements for farming considerably higher than when they went into the service (see Table 15). Machinery prices increased by 17 percent from 1941 to 1946, livestock prices were 75 percent higher,

TABLE 15. CHANGES IN FARM SIZE AND CAPITAL INVESTMENT FOR SELECTED
TYPES OF FARMS, 1937–41 AND 1956–58

| | 1937–41 | 1947–49 | 1957–58 |
|---|---|---|---|
| | HOG-BEEF FATTENING FARMS—CORN-BELT | | |
| Acres in farm . . . . . . . | 178 | 192 | 207 |
| Total capital, Jan. 1 . . . . . | $20,380 | $46,930 | $65,905 |
| Land & buildings . . . . . | 14,100 | 26,950 | 42,855 |
| Machinery & equipment . . | 1,840 | 4,100 | 7,070 |
| Livestock . . . . . . . . . | 2,810 | 9,940 | 9,595 |
| Crops, feed, seed . . . . . | 1,630 | 5,940 | 5,385 |
| Cash expenditures . . . . . . | 3,222 | 9,816 | 13,856 |
| | WHEAT, SMALL GRAIN, LIVESTOCK— NORTHERN PLAINS | | |
| Acres in farm . . . . . . . | 497 | 621 | 702 |
| Total capital, Jan. 1 . . . . . . | $11,610 | $31,090 | $49,025 |
| Land & buildings . . . . . . | 8,190 | 17,050 | 29,420 |
| Machinery & equipment . . . | 1,660 | 5,430 | 10,395 |
| Livestock . . . . . . . . . | 1,020 | 2,610 | 2,885 |
| Crops, feed, seed . . . . . | 740 | 6,000 | 6,325 |
| Cash expenditures . . . . . . | 1,614 | 5,104 | 5,607 |
| | WHEAT, CORN, LIVESTOCK— NORTHERN PLAINS | | |
| Acres in farm . . . . . . . | 427 | 460 | 504 |
| Total capital, Jan. 1 . . . . . | $11,900 | $30,600 | $50,060 |
| Land & buildings . . . . . . | 8,680 | 17,130 | 28,420 |
| Machinery & equipment . . . | 1,210 | 4,500 | 8,965 |
| Livestock . . . . . . . . . | 1,300 | 4,390 | 7,925 |
| Crops, feed, seed . . . . . | 710 | 4,580 | 4,750 |
| Cash expenditures . . . . . . | 1,431 | 4,336 | 4,443 |
| | WHEAT, ROUGHAGE, LIVESTOCK— NORTHERN PLAINS | | |
| Acres in farm . . . . . . . | 562 | 687 | 792 |
| Total capital, Jan. 1 . . . . . . | $8,690 | $27,630 | $44,665 |
| Land & buildings . . . . . . | 6,420 | 14,710 | 26,065 |
| Machinery & equipment . . . | 1,060 | 4,030 | 8,475 |
| Livestock . . . . . . . . . | 800 | 3,990 | 4,915 |
| Crops, feed, seed . . . . . | 410 | 4,900 | 5,210 |
| Cash expenditures . . . . . . | 1,306 | 4,363 | 4,604 |

Source: *Farm Costs and Returns*, USDA Research Service Information Bulletin 176 (rev.),
August, 1959.

and land prices had gone up 60–75 percent. Likewise the costs of operation had also
increased considerably with increases in general price levels. Not only had operating
expenses gone up, but a larger proportion of these expenses involved cash expenditures.
The same was true of living expenses. Under dry-land conditions, such as those in the
Northern Plains, the relatively high cash costs were particularly significant, for in the
case of drought the chances of actual out-of-pocket losses were greater. Some of the
flexibility of horse-powered farming and kerosene-lighted houses had been lost, and
risks had been increased, as farming became more commercialized.

In effect, some of the more conservative aspects of farming and farm living had been laid aside in a new version of an old game; the stakes were higher than they had been before. If everything went well, a farm family could expect to make more than under the old scheme of things, but if drought, hail, disease, or heavy insect damage struck, there was less likelihood of surviving the experience unscathed. The proverbial belt could not be tightened as readily, nor as much, under the new rules.

Where crop production depends on the unpredictable ups and downs of weather around a critical level, high cash operating costs soon spell financial loss in years when rainfall or weather conditions are much below average, especially if several such years should occur in succession. Such an unfortunate occurrence can easily be disastrous to the farmer who must meet substantial fixed principal and interest payments, particularly if he does not have a substantial initial equity.

### BIG INCREASE IN LABOR EFFICIENCY

One of the most remarkable things that has taken place in agriculture is the big increase in output per man and per man-hour in the years since 1940. In 1940, one U.S. farm worker produced enough for himself and ten other people; by 1949 he could produce enough for himself and fourteen others. A comparison of output per hour shows an even greater increase, 66 percent for the United States as a whole, between 1939–40 and 1949–50. During the same years, output per man-hour in the Northern Plains states increased by more than 100 percent, a larger increase than for any other group of states.[5] This large increase in efficiency reflects the comparatively low level of productivity in 1939–40 (partly as a result of drought), the large out-movement of farm population during the forties, and the associated increase in size of farm.

### POPULATION MOVEMENTS

Because of limited industrial development in the Northern Plains, job opportunities for those who left the farm during the forties were comparatively scarce within the area itself. Some found jobs in the larger cities along the eastern edge of the region, but many moved elsewhere. From 1940 to 1950 the Northern Plains states experienced an average decline in farm population of 19.5 percent while their total population increased by about 2 percent. The latter figure may be compared to a 15 percent increase for the United States as a whole.

By the end of the decade, population density in the Northern Plains had declined to an average of 4.5 persons per square mile, only slightly more than half of that for the United States as a whole. The rapidly diminishing population in the rural areas served to create and to emphasize serious problems for schools and churches serving rural areas. Likewise, costs of maintaining roads and of other services increased on a per capita basis since fixed costs now had to be borne by fewer tax payers. It was during this decade that people first began to give serious thought to the need and the possibility of consolidating schools and churches.

[5] "Changes in Farm Production and Efficiency: A Summary Report," USDA Statistical Bulletin 233 (1958), p. 24.

# CHAPTER 7

# The 1950's: Peace, Drought, and Adjustments

FARM PRODUCTION increased much more rapidly than population in the early 1940's. After that, it simply kept pace with population growth, but the basis for future surpluses had been established (Figure 18). By the end of World War II, surpluses of agricultural products had once more begun to accumulate. Korean War requirements helped to reduce them, but only temporarily. Carryover stocks that had loomed over the product market were soon reflected in lower prices to farmers, yet costs continued to rise—largely owing to inflation but also because of higher taxes and the increased use of fertilizer, machinery, and other purchased inputs. For the first time since the early forties, farmers became generally aware of a price-cost squeeze.

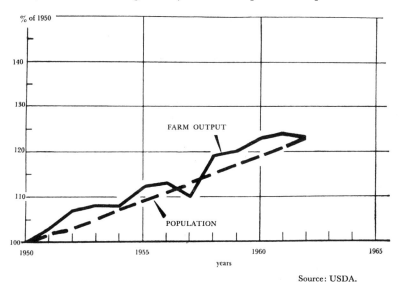

Source: USDA.

FIG. 18.   FARM OUTPUT AND POPULATION CHANGES, 1950–62

### IMPACT OF NEW TECHNOLOGIES

Farmers' use of purchased inputs increased substantially from 1940 to 1960 while that of non-purchased inputs declined, especially after 1944. By 1959, farmers in the

United States were purchasing 63 percent of their inputs, compared to less than half in 1940. The real shift to purchased inputs is somewhat overstated in value terms since prices rose more in the 1950's than those of non-purchased items (Figure 19). However, power and machinery made up 22 percent of all inputs in 1959, compared to 10 percent in 1940. We had four times as many cornpickers on farms as in 1945, more than fourteen times as many forage harvesters, and more than 15 times as many pickup balers. These items, as well as fertilizers and pesticides, came from non-farm sources.

This increase in the cash costs of operation in relation to income not only intensified the need for capital but also heightened risk in areas—such as the Northern Plains states—where weather, and hence yields and income, are subject to wide variations. A few successive years of drought, coupled with high cash costs of operation, could

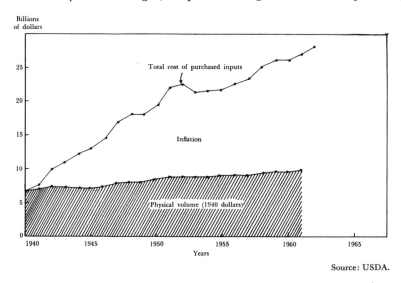

FIG. 19.   FARM INPUTS IN THE U.S. AS MEASURED IN PHYSICAL TERMS AND CURRENT DOLLARS, 1940–61

severely cripple the capital and credit position of farmers who might be struggling to get established and who had comparatively small initial equities.

Nevertheless, these changes in price-cost relationships did not seem to dampen the upward trend in farm output. As indicated in Figure 18, total farm output in the United States increased by approximately 25 percent from 1940 to 1950, and by about the same proportion during the 1950's. By 1960, the average American farm worker was supplying the needs of twenty-six other persons, compared to fourteen persons ten years earlier. Output per man-hour in 1960 was more than two and a half times its 1944 level.

Farmers who had sufficient moisture available, either in the form of natural precipitation or irrigation water, increased their use of the newer technologies—especially commercial fertilizer—to increase production and lower their total cost per unit of output. Farmers with inadequate and undependable moisture supplies were at a

TABLE 16. COMPARISON OF FERTILIZER USE BETWEEN 1939 AND 1954
IN THE U.S., THE CORN BELT* AND THE NORTHERN PLAINS

| | United States | | Four Corn-Belt States | | Four Northern Plains States | |
|---|---|---|---|---|---|---|
| | 1939 | 1954 | 1939 | 1954 | 1939 | 1954 |
| Tons of fertilizer used . . . | 8,249,000 | 22,283,975 | 690,000 | 4,033,680 | | 543,663 |
| Percent of farmers using . . | 38.3 | 61.2 | 30.8 | 67.8 | 2.1 | 32.3 |
| Tons used per farm†. . . . | 2.9 | 6.5 | 2.6 | 7.7 | 1.7 | 4.7 |
| *Corn* | | | | | | |
| Percent of acres fertilized . . | | | | 64.5 | | 19.9 |
| Amount per acre . . . . . | | | | 232 | | 137 |
| Percent of total fertilizer used | | | | 57.0 | | 33.2 |
| *Wheat* | | | | | | |
| Percent of acres fertilized . . | | | | 83.5 | | 14.1 |
| Amount per acre . . . . . | | | | 134 | | 96 |
| Percent of total fertilizer used | | | | 12.8 | | 25.1 |

\* Iowa, Illinois, Indiana, Ohio.
† Per farm using fertilizer.
Source: "Fertilizer Summary Data," Tennessee Valley Authority, September, 1958.

comparative disadvantage in the use of technologies that depended on moisture for optimum benefits. As is indicated in Table 16, a much smaller proportion of the farmers in the Northern Plains states were using commercial fertilizer in 1954 than in four of the principal corn-belt states. Moreover, the amount used per farm and per acre was smaller. Nearly two-thirds of the corn acreage and more than 80 percent of the wheat acreage was fertilized in the four corn-belt states, compared with one-fifth of the corn acreage and about one-seventh of the wheat acreage in the Northern Plains states.

The increase in fertilizer utilization is understated by a consideration of tonnage data alone, since the nutrient content was also on the rise. Most of the improvement in nutrient content took place after 1950.[1]

By the late 1950's, crop yields had increased substantially. Most of the increase can be attributed to (1) improved varieties, (2) increased use of commercial fertilizer, (3) shifting of crop production to more productive land, and (4) favorable weather conditions.[2] Rapid increases in the use of weed and insect sprays also made substantial contributions toward higher production, both on a per acre and total basis.

## CROP CONTROLS REAPPEAR

As a result of mounting surpluses and falling farm prices, acreage allotments came back into the picture in 1954. Acreages of crops grown in 1951–53 were used as a basis for assigning allotments. Farmers were free to decide whether they wished to abide by the allotments assigned them, but, to qualify for commodity credit loans, they had to stay within their allotments.

[1] Louis M. Thompson, Iver J. Johnson, John T. Pesek, Jr., and Robert H. Shaw, "Some Causes of Recent High Yields of Feed Grains," *Proceedings of the Iowa State College Feed-Livestock Workshop*, Center for Agricultural Adjustment Special Report 24, 1959, p. 16.
[2] *Ibid.*

*Corn Program*

The number of farmers who complied with corn allotments was relatively low.[3] Cash grain farmers in the corn belt were more inclined to comply than livestock farmers. The latter fed a considerable portion of their corn crop to livestock and were much less interested in commodity credit loans as a "market" for their crop. Those who complied used the acres taken out of corn for the production of other feed grains: soybeans, wheat, and hay.

Restrictions on corn acreage (Table 17) spurred farmers who chose to comply to use still more commercial fertilizer, since there was no restriction on the number of bushels that could be marketed from the alloted acreage. By substituting fertilizer for land, many succeeded in maintaining their total production of corn. In addition, they increased their production of other crops (Table 18).

Acreage allotments for corn were assigned only to commercial corn counties.[4] The producer who complied with his allotment could either obtain a commodity credit loan on his crop or sell on the open market. Thus he was assured of a minimum price

TABLE 17.   ACREAGE HARVESTED IN U.S., 1950–58

| Years | Corn and Wheat (Acres Harvested) | | Oats, Barley, Grain Sorghum* and Soybeans† (Acres Harvested) | |
|---|---|---|---|---|
| | (Acres) | Percent (1951–53 = 100) | (Acres) | Percent (1951–53 = 100) |
| 1951–53 . . . . | 147,657,000 | 100 | 71,946,000 | 100 |
| 1954 . . . . . . | 134,542,000 | 91 | 89,098,000 | 124 |
| 1955 . . . . . . | 126,657,000 | 86 | 92,961,000 | 129 |
| 1956 . . . . . . | 125,015,000 | 85 | 83,613,000 | 116 |
| 1957 . . . . . . | 115,618,000 | 70 | 95,456,000 | 133 |
| 1958 . . . . . . | 125,271,000 | 85 | 90,091,000 | 125 |
| 1959 . . . . . . | 133,683,000 | 91 | 84,354,000 | 117 |

\* Grain, syrup, and silage.
† Soybeans for beans.
Source: *USDA Agricultural Statistics*, 1962.

for his corn crop. If the market price remained below the "loan rate," as was usually the case, the farmer had the privilege of forfeiting his corn in settlement of his "loan." On the other hand, if the market price went above the "loan rate," he had the privilege of paying off the loan and selling his corn at the higher price.

In non-commercial counties, corn producers were free to produce as much corn as they liked. Loans were also available to these producers, but at a lower rate.

Late in 1956 a new feature was added to the price-support program for corn when supports were announced for non-allotment–grown corn in commercial corn counties. The loan rate announced was $1.25 per bushel (national average), compared with $1.50 for corn grown under allotment. Loans were again available on non-allotment corn in 1957 and 1958.

[3] *Ibid.*
[4] A commercial corn county was defined, at that time, as one in which 25,000 acres of corn or more were grown. Presently, no differentiation is made between counties.

TABLE 18. TOTAL PRODUCTION OF WHEAT AND FEED GRAIN CROPS IN 1951–53 TO 1959

| Year | Corn | Oats | Barley | Grain Sorghum | All Feed Grains* | Wheat |
|---|---|---|---|---|---|---|
| | | | (Millions of Bushels) | | | |
| 1951–53 . . . | 2,830 | 1,216 | 244 | 123 | 113.6 | 1,156 |
| 1954 . . . . . | 2,708 | 1,410 | 379 | 236 | 119.5 | 984 |
| 1955 . . . . . | 2,873 | 1,496 | 403 | 243 | 126.6 | 937 |
| 1956 . . . . . | 3,075 | 1,151 | 377 | 205 | 125.5 | 1,005 |
| 1957 . . . . . | 3,045 | 1,290 | 443 | 568 | 138.5 | 955 |
| 1958 . . . . . | 3,356 | 1,401 | 477 | 581 | 150.8 | 1,457 |
| 1959 . . . . . | 3,824 | 1,052 | 422 | 555 | 157.2 | 1,121 |

* Millions of tons.
Source: *USDA Agricultural Statistics*, 1962.

In 1959, acreage allotments on corn were withdrawn. Loans were made available to all farmers at $1.12 per bushel, the national average. This compared with $1.06 for non-allotment–grown corn and $1.30 for corn grown under allotment in 1958. Since only 11 or 12 percent of the corn grown in 1958 was under allotments, this meant in effect that support prices were higher in 1959 than in 1958.

Support prices for other feed grains in 1959 were disproportionately low in relation to corn. As a result of the withdrawal of acreage restrictions, the higher support for non-allotment corn, and the relatively low price supports for other feed grains, acreage of oats and grain sorghum were reduced while corn acreage was increased in 1959.

### Wheat Program

Acreage allotments for wheat were declared again in 1954 and have remained in effect since that time. These allotments, established by the Secretary of Agriculture, applied to all farmers in states designated as commercial wheat-producing states, those having 25,000 acres of wheat or more. (This differentiation is no longer made.) Commodity credit loans were available to all producers in commercial producing states who stayed within their allotments. In non-commercial states, allotments did not apply, and producers in these states were eligible for loans—but only at 75 percent of the level in commercial states.

Marketing quotas for wheat were also introduced with the 1954 crop. Like the acreage allotments, they did not apply in non-commercial states. In commercial states, producers who had allotments of less than 15 acres could disregard their allotments and plant up to 15 acres. By so doing, they became ineligible for a loan but could obtain a marketing certificate for their entire crop without any penalties.

Farmers in commercial wheat-producing states who had allotments of more than 15 acres could not market wheat produced on acres in excess of their allotments without being subject to a penalty equal to 45 percent of parity for every bushel marketed in excess of those bushels produced on their alloted acres. They had only one other option: if they overplanted their allotment, they could store the wheat from these excess acres, furnish acceptable proof to the local ASC office that such wheat was in storage, and then obtain a marketing card which would permit them to market the wheat grown on their alloted acres. In years when yields dropped below the long-time average, so that their actual production was less than their "normal" production, they could market part of the "excess" wheat produced in prior years—enough to bring their total marketings for that year up to their "normal" quota.[5]

Later a provision was made whereby a farmer could grow up to 30 acres of wheat without any penalties, provided he fed his production to livestock.

Starting in 1959, under the Anfuso Amendment, wheat farmers who overplanted their allotments became liable to an additional penalty. Under this provision, allotments for a given year would depend on a farmer's acreage "history" during the preceding three years. Those who planted within their allotment were credited with an annual "history" equal to the acreage grown in 1951–53, called their "base." Those who overplanted were penalized not only in terms of 45 percent of the parity price for each bushel of wheat marketed from non-allotted acres but also in terms of "history." Instead of maintaining his base acreage as of 1951–53, a violating producer would have his base reduced. Allotted acres were substituted for actual acres in one of the base years for purposes of establishing a new base acreage. Under this method of determining history for allotment purposes, the penalties became increasingly severe with repeated violations.

Controls have apparently been more successful in reducing wheat acreage than that of corn (Table 19). Actual production of wheat has varied, from year to year,

TABLE 19.   ACREAGE OF CORN* AND WHEAT HARVESTED IN U.S., 1951–53 TO 1959

| Year | Corn (1,000 acres) | Percent of 1951–53 | All wheat (1,000 acres) | Percent of 1951–53 |
|---|---|---|---|---|
| 1951–53 . . . | 80,709 | 100 | 66,947 | 100 |
| 1954 . . . . . | 80,186 | 99 | 54,356 | 81 |
| 1955 . . . . . | 79,367 | 98 | 47,290 | 71 |
| 1956 . . . . . | 75,247 | 93 | 49,768 | 74 |
| 1957 . . . . . | 71,864 | 89 | 43,754 | 65 |
| 1958 . . . . . | 72,224 | 89 | 53,047 | 79 |
| 1959 . . . . . | 81,902 | 101 | 51,781 | 77 |

\* Includes grain, silage, and forage.
Source: *USDA Agricultural Statistics*, 1962.

around the amount produced in the base period. Average annual production has been 5 to 10 percent below production during the base years. Actual production of corn, however, has been increasing rather steadily since the base period, in spite of the reduction in acreage. During the years 1954–59, average annual production was 13 percent higher than during the base years 1951–53.

### The Soil Bank Program

The soil bank program, authorized under the Agricultural Act of 1956, was an attempt to control production of allotment crops by a different method. There were two parts to this program, the acreage reserve and the conservation reserve.

The *acreage reserve* provided for direct payments to a farmer if he planted less than his permitted acreage of allotment crops. Payments were based on the productivity

[5] Charles W. Nauheim, Warren R. Bailey, and Della Merrick, *Wheat Production*, ARS, USDA Agricultural Information Bulletin 179, pp. 58–62.

of the soil and the number of acres taken out of production. No crop could be harvested or grazed on the land taken out of production during the year, except under specially designated emergency conditions. This program was available to producers of both wheat and corn in 1956 and 1957.

In the drought area of the Great Plains, participation was heavier—because of drought conditions—than it might have been otherwise. A guaranteed income per acre was provided by the program at a time when moisture conditions were generally poor. The chances of producing a crop that would net as much per acre were slim.

Farmers were paid a higher rate per acre for leaving the same acres out of production the second year. However, many took advantage of the opportunity to plant sweet clover on the "acreage reserve" land in an effort to build up a supply of nitrogen for a crop to be grown on these acres in the following year. Others chose to use the acreage reserve acres as fallow land, in the hope of accumulating both nitrogen and moisture for the crop to follow. Land that was dry and without cover when placed in the acreage reserve was particularly susceptible to wind erosion, and, to this extent, posed a threat to the conservation of soil resources.

The *conservation reserve* was an attempt to control production of non-allotment crops. Farmers could enter into contract agreements with the government to take certain specified acres out of production for specified periods of time (three to ten years). Some kind of cover had to be established and certain conservation measures had to be carried out. Payments were made at specified rates each year during which the contract was in effect. In order to encourage permanent retirement of such land from crop production, additional payments were made to farmers for up to 80 percent of the cost of establishing permanent grass cover or of carrying out conservation practices. Higher rates of payment were made in those instances where all the cropland in a particular farm was placed in the "conservation reserve." Participation in the conservation reserve program reached a peak in 1960, when the equivalent of 9 percent of the harvested acres were under contract in the Northern Plains states.

A third variation of the soil bank was introduced in 1958, on an experimental basis in four states: Illinois, Maine, Nebraska and Tennessee. Under this program, farmers were invited to submit "bids" indicating the amount per acre they would be willing to accept as an annual rental for all their cropland. Had the bid been accepted, all the cropland in the farm would have been placed under contract for a specified period of time. Interest in this program by Nebraska farmers was much higher than anticipated, but the program never went into effect. Reasons for the withdrawal of the program were never adequately explained. The stated reason was that the bids were too high to be acceptable—but a review of some of the bids offered in Nebraska indicated that many were quite realistic.

There may have been other reasons that have never been fully disclosed. Businessmen in rural areas were concerned about the possibility that the program might meet with general acceptance and thus pose a serious threat to the continued existence of their businesses. Widespread acceptance of such a program would have presented similar but less severe problems to public schools, rural churches, and utility companies.

It cannot be known, of course, how many farm families would have actually left their farms had this program become operative. At least a part of the adjustment that would have occurred as the result of such a program would simply represent a speeding up of changes that were bound to come eventually.

## THE GREAT PLAINS PROGRAM

With the advent of drought in Texas and New Mexico in 1950, its spread northward, and the progressively less favorable price-cost situation, more and more concern was again directed toward the overall economy of the Plains. A special conference was called at Denver, May 31–June 2, 1955, by the U.S. Department of Agriculture. Attending were Plains governors, state agricultural commissioners, deans and directors of land-grant colleges, and representatives of USDA and other federal agencies.

Out of this conference came a series of recommendations for a long-range program for the Plains. The report recommended the acceleration of soil surveys, land classification, and water surveys in the Plains; changes in credit policy and practices, including expansion of intermediate and long-term credit, and establishment of a permanent emergency credit program; changes in and expansion of the crop-insurance programs; changes to bring acreage allotments and price supports into line with desirable long-run land-use adjustments; aids to the adjustment of land use in severe problem areas; expanded research, particularly directed at dry-land areas; and expanded educational programs in the Plains. It called for expansion of conservation measures, particularly those necessary to bring about land-use adjustment, and for changes in legislation enabling the ACP to make forward commitments with respect to cost sharing in the establishment of permanent cover.

An outgrowth of this conference was a message to Congress from President Eisenhower, on January 11, 1956, entitled "Program for the Great Plains."[6] It included many of the recommendations made at the Denver meeting. It called for the acceleration of soil survey work in the drought area of the Southern Plains, for the acceleration of technical assistance to farmers and ranchers for soil and water conservation, for cost sharing for new conservation practices, for expansions in the credit program of the Farmers Home Administration to cover financing of reseeding, erosion control practices, irrigation development, emergency purchases of supplies in drought areas, and loan refinancing. Expansion in federal crop insurance was recommended. The importance of weather research was noted, and expansion in agricultural research on problems particularly characteristic of the Plains was suggested.

## THE GREAT PLAINS CONSERVATION PROGRAM

Another result of the Denver conference and the renewed interest in Great Plains problems was the Great Plains Conservation Program, PL 1021, which was passed by Congress in July of 1956. It was designed "to amend the Soil Conservation and Domestic Allotment Act and the Agricultural Adjustment Act of 1938."[7] Under this law the Secretary was authorized

---

[6] *Program for the Great Plains*, USDA Miscellaneous Publication 709, 1956, pp. 1–11.

[7] *United States Statutes at Large—84th Congress, 2d Session, 1956*, Vol. 70 U.S. Government Printing Office, 1957, p. 115.

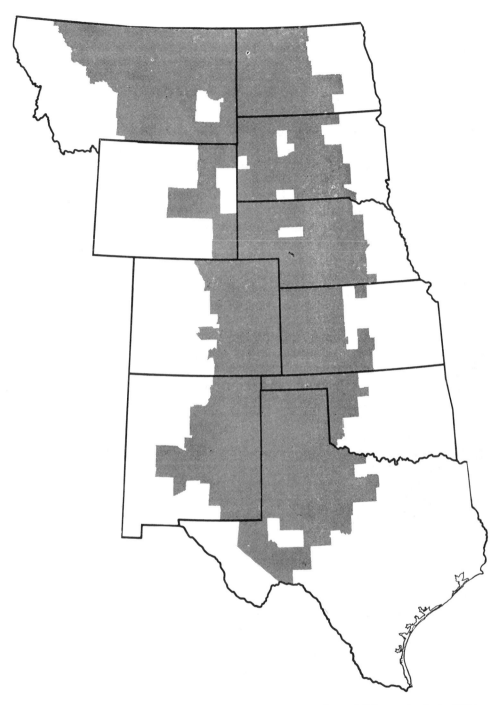

Source: Soil Conservation Service, USDA.

Fig. 20. Area Approved for the Great Plains Conservation Program (as of Sept. 30, 1960)

... to enter into contracts of not to exceed ten years with producers in the Great Plains. ... Such contracts ... [were] designed to assist farm and ranch operators to make, in orderly progression over a period of years, changes in their cropping systems and land uses which were needed to conserve the soil and water resources of their farms and ranches and to install the soil and water conservation measures needed under such change systems.

The program was to apply to the designated Great Plains area (Figure 20).

As set up by SCS, which was assigned its administration, the Great Plains Conservation Program called for complete programs of soil and water conservation for whole farms and ranches, with cost sharing contracts of three to ten years in duration for the adoption of the practices called for. These practices included the seeding of marginal cropland to grass, erosion control, and wind erosion. The farm plans called for a time schedule for land-use changes and installation of these practices, a major innovation. The cost-sharing rates payable by the government could not exceed 80 percent of the cost of the practices.

There were no restrictions on the farmer's use of land that was placed in either the conservation reserve or the Great Plains conservation program *after* the contract period was ended. It could be plowed up and used as cropland again, if the farmer so desired.

### Federal Crop-Insurance Program

One of the greatest problems confronting farmers in the Plains is the risk of crop failure due to the great variability in moisture conditions. Although Plains agriculture does not have a corner on all the risks in farming, it has more than its share of those that are weather-induced. As previously noted (Chapter 5), federal crop insurance was introduced in 1939. Its purpose was to protect the farmer against all natural hazards between the time the crop was planted and the time it was harvested. (Coverage for different crops is being added gradually.) Grain sorghums were included for the first time in 1959, on an experimental basis, in five counties in the Great Plains.

Over 56,000 policyholders in the Great Plains held policies amounting to more than $60 million in 1958. During the years 1939–57, indemnities of $108,731,088 were paid to Great Plains farmers. Premiums paid in during this same time amounted to $110,380,324. The net cost to farmers amounted to $86,802 a year.

In 1956, when the soil bank program came into being, crop insurance was dropped in fourteen counties of the dust bowl area. Premiums collected in these counties had not been in line with loss experience. Premiums collected amounted to $9 million, compared with indemnity payments of $27 million. A more realistic insurance rate had to be determined for these counties, so the program was halted there until this could be done.[8]

### Drought and High Operating Costs Hit Hard

In 1952, serious drought conditions occurred in the Southern Plains. These conditions persisted and spread over a large part of the Great Plains during the next four years. According to the U.S. Weather Bureau, the 1952–56 drought in the

---

[8] Earll H. Nikkell, "Federal All-Risk Crop Insurance in the Great Plains," *Proceedings* of the Great Plains Agricultural Council, 1958, pp. 97–106. Also see Tables 8 and 9 and Figure 11.

Southern Plains was one of the most severe since the beginning of reliable records.[9] Moreover, upward trends in capital requirements for farming and ranching made its economic effects more apparent and more severe than in the past.

Average capital investment per farm or ranch was roughly two and half to three and a half times as large in the Plains in the early 1950's as it was at the end of the drought period during the thirties. Operating expenses also had sharply increased. Even more critical was the rise in cash expenses of farm operation, as much as 150 percent.[10] Because financial outlays were much higher, the risk of financial loss was correspondingly greater.

*Credit Problems Come to the Front*

The combination of high costs and drought was disastrous to farm families who had only a small equity in their business. Many found their money and credit exhausted before the drought was ended. Those who saw better opportunities for jobs elsewhere sold out, salvaging what equity they could. The number of farm sales ran high; young families, tenants, and those who had high principal and interest payments to meet were particularly hard hit.

Farmers in their forties and fifties who had to quit found it especially difficult to adjust to their new situations. Most of these people were too old to compete advantageously in the labor market. Few of them had much knowledge or training for any work other than farming. Relatively little information was available to them as to where jobs could be had, as to living conditions, etc. Their financial needs tended to be at least as great as at any other time in the family cycle. Despite these limitations, many of them had little choice except to find a job of some kind off the farm and away from their home community.

Machinery has never been accepted by credit institutions as desirable collateral; hence crops and livestock form the backbone of the tenant's claim to credit. The drought and near or complete crop failures severely taxed the credit of the tenant who depended largely on crops for income. Good wheat crops in the summer of 1956, coupled with the cooperative attitudes of lenders, made it possible for many to hang on. Others were less fortunate.

Similarly, the tenant who depended largely on cattle as a basis of credit found himself in trouble. As the drought spread, pastures and ranges were severely strained. It soon became evident that many farm pastures, overstocked even during periods of normal rainfall, would be unable to supply enough feed for the roughage-consuming livestock on hand. Hay was scarce and high-priced. Few farmers had any appreciable amount of feed reserves. Herds had to be reduced. The extent of the required reduction on a particular farm depended on the condition of the pasture at the onset of drought, existing stocking rates, supplemental feed available, local moisture conditions, and the immediate need for money. Some sold only a few head, while others found it necessary to sell entire herds.

Those with breeding herds were more reluctant to sell than those who handled

[9] "Drouth," a report on drought in the Great Plains and the Southwest (October, 1958), prepared under the direction of the Special Assistant to the President for Public Works Planning, p. 12.

[10] *Farm Costs and Returns, Commercial Family-Operated Farms by Type and Location*, ARS, USDA Agricultural Information Bulletin 176, June, 1957.

TABLE 20.   EFFECT OF DROUGHT ON TENANT'S EQUITY

|  | 1951 | 1954 | 1956 |
|---|---|---|---|
| Assets |  |  |  |
| 20 cows . . . . . . | $ 5,000 | $ 2,500 |  |
| 15 cows . . . . . . |  |  | $1,650 |
| Crops on hand . . . | 2,500 | 2,500 | 600 |
| Machinery . . . . . | 5,000 | 4,800 | 3,000 |
| Total . . . . . | $12,500 | $9,800 | $5,250 |
| Liabilities |  |  |  |
| Debts . . . . . . . | $3,000 | $1,000 | $2,500 |
| Net Worth . . . . . | $9,500 | $8,800 | $2,750 |

Source: University of Nebraska Agricultural Experiment Station.

steers. In either case, they were inclined to hold on longer than they should have—hoping that next week or next month would bring rain and make it possible to keep their cattle.

The tenant who might have been well off had he sold out in 1951, now found that he had little basis for credit. Table 20 shows how a tenant's equity and basis for credit might have been affected as a result of drought and price changes, both of which were largely beyond his control.

Credit institutions differed in their reactions to these situations. For the most part, they made sincere efforts to help their clients weather the drought. Borrowers were permitted to postpone principal payments in many instances. Lenders went beyond their usual limits in carrying a borrower as long as the borrower and his family evidenced a willingness and determination to confine their spending to essentials. Few credit institutions were interested in getting into the farming business through foreclosures.

The usual nongovernmental sources of credit were scarcely adequate, however, to meet the total credit needs of farmers confronted by a combination of drought, high cash operating expenses, and falling prices for commodities to be sold. Commercial banks and production credit associations referred their borrowers to the Farmers Home Administration in instances where they felt they could no longer legitimately carry a borrower's loan. Federal legislation allowed FHA to make emergency loans to established farmers who could not get credit elsewhere.

Beginning in 1954, counties could apply for drought relief. If the application was approved, and many were in the Great Plains, farmers in that county could obtain grain and hay for breeding livestock at reduced prices through local FHA offices.

### Drought Spurs Irrigation Development

Desperation drove farmers to explore new possibilities. Deep-well irrigation held promise for those who were fortunate enough to have underground water in sufficient quantity to justify an irrigation well. But the development of irrigation requires capital in relatively large amounts. Insurance companies, production credit associations, commercial banks, and FHA devised special kinds of loans for the purpose of financing irrigation development. If necessary, insurance companies could and did lend money for irrigation development—over and above their usual limits on real estate.

Similarly, FHA could make a "soil and water conservation loan" to a farmer who could not obtain such credit elsewhere. This type of loan could be used for irrigation development, to carry out approved soil conservation practices, and to develop or improve permanent pastures.[11]

The outcome of irrigation ventures is not always certain. No doubt, some acted unwisely in going into irrigation. Failure to explore all the angles, such as depth to water, probable amount of water available, proper equipment for the job, labor requirements, nature of the soil to be irrigated, etc., spelled doom for others. But far more found it to be a real salvation. Of the states in the transition area, Nebraska seems to be particularly well endowed with underground water.

## New Development in Research and Education

Experiment stations and the U.S. Department of Agriculture continued their search for new ideas, substances, and techniques that would increase the efficiency of agricultural production. Agricultural chemistry played a prominent role in the achievements. New feed additives (such as stilbestrol), tranquilizers, systemic means of controling cattle grubs, new insect sprays, new selective weed sprays, gaseous and liquid forms of fertilizer—these are among the many new technical developments that sprang into use as the result of the combined efforts of research workers, largely in educational and governmental institutions.

The drought stimulated further interest in research directed at water conservation. Stubble-mulch farming received more attention as a means of conserving moisture and preventing erosion.

Perhaps the greatest development in the agronomic area for the Great Plains was the rapid strides made in the perfection of hybrid sorghums. By nature, grain sorghums are more flexible in their moisture requirements from the standpoint of timing, and hence are better adapted to areas with variable rainfall and semiarid climate than is corn.[12] The successful development of male sterile plants, which made hybridization of sorghums possible, was especially important to the transition-area farmer.

At the close of the 1950's, experiment stations and extension services alike were being challenged by taxpayers and farmers about how continued production research could be justified in the face of growing surpluses. Much confusion existed in the minds of farmers, consumers, and educators concerning the dilemma of agricultural price policies, mounting surpluses, and the struggle for survival among farm families.

As new technologies were introduced and adopted, dry-land farmers in the Plains became increasingly aware of the limiting effect of a scarce moisture supply. Researchers also were cognizant of the problem. At a conference in Denver, in 1955, a proposal was made to establish a regional laboratory where weather could be simulated, permitting research on crop-weather responses. Much interest has been evidenced in rain making, and interest in irrigation has been tremendous—especially during the dry years of the fifties.

With the rapid growth in new technologies, farmers and farm families were confronted with the job of keeping up with all the new information. Means of communicating ideas were changing too. Most farm homes now had radios; many had television. While these offered new avenues for getting information to farm people,

[11] "Loan Program of the Farmers Home Administration," FHA, USDA (January, 1960), No. PA360.
[12] K. W. H. Klages, *Ecological Crop Geography* (New York: Macmillan Co., 1942), p. 409.

they also offered competition. Watching an "adult western" or a favorite weekly comedy program is much more appealing to many than going to an educational meeting that is not intended to be entertaining. At any rate, county agricultural extension agents seem to find it more and more difficult to get people to attend meetings.

Like the farmer, the county agricultural agent was having difficulty in keeping up with the vast amount of new, highly technical information available. Few Plains counties could hire enough personnel to permit much specialization within a county. County agents found themselves in competition with magazines, feed dealers, fertilizer dealers, and equipment salesmen as sources of technical information. More and more, agents found that these "competitors" were as well versed on these subjects as they were.

Not only did farm people have difficulty in keeping informed, an even greater problem for many was How can we make use of this in *our* business or in *our* homes? Adoption of a new technology frequently meant the need for more capital and, perhaps, less labor. If a farm family used money for one purpose, it obviously wasn't available for another. What could and should be done with the labor freed by the adoption of a new technique? Decisions of some kind had to be made as to how resources were to be used.

### FARM AND HOME DEVELOPMENT

Extension leaders were aware of the difficulty many families have of assimilating new developments. They were aware, too, that there was a certain amount of competition between the home and the farm business for available resources. People needed help in evaluating their resources, in identifying alternatives, and in deciding on a course of action which would yield the greatest satisfaction. Various sources of information indicated that large numbers of families were not succeeding in making very high incomes.

Awareness of these situations led to the initiation of the Farm and Home Development Program within the agricultural extension service in 1954. The program was designed to help farm families (supposedly low-income families) learn how to make decisions relative to the use of their particular resources to achieve their particular goals. Although it has been commonly referred to as a "program," many administrators prefer to think of it as a means of doing extension work—a unit (farm and home) approach with emphasis on the management aspects.

Accomplishments under the program varied greatly from state to state, depending on the interpretation of objectives, the kind of work done, the enthusiasm and ability of the workers, and numerous other factors. In many states the farm families who cooperated with extension workers in the program were not the lowest-income families. To this extent, the program failed to accomplish one of its primary objectives, in the minds of many people.

By the end of the 1950's it was apparent that many administrators were even less pleased with the results. Objectives were reexamined, and the type of work done under the name of Farm and Home Development has been changing. Whether the new approaches will be more successful remains to be seen.

## Rural Development

Some parts of the United States have developed economically much more than others. Some areas have developed rapidly along industrial lines while others have developed agriculturally. Unfortunately, there are areas—especially in the southeastern United States—where neither industry nor agriculture has developed very strongly. Incomes of families—both town and country—tend to be low. In an effort to deal with situations of this kind, a new program, Rural Development, was launched in 1955. Although the agricultural extension service was actively engaged in the program in the states where Rural Development projects were located, it was not intended to be strictly an agricultural extension service program. All federal and state agencies were to be drawn in on a cooperative basis—usually under the leadership of agricultural extension—in an effort to help low-income communities or counties analyze their situation and make whatever improvements were possible.

Broadly speaking, the job of Rural Development was to do for the low-income community about the same thing as Farm and Home Development was expected to do for low-income farm families.

## Program Projection

Larger and fewer farms, more mechanization, new crop varieties, new livestock feeding techniques, rising taxes and operating costs, leasing problems, more home conveniences, changes in methods of communication, and other similar developments had brought about a vastly different situation in many parts of the country since extension first came into being. Some felt it was time for farm people to take a fresh look at themselves, at the situation in their counties, and at the direction in which agricultural extension was moving.

Out of this came Program Projection on the state and county level. Here again was an effort to get agricultural leaders to apply the decision-making process; that is, inventory and evaluate the situation at hand, identify and evaluate various alternatives, and decide on a course of future action.

On the national level, work of the national Extension Committee on Policy (ECOP) led to the "Scope" report—a somewhat detailed consideration of the future role of the agricultural extension service.

## Farm Prices and the Cost of Living

Toward the close of the 1950's, complaints were often voiced about the rising cost of living. Farmers were at times singled out as being responsible for at least a part of the increase. The publicity given to large surpluses and high price supports was undoubtedly a factor that led consumers to blame the farmer for their high grocery bills. Few consumers were aware, however, of the relationship between their grocery bills, the prices they paid for food items, and what the farmer received (Figure 21).

More packaging, higher wage rates, and higher transportation costs made for an increasing spread between what the consumer paid and what the farmer received. The amount the farmer received for food products was actually less at the close of the 1950's than it had been ten years earlier, but retail food prices failed to reflect this.

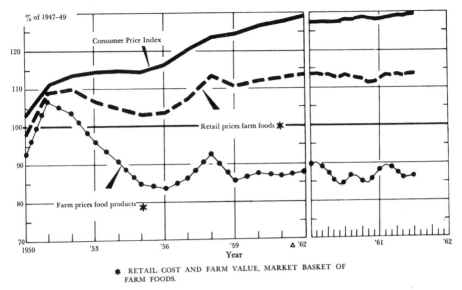

Source: *USDA Agricultural Chartbook*, 1963.

FIG. 21. CONSUMER PRICES, RETAIL FOOD PRICES, AND FARM PRICES FOR FOOD PRODUCTS, 1950–62

As a whole, farmers were hard put to hold their own in terms of income. The average incomes of commercial farms declined moderately over the period (Figure 22); in real terms—adjusted for purchasing power—the decline was still greater, leaving them in the same position as in the early forties.

Thanks to favorable weather, good crops, and good livestock prices, net farm incomes rose in 1958. This upturn probably does not presage a continued improvement during the 1960's, however. That would require some means of bringing production more nearly in line with demand.

Although farm incomes fluctuated around the 1947–49 level during the 1950's, land values continued to rise. Farmers and ranchers actively competed with each other

TABLE 21. FARM DEBTS IN RELATION TO TOTAL FARM ASSETS

|  | Total Assets | Total Indebtedness | Indebtedness as Percent of Assets |
|---|---|---|---|
|  | (Billions) | (Billions) |  |
| 1940. . . . . . | $ 48.8 | $ 9.6 | 20 |
| 1945. . . . . . | 80.6 | 7.6 | 10 |
| 1950. . . . . . | 115.7 | 10.8 | 13 |
| 1955. . . . . . | 146.7 | 15.6 | 15 |
| 1959. . . . . . | 181.3 | 20.3 | 16 |

Data from Agricultural Credit and Related Data, 1959, Agricultural Commission, American Bankers Association.

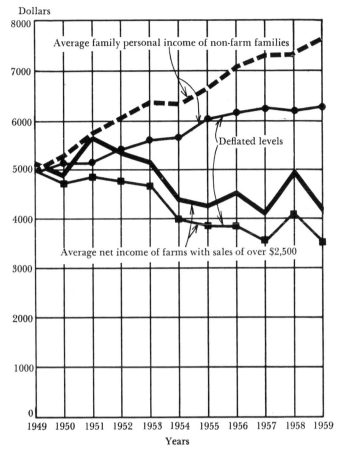

Source: Estimates from Dept. of Agriculture and Dept. of Commerce data.

FIG. 22. NET INCOMES FOR COMMERCIAL FARMS* AND FOR NON–FARM FAMILIES, 1949–59

\* Families on farms with sales of more than $2,500 also received income from non-farm sources, averaging $800 to $1,600 per family during this period.

for additional land; hence a considerable portion of the price increase was due to competition for additional land to add to existing units.

Both farm-mortgage and non-real–estate indebtedness of farmers increased substantially during the 1950's. Nevertheless, farm indebtedness was smaller in proportion to the value of all farm assets in 1959 than it was in 1940, though it had risen since the low point in 1945 (Table 21). The downward trend in farm tenancy continued in the 1950's, but at a much slower rate than in the 1940's.

# Part II

## THE TRANSITION AREA TODAY

# CHAPTER 8

# Factors Affecting the Development of Regional Economies

WE HAVE REVIEWED the history of the Northern Plains and have traced its agricultural development since early settlement. This survey has given us some notion of how the economic development of a region speeds up, slows down, and even regresses at times. We have also seen that all parts of a large region like the Northern Plains do not develop alike, or at the same rate. Before going on to more detailed consideration of the Nebraska pilot area, we will pause and examine more thoroughly the notions of economic development and area economies. Then, in Chapter 9, we shall review some of the relevant data for the Northern Plains states to see how these concepts apply to the region. It should perhaps be emphasized at the outset that area economies do not develop automatically but in response to the actions of men. Thus development of an area can be deliberately influenced by planning and action, and therefore is a legitimate concern of the people.

## WHAT IS AN ECONOMIC REGION?

To define an economic region is to draw a boundary around an area that is associated with certain of its economic characteristics. There are many kinds of economic regions; one type often overlaps another, and collections of overlapping regions whose characteristics are interrelated form general regions, such as the Northern Plains. These general regions are no respecters of state lines. For example, the western part of the corn-belt overlaps the state boundaries of Kansas, Nebraska, and South Dakota; the Missouri Valley traverses parts of the Northern Plains region, but many other states as well; and so on.

What are the various types of economic regions?[1] A first type is a *physiographic* or natural resource region. Here, natural features like climate, topography, and soil characteristics are similar; and these give rise to a common natural vegetation or a primary economic activity, such as particular types of farming. The Great Plains is one such region. A more specialized type of natural region is the *river valley*, which is tied together by a river and is bounded by the highlands on either side. Topography

---

[1] See Joseph Fisher, "Concepts of Regional Economic Development," RRF reprint No. 2 (Washington: Resources for the Future, Inc., 1958); reprinted from *Papers and Proceedings of the First Annual Meeting of the Regional Science Association* (December, 1954), pp. 27–29.

is the chief link, and, where the river is navigable, waterborne transportation and trade may be another link.

A second group of regions includes those based chiefly on economic relationships. Such a type is the *urban* area, which includes a densely populated center and its supporting service area. A specialized type of urban area is the *industrial complex*, such as the Pittsburgh area, the Chicago area, or, more locally, the Wichita area. It includes a center of intensive production plus the surrounding area in which the workers live. Another specialized type is the *transportation complex*, which develops as a logistical center and transfer point for transportation services. Denver, Kansas City, and Chicago are economic regions of this kind. Grand Island, Nebraska, is a much smaller city than these but its economic life probably depends even more heavily, in relative terms, on transportation. This is true of a number of other cities in the Plains area today. Many more communities sprang into existence during the settlement period in anticipation of serving such a function, only to die when the railroad they depended on took another route.

A third specialized type of urban area is the *trade* area. This is the "economic community" of Vining, which

> seems to be organized around its "export" industry, this being the source of the flows which this community injects into the larger interdependent system and which acts as a balance for the flows diverted from the larger system and channeled into this community . . . the region, then, is the area including this primary unit, and it corresponds approximately to the familiar primary trade area.[2]

Losch, along similar lines, begins with a plain on which population is located, division of labor takes place, and transportation costs have to be overcome.[3] This type of area with the out-movement of surplus products and the importation of consumption and production goods, seems to describe the economic organization of the Northern Plains quite well.

A *type-of-farming* area is an economic region specialized for application to agriculture. It is delineated to include farms producing a fairly homogeneous collection of products, as well as fringe or *transition* areas in which the collection of products for one region gradually becomes like that of its neighbor, as one moves geographically from one to the other. Type-of-farming areas usually have many underlying economic characteristics in common, such as soils, climate, and transportation, or even cultural characteristics—such as nationality and religion—which add to their cohesiveness. The Northern Plains includes such "core areas," centering on specialized wheat or range livestock production on the one hand and corn-belt farming on the other, with transitional areas between them.

Another kind of region that often interests economists is the cultural region where such factors as nationality, rates of population growth, level of living, tenure, and race are relatively homogeneous. Distinct cultural regions were formed in the Northern

---

[2] From Rutledge Vining, "The Region as an Economic Entity and Certain Variations to Be Observed in the Study of Systems of Regions," *Papers and Proceedings of the American Economic Association*, 39 (May, 1949), 90–92, as quoted in Fisher, *op. cit.*, p. 2.

[3] A. Losch, "The Nature of Economic Regions," *Southern Economic Journal*, 5 (July, 1938–April, 1939), 71–78, as quoted in Fisher, *op. cit.*, p. 2.

Plains states with the entry of distinct ethnic groups, such as the Scandinavians and Germans, at the time of settlement.

There are several other types of regions. *Data regions* are defined as the basis for the collection of data by government agencies. These include states, counties, state economic areas, metropolitan statistical areas, etc. Their utility is influenced by their correspondence, or lack of it, with economic regions.

States and counties are also *political regions*, as are other administrative units used by federal agencies—such as the Great Plains. Economic repercussions tend to follow legislative or administrative measures taken by a unit of government in a political region; and the impact is sometimes great enough to alter the basic type of economic activity. For example, the political decision to initiate an irrigation development project would probably lead to the supplanting of dry-land farming by irrigation farming. This has happened in many parts of the Plains.

Finally, the *problem* area is just what the name implies, a place that people are concerned about because it is not functioning well in terms of commonly accepted criteria. Thus the corn-belt–Plains transition area, in which we are chiefly interested, is a problem area, particularly from the standpoint of economic development. Within this broad area there are also distinct trade areas, transportation complexes, type-of-farming areas, and cultural regions.

## MISCONCEPTIONS ABOUT ECONOMIC DEVELOPMENT

Several misconceptions about economic development should be clarified before we delve into the subject. These are important because they are widely held by people in rural communities, and frequently even at state and national levels; they thus affect public policies.

First, many local people, with newspaper publishers in the vanguard, believe that economic development depends on population density. They fear emigration and cast about for ways to stop it. Yet some rural areas with rather high population densities—such as parts of the southern mountain states—have low per capita incomes, while some thinly populated areas—for example, the Nebraska Sandhills—have high per capita incomes. Persons most affected by decreasing population density, of course, are those who provide services on a per head basis in an area—such as newspaper publishers—or those for whose products the *income elasticity* (percent increase in expenditure for an item associated with a percent increase in income) is low—for example, grocers.

However, if average size of farm is such that, assuming other resource adjustments have been made, income levels are below "standard," an area is overpopulated; that is, there is too much labor available in relation to other resources. In this case, a decrease in farm population probably will reduce neither the production of farm products for the whole area nor total farm income. It will result in greater per capita incomes and higher levels of living.

This does not imply that employment of surplus farm people in local nonfarm businesses is undesirable. On the contrary, where such opportunities exist they should be properly exploited. But this is a far cry from saying that merely keeping people in an area increases the area's economic development.

A second misconception is that economic development is a function of the distribution of workers between farm and nonfarm activity; that is to say, the higher the proportion in nonfarm activity, the higher the level of development. Superficially, this appears to be true, and we can find evidence supporting it. In the United States, agriculture's share of the labor force has been declining for many years while the national average per capita income has been rising. At the other end of the economic spectrum, incomes are shockingly low in many underdeveloped countries that are almost wholly dependent on agriculture. In the same vein, per capita income in New York state, with less than 2 percent of its people in agriculture, is more than double that of Mississippi, with 25 percent of its people in agriculture. Yet these relationships are not universally observed; there are many examples that are directly opposed to them. For example, Australia and New Zealand are agricultural countries with rather high per capita incomes. The income level in Iowa, with 24 percent of its people in agriculture in 1960, was higher than that in Maine, with only 5 percent of its people in agriculture.

This misconception leads to serious errors in economic development. First, it causes agriculture to be viewed as a "drag." [4] Second, it may result in undue emphasis on attracting new industry, regardless of its economic justification. Third, it often makes people feel that adequate local services can be financed only if industry is brought in to support them.

The crux of the matter is the productivity of workers rather than the kind of work they do. There is no reason why per capita income levels, services, and levels of living cannot be as satisfactory in a farming area as in an industrial area. It is a matter of proper adjustment to the available resources.

A third misconception concerns the identification of problem areas in agriculture, and has been voiced by specialists—sociologists and economists—rather than by lay people. The former have held that "good farmers end up on the good land." Some instances of this can undoubtedly be found in a local area, but over broad regions it can be supported by neither logic nor evidence. Given the same training and other cultural opportunities, the average farmer from the Northern Plains transition area cannot be judged inferior in ability to the corn-belt farmer in central Iowa. The Sandhills of Nebraska also furnish a counter example since their unusually "poor" land apparently is operated by rather effective managers.

A related notion is that problem areas can be identified by low land values per acre. Land values undoubtedly reflect soil productivity on a per acre basis, but agricultural prosperity is a matter of income per family rather than income per acre. Again it is a matter of resource adjustments.

Another related fallacy is that tenancy causes low incomes and maladjustments in farming. Although many areas of high tenancy have low incomes, there are others where incomes are high. Farm ownership does not assure high or stable incomes; on the contrary, undue emphasis on the presumed benefits of ownership can lead farmers to buy land and pay dearly for it in lost opportunities; that is, in a reduced volume of business that results from a shortage of capital for other uses. The percentage of owner-operated farms in some problem areas is relatively high. Tenancy arrangements can

[4] Harvey S. Perloff, "Interrelations of State Income and Industrial Structure," *Review of Economics and Statistics*, 34 (May, 1957) 162.

be used conveniently by beginning operators if they are established on units large enough to provide adequate incomes as well as efficient production and reasonable security. Again, it is a matter of adapting useful institutional arrangements, including tenancy, to local conditions.

## NATURE OF REGIONAL ECONOMIC DEVELOPMENT

What, then, constitutes economic strength, development, and growth? To answer this question we must distinguish four closely related concepts. These include economic growth, economic stability, cultural maturity, and economic self-sufficiency.

### Economic Growth

Economic growth might be defined as the increase in average per capita real income. In other words, it relates to the goods and services produced by the people of an area, some of which can be exchanged for other goods and services produced in some other region. The distribution of income between individual families, or between different types of industries, is not of immediate concern at this point; rather, the concept relates to the increase in real income of all the people for a region as a whole.

There is no single satisfactory measure of economic growth. Net annual income per capita is commonly used as a measure, adjusted for changes in the purchasing power of the dollar if comparisons are made between years. Higher net incomes permit greater spending for both consumption goods and capital accumulation or saving. It must be recognized that net incomes, as commonly estimated, do not include all sources of real income. For example, no accounting is made of the use of leisure time. Also, in dealing with net farm income, such items as farm-raised food and the value of farm housing are usually undervalued.

A second measure of economic growth is level of living. The common level-of-living indexes include indicators of production and consumption, and so reflect both the degree to which people are achieving satisfactory incomes and the degree to which the income is being used to achieve standards of living commonly accepted as desirable. As applied to farms, these indexes include four components: (1) the value of products sold or traded, (2) the percent of farms with electricity, (3) the percent of farms with telephones, and (4) the percent with automobiles.[5] Of course the level-of-living indexes do not include all the items families buy, but those excluded are frequently closely related to those included. Thus farmers with electricity probably spend more money for electrically powered conveniences than those without; the possession of a car means that the family can use the services available to it in the community to a fuller extent than would otherwise be possible. The gross value of products, while not the same as net income, reflects the amount of money available for family living.

Economic growth is a relative concept. Measures of growth mean little on an absolute basis; they require standards for comparison. For example, the present level of living in a community can be compared with what it had been in the past to see how much progress has been made. But we are most interested in comparing a given

---

[5] *Farm Population, Employment, and Levels of Living. Major Statistical Series of the U.S. Department of Agriculture.* USDA Agriculture Handbook No. 118, 1957.

area with other areas, or with the country as a whole, to make some judgment of its relative progress. For example, income per person in agriculture is often compared with income per person in nonfarming activity over a period of years—as was done in Figure 22. Such a comparison gives a notion of the relative position of farm people with respect to income, over time. Thus the growing difference between farm and nonfarm income during the 1950's would seem more important to farmers than the slight decline in their own incomes. This is what hurts; the additional things our neighbors can now afford become necessities to us.

In earlier times, regions were much more alike than they are now. The differences in income and level of living between regions did not arise because some communities fell behind in the absolute sense but because other communities drew ahead of them in per capita real incomes. The people of all regions have similar inherent capabilities —the critical questions for economic development are how much education and training they have, how much capital they have to work with, and how well they are organized to produce goods and services.

### Economic Stability

Economic stability is the degree to which economic growth is smooth and steady. It refers to the extent to which employment, prices, incomes, and financial transactions move up and down. Each area is linked to the national economy, so its own stability is partially tied to that of the national business cycle, which it cannot change at will. In addition, each area has its own sources of instability, depending on the diversity of economic activity, the vagaries of weather and prices, and the policies employed to counteract the effects of these variable phenomena. Instability, and the threat of it, "costs" an area. Stability also costs something. A balance must be struck between how much stability an area wants and how much it can afford.

### Cultural Maturity

Cultural maturity is related to economic growth. In one sense, it relates to how a community or an area organizes to provide needed services in line with the cultural value structure of our society. In another sense, it is measured by those elements of the living level that are consumed by the community as a whole, rather than on an individual family basis. For instance, the amount spent per pupil for education is one index of cultural maturity. This has certain weaknesses, since one community may have to spend more to obtain the same physical service. Better indexes might be the proportion of the young people of an area who go to college, or the average grade attained by all children. In the field of health, the number of hospital beds or the number of doctors per 1,000 people may be useful. Similarly, the dollars per capita spent for outdoor recreational facilities might be another useful measure of cultural maturity.

Some people think there is a fundamental economic difference between goods or services produced privately, such as automobiles or farm products, and those produced at public expense, such as education, roads, and recreation. They think of the one as being natural and therefore good, while the other is unnatural, wasteful, and a necessary evil.

It is true that a farmer is interested in producing as much net production as possible, which he can *exchange* for other goods and services his family wants; but it is equally true that the teacher working in a public school or the trucker who hauls the farmer's products to market is also producing services in *exchange* for which they can obtain other things, like food. The farmer buys trucking service by paying his trucking bill; he buys public education service or road service by paying taxes. Yet those who carp most about taxes are often the first to complain about poor roads or streets. There is no fundamental difference between private goods and services and public goods and services; one is not economic and the other uneconomic. Good roads cannot be obtained without taxes any more than good food can be procured without paying its price.

Thus the sum total of all of the activities of all of the people of an area, translated into a standard unit of measurement, like the dollar, comprise the economic status of an area.

### Self-sufficiency

It is easy to overemphasize economic self-sufficiency in an area, like the transition zone of the Northern Great Plains, that is heavily specialized in agriculture. Self-sufficiency refers to the balance of the economic activities of an area—to its ability to operate as an independent unit isolated from the rest of the economy. An area may try to become self-sufficient to avoid the disruptions that could occur in the economic system in the event of a military attack, a valid reason that should be considered by the people of any area. A second reason sometimes advanced for self-sufficiency is to prevent exploitation of the area in question by some other area. For example, a community may decide to build its own packing plant to prevent exploitation by plants in some distant packing center. This is a purely economic reason that should be evaluated in economic terms.

Frequently, hidden costs are overlooked, such as the benefits of specialization and trade that will be sacrificed by moving toward self-sufficiency. There may be cheaper ways to prevent bona fide exploitation, such as government intervention—either to enforce antitrust legislation or to eliminate discriminatory freight rates. There are, of course, some new activities that increase self-sufficiency and also have economic merit. Thus it may be more efficient to establish cattle feeding in a grain-producing area located near a source of feeder cattle than to export both grain and cattle to be fed elsewhere.

No discussion of economic development would be complete without a warning to those people who want to accelerate their area's growth rate: There is no economic jusification for regional economic development that, in the long run, comes only at the expense of either the development of the national economy or of the more efficient development of some other region or sector of the economy. This does not imply that a region cannot be lent resources by the public to be used in development, or given resources to start development, if this is in the national interest. However, the investment should be self-liquidating in the long run.

In areas seeking faster growth rates, a popular and simple method is to "go after a government project." Such a solution means new money spent in the community, more payrolls, more employees, more consumers buying goods, larger tax bases, and other desirable consequences—from the *standpoint of that community*. The basic economic question, however, is the effect of such a project on the national economy. Would the same funds, applied in some other region, or in *some other use* (possibly in the same region), have resulted in more economic growth, that is, in a greater contribution to the national product? This question, and the interests of other regions (and their taxpayers) in it, are often neglected.

### Factors Affecting the Rate of Economic Development

An area's rate of economic development is affected by what goes on outside it as well as within it. The internal factors include the resources available in the area and the adaptations local people have made to them. The external factors are both socio-cultural and economic. The economic factors affect the terms under which one area trades with another, and some of these relate to the nature of demand for the products or services of an area, others to the supply of factors used in production.

As farm families in agricultural areas have become less self-contained or self-sufficient, their reliance on exchange—buying and selling—has increased. Consequently, farmers have become more vulnerable to such external economic factors as inflation, deflation, unemployment, foreign trade, and the general demand for food.

From the demand side, the terms of trade depend on the existence of an effective (that is, money) demand for the products of an area. This demand must be reflected through a market organization in terms of prices to be paid, or, alternatively, in the amount of other goods to be exchanged for the goods produced in the area. Since costs of transportation must be deducted, an area near a consuming center usually has an advantage over an area farther away, particularly in the production of bulky or perishable goods. The effect of transportation costs is complicated by the varying rate structure which sometimes makes it cheaper to ship goods in one direction than another, even when the distance involved is the same.

Similarly, from the factor supply side, the terms of trade depend on the existence of a supply of the required materials used for production—available at some price—to which the cost of transportation must be added to get the real cost in a particular area.

Nor are these the only important external factors. The availability of outside capital affects producers' ability to finance their various activities. This capital may be in the form of loans or investment capital from private sources, or it may be in the form of government payments (loans and subsidies) for such things as roads, education, transportation, and development projects.

In the United States, every economic region is connected with other regions by almost incomprehensibly complicated sets of demand and supply relationships for products and factors. No region is completely self-sufficient.

Typically, agricultural regions have exported to the rest of the economy not only products but labor, since birth rates have been higher in country areas. Unless this surplus labor can be employed within the area at other things besides farming, per capita income within the area will be influenced by the employment opportunities available for this labor outside the area. The movement of people out of an area will tend to raise the wages of those remaining; also, capital will probably be substituted for labor. These two phenomena are reflections of economic growth.

Another imported factor is technology—new methods and techniques for doing things. An area's productivity ability depends on the availability of new technology from centers specializing in its development: universities, and governmental and private research agencies. Technology is another source of interdependence between areas. Whether it is an economic or a cultural factor is a moot point.

Several socio-cultural factors from outside a region affect its rate of development. Whether this effect is favorable depends on the extent to which the particular importation was designed for, or adapted to, the conditions and resources of the importing area.

The standards of living of the Northern Plains states are imported for the most part. They are largely of urban origin, and, as a consequence, are somewhat unsuitable for measuring goals of rural people. If the standard specified a store or theater within walking distance, a rural region may well be judged deficient, but only because of how the standard was devised. Nevertheless, urban values are paramount in our society. Such standards are carried by all communications media—radio, television, magazines, and newspapers—as well as by the many individual contacts made by travelers. These standards become norms of achievement for the residents of an area, and provide incentives that affect the nature and rate of economic development.

Historically, another carrier of culture into the Northern Plains was the movement of settlers, who brought with them the traditions, customs, and habits of their parent areas. Thus the corn-belt was settled by New Englanders, many of whom—after a few decades—moved on to Nebraska and South Dakota; they carried with them a corn-belt culture, with vestiges of their New England background, such as the design of farm buildings. On the other hand, some parts of North and South Dakota were settled more heavily by Scandinavians, who imported different cultural orientations, not the least of which may be the dynamic politics of North Dakota, occasionally still evident.

Educational values and objectives are still imported from the east; witness the many college and university staff members trained in schools east of the Missouri. Even the agricultural colleges have been traditionally oriented toward the corn-belt, although—since the 1930's—this has been tempered by a developing sense of unity with the other Plains states.

Federal agencies whose mission is national in scope also bring into a region their particular ideas, practices, and standards. Sometimes these are ill suited at the beginning, but they improve through a process of regional adaptation. In the private sector, we have noted the effects of the railroads crossing the Plains; they, too, were eastern in orientation. Other "foreign" corporate groups, such as machinery companies, have undergone processes of regional adaptation. Nearly all the institutions under which the Northern Plains region was organized—state governments, school organization, churches, local government, and finance institutions—were of external origin.

## INDIGENOUS FACTORS AFFECTING DEVELOPMENT

In one sense, the only truly indigenous factors affecting an area's development are the endowments of nature. However, in assessing its development potential, all social factors that must have been imported at one time or another—people, customs, institutions, capital—are also classified as indigenous; they are considered an integral part of the local scene.

In a primarily agricultural area, soil and climate represent limitational factors on development. Soil includes all attributes of the land that affect farm production, such as topography, plant nutrients, and drainage—soil technicians even include climate as part of soil. Granted that other resources, such as water and fertilizer, can be added to soil, it is still true that a soil's extent is spatially limited. There are, first, economic limits, and, finally, there are physical limits to the amounts of other resources that can be applied to increase yields. In a nonirrigable area, with relatively low rainfall, the *capacity* of the soil to absorb other resource inputs is more limited than in more humid farming areas. Thus there are definite economic and physical limits to crop production, and consequently to the number of livestock that can be fed from local sources. Irrigation water, where available, raises these limits.

The second resource factor affecting economic development is the availability of capital, a word that can have a number of meanings and can therefore be confusing. In its narrowest sense, it refers to money, including credit. Most broadly, it includes all nonlabor resources used in production, including land. We shall use it to denote all nonlabor resources used in production *other* than land. Because of its fixed nature, land is often considered separately.

Personal income is derived from two sources: payments to people for the work they do or payments to them for something they own, whether land or capital. These two components are intertwined: the more labor associated with a given amount of capital, the greater the returns to capital. Conversely, the more capital associated with a given amount of labor, the higher the returns to labor.

Since all income ultimately comes to rest in some person's hands, it follows that the more capital used per person in a region, the higher the expected per capita income in that industry or region. When we look at various regions in the United States, this appears to be generally true. High-income regions use large amounts of capital per worker. Differences in capital use per worker (including land) explain much of the difference in income levels between areas. Nonland capital in agriculture includes livestock, seed, feed, machinery, tools, power, fertilizer, spray materials, and all the other items used in production, as well as money that can be exchanged for these things.

Where does the money come from? The answer is, by saving or borrowing. Thus the financial institutions in a region are of critical importance in supplying capital to its people. The financial institutions ministering to agriculture include commercial banks, production-credit associations, national farm-loan associations, the Farmers Home Administration, and Banks for Cooperatives—as well as supply and marketing firms that provide credit. While farmers have traditionally depended more on their own savings than on financial institutions, the terms of credit available from the latter still influence the directions farming will take. In speaking of finance and credit, it is assumed, of course, that the capital goods for which credit will be used are available for purchase.

It should be noted that finance is just as important to other types of economic activities—transportation, retailing, and manufacturing—as it is to farming.

The third of the three resource "legs" supporting per capita income in an area is labor. In this context, people are viewed as a resource factor in production that is combined with land and capital. Labor has a qualitative as well as a quantitative side. It refers not merely to numbers of workers but also to their ability and training.

In considering the adjustment of labor to other resources—that is, the way in which land, capital, and labor are combined—there are several quantitative shifts for improving per capita incomes. First, we can increase the amounts of land that is combined with a given amount of labor in production. In the Northern Plains states, this process has been approaching its upper limit, although some small amounts of land can still be added in certain areas; for example, where irrigation can be developed. The second possibility is to add more nonland capital to given quantities of labor and land, which also has been done on farms in the Northern Plains. The economic and physical limits of this process were noted earlier.

When these possibilities are exhausted, an opposite type of adjustment can be made: *to reduce the amount of labor combined with land and capital in farming.* This can be done in several ways. First, farmers may work off the farm on a part-time basis; or they can seek full-time work off the farm, but in the same area. Both of these adjustments reduce the number of labor's income claims on farming, increasing the returns per hour to those remaining. Failing either of the above, they may seek nonfarm employment outside the area, which again increases the income per worker of those workers who are left. This kind of resource adjustment is frowned upon by those who equate development with population density, but it has been going on for many decades and will surely continue.

In addition to the quantitative aspects of resource combination, the effectiveness of resource utilization affects the real incomes of an area's people. We refer to such things as the combinations of crops raised, the extent of soil and water conservation, the combinations of livestock enterprises in relation to feed and labor resources, the efficiency with which machinery is used, the efficiency with which labor is used, and the use of strategic resources such as fertilizers, sprays, and other outgrowths of technological development. The effectiveness of resource utilization depends first upon the state of the arts, and secondly on the awareness of it on the part of farmers. These are related to their education and training.

As might be deduced from the preceding paragraph, another factor affecting development is the state of local nonfarm industry. Nonfarm firms are of two general types: first, those that provide farmers with consumption and production supplies, and process and market their products; and second, those that are not related to agriculture but manufacture other products for export as an independent activity.

The first type includes retail stores, machinery and farm supply firms, elevators, trucking and other transportation facilities, and packing plants. At the minimum, these facilities provide the means of importing supplies and exporting farm produce, including the transportation services required plus such processing as is associated with transportation. The effectiveness of these services directly affects farm incomes.

To this minimum may be added activities that represent the second type of production: packaging and processing of produce, or the manufacture of consumption goods for local consumption. Farm incomes are affected by the efficiency of these firms, which also provide a market for surplus labor. An example of an independent industrial activity, producing primarily for export from the area, might be a machinery company or an aircraft factory. It provides a market for suplus labor from the farm sector—assuming that the real income per person involved in it is greater than that in the agricultural sector.

Education also affects development. Education includes all available training facilities: primary and secondary schools, agricultural extension, evening classes, and junior colleges. In the first place, the efficiency with which the educational facilities are organized and operated affects the average real income of the area. Second, the types and quality of the training provided directly influence the effectiveness of the students as they become workers in the area, whether it be in farming, in agricultural business activity, or in nonagricultural industry. Their effectiveness as workers in turn affects the level of real incomes which they—and, in fact, all people of the area—will achieve. This depends not only on the general knowledge they have acquired but on the specific skills and knowledge they have, as related to the particular characteristics of the area.

The Northern Plains has a peculiar problem in this regard since, after it makes an educational investment in its people, large numbers of them migrate to other regions. This poses a good argument for expecting other areas to share its educational burden. On the other hand, it is in the region's own interest to train its people to be flexible, so that some will be willing to migrate, adapt to other situations, become productive in their new locations, and cease to need support from their parent area as soon as possible.

Local government also affects economic development. First, the speed of development depends on the imagination and ingenuity of local government leaders in identifying the problems involved with development and in using available means to solve them. Also, local governments, by their efficiency in providing the requisite local services, affect their per unit costs to consumers.

The role of technology as an imported factor affecting development has been discussed. It also has indigenous aspects. First, imported technologies may be adopted rapidly or slowly, depending on the ingenuity and training of the people. Second, it may be necessary to adapt imported technologies, or even to invent new ones—such as crop varieties, irrigation techniques, water conservation, and specialized machinery —for the particular area if development is to progress.

Hard to measure, but undoubtedly important in affecting development, is the motivation of the people. An area may become stagnant because of low morale; the people of another area may prosper because their desire and drive enhance the effectiveness of their judgment. They become more efficient and ingenious at exploiting strategic possibilities. Motivation originates in the whole socio-cultural environment, and is affected by some of the factors mentioned above—as well as by such social phenomena as church affiliation and nationality.

Land tenure arrangements—tenancy, credit provision, etc.—can affect an area's income distribution and can impede or encourage production efficiency. For example, landlord-tenant relationships in agriculture can influence the use of strategic inputs, like fertilizer. Frequently, new arrangements must be evolved to adapt to an area's unique conditions. Probably no better example of the critical influence of land-tenure arrangements on development could be found than the homestead laws and their effects on settlement of the Plains.

# CHAPTER 9

# The Differential Development of Area Economies

## THE NORTHERN PLAINS VERSUS OTHER REGIONS

*Income Levels and Economic Structure*

SINCE changes in per capita incomes are an index of economic growth, Table 22 presents selected income data for 1940, 1950, and 1960. Growth in the national economy during these twenty years appears impressive on first glance, with 1960 incomes almost four times what they were a mere two decades earlier; but more than half of this gain was illusory, a reflection of the higher price levels (or lower purchasing power of the dollar) in 1960. When incomes are expressed in terms of 1957–59 dollars, the 1960 level is about 1¾ times the 1940 level. In real terms, then, per capita incomes had almost doubled in those twenty years—a respectable rate of growth, nearly everyone would agree.

The growth pattern had not been smooth and regular; it was sharply influenced by World War II. Nor have all states shared equally in this development. The table shows per capita incomes of the Northern Plains states, together with those of a few neighboring states for comparison. In 1940, only Illinois and Wyoming—of the eight

TABLE 22.  PER CAPITA PERSONAL INCOME (IN CURRENT AND CONSTANT DOLLARS), 1940, 1950, AND 1960 (1957–59 = 100)

| | 1940 | | 1950 | | 1960 | |
| | Current Dollars | Constant Dollars | Current Dollars | Constant Dollars | Current Dollars | Constant Dollars |
|---|---|---|---|---|---|---|
| U.S. . . . . . . | 595 | 1,219 | 1,491 | 1,780 | 2,215 | 2,151 |
| Illinois . . . . . | 754 | 1,544 | 1,826 | 2,180 | 2,624 | 2,548 |
| Iowa . . . . . | 501 | 1,026 | 1,449 | 1,730 | 2,017 | 1,959 |
| North Dakota . . | 350 | 717 | 1,268 | 1,514 | 1,744 | 1,693 |
| South Dakota . . | 359 | 735 | 1,216 | 1,452 | 1,853 | 1,799 |
| Nebraska . . . . | 439 | 899 | 1,472 | 1,758 | 2,137 | 2,075 |
| Kansas . . . . . | 426 | 872 | 1,380 | 1,648 | 2,057 | 1,997 |
| Wyoming . . . | 608 | 1,245 | 1,623 | 1,938 | 2,295 | 2,228 |
| Colorado . . . . | 546 | 1,118 | 1,444 | 1,724 | 2,296 | 2,229 |

Source: Current dollars from U.S. Bureau of the Census, *Statistical Abstract of the U.S., 1963*, table 441; converted to constant dollars by "Purchasing Power of the Dollar," in U.S. Office of Business Economics, *Business Statistics*, 1963 ed., p. 45.

states shown—had incomes above the national average. By 1960, Colorado had also joined this circle; yet Illinois failed to keep up with the national growth, and Wyoming only barely exceeded it.

This is another illustration of a widely observed phenomenon; namely, that inequality between states and regions is gradually being reduced. Thus the poorest states in 1940 improved their positions most, in relative terms, and the richest gained least. The substantial rate of increase for the Northern Plains states is largely a reflection of the very poor position they were in at the end of a decade of depression. The data shown also mask the instability of incomes in the Plains states. During the fifties, per capita incomes in these states declined until after 1956, probably owing to drought and declining farm prices, but by 1960 they were on the rise again. In contrast, Iowa and Illinois (to the east) showed much more moderate rates of growth over the decade, but this growth was steady year by year. The data shown are of course not in terms of relative growth but in absolute dollars. This is appropriate since we buy goods with actual incomes rather than with rates of increase. Thus per capita incomes in Nebraska and Kansas increased about equally from 1940 to 1960, but Nebraska's average income still surpasses that of Kansas because it was higher in the beginning.

To understand why these differences in real income persist, we note first how these states are organized for production of goods and services. One indicator of economic organization is the distribution of employed persons by major industry groups, as shown in Table 23. Nearly one-third of the working population in the heavily industrial state of Illinois is engaged in manufacturing and less than 10 percent is in agriculture.

This can be compared with the Northern Plains states, where the structure is almost reversed. There, manufacturing occupies about 12 percent of the employed labor force while agriculture occupies 20 percent. In all the states shown, as in the nation as a whole, agriculture has been dropping in relative importance and manufacturing has been rising. Colorado is an interesting case in point. In 1940, more than twice as many people in that state were employed in agriculture as in manufacturing. In 1950, agriculture was still ahead, but only slightly. By 1960, a complete turnabout had occurred, with employment in manufacturing more than double that in agriculture. Iowa, to the east, is following a similar pattern, but is now where Colorado was in 1950, with agriculture only very slightly ahead of manufacturing as a source of employment. By 1970, if these trends continue, manufacturing will employ substantially more Iowans than farming will.

The Northern Plains states are subject to these same inexorable economic forces, but the pace of change is much slower because the growth in manufacturing is less dramatic. Wyoming shares many of the Plains' characteristics. Employment in agriculture has been sharply reduced, but very little expansion in manufacturing has taken up the slack. Instead, employment has risen in a host of other activities, such as transportation and communications, trade, mining, and public service.

Given the industrial structure of a state, earnings per worker in the major industry groups determine average per capita income for the state as a whole. Data for six industry groups are shown in Table 24, for the United States and for selected states.

Income levels in manufacturing are higher than those in other industries, but they are generally lower in the Northern Plains states than in the other states compared or

TABLE 23. DISTRIBUTION OF EMPLOYED PERSONS BY INDUSTRY GROUP, 1940, 1950, AND 1960

| | Agriculture | | | Manufacturing | | | Transportation, Public Utilities, & Communication | | | Wholesale & Retail Trade | | | Business, Professional & personal Service | | | Public Service | | | Other | | |
|---|---|---|---|---|---|---|---|---|---|---|---|---|---|---|---|---|---|---|---|---|---|
| | '40 | '50 | '60 | '40 | '50 | '60 | '40 | '50 | '60 | '40 | '50 | '60 | '40 | '50 | '60 | '40 | '50 | '60 | '40 | '50 | '60 |
| | PERCENT | | | | | | | | | | | | | | | | | | | | |
| U.S. | 18.7 | 12.2 | 6.6 | 23.7 | 26.0 | 27.1 | 6.9 | 7.9 | 7.0 | 16.9 | 18.7 | 18.2 | 14.8 | 12.7 | 13.5 | 10.6 | 13.0 | 16.6 | 8.4 | 9.4 | 11.0 |
| Illinois | 10.0 | 7.1 | 4.4 | 28.9 | 32.2 | 31.8 | 9.0 | 9.5 | 7.9 | 22.4 | 19.4 | 18.0 | 15.0 | 12.3 | 12.2 | 10.4 | 11.9 | 14.9 | 7.2 | 7.5 | 10.8 |
| Iowa | 35.9 | 28.4 | 20.6 | 11.6 | 15.3 | 18.6 | 6.7 | 7.0 | 6.2 | 16.7 | 19.1 | 19.4 | 11.7 | 10.4 | 11.0 | 10.5 | 11.9 | 16.0 | 6.7 | 7.9 | 7.9 |
| N. Dak. | 53.5 | 44.2 | 32.8 | 2.5 | 3.0 | 3.7 | 5.1 | 7.1 | 6.4 | 13.8 | 18.6 | 20.2 | 10.0 | 8.6 | 10.6 | 11.3 | 12.3 | 18.1 | 4.0 | 7.1 | 8.0 |
| S. Dak. | 48.2 | 40.4 | 30.5 | 4.6 | 5.0 | 6.6 | 4.2 | 5.5 | 5.1 | 14.6 | 17.6 | 18.9 | 9.9 | 9.2 | 11.1 | 12.2 | 13.1 | 17.8 | 6.0 | 9.1 | 10.0 |
| Nebraska | 37.6 | 29.6 | 21.2 | 7.0 | 9.3 | 12.2 | 8.3 | 9.3 | 7.9 | 17.1 | 19.0 | 19.6 | 13.2 | 11.4 | 12.6 | 11.9 | 12.6 | 17.2 | 5.4 | 8.9 | 9.0 |
| Kansas | 31.7 | 23.0 | 13.3 | 9.2 | 12.7 | 16.6 | 8.6 | 9.6 | 8.6 | 17.4 | 19.3 | 19.9 | 12.8 | 11.0 | 12.0 | 11.8 | 13.3 | 18.4 | 8.5 | 11.1 | 11.2 |
| Wyoming | 30.9 | 20.5 | 13.3 | 5.6 | 6.1 | 7.7 | 11.0 | 13.0 | 10.4 | 15.1 | 17.0 | 19.2 | 11.2 | 11.0 | 12.5 | 12.0 | 13.9 | 17.8 | 14.9 | 18.4 | 19.1 |
| Colorado | 21.1 | 15.1 | 7.6 | 10.3 | 12.4 | 15.8 | 8.5 | 9.6 | 8.0 | 19.4 | 20.9 | 20.5 | 15.0 | 13.9 | 14.4 | 13.8 | 16.5 | 20.9 | 11.8 | 11.8 | 12.8 |

Source: U.S. Census of Population, 1960, tables 62 and 92.

in the United States. The wholesale trades ranked second, the retail and public service trades occupied a somewhat intermediate position, while agriculture and personal service were at the bottom. It is apparent that the states most dependent on agriculture would have relatively low average per capita incomes, while those with more people in manufacturing or wholesale trade would rank higher in per capita incomes. As noted in Table 23, the proportions in the wholesale and retail trades do not vary much between states, and this is also generally true for transportation and services. Agriculture and manufacturing tend to be the most variable. Thus Illinois ranks high in people employed in manufacturing, and also has high per capita incomes. North and South Dakota ranked highest in agriculture, and had the lowest incomes.

This seems to support the idea (labeled as a misconception in Chapter 8) that industrialization is the high road to economic development, but among the states cited, Wyoming contradicts this assumption. Although earnings per worker in

TABLE 24.  MEDIAN ANNUAL EARNINGS PER WORKER BY INDUSTRY GROUP, 1959

| | Agri-culture | Manu-facturing | Wholesale Trades | Retail Trades | Personal, Business, & Repair Services | Public administration, professional, & Related Services |
|---|---|---|---|---|---|---|
| U.S. . . . . . . . . | $1,925 | $4,434 | $4,699 | $2,697 | $1,762 | $3,937 |
| Illinois . . . . . . . | 2,479 | 4,865 | 5,118 | 3,050 | 2,559 | 4,193 |
| Iowa . . . . . . . | 2,395 | 4,665 | 4,361 | 2,493 | 1,495 | 3,216 |
| North Dakota . . . . | 2,504 | 3,697 | 4,228 | 2,533 | 1,375 | 3,128 |
| South Dakota . . . . | 2,138 | 4,261 | 4,019 | 2,278 | 993 | 3,106 |
| Nebraska . . . . . . | 2,373 | 4,200 | 4,252 | 2,453 | 1,441 | 3,120 |
| Kansas . . . . . . . | 2,386 | 4,814 | 4,535 | 2,465 | 1,495 | 3,353 |
| Wyoming . . . . . | 2,699 | 5,244 | 4,691 | 2,659 | 1,606 | 3,834 |
| Colorado . . . . . . | 2,625 | 4,846 | 4,539 | 2,773 | 1,900 | 3,985 |

Source: *U.S. Census of Population, 1960.*

manufacturing are very high in that state, the number of people employed is small. It appears that above-average incomes in agriculture and average incomes in wholesale and retail trades—as well as the relatively high wages in mining—all contribute to Wyoming's favorable per capita income. There also are counties in each of the Northern Plains states that have comparatively high farm incomes.

Agricultural incomes in Iowa and Illinois are also somewhat higher than those in the Northern Plains states. Agriculture did not have the same "down-pulling" effect on per capita incomes in these states as it did in the Plains states. This is important in a farm state like Iowa, which has a higher proportion of its people engaged in farming than Kansas.

It is not possible to investigate here the many reasons for variation in nonfarm incomes from one industry or state to another, although some were suggested in Chapter 8. Undoubtedly, such things as the productivity of labor, its supply and demand, the extent of unionization, and the amounts and types of capital used affect these variations. We shall shortly take a closer look at agriculture. However, we should point out that comparisons between farm and nonfarm incomes are complicated by two factors: weather and price-cost relationships. Farm incomes in any one year may vary considerably from their normal levels.

Real wages in manufacturing in the United States rose more than 22 percent from 1950 to 1960 at a steady annual pace. The same trend and stability was evident in the selected states in Table 24, although there were some changes in relative position among them. At the beginning of the decade, only Wyoming and Illinois were above the national average; by 1960, only Nebraska and North Dakota were below it. Wyoming and Illinois had maintained their high positions, and Colorado, Kansas, South Dakota, and Iowa had moved up strongly to join them.

In contrast, real farm incomes in the United States were only 3 percent higher in 1960 than in 1950. These incomes include cash income from farming, the value of food raised, government payments, and the estimated value of farm dwellings. They do not, however, include income from nonfarm sources. Farmers are doing more off-farm work than ever before, and this is contributing an ever larger share of their total earnings. When this nonfarm income is included, per capita farm incomes in constant dollars rose by 15 percent from 1950 to 1960. Even this improvement is not enough to put farm incomes on a par with nonfarm incomes.

Farm incomes in the Northern Plains states showed the same general trend, although with more variation (Figure 23). The effects of falling beef prices can be seen in 1952. Drought made its impact felt in Kansas in 1953–55, Nebraska in 1954–56, South Dakota in 1955–56, and in North Dakota in 1952 and 1957–58.

Excess moisture hurt Kansas wheat in 1957. Similarly, Colorado was affected by a combination of declining beef prices and drought during the entire period of 1952 to 1956. The effects of drought can also be seen in Wyoming and Iowa in 1956.

If we overlook the short-run effects of weather, the basic trouble with agriculture during the 1960's was the prices received, as is illustrated by the case of Illinois. Despite the year-to-year stability shown by farm incomes in that state, its agriculture followed the national trend in income per farm. After the upturn of 1957, incomes per farm were down again in 1958 and 1959. However, they improved somewhat in the following year, and more since that time because of the combined effects of farm programs and the continuing movement of people out of agriculture.

To summarize, one basic reason for the disadvantaged position of the Northern Plains during the 1950's with respect to economic growth has been the combination of increasingly unfavorable price-cost relations—coupled, to a lesser extent, with drought. The economic condition of agriculture in these states is basically better than that in some other sections of the country, but this is small consolation when agriculture as an industry is in such a disadvantaged position.

One cannot measure economic growth in physical terms alone, like bushels of wheat or pounds of beef; it depends on physical units multiplied by prices. In this context, prices are the values that the consuming public places upon the products of a region. The agricultural industry has shown a rather remarkable ability to produce more units than it can market at prices that will keep in step with other values in the economy.

Having recognized this, however, we shall not—in the context of this book—deal further with farm prices. We shall examine other evidence bearing on economic

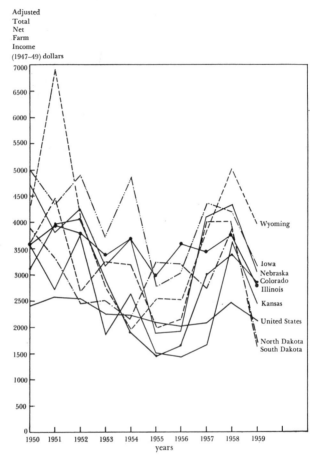

Based on data in USDA's "Farm Income Situation" (FIS. 179), August, 1960.

FIG. 23.   NET FARM INCOME IN THE NORTHERN PLAINS,
SELECTED STATES, AND THE U.S., 1950–59 (1947–49
DOLLARS)

growth in farming in the Northern Plains, and then turn our attention to economic conditions in farming in specific areas within the region.

### Economic Stability

Stability was suggested earlier as one of the objectives of economic development. It is apparent in the data presented that economic growth does not progress steadily but tends to spurt and then slow down. Moreover, these spurts and lags do not occur simultaneously in all areas. Professor Hanna has devised a sensitivity index with which to measure the stability of state income.[1] His index is the ratio of the percentage change in state per capita income to the percentage change in per capita income for the country as a whole. The indexes for the states we have been comparing are as follows:

[1] Frank A. Hanna, "Cyclical and Secular Changes in State Per Capita Incomes, 1929–50," *Review of Economics and Statistics*, XXXVI (Harvard University Press, 1954), 320.

| | | | |
|---|---|---|---|
| Illinois . . . . . . . . . . . | 1.087 | Nebraska . . . . . . . . . . . | 1.400 |
| Iowa . . . . . . . . . . . . | 1.292 | Kansas . . . . . . . . . . | 1.276 |
| North Dakota . . . . . . . | 1.560 | Wyoming . . . . . . . . . | 1.016 |
| South Dakota . . . . . . . | 1.383 | Colorado . . . . . . . . . | 1.071 |

These data are based on the years 1929–50. A highly sensitive index means that income in the state in question is overcompensating; when national income rises, the state income rises more than proportionately, and, when it falls, the state income falls even more. A sensitive index results from the influence of agriculture, which is highly responsive to cyclical influences; the greater the proportion of the labor force in agriculture, the greater the sensitivity index. Also, a higher index is associated with agricultural products for which demand is more inelastic, and therefore more subject to price variation. The Northern Plains states rank among the highest in the country in the sensitivity index. Iowa also shows some economic sensitivity—in contrast to Illinois, Wyoming, and Colorado, which show medium stability.

### A Closer Look at Northern Plains Agriculture

We can get a bird's-eye view of the development of the Plains states, compared with the corn-belt states of Iowa, Illinois, Indiana, and Ohio, by observing the number of people engaged in agriculture over the years. The proportion of United States farm workers in the Northern Plains states has held remarkably constant for more than half a century, at around 6 percent (Table 25). The corn-belt started

TABLE 25. Persons Engaged in Agriculture, 1880–1959 (in Thousands)

| | 1880 | 1890 | 1900 | 1910 | 1920 | 1930 | 1940 | 1950 | 1959 |
|---|---|---|---|---|---|---|---|---|---|
| U.S. . . . . . . . | 8,585 | 9,938 | 10,912 | 11,592 | 11,449 | 10,472 | 9,163 | 6,906 | 6,332 |
| Corn-belt. . . . | 2,044 | 2,157 | 2,199 | 1,885 | 1,787 | 1,616 | 1,461 | 1,176 | 1,178 |
| Plains states . . | 364 | 615 | 657 | 685 | 671 | 692 | 596 | 511 | 492 |
| Percent of U.S. in Plains states . . | 4.3 | 6.2 | 6.0 | 5.9 | 5.9 | 6.6 | 6.5 | 7.4 | 7.8 |

Sources: 1880–1950 data reprinted from *Capital in Agriculture: Its Formation and Financing since 1870*, by A. S. Tostlebee, by permission of the Princeton University Press, copyright 1957, by Princeton University Press, all rights reserved; 1959 data from *U.S. Statistical Abstract, 1963*, table 889, p. 642.

reducing its farm labor force by 1910, while the Northern Plains did not enter upon a consistent decline until 1940. Similarly, the number of farms began to diminish in the corn-belt in 1910, and in the Plains states by 1940 (Table 26).

TABLE 26. Number of Farms in the U.S., Corn-belt, and Northern Plains States, 1880–1959 (in Thousands)

| | 1880 | 1890 | 1900 | 1910 | 1920 | 1930 | 1940 | 1950 | 1959 |
|---|---|---|---|---|---|---|---|---|---|
| U.S. . . . . . . . | 4,009 | 4,565 | 5,737 | 6,362 | 6,448 | 6,289 | 6,097 | 5,382 | 3,708 |
| Corn-belt. . . . | 1,098 | 1,130 | 1,276 | 1,234 | 1,176 | 1,086 | 1,101 | 995 | 767 |
| Great Plains . . | 219 | 358 | 393 | 460 | 442 | 457 | 424 | 370 | 305 |
| Percent of U.S. in Northern Plains | 5.5 | 7.9 | 6.9 | 7.2 | 6.8 | 7.3 | 7.0 | 6.9 | 8.2 |

Sources: 1880–1950 data reprinted from *Capital in Agriculture: Its Formation and Financing since 1870*, by A. S. Tostlebee, by permission of the Princeton University Press, copyright 1957, by Princeton University Press, all rights reserved; 1959 data from *U.S. Statistical Abstract, 1963*, table 852, p. 619.

The resource adjustments that have taken place in the Northern Plains can also be illustrated by the changes in size of farm. Starting with 160 acres in 1880, Northern Plains farmers more than tripled the size of their farms by 1950, while corn-belt farms expanded their acreage by only 20 percent. Although acreage is a poor way of comparing size of farm business between areas like these, the comparisons illustrate both the inadequacy of farm size in the Northern Plains at the time of settlement and the drastic reshuffling and consolidation of farm units that has occurred since that time.

The relationship between resources and income in the Northern Plains, as compared with other areas, is revealed in Figure 24. In this chart, average gross farm incomes per person engaged in farming are plotted (for each census year) against the amounts of capital used per worker in farming. Constant (1910–14) dollars have been used to remove the effects of inflation. Capital includes land, buildings, machinery, workstock, and crop inventories. We can see first that the growth of all capital per worker in the Plains states was quite steady until 1920, slight until 1940, and then very rapid between 1940 and 1950. In fact, a comparison of the round dots and the square ones (using the bottom scale) shows that the Northern Plains states surpassed the corn-belt states in capital used per man by 1890, and have kept ahead of them ever since. The Northern Plains farmers were adding capital in the form of more land, while the Corn-belt farmers were adding non-land capital to farm more intensively. Capital per man in farming for the United States as a whole grew much more slowly, until 1940. Between 1940 and 1950 it grew by 45 per cent, however, compared with 31 percent in the corn-belt and 30 percent in the Plains states.

Gross income per farm worker in the Northern Plains also passed that of Corn-belt farmers in 1890, and kept ahead of them through 1940. Between 1940 and 1950, however, gross income per farm worker rose 145 percent in the corn-belt, compared with 65 percent in the Northern Plains; and, by 1950, the corn-belt was ahead.

By connecting the dots for each area, we can also see that—*with the same capital*—a corn-belt farm worker can produce more gross income than a farm worker in the Northern Plains. (The observation for 1940 was omitted since it was so far off what was otherwise a smooth upward trend; 1940 was an unusually poor year.) This has been true only since 1930, but the tendency seems to be strengthening. Why should this be? The new technology flowing into agriculture has been largely the kind that could "take root" on corn-belt farms. New fertilizers and spray materials for corn, as well as hybrid corn itself, benefit corn-belt farming more than Plains farming. Of course, irrigation is an example of technology that has increased the productivity of some Plains land. In general, however, the Plains has failed to share equally in the benefits of new technology, so that capital (on the average) now earns more in the corn-belt, given the same labor. Plains farmers have been counteracting this by using more capital per worker, a sensible course of action as long as the additional capital returns more than its annual cost.

The U.S. line in the chart also is steep enough to raise some questions. It reflects very rapid increases in efficiency and adoption of technology in farming on the west coast, in the northeast, and in the south.

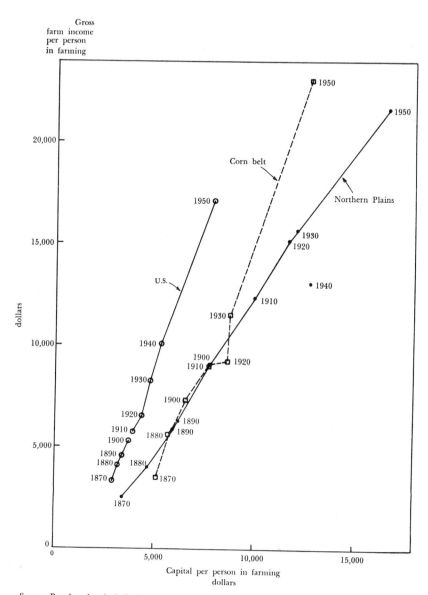

Source: Based on data in A. S. Tostlebee. *Capital in Agriculture: Its Formation and Financing since 1870.* (Princeton: Princeton University Press, 1957.)

FIG. 24. GROSS FARM INCOME AND CAPITAL PER PERSON, 1870–1950 (IN 1910–14 DOLLARS)

139

ECONOMIC DEVELOPMENT IN SELECTED COUNTIES

County data give a sharper picture of some of the differences between the Northern Plains transition area and its neighboring areas to the east and west with respect to economic development. As data sources, four transition-area counties were selected, one in each of the Northern Plains states, as shown on the map in Figure 25. Of the counties lying to the west of the transition area, five that represent favorable stages of farm resource adjustment were selected for comparison. Bowman County, North Dakota, is a cash grain county, as are Cheyenne County in Nebraska and Thomas County in Kansas; Haakon County, South Dakota, and Cherry County, Nebraska, are dominated by livestock ranching. Finally, three eastern counties represent more

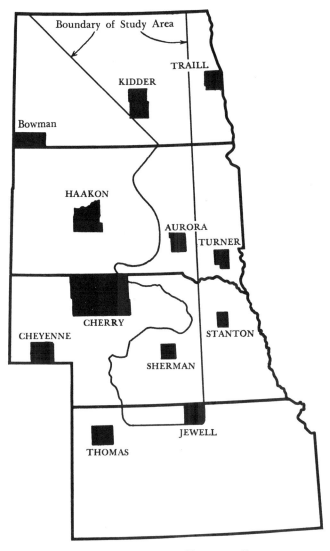

FIG. 25.   COUNTIES USED FOR ECONOMIC COMPARISONS

intensive farming in comparatively adjusted situations: Traill County in North Dakota, Turner County in South Dakota, and Stanton County in Nebraska. We chose no county in eastern Kansas because that area has a "small farm" problem, somewhat like that of southern Iowa and Missouri, and is not really representative of adjusted corn-belt farming. Counties near urban centers—like Omaha, Nebraska, or Fargo, North Dakota—were also avoided.

The general characteristics of the economy of these selected counties are shown in Table 27. All of these counties are truly agricultural; nearly all of them experienced out-migration during the decade of the forties. The income disadvantage of the transition counties is quite clear, in their low–median income levels and in the small portion of the population with incomes of more than $5,000.

The economic characteristics of farming in the selected counties are summarized in Table 28. Although differing in the amounts of capital used, these counties are quite uniform in their average labor force per farm. The percentages of the commercial farms in the various economic classes give a clearer picture of the income structure of farming in these counties. There is a large variation in income levels among farms in each of the counties. However, the higher levels of the entire income structure in the nontransition counties are also obvious.

With this glimpse at the differences between transition-area and nontransition-area counties, we can examine the process by which they developed through time. The comparative development rates of the selected counties, measured in terms of value of product per farm (in 1910–14 dollars), are shown in Figure 26. The four transition-area counties of Kidder, Aurora, Sherman, and Jewell have generally had lower levels of production per farms than have either the selected eastern or western counties of the Northern Plains. It is not that their average production has decreased in absolute terms; rather, they have fallen behind, relatively, because other counties made more progress.

Particularly impressive have been the rates of growth of gross-value product in Thomas, Cherry, Cheyenne, Stanton, and Haakon counties. Traill County has shown stability at a rather high level of income; Turner and Bowman counties have tended to be only slightly above the transition counties. The latter have shown growth per farm since 1939, but the dollar differences between them and the other counties have also tended to widen since that time.

Partial explanation of the differences in income growth between counties can be seen, in Figure 27, in the average acreage per farm for the same ten-year periods. Compare the increases in size of farm in Cherry, Haakon, and Bowman counties with those in Thomas, Kidder and Cheyenne. The sizes of farms in the other counties have been much more stable. However, Stanton and Turner counties apparently did not "have as far to go"; they also were able to take other measures besides adding acres to increase incomes per farm.

Acres are a poor measure for comparisons of size of farm between areas, however. A better idea of the growth in real size of farm is given in the average values of land and buildings per farm, which are given in constant, 1910–14 dollars in Figure 28. Productivity is presumably reflected in land values. A small farm of very productive, high-priced land may be the same "size"—in terms of resources—as a large farm that has land of low productivity and low price. Again, the western counties exceeded

TABLE 27. SOCIO-ECONOMIC CHARACTERISTICS OF THE SELECTED COUNTIES

| | High Plains Counties | | | | | Transition Counties | | | | Eastern Area Counties | | |
|---|---|---|---|---|---|---|---|---|---|---|---|---|
| | Cheyenne Neb. | Bowman N.D. | Haakon S.D. | Cherry Neb. | Thomas Kan. | Kidder N.D. | Aurora S.D. | Sherman Neb. | Jewell Kan. | Traill N.D. | Turner S.D. | Stanton Neb. |
| Population, 1950 | 12,081 | 4,001 | 3,167 | 8,397 | 7,572 | 6,168 | 5,020 | 6,421 | 9,698 | 11,359 | 12,100 | 6,387 |
| Population per sq. mi. | 10 | 3 | 2 | 1 | 7 | 5 | 7 | 11 | 11 | 13 | 20 | 15 |
| Population changes 1940–50 | 27.1% | 3.7% | −9.9% | −12.9% | 17.9% | −7.8% | −6.8% | −17.3% | −19.0% | −7.7% | −8.8% | −7.3% |
| Percent employed in manufacturing | 2.2 | 1.3 | 0.9 | 0.8 | 0.9 | 0.5 | 1.5 | 1.2 | 1.5 | 1.2 | 1.7 | 1.3 |
| Percent employed in agriculture | 28.4 | 50.9 | 64.7 | 55.3 | 48.3 | 70.7 | 64.7 | 60.4 | 58.4 | 51.5 | 58.2 | 73.0 |
| Median income per family, 1949 | $3,179 | $3,038 | $3,682 | $2,500 | $2,625 | $2,034 | $2,125 | $2,216 | $1,966 | $2,770 | $2,980 | $2,340 |
| Percent of families with incomes greater than $5,000, 1949 | 24.6 | 25.4 | 32.5 | 19.8 | 19.5 | 8.5 | 11.6 | 7.0 | 11.0 | 19.0 | 10.7 | 16.0 |
| Estimated annual wages per worker, 1949: | | | | | | | | | | | | |
| Retail trade | $2,366 | $2,445 | $2,233 | $2,377 | $2,444 | $2,245 | $1,591 | $2,096 | $1,932 | $1,979 | $1,793 | $2,286 |
| Wholesale trade | 3,427 | n.a.* | n.a. | 2,241 | 3,000 | n.a. | 2,937 | n.a. | 1,633 | 2,243 | 2,764 | n.a. |
| Service trades | 2,086 | 2,227 | 1,750 | 1,500 | 1,447 | 1,000 | 571 | 1,556 | 1,692 | 1,348 | 1,278 | 1,400 |
| Manufacturing | 3,425 | n.a. | n.a. | 3,192 | 2,200 | n.a. | 3,000 | 2,944 | 2,333 | 2,514 | 2,667 | 3,250 |

Source: *County and City Data Book, 1956.*

* Not available.

142

|  | High Plains Counties | | | | | Transition Counties | | | | Eastern Area Counties | | |
|---|---|---|---|---|---|---|---|---|---|---|---|---|
|  | Bowman N.D. | Haakon S.D. | Cherry Neb. | Thomas Kan. | Cheyenne Neb. | Kidder N.D. | Aurora S.D. | Sherman Neb. | Jewell Kan. | Traill N.D. | Turner S.D. | Stanton Neb. |
| Number of farms | 537 | 431 | 812 | 731 | 953 | 871 | 817 | 1,021 | 1,553 | 1,326 | 1,866 | 1,150 |
| Average size of farm (acres) | 1,354.2 | 2,655.8 | 4,577.7 | 1,014.1 | 832.8 | 948.3 | 543.3 | 336.8 | 336.0 | 409.1 | 207.1 | 229.0 |
| Value of farmland per acre (dollars) | 20.96 | 15.85 | 19.54 | 71.64 | 76.04 | 15.45 | 32.16 | 52.05 | 63.54 | 88.49 | 142.81 | 137.90 |
| Percent of total sales from crops | 53 | 27 | 21 | 76 | 82 | 45 | 27 | 23 | 60 | 80 | 29 | 10 |
| Total labor used per farm (man-years) | 1.57 | 1.70 | 1.79 | 1.53 | 1.75 | 1.84 | 1.72 | 1.83 | 1.51 | 1.47 | 1.60 | 1.69 |
| Investment per farm (dollars): | | | | | | | | | | | | |
| Land & buildings | 27,563 | 39,850 | 82,950 | 77,812 | 64,277 | 15,617 | 22,412 | 18,602 | 22,345 | 39,084 | 30,655 | 32,947 |
| Livestock | 6,498 | 16,371 | 35,250 | 5,134 | 3,186 | 8,000 | 8,069 | 5,546 | 3,770 | 2,231 | 4,676 | 7,653 |
| Machinery & power | 7,279 | 6,079 | 8,190 | 7,234 | 6,623 | 6,071 | 5,894 | 4,646 | 5,735 | 7,446 | 5,523 | 5,997 |
| Total | 41,340 | 62,300 | 126,390 | 90,180 | 74,086 | 29,688 | 36,375 | 28,794 | 31,850 | 48,761 | 40,854 | 46,597 |
| Investment per worker (dollars) | 26,331 | 36,647 | 70,609 | 58,941 | 42,335 | 16,135 | 21,148 | 15,734 | 21,093 | 33,171 | 25,534 | 27,572 |
| Percent of commercial farms in various economic classes: | | | | | | | | | | | | |
| I (Gross sales of $25,000 or more) | .9 | 6.8 | 21.5 | 9.8 | 8.1 | .7 | 2.2 | .2 | 3.2 | 4.8 | 1.5 | 8.4 |
| II (Gross sales of $10,000 to $25,000) | 10.8 | 21.7 | 27.4 | 35.7 | 41.3 | 8.0 | 11.8 | 6.2 | 16.9 | 28.0 | 14.0 | 17.7 |
| III (Gross sales of $5,000 to $10,000) | 24.1 | 29.8 | 19.8 | 26.2 | 29.0 | 27.1 | 43.0 | 32.3 | 36.9 | 38.6 | 42.8 | 38.9 |
| IV (Gross sales of $2,500 to $4,900) | 38.2 | 24.5 | 18.0 | 14.9 | 13.1 | 41.1 | 28.1 | 32.3 | 21.9 | 21.1 | 28.0 | 27.2 |
| V & VI (Gross sales of less than $2,500) | 26.0 | 17.2 | 13.3 | 13.4 | 8.5 | 23.1 | 14.9 | 29.0 | 21.1 | 17.5 | 13.7 | 7.8 |

Source: *Census of Agriculture, 1954.*

143

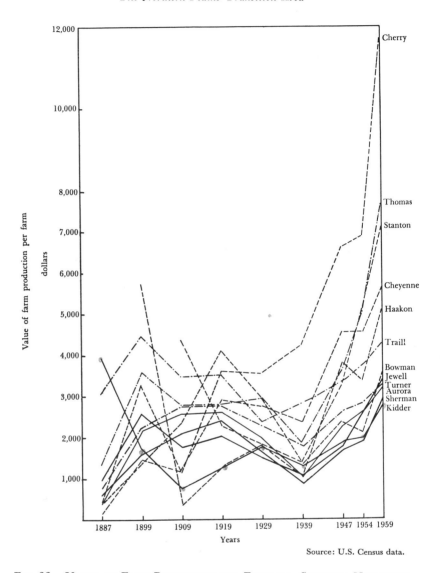

FIG. 26. VALUE OF FARM PRODUCTION PER FARM FOR SELECTED NORTHERN PLAINS COUNTIES (IN 1910–14 DOLLARS), 1887–1959

both the eastern and the transition counties in rates of increase. The eastern counties also show somewhat larger investments in land and buildings than the transition-area counties. It is apparent that a source of the growth shown by some of the nontransition counties, and the greater relative (but stable) prosperity of the others, has been the greater amounts of capital their farmers could combine with manpower—with land and buildings being a major class of capital in farming.

This is illustrated more clearly in Figure 29, where the estimated values of farm

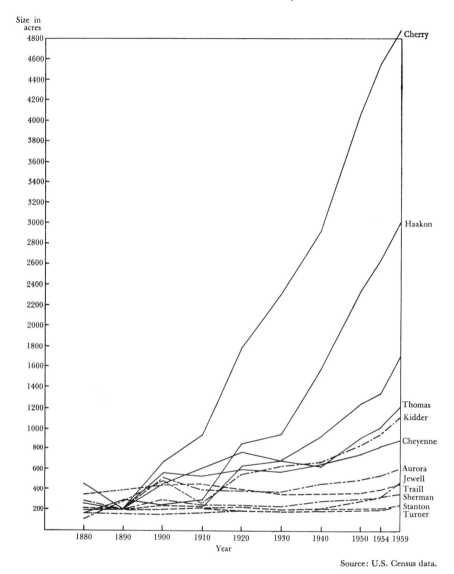

Source: U.S. Census data.

FIG. 27. AVERAGE SIZE OF FARM IN SELECTED NORTHERN PLAINS COUNTIES, 1880–1959

production per farm worker in 1954 have been plotted against the estimated investment in land, buildings, machinery, and livestock per worker in the same year. The degree of resource adjustment in terms of resources per man that has taken place in the western areas is illustrated, as well as that of some of the eastern counties. We can also see more clearly why Turner and Bowman counties occupied intermediate positions in these comparisons, along with the transition counties of Jewell and Aurora, and why Kidder and Sherman run a poor third.

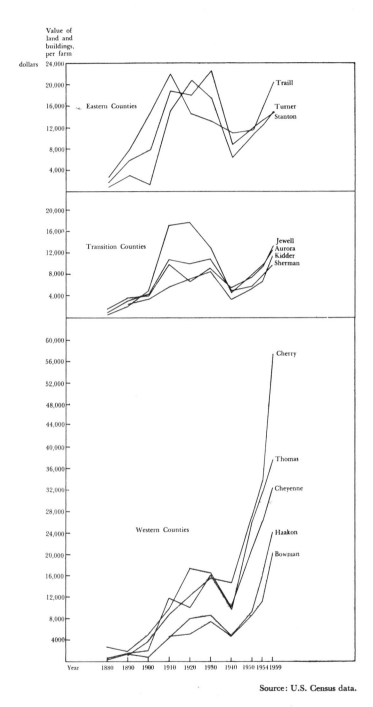

Source: U.S. Census data.

Fig. 28.   Value of Land and Buildings per Farm in Selected Northern
Plains Counties (1910–14 Dollars)

146

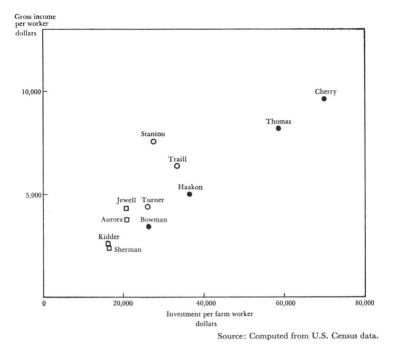

Source: Computed from U.S. Census data.

Fig. 29. Relationship between Gross Income per Farm Worker and Investment per Farm Worker in the Selected Counties, 1954

# CHAPTER 10

# Inheritance of the Transition Area from other Economies and Cultures

AFTER EXAMINING the characteristics of economic development in the last chapter, we ended with some preliminary probing of the Plains transition area. Comparing its agriculture with that of other neighboring areas, we became aware that the area has fallen behind economically over the years. In the rest of Part II we shall devote our attention to a detailed analysis of the agricultural and social problems of this transitional area. These arose out of the conflict between the practices, institutions, knowledge, and cultures imported by the settlers, on the one hand, and the environment—that is, the resources of the area—on the other. An understanding of these importations, and of how they were introduced, provides perspective for a view of the area's current problems.

## THE NATURAL RESOURCES

It is no wonder that settlers were favorably impressed by the land of the Northern Plains transition area. On it grew heavy stands of the tall grasses, shading off into the short grasses at the western fringes. It seemed to be made for farming; the land was flat or gently rolling, and, for the most part, plowable. The absence of trees and the gentle landscape must have appealed to farmers accustomed to the small fields in New York or Ohio—after they conquered their initial impulse to flee from so much open sky. The chernozem soils, when plowed, appeared very productive, with their deep colors ranging from dark brown to black, and there were no rocks or other impediments to implements. On the western fringes, the chestnut soils of the western Dakotas, Nebraska, and Kansas would have seemed only slightly less inviting.

Most of the differences in soils a settler might have noticed in traveling across the 98th meridian were due to climate, yet rare was the settler who realized this. Nor did he visualize climate in terms of long-run average rainfall. More likely he had an impression of particular conditions that he found on his first trip out, or those met by some acquaintances during the previous year, or even those described to him by some promoter or outlined in the colorful and widely distributed literature about the region.

From the evidence immediately at hand, a settler had no way of knowing that annual rainfall decreased by about 1 inch for every 30 miles he traveled west of Lincoln, Nebraska. In fact, in a wet year, and under the native grass cover, the landscape in Howard County, 84 miles to the west as the crow flies—or in Custer

County, 140 miles to the west—would have seemed very much like Lincoln's. Even if he had known that in this journey he had passed from a region of 27-inch average rainfall to one of 23 or 22 inches, he might not have been greatly impressed, since these differences seem insignificant; larger ones can be observed in various parts of Illinois and Iowa. However, when we assume an average annual rainfall of 20 to 24 inches as the lower margin of corn-belt-type crop production, these differences become critical.

Yet low average rainfall is not the only important climatic feature; its variability is also of some moment. The common belief that rainfall varies more as one moves west across the Plains is fallacious, as data from several Nebraska weather stations show.

| Stations | | Coefficient of Variability of Rainfall (Percent)* |
|---|---|---|
| Eastern | | |
| West Point | (Cuming Co.) . . . . . . . . | 20.1 |
| Ashland | (Saunders Co.) . . . . . . . . | 25.7 |
| Transition Area | | |
| St. Paul | (Howard Co.) . . . . . . . . | 18.2 |
| Broken Bow | (Custer Co.) . . . . . . . . . | 20.3 |
| Western Area | | |
| Lodge Pole | (Cheyenne Co.) . . . . . . . | 25.6 |
| Hay Springs | (Sheridan Co.) . . . . . . . . | 21.7 |

\* Weather Bureau data. Coefficient of variability is the percentage range, on each side of the average, in which two-thirds of the individual observations occur.

Nevertheless, when this variability is coupled with the lower average rainfall in the west, the likelihood of crop failure in any given year is increased.

Crop failure can stem from either physical or economic characteristics of production. Crop farming involves the application of certain fixed factors—investment in land, buildings, and equipment—and other variable ones, such as gasoline, seed, and sprays, to bring plants to the stage of growth where they will yield some product. Crop failure in the physical sense occurs when the plants yield little or no product at all, and in the economic sense when the resulting product fails to cover the costs of production—either the cash costs in the short run, or, in the longer run, the costs of all resources used, including opportunity costs. Thus there is a level of rainfall below which economic crop failure will result.

### INHERITANCES OF THE TRANSITION AREA FROM OTHER ECONOMIES

The problems created by the interaction of imported practices and ideas with the particular natural conditions in the Plains were recognized by President Roosevelt in 1937, in transmitting the report of his Great Plains Committee to Congress.

> I transmit herewith for the information of the Congress the report of the Great Plains Committee under the title, "The Future of the Great Plains."
> ... Depression and drouth have only accentuated a situation which has been long developing. ...

The settlers of the Plains brought with them agricultural practices developed in the more humid regions from which they came. . . . The long-run experience, however, has disclosed that the rainfall of the area hovers around, and, for considerable periods, falls below the critical point at which it is possible to grow crops by the agricultural methods common to humid regions. A new economy must be developed which is based on the conservation and effective utilization of all of the water available, especially that which falls as rain and snow; an economy which represents generally a more rational adjustment of the organization of agriculture and cropping plans and methods to natural conditions. . . .[1]

### Frontier Optimism

The fortitude of the pioneers who staked out homesteads and took up life in the Plains country is legendary, and rightly so. It must have taken courage of a high order to make families pile all their possessions into covered wagons and travel for hundreds of miles to a mysterious new land. A rash, devil-may-care confidence in the future manifested itself on all sides. The spirit of the boomers was contagious, as they created "paper" towns along the rail lines and sold lots to the people back east. Free land, a powerful incentive to settlement, helped compensate for the astounding lack of information characteristic of the whole process. Many settlers took up claims not to remain on them but to sell them later at a profit. Speculators bought railroad land for the same purpose. More serious settlers mistook a series of high rainfall years in the decade of the 1870's for a permanent phenomenon, or considered this proof that the climate changed with settlement. These great expectations were capitalized into land values, with disastrous effects for those who had borrowed money under real estate mortgages.

A residual of this frontier optimism remains in the Plains today. In areas of variable rainfall, farmers are inclined to remember the years of above-average rainfall; they come to be regarded as "normal," which means that crop yields are "below normal" most of the time. An aura of disaster looms over the countryside when a sequence of two or three dry years occurs, but this could be eliminated if such events were correctly recognized as normal phenomena, to be taken into account in business planning and in community life.

### Rectangular Survey

The rectangular survey was an inheritance of the land ordinance of 1785. Although there had been a debate preceding its adoption, when it was pointed out that "if the country was not square, the lines could not be run in squares,"[2] its ease and simplicity apparently won out. Surveyors usually preceded the settlers, and they charted the frontier country with series of parallel lines, ignoring topography, rivers, climate, or soil differences. Farms and roads were laid out on the same basis, and the later addition of fences rendered them permanent. These boundaries have since hampered the planning of irrigation and the arrangement of fields and farm units; they have aggravated the general problems of land use.

Obviously, the rectangular survey was convenient; it was easy to train surveyors to do the job since it called for little knowledge about the areas involved; and the

[1] Elmer Starch, "The Great Plains Missouri Valley Region," in Merrill Jensen (ed.), *Regionalism in America* (Madison: The University of Wisconsin Press, 1951), p. 348.

[2] B. H. Hibbard, *A History of the Public Land Policies* (New York: The Macmillan Company, 1924), p. 66.

administration of the survey became a simple task. This single advantage was not enough to outweigh the many unfortunate consequences of its use in the Plains.

## The Preference for Private Ownership

The concept of private property has been basic in the nation's history, and has underlain its public land policies since independence. It was implicit in the policies encouraging the development of the west by establishing settlers in large numbers, the objective being to increase national strength, trade, and the demand for manufactured products. More recently the concept has been involved in the debates on publicly owned grazing land.

The preference for private ownership is based on the notion that land in private hands is automatically used for its best purposes, and that public control is necessarily less efficient. In the Plains, these beliefs have been tempered considerably in response to special problems, as evidenced by various kinds of group undertakings: drainage, reclamation, grazing, and conservation districts. Activities like these represent the surrender of some private property rights to the group, but testify to the superiority of group control in some situations.

## The Homestead Concept

The success of the homestead provision in stimulating settlement in Iowa and Missouri prompted the "free-soilers" of the corn-belt to back its extension to the Plains states. Its importation to the Plains—though seemingly based on proven performance—was ill advised, to say the least. The act did not attempt to ease settlement difficulties nor to cope with problems that might later arise. As Clawson puts it:

> The land laws simply were not well designed to meet their ostensible objectives. The Congress did not have adequate personal contact with natural conditions in the public land areas to make wise decisions . . . and they were unwilling to appropriate adequate funds to make the necessary investigations.[3]

The act's unsuitability to the Plains was clearly shown in its requirement that farmers plow their lands, even where this was wholly undesirable. Fifty-four years later, in 1916, the Stock-raising Homestead Act finally recognized that some land was uniquely suited to grazing. The settler had to establish residence on his homestead. This requirement, when coupled with the rectangular survey, inevitably encouraged the scattering of farmsteads over the countryside, with no reference to such broad considerations as natural roadways, watercourses, or other features of the topography.

The Timber Culture Act not only assumed that one could raise timber in the Plains but that one could do it in almost any eight-year period! Its failure was evidenced by the continued lack of any appreciable timber in either the semiarid or the subhumid regions.

Nebraska's designation, the "Tree Planter's State," is significant; it implies not that trees abound, nor even that they grow, but merely that they are planted. The impossible was attempted, in keeping with the act's directives. Yet the Timber Culture Act had one desirable, though unintended, result: its fraudulent application enabled settlers to add land to their units.[4]

[3] Marion Clawson, *Uncle Sam's Acres* (New York: Dodd, Mead & Co., 1951), p. 85.

[4] Hibbard, *op. cit.*, pp. 421–22.

The Desert Land Act was directed chiefly at land not fit for cultivation, since most of the tillable land had been taken up. It was not until 1904—with the Kinkaid Act, which applied only to Nebraska—and 1909—with the expansion of the homestead to 320 acres—that Congress officially recognized the difficulty of making a living on small homesteads in the Plains.

## The Family Farm Concept

The preference for small landholdings owned and operated by farm families is another embodiment of the Jeffersonian agrarianism of the east, which has been carried down through the discussions and policies concerning free land.[5] The unpopularity of large-scale farming and the villain's role played by the cattlemen—in the popular conception of the troubles between the homesteaders and the cattlemen—spring partly from the same orientation. During the depression, as we have seen, an emphasis on the inherent worth of small farms and the assumption that national welfare is promoted by keeping the largest possible number of families on the land as family farmers influenced some of the programs of the Farm Security Administration.

Differences of opinion on the definition of a family farm have arisen in recent years; the following comment illustrates one man's opinion.

> We can use, develop, and conserve our resources most efficiently on small farms. . . . Small farms have been the development of the common man. They foster the well-being of the ordinary family. They form the background for a sound community life.[6]

Even the orientation of the farm organizations reflect differences in definition. The Farmers Union defines the family farm as "an agricultural production unit which can be efficiently operated by a typical full-time operator or family that furnishes most of its own labor."[7] It is worried about the increase in farm size. The Farm Bureau, on the other hand, has not emphasized family labor as part of the definition; its concept of a family farm implies less concern with the size of farm.

The difficulties associated with the family farm concept have not arisen because of any demonstrated inability of family farms to compete with other types. On the contrary, the "bonanza" farms gave way before them. The argument arises because of (1) differences in the amount of nonfamily labor that can be allowed in defining a

[5] Jefferson stated that "The small land holders are the most precious part of the state"; quoted in Hibbard, *op. cit.*, p. 143.

[6] J. G. Ligutti, "Small Farms—We Need More of Them," *Farm Policy Forum* (Iowa State University Press), 1, No. 1 (January, 1948), 47.

[7] "The Modern Family Farm," Farmers Union Policy Leaflet No. 10. Land economists have devoted considerable thought to the definition of a family farm. One definition which has been quite widely accepted is found in Joseph Ackerman and Marshall Harris, *Family Farm Policy* (Chicago: University of Chicago Press, 1947), p. 389:

1. The entrepreneurial functions [are] vested in the farm family.

2. The human effort required to operate the farm [is] provided by the farm family with the addition of such supplementary labor as may be necessary, either for seasonal peak loads or during the developmental and transitional stages in the family itself. (The amount of such regular outside labor should not provide a total labor force in excess of that to be found in the family of "normal" size in the community.)

3. A farm [that is] large enough, in terms of land, capital, modern technology, and other resources, to employ the labor resources of the farm family efficiently.

family farm, and (2) the interpretation of concern over the *size of farm* problem as evidence of a desire to do away with family farms.

Family farm issues and those related to farm size in acres need to be very carefully distinguished. Acres have little meaning as a measure of scale of operations in an area as diverse as the Plains; their usefulness is limited to a comparison of farms of similar types on the same kind of soil. Community leaders, including some rural editors, often bridle at any suggestion of the need for larger farms; they think such a policy will inevitably lead to the ruin of rural communities. Out-movement of farmers associated with increased size of farms is not necessarily evidence of the economic downfall of the community, if we assume average rather than gross income as the appropriate index of community welfare.

Despite the many predictions of its demise, the family farm has shown considerable resilience in the Plains in terms of its ability to survive and to achieve efficient production. If we are liberal in our restriction on the use of hired labor, we find that most farms in the Plains, including ranch operations, are family units.

This is illustrated by Nebraska data. The census economic classes given an indication of farm size, although they are based on output rather than inputs. The number of Class I and II farms increased substantially in the five-year period between 1949 and 1954. By 1959 there were more farms with products worth $40,000 or more in Nebraska than there were with products worth $25,000 or more in 1950. Class I farms are considered by some to be larger than family farms. However, if one assumes that 70 percent of gross income goes to cover cash costs in farming, there should be little concern—from the family farm standpoint—about a farmer who grosses $25,000 and consequently nets $7,500.

Only 10 percent of Nebraska farms spent $2,500 or more for hired labor in 1959; less than 4 percent spent $5,000 or more. Expenditures of less than $5,000 probably do not represent a larger hired labor force than a liberal definition of family farms would permit, since this would represent not more than two and one-half full-time worker equivalents. Even in Cherry County, where there is a concentration of large ranch units, less than half of the farms spent more than $2,500 for hired labor.

We need a flexible concept of size of farm in the Plains area. Plains people have sometimes been criticized by corn-belt people for their interest in large farms; however, it probably takes a larger investment in land for a family to make a living in the Plains than it does in more humid sections farther east. Plains farmers do not have the same opportunity to apply other variable inputs to enhance yields, as do their neighbors to the east. Also, their heightened dependence on reserves, in the face of greater weather risks, necessitates a farm large enough to accumulate them rapidly during favorable periods so the family can be sustained in adverse times.

### Corn-belt Practices

Plains settlers naturally brought with them the practices they knew, chiefly those of the corn-belt. They took pride in their deep plowing and clean cultivation. A straight furrow was praised as evidence of a man's skill in handling a team of horses and a walking plow. Yet deep tillage and dust mulching—another common practice —were expensive and wasteful of moisture. This was a perilous course to follow in the Plains.

The western areas have since adjusted. Subtillage and stubble mulching leave crop residues on top of the soil—practices that prevent the soil from blowing and that help retain moisture. Cultivation costs have thus been cut and yields increased. However, the appearance of a stubble-mulched field is almost repulsive to farmers of an older era, and clean tillage is still approved by many farmers in the transition area.

Coming from the corn-belt states of Iowa and Illinois, many of the settlers were naturally interested in raising corn. They first planted sod corn as a "soil conditioner," and then planted corn in orthodox corn-belt fashion—after plowing up the sod. For example, Graham County in northwestern Kansas and Frontier County in south-western Nebraska had five times as many acres of corn as wheat during the 1880's.[8] These counties have about 20 inches of annual rainfall. Farther west and south, in Greeley County, Kansas, with a 16-inch average rainfall, there were nearly ten times as many acres of corn as of wheat during this period.

Part of the reason for the early spread of corn was the lack of satisfactory wheat varieties. The introduction of hard winter wheat, coupled with drought years, pushed corn east fairly rapidly. Yet even today a surprisingly large acreage is still devoted to corn in the transition area of central Nebraska.

Another inheritance from the east was the notion of diversification. It was imported to the Plains not so much by the settlers as by their leaders—editors, and others. It held that farming should rest on many enterprises—crops and livestock—to become more self-sufficient and to withstand weather and price risks. The notion breaks down because several enterprises imply a small size for each, and low returns per hour of labor. A man has to move fast, and cover large acreages in the Plains, if he is to get a high return from his labor, since the return per acre is lower than in the corn-belt.

An allied notion, springing from corn-belt agronomic research around the turn of the century, was the advocacy of regular crop rotations, including corn, with legume hay to provide nitrogen and small grain to bridge the gap involved in shifting land from one to the other. This was a valid idea for regions with more regular rainfall, but not for the Plains. Legumes are heavy moisture users, and finding a place for them in a cropping system takes careful judgment. Some land is more economically left under native grass cover, and hence does not enter into a rotation.

On soil which can be economically tilled, Northern Plains farmers pay less attention to what crop they raised last year in deciding what to raise this year, and more to the number of inches of soil moisture. In the westerly areas the alternatives on tilled land have been quite clear; it has been a matter of wheat and fallow, with sorghum as the next best alternative. The most flexible arrangement is where wheat may follow wheat, and fallow may on occasion succeed fallow, depending upon moisture. In the transition area, however, farmers have tried to imitate their corn-belt neighbors, with more diversified farming systems. They are still grappling with farming problems that were long ago solved by their neighbors to the west.

In a sense, diversification reappears in a new form in the Plains. Native pasture leads to livestock; and wheat, pasture, and livestock provide an important degree of diversification. In addition to the raising of feeder cattle, feeding may also be economical in these areas, using wheat and sorghum. (Hybrid sorghum promises to increase the competitiveness of this crop with wheat.)

[8] Robert P. Marple, "The Transition Zone between the Corn Belt and Hard Winter Wheat Belt" (unpublished Ph.D. thesis, University of Nebraska, 1958), p. 34.

In a nutshell, there has been a compromise between diversification and specialization. The small dairy herd, the small poultry flock, the family garden, the small orchard, the small flock of sheep or hogs, all on one farm, this romantic picture has been discarded.[9] The new diversification has a commercial rather than a subsistence orientation; it provides for sufficient specialization to let a man cover enough ground so his returns per hour and per dollar of working capital can be satisfactory. What has happened in the High Plains may well foreshadow solutions for farmers in the transition area.

### Buildings and Fences

Despite its colorful publicity, the sod shanty was but a fleeting expedient; the settler replaced it as soon as he could with a traditional house of lumber or brick, such as he had known in his childhood. He followed the patterns of the eastern humid environment to which he was accustomed. As with houses, so with other buildings; the erection of a large barn, with hay storage and a warm shelter for livestock, was viewed as proof of success. In Kansas, a Pennsylvania-style barn was also related to good farm management:

> Whenever Pennsylvania barns are seen all over our Prairies, we shall not fear insect pests, or any other disaster, for our farmers will always have enough in store to tide a bad year.[10]

The concern about reserves seems rational enough, but alternative approaches to this goal were not entertained.

The crucial aspect of the construction of farm houses and buildings is the amount of investment they represented, not only in total but in relation to the land resources to which they were attached. Vacant buildings thus were the inevitable heritage of adjustments of people to land, which came soon after settlement. In retrospect, this overinvestment in costly buildings ill suited to their environment represents wasted resources. The limited financial resources of the time could have been used much better in other ways.

The introduction of barbed wire fencing solidified the farm boundaries that had been established under the homesteading procedure. Straight field lines were fenced parallel to quarter lines, regardless of topography or soil type. Fencing kept the homesteader's cattle in and the rancher's cattle out. It spelled the end of the free range, as is well known. Less appreciated is the role it played in shutting farmers' cattle off from the undeveloped railroad lands that had been used as common pasturage. Barbed wire encouraged the entry of still more settlers and the taking up of land that had been bypassed in the first waves.

---

[9] In 1881 the average farm in Dickinson County, in central Kansas, had "160 acres, grew 50 acres of wheat, 36 acres of corn, one acre of potatoes, 3 or 4 acres of other crops, 4 horses or mules, 7 or 8 head of cattle, 12 hogs, 6 sheep, some plum and pear trees and raspberry, gooseberry, and blackberry bushes, besides some grape vines." From James C. Malin, *Winter Wheat in the Golden Belt of Kansas* (Lawrence: University of Kansas Press, 1944), p. 129.

This illustration is cited here not with the intention of criticizing what was the case in another age but because there are still romanticists who suggest the type of diversified, subsistence type of farming that was already on the way out in that area at that time. By 1954 the average-size farm in Dickinson County was 291 acres. Farms, on the average, had 35 head of cattle, 21 acres of corn, 22 acres of sorghum, 97 acres of small grains—mostly wheat—27 acres of tame hays, and 98 acres of permanent pasture. One-third of the farms had hogs, 8 percent had sheep, and 3 percent had fruit trees.

[10] Malin, *op. cit.*, p. 134.

Fencing also represented a heavy investment of resources; moreover, it cost as much to fence a poor quarter as a good one. As in the case of buildings, the process of *disinvestment* began almost immediately.

*Notions about Water*

Earlier, we noted conflicting views of the Plains. First came the "Great American Desert" concept, which implied a dismal future for the area. At the other extreme was the later "garden of the world" idea, which saw the Plains as a potential Nile River valley, based on irrigation. The first arose out of the observations of early explorers in the Southern Plains and hasty judgments of some easterners, like Horace Greeley, who traversed the Plains later. The second idea resulted from exaggerated notions of the amount of water available in the west for irrigation.

These varying concepts both stem from considerations of the same resource: water. Although water problems, as such, are not the focus of this book, it is appropriate to note the implications for Plains farming of imported ideas about water. While land use has improved considerably since the early days, our policies on water—particularly ground water—have remained at an immature stage.

The body of laws regulating the use of water in the Plains states is primarily riparian doctrine; it had its origin in English common law, and is an importation from the humid states to the east where competition for water was no problem. Under this doctrine, all the landowners along a stream have equal rights to the use of its water; however, the water in the stream cannot be diverted, and what is not used must be returned to the stream. Nor can the stream flow be appreciably diminished by its use. Owners whose land does not adjoin the stream have no right to its water, even though the water originates in the hydrographic area common to both types of owners. The law works well enough for such uses as milling, or watering stock, or even for use by a small factory or city, but difficulties arise when an irrigation development by an owner along the stream reduces the stream flow, since little irrigation water returns to the stream after use.

Riparian doctrine broke down in the semiarid states, as in Colorado and New Mexico, and has been replaced by another concept: the appropriation doctrine. This doctrine is of Mexican origin—and more remotely of Spanish and Roman origin. It requires that water be devoted to "useful" purposes, thus involving the concept of priority of use. It permits diversion from the stream to nonriparian lands, and grants the first appropriator exclusive use of the water right granted him—as opposed to the rights of later appropriators. Finally, non-use of a right means its eventual forfeiture.[11]

In the Plains states, the common law doctrine has been kept, but it has been modified by application of appropriation concepts to irrigation problems through the so-called California doctrine, or the Western doctrine of riparian rights.

The fundamental difficulty in land development in the Plains has been the imported concept of land as the scarce resource, rather than water. Consequently, thought has focused on the disposition of land, letting water follow as it might, rather than on the proper use of the water, and the organization of land around it.

[11] Walter P. Webb, *The Great Plains* (Boston: Ginn & Company, 1931), p. 437.

Much attention has been given to the legal problems surrounding stream irrigation in the Plains area. Yet ground water law is still a sort of no-man's land. The ground water under a particular tract of land is not a self-contained entity, unaffected by the operations around it. However, much investment in ground water facilities has been made as though this were the case. Water moves through the soil, although slowly, and the number of wells and the intensity of use on one farm can affect the volume of water available to another. The total supply of ground water under a particular tract can increase, remain static, or decrease—depending upon volume of use. We have seen only the beginning of economic and legal problems that will arise in the Plains as competition for ground water supplies increases.

*Financial Arrangements*

A prospective settler was not warned of financial problems, and most of the literature assumed they were nil. To quote one example:

> Any active young farmer who can control $500 to $1,000 or has that much invested in stock and farm machinery can come here, buy a home on time, or take up a piece of government land, and in a few years, providing he works as hard as he did in the east, be independent, owning his own home, free of debt, plenty of stock around him, good farm buildings, and preparing to live a life of ease and comfort.[12]

This rosy picture was something less than accurate, as the settler discovered when he tried to get a loan. Feelings ran high against the infamous eastern money lenders. Yet their high interest rates, considered exorbitant by the settlers, could be largely justified by the lack of indigenous financial resources and the admittedly large risks involved. Much of the early distress occurred because people were trying to make a living on farms that were too small. However, some basic difficulties in farm credit did stem from mortgage terms.

Farmers were expected to pay off "long-term" mortgages in three to five years. Annual payments of principal and interest were to be made on a regular basis, without recognition of the irregular way in which incomes accrue from one year to the next in Plains farming. The local lending institutions had limited resources since they derived their capital from deposits or other short-term obligations, and thus were themselves vulnerable to the variable climate. If these facts are coupled with the kind of optimism that typically pervaded these areas, it is easy to see how enthusiastic overexpansion of farm credit could lead to disaster.

Later federal institutions, including the Land Banks of 1916 and various agencies created under the Farm Credit Administration of 1933, provided credit of much longer term for farmers. The Farm Security Administration—later the Farmers Home Administration—instituted flexible repayments geared to farm income fluctuations. (The latter agency deals, however, only with farmers unable to obtain credit elsewhere.) These agencies, as well as the commercial banks, have learned much about lending in the Plains, but they still have much more to learn.

Commercial banks even now cannot grant mortgage loans with terms of more than five to ten years. (They do, of course, handle loans for insurance companies that lend

[12] M. W. M. Hargreaves, *Dry Farming in the Northern Great Plains, 1900–1925* (Cambridge: Harvard University Press, 1957), p. 519.

on a longer-term basis.) Flexible payment provisions are not available to most farmers from private, cooperative, or public credit agencies. In view of the large real estate capital requirements in relation to other resources in Plains farming, the notion that a farm family should pay off an entire farm's mortgage during the course of a single farming career may be increasingly unrealistic.

### *The Property Tax*

Notwithstanding the Plains states' heavy reliance on it, the property tax is actually one more heritage from eastern states of an earlier era. It is not well adapted to Plains farming because of its fixed nature in the face of variable income. Farmers are least able to pay their taxes in years of low farm incomes, just when the revenue needs to state and local governments are greatest. This becomes particularly serious when two, three, or more low-income years follow in succession. Plains governments, like Plains farmers, should operate in the longer run, rather than on a year-to-year basis. They should build up reserves for lean years during years when taxpayers are best able to pay their taxes. This is true whether their reliance is chiefly or only partially on property taxes as a source of revenue.

A corollary difficulty with the property tax is its effect on farm reserves. For example, a farmer or rancher who accumulates extensive reserves of feed over a series of good years will be penalized for doing so because tax rates on tangible property discriminate against such physical reserves.

Finally, the relationship between the assessed value of farmland and its productivity is frequently only slight. If we are interested in relating taxes to the land's ability to produce income, this means that land of low productivity is overtaxed in relation to more highly productive land.

# CHAPTER 11

# Farm Organization and Income in the Transition Area

WE CAN ASSUME that most farm people, including those in the transition area, want higher financial returns to their labor, management, and accumulated capital—consistent with a reasonable degree of stability in earnings. Nonmonetary returns and resource immobility may weaken this assumption; nevertheless, the idea is sufficiently accurate to justify the use of monetary measures to appraise present farming operations and to evaluate possible alternatives. Money earnings can be compared with those of other farms, with estimated requirements for family living, and with earnings of nonfarm people.

Thair states that dry-land farmers on the Great Plains have a twofold objective: to maximize their incomes and to avoid insolvency and substandard living conditions. Both goals can exist simultaneously in farmers' minds, and either one may dominate at a given point in time. Thair believes both objectives are essential to a satisfactory explanation of rational behavior in agriculture. He points out that uncertainty (presumably as found in the Great Plains) is more than a deductible cost; it can disrupt operations when continuity is required to realize maximum profits and a satisfactory livelihood.[1] This point is extremely important; research workers and educators cannot afford to overlook it. Farm planners and those engaged in agricultural policy formulation must also be conscious of the serious errors that can result from failing to take the second goal into account.

The farmer who encounters severe losses early in his career may be forced out of business before he can realize any of the compensatory higher earnings that would be forthcoming in later, more favorable years.[2] For him, the second objective—maintaining solvency—may be of the utmost importance in determining the enterprises selected, the size of operation, and the practices used. Under our present systems of tenure and financing, such behavior is rational.

Thair also points out that these two goals may occasionally conflict, and at other times complement each other. For example, some farmers may elect to use their feed resources through a beef breeding-herd rather than through steers, even though they

[1] Philip J. Thair, *Meeting The Impact of Crop-Yield Risks in Great Plains Farming*, North Dakota Experiment Station Bulletin 392 (June, 1954), p. 9.

[2] E. Lloyd Barber, *Meeting Weather Risks in Kansas Wheat Farming*, Agricultural Economics Report No. 44, Kansas Agricultural Experiment Station and USDA (September, 1950).

159

recognize that the latter would probably yield higher average returns. This behavior is not necessarily irrational. The greater risks that accompany the higher earnings from steers may be more than they are willing to assume. Whether a farmer will hazard such a risk depends on many factors: the amount of capital (both absolute and relative) at stake, the effect of a possible loss on his ability to stay in business or on his future operation if he does stay in business, alternative opportunities for the use of resources if he should be forced out of business, etc. Such considerations may cause some farmers to choose the safer enterprise in spite of its low returns.

Some efforts to lessen uncertainty also enhance earnings. For example, the practice of summer fallowing land in an area of low rainfall promotes storage of needed soil moisture and the accumulation of nitrogen, and hence lessens the likelihood of poor crop yields. Experience shows that fallowing not only reduces yield variability but increases net earnings.

## NONMONETARY CONSIDERATIONS

It is often said that farming is a "way of life." It cannot be denied that farm life has certain characteristics that tend to set it apart. Presumably, those who farm believe that farmlife, with its psychic values as well as money income, gives them a greater total return than any other occupation. In their eyes, the income disadvantage in farming is more than offset by nonmonetary rewards. Some of these rewards are: being one's own boss, working with plants and animals, being away from the noisy confusion of the city, rearing a family where children have a simple play area and yet can be kept under close parental control, and providing youngsters with the opportunity to work and to assume responsibility.

To other families, the disagreeable features loom large. Drought, crop failures, livestock disease, and ravages of weeds and insects are experiences never to be forgotten. The struggle against the elements—snow, rain, hail, mud, bitter cold, and scorching heat—is a personal battle on a farm and it admits no conscientious objectors. Those who see chiefly this aspect of farmlife are among the many who have already left the farm, or who will soon do so, to seek employment elsewhere.

In short, it is difficult to measure the values people place on these nonmonetary rewards of farmlife, although it is clear that they do possess some value. The relative values of both monetary and nonmonetary characteristics of farmlife also differ from one person to another. Nevertheless, it can be said that farming, as a way of life, is becoming less important in determining whether a family stays on the farm.

Since nonmonetary considerations are virtually impossible to measure, this discussion will focus on an appraisal of the monetary returns to land, labor, capital, and management in the Northern Plains states, and especially in their transition area.

## INCOME NEEDS

To evaluate the adequacy of farming operations, some kind of measuring stick is required. Since one of the primary objectives of any occupational endeavor is to make a living, it seems logical to compare farm earnings with the amount of money required to provide a moderate, modern living to farm families. In addition to current living needs, some allowance must be made for savings to be used for children's education, for retirement, for the accumulation of property (as a source of retirement income), and for reserves to be drawn upon in emergencies.

*Family Living*

According to Anderson, the average amount required by Nebraska transition-area farm families for family living in the 1950's was about $2,400—for a family with three children. This was the annual average required during the forty years during which the household head was between twenty-five and sixty-five. Specific annual requirements varied within this span according to the stage of family development. The $2,400 figure included no provision for savings toward purchase of a farm, nor did it include much for any capital requirements associated with retirement.[3]

Records kept by Kansas farm-management association families during the years 1959–62 revealed that these families spent an average of $3,563, in addition to the value of farm-raised products used in the home.[4] During the years when teenage children were at home, these expenses were substantially higher. These findings were similar to those in Iowa. The average annual cash expenditure by Iowa farm families was $3,494 for the same years.[5]

A study committee, composed of agricultural extension leaders in central Nebraska, estimated that a young couple just starting to farm in 1956, with either no children or with one or two very young ones, might be able to live on $2,000. As the children grew older, the committee felt $2,800–$3,000 would be required. After the children had left home, it was estimated that the cost might drop somewhat, but not as low as the original level. In terms of early 1964 prices, these figures would have to be raised 11 or 12 percent.

On the basis of the foregoing data, it seems that an allowance for average day-to-day family living expenses of $3,000–$4,000, or an average of $3,500, would not be excessive under 1964 conditions.

*Saving for Future Needs*

Under the influence of private enterprise and ownership, the financial success of a farm family has come to be judged by the amount of property accumulated during the farmer's lifetime. Moreover, the property accumulated during its working lifetime serves as the basis of its income during retirement years. Thus, at least until social security came along, most young couples who set out to farm hoped to own a place of their own by the time they retired.

Many farm families receive assistance from parents when they are getting started. They may be given furniture or machinery, at least for temporary use, but they are soon faced with the necessity for saving, and their first savings usually go toward the purchase of household goods and machinery. How much they need depends on their goals. Since most young couples have more of the labor resource than any other, they can often economize their limited supply of capital by buying used furniture and

[3] Anton H. Anderson, *Agricultural Economics Departmental Report No. 24* (Lincoln: University of Nebraska [August], 1961), p. 6.

[4] *Kansas Farm Management Summary and Analysis Report*, Agricultural Extension Service, Kansas State University, Annual Reports, 1959–63.

[5] *Family Living Expenditures of 183 Iowa Farm Families*, Iowa State University, FM–1426 (1962), p. 3.

machinery and by doing the necessary repair work themselves. The scale of farming contemplated and the combination of enterprises considered have an important bearing on the amount and type of machinery needed. A total of $10,000–$20,000 for household goods and farm machinery is probably a conservative estimate of the capital required during the first fifteen years of farming.

As the business of farming becomes more complex, an increasing proportion of farm children seeks jobs in other parts of our economy. The need for a college education has intensified. Thus many farm families now include a college education for their children among the goals calling for savings. If the parents provide all or most of the money needed, the amount is substantial, particularly if more than one child is involved. A couple would have to set aside about $165 a year (at 5 percent interest) from the time a child was born (at parents' age twenty-five) until he completed high school if they were to provide him about $4,800 during the four college years. Two children would necessitate annual savings of $305; three, $426; and four, $530.

A study by the U.S. Agricultural Research Service concluded that an investment of about $70,000 (exclusive of machinery) would be required under Central Plains conditions in Kansas (a beef-wheat farm) to enable the operator to earn $2,500 annually.[6] This assumed 1955 cost-price relationships. To bring his annual earnings up to $3,500, an additional investment of $20,000 would be needed. Another study revealed that capital assets used in farming ranged from $40,000 to $76,000 in two regions that correspond roughly to the transition area discussed in this book.[7] The value of assets used by tenants was just as large as that of full owners, and part owners used considerably more than either of them. Annual summaries of farm records in north-central Kansas and Nebraska show that investments of $50,000–$100,000 are not uncommon.

It is clear from these data that the young farmer who expects to become a debt-free owner must make substantial savings during his working years. Nor is this the only goal for which he must save. Such items as life insurance, accumulation of a cash reserve, and, in more recent years, social security payments all have a bearing on a family's savings. Table 29 gives some estimates of the annual savings required to achieve certain designated goals. These figures are somewhat conservative since no allowance is made for future inflation.

It is apparent that farmers must earn substantially more than the amount needed for living expenses if their lifetime goals are to be achieved. In fact, a farm would have to net $5,000 a year to provide $3,500 for living expenses and $1,500 for savings. Comparatively few farms in the Northern Plains do this. During the early sixties, operating expenses were taking 65–75 cents of each dollar of income received. To net $5,000, a farm would have to gross $14,286 if operating expenses took 65 per-cent of income, $16,667 if they took 70 percent, and $20,000 if they took 75 percent. Only one Nebraska farm in six received as much as $20,000 in 1959, among commercial farms.

[6] John M. Brewster, *Farm Resources Needed for Specified Income Levels*, Agriculture Information Bulletin No. 180, U.S. Agricultural Research Service (December, 1957), p. 20.

[7] Russell W. Bierman, "Farm Credit and Farm Debts in the Great Plains," ch. 7 in *Farming in the Great Plains—a Survey of the Financial and Tenure Situation in 1957*, USDA Production Research Report No. 50, USDA Agricultural Research Service, p. 27.

TABLE 29. APPROXIMATE ANNUAL SAVINGS (BEGINNING AT FATHER'S AGE 25) REQUIRED TO ACHIEVE CERTAIN GOALS

| Goal | Savings assumed to compound at: 3½% | 5% |
|---|---|---|
| Education: $4,800 for child's education, available at father's age 42 . . . . . . . . . . . . . . . . | $ 190 | $165 |
| Household goods & machinery: $15,000 available at father's age 40 . . . . . . . . . . . . . . . | 777 | 695 |
| Cash reserve: $1,000 available at father's age 35 . . . | 85 | 80 |
| Life insurance: $10,000 ordinary life policy, begun at father's age 25, dividends paid toward premium . . | 85 | 85 |
| Accumulation of down-payment on farm: $20,000 available at father's age 40 . . . . . . . . . . . | 1,037 | 927 |

Source: Neb. Agr. Exp. Sta. data.

### ALTERNATIVE OPPORTUNITIES FOR USE OF RESOURCES

The need for farm income can be approached from still another angle. If resources fail to earn as much in the current use as in another one, a tendency to transfer resources should result.

Until quite recently, the tendency of farm families to regard farming as a way of life rather than as a strictly money-making activity served to hold both human and capital resources in farming longer than monetary considerations alone would justify. Today, however, farm people have become increasingly aware of job and income opportunities elsewhere. To a more limited extent, they have learned what their capital might earn if invested in something other than farm property. Young people especially have been inclined to make comparisons. Per capita incomes of farm people have averaged only about half of those of nonfarm people during the last twenty years.

Alternative uses of capital are more difficult to evaluate. Several aspects should be considered, including not only annual earnings but also opportunities for investment of additional capital, comparative effects of inflation or deflation, amounts of capital required, amount of management required on the part of the investor, stability of year-to-year earnings, and others.

Generally speaking, farmers are not familiar with other types of investment and are hesitant to venture into these fields. This lack of familiarity is not an insurmountable obstacle, however. The possibilities of investing in government bonds are probably most familiar to farm families. They are aware that they could get 3 to 4 percent interest on their money. Most of them are familiar with rates paid on savings accounts. Such opportunities offer safety of principal, with few (if any) worries to the investor. They have the distinct disadvantage, however, of offering no hedge against inflation. Although most farm people are reasonably well informed about the rate of interest being paid on real estate mortgages, many either do not have or could not acquire enough capital to make loans of this kind. Furthermore, many would hesitate to make such loans even if they had the capital readily available; they are not prepared to evaluate either the purpose of the loan or the character of the person seeking it.

Similarly, most farm people are hesitant to put money into stocks. They tend to suspect anyone who deals in or invests in common stocks; he is not quite "honest and above-board" somehow. In their minds, common stocks are associated with "playing the board of trade" or gambling on a big scale. The fear of financial losses, and of the reactions of their neighbors, and a general lack of information make most farm people look at stocks with a wary eye. Actually, common stocks of some of the well-established companies in industry probably offer them one of the best long-run alternative uses for capital. Those who need the help of someone trained in the field of investments can secure such assistance through reputable brokers or by investing in some of the mutual investment companies. In either case, earnings have amounted to 4 to 8 percent in recent years.

### INCOMES OF FARM FAMILIES IN THE NORTHERN PLAINS STATES

Various estimates have been made of the long-term earnings of capital in agriculture. Goodsell and others in the U.S. Department of Agriculture have estimated the average returns per $100 invested for various types of farms in the Plains area for the period 1951–60 to be about $4.25.[8] In making this estimate, an allowance was made for the value of labor supplied by the operator and his family on the basis of going wage rates for hired farm labor. It does not include any allowance for the effect of changing prices on inventory values of capital items.[9]

Use of the going wage rate for farm labor as a basis for the value of the operator's time means that the return per $100 invested covers both the return to capital and to management since no allowance was made for management in the value placed on the operator's time. It is obvious, therefore, that the strict return to capital is something less than $4.25.

Cook used census data for Nebraska to estimate the return to capital resources in Nebraska counties.[10] His figures for eight counties within the transition zone show very low returns to capital, labor, and management in all three years (Table 30). As a result of the method used to estimate the capital investment, the rate of return to capital, as shown in Table 30, may be higher than was actually realized.

Examination of the distribution of farms within the transition zone of the Northern Plains states according to economic classes reveals that roughly 75–85 percent of the farms received less than $10,000 from the sale of all products in 1954 (Table 31).

[8] *Farm Costs and Returns*, USDA Economic Research Service Agricultural Information Bulletin No. 230 (revised August, 1963), p. 16.

[9] Disregard of changes in value resulting from such price changes is justifiable in measuring the operating earnings of farms or ranches. It should be recognized, however, that per capita incomes of people owning farm real estate or livestock are effected by changing prices insofar as the real estate or livestock is sold at a price different from the one at which it was acquired. Farm real estate in the Northern Plains has more than trebled in value since the low point in 1940–41. People who purchased land in the early forties and sold it during the next twenty years have realized a substantial appreciation on their investment. This appreciation alone has been at least as great as might have been earned by money placed in a savings account. The opposite relationship of course prevails during periods of falling prices.

[10] Capital invested was calculated as follows: Value of land and buildings was taken from the 1954 census; capital investment in machinery was estimated on the basis of assumed average values for only the machines specified in the 1954 census; livestock investment was based on numbers of livestock reported in the census and on values used as the basis for tax assessment.

TABLE 30. ESTIMATED RETURNS TO CAPITAL, LABOR, AND MANAGEMENT IN EIGHT NEBRASKA COUNTIES IN THE TRANSITION AREA, 1949, 1954, AND 1959

| | Nuckolls | Webster | Custer | Valley | Greeley | Howard | Sherman | Franklin |
|---|---|---|---|---|---|---|---|---|
| **1949** | | | | | | | | |
| Total investment | $25,247 | $20,107 | $27,737 | $26,794 | $24,585 | $24,284 | $19,610 | $24,809 |
| Gross receipts | 6,322 | 4,188 | 6,452 | 6,785 | 6,028 | 5,247 | 4,536 | 4,778 |
| Expenses | 3,988 | 2,183 | 3,402 | 4,755 | 3,117 | 3,123 | 2,205 | 2,379 |
| Farm income | 2,334 | 2,005 | 3,050 | 2,030 | 2,911 | 2,124 | 2,331 | 2,399 |
| Labor income | 2,163 | 1,201 | 1,941 | 962 | 1,879 | 1,152 | 1,547 | 1,403 |
| Value of unpaid family labor | 2,237 | 2,354 | 2,315 | 2,428 | 2,429 | 2,580 | 2,398 | 2,273 |
| Rate of return on investment | 3.7 | — | 2.7 | — | 2.0 | — | — | 0.5 |
| **1954** | | | | | | | | |
| Total investment | $33,654 | $30,312 | $42,402 | $37,466 | $37,964 | $32,837 | $31,163 | $38,836 |
| Gross receipts | 8,032 | 5,559 | 6,816 | 7,181 | 7,349 | 5,717 | 4,804 | 6,637 |
| Expenses | 4,936 | 2,789 | 4,380 | 5,684 | 4,459 | 3,860 | 3,084 | 2,950 |
| Farm income | 3,096 | 2,770 | 2,436 | 1,497 | 2,890 | 1,857 | 1,720 | 3,687 |
| Labor income | 1,670 | 1,557 | 739 | −2 | 1,371 | 544 | 474 | 2,133 |
| Value of unpaid family labor | 2,843 | 2,936 | 2,885 | 2,868 | 3,008 | 3,150 | 2,817 | 2,800 |
| Rate of return on investment | 0.7 | — | — | — | — | — | — | 2.3 |
| **1959** | | | | | | | | |
| Total investment | $51,694 | $42,621 | $65,294 | $57,031 | $54,923 | $47,270 | $40,913 | $53,834 |
| Gross receipts | 12,286 | 7,151 | 11,181 | 9,916 | 11,068 | 8,174 | 8,250 | 8,139 |
| Expenses | 7,450 | 3,385 | 5,973 | 6,984 | 6,866 | 5,430 | 4,948 | 4,108 |
| Farm income | 4,836 | 3,766 | 5,208 | 2,932 | 4,202 | 2,744 | 3,302 | 4,031 |
| Labor income | 2,768 | 2,061 | 2,596 | 770 | 2,006 | 853 | 1,666 | 1,884 |
| Value of unpaid family labor | 3,433 | 3,383 | 3,371 | 3,504 | 3,584 | 3,518 | 3,712 | 3,267 |
| Rate of return on investment | 2.7 | 0.9 | 2.8 | — | 1.1 | — | — | 1.4 |

Neil Cook, " Labor Productivity on Nebraska Farms" (unpublished M.S. thesis, University of Nebraska, 1961).

TABLE 31. PERCENTAGE DISTRIBUTION OF FARMS, WITHIN VARIOUS TYPES, ACCORDING TO ECONOMIC CLASSES, 1954

| | Economic Class* | | | | | |
|---|---|---|---|---|---|---|
| | I | II | III | IV | V | VI |
| **Subregion 90** | | | | | | |
| Cash grain . . . . . . . . | .8 | 12.9 | 33.4 | 35.3 | 13.8 | 3.8 |
| General crop & livestock . . | .4 | 5.4 | 28.0 | 42.9 | 20.3 | 3.0 |
| **Subregion 91** | | | | | | |
| Livestock . . . . . . . . . | 3.1 | 18.7 | 33.8 | 28.6 | 12.3 | 3.5 |
| Cash grain . . . . . . . . | 1.5 | 15.8 | 33.6 | 33.5 | 12.5 | 3.1 |
| General crop & livestock . . | .7 | 7.8 | 32.0 | 43.1 | 13.7 | 2.7 |
| **Subregion 92** | | | | | | |
| Livestock . . . . . . . . . | 4.2 | 19.2 | 33.7 | 27.2 | 11.7 | 4.0 |
| Cash grain . . . . . . . . | 1.2 | 15.2 | 39.0 | 30.2 | 11.5 | 2.9 |
| General crop & livestock . . | 0.8 | 11.3 | 38.1 | 33.9 | 13.8 | 2.1 |
| **Subregion 93** | | | | | | |
| Livestock . . . . . . . . . | 7.6 | 21.3 | 29.0 | 21.3 | 13.3 | 7.5 |
| Cash grain . . . . . . . . | 1.4 | 19.5 | 39.1 | 28.2 | 9.6 | 2.2 |
| General crop & livestock . . | 0.6 | 10.2 | 32.7 | 34.5 | 16.6 | 5.4 |

Source: U.S. Bureau of the Census, *1954 Census of Agriculture.*

\* Defined in the 1954 census as follows:

| Class of farm | Value of Products Sold | Class of farm | Value of Products Sold |
|---|---|---|---|
| I . . . . . . . . . | $25,000 or over | IV . . . . . . . . . | $2,500–4,999 |
| II . . . . . . . . . | 10,000–24,999 | V . . . . . . . . . | 1,200–2,499 |
| III . . . . . . . . . | 5,000–9,999 | VI . . . . . . . . . | 250–1,199 |

From 40 to 60 percent sold less than $5,000 worth of farm products. With operating expenses taking approximately 65 cents out of every dollar received in 1954, it is obvious that a large proportion of the farm families within the transition zone was not receiving very high returns for their labor, management, and capital. Farmers selling $10,000 worth of farm products had farms worth at least $25,000 to $30,000, according to the census. Undoubtedly, investments in machinery and livestock would have raised the total to $35,000, or more. If one credits capital with interest at 4 percent, returns to labor and management would have been no greater than $2,100. Top farmers in economic Class IV (gross sales of $2,500–$4,999) would have received about $825 for their labor and management. Comparable groupings of census data for 1959 are not available. Since 1954, however, operating expenses have risen in relation to receipts. They now take more nearly 70–75 cents of every dollar received —on the average.

The Agricultural Research Service found that 55 percent of the farm families in the wheat-corn area in the Great Plains had net cash incomes of less than $2,500 in 1956. In the spring wheat area, 34 percent had incomes of this kind. These figures do not take changes in inventory into account, nor do they make any allowance for depreciation or for interest on the family's equity. They represent amounts available for family living, saving, and capital purchases.

Very low incomes accrued to capital, labor, and management on farms in the transition area of central Nebraska in 1955, a drought year (Table 32). With average crop yields, it was estimated that net returns to labor, capital, and management

TABLE 32.   FINANCIAL SUMMARY OF CENTRAL NEBRASKA DRY-LAND FARMS
IN A SEVERE DROUGHT YEAR (1955)

| | Size of Farm | | | | |
|---|---|---|---|---|---|
| | *160*<br>*Acres* | *320*<br>*Acres* | *480*<br>*Acres* | *640*<br>*Acres* | *1,280*<br>*Acres* |
| Capital investment | | | | | |
| Land . . . . . . . . . . | $ 8,944 | $16,071 | $23,646 | $29,386 | $59,776 |
| Livestock . . . . . . . . . | 1,747 | 3,266 | 5,479 | 6,661 | 15,308 |
| Machinery . . . . . . . . | 1,108 | 2,497 | 3,352 | 3,778 | 5,529 |
| Crops . . . . . . . . . . | 559 | 686 | 1,054 | 1,526 | 1,832 |
| Total . . . . . . . . | $12,338 | $22,520 | $33,549 | $41,358 | $82,445 |
| Total receipts . . . . . . . | $2,243 | $4,192 | $4,034 | $6,898 | $13,388 |
| Total expenses . . . . . . | 1,575 | 3,393 | 3,986 | 6,306 | 10,344 |
| Net cash income . . . . . . | 668 | 799 | 2,048 | 2,592 | 3,044 |
| Inventory change . . . . . | −458 | −325 | −893 | −1,067 | +607 |
| Depreciation . . . . . . . | 178 | 295 | 376 | 439 | 469 |
| Net farm income . . . . . | 32 | 179 | 779 | 1,056 | 3,182 |
| Interest on capital @ 5% . . . | $617 | $1,126 | $1,679 | $2,068 | $4,135 |
| Return to labor & management | −585 | −947 | −900 | −1,012 | −953 |
| Nonfarm income . . . . . . | 327 | 186 | 164 | 175 | 230 |

Source: Nebr. Agr. Exp. Sta. data.

TABLE 33.   AVERAGE NET FARM INCOME AND VARIATION IN
INCOME FOR SELECTED STATES, 1949–59

| | Average net<br>Farm Income<br>(Million Dollars) | Coefficient<br>of<br>Variation* |
|---|---|---|
| South Dakota . . . . . | 221.9 | *44.6* |
| Wyoming . . . . . . | 52.1 | 38.7 |
| Maine . . . . . . . | 64.1 | 36.5 |
| Kansas . . . . . . . | 360.0 | *33.1* |
| New Mexico . . . . . | 78.0 | 28.3 |
| Nebraska . . . . . . | 411.8 | *25.8* |
| North Dakota . . . . . | 205.5 | *22.5* |
| Vermont . . . . . . . | 28.4 | 21.1 |
| Texas . . . . . . . | 883.4 | 20.8 |
| Iowa . . . . . . . . | 896.3 | 19.6 |
| Florida . . . . . . . | 289.4 | 18.0 |
| Alabama . . . . . . . | 266.2 | 16.9 |
| Wisconsin . . . . . . | 447.6 | 16.4 |
| Oregon . . . . . . . | 162.9 | 15.3 |
| Pennsylvania . . . . . | 254.0 | 15.0 |
| New York . . . . . . | 283.8 | 14.5 |
| Michigan . . . . . . . | 312.5 | 13.8 |
| North Carolina . . . . | 598.0 | 12.3 |
| Indiana . . . . . . . | 441.8 | 11.3 |
| California . . . . . . | 996.3 | 10.4 |

* Coefficients for Northern Plains states italicized.
Based on data from *State Estimates of Farm Income, 1940–59*, FIS–179, Agricultural Marketing Service, USDA.

would have been a little more than twice as high on most farms. Nevertheless, it must be recognized that drought has occurred repeatedly in the Plains and will continue to recur. Hence, years of lower-than-usual income must be anticipated.

Incomes in the Plains area vary widely from farm to farm and from year to year, depending on weather, crop yields, prices received for commodities sold, and price-cost relationships. Variations in weather cause large variations in crop production, gross farm income, and net income per farm. The relative variation in net income to agriculture in the Northern Plains states, compared with other selected states, is shown in Table 33.

The introduction of new technologies, including hybrid seed, commercial fertilizer, or mechanized methods of production, apparently has had little effect on crop yields in dry years. Farm incomes may even be more variable than before such technologies were introduced. While incomes drop, expenses also are higher because the new technologies were used. In years of average or above-average rainfall, however, the use of these new technologies improves the competitive position of the dry-land transition-area farmer.

## OVERALL EFFICIENCY OF TRANSITION-AREA FARMS

An appraisal was made of resource productivity on farms in the five-county survey area in central Nebraska. By use of these data, as well as data from other regions, it is possible to draw some conclusions about the efficiency of farming in the transition area. First, however, it is useful to explore the concept of efficiency.

### What Is Efficiency in Farming?

In the classical sense, efficiency refers to the returns that arise from each of the resources used in farming. What standards can be used to decide whether these returns are acceptable? One such standard is "opportunity cost," defined as the returns that are forgone in committing a particular resource to a given use as opposed to all of the alternative uses for it. Thus we say that labor used in a farm business ought to earn as much as it would if used on other farms, elsewhere in the community, in some other farming area, or in some other industry. Similarly, money capital is expected to return as much when applied on a farm in some specific form, such as machinery or fertilizer, as it would in some other use. Land presents peculiar problems, since it cannot be moved, yet its control can be transferred from one farm to another. Also, money invested in land is expected to earn as much as it would in some other use. Because of its special characteristics, we commonly distinguish between land and other forms of capital goods in economic analysis.

If labor, capital, or land do not return their opportunity costs in their present use, this use is considered inefficient—on the premise that they would contribute more to the economy if shifted to some use where they would earn a greater return. The opposite also holds true; if a resource earns much more in its present use than in any alternative use, it is considered scarce; the total product of the economy would increase if more of it were shifted to this use.

Average and marginal returns must be distinguished. The average returns for a resource, with other resources held constant, is the average contribution each unit of it makes to production. Thus we say that twelve man-months of labor in a farm business return an average of $X$ dollars per month. The marginal return, on the other hand, is the earning or production of the twelfth month of labor—assuming that the months used might have been eleven, or thirteen, instead of twelve. In speaking of resource adjustments in the classical sense, we are concerned with marginal rather than average returns. They indicate whether there is a scarcity or a surplus of a resource in a certain use; that is, whether or not the marginal returns are greater or less than the opportunity cost; that is, what the last month would have earned elsewhere.

There are some problems here with "lumpy" resources. A farmer may consider the whole year of his own labor to be committed to farming, whether or not he is fully employed. Even though he is not fully employed, it may be too far to drive to a part-time job, or he may choose not to work off the farm for other reasons. Similarly, we cannot use one-half a combine instead of a whole one. Of course, we can choose between different sizes of machines, or buy one in partnership. We can also obtain combine service by hiring custom work.

Thus the task of analyzing farming efficiency is difficult and the answers may not apply to a single farm. Efficiency analyses are useful chiefly in evaluating the present situation in a general way. They are less useful in suggesting solutions to resource problems. An understandable parallel is that of a thermometer, which suggests to a doctor that a patient is sick but is not effective in prescribing medicines to treat the illness.

*Method of Analysis*

The data used were obtained by a survey in 1955, a drought year when yields were much lower than average. Since yields were more normal in 1954, incomes from crops in 1954 were combined with income from livestock in 1955 to obtain a less distorted estimate of normal 1955 income. Input items for 1955 were used. The Cobb-Douglas technique was applied to these data to estimate marginal productivity of labor, land, and other capital in the central Nebraska transition area.

*Productivity of Labor*

Estimates of marginal productivity of various quantities of farm labor on four sizes of transition-area farms are shown in Figure 30. These curves indicate how much additional income the last man-month of labor would be expected, on the average, to produce at a given level of use, with other resources held constant.

On the 320-, 480-, and 640-acre dry-land farms, the last month of labor produced less than $100 in additional income at the average levels of labor use.[11] The income contribution of an additional month of labor on 1,280-acre farms was greater: $130 per month. These data can be compared with the monthly farm-wage rate in Nebraska in 1954, which was about $174, with house furnished. We estimated the opportunity charge for family labor, including board and room, at $214 per month,

[11] The average referred to is the geometric rather than the arithmetic average. A geometric average is not influenced as much by numbers at the "tails" of a distribution as the arithmetic or simple average. In an asymmetrical distribution it will be nearer to the typical figure than the simple arithmetic average.

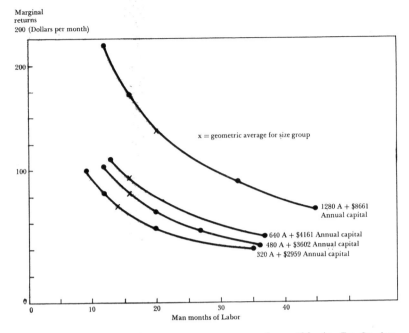

Source: Nebr. Agr. Exp. Sta. data.

Fig. 30. Marginal Returns to Labor on Farms of Different Sizes in the Central Nebraska Transition Area, 1954–55

which is much higher than the marginal productivities of labor at average levels of use, or even at the lower levels reported.

Our conclusion is that farm labor was earning rather low returns on the average in the Central Nebraska transition area during 1954–55. The critical reader may note that these years might not be typical of a longer-run period. However, they are quite representative of the decade of the 1950's in Central Nebraska.

The effect of additional capital and land on the productivity of labor also can be estimated (Figure 30). For example, each 100 acres of additional land and associated capital necessary to operate it—combined with sixteen months of labor—increased the marginal productivity of labor by from $8.00 to $10.00 per month for the various size groups.

## Productivity of Non-land Capital

The marginal productivities of various amounts of non-land capital on transition-area farms in the major size groups are shown in Figure 31. First, what is non-land capital? The data used here are not amounts of capital invested but are rather the *annual non-land capital services*; they include the cost of feed purchased, the cost of feeder cattle bought, depreciation on machinery, and other operating items—as well as interest charges on fixed items, such as buildings, machinery, and breeding stock. In other words, they are the dollars committed during a particular year for production, except for land. No interest has been charged for operating items; for these

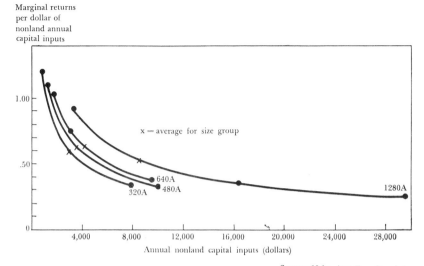

Marginal returns
per dollar of
nonland annual
capital inputs

x = average for size group

640A
480A
320A

1280A

Annual nonland capital inputs (dollars)

Source: Nebr. Agr. Exp. Sta. data.

FIG. 31. MARGINAL RETURNS TO NON-LAND CAPITAL ON TRANSITION-AREA FARMS OF DIFFERENT SIZES, 1954–55

dollars to pay their way, they have to return an interest charge. Thus, to break even, with the going rate of interest at 7 percent, the return per dollar must be $1.07.

The average inputs of non-land capital were surprisingly close on the three smaller sizes of farm, while that on the 1,280-acre farms was about twice that of the 640's. The range in non-land capital inputs was extremely long on the 1,280-acre farms, as is shown in Figure 31. However, on only five out of forty-two of these farms were these inputs greater than $16,000.

The striking thing about Figure 31 is the very low productivity of non-land capital. For the three smaller sizes, the marginal returns per dollar were only about 60 cents, and they were about 50 cents for the 1,280-acre farms. This is subject to a variety of interpretations. First, we might be in error because 1954–55 production data might be lower than normal. Second, the capital inputs might have been overvalued. Just to be safe, we might add a margin of 20 percent for underestimation of returns, and 10 percent more for overestimation of annual inputs; but we would still have to conclude that returns to capital on the sample farms—on the average—were extremely low.

Of course, this analysis does not tell us why they are low. One could suggest that if less capital were used on a given size of farm, marginal returns to capital would be higher. But what capital? How does one reduce capital? Can one actually reduce farm capital? These questions will be considered later.

*Productivity of Land*

The marginal productivity of land in different sizes of farm, estimated at the geometric averages of labor and capital for all farms in the transition-area sample, is indicated in Figure 32—both in terms of returns per acre and in returns per 100 acres

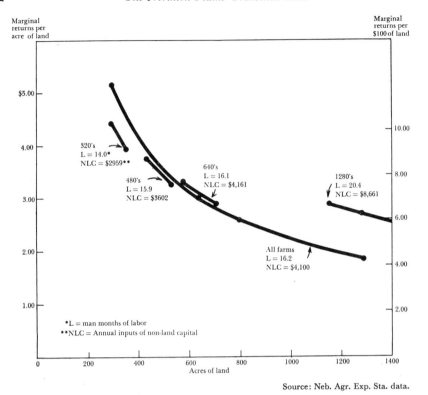

Marginal
returns per
acre of land

Marginal
returns per
$100 of land

$5.00

4.00

3.00

2.00

1.00

320's
L = 14.0*
NLC = $2959**

480's
L = 15.9
NLC = $3602

640's
L = 16.1
NLC = $4,161

1280's
L = 20.4
NLC = $8,661

All farms
L = 16.2
NLC = $4,100

*L = man months of labor
**NLC = Annual inputs of non-land capital

10.00

8.00

6.00

4.00

2.00

0    200    400    600    800    1000    1200    1400

Acres of land

Source: Neb. Agr. Exp. Sta. data.

Fig. 32.    Marginal Returns* per Additional Acre of Land, and per $100 Invested in
Land, for Various Acreages in Transition Area, 1954–55

* Estimates are based on specified quantities of non-land capital and labor inputs.

invested in bare land. Land without buildings was valued at $43.00 per acre. Investment in land returned more than 5 percent on the funds invested, even for sizes of farm as large as 1,000 acres, with capital and labor held constant.

The amounts of non-land capital and labor affect the returns to land, of course. With the averages of twenty man-months of labor and $8,661 of non-land capital actually used on the 1,280-acre farms, each additional acre returned $2.72, or $6.30 per $100 invested—as is shown by the short curve to the right in Figure 32. This exceeds $1.87 per acre, or $4.30 per $100, estimated from the long curve, which is based on sixteen months of labor and $4,161 of non-land capital. In other words, the more labor and non-land capital used per 100 acres, the higher the additional income accruing to land.

*Implications for Resource Adjustments*

The data just examined suggest certain tentative generalizations about the direction of farming adjustments in the transition area. First, it is apparent that land contributed to farm earnings, during the period examined, at rates equal to or above its opportunity costs. This implies that farmers could increase income by increasing acreage. On the other hand, marginal returns to capital were low; variations in non-land capital inputs had much less effect on gross income during the period studied than variations in land investment. The contribution of a given amount of farm labor depended on the amount of land and other capital with which it was used. Whether its contribution to earnings is acceptable depends on the definition of "acceptable." However, in no size group were the average contributions of labor equal to the average hired wage rates for the period.

Economic theory would suggest that the way to increase income would be to increase land relative to labor and non-land capital. The question is: How do you increase land? Land in an area is fixed in supply, a feature that distinguishes it from other resources. An individual farmer can increase the proportion of land to his other resources by adding acres; however, it is impossible for all farms in an area to expand in acreage. Increasing land relative to other inputs must mean the release of some non-land inputs from farming. Increasing the average of some farms means decreasing the acreage of others; in other words, it necessitates the extinction of some farms.

The above data suggest that the area, as a whole, has too much labor and non-land capital in farming. To decrease the amount of labor, some people will have to emigrate. The amount of capital used can be decreased by not replacing certain capital items when they wear out. This implies more extensive farming, with the use of less labor and non-land capital per acre.

That is as far as these data can take us. However, they "square" with what has been happening in the area's agriculture. They undergird the specific suggestions (made in the next part of the book) for how the process can be made more orderly and how its inevitability can be understood.

### Comparisons with Other Farming Areas

The implications of the above data are reinforced by findings in other areas. The map in Figure 33, for instance, shows smaller annual inputs of capital per worker in the transition area than in neighboring areas. Of course, it must also be noted that capital per man in the south is much less than that in the transition area.

Other figures tell the same story. Table 34 shows several types of farm efficiency data for four sizes of farm in the central-Nebraska transition area as compared with a wheat farming area in north-central and eastern Montana, with a prosperous farming area in northern Iowa, and with the part of southern Iowa generally considered to be a problem area. One difficulty is that the data for the Nebraska transition area are for 1954–55, while the rest are for 1950. This probably doesn't affect the organization and resource data very much, but it makes the income comparisons less reliable.

At any rate, not even the 1,280-acre Nebraska transition-area farms were as large as the average-size wheat farms in the Montana area in terms of the total capital investment or in investment per man. The average farm in northern Iowa was comparable to a farm of about 900 acres in the transition area in total investment and investment per man, if one interpolates between the 640's and the 1,280's. However, since the Iowa farms used more working capital, particularly feed and livestock, the annual capital inputs per man-year were even larger than those in Montana. Finally, the average farm in southern Iowa was comparable to the 640-acre farms in the

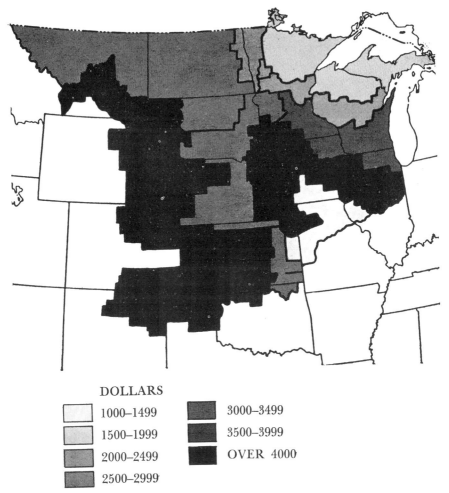

**DOLLARS**

| | | | |
|---|---|---|---|
| ☐ | 1000–1499 | ▨ | 3000–3499 |
| ☐ | 1500–1999 | ▨ | 3500–3999 |
| ▨ | 2000–2499 | ■ | OVER 4000 |
| ▨ | 2500–2999 | | |

Source: Earl O. Heady and Edwin G. Strand, "Efficiency within American Agriculture," *Journal of Farm Economics*, 37 (August, 1955), 524–37.

Fig. 33.   Value of Annual Input of all Capital per Worker on Commercial Farms, 1949

transition area in investment characteristics. However, the capital inputs per man-year in southern Iowa were nearest to those of the 1,280's in the Nebraska transition area.

The residual returns or over-all costs at the bottom of the table must be viewed with caution. They depend not only on cash income and cash expenditures but also on the valuations placed on noncash inputs, like land, breeding stock, and machinery. Also, the economic conditions of 1954–55 were less favorable than those of 1950, particularly in the relationship of prices paid and prices received by farmers. It is clear, nevertheless, that resources in the transition area of Nebraska were not paying their opportunity costs in 1954–55 on any of the four sizes of farm.

TABLE 34. SELECTED CHARACTERISTICS OF CENTRAL–NEBRASKA TRANSITION AREA AND OTHER FARMING AREAS

| | Nebraska Transition-Area Sample Groups | | | | North-central* and Eastern Montana | Northern* Iowa | Southern* Iowa |
|---|---|---|---|---|---|---|---|
| | 1954–55 DATA | | | | 1950 DATA | | |
| Average size of farm (acres) | 320 | 480 | 640 | 1,280 | 2,325 | 203 | 194 |
| Total investment ($) | 22,500 | 33,600 | 41,500 | 82,500 | 90,400 | 61,400 | 32,700 |
| Investment per man-year ($) | 19,400 | 24,700 | 28,800 | 44,500 | 46,600 | 39,900 | 24,500 |
| Labor used (months) | 14.6 | 16.5 | 17.1 | 22.3 | 20.3 | 17.5 | 16.1 |
| Annual non-land capital inputs ($) | 3,414 | 4,087 | 4,545 | 10,446 | 11,747 | 13,535 | 9,035 |
| Annual inputs of land† ($) | 833 | 1,218 | 1,490 | 3,316 | 2,994 | 2,175 | 983 |
| Total annual capital inputs ($) | 4,247 | 5,305 | 6,035 | 13,762 | 14,741 | 16,710 | 10,018 |
| Annual capital inputs/man-years ($) | 3,481 | 3,844 | 4,226 | 7,398 | 9,698 | 11,445 | 6,633 |
| Output ($) | 4,680 | 6,550 | 7,765 | 14,517 | 30,634 | 22,718 | 14,339 |
| Value of all services‡ ($) | 6,802 | 8,193 | 9,028 | 17,664 | 19,372 | 20,062 | 13,162 |
| Residual over-all costs ($) | −2,112 | −1,643 | −1,263 | −3,147 | 11,263 | 2,656 | 1,177 |

* From Earl O. Heady and Russell Shaw, *Resource Returns and Productivity Coefficients in Selected Farming Areas of Iowa, Montana, and Alabama,* Iowa Agricultural Experiment Station Research Bulletin 425, 1955; *idem,* "Resource Return and Productivity Coefficients in Selected Farming Areas," *Journal of Farm Economics,* 36 (1954), 243–57.
† Estimated for Nebraska at 6 percent of estimated value of bare land; estimated for Montana and Iowa at rental value.
‡ Includes estimated value of labor, figured at $175 in Nebraska.

175

*Labor Returns*

Deducting the annual costs of capital from net farm returns gives the return to labor. Table 35 presents labor earnings for the portion of the transition area included in southern South Dakota, Nebraska, and Kansas, compared with those from the prairie corn-belt region of southern Minnesota, central Iowa, northwestern Illinois, and from the Northern Plains ranching area and the winter wheat area. (See Figure 33.) They were estimated by subtracting from gross income and annual crop and livestock expenses, depreciation, and charges on land and other capital, and by dividing the remainder by the man-years of labor. The central corn-belt and the wheat areas rank considerably above the transition area in returns to labor. The ranching area also showed returns to operator's labor almost $400 per year higher than those of the transition area. The ranch data would normally be even higher, but they were influenced by the lower prices for feeder cattle in 1949.

TABLE 35.   RESIDUAL PRODUCT PER FARM WORKER ON COMMERCIAL FARMS
IN SELECTED FARMING REGIONS, 1949

|  | Transition Area* | Iowa-Illinois Corn-belt | Neb., S. Dak., Wyo., Mont. Ranch Area | Neb., Colo., Kansas Wheat Area |
|---|---|---|---|---|
| Residual income per worker |  |  |  |  |
| All labor . . . . . . | $1,282 | $1,855 | $1,539 | $1,720 |
| Operator & family labor . . . . . . | 1,238 | 1,899 | 1,490 | 1,822 |
| Operator labor . . . | 1,026 | 2,000 | 1,391 | 1,982 |

Source: Earl O. Heady and Edwin G. Strand, "Efficiency within American Agriculture," *Journal of Farm Economics*, 37 (August, 1955), 524–37.
* Portion of the Northern Plains transition area extending from the middle of South Dakota through Nebraska and northern Kansas.

For a final look at residual labor returns, the benchmark counties of the Northern Plains states were examined again for 1954. Residual returns per man were estimated by subtracting from 1954 gross incomes (as reported by the Census of Agriculture) the amounts spent for feed, gasoline, fertilizer and lime, and 5 percent of the investment in land, buildings, machinery, and livestock. These expense items do not include all farming costs, but most are represented; the results are shown in Table 36.

TABLE 36.   ESTIMATED RETURNS PER MAN IN FARMING IN SELECTED COUNTIES
OF THE PRAIRIE STATES, 1954

|  | High Plains Counties |  | Transition Counties |  | Eastern Area Counties |  |
|---|---|---|---|---|---|---|
| North Dakota . . . . . | Bowman | $1,400 | Kidder | $1,240 | Traill | $2,908 |
| South Dakota . . . . . | Haakon | 2,518 | Aurora | 1,898 | Turner | 1,381 |
| Nebraska . . . . . . . | Cherry | 4,320 | Sherman | 1,085 | Stanton | 2,944 |
|  | Cheyenne | 3,508 |  |  |  |  |
| Kansas . . . . . . . . | Thomas | 4,258 | Jewell | 2,732 |  |  |

Based on data from *U.S. Census of Agriculture, 1954.*

Generally, the returns to labor are lower in the transition counties than in the benchmark counties to the west and to the east, with the exception of Turner County, South Dakota. These comparisons are consistent with those shown previously.

### Comparisons with Other Industries

A final test for the relative efficiency of farming is to compare the returns to the resources used in farming with the returns they might earn in other industries. Table 37 shows the average wages paid per full-time employee in five types of non-farm industries in the states of Nebraska, Colorado, Iowa, and Illinois in 1954.

The table also includes net returns per farm family worker for labor, management, and the operator's equity, based on crop returns from 1954 and livestock returns for 1955 plus wages from nonfarm work. Only the returns on the 1,280-acre farms equal or exceed the wages received in other industries. However, the nonfarm data are not comparable with those from agriculture in one important respect. The farm returns include a return on the farmer's equity, that is, a return to his own capital; no such capital return is involved in industrial wages. Accordingly, we have subtracted a capital charge on the operator's equity of 5 per cent, which yields farm returns in the transition area—shown in the right-hand column of the table—in a much less favorable light.

It might be argued that the net for labor and management per family worker underestimates the real income to farm workers because of the computational methods

TABLE 37. Comparison of Wages Paid in Nonfarm Industries in Selected States with Net Farm Income per Worker in the Central Nebraska Transition Area, 1954–55

| | *Wages Paid per Full-time Worker, 1954** | | | | |
|---|---|---|---|---|---|
| | | *Industry* | | *Wholesale & Retail* | *Service & Misc.* |
| | *Mining* | *Manufacturing* | *Transportation* | | |
| | DOLLARS PER YEAR | | | | |
| Illinois . . . . . . | 4,413 | 4,500 | 3,155 | 3,701 | 3,450 |
| Iowa . . . . . . | 3,792 | 3,956 | 2,626 | 2,836 | 2,689 |
| Nebraska. . . . . | 4,117 | 3,793 | 3,063 | 2,937 | 2,556 |
| Colorado . . . . . | 3,724 | 4,108 | 2,853 | 3,176 | 2,716 |

| *Net Incomes by Size of Farm in Nebraska Transition Area, 1954–55†* | | | |
|---|---|---|---|
| *Size of Farm (Acres)* | *Net Operating Income per Family Worker†* | *5% of Operator's Equity* | *Net Return per Family Worker* |
| 160 . . . . . . . . . . | $1,037 | $455 | $ 572 |
| 320 . . . . . . . . . . | 1,907 | 620 | 1,387 |
| 480 . . . . . . . . . . | 2,201 | 1,120 | 1,081 |
| 640 . . . . . . . . . . | 2,398 | 1,034 | 1,364 |
| 1,280 . . . . . . . . . . | 3,760 | 2,402 | 1,358 |

\* Based on data in *Statistical Abstract of the United States* for 1955 and 1956.

† Computed by combining net crop income for 1954, net livestock income for 1955, and wages from off-farm work, and by deducting interest of 5 percent on farm capital not owned by operator. Includes value of home-produced meat and dairy products consumed on the farm.

used. There is some basis for this criticism; however, in the farm data in Table 37 the value of home-raised meat and dairy products consumed has been included. If we added another $400 for the value of living in the farm dwelling, and $100 for the farm garden, the data in the right-hand column would be more comparable. Even so, the comparison of labor returns in industry versus those in transition-area farming is definitely in favor of industry.

### Competitive Position and Technological Advance

Changing technologies can affect an area's relative efficiency. In agriculture, technologies are usually divided into two classes: those that reduce costs of production, such as labor-saving machinery, and those that increase output on a given resource base, such as fertilizer.

One would suppose that the Northern Plains area would be as competitive as any other with respect to cost-reducing technologies; in fact, with its typically larger scale of operations, it might even have a slight advantage. On the other hand, some output-increasing technologies may tend to discriminate against the Northern Plains as compared with more humid areas. This would be particularly true of fertilizer, but might also pertain to new crop varieties, insect control, or other technologies whose yield-effect is partially dependent on rainfall.

Livestock technologies should be as advantageous to the Plains as to any other region; dryer, more sanitary conditions in the Northern Plains may give them a slight advantage from the standpoint of technological advance.

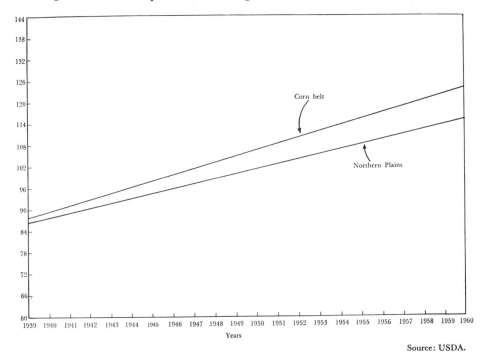

Source: USDA.

Fig. 34.   Index of Crop Production per Acre, 1939–60 (1947–49 = 100)

TABLE 38. MAN-HOURS USED FOR FARM WORK PER CROP-ACRE,
NORTHERN PLAINS AND CORN–BELT, 1940–44 AND 1955–59

|  | *1940–44* | *1955–59* | *Percent of Change* |
|---|---|---|---|
| Northern Plains . . . . | 19 | 10 | −47 |
| Corn-belt. . . . . . . | 46 | 29 | −37 |

Source: *Changes in Farm Production and Efficiency*, USDA Statistical Bulletin No. 233 (Washington: U.S. Government Printing Office, 1961).

Specific kinds of agronomic research can work in favor of the Plains' competitive position, namely those on specialized crop enterprises. Such types would include hard winter wheat breeding, sorghum breeding, range grass breeding, and soil and water conservation.

Perhaps the region with which competitive relations are the most crucial for the Northern Plains area is the corn-belt. There is some evidence that during recent decades the Northern Plains has lost ground in production efficiency (Figure 34). The index of crop production per acre in the corn-belt per year has been increasing about .4 of a point faster per year than in the Northern Plains.

The Plains has shown a more rapid reduction in the amount of labor combined with land (Table 38). And, in livestock enterprises, production per hour has increased slightly faster in the Northern Plains than in the corn-belt. In crop production per hour, where efficiency has increased much more rapidly, the Plains lost considerable ground. An important reason for this was the corn-belt's ability to use more fertilizer. Between 1940–44 and 1955–59 the application of fertilizer nutrients in the Northern Plains increased from .2 pounds to 5.5 pounds per acre. During the same period it rose from .7 pounds to 40.6 pounds per acre in the corn-belt. The upper limits of the process are also probably proportionately higher in the corn-belt than in the Plains. As. a net result of these changes, farm production per hour increased somewhat less rapidly in the Plains than in the corn-belt (Table 39).

The data in Table 40 provide additional insight along the same line. Capital per worker in the Northern Plains still exceeds that in the corn-belt, although the latter is gaining. By 1950, gross income per worker in the corn-belt was substantially ahead, having gained during the 1940's. While the productivity of capital did not increase between 1920 and 1950 in the Plains, it showed a fairly steady increase in the corn-belt, as in the country as a whole. The capital investment to produce one dollar of gross income had been nearly halved in the corn-belt during the thirty-year period. By 1950 the average gross income productivity (return per dollar of capital) was 40 percent higher in the corn-belt than in the Northern Plains. The ratio of land value

TABLE 39. CHANGES IN FARM PRODUCTION PER HOUR (1947–49 = 100)

|  | *1940–44* | *1955–59* | *Percent of Change* |
|---|---|---|---|
| Northern Plains . . . . | 70 | 151 | 116 |
| Corn-belt. . . . . . . | 74 | 166 | 124 |

Source: *Changes in Farm Production and Efficiency*.

TABLE 40.　SELECTED PRODUCTION COEFFICIENTS FOR NORTHERN PLAINS, CORN–BELT, AND U.S., 1920 AND 1950

| | *Northern Plains* | *Corn-belt* | *U.S.* |
|---|---|---|---|
| Value of physical assets* per worker, 1950 (current prices) . . . . . . . . . . . . | $25,000 | $22,900 | $15,554 |
| Change in value of physical assets per worker, 1920–50 (1910–14 prices) . . . . . . . . | +42% | +48% | +78% |
| Gross farm income per worker† (1910–14 prices): | | | |
| 1920 . . . . . . . . . . . . . . | $1,560 | $920 | $660 |
| 1950 . . . . . . . . . . . . . . | 2,160 | 2,300 | 1,700 |
| % change . . . . . . . . . . . . . . | 44 | 150 | +158 |
| Ratio of physical farm capital* to gross farm income (1910–14 prices): | | | |
| 1920 . . . . . . . . . . . . . . | 7.75 | 9.29 | 6.61 |
| 1950 . . . . . . . . . . . . . . | 7.70 | 5.52 | 4.57 |
| % change . . . . . . . . . . . . . . | −0.01 | −41 | −31 |
| Ratio of land value to gross farm income* (1910–14 prices): | | | |
| 1920 . . . . . . . . . . . . . . | 5.54 | 6.34 | 4.24 |
| 1950 . . . . . . . . . . . . . . | 5.87 | 3.65 | 2.94 |
| % change . . . . . . . . . . . . . . | +6 | −42 | −31 |

* Source: Data reprinted from *Capital in Agriculture: Its Formation and Financing since 1870*, by A. S. Tostlebee, by permission of the Princeton University Press, copyright 1957 by Princeton University Press, all rights reserved.

† Computed from data in the source above: table 5, p. 48; and table H–3, p. 214.

to gross farm income—a measure of the productivity of land—shows the same trend, with the corn-belt showing a steadily more favorable land-value income ratio while the Plains ratio increased only slightly.

These data support the hypothesis that technological advance and farming adjustments during the past decades have left the Plains in a less favorable competitive position in certain respects. To maintain and improve its position, the area must capitalize on cost-reducing technologies as well as on output-increasing technologies that are well adapted to the region. In addition, it will have to be particularly ingenious in its resource adjustments—the combinations of land, labor, and capital—in farming.

# CHAPTER 12

# Farm Finance in the Plains Transition Area of Nebraska

FARMERS' financial arrangements describe the various ways they control all the different resources they use; they can tell us much about the degree of risk a farmer faces and the economic progress he is making. In this chapter we shall examine the financial arrangements of farmers in the Nebraska transition study area during 1956.

Most of the discussion is based on survey data collected from a subsample of 135 farms selected from a larger Nebraska transition-area sample. This farm finance subsample was limited to those who began farming between 1924 and 1949, and who had previously had less than two years of nonfarm employment. These restrictions were imposed to keep the group as homogeneous as possible.

## FARM CAPITAL IN THE TRANSITION AREA

*Sources of Capital*

Four classes of capital can be distinguished in the transition area: owned, rented, short-term borrowed, and long-term borrowed. As a group, the farmers studied owned at least half and rented about a third of the capital they used in farming in 1956 (Figure 35). The proportion of total capital that was rented ranged from a low of 21 percent on the 160-acre farms to a high of 40 percent on the 320-acre farms. In terms of land alone—that is, excluding non-land capital—38 percent of the acreage operated by the sample farmers was rented. The proportions of borrowed capital are much smaller than might be expected, particularly in view of the conditions of the area at the time of the survey. About 7 percent of the farm capital was in the form of long-term loans, and about 5 percent of the capital originated in short-term loans, with the percentages varying among size groups from 6 to 2 percent. As a group, the farmers thus were in good shape financially in 1956, as far as the percent of farm equity owned by the operators is concerned. If one excludes the 160-acre farms as a somewhat unique class that includes a large proportion of older operators nearing retirement, the pattern of capital source for the other sizes is fairly uniform.

*Types of Lenders Supplying Credit.* Most of the short-term credit used by sample farmers in the transition area was secured from commercial banks (Table 41). More than two-thirds of the farmers borrowed short-term money in 1956; less than half of

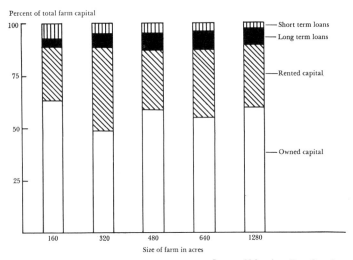

Source: Nebr. Agr. Exp. Sta. data.

Fig. 35.    Sources of Capital by Size of Farm on 135
Sample Farms in the Nebraska Transition Area, 1956

those who did, still had short-term debts outstanding at the end of that year. Of the amount carried over, 96 percent was owed to commercial banks, 2 percent to Production Credit Associations, and 2 percent to individuals; charge accounts of an informal, unsecured nature were not considered in the study. The ratio of PCA loans to commercial bank loans was surprisingly low in the Nebraska transition area. It was only one-fourth of the ratio for the entire state and only one-eighth of the national ratio.

About 40 percent of the 135 farmers interviewed had long-term loans in 1956 (Table 42). The largest single source of long-term credit was individuals, followed by National Land Bank Associations and insurance companies. These three types of lenders accounted for 85 percent of the long-term credit. The distribution among

Table 41.    Nature of Short-term and Intermediate Credit Used, by Source of Credit, by 135
Sample Farmers in the Nebraska Transition Area, 1956

| Source of Credit | Number of Farmers | Number of Loans | Average Size of Loan | Average Interest Rate | Loans Out-standing at End of Year | Average Size of Loans Outstanding |
|---|---|---|---|---|---|---|
| Farmers using credit . . . | 93 | 93 | $1,567 | 6.2% | 38 | $  962 |
| Banks . . . . . . . . | 75 | 75 | 1,166 | 7.1 | 33 | 2,578 |
| Farmers Home Administration . . . . . . | 1 | 1 | 6,850 | 5.0 | — | — |
| Production Credit Association . . . . . | 12 | 12 | 3,350 | 5.6 | 3 | 650 |
| Individuals & Dealers . | 5 | 5 | 2,250 | 3.0 | 2 | 1,200 |
| Farmers not using credit . | 42 | 0 | — | — | 0 | — |

Source: Nebr. Agr. Exp. Sta. data.

TABLE 42. NATURE OF LONG-TERM CREDIT USED, BY SOURCE OF CREDIT, BY 135 SAMPLE FARMERS IN THE NEBRASKA TRANSITION AREA, 1956

| Source of Credit | Number of Farmers | Number of Loans | Average Size of Loan | Percentage Distribution of Long-term Credit |
|---|---|---|---|---|
| Farmers using credit . . . . . | 52 | 52 | $6,468 | 100% |
| Commercial banks . . . . . | 1 | 1 | 3,500 | 1 |
| National Farm Loan Association . . . . . . . | 14 | 14 | 7,103 | 29 |
| Insurance companies . . . . | 11 | 11 | 7,218 | 24 |
| Individuals . . . . . . . . | 17 | 17 | 6,244 | 32 |
| Loan & trust companies . . | 7 | 7 | 4,430 | 9 |
| Farmers Home Administration . . . . . . . . . . | 2 | 2 | 8,409 | 5 |
| Farmers not using credit . . . | 83 | 0 | — | — |

Source: Nebr. Agr. Exp. Sta. data.

types of lenders was similar to that for the state as a whole. The average size of loans, $8,468, was not particularly large. Of course, some loans were quite high. In the 320-acre group, for example, the largest loan was $14,000, and several loans were at the $7,000 or $8,000 level. But even among the biggest farms, those with 1,280 acres, the largest loan was only $21,500. The size of loan was related to size of farm, but there was no undue concentration of borrowed funds in any size group. In fact, the use of credit was not nearly as extensive as circumstances might indicate, especially in view of the hard times occasioned by drought in the area that year.

*Knowledge of Credit Sources.* Their restricted use of credit may well have been partly due to ignorance. The farmers interviewed knew surprisingly little about the sources of credit available to them. When asked about the location of various credit offices, more than half of them couldn't place the Farmers Home Administration; almost half didn't know the location of the NLBA; and more than a third didn't know where the PCA was. Only one in five knew that insurance companies made loans (Table 43). Commercial banks were by far the best-known sources of credit.

TABLE 43. FARMERS WHO INDICATED KNOWLEDGE OF SPECIFIED ITEMS CONCERNING SOURCES OF CREDIT, 135 SAMPLE FARMERS, NEBRASKA TRANSITION AREA, 1956

| Source of Credit | Agency's Location | Name of Agency's Agent | Agency's Interest Rate | Type of Credit Agency Provides | Agency's Function as Credit Source |
|---|---|---|---|---|---|
| Commercial banks . . . . . . | 135 | 134 | 132 | 128 | 96 |
| National Land Bank Association . . . . . . . . . . . | 78 | 57 | 64 | 61 | 35 |
| Production Credit Association . | 87 | 41 | 47 | 48 | 31 |
| Farmers Home Administration | 62 | 40 | 39 | 37 | 28 |
| Insurance company . . . . . | 28 | 26 | 25 | 22 | 20 |

Source: Nebr. Agr. Exp. Sta. data.

*Resource Structure*

The structure of the resources controled by the 135 farmers interviewed in the transition area is shown in Figure 36. As one would expect, total capital per farm was closely related to farm size; the 1,280-acre farms, for example, had twice as much capital investment as the 640-acre farms. The average capital for the latter, $41,323, was about equal to the average for all farms in the entire transition area in Nebraska. This is somewhat less than the average investment for the eastern benchmark counties in the Plains states (shown in Chapter 9), and much lower than that for most of the western benchmark counties. For example, the average capital investment on farms in Cheyenne County, Nebraska, is equivalent to that on farms of 1,100 acres in the transition-area sample.

The lower investment typical of transition-area farms is further confirmed in Table 44. The spring wheat and wheat-corn areas designated by the U.S. Department of Agriculture approximate the area delineated in this study as the Northern Plains transition area; the northern range and winter wheat areas include the western portion of the Northern Plains states, as well as the eastern part of a few Mountain states. The western areas have much larger investments per farm than the transition area, as the table clearly shows.

*Owners of Rented Land*

Business interests are sometimes feared to be taking over the ownership of farmland. This notion is not supported by evidence from the Nebraska transition area. First,

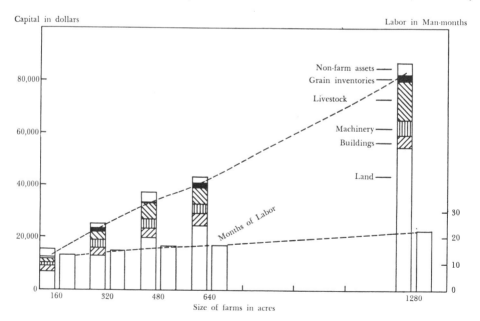

Source: Nebr. Agr. Exp. Sta. data.

Fig. 36.   Resource Structure on 135 Sample Farms, by Size of Farm, Nebraska Transition Area, 1956

TABLE 44.  ASSETS USED IN FARMING: AVERAGE VALUE PER FARM BY TYPE OF ASSET, AREAS OF THE GREAT PLAINS AND U.S., 1957

| | | Plains Transition Area | | Plains Western Area | |
|---|---|---|---|---|---|
| Type of asset | U.S. | Spring Wheat | Wheat- Corn | Northern Range | Winter Wheat |
| Total assets . . . . . | $31,080 | $53,720 | $59,320 | $82,190 | $93,000 |
| Farm real estate. . | 23,250 | 39,240 | 47,550 | 59,120 | 79,500 |
| Livestock . . . . . | 2,620 | 4,910 | 5,170 | 15,480 | 4,750 |
| Motor vehicles & machinery . . . | 3,580 | 8,550 | 5,850 | 6,750 | 8,070 |
| Stored crops . . . | 1,630 | 820 | 570 | 600 | 410 |
| All other . . . . . | — | 200 | 180 | 240 | 270 |

Sources: Great Plains areas: U.S. Agricultural Research Service, *Farming in the Great Plains*, USDA Production Research Report No. 50 (May, 1961); United States: Computed by dividing assets shown in the balance sheet of agriculture (average of January 1, 1957, and January 1, 1958) by number of farms in 1957, as estimated by the U.S. Agricultural Marketing Service.

as was noted earlier, almost two-thirds of the land included in the sample was owner-operated; this compares with 53 percent for the state as a whole. Secondly, the land that is rented is—more often than not—owned by another farmer (Table 45). The most important single group of landlords in the transition area is composed of retired and operating farmers. Together, they include more than half the landlords, and they probably own more than half of the rented land.

Business and professional workers were a close second, it is true, but their ownership of a third of the rented land represents control of only 12 percent of all the land in the sample, hardly enough to herald a takeover. The notion of a businessmen's conspiracy is further refuted by the great diversity of interests among the business and professional people who rent out their land; the twenty-one such landlords mentioned in the study represented twenty different occupations. As long as leasing arrangements are equitable, there is no reason why people like these cannot be a good source of capital in farm areas.

TABLE 45.  PERCENTAGE DISTRIBUTION OF RENTED LAND BY OCCUPATION OF OWNER, 135 SAMPLE FARMS, NEBRASKA TRANSITION AREA, 1956, AND STATE OF NEBRASKA, 1958

| Occupation of owner | Nebraska Transition Area | Nebraska* |
|---|---|---|
| Total . . . . . . . . . . . . . | 100% | 100% |
| Retired . . . . . . . . . . | 35 | |
| Farmers . . . . . . . . . . | — | 22 |
| Others . . . . . . . . . . | — | 13 |
| Active farmer . . . . . . . . | 17 | 32 |
| Business or professional worker . . | 32 | 13 |
| Housewife . . . . . . . . . | 10 | 8 |
| Other . . . . . . . . . . . | 6 | 12 |

* Computed from data in *Land Ownership in the Great Plains*, USDA Agricultural Research Service ARS 43–93 (June, 1959).

*Resources in Relation to Size of Farm.* As Figure 36 indicates, investment in specific capital items on the farms studied generally increased as size of farm increased, though there was some tendency for this process to slow down above the 640-acre size. An exception was machinery; investment in machinery represented a proportionately smaller share of total investment on the larger farms.

The use of labor on the sample farms, as shown in Figure 36, was remarkably uniform over all size classes. Of course, the 320-acre farms used 1½ months' more labor than the 13 months used on 160's, and each additional 160 acres—up through the 640-acre group—took slightly more than 1½ months' additional labor. However, only 22 months were used on the 1,280's, or 30 percent more than on the 640's. The available labor is probably kept more fully occupied on the larger farms. These data show how capital replaces labor on the larger farms; its efficiency must be considerably greater there than on smaller units.

Farmers hold some assets that are not directly related to their farm business. In times of stress, these nonfarm assets can serve as reserves, or they can provide a way to expand the farm business when conditions for the purchase of a new machine or breeding stock seem propitious. Finally, they represent part of the resources farmers depend upon when they retire. In Figure 36 the value at the top of the bars represents the amount of nonfarm investments held by the sample farmers in 1956. There was little relation between the value of these assets and size of farm. For all farms surveyed, the distribution of these nonfarm assets by type was as follows:

| Type | Average per Farm | Percent |
|---|---|---|
| Total . . . . . . . . | $2,694 | 100 |
| Cash (including checking accounts) . . . . | 927 | 35 |
| Bonds . . . . . . . . | 425* | 15 |
| Insurance (cash value) . | 561 | 21 |
| Stocks . . . . . . . . | 60 | 2 |
| Real estate (nonfarm) . | 675 | 25 |
| Savings . . . . . . . | 46 | 2 |

\* Half of the bonds reported were held by one farmer.

There is no way to check the accuracy of these data; they were estimated by the respondents. However, assuming they are reliable, these figures indicate a lower financial reserve held by farmers in this area than has been commonly supposed. This varied considerably from one farmer to another, as the following frequency distribution shows:

| Amount of Nonfarm Assets | Number of Farmers |
|---|---|
| None . . . . . . . . . . | 10 |
| Less than $1,000 . . . . . | 57 |
| 1,000– 1,999 . . . . . . . | 30 |
| 2,000– 2,999 . . . . . . . | 10 |
| 3,000– 3,999 . . . . . . . | 8 |
| 4,000– 4,999 . . . . . . . | 5 |
| 5,000– 9,999 . . . . . . . | 7 |
| 10,000–19,999 . . . . . . . | 3 |
| 20,000–29,999 . . . . . . . | 4 |
| 30,000–39,999 . . . . . . . | 1 |
| Total . . . | 135 |

Thus half the farmers surveyed had nonfarm assets of less than $1,000 at the time of the interviews. Only 11 percent had as much as $5,000.

*Insurance carried*

The amount of insurance carried by transition-area farmers was related to size of farm (Table 46). Nearly all farmers had some fire and auto insurance; yet less than half of the respondents reported holding health insurance. Just over half had life insurance.

TABLE 46.   INSURANCE PREMIUMS PAID BY 135 SAMPLE FARMERS, NEBRASKA TRANSITION AREA, 1956

| | *Size of Farm, in Acres* | | | | |
| Type of Insurance | 160 | 320 | 480 | 640 | 1280 |
|---|---|---|---|---|---|
| Total . . . . . . . . . . | $54.37 | $127.34 | $161.29 | $217.76 | $356.76 |
| Fire . . . . . . . . . . . | 10.93 | 15.97 | 21.40 | 32.63 | 27.05 |
| Life . . . . . . . . . . . | 17.69 | 47.24 | 88.17 | 97.70 | 231.10 |
| Health . . . . . . . . . . | 4.00 | 28.74 | 17.34 | 42.73 | 25.50 |
| Auto . . . . . . . . . . . | 21.75 | 35.39 | 34.38 | 43.70 | 72.63 |

Source: Nebr. Agr. Exp. Sta. data.

*Capital and Volume of Business*

The capital-investment data in Figure 36 can be compared with the gross income, or volume of business, data in Figure 37. The lower dotted line represents income in 1955, a drought year when yields were much lower than average. Since yields were more nearly normal in 1954, income from crops in 1954 was combined with income from livestock in 1955 to obtain a less distorted estimate of normal 1955 income, represented by the upper dotted line in Figure 37. If we assume that 70 percent of

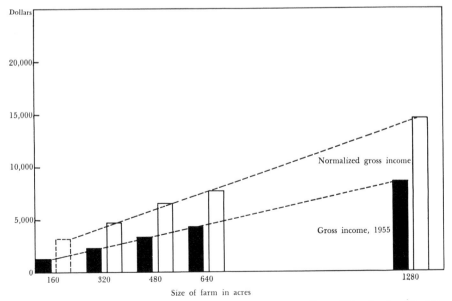

Source: Nebr. Agr. Exp. Sta. data.

FIG. 37.   GROSS INCOMES IN 1955 AND "NORMALIZED" GROSS INCOME ON 135 SAMPLE FARMS IN THE NEBRASKA TRANSITION AREA

gross income is spent for farm operation, we can estimate net income for each of the farm sizes. All farms had very low net incomes in 1955, but, even under more normal conditions, their income levels would not be spectacular. Estimated normal net income, even for 1,280-acre farms, was well under $5,000.

*Resource Combinations*

Resource structure is also reflected in certain useful resource ratios; several of the more important ones are shown in Table 47. As might be expected, capital investment per man among the sample farms is related to size. In fact, from $4,000 to $5,000 more capital is associated with a man-year of labor with each increase of 160 acres beyond the 320-acre size. These investments per man can be compared with those for the benchmark counties mentioned in Chapter 9.

For example, the $28,000 for the 640-acre group is almost the same as the average for the benchmark transition counties of the Northern Plains states. The investment per man of $44,500 for the 1,280-acre farms was about equal to the average in Stanton County, Nebraska; somewhat more than that in Turner County, South Dakota; and less than that in Traill County, North Dakota—all in the eastern benchmark group. It was much less than the average in all but one county of the western benchmark group. The average for the 480-acre group was less than that for the entire Northern Plains region in 1950. These data imply that the sample farms of up to 480 acres are small by comparison with nontransition county or regional averages. The 640-acre farm is average, from the investment standpoint, while the 1,280-acre size, in terms of investment, could fairly be called only moderately large.

The resource ratios indicate the slight measure of building economy evident in the larger farms, the more discernible machinery economy, and the fact that the large farms were not less intensive in the use of livestock than the smaller units.

We also investigated resource structure between tenure groups among the 480-acre farms; the data are presented in Figure 38. Most of the tenants were operating under crop-share or crop-share–cash-lease arrangements. On these rented farms, productivity per acre, or the investment in buildings, or both, appear to be somewhat lower than on the owner-operated farms, at least as reflected in the farmers' estimates of value. The amounts of machinery investment were about the same, $3,700 for the

TABLE 47.  RESOURCES PER MAN AND PER ACRE, BY SIZE OF FARM, FOR 135 SAMPLE FARMS IN THE NEBRASKA TRANSITION AREA, 1956

| Resource Ratio | Size of Farm, in Acres | | | | |
| --- | --- | --- | --- | --- | --- |
| | 160 | 320 | 480 | 640 | 1,280 |
| Acres per man . . . . . | 148 | 261 | 387 | 448 | 690 |
| Capital per man . . . . | $11,300.00 | $19,400.00 | $24,700.00 | $28,000.00 | $44,500.00 |
| Real estate investment per acre. . . . . . . | 55.60 | 50.40 | 49.30 | 46.00 | 47.60 |
| Livestock investment per acre . . . . . . . . | 10.70 | 10.20 | 11.40 | 10.40 | 12.10 |
| Machinery investment per acre. . . . . . . | 6.79 | 7.83 | 6.89 | 5.89 | 4.38 |

Source: Nebr. Agr. Exp. Sta. data.

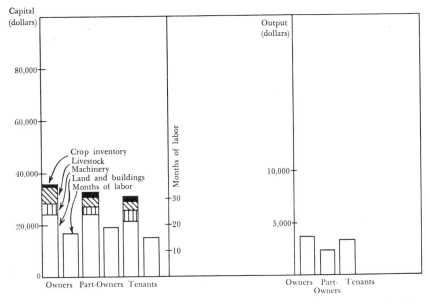

Source: Nebr. Agr. Exp. Sta. data.

FIG. 38.  RESOURCE STRUCTURE AND GROSS OUTPUT ON 480-ACRE FARMS OPERATED BY OWNERS, PART-OWNERS, AND TENANTS, NEBRASKA TRANSITION AREA, 1955

owners and $3,800 for the tenants. Owner-operators had $2,100 more invested in livestock, which probably accounts for the somewhat lower level of gross income for the tenants as compared with the owners. We are inclined to place less confidence in the data for part-owners, since only ten such cases were studied.

### FACTORS AFFECTING CAPITAL ACCUMULATION

One of the goals of farm operators is to accumulate capital to increase their net worth. Such an increase occurs in any given year when the value of an operator's income exceeds the amount he spends for cash production and fixed expenses, the depreciation of nonvariable assets he owns, and the cash operating expenses involved in family living. The degree to which his net worth, or accumulated capital, increases from one year to the next is one indicator of the success of a farmer's operations. Of course, capital is not accumulated simply for the sake of more "money in the sock," or merely to improve farming operations—people also have personal and family goals.

In Sherman County, Nebraska, 196 randomly selected farm families were asked about their goals relating to both farm operations and family living. They were also asked to rank goals of each type in order of importance. The results are summarized in Table 48. Eleven of the sixteen farming goals mentioned involve the need for capital. Particularly noticeable was the number of specific goals involving a desired expansion of the business, by increasing either acreage or intensity. On the family side, the value these people place on educating their children is clear; they also put house and farm improvements and security in old age rather high in their rankings.

Accumulated capital can take many forms, such as farm assets like land and

TABLE 48.    RANKING OF FARM AND FAMILY GOALS MENTIONED BY 196 SAMPLE FAMILIES,
SHERMAN CO., NEBRASKA, 1956*

| Goal | 1st | 2d | 3d | Total Times Mentioned |
|---|---|---|---|---|
| *Farm Goals* | | | | |
| A.  To improve productivity of farm . . . . . . | 35 | 21 | 20 | 86 |
| B.  To buy a farm. . . . . . . . . . . . . . | 32 | 11 | 6 | 49 |
| C.  To get operations adapted to uncertainty . . | 28 | 31 | 12 | 71 |
| D.  To increase farm size (acreage) . . . . . . | 16 | 17 | 6 | 39 |
| E.  To replace old machinery with new . . . . | 18 | 29 | 20 | 67 |
| F.  To increase landholdings (own) . . . . . . | 12 | 11 | 4 | 27 |
| G.  To shift to good livestock enterprise . . . . | 10 | 2 | — | 12 |
| H.  To "make a living" (economic survival) . . | 6 | 1 | 1 | 8 |
| I.  To change occupation . . . . . . . . . . | 9 | 8 | 15 | 32 |
| J.  To move to other area . . . . . . . . . . | 6 | 10 | 9 | 25 |
| K.  To get out of debt . . . . . . . . . . . . | 6 | 1 | 0 | 7 |
| L.  To get into irrigation farming . . . . . . . | 4 | 1 | 4 | 9 |
| M.  To expand present irrigation enterprise . . . | 1 | 2 | 1 | 4 |
| N.  To rent out land. . . . . . . . . . . . . | 4 | 3 | 0 | 7 |
| O.  To sell land . . . . . . . . . . . . . . . | 3 | 1 | 1 | 5 |
| P.  To adopt sound credit program . . . . . . | 0 | 1 | 2 | 3 |
| *Family Goals* | | | | |
| A.  Education for children . . . . . . . . . . | 79 | 24 | 7 | 110 |
| B.  Farmstead improvement . . . . . . . . . | 56 | 37 | 17 | 110 |
| C.  Retirement . . . . . . . . . . . . . . . | 38 | 42 | 35 | 115 |
| D.  Home furnishings . . . . . . . . . . . . | 10 | 26 | 9 | 45 |
| E.  To help boys start farming . . . . . . . . | 6 | 1 | 0 | 7 |
| F.  Estate for children . . . . . . . . . . . . | 3 | 18 | 22 | 43 |
| G.  Support for household (make living) . . . . | 4 | 1 | 1 | 6 |
| H.  Travel . . . . . . . . . . . . . . . . . | 3 | 11 | 12 | 26 |
| I.  Security for old age . . . . . . . . . . . | 2 | 3 | 1 | 6 |

* Arrayed according to first-goal frequency.          Source: Nebr. Agr. Exp. Sta. data.

buildings, machinery, livestock, and inventories of feed and seed. It can also be home equipment, house, clothing, and car. Finally, such intangibles as cash, stocks, bonds, savings accounts, and the cash value of insurance should be included. The value of all these items, minus the debts of the family, is the net worth or accumulated capital.

Many factors interact to affect the rate at which any given farm family accumulates capital. These include the amount of assets they had when they started farming, the amounts and kinds of credit they used, their education, the type and size of farm enterprises, their experience and managerial ability, the size of the family, and how much they spent for family living each year. Not the least would be the general economic conditions they experienced during their careers, and particularly at the time of starting. The section to follow presents the results of our investigation into some of the factors affecting the rate of capital accumulation by the farm families in the 135-farm finance sample in the Nebraska transition area.

We defined accumulated capital as the increase in farm net worth from the year of starting up to 1956—after subtracting unusual gains or losses occurring during that time. Unusual losses were those from fire, tornado, illness, and other things beyond the operator's control. Unusual gains included veterans' payments, income from nonfarm work, and gifts after starting—which also were randomly distributed among operators, and irrelevant to our analysis. All data were converted to 1950 dollar values to remove the effect of changes in the purchasing power of money.

## Amounts of Capital Accumulated

Among the finance-sample farmers, the amounts of capital accumulated ranged from a high of $76,510 down to a loss of $23,690 from the time of starting until 1956 (Table 49). This averaged $14,670 per farmer or $860 per year for 18 years. Farmers in the second capital-accumulation class were most numerous; they had farmed an average of 17 years, and had accumulated about $381 per year. Group 1, averaging 13 years in farming, had lost capital at the rate of $495 per year, while groups 3, 4, and 5 had accumulated capital at very high rates: namely $1,050, $1,650, and $2,430 per year.

These data must be interpreted with caution since farmers were asked to recall facts from thirty or more years in the past. Their investments in durable consumption goods, such as refrigerators and furniture, etc., were not included, so the accumulated capital was underestimated to this extent. Also, such unusual financial drains as sending children to college or helping them get established in farming could not be accounted for, and these could have made a big difference, especially among the older operators. Finally, the farmers studied represent only the "success" cases. Those who had started during the period 1924–49 but had quit farming were not included in the study.

## Effect of Time of Starting

The economic conditions prevailing when a man begins farming will affect his financial progress; variations in farm prices and weather will enable him to save

TABLE 49. OPERATORS AND FAMILY CHARACTERISTICS OF 135 SAMPLE FARMS IN THE NEBRASKA TRANSITION AREA, BY CAPITAL ACCUMULATION CLASSES, 1956

| | Capital Accumulation Class | | | | |
|---|---|---|---|---|---|
| | *1* | *2* | *3* | *4* | *5* |
| Total capital accumulation: range ($) . . | −23,690 | −1,499 | 13,501 | 28,501 | 43,501 |
| | to | to | to | to | to |
| | −1,500 | 13,500 | 28,500 | 43,500 | 76,510 |
| Average capital accumulation ($) . . . . | −6,622 | 6,448 | 19,597 | 35,715 | 54,578 |
| Number of farms . . . . . . . . . . . | 14 | 67 | 28 | 13 | 13 |
| Operator age . . . . . . . . . . . . . | 45.86 | 43.01 | 44.54 | 47.18 | 52.38 |
| Years of operator's education . . . . . . | 8.21 | 9.06 | 9.79 | 9.11 | 9.92 |
| Number of years farmed . . . . . . . . | 13.14 | 16.91 | 19.07 | 21.96 | 22.53 |
| Credit-knowledge index* . . . . . . . . | 29 | 41 | 39 | 48 | 48 |
| Family consumption expenses per year ($)† | 1,512 | 1,863 | 2,010 | 2,237 | 2,556 |
| Number of "child units" raised‡ . . . . | 1.25 | 2.41 | 2.54 | 1.94 | 3.07 |

Source: Nebr. Agr. Exp. Sta. data.

* This is a rating of the operator's general knowledge of credit. The highest possible score was 85.
† These data are an average of estimates for 1952 and 1956.
‡ Children of ten years or older counted as one unit each. Younger children were weighted in proportion to age.

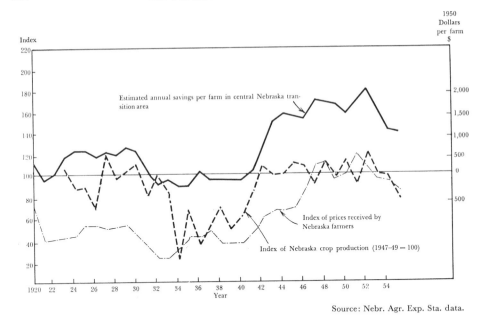

FIG. 39. ESTIMATED SAVINGS OPPORTUNITY AS RELATED TO PRICES RECEIVED AND INDEX
OF CROP PRODUCTION, CENTRAL–NEBRASKA TRANSITION AREA, 1920–55

large amounts in some years and in others to save little or even lose money. The
opportunity that farmers in the transition-area counties had, *on the average*, to accumulate savings was estimated for each year since 1920 for two reasons. First, we were
interested in how this opportunity varied from one year to the next; second, in
analyzing the effects of other factors affecting financial progress, we wished to remove
the influence of the specific year in which each farmer started.

The year-to-year variation in the average opportunity to save in central Nebraska
is shown in Figure 39, along with indexes of prices received by Nebraska farmers and
of crop production in Nebraska. The effects of prices and weather can be seen in the
opportunity-to-save index. This index was estimated by subtracting the estimated
production and farm family living expenses for all farms in each year from the estimated gross farm incomes for the transition-area counties.[1] In summary, then, the
opportunity to save was used as an index of the varying economic conditions over
time which would affect all farmers alike.

An illustration of what this index means in terms of farm capital accumulation in
Sherman County is given in Figure 40. The top scale indicates the year since starting
farming while the bottom one indicates the number of years a farmer starting in any
year since 1920 would have farmed by 1955. The top line shows the average capital
a typical farmer in Sherman County starting in any year between 1920 and 1955
would have accumulated by 1956. Thus those starting in 1923 would have been no

[1] For a complete description of methodology, see Roger H. Willsie and H. W. Ottoson, *Factors
Affecting the Financial Progress of Dryland Farmers in Central Nebraska, 1924 to 1956*, Nebraska Agricultural
Research Bulletin No. 201, 1961.

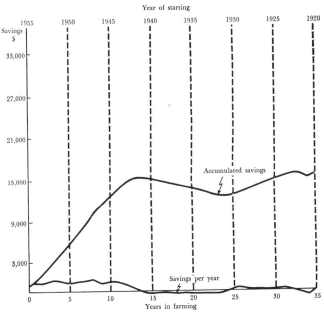

FIG. 40. HYPOTHETICAL TOTAL SAVINGS POSSIBILITY PER FARM, BASED ON YIELDS, PRICES, AND ESTIMATED LIVING EXPENSES, SHERMAN CO., NEBRASKA

better off in 1956 than those starting in 1942; those who started in the thirties had to make up losses and were thus at a disadvantage.

Analysis of the data on capital accumulation for the 135-farm sample indicated that the opportunity-to-save index was the most important factor explaining the rate at which farmers made financial progress. It accounted for 22 percent of the variation in rates of saving when other selected factors were held constant. Even so, we apparently understated the effect of general farm economic conditions since, for each dollar estimated as a savings opportunity, the sample farmers actually saved an average of $2.29.

*Effect of Size of Farm*

Size of farm can also affect financial progress. With no change in per unit efficiency, net income can increase with more acres. Savings would rise even faster since family living expenses tend to increase more slowly than income. In addition, there are certain economies in the use of machinery, buildings, and labor associated with larger acreages. For example, the average machinery investment on 640-acre farms was only 53 percent greater than on 320-acre farms in the transition-area sample.

The average size of farm operated by the farmers in the farm finance sample during the period was 466 acres; the smallest size operated by anyone at any time was 160 acres; the largest size was 1,440 acres. As shown in Figure 41, each additional acre of land resulted in $15.38 of accumulated capital for the average period of 17.8

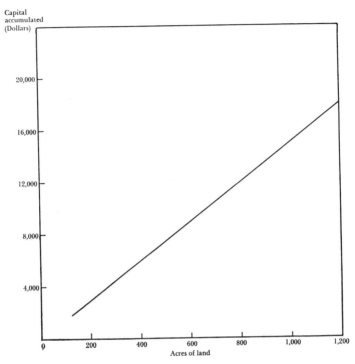

Source: Nebr. Agr. Exp. Sta. data.

FIG. 41.   EFFECT OF SIZE OF FARM ON CAPITAL ACCUMULATED BY THE 135 FARMERS DURING AN AVERAGE OF 18 YEARS IN FARMING, NEBRASKA TRANSITION AREA

years farmed by all operators. This amounts to 86 cents per acre per year, with other factors held constant. Size of farm explained about 7 percent of the total variation in the amounts of capital accumulated.

### Effect of Size of Livestock Enterprise

Other things being equal, income levels and financial progress should be affected by the size of the livestock enterprise. Having livestock makes it possible to operate a bigger business on a given acreage and use fixed factors, like labor and machinery, more efficiently. In the analysis, we converted all types of livestock into standard units, equivalent to one dairy cow in feed consumption. The number of these standard animal units kept by sample farmers during the period studied ranged from 4 to 411 per farm, with an average of 85.5.

We found that, for the average of 17.8 years farmed, each additional animal unit contributed $85.44 to savings (Figure 42). This amounts to $4.80 per animal unit per year. The size of the livestock enterprise explained 10 percent of the variation in capital accumulation. The size of the livestock enterprise was, of course, interrelated with size of farm, but not so much so that the two effects could not be separated. (The "joint" variation between them was about 25 percent of the total.)

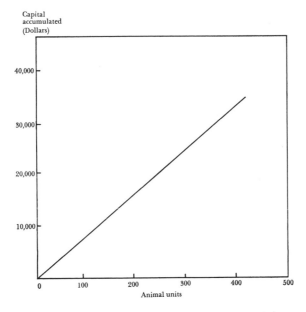

Source: Nebr. Agr. Exp. Sta. data.

FIG. 42. CONTRIBUTION OF ANIMAL UNITS ON CAPITAL
ACCUMULATED BY 135 FARMERS DURING AN AVERAGE OF
18 YEARS, NEBRASKA TRANSITION AREA

### Effect of Education

Additional training in school frequently makes a person a better manager. Also, the traits that lead a person to further his education are often those that contribute to his managerial ability. For both these reasons we expected education to have some bearing on the rate of financial progress achieved by the sample farmers. The range in education among the sample operators was 3 to 12 years, with an average of 9 years. Their capital accumulation was associated with years of schooling, but not as much as we had anticipated. Each year of education "explained" about $47.00 per year of capital accumulated. In other words, a farmer with three years of high school, who had farmed the average span of 17.8 years, would have accumulated about $2,500 more than the farmer with one year. Or, to put it another way, the value of an extra year of schooling, if the annual additional saving were capitalized at 5 percent, would be $940. But educational level was much less influential than the three factors mentioned earlier; it was about one-fourth as important as size of farm and one-fifth as important as animal units.

### Resources at Time of Starting

The initial stake possessed by a farmer might conceivably affect his financial progress. Such resources might have been furnished by parents or saved from wages earned in other occupations. There was a wide range in the net worths of the farmers when they started farming, from $290 to more than $43,000. Most of them started with less than $5,000, with an average of $4,510. We found no relation between financial progress and the amount of beginning worth. On the average, farmers starting with very low investments made just as fast progress as those who were more fortunate in this respect. Of course, the effect of a substantial net worth may be masked in this study, since it may enable a farmer to hold out in adverse times. People who had been forced out of farming were not included in this study, so we observed only the success cases.

## CAPITAL ACCUMULATION AND FAMILY LIVING

How does net worth affect expenditures for family living? It has been suggested that such expenditures are associated with increases in family capital. In 1956 the average expenditures of all sample farmers for family living were $2,309. To sort out the effects of net worth on family living it was necessary to remove the effect of another important factor, the size of family. The sample farmers spent $146 more per year for family living for each adult male equivalent member in the family above the average size of 3.6 members, and $146 less for smaller-than-average families. Families ranged in size from one to nine adult equivalents. For each additional dollar of net worth above the average of $25,000, the families spent 1.7 cents, or about 2 percent, for family living. Net worth explained twice as much of the variation in family living expenditures as did size of family.

## IMPACT OF DROUGHT IN THE TRANSITION AREA

A soil-moisture deficiency began to develop in the Nebraska transition area in 1954. In that year county corn yields averaged 16–18 bushels, compared with the long-run average of about 20 bushels. The drought worsened in 1955, when yields of corn went down to 3–6 bushels; and they continued at these low levels through 1956. Wheat yields were not affected quite so early, but they dropped substantially in 1956. Because these drought conditions were coupled with declining price levels for farm commodities, it was anticipated by the study group that the resulting combination would have noticeable impacts on farming in the area. Consequently a special effort was made to analyze the effects of these drought conditions—with worthwhile results. Of course, this drought was not as serious as the one in Texas and Oklahoma in the immediately preceding years, nor in northwestern Oklahoma during the period in which we are interested.

Besides its effects on corn and wheat yields, the drought seriously cut hay production in the study area, while pasture conditions were down to as low as 70 percent of the average of 1942–51. Cattle numbers were reduced as farmers culled their herds, at a time when cattle numbers in the country as a whole increased. Hog production was down 30 percent on the average. Gross incomes in 1955 were only slightly more than half of "normal" income levels. Net incomes, counting inventory changes, were minus-values on many farms.

### Adjustment by Selling Out

One major adjustment farmers can make to drought is to sell out. During the last half of 1956 and the spring of 1957, more than 300 farmers in central Nebraska listed their farms for sale. We sent mail surveys to 285 (90 per cent) of them to study the circumstances surrounding their decision to sell their farms. Though not everyone who left his farm under duress was represented, the 131 who returned the questionnaire revealed some significant facts.[2]

The people who sold out were operators of somewhat smaller-than-average farms. They were likely to be tenants; 57 percent of them were tenants as compared with 47 percent in the area as a whole. Owners and part-owners were proportionately fewer in number among those who sold out. Contrary to popular assumption, most of those selling were not young people. Actually, their age distribution was very similar to that of all farmers in the area, with about one-fourth of them less than thirty-five years old, half of them between thirty-five and fifty-four, and the other one-fourth over fifty-five years of age.

Why did they sell? The major reasons given were financial difficulty, the drought, and the better opportunities they visualized outside of agriculture (Table 50). Financial difficulty and drought were obviously related. With these combined, over one-third of the responses were related to drought. These two reasons, along with better opportunities elsewhere, constitute a class that might be termed economic factors. These economic factors represented two-thirds of the reasons given for selling out by people on farms of 480 acres or less. The frequency was less on the larger farms, where retirement, health, and other factors became more important. Tenure was a factor, too. Economic factors played a heavier part in the decisions to sell among tenants than among owners.

What happened to their farms? The answer to this question is most important. Of the farms released by sale, over 53 percent of the owned units and 65 percent of

TABLE 50. REASONS FOR SELLING, BY SIZE OF FARM, NEBRASKA TRANSITION AREA, 1956–57

| | | Size of Farm, in Acres | | | |
|---|---|---|---|---|---|
| Reasons for Selling | Total | Less than 250 | 250 to 349 | 350 to 480 | More than 480 |
| Number of respondents . | 131 | 47 | 38 | 21 | 25 |
| Total reasons*  . . . . | 209 | 71 | 59 | 33 | 46 |
| Financial difficulty. . . | 51 | 16 | 16 | 10 | 9 |
| Drought . . . . . . . | 38 | 13 | 15 | 4 | 6 |
| Better opportunities out- side of farming  . . . | 36 | 13 | 7 | 8 | 8 |
| Retirement . . . . . . | 18 | 10 | 4 | 1 | 3 |
| Poor health . . . . . . | 29 | 12 | 8 | 4 | 5 |
| Other†. . . . . . . . | 37 | 7 | 9 | 6 | 15 |

Source: Nebr. Agr. Exp. Sta. data.

* The total reasons, in this and subsequent tables, are greater than the number of respondents because many sellers gave more than one reason.

† Including poor leasing arrangements, dissatisfaction with government programs, landlord selling farm, capital gain on farm, dissolving partnership, move to better farm, and death in family. "Other" will include these same reasons in subsequent tables.

[2] Roger H. Willsie, *Why Farmers Sold Out in Central Nebraska in 1956–57*, Nebraska Agricultural Experiment Station Bulletin No. 445, 1958.

TABLE 51.   Disposition of Farms Released by People Selling Out,
Nebraska Transition Area, 1956–57

| Tenure of Land Farmed in 1956 | Disposition of Farm Units Released | | | | | |
|---|---|---|---|---|---|---|
| | Rented as a Unit | Rented as Addition to a Unit | Sold as a Unit | Sold as Addition to a Unit | Idle or Soil Bank | Total |
| Rented. . . . . | 15 | 55 | 3 | 4 | 8 | 85 |
| Owned. . . . . | 8 | 17 | 10 | 10 | 6 | 51 |
| Total . . . . | 23 | 72 | 13 | 14 | 14 | 136 |

Source: Nebr. Agr. Exp. Sta. data.

the rented farms were transferred as additions to farms already existing in the area. In other words, they were used for farm enlargement (Table 51).

These data illustrate the process by which farm consolidation occurs. Some people selling out were squeezed out; others had opportunities to which to go. In fact, the pull for some was greater than the push. Finally, over half the farms released lost their identity as they were merged with going operations. Thus the broad problem of farm size was being solved in the process.

How large were these sales? The information obtained in the survey indicated that the farmers who were selling out did not, for the most part, realize large proceeds from their sales. This is illustrated by data on three property items. Fifty-eight percent of the people selling livestock realized less than $2,000 from them. Seventy-two percent received less than $2,000 for their machinery. Only twenty-one people sold land in these sales, of whom fourteen received less than $20,000 for it. We had no data on the indebtedness of the sellers. However, Nebraska state data in 1956 indicated that the number of forced sales through foreclosure or for taxes was small compared with the thirties: 2.3 per thousand farms. This was an increase over the rate of 0.3 per 1,000 farms in 1955, however. From the debt data mentioned previously, we would conclude that these people were selling out before they were forced to do so. The amount of cash they took with them was not large, but they did acquire some.

A fact to be recognized is that these farm-sales data related only to farms involved in advertised auction sales. Some farms are transferred directly between buyer and seller, with or without the use of an agent. We feel that our data are quite representative of sales involving non-real-estate assets; most of these are probably sold in auction sales. However, in the state as a whole, only a fifth of the real estate transfers involve auction sales; thus our data involve only a small proportion of the transfers of land in the area. More will be said about land transfers later in this chapter.

Where did the sellers go? The future plans of the people selling out in 1956–57 seemed quite definite. One-third of them were leaving the state, representing part of the labor that has been one of the state's important exports in recent decades. Most of those leaving the state had definite jobs to which to go. Of the small number who were leaving the state without jobs, some were going for health reasons or to retire, rather than to seek employment. Eighteen states were represented in the plans of those leaving Nebraska, with the west coast being the destination of one-fourth of them. Only two-thirds of those remaining in the state had obtained jobs by the time of the survey—which was September, 1956, to April, 1957. The plans of about 10 percent of all the respondents were indefinite.

All the respondents selling out were leaving farming at the time. They were asked whether they planned to return to farming some time in the future. The majority of them said no, regardless of their reason for leaving. Only one-fifth of them gave an affirmative answer to the question.

*Impact of Drought on Those Who Stayed*

The first tangible effect of drought in the transition area was the shrinking of capital assets. This occurred through lower income levels, the resulting lower rates of replenishment, and a general decline in values. The net effect was a reduction in the total assets of these transition farms of $5,154 between 1952 and 1956 (Table 52). Their net worths decreased by $5,389, or 16 percent.

Land values in the central-Nebraska transition area rose by 22 percent from January 1, 1952, to January 1, 1956. Thus the entire increase shown for land in Table 52 could be accounted for by land prices. However, the average size of farm among the sample farmers also increased, from 537 to 551 acres, during that time.

The land-value figures are farmer estimates. They probably underestimated the actual increases in value of their land and buildings during this period, most of which took place during 1952. There was a slight rise in land prices during the next three years, and a decline in 1956. The effects of drought and falling prices are reflected in the other assets. Machinery depreciated and was not replaced, and livestock were sold off as feed shortages developed in 1955. Crop inventories for the two years reflect the liquidation of feed stocks in the face of lowered production.

The data in Table 52 indicate that tenants suffered more heavily from financial attrition during the period 1952–56 than did owner-operators, whose investments in land partially offset their capital losses. The subtraction of land and long-term liabilities from the capital structures in the table leaves a comparison which indicates the

TABLE 52.  CAPITAL STRUCTURES ON 135 SAMPLE FARMS, 1952 AND 1956,
NEBRASKA TRANSITION AREA (CURRENT DOLLARS)*

|  | January 1 | |
|---|---|---|
|  | *1952* | *1956* |
| Assets |  |  |
| Land . . . . . . . . | $12,849 | $15,216 |
| Livestock. . . . . . . | 11,113 | 6,150 |
| Machinery . . . . . . | 4,677 | 3,513 |
| Crop inventory . . . . | 2,742 | 811 |
| Cash & other assets . . | 2,194 | 2,731 |
| Total . . . . . | $33,575 | $28,421 |
| Liabilities . . . . . . | $3,781 | $4,016 |
| Net worth . . . . . . | 29,794 | 24,405 |
| Total . . . . . | $33,575 | $28,421 |

Source: Nebr. Agr. Exp. Sta. data.

* Not a random sample, but reasonably representative.

financial condition of tenants. Their net worth shrank from $19,176 on the average in 1952 to $11,560 in 1956, a decrease of 40 percent.

The drought of 1955–56 broke dramatically in the spring of 1957. Instead of the 15 inches of rainfall the transition area received in 1956, precipitation ranged from 30 to 35 inches the following year. The rains started in March, early enough to give yields of 32 bushels of dry-land corn and 25 bushels of wheat per acre, as compared with 5 and 15 bushels, respectively, the previous year. Fortunately, livestock prices also rose suddenly, by about one-fifth.

Thus the financial problems that were becoming severe in transition-area farming in 1956 were suddenly alleviated. The improved morale of the people in the area was obvious between the time of our first field survey in 1956 and the second one in 1957. However, we still attempted to capture the farmers' reaction to the drought in our second survey in 1957, even though they were already viewing it from the perspective of some months of favorable weather.

### Measures Taken in Response to Depression

Table 53 shows how the sample farmers took various measures to safeguard their farm businesses. The money they borrowed was chiefly of a short-term nature, from commercial banks and dealers. Many dealers became concerned over the increase in their outstanding accounts. Machinery dealers apparently were most severely affected with increased credit and reduced sales. Feed dealers reported less protein feed being sold, and fertilizer dealers also made lower sales to dry-land operators. The farmer responses clearly reflect a concerted effort to cut cash costs. Some farmers even tried part-time nonfarm work, moving temporarily to such places as Omaha, Lincoln, Kansas City, and Wichita.

Farmers also tried to adjust family living expenses to the bleak prospects afforded by the drought, as is shown in Table 54. A few also tried to reduce their food costs by substituting cheaper foods and even by attempting to raise some of their own food. Some nonfarm people have suggested that during such difficult times farmers might reduce living expenditures even more by giving up gas, electricity, and other con-

TABLE 53. FARM BUSINESS MEASURES TAKEN BY 135 FARMERS TO REDUCE EFFECTS OF DROUGHT, NEBRASKA TRANSITION AREA, 1956–57

| Measure Taken | Number of Farmers |
|---|---|
| Total . . . . . . . . . . | 135 |
| Borrowed for farm operations . | 78 |
| Reduced machinery expenses . | 71 |
| Reduced livestock inventory. . | 64 |
| Cultivated less land . . . . . | 42 |
| Used cash reserves to buy feed. | 39 |
| Held over feed reserves . . . . | 38 |
| Worked off the farm . . . . . | 35 |
| Used lower-protein feeds . . . | 23 |

Source: Nebr. Agr. Exp. Sta. data.

TABLE 54.  HOME-RELATED MEASURES USED BY 135 FARMERS TO OFFSET THE EFFECT
OF DROUGHT, NEBRASKA TRANSITION AREA, 1956–57

| Measure Taken | Number of Farmers |
| --- | --- |
| Total . . . . . . . . . . . . . | 135 |
| Reduced clothing expenditures  . . | 76 |
| Reduced transportation expenditures | 66 |
| Borrowed for living expenses  . . . | 36 |

Source: Nebr. Agr. Exp. Sta. data.

veniences adopted during the last two decades. However, the farmers interviewed clearly implied that living standards are fairly inflexible; many said they would quit farming rather than change their living patterns to that extent.

*The Role of Reserves.*   Most of the sample farmers maintained some reserves as a potential defense against drought. They were more prevalent on larger farms than on the 160-acre and 320-acre units, since farmers in the latter classes cannot well afford them. The most widely used reserve was maintaining feed stocks in excess of livestock needs as a hedge against dry weather; 82 percent of the sample farmers practiced this. Reserves in the form of cash or of easily converted items, such as bonds or wheat, were held by 60 percent of the farmers. This is reflected in the capital structure comparisons of Table 52. Also, 55 percent of the farmers tried diversifying their crop and livestock enterprises to reduce risk.

*Postponed Investments.*   Since the sample farmers were trying to reduce cash outflow during the difficult period 1952–56, they tended to postpone necessary investments, as follows:

| Size of Farm (Acres) | Farmers Indicating Postponed Items | Average Amount of Postponed Investment (All Farms) |
| --- | --- | --- |
| 160 | 31% | $  610 |
| 320 | 62 | 2,645 |
| 480 | 72 | 922 |
| 640 | 59 | 2,295 |
| 1,280 | 74 | 2,068 |

Buildings, machinery, land, and land improvements were most frequently subjected to this postponement (Table 55). The 160-acre farmers seemed less affected by the drought in this respect, but this was chiefly due to their being older and nearer to retirement. Most of their postponements related to building repairs. In the other size groups there was no particular relation between type and amount of postponed investment and size of farm.

The farmers said they postponed these investments because of dry weather and lack of finances. We had no way of knowing to what extent they felt that dry weather temporarily removed the need for the improvements, as opposed to its influence in limiting their financial resources.

TABLE 55.   TYPES AND AMOUNTS OF INVESTMENTS POSTPONED DURING 1952–56 BY
135 SAMPLE FARMERS, NEBRASKA TRANSITION AREA (1956–57)

| Type of Postponed Investment | Farmers Indicating Type | Average Amount of Postponed Investment | |
|---|---|---|---|
| | | For Farms Indicating Postponement | For all Farms |
| Buildings. . . . . . . . | 21% | $2,720 | $580 |
| Machinery . . . . . . . . | 16 | 2,010 | 310 |
| Land and improvements other than buildings . . . | 9 | 5,000 | 440 |
| Home improvements. . . . | 7 | 1,000 | 70 |
| Livestock. . . . . . . . . | 6 | 2,130 | 130 |

Source: Nebr. Agr. Exp. Sta. data.

*How Much More Drought Would Farmers Stand?*   To determine their mobility in the face of continued adverse conditions, the 135 farmers in the 1957 survey were asked how many more bad years they would take before leaving farming. This question was asked of people who had already withstood two years of drought. The responses of each size group are shown in Table 56. The 160-acre farmers showed surprising resistance to shift, undoubtedly owing to their older age and nearness to retirement. Among the rest, the inclination to "take it" was greater with larger size of farm, as one would expect. If we combine those who would never quit with those who would

TABLE 56.   RESPONSES OF 135 SAMPLE FARMERS, BY SIZE GROUP TO QUESTION
"HOW MANY MORE YEARS WOULD YOU TAKE BEFORE LEAVING FARMING?"
NEBRASKA TRANSITION AREA, 1957

| Type of Response | Size of Farm in Acres | | | | |
|---|---|---|---|---|---|
| | 160 | 320 | 480 | 640 | 1,280 |
| None . . . . . . . . | 1 | 1 | 3 | 0 | 0 |
| 1 year . . . . . . . . | 4 | 8 | 12 | 5 | 1 |
| 2 years. . . . . . . . | 1 | 8 | 7 | 1 | 2 |
| 3  ,, . . . . . . . . | 2 | 2 | 5 | 4 | 1 |
| 4  ,, . . . . . . . . | 1 | 1 | 0 | 4 | 0 |
| 5  ,, . . . . . . . . | 0 | 0 | 2 | 1 | 0 |
| 6  ,, . . . . . . . . | 0 | 0 | 0 | 0 | 1 |
| 7  ,, . . . . . . . . | 0 | 0 | 1 | 0 | 0 |
| 8  ,, . . . . . . . . | 0 | 0 | 0 | 0 | 0 |
| 9  ,, . . . . . . . . | 0 | 0 | 0 | 0 | 0 |
| 10 ,, . . . . . . . . | 1 | 0 | 0 | 1 | 1 |
| Several years . . . . . | 5 | 5 | 7 | 3 | 5 |
| Would never quit . . . | 2 | 2 | 4 | 1 | 2 |
| Don't know . . . . . . | 2 | 2 | 4 | 2 | 5 |
| Average years for those indicating years . . . | 2.6 | 1.8 | 2.1 | 3.1 | 4.0 |

Source: Nebr. Agr. Exp. Sta. data.

last four or more years, or several years, we find that the proportion of farmers who would withstand the drought increases somewhat with size of farm.

| Size (Acres) | Proportion who would withstand drought |
|---|---|
| 320 . . . . . . . . . . . . . . . | 28% |
| 480 . . . . . . . . . . . . . . | 47 |
| 640 . . . . . . . . . . . . . . | 45 |
| 1,280 . . . . . . . . . . . . . . | 52 |

To probe their thinking further, we asked these farmers what they would do if they were forced out by drought. The results indicate how much they have considered alternatives to farming, as well as the forms these alternatives might take (Table 57).

The commitment to farming, as indicated by "don't know" and "no response," was heaviest among the 160's and the 1,280's, undoubtedly for different reasons. It is interesting to note that of those who might leave farming, nearly twice as many would leave their local community as would stay there to work at nonfarm jobs.

TABLE 57. FARMERS' ALTERNATIVES IF FORCED OUT OF FARMING BY DROUGHT, NEBRASKA TRANSITION AREA, 1956

| Size of Farm | Don't Know | No Response | Labor | | | Another Farm | White-collar | Other | Total |
|---|---|---|---|---|---|---|---|---|---|
| | | | Farm | Common | Skilled | | | | |
| (Acres) | | | | | | | | | |
| 160 . . | 21% | 47% | — | 16% | 16% | — | — | — | 100% |
| 320 . . | 18 | 37 | 3% | 11 | 11 | 11% | 3% | 6% | 100 |
| 480 . . | 10 | 47 | 4 | 6 | 10 | 13 | 6 | 4 | 100 |
| 640 . . | 18 | 37 | — | 18 | 23 | 4 | — | — | 100 |
| 1,280 . . | — | 74 | — | — | 5 | 16 | — | 5 | 100 |

Source: Nebr. Agr. Exp. Sta. data.

*Operators' Ideas on Additional Capital.* The 135 farmers in our finance sample were asked what additional capital items for farming they thought could be profitably added on their farms, and what home improvements they would make if funds were available—without considering their financing or any other problems involved in obtaining them. The pattern of responses was quite consistent between sizes of farm, but the average estimated amounts were proportionately much greater on the smaller farms than on the larger ones (Table 58). For example, the total of the suggested farm improvements averaged $22.00 per acre on the 320-acre farms, $13.00 on the 480-acre farms, and only $8.00 per acre on the 1,280-acre farms. Additional investments in land and buildings represented the largest class of these estimates.

When this class was further broken down into additional cropland, improvements, and buildings (Table 59) we found that the smallest and largest farms mentioned more additional acres than the other groups. However, all size groups recognized additional land as a profitable investment. This is consistent with the average increase of 14 acres in size of farm in the transition-area sample during the four-year period 1952–56. Additional building items were the most common of those in the

TABLE 58.   POTENTIALLY PROFITABLE ADDITIONAL INVESTMENTS, BY SIZE OF FARM, 135
SAMPLE FARMERS, NEBRASKA TRANSITION AREA, 1956–57

| | Size of Farm (Acres) | | | | |
|---|---|---|---|---|---|
| | 160 | 320 | 480 | 640 | 1,280 |
| | *Percent of each group indicating profitable investments:* | | | | |
| Land & Buildings . . . . . | 68 | 62 | 72 | 59 | 73 |
| Machinery . . . . . . . . | 53 | 76 | 73 | 73 | 42 |
| Other farm investments. . . | 5 | 24 | 26 | 33 | 5 |
| Home improvements . . . . | 79 | 62 | 63 | 64 | 47 |
| | *Amount per farm reporting:* | | | | |
| Land & buildings . . . . . | $9,177 | $7,512 | $4,715 | $8,363 | $12,314 |
| Machinery . . . . . . . . | 1,840 | 2,072 | 2,197 | 3,241 | 3,088 |
| Other farm investments. . . | 1,800 | 1,553 | 3,053 | 3,806 | 1,900 |
| Home improvements . . . . | 675 | 1,959 | 1,285 | 2,241 | 3,756 |
| | *Amount per farm, all farms:* | | | | |
| Land and buildings . . . . | $6,280 | $4,317 | $3,280 | $ 5,322 | $ 9,074 |
| Machinery . . . . . . . . | 968 | 1,572 | 1,624 | 2,357 | 1,300 |
| Other farm investments. . . | 95 | 375 | 796 | 1,211 | 100 |
| Home improvements . . . . | 426 | 1,216 | 782 | 1,324 | 1,779 |
| Total . . . . . . . | $7,769 | $7,480 | $6,482 | $10,214 | $12,253 |

Source: Nebr. Agr. Exp. Sta. data.

land and buildings group. Although they were on the average much smaller, they were mentioned more frequently than all the other items combined, regardless of size class.

A variety of machinery was indicated as being profitable. The most common were tractors, suggested by 30 percent of the 135 respondents. Second were combines, mentioned by 22 farmers; followed by loaders, 19 responses; grain drills, 14 responses; balers, 10 responses; and all other types of farm machinery in smaller numbers. Altogether, 89 farmers mentioned at least one machinery item they thought might be profitable.

The "other farm investments" they were asked about included livestock and items other than land, buildings, and machinery. Only one non-livestock item was men-

TABLE 59.   POTENTIALLY PROFITABLE ADDITIONAL INVESTMENTS IN LAND AND BUILDINGS,
BY SIZE OF FARM, 135 SAMPLE FARMERS, NEBRASKA TRANSITION AREA, 1956–57

| | | Bare Land | | |
|---|---|---|---|---|
| *Acreage* | *Cost* | *Acre equivalent** | *Land Improvement* | *Buildings* |
| 160 . . . . . . | $4,706 | 109 | $1,053 | $ 521 |
| 320 . . . . . . | 2,045 | 47 | 903 | 1,369 |
| 480 . . . . . . | 1,730 | 40 | 598 | 952 |
| 640 . . . . . . | 1,023 | 24 | 2,454 | 1,845 |
| 1,280 . . . . . . | 4,611 | 105 | 2,316 | 2,147 |

Source: Nebr. Agr. Exp. Sta. data.

*Based on average value of land without buildings of $43 per acre.

tioned under this heading by any respondent: a bunker silo. Of the 135 farmers, 31 suggested additional investments in cattle as being profitable. Of these, 16 suggested investments in better beef cows, 3 in better dairy cows, 3 would buy bulls, one would add more beef cows, one would add more sheep, and one would buy a boar. The small size of the average estimates for cattle per farm, as compared with machinery, was surprising. It probably reflects the fact the farmers had passed through a period when they had been liquidating livestock inventories. It probably also reflects the orientation of many farmers toward a cash-grain type of operation.

Ninety-eight of the farmers said they would make home improvements if they had the money. The most common type suggested was remodeling the house (31 responses); the next most common was a new bathroom (28), followed by electrical fixtures and appliances (15), running water (14), cellar, and electricity. Six indicated they would build a new house.

When they had discussed these desired acquisitions, the farmers were asked what investments they actually planned to make during the next three years. The responses in Table 60 show that only about one-third of the farmers who had found some acquisition desirable actually planned to spend money on it in the next three years. These planned investments were much more modest in size than the desired ones but this is no surprise, since "a man's reach should exceed his grasp." Yet the gap between dream and reality was not the same for all types of investments. Land, for example, tended to fade out of their plans while land improvements did not. The modest expansion of livestock also failed to materialize on the smaller units. Apparently, machinery was truly wanted by the sample farmers; planned machinery expenditures represented larger proportions of the "profitable or desired" estimates than those for other items. On the other hand, home improvements suffered most severely.

Of course, these results are based on conjectures the respondents were asked to

TABLE 60. INVESTMENTS DEFNITELY PLANNED FOR NEXT THREE YEARS, BY TYPE AND SIZE OF FARM, 135 SAMPLE FARMERS, NEBRASKA TRANSITION AREA, 1956-57

|  | Size of Farm (Acres) | | | | |
|---|---|---|---|---|---|
|  | 160 | 320 | 480 | 640 | 1,280 |
|  | *Percent of farmers in each group indicating investment:* | | | | |
| Land & buildings . . . | 21 | 14 | 22 | 23 | 26 |
| Machinery . . . . . . | 26 | 28 | 35 | 46 | 26 |
| Other . . . . . . . . | 5 | 3 | 7 | 13 | 16 |
| Home . . . . . . . . | 16 | 17 | 22 | 23 | 26 |
|  | *Average investment, by size of farm:* | | | | |
| Land . . . . . . . . | — | $ 414 | — | — | — |
| Land improvements . . | $ 368 | 379 | $ 326 | $1,136 | — |
| Buildings . . . . . . . | 295 | 38 | 377 | 341 | $ 737 |
| Machinery . . . . . . | 284 | 540 | 483 | 1,005 | 947 |
| Livestock . . . . . . . | — | — | 32 | 373 | 247 |
| Home . . . . . . . . | 89 | 393 | 261 | 204 | 292 |
| Total . . . . . . | $1,036 | $1,764 | $1,479 | $3,059 | $2,223 |

Source: Nebr. Agr. Exp. Sta. data.

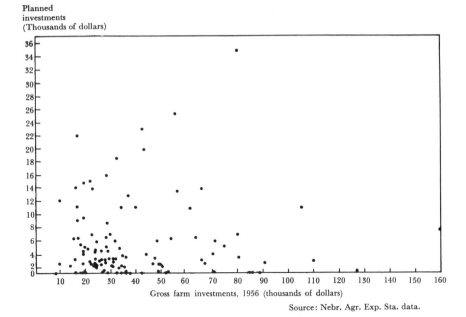

Source: Nebr. Agr. Exp. Sta. data.

FIG. 43.   RELATIONSHIP BETWEEN PLANNED INVESTMENTS AND PRESENT GROSS FARM
INVESTMENTS AMONG TRANSITION–AREA FARMERS, 1957

make on short notice, with all the limitations therein, yet they appear to be consistent
between size groups. Figure 43 indicates an inverse relationship between present
gross farm investment and planned investments, as one would expect. It appears that
farmers' investment plans lean mostly toward labor-saving equipment, which increases cash costs. Additional investments in land and livestock, which permit
expanded output from a fixed resource base, were given second place.

*Productivity of Planned Investments*

The investments planned by the survey farmers bring to mind the analysis of
resource productivities in the central-Nebraska transition area discussed in Chaper 11.
What do those results imply concerning these planned investments?

The interest of the sample farmers in more machinery seems unjustified by the
potential returns. Might not more livestock offer more opportunity for expanding
volume than additional investment in labor-saving equipment? Even additional land
seems more promising.

Figure 44 shows the additional returns forthcoming from increments of land for
each of the four size groups. For this analysis, labor and non-land capital were held
constant at the geometric average for each size group. Of course, when a farmer adds
land he probably adds some other capital items as well; he may hire more labor, or
he may work harder. However, in the long run he *could* reorganize his business to
use the additional land without changing the amount of labor or non-land capital
items used. This means he would operate less intensively; this is the situation
represented by these data.

Annual
returns

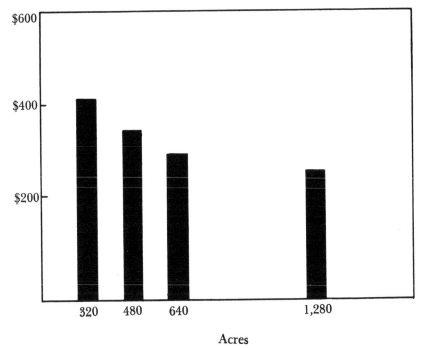

Acres

Source: Nebr. Agr. Exp. Sta. data.

Fig. 44. Additional Returns for Additional 100 Acres of Land Added to Given-size Farms in the Transition Area, 1953–54

Returns to land appear to be quite substantial. From an investment standpoint, we must convert acres to dollars. Using the farmers' estimate of $43.00 per acre of land without buildings, the rates of return on an additional $100 invested in land for the various size groups work out as follows.

| Acreage | Return per $100 Invested |
|---|---|
| 320 | $9.70 |
| 480 | 8.20 |
| 640 | 7.00 |
| 1,280 | 6.30 |

These returns would have to cover the cost of owning the land, such as taxes, of course. However, they cast land in a rather favorable light, and bear out the farmers' ideas on land as a profitable investment. They also raise a question about the absence of land in the three-year investment plans of most operators.

It might be argued that farmers underestimated the value of their land when they were in the position of buying additional acres. Were this the case, the returns per $100 invested would be proportionately smaller. For example, if this land actually was worth 50 percent more, the marginal returns per $100 invested would be $6.60 for the 320's, $5.50 for the 480's, $4.90 for the 640's, and $4.30 for the 1,280's.

*The Process of Getting Started in Farming in the Transition Area*

In the 135-farm sample in the Nebraska transition area we obtained data for sixty-three farmers who had become established in farming between 1940 and 1949 and were still farming at the time of the survey. We were interested in the circumstances under which they had become established, the amount of financial progress they made from the time they started (1945, on the average) until 1952, and the impacts of drought and unfavorable prices on this group after 1952. These farmers started in a highly favorable period. In the four years between 1952 and 1956, they were subjected to adversity; however, they are success cases in that they remained in farming. We have already discussed another group that left farming during the same time. We did not study farmers who started after 1949 because their tenure in farming would have been too short to give us any conclusive results.

*Time of Starting*

Despite the war, some men started farming each year, beginning with 1940. However, most began at the close of the war.

| *Year in which Sample Farmers Began Farming*, 1940–49 | *Number of Farmers* |
|---|---|
| 1940 | 4 |
| 1941 | 3 |
| 1942 | 3 |
| 1943 | 3 |
| 1944 | 8 |
| 1945 | 13 |
| 1946 | 13 |
| 1947 | 5 |
| 1948 | 5 |
| 1949 | 5 |

The number tapered off in the last three years of the period. These men averaged 29.6 years of age when they started, and had the equivalent of 9.4 years of education.

*Size of Farm*

As is shown in Figure 45, the farmers starting in the decade of the forties began with an average of 415 acres of land. Those starting as owners had 300 acres; part-owners had 512 acres, and tenants had 423 acres.

As Figure 46 shows, most of the operators started as tenants. The beginners, as a group, added an average of 9 acres to their farms each year. At the same time, there was a shift from the tenant group to the owner-operator and part-owner groups. The size of owner-operator farms increased much faster than average while the farms of those who remained tenants stayed about the same size.

A word of caution: The most significant parts of Figures 45 and 46 is to the left of the year *13*. This range includes the bulk of the beginning farmers of the forties; to the right of that point, the number of farms represented shrinks down to 4 for year 17, since only the operators starting in 1940 would have had 17 years in farming at the end of 1956.

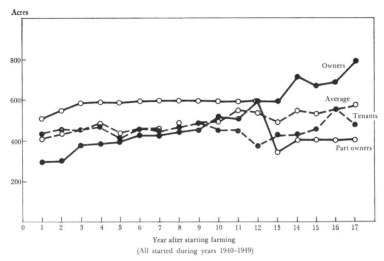

Source: Nebr. Agr. Exp. Sta. data.

Fig. 45.    Change in Size of Farm, by Tenure, during Each Year after Starting in 1940–49, for 63 Farmers in the Nebraska Transition Area

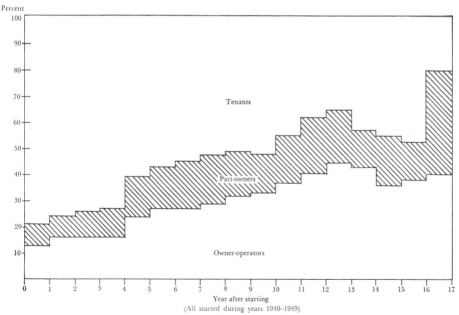

Source: Nebr. Agr. Exp. Sta. data.

Fig. 46.    Percentage of 63 Operators, by Tenure, in Each Year after Starting

*Circumstances in Beginning Farming*

Family assistance played an important role in the establishment of these farmers. One-third of them rented land from relatives when they started. Fourteen inherited assets—land or cash—in amounts ranging from $100 to $32,500. Most of these inheritances were in the form of land. For the entire group of beginning farmers, the average inheritance was $1,619. Families helped in other ways, too. For example, eight of the group of 63 operators had obtained machinery from relatives, six had received livestock, three cash, and one a higher education. Assistance of this kind averaged $288 per farm. Altogether, 39 farmers, or two-thirds of the total, had received some family assistance in getting started.

These beginning operators gained in other ways not connected with their farming efforts. Twelve of them had been registered in the federal on-the-job training program for veterans and had received sizable subsidies, ranging from $1,000 to $7,500. Nineteen had received payments from the Agricultural Conservation Program or the Soil Bank Program. Assistance of this kind from federal sources averaged $958 per farm.

Balanced against these windfalls were unusual losses. In the long run, or among a large group of farms, such losses as those from hail or disease are not unusual. Nevertheless, to individual operators, particularly when starting with short funds, such losses may be critical. Half of the beginning operators experienced unusual losses during the period considered. These were chiefly from hail, but they also included livestock diseases, personal illness, tornado, and fire. The average loss for all farms was $1,394.

Altogether, then, these beginning operators had received assistance from various sources averaging $2,865, excluding such nonmonetary advantages as the opportunity to rent land from relatives. Not quite half of this assistance was offset by unusual losses.

The beginning operators made financial progress between the year of starting and 1952. Most of the capital used in starting was in the form of rented land and buildings; the average net worth of the operators at the time of starting was $6,674 (in 1950 dollars). By renting, and some borrowing, they managed to *control* businesses averaging nearly $25,000 at the time of starting (Figure 47). They accumulated capital at the rate of more than $2,000 per year up to 1952, when they owned two-thirds of the value of their businesses.

It is surprising that only two of the beginning operators used mortgage capital in getting started; these two loans were very small, $2,500 and $3,000, respectively. However, thirty-seven farmers, or 60 per cent of them, had short-term loans, averaging about $3,000 each. The types of lenders from whom these loans were obtained were as follows.

FHA . . . . . . . 9
Bank . . . . . . . 21
Individual . . . . . 6
PCA . . . . . . . 1

By 1952, however, more of them had used mortgage credit, as well as their own capital, in buying land. One-third of them had mortgage loans averaging $7,458. The amount of short-term credit used in that year was incidental.

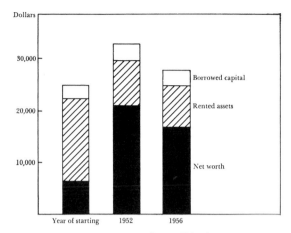

Source: Nebr. Agr. Exp. Sta. data.

Fig. 47. Financial Progress of Farmers from the Year of Starting in 1940–49 to 1952 and 1956 (in 1950 Dollars) Nebraska Transition Area

The effect of drought and depressed relative prices in 1956 is evident in Figure 47. In that year they were renting about $400 less capital and borrowing about $430 less capital than in 1952 (in constant 1950 dollars). Their own net worths had shrunk by $4,293, or about $1,073 per year, during the four-year period—decreasing the size of their businesses on the average by the same amount per year, for a total decrease of 20 per cent in equity during the period.

Farmers' Ideas on Financial Management

The sample farmers were questioned on several aspects of financial management to assess their awareness of the problems hypothesized by the research group.

*Minimum Size of Farm for Adequate Living*

The minimum size of farm they considered necessary for an adequate living was related to the size of farm they operated (Table 61). There was general recognition by all farmers that farms up to 320 acres in size were too small. However, all but the operators of 1,280-acre farms seemed too modest in their estimate of minimum size, in light of the study data.

Table 61. Size of Farm Recommended as Minimum for Adequate Living by 135 Sample Farmers, by Present Farm Size, Nebraska Transition Area, 1956–57

| Present Acreage | Recommended Size |
|---|---|
| 160 . . . . . . . | 333 |
| 320 . . . . . . . | 361 |
| 480 . . . . . . . | 432 |
| 640 . . . . . . . | 462 |
| 1,280 . . . . . . . | 618 |

Source: Nebr. Agr. Exp. Sta. data.

*Minimum Beginning Equity*

As expected, the farmer who started farming before World War II tended to suggest a rather high equity in the farm business for beginning farmers, in the interest of financial safety (Table 62). It was much more surprising to find that the group starting in 1940–49 with about 25 percent equity in its businesses suggested more than twice this share as a safe minimum. Perhaps they were conscious of the increased risks of 1952–56; also, they had observed other farmers leaving the occupation during those years.

TABLE 62. Percent Equity Considered Adequate for Beginning Farmers, by the Time at which Respondents Started, 135 Sample Farmers, Nebraska Transition Area, 1956–57

|  | *Average percent of equity recommended for:* | |
|---|---|---|
| *Time of Starting* | *Beginning Owners* | *Beginning tenants* |
| 1924–29 . . . . . . | 59 | 54 |
| 1930–39 . . . . . . | 57 | 63 |
| 1940–49 . . . . . . | 58 | 52 |

Source: Nebr. Agr. Exp. Sta. data.

*Financial Management and Credit*

Operators in the transition area sample were queried about their ideas on financial management and credit. About 33 percent of them felt that supplies of operating credit were adequate and had not been pushed to the limit (1957). Only 9 percent were aware that such credit was tighter than before the drought. Eleven percent, on the other hand, felt that the supply of short-term credit was inadequate, while only 6 percent considered the supply of long-term credit inadequate.

The sample farmers were asked what improvements in credit policies they would suggest in the agencies from which they borrowed. The responses were as follows:

No response or don't know . . . . .    47
None recommended. . . . . . . . .    66
Recommended one or more changes. .    22
                                    ——
Total . . . . . . . . . . . . . .   135

These responses indicate a surprising lack of suggestions, or at least a tacit acceptance of the status quo, in view of the hardships these people had suffered. Of the few suggestions on changes that were proferred, the most frequent was to lower the interest rate. A very few others suggested variable payments, longer-term loans, a less tight money policy, and more technical experience on the part of the lender.

The farmers were also asked whether lenders had influenced their crop and livestock program, family living, or their size of farm. Again, the number of affirmative responses was low.

No . . . . . . . . . . .    82
No response . . . . . .    37
Yes . . . . . . . . . .    16
                          ——
Total . . . . . . .   135

The most common type of influence by creditors concerned the livestock program, chiefly encouraging expansion. A few indicated influence toward better breeding. A little influence had been exerted on the cropping system, while almost none was felt on family living or size of farm. In one sense, these are happy results, since they indicate little or no interference by outsiders in the farm business. On the other hand, these farmers might have benefited by more guidance from their creditors.

## LAND VALUES AND THE LAND MARKET

The land market has been a phenomenon of particular interest in the transition area since World War I, and the reasons for this interest are several. First, it is thought that people who buy land in the area, farmers and others, tend to overestimate the land's long-run productivity; they are too much influenced by crop yields in years of above-average rainfall and consequently bid up land prices speculatively. Then, when yields and prices become less favorable, people who have borrowed money to buy land find themselves caught in a trap. One jaw of this trap is the fixed financial commitments they have made to creditors; the other is the decline in values—and consequently in their equities—when people in general no longer care to invest in the area's land.

The second concern is that the crop systems also become geared to these speculatively high values, and to optimistic opinions about the climate as well. Marginal land is tilled and credit commitments become geared to tilled-crop systems. Then, when drought and low prices come, farmers are not only vulnerable because of these fixed commitments but they are not inclined to invest further funds in shifting marginal lands to cropping systems of a more extensive nature, particularly to permanent grasses.

A third concern is that nonfarm investors enter the land market with the long-run objective of hedging against inflation. They bid up prices and provide the basis for increased tenancy.

Our evidence concerning these hypotheses is not complete, but we investigated land sales and land values in our study to a limited extent.

### General Trends in Land Values

Land prices in the transition area during the last three decades fluctuated more than those in some other parts of Nebraska, or in the state as a whole (Figure 48). The decline in land values was more rapid from 1930 to 1941 in the study area than in the state generally. After closely following the state trend during the prosperous and the "wet" war years, land prices in the transition area took a sudden spurt in 1950–51. Between 1950 and 1954, land prices in the transition area rose 61 percent, or about 12 percent a year. The state increase was only 36 percent. This inflation continued through 1954, in spite of the price break in 1952. The drought of 1955 brought a sudden reversal, with a price decline of 15 percent in one year. Recovery was rapid enough, though, to bring prices to a new high by 1957.

The data in Figure 48 apply only to a small portion of all the land in the transition area. It is true that the transfer rate there jumped from 1.4 percent of all farmland in 1954 to 2 percent in 1955, the highest in the state, but these figures relate only to bona fide sales. Many land transfers are not classed as bona fide sales; and within-family transfers are the most important of these.

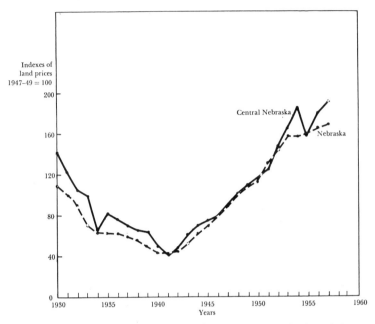

Source: Loyd K. Fischer and John Muehlbeier (unpublished data), Nebraska Agricultural
Experiment Station.

FIG. 48.    INDEXES OF PRICES OF LAND SOLD IN NEBRASKA, AND IN
CENTRAL NEBRASKA, 1930–56

The increase in land prices in the study area at a time when farm incomes were
falling off is puzzling. It raises questions about what kind of buyers were in the market
for land at this time and why they were buying.

*The Land Market*

A special study was made of the real estate market in Greeley and Valley counties
in 1956–57 as a part of a larger study in Nebraska.[3] It concerned all bona fide sales
of farmland between January 1, 1956, and April 1, 1957, excluding family transfers,
transfers for title clearance, and the like. Information was obtained from the buyers
and sellers of these lands about the circumstances of the transfers.

The land transfers in the two counties by bona fide sale represented 1.2 per cent
of the total land area. This consisted of 53 tracts of land, averaging 231 acres, and
selling for an average price of $55.00 per acre. Half of the land sold was in crops, and
5 percent was irrigated. Most of the buyers and sellers of land considered it to be of
average quality compared with that of surrounding farms. Of the tracts transferred,
66 percent had a house and other buildings, 28 percent had no buildings, and the
remaining 6 percent was partially improved.

As Table 63 reveals, the result of these transactions was a slight decrease in the
number of nonfarm landowners in the area. Most of the sales were between farmers,

[3] Loyd K. Fischer, Richard Burkholder and John Muehlbeier, *Farm Real Estate Market in Nebraska*,
Nebraska Agricultural Experiment Station Bulletin No. 456, 1960.

TABLE 63. OCCUPATIONAL STATUS OF BUYERS AND SELLERS OF FARM REAL ESTATE IN
GREELEY AND VALLEY COUNTIES, NEBRASKA, JANUARY 1, 1956, TO APRIL 1, 1957

| Occupation | Buyers | | Sellers | |
|---|---|---|---|---|
| | Number | Percent | Number | Percent |
| Active farmers . . | 38 | 70 | 28 | 52 |
| Retired farmers . . | 3 | 6 | 8 | 15 |
| Others (nonfarm) . | 12 | 24 | 14 | 27 |
| Unknown . . . . | 0 | 0 | 3 | 6 |

Source: Nebr. Agr. Exp. Sta. data.

including some transfers between retired and other farmers. Thus farmers were the main influence on the land market during the fifteen-month period studied.

The other nonfarm buyers of farmland, who were so classified if more than half their income came from nonfarm sources, were equally divided between professional people, businessmen, laborers, and salaried people.

*Reasons for Selling Land.* In view of the depressed conditions of the preceding two years, it is not surprising that financial reasons were prominent in the decisions to sell. Of the twenty-eight sellers of land who indicated their motivation, eight referred to financial considerations and six referred to health and age imperatives.

*Reasons for Buying Land.* The most common reason given for buying land in Greeley and Valley counties was to enlarge the present farm; this was the primary purpose of more than one-fourth of the fifty-three buyers. Another fifth of them bought land in order to change from tenant to owner. Another fifth bought land for investment purposes; some of these also were farmers. Most of these investors had no other important investments. Of all the people who bought land, nearly two-thirds lived on a farm, which was typically within five miles of the tract purchased. Half of these land buyers planned to add the purchased land to farms they already owned, even though this was not always their principal reason for buying.

Although half of those who bought land for farm enlargement said they could not have rented land if they had wanted to, and one-fourth of the tenants who bought land said they could not have continued to rent their present land, there was little evidence of specific compulsion to buy. Typically, the decision was unhurried and voluntary. Half of the buyers were unaware of any competition for the land they bought.

Typically, the buyer was younger than the seller. Although the buyer had not previously operated the land he purchased, he knew the seller and had some notion of the yields on the farm. He used cash he had accumulated from his farming operations either for the full purchase price or for his down-payment. One-third of the buyers paid in cash for the entire farm; the rest borrowed funds from a variety of sources, typically under a mortgage whose term was less than ten years, and whose amount was equivalent to 50 to 74 percent of the purchase price. The buyers planned to pay the debt with income from farming. Most buyers were satisfied with the price they had paid.

The typical buyer did not consider farms other than the one he bought. His knowledge was sketchy; he received no specific appraisal of the farm's potential nor any record of the income it had produced in the past. Apparently, his main criterion of market value was knowledge of other land sales in the community. The sellers of land suggested that the principal factor considered by the buyer was location of the particular tract. This was followed in importance by the type of land, and then by buildings. This evaluation is consistent with the use of the purchased land for farm enlargement.

The data reviewed here also refute the idea that outside investors are taking over the land in the transition area. The transactions noted appear, instead, to be part of the trend toward farm enlargement that has been continuing at a steady rate in the entire nation during the past decade. The process is unhurried but deliberate. The steady rise in land prices can be largely attributed to this.

*Land Prices*

Land prices in the study area were available from several sources. Each county's Registrar of Deeds submits annually to the state tax commissioner the prices involved in all land transfers in this county. The special study in Greeley and Valley counties also included land prices. Finally, the survey farmers in the transition area were asked to estimate the per acre market values of their farms; first, as they existed in 1956, and second, assuming the buildings were removed. Real estate dealers in the study area who were familiar with these farms were also asked to make similar pairs of estimates.

The consistency among these various sets of price estimates, which are given in Table 64, is rather impressive. Although there was considerable disagreement between individual real estate men and farmers about the worth of single farms, the average estimates made by the two groups were practically identical. The farmers knew more about land values than is commonly supposed. A statistical analysis of the data indicated that the two principal factors influencing these values were the buildings and the longitude at which the farm is located; that is, whether it is east, west, or in the central portion of the survey area. The farms had quite homogeneous soil combinations; thus little of the variation in price was explained by yield variation. On the basis of the difference in the estimates between improved land and land without buildings, it appears that the operators of 480-acre farms valued their buildings at an average of about $3,400.

For Greeley and Valley counties, the land-value study data for land with buildings were over $30.00 per acre higher than the farmers' estimates. Of course the land-value study data represent a span of 1⅓ years; and land values rose considerably between 1956 and 1957 in those two counties. However, the land-value study data are also higher on the average than the data from the state tax commissioner: $55.00 as compared with an average of about $48.00 per acre for the two years.

The gap would have been wider had the study data included two full years. However, the difference may be due to the exclusion from the land-value study of all sales that were not bona fide sales, such as those between relatives and other transfers where market price would not be established in the usual way. In turn, the somewhat higher structure of prices shown in the tax commissioner data, as compared with the farmers' estimates, might be explained by the smaller average size of tract represented in the former.

TABLE 64. SUMMARY OF LAND-VALUE DATA IN THE NEBRASKA TRANSITION AREA, BY SPECIFIED SOURCE, 1956–57 (DOLLARS PER ACRE)

| Source of Data | Land & Buildings | | All Land Sold | | Unimproved Land | |
|---|---|---|---|---|---|---|
| | 1956 | 1957 | 1956 | 1957 | 1956 | 1957 |
| *Transition area—480-acre farms* | | | | | | |
| Transition survey farmers' estimates . . . . | 49.30 | | | | 42.30 | |
| Real estate dealers' estimates . . . . . . | 49.94 | | | | | |
| *Transition area—all farms* | | | | | | |
| Transition survey farmers' estimates . . . . | 49.70 | | | | 42.80 | |
| Real estate dealers' estimates . . . . . . | 48.31 | | | | | |
| Sales data reported to tax commissioner, transition counties . . | | | 51.40* | 52.00* | | |
| *Valley-Greeley counties* | | | | | | |
| Land value study of bona fide sales . . . | 83.00† | | | | | 44.00† |
| Transition survey farmers' estimates: | | | | | | |
| Valley County . . . | 53.07 | | | | | |
| Greeley County . . . | 49.61 | | | | | |
| Sales data reported to state tax commissioner: | | | | | | |
| Valley County . . . | | | 44.00* | 51.00* | | |
| Greeley County . . . | | | 41.00* | 55.00* | | |

Source: Nebr. Agr. Exp. Sta. data.

\* Includes both improved land and land without buildings.
† From January 1, 1956, to April 1, 1957. The average value of all land sold was $55.00 per acre during this period.

We also examined farmers' estimated land values in relation to incomes received from their cropping operations. Long-run data on land earnings were not available; however, in a 1956 survey of 261 farms, crop-production data were collected for 1953, 1954, and 1955. The first two years may be regarded as average from the yield standpoint, while 1955 was far below par. For these years, we estimated the gross crop income from the cash sales, feed fed less feed purchased, inventory change, and rental value of pasture. From this were deducted cash-crop expenses and the share of machinery, building repairs, and depreciation allocable to the crop enterprises to give the net crop income per acre (Table 65). We estimated that 45 percent of the family labor was chargeable to crop production on 480-acre farms (based on standard labor requirements for crops and livestock). This was valued at $214 per month. By deducting this, and a charge of 6 percent on investment in machinery, we arrived at a residual estimate of the earning of land per acre. Of course these data are only rough estimates, subject to several kinds of error; on the other hand, they are probably as good as possible, given the limitations of available data.

For 1955 there was a net loss to land (Table 65). Capitalizing the net return for

TABLE 65. Estimated Net Income to Land, and Capitalized Value on Forty-six 480-acre Sample Farms, Nebraska Transition Area, 1953–55

|  | 1953–54 | 1955 |
|---|---|---|
| Gross crop income. . . . . . . . | $4,610 | $1,729 |
| Crop expenses. . . . . . . . . . | 1,780 | 2,029 |
| Net crop income . . . . . . . | $2,830 | — $300 |
| Net crop income per acre. . . . . | $5.91 | — $ .59 |
| Family labor & interest on crop machinery per acre at 6% . . | 3.68 | 3.68 |
| Net return to land per acre . . . | $2.23 | — $2.23 |
| Return to land capitalized at 6% . | $37.00 | 0 |

Source: Nebr. Agr. Exp. Sta. data.

1953–54 at 6 percent, assuming that this is an appropriate opportunity cost for the capital funds tied up in land and buildings, we obtain a capitalized value for land of $37.00 per acre, which is $12.00 per acre less than the farmers' estimates of sale values for the sample farms.

These data would suggest that land is overvalued in the sample area in terms of its *whole farm* earning power. Note, however, that an interest rate of 5 rather than 6 percent would raise the capitalized value to $44.60 for 1953–54. Also, the correctness of the capitalized values depends on the values assigned to labor and non-land capital used in crop production. If the assigned wage of $214 per month were greater than what labor actually earns at the margin, the capitalized value of land would be penalized accordingly.

In the long run, of course, labor is not necessarily entitled to its opportunity cost; that is, what it could earn in other kinds of activity. If its earnings in farming are less than the opportunity costs, this implies that too much labor is being used. Reducing the proportion of labor combined with land will increase its earning at the margin. By this means, labor's earnings will be brought into line with opportunity costs. With less labor claiming a wage, the residual remaining for land will be increased.

The degree to which farmers know the opportunity costs for their labor—and whether some even know that this opportunity exists—is open to conjecture. Where part-time work opportunities off the farm are few, a farmer is probably inclined to treat his own labor as a residual claimant, as a sunk investment. Thus he may capitalize the returns actually earned by *both* his labor and capital into land when he is at the point of decision about buying more land. Land values are inflated accordingly.

The economies of buying a tract to add to an existing farm unit to make the whole operation more profitable are more conducive to inflation of land values than those involved in buying a whole farm, which must be justified on the basis of its costs and returns. It appears that land was being overvalued in terms of its earnings in 1954.

# CHAPTER 13

# The Rural Community in Transition

## THE IMPACTS OF COMMERCIALIZED FARMING

THE DRIVE toward commercialization of agriculture has been strong, steady, and complex. Farming as a way of life is being gradually eroded and farming on a business-like basis is taking its place. This change has been reflected in the trend to larger farms, mechanization, and heavier dependence on nonfarm sources for production inputs and markets. Farmers in the United States have always had a definite market orientation rather than a goal of self-sufficiency. Yet the little economic self-sufficiency they had has been almost eliminated. The pressure toward efficiency has been forcing farmers to perform highly specialized functions.

We have noted the increasing reliance of farmers on nonfarm sources for production inputs. Their dependence on the rest of the economy is also indicated by the increased reliance of farmers on processors as potential markets for their crops. Factory production of farm foods has been rising faster than the volume of farm marketings, reflecting the continued expansion in the proportion of farm foods that pass through a processing stage before reaching the final consumer.

Our era of technological change has encouraged mobility of people in agriculture. As farm people have left the country for the city, our relatively fixed supply of land has been divided up into larger units. In addition to this, the substitution of machinery for labor has tended to make farm labor an underemployed or oversupplied resource. The surplus of people in agriculture is further intensified by farm birth rates, which exceed those in the nonfarm sector. Despite the wellknown rise in urban birth rates, farm women are still bearing more than one and a half times as many children, per woman, as are urban women. Clearly, one of agriculture's most important products is its people. This "export" has been instrumental in producing the expanded range of nonfarm goods and services we all enjoy. Our nation has been able to grow because of this additional labor which it could draw upon for its economic expansion.

The size of this "agricultural surplus" has been substantial. In the past half century, farm population in the United States dropped by more than two-fifths, from a peak of more than 32 million in 1910 to the 1960 level of 13.4 million.[1] Since total

[1] There is some controversy about this figure, which was obtained by the census enumeration. The *Current Population Survey* yields an estimate of 15.6 million for 1960. There has also been a change in the definition of a farm, which affects the comparability of the data.

population has just about doubled during this period, the relative importance of farm residents to the total has declined precipitously. While in 1910 one out of three Americans lived on a farm, by 1960 only one in fourteen was a farm resident. Most of this sharp drop in farm population, 17.2 out of 18.8 million, has occurred since 1940 in response to favorable nonfarm opportunities associated with World War II and the postwar expansion of the economy. Nonfarm workers increased from about 26 million in 1910 to more than 60 million in 1960. Those employed in agriculture declined from more than 12 million to 4.3 million.

Since this substantial migration has occurred as a response to economic stimuli, it is not surprising that it has altered the age composition of those left on farms. It is largely the young adults, those between nineteen and forty-five, who have been leaving the farm to seek better opportunities elsewhere. Thus, children and youths are relatively more numerous on farms than in urban areas. In 1960 the proportion of the population represented by people less than twenty years of age was 37 percent in cities, but 42 percent on farms.

In the young adult group, the difference is even more striking. The important 20–44 age group is only 25 percent on farms, compared with 33 percent in urban areas. The contrast between the two age groups is dramatic indeed. For every ten people between 20 and 29 on farms, there are thirty-four between 10 and 19. In cities the corresponding ratio is only 13 to 10. Older people are also somewhat more numerous on farms, relatively speaking, than in cities, but their actual number is not as large as one might expect because many of them also migrate from farms.

The recent burgeoning of our total population, with its attendant problems of overcrowded schools and housing and inadequate water supplies in some cities, has had a massive effect on the economy of the nation. However, not all areas of the country are affected similarly and not all sectors of the economy are reacting in the same way. The far west is growing, but parts of New England are dying; the electronics industry is expanding, but farming is contracting. Thus rural farm areas, particularly in the more slowly growing sections of the country, are facing problems diametrically opposite those of most heavily industrialized cities. People are moving from farms to nearby towns and cities, and even those who remain in farming are increasingly linked with the nonfarm world.

As one instance of this, consider the nonfarm work done by farm operators in the course of a year. The proportion of farmers who do any nonfarm work has risen only moderately in the past two decades, going from 26.3 percent in 1940 to 28.5 percent in 1959. But the big change has come in the amount of such work they do. Farmers working only part-time off their farms (less than 200 days a year) have decreased slightly in importance, from 22.7 percent to 20.6 percent of all farmers. But those who worked at full-time nonfarm jobs (200 or more days a year) more than doubled in relative importance, from 3.6 percent of all farmers in 1940 to 7.9 percent in 1959. As a proportion of farmers who did any off-farm work, they increased from 13.7 percent in 1940 to 27.7 percent in 1959. These farm operators may well represent an intermediate stage between actual farming and outright migration.

*Population Shifts*

Open country or farm areas are losing population faster than any other parts of the nation. As farmers decline in number, the smallest rural trade centers (those of less than 1,000 population) lose their economic base and shrink in size and importance. Urban areas, on the other hand, are growing at a rapid pace; and the larger rural centers—what we have been calling farm-cities (those with 1,000–2,500 population)—are also expanding, though at a much more moderate rate. Table 66 shows the pattern of these changes over the past thirty years.

Nebraska has shared, of course, in all these trends. Average farm size, which was much larger than the national figure even in 1900, rose from 246 acres to 514 in 1959, slightly faster than in the nation as a whole, and it has continued on its upward climb to 536 acres in 1961. Mechanization has proceeded apace. Nebraska farms in 1959 had more than two and a half times as many grain combines as they had in 1945, almost two and a half times as many trucks, and about 87 percent more tractors.

In terms of population changes, Nebraska, and indeed the entire Northern Plains region, is especially interesting because here both geographical and occupational forces act in concert as a depressant to growth. The situation is precisely the reverse of that in California, where both coastal location and climatic factors on the one hand, and the presence of huge urban centers with many industrial opportunities on the other, combine to stimulate rapid population expansion. The Northern Plains region has shared in the national trend toward urbanization, but the declines in agriculture have largely offset the growth of the cities. Table 67 gives a historical perspective on some regional population changes.

Note that here the Northern Plains are compared only with adjoining states. Contrasts with other states would be much sharper. States in some other regions showed a greater percentage increase in the past decade than the United States experienced even in thirty years. But the Northern Plains region has expanded only moderately;

TABLE 66. POPULATION IN U.S. URBAN AND RURAL TERRITORY, BY SIZE OF PLACE, 1930–60 (IN THOUSANDS)

| Size & Class | 1930 | 1950 | 1960 | Percent Change | |
|---|---|---|---|---|---|
| | | | | 1930 to 1960 | 1950 to 1960 |
| Urban territory . . . . . . | 68,955 | 96,468 | 125,269 | +81.7 | +29.9 |
| Rural territory . . . . . . | 52,820 | 54,230 | 54,054 | + 0.4 | − 0.3 |
| Places of 1,000–2,500. . . . | 4,821 | 6,473 | 6,497 | +34.8 | + 0.4 |
| Places under 1,000. . . . . | 4,363 | 4,031 | 3,894 | −10.7 | − 3.4 |
| Other rural territory . . . . | 44,637 | 43,725 | 43,664 | − 2.2 | − 0.1 |
| On farms. . . . . . . . . | 30,529 | 25,058 | 15,635* | | |

| | Percentage Distribution | | |
|---|---|---|---|
| | 1930 | 1950 | 1960 |
| Total population . . . . . . . . | 100.0 | 100.0 | 100.0 |
| Urban territory . . . . . . . . . | 56.2 | 64.0 | 69.9 |
| Rural territory . . . . . . . . . | 43.8 | 36.0 | 30.1 |
| Places of 1,000–2,500. . . . . . | 3.9 | 4.3 | 3.6 |
| Places under 1,000 . . . . . . . | 3.6 | 2.7 | 2.2 |
| Other rural territory . . . . . . . | 36.4 | 29.0 | 24.3 |
| On farms. . . . . . . . . . . . | 24.9 | 16.6 | 8.7 |

Source: U.S. Bureau of the Census, *Statistical Abstract of the United States, 1961*, table 13, p. 23, and table 840, p. 613.

* New definition. This would have been 20,541 under the old definition.

TABLE 67.  CHANGES IN POPULATION OF THE NORTHERN PLAINS REGION, WITH
COMPARISONS, 1910–60

| Region | Change in Total Population from: | | |
|---|---|---|---|
| | *1910 to 1960* | *1930 to 1960* | *1950 to 1960* |
| Northern Plains | | | |
| Kansas, Nebraska, South Dakota, | | | |
| North Dakota. . . . . . . . | +21.2% | + 5.8% | + 8.9% |
| Mountain | | | |
| Colorado, Wyoming, Montana . | +108.9 | +53.3 | +25.0 |
| Central | | | |
| Missouri, Iowa, Minnesota . . . | +38.2 | +21.1 | + 9.8 |
| United States . . . . . . . . . . | +94.4 | +45.6 | +18.5 |

Source: U.S. Bureau of the Census, *Statistical Abstract of the United States, 1961*, table 9, p. 12.

two of its states actually experienced a net decline in population over the three decades. In all regions, the urban population has increased more rapidly than the total. Both the number and size of urban areas vary by regions. Thus the population trends largely reflect the incidence and importance of metropolitan complexes.

Nebraska, approximating a cross-section of the Plains, is an agricultural state in a region of extensive farming. Its population density of 18.4 persons per square mile is less than a third as large as that of the continental United States. The state's economy is largely dependent on agriculture. For example, only 7.9 percent of the nation's residents were living on farms in 1960, but in Nebraska the proportion was 21.9 percent. Or, to look at it another way, for the country as a whole about 8.3 percent of all employed males are working on farms, but the figure for Nebraska is 28.0 percent.

In terms of income effects, too, agriculture is quite important to the state. Of all the personal income in the nation in 1959, only 3.8 percent was classified as farm income. In Nebraska, 14.6 percent of all personal income originated on farms. In this respect Nebraska even surpassed its own Northern Plains region, where the ratio of farm income to the total is 11.8 percent. Thus, when agriculture is in a process of adjustment, Nebraska is affected much more profoundly than most other states, especially in view of its low level of industrialization.

The state as a whole shows very slight changes in total population over the past two decades. From 1940 to 1950 the increase was less than 1 percent, but there was some expansion during the 1950's, so 1960 shows a moderate growth of 7 percent over 1940 (as Table 68 indicates).

TABLE 68.  CHANGES IN URBAN AND RURAL POPULATION IN NEBRASKA, 1940, 1950, AND 1960

| Residence | Population | | | Percent Change from: | | |
|---|---|---|---|---|---|---|
| | *1940* | *1950* | *1960* | *1940–50* | *1950–60* | *1940–60* |
| Total . . . . . . | 1,315,834 | 1,325,510 | 1,411,330 | + 0.7 | + 6.5 | +7.3 |
| Urban . . . . . . | 514,148 | 621,905* | 766,053 | +21.0 | +23.2 | +49.0 |
| Rural . . . . . . | 801,686 | 703,605* | 645,277 | −12.2 | − 8.3 | −19.5 |

Source: U.S. Bureau of the Census, *U.S. Census of Population, 1960*, Nebraska, Number of Inhabitants, PC(1), 29A, table 1, p. 7.

* New definition. Under previous definition, urban population was 606,530, rural was 718,980.

*Effect of Rurality*

The urban and rural components of the population have moved in exactly opposite ways, with the urban sector increasing by almost one-half over the past twenty years and the rural population declining by about one-fifth. A small part of the population gain in urban areas is due to their higher birthrates, as shown in Table 69. If the relative importance of the rural-farm component of the population is used as an indicator of a county's "rurality," it is clear that highly rural counties tend to have the lowest birth rates and that birth rates generally rise as the degree of rurality decreases—so that the least rural (or most urban) counties have the highest birth rates.

This pattern of birth rates is exactly the opposite of what we should expect, based upon the national picture and the situation in the past. But the data must be interpreted with caution. These are "crude" birth rates; that is, unadjusted for age differences in the population. As such, they are heavily influenced by the differential age distributions. In fact, the higher birth rates in the urban counties probably reflect the selective migration of young farm adults toward the cities, and the low birth rates in the very rural counties can be explained by their relatively small population in the child-bearing age groups.

Similar considerations undoubtedly attach to the death rate pattern. The death rates probably reflect the relative importance of the aged in the population. For example, the pattern evidenced in Table 69 could be explained as follows. Death rates are lowest in heavily rural counties because older persons migrate from these areas; death rates are highest in medium-rural counties because the aged tend to settle in these counties in or near medium-size cities; and, finally, death rates are somewhat lower in the most urban counties (though not as low as in rural areas) because the influx of youths and young adults into cities tends to lower the relative importance of the aged in the urban population.

TABLE 69. CRUDE ANNUAL BIRTH AND DEATH RATES FOR NEBRASKA COUNTIES, GROUPED BY DEGREE OF RURALITY OF EACH COUNTY, 1950–60

| Degree of Rurality* | Counties | Average % Rural-farm in 1950 | Crude annual Birth Rate (per thousand population) | Crude annual Death Rate (per thousand population) |
|---|---|---|---|---|
| Percent rural-farm in 1950: | | | | |
| Less than 15 . . . . | 2 | 3.4 | 25.5 | 9.3 |
| 15–24.9 . . . . . | 7 | 20.5 | 25.1 | 9.5 |
| 25–34.9 . . . . . | 10 | 28.9 | 24.9 | 8.7 |
| 35–44.9 . . . . . | 20 | 39.6 | 22.0 | 10.7 |
| 45–54.9 . . . . . | 25 | 49.7 | 22.3 | 10.4 |
| 55–64.9 . . . . . | 18 | 57.8 | 23.5 | 10.1 |
| 65–74.9 . . . . . | 7 | 71.2 | 21.4 | 7.8 |
| 75 or more . . . . | 4 | 83.0 | 18.7 | 5.8 |

Source: U.S. Bureau of the Census, *1950 Census of Population,* and University of Nebraska, Bureau of Business Research, *Business in Nebraska,* No. 201 (June, 1961).

* Based upon relative importance of rural-farm population to total population in 1950, expressed as a percentage.

The state's population increased by 85,820 from 1950 to 1960. Since Douglas and Lancaster counties (containing Omaha and Lincoln, respectively) gained 98,000 people during the same period, it is clear that most of the remainder of the state lost population. Not all other counties lost, but the great majority did. Of the 93 counties in the state, only seven had rates of growth in excess of 19 percent; two gained between 10 and 19 percent, fourteen gained less than 10 percent, and seventy counties lost population.

Figure 49 shows the geographical pattern of these changes. It is clear that all the counties showing population increases were strongly affected by the presence of cities within or near them that were growing. Thus Omaha's expansion affected not only its own Douglas County but also the surrounding counties of Cass, Sarpy, Saunders, and Washington. In addition to the counties around Lincoln and Omaha, thirteen others had population gains (excluding Adams, Clay, and Dawson, which increased less than 1 percent). Table 70 presents the population data for these counties and for the principal towns or cities within them.

In virtually all these instances the remaining areas within these counties—including smaller towns as well as open country—lost population while the principal urban

TABLE 70. POPULATION OF SELECTED COUNTIES AND THEIR PRINCIPAL
URBAN PLACES, NEBRASKA, 1950 AND 1960

| County & Urban Place | 1950 | 1960 | Change |
|---|---|---|---|
| Buffalo County . . . . . . . | 25,135 | 26,236 | 4.4% |
| Kearney . . . . . . . . . | 12,115 | 14,210 | 17.3 |
| Cheyenne County . . . . . . | 12,081 | 14,828 | 22.7 |
| Sidney . . . . . . . . . . | 4,912 | 8,004 | 62.9 |
| Dakota County . . . . . . . | 10,401 | 12,168 | 17.0 |
| South Sioux City . . . . . | 5,557 | 7,200 | 29.6 |
| Dodge County . . . . . . . | 26,265 | 32,471 | 23.6 |
| Fremont . . . . . . . . . | 14,762 | 19,698 | 33.4 |
| Hall County . . . . . . . . | 32,186 | 35,757 | 11.1 |
| Grand Island . . . . . . . | 22,682 | 25,742 | 13.5 |
| Hooker County . . . . . . . | 1,061 | 1,130 | 6.5 |
| Mullen. . . . . . . . . . | 652 | 811 | 24.4 |
| Kearney County . . . . . . | 6,409 | 6,508 | 2.7 |
| Minden . . . . . . . . . | 2,120 | 2,383 | 12.4 |
| Keith County . . . . . . . | 7,449 | 7,958 | 6.8 |
| Ogallala . . . . . . . . . | 3,456 | 4,250 | 23.0 |
| Kimball County . . . . . . | 4,283 | 7,975 | 86.2 |
| Kimball . . . . . . . . . | 2,048 | 4,384 | 114.1 |
| Lincoln County . . . . . . | 27,380 | 28,491 | 4.1 |
| North Platte . . . . . . . | 15,433 | 17,184 | 11.3 |
| Madison County . . . . . . | 24,338 | 25,145 | 3.3 |
| Norfolk . . . . . . . . . | 11,335 | 13,111 | 15.7 |
| Phelps County . . . . . . . | 9,048 | 9,800 | 8.3 |
| Holdrege. . . . . . . . . | 4,381 | 5,226 | 19.3 |
| Platte County. . . . . . . | 19,910 | 23,992 | 20.5 |
| Columbus . . . . . . . . | 8,884 | 12,476 | 40.4 |

Source: U.S. Bureau of the Census, *U.S. Census of Population, 1960*, Nebraska, Number of Inhabitants, PC(1), 29A.

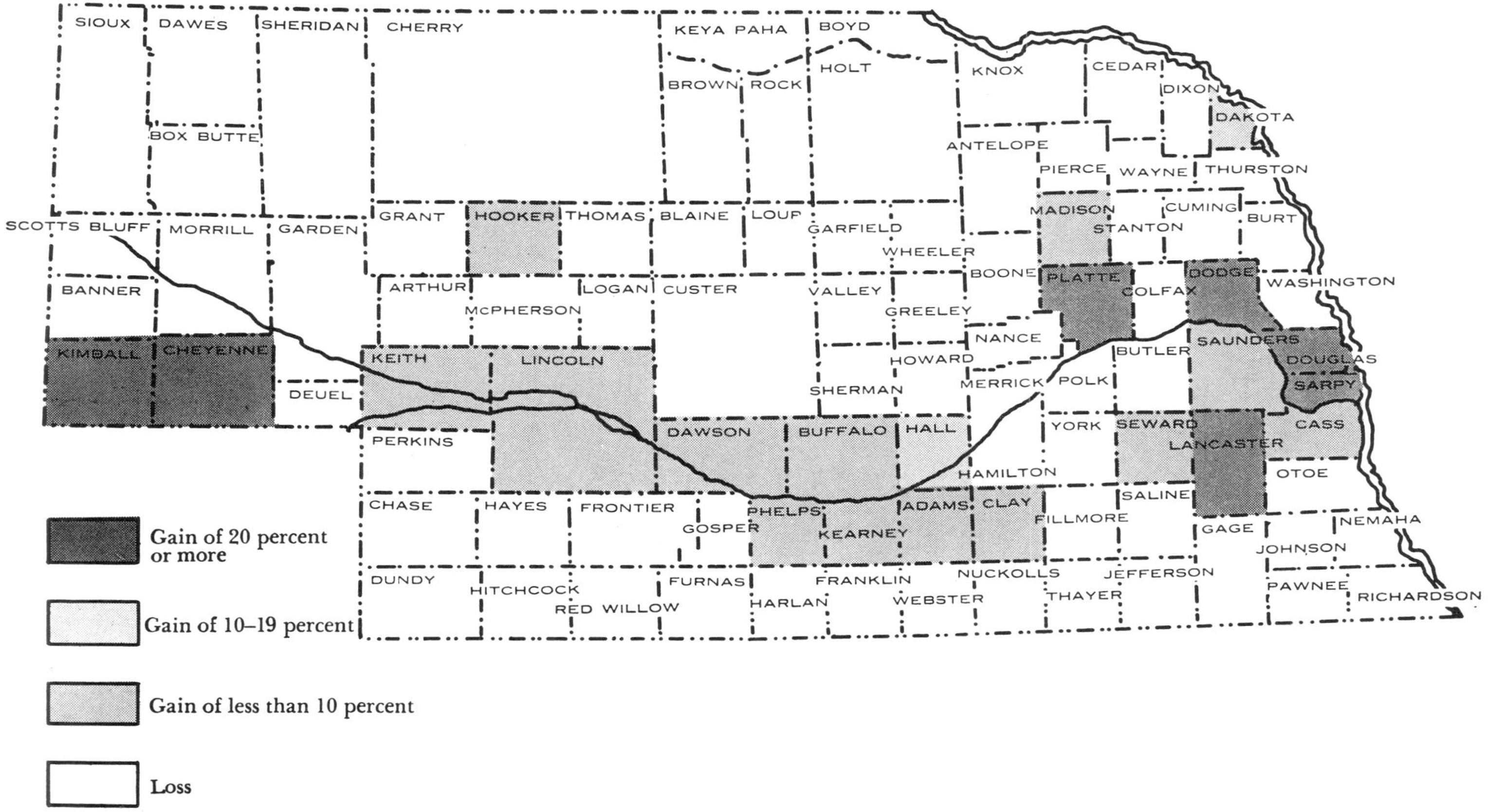

Source: Nebr. Agr. Exp. Sta. data.

FIG. 49. PERCENTAGE CHANGE IN POPULATION, NEBRASKA COUNTIES, 1950–60

Gain of 20 percent
or more

Gain of 10–19 percent

Gain of less than 10 percent

Loss

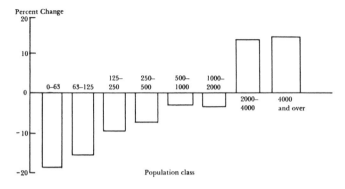

Source: Nebr. Agr. Exp. Sta. data.

FIG. 50. MEDIAN CHANGE IN POPULATION, 1950–60, IN
NEBRASKA TOWNS, CLASSIFIED BY 1950 SIZE

places, as shown in Table 70, gained substantially. The correlation between size of town and population growth is quite marked, as Figure 50 shows. The smaller the town in 1950, the greater the percentage loss it was likely to experience by 1960. Similarly, the larger the town the greater the relative gain to be expected. Although 23 counties gained in population from 1950 to 1960, the growth in many of them was not as large as might have been expected from their rates of natural increase.

In other words, even many of the counties with population gains showed net out-migration during this period. In fact, only five counties in the state had net in-migration: Douglas (Omaha), Lancaster (Lincoln), Dodge (Fremont), Sarpy (Omaha), and Kimball (Kimball). The heaviest out-migration was from the more rural areas. As Table 71 shows, county migration rates in the 1950–60 period were inversely associated with the county's degree of rurality. In the least-rural class—those with a rural-farm population of less than 15 percent in 1950—were two counties, Douglas and Lancaster, whose combined net migration during the decade was 24,850, or 6.2 percent. This was the only group that evidenced in-migration.

Migration rates generally tend to decrease—or, more realistically, out-migration rates tend to rise—as the degree of rurality increases. Thus, in counties whose rural-farm population represented 65 percent or more of their 1950 total, out-migration averaged more than 25 percent. These relationships are fairly strong on a grouped basis, as Table 71 clearly indicates, but they do not hold strictly for every county. For example, three counties other than Douglas and Lancaster also experienced net in-migration, as mentioned previously, but their gains were not enough to offset the losses of other counties in their class.

Certain other counties are in unique situations. Cheyenne and Kimball counties have benefited from the development of their oil deposits. Also, agriculture in several south-central counties has been greatly enriched by the development of irrigation in the past two decades. According to a study of the influence of irrigation on farm sizes in two of these counties, long-term trends there have been reversed. While dry-land farms increased in size by 13 percent from 1940 to 1950, farms with supplemental

TABLE 71. Population, Natural Increase, and Net Migration for Nebraska Counties, Grouped by the Degree of Rurality of Each County, 1950–60

| Degree of Rurality | Counties | Average Degree of Rurality | Rural Farm Population, 1950 | Total Population, 1950 | Births & Deaths | | Expected Population, 1960 | Actual Total Population, 1960 | Net Migration, 1950–60 | Migration Rate (based on 1950 Population) |
|---|---|---|---|---|---|---|---|---|---|---|
| | | | | | 1950 | 1959 | | | | |
| Percent rural farm (1950): | | | | | | | | | | |
| Under 15 . . . . . . . . | 2 | 3.4% | 13,628 | 400,762 | 114,885 | 41,735 | 473,912 | 498,762 | +24,850 | +6.2% |
| 15–24.9 . . . . . . . . | 7 | 20.5 | 30,748 | 150,343 | 39,251 | 14,803 | 174,791 | 162,459 | −12,332 | −8.2 |
| 25–34.9 . . . . . . . . | 10 | 28.9 | 51,182 | 176,848 | 46,366 | 16,297 | 206,917 | 196,146 | −10,771 | −6.1 |
| 35–44.9 . . . . . . . . | 20 | 39.6 | 76,510 | 193,215 | 41,648 | 20,242 | 214,621 | 185,499 | −29,112 | −15.1 |
| 45–54.9 . . . . . . . . | 25 | 49.7 | 112,597 | 226,451 | 48,639 | 22,628 | 252,462 | 209,420 | −43,042 | −19.0 |
| 55–64.9 . . . . . . . . | 18 | 57.8 | 89,082 | 154,052 | 34,355 | 14,822 | 173,585 | 138,512 | −35,073 | −22.8 |
| 65–74.9 . . . . . . . . | 7 | 71.2 | 12,643 | 17,762 | 3,529 | 1,287 | 20,004 | 15,273 | −4,731 | −26.6 |
| 75 or more . . . . . . . | 4 | 83.0 | 5,045 | 6,077 | 1,059 | 331 | 6,805 | 5,259 | −1,546 | −25.4 |

Source: U.S. Bureau of the Census, *1950 Census of Population*, and University of Nebraska, Bureau of Business Research, *Business in Nebraska*, No. 201 (June, 1961)

irrigation declined in acreage nearly 9 percent.[2] Such factors would presumably also upset normal migration patterns.

The technological advancement of American agriculture, with its concomitant population adjustments, is impinging with great force upon the Northern Plains transition area that, to start with, had an all too generous ratio of people to land. The five central-Nebraska counties in the study area experienced a 26.3 percent decline in total population from 1940 to 1960 while their rural-farm population dropped by 41.2 percent (Table 72). For the region as a whole, the rural-farm component of the population has declined sharply in relative importance, going from 61.2 percent in 1940, to 54.9 percent in 1950, and to 48.8 percent in 1960. The area is sparsely populated, with only 8.2 persons per square mile, less than half the population density in the state.

This 4,800-square-mile region consists of thirty-one farm communities, each centered on a small village or town, only one of which has a population of more than 2,500. More than half of these towns lost over a quarter of their population from 1940 to 1960, and the bulk of this loss occurred in the single decade 1950 to 1960. The very smallest towns, those with fewer than 500 people, have been especially hard hit; many of them lost 30 or 40 percent of their population between 1940 and 1960.

These changes are common, of course, to rural Nebraska, and indeed to the Northern Plains, but they seem to be more severe in the transition area than in either the extreme eastern or western parts of the state. These towns are directly and almost exclusively dependent upon agriculture, and their population trends follow those in farming. Their future is further clouded by modern transportation methods, which lead to their being bypassed in favor of larger service centers.

Migration patterns in the transition area, as in the state of Nebraska, are more severe than the changing levels of population indicate. Migration rates in the five transition-area counties during the 1950–60 decade were almost double the percentage

TABLE 72.  POPULATION CHANGES IN 5 CENTRAL NEBRASKA COUNTIES IN THE TRANSITION AREA, 1940–60

| | | | | | | | % Change | | | |
| | | | | | | | Total Population | | Rural-farm Population | |
| | Total Population | | | Rural-farm Population | | | 1940 to 1960 | 1950 to 1960 | 1940 to 1960 | 1950 to 1960 |
| County | 1940 | 1950 | 1960 | 1940 | 1950 | 1960 | | | | |
|---|---|---|---|---|---|---|---|---|---|---|
| Total . . | 53,785 | 45,644 | 39,625 | 32,924 | 25,037 | 19,354 | −26.3 | −13.2 | −41.2 | −22.7 |
| Custer . . | 22,591 | 19,170 | 16,517 | 13,944 | 10,321 | 7,081 | −26.9 | −13.8 | −49.2 | −31.4 |
| Greeley . | 6,845 | 5,575 | 4,595 | 4,042 | 3,034 | 2,460 | −28.7 | −17.6 | −39.1 | −18.9 |
| Howard . | 8,422 | 7,226 | 6,541 | 5,429 | 4,204 | 3,567 | −22.3 | −9.5 | −34.3 | −15.2 |
| Sherman . | 7,764 | 6,421 | 5,382 | 4,796 | 3,855 | 3,169 | −30.7 | −16.2 | −33.9 | −17.8 |
| Valley . . | 8,163 | 7,252 | 6,590 | 4,713 | 3,623 | 3,077 | −19.3 | −9.1 | −34.7 | −15.1 |

Source: Nebr. Agr. Exp. Sta. data.

[2] A. H. Anderson and Paul J. Jehlik, *Irrigation and the Community*, University of Nebraska, Agricultural Economics Progress Report No. 6 (July, 1952), p. 12.

TABLE 73. POPULATION, NATURAL INCREASE, AND NET MIGRATION FOR FIVE CENTRAL NEBRASKA COUNTIES IN THE TRANSITION AREA, 1950–60

| County | Degree of Rurality* | Rural Farm Population, 1950 | Total Population, 1950 | 1950–1959 Births & Deaths | | Expected Total Population, 1960 | Actual Total Population, 1960 | Net Migration, 1950–60 | Migration Rate (Based on 1950 Population) | Change in Total Population, 1950–60 |
|---|---|---|---|---|---|---|---|---|---|---|
| Total . . . . | 54.9% | 25,037 | 45,644 | 9,490 | 4,567 | 50,567 | 39,625 | −10,942 | −24.0% | −13.2% |
| Custer . . . | 53.8 | 10,321 | 19,170 | 3,778 | 1,887 | 21,061 | 16,517 | −4,544 | −23.7 | −13.8 |
| Greeley . . | 54.4 | 3,034 | 5,575 | 1,366 | 561 | 6,380 | 4,595 | −1,785 | −32.0 | −17.6 |
| Howard . . | 58.2 | 4,204 | 7,226 | 1,488 | 752 | 7,962 | 6,541 | −1,421 | −19.7 | −9.5 |
| Sherman . . | 60.0 | 3,855 | 6,421 | 1,311 | 584 | 7,148 | 5,382 | −1,766 | −27.5 | −16.2 |
| Valley . . . | 50.0 | 3,623 | 7,252 | 1,547 | 783 | 8,016 | 6,590 | −1,426 | −19.7 | −9.1 |

Source: U.S. Bureau of the Census, 1950 Census of Population, and University of Nebraska, Bureau of Business Research, Business in Nebraska, No. 201 (June, 1961).

* Based upon relative importance of rural-farm population to total population in 1950.

change in total population, as Table 73 indicates. The migration rate for the five counties combined was − 24.0 percent, while the decrease in total population was only 13.2 percent.

This level of out-migration could have been predicted fairly closely from the patterns shown in Table 71, where the relationship between migration rates and degree of rurality is presented. There is one group of counties shown in that table whose degree of rurality, or proportion of rural-farm to total population, averaged 57.8 percent in 1950 and whose migration rate averaged − 22.8 percent in the 1950–60 decade. The five transition-area counties had an average degree of rurality or 54.9 percent, rather close to the group in Table 71. On this basis, we should expect their migration rate also to be similar and to average around 23 percent, or perhaps a little less, since they are slightly less rural than the other group. Their actual migration rate for 1950–60 was quite close to this estimate, averaging 24.0 percent. It was a trifle higher than would have been anticipated, but this may reflect the particularly severe adjustments required in the transition region.

It is interesting to speculate on what changes may occur in the decade of the sixties in this area. If the same relationships hold in the 1960's that were operative during the 1950's, we should expect an out-migration from these five central-Nebraska counties of about 19 percent, and a further decline in total population of around 10 percent.

A survey of four of the 16 precincts in Sherman County, Nebraska, in the heart of the study area, shows how profoundly farm family life has been affected by the developments discussed above. The survey covered the period 1946 to 1956 and included 502 families; that is, all families living on farms in these precincts at any time during the period. The families were distributed as follows.

Total families in 1946 . . . . . . . . . . 356
Families present in 1946 and 1956 . . . . 164
Total movers . . . . . . . . . . . . . 338

Families present in 1946 but not in 1956 . 192
Families coming and going, 1946–56 . . 146

These figures reflect a rather surprising mobility of farm people. They also indicate the extent to which the human community can change in a decade. Of the 338 families leaving farms, 27 percent were deaths or retirements; the rest were moves to other farms and moves out of agriculture. Twice as many of the total moves were by tenants as by owners. More than half (53 percent) of all moves by farmers were to nonfarm occupations; two-thirds of the farm tenants who moved from farms went out of agriculture.

*Adjustments of Rural Youth*

Many farm youth have, of course, been going into careers outside agriculture— and for several reasons quite apart from personal preference. In the first place, more farm males enter the 25–69 age group than leave it, according to the 1950–60 replacement rate for Nebraska. Even if total farm labor requirements remained constant over the ten-year period, a labor surplus of about 10 percent would accumulate. But an important factor in the migration of farm youth is farm-size adjustments due to increasing mechanization and changing technology, as we have seen.

Sherman County is affected by these developments. It had 1,444 farms in 1935 and only 919 in 1959, a decline of nearly 37 percent in twenty-four years. Hence the local vocational opportunities for maturing farm youth have declined. In Sherman County, seven out of ten of the present farmers' sons away from home are in occupations outside agriculture. One reason for this may be the rising educational status of farm youth. Table 74 shows the educational attainment of those sample farmers for whom such information was available. These data clearly show a rising level of education among farm youth. Such preparation broadens opportunities for occupational adjustment and gives more latitude in the choice of careers. Thus education trends may be a factor in mobility.

A survey of nearly three hundred students enrolled in the four high schools in Sherman County in 1957 indicates something of the future occupational mobility patterns in a rural area of central Nebraska. A summary of their vocational interests shows that professional careers were favored by more than one-third of the students. Indicated plans or preferences of high school students show that only 41 percent of the farm boys were looking toward farming as their lifework. A professional career was indicated by 50 percent of the town boys and by 15 percent of the farm boys. Of the town girls, 47 percent looked forward to a professional career, while 42 percent of the farm girls had this objective. Twenty-seven percent of all girls indicated clerical work, and 17 percent social work (Table 75).

This survey of students' educational and vocational plans presumably reflects many socio-economic factors, such as rural cultural values, information about alternative vocational opportunities, and the influence of the schools. Substantial differences between rural town and farm youth may be seen. Obviously, actual decisions may not follow the present plans, but the summary gives some insight into the thinking of this part of the Sherman County population.

About two-thirds of the high school students indicated an interest in college, and more than 40 percent had some plans for higher education. The following summary

TABLE 74. EDUCATIONAL ATTAINMENT OF SAMPLE FARM PEOPLE, AGE 18 OR MORE (FOR WHOM COMPLETE DATA WERE AVAILABLE), SHERMAN CO., NEBRASKA, 1956

| | *% Distribution of People by Highest Grade Completed* | | | | |
| *Age* | *Total* | *Less than 9* | *9–11* | *12* | *More than 12* |
|---|---|---|---|---|---|
| Total . . . . . . | 100 | 23 | 10 | 51 | 16 |
| 18–23 . . . . . . | 100 | 13 | 6 | 62 | 19 |
| 23–30 . . . . . . | 100 | 20 | 10 | 60 | 10 |
| 31 or older . . . . | 100 | 32 | 15 | 34 | 19 |

Source: Nebr. Agr. Exp. Sta. data.

TABLE 75.  DISTRIBUTION OF HIGH SCHOOL STUDENTS BY VOCATIONAL PLANS OR FIRST PREFERENCE,
BY SEX AND BY FATHER'S OCCUPATION, SHERMAN CO., NEBRASKA, 1957

| Father's Occupation | All Students | Farm-ing | Pro-fession | Busi-ness | Clerk or Office Worker | Trades and Manual | Service and Pro-tective | Military Career | Other |
|---|---|---|---|---|---|---|---|---|---|
| Male students, total . . | 151 | 41 | 41 | 3 | 0 | 10 | 5 | 16 | 35 |
| Farmer . . . . . . | 99 | 41 | 15 | 1 | 0 | 5 | 2 | 10 | 25 |
| Business or profession | 11 | 0 | 7 | 0 | 0 | 2 | 0 | 1 | 1 |
| Service or protective . | 13 | 0 | 7 | 2 | 0 | 0 | 2 | 0 | 2 |
| Business or industry employee . . . . . | 18 | 0 | 7 | 0 | 0 | 2 | 0 | 4 | 5 |
| Other . . . . . . . | 10 | 0 | 5 | 0 | 0 | 1 | 1 | 1 | 2 |
| Female students, total . | 134 | 0 | 59 | 2 | 37 | 0 | 16 | 1 | 19 |
| Farmer . . . . . . | 94 | 0 | 40 | 2 | 25 | 0 | 10 | 0 | 17 |
| Business or profession | 10 | 0 | 3 | 0 | 3 | 0 | 4 | 0 | 0 |
| Service or protective . | 8 | 0 | 6 | 0 | 1 | 0 | 0 | 1 | 0 |
| Business or industry employee . . . . . | 11 | 0 | 7 | 0 | 1 | 0 | 2 | 0 | 1 |
| Other . . . . . . . | 11 | 0 | 3 | 0 | 7 | 0 | 0 | 0 | 1 |

Source: Nebr. Agr. Exp. Sta. data.

indicates the interests and plans of 285 high school youths in the four systems of Sherman County, Nebraska, as of 1957:

|  | Boys | Girls |
|---|---|---|
| Total students. . . . . . . . . . . . | 151 | 134 |
| Number with college interest . . . . . | 78 | 115 |
| With college plans . . . . . . . . . | 48 | 74 |
| No college plans . . . . . . . . . . | 30 | 41 |
| Reasons for college interest: |  |  |
| General economic . . . . . . . . . | 46 | 50 |
| Self-improvement . . . . . . . . . | 14 | 29 |
| Professional interest . . . . . . . . | 11 | 34 |
| No reason defined . . . . . . . . . | 7 | 2 |

Among the reasons for no interest in college, the most frequently cited by farm youth was financial; but about half of this group evidenced some desire for a college education. Obviously, the above represents varying degrees of maturity of judgment, but it does reflect a broadening career outlook among rural youth—with increasing consideration of nonfarm alternatives. The level of education appears to be a factor in occupational mobility of the young adult, along with a general broadening of contacts and modern communication.

## FARM LIVING STANDARDS

The growing contact between town and country has led not only to increased mobility of farm people, as we have seen, but it has also exerted a subtle influence on many other aspects of farm family life. Living standards of farm people, for example, have traditionally lagged behind those of city dwellers, but the gap appears to be narrowing. Modern conveniences and amenities are increasingly regarded as necessities by farm families—but this is not to say that farm people have caught up with the urban population. Standards of living have been rising in the whole nation, and farmers no longer live in a separate world when it comes to concepts of the good life.

A standard of living is, of course, a social and cultural concept; it refers to wants rather than to their realization. The fulfillment of wants is reflected in the level of living, which has also been rising for farm families, though it is affected by many factors other than contact with urban ideas. A very low income, for example, will clearly keep one's level of living low even though one's living standard may be high. Yet there is a connection between levels and standards of living. When we become accustomed to a way of life, we tend to regard it as proper. Thus, living requirements of farm families—their standards of living—are related to the general level of living in their communities or the general economic status of their area. Areas of high average income tend to have high levels and standards of living.

A study of U.S. farmers in 1946 revealed a general relationship between their incomes and their expenditures of various types (Table 76). Savings tended to be highly responsive to income, and farm production expenses increased sharply at successively higher income levels. Farm-family living expenditures also rose with increasing income, but not nearly so rapidly. These general findings have been confirmed by other studies, notably one published in 1957 concerning farm families in Illinois, where the expenditures were related to gross cash receipts rather than income.[3] As we observe farm families at different income levels, it is clear from

TABLE 76. AVERAGE EXPENDITURES FOR FAMILY LIVING AND FARM PRODUCTION, AND AVERAGE SAVINGS OF FARM FAMILIES BY GROSS INCOME, 1946*

| Classified Gross Cash Income | Average Income | Average Expenditure on | | Average savings (or dissavings) |
| | | Farm Production | Family Living | |
|---|---|---|---|---|
| Total . . . . | $ 4,330 | $ 2,289 | $1,629 | $ 412 |
| $ 0– 499 . . . . | 293 | 353 | 656 | — (716) |
| 500– 999 . . . . | 755 | 363 | 759 | — (367) |
| 1,000– 1,499 . . . . | 1,261 | 591 | 931 | — (267) |
| 1,500– 1,999 . . . . | 1,728 | 792 | 1,129 | — (193) |
| 2,000– 2,999 . . . . | 2,430 | 1,091 | 1,462 | — (123) |
| 3,000– 3,999 . . . . | 3,463 | 1,608 | 1,704 | 151 |
| 4,000– 4,999 . . . . | 4,361 | 2,067 | 1,942 | 352 |
| 5,000– 7,499 . . . . | 5,972 | 2,854 | 2,237 | 881 |
| 7,500– 9,999 . . . . | 8,519 | 4,202 | 2,566 | 1,751 |
| 10,000–19,999 . . . . | 12,890 | 7,745 | 3,025 | 2,120 |
| 20,000 and over . . . | 33,585 | 20,449 | 5,379 | 7,757 |

Source: T. Wilson Longmore and Carl C. Taylor, "Elasticities of Expenditures for Farm Family Living, Farm Production, and Savings, United States, 1946," *Journal of Farm Economics*, XXXIII. No. 1 (February, 1951), table I, 6.

* Includes farm and nonfarm cash income.

[3] Ruth E. Deacon and Ruth Crawford Freeman, *Family Cash Living and Other Outlays as Related to Gross Cash Receipts for 48 Illinois Farm Families, 1938–1953*, University of Illinois, Agricultural Experiment Station Bulletin 614 (July, 1957), p. 4.

Table 76 that, in each successive income class, living expenses are larger than in the preceding one. But if they are expressed in relative terms, say, as a percentage of income, they actually decline—as Table 77 shows.

This general tendency for consumption to increase at a lower rate than income was suggested by Engel in 1854. It reflects the fact that basic consumption requirements tend to be fairly uniform over the entire population. When income doubles, we do not eat twice as much or wear twice as much as we did before. There is a limit to how much we can eat and wear, and, after we satisfy our broadened tastes and add a few frills, the bulk of our increased income tends to be spent on quite different things, such as recreation, education, or investments.

Farm-family living expenditures thus tend to be somewhat rigid as compared with expenses on farm production or savings. At low income levels, the amount required for family living drastically restricts the quantity available for farm production. Also, as other studies have shown, living standards are to some degree irreversible. That is, living expenses tend to respond more to increases than to decreases in income. People accustomed to a high level of living find it difficult to adjust their consumption downward when their incomes are reduced. The level of living to which they are accustomed becomes a standard of living that they tend to maintain.

These findings are particularly relevant to Nebraska farm families, especially those in the transition area, whose incomes tend to be both low and variable. Table 78 shows 1950 and 1959 farm-operator level of living indexes for Nebraska and for the five counties in the heart of the transition area. Of the 93 counties in the state, only 11 others had indexes as low as these six, and all but one of them are also in the transition area. These data indicate that the farmers in this region clearly are not doing as well as those in the rest of the state. This could be deduced from their incomes, too. In Sherman County, for example, gross farm income per farm averaged only 58 percent of the state figure in five census years (Table 79).

TABLE 77.　RATIO OF AVERAGE EXPENDITURES AND SAVINGS TO AVERAGE GROSS CASH INCOME OF FARM FAMILIES, 1946

| Classified Gross Cash Income | Ratio of Specified Item of Expenditures to Income | | Ratio of Savings (or Dissaving) to Income |
|---|---|---|---|
| | Farm Production | Family Living | |
| Total . . . . . . . . | .53 | .37 | .10 |
| $　　0– 　499 . . . . | 1.20 | 2.24 | −2.44 |
| 　500– 　999 . . . . | .48 | 1.01 | −.49 |
| 1,000– 1,499 . . . . | .47 | .74 | −.21 |
| 1,500– 1,999 . . . . | .46 | .65 | −.11 |
| 2,000– 2,999 . . . . | .45 | .60 | −.05 |
| 3,000– 3,999 . . . . | .46 | .49 | .04 |
| 4,000– 4,999 . . . . | .47 | .45 | .08 |
| 5,000– 7,499 . . . . | .48 | .37 | .15 |
| 7,500– 9,999 . . . . | .49 | .30 | .21 |
| 10,000–19,999 . . . . | .60 | .23 | .16 |
| 20,000 and over . . . | .61 | .16 | .23 |

Source: Longmore and Taylor, *op. cit.*, table VI, p. 15.

TABLE 78. Farm–operator Level of Living Index for 5 Central Nebraska Counties in the Transition Area, and for Nebraska, 1950 and 1959

| | (U.S. County Average in 1959 = 100) | |
| --- | --- | --- |
| | 1950 | 1959 |
| Nebraska . . . . . . . . . . . | 82 | 123 |
| Custer . . . . . . . . . . . | 77 | 114 |
| Greeley . . . . . . . . . . | 73 | 109 |
| Howard . . . . . . . . . . | 78 | 116 |
| Sherman . . . . . . . . . . | 64 | 97 |
| Valley . . . . . . . . . . . | 79 | 110 |

Source: U.S. Economic Research Service Statistical Bulletin No. 321, *Farm Operator Level-of-Living Indexes for Counties of the United States, 1950 and 1959* (September, 1962), table 2, p. 44.

This does not mean that all farmers had low incomes; but the proportion of low-income farms is rather high. In recent years, more than a third of all farms in the county had gross incomes of less than $2,500.

More detailed information on family living and farm business expenses was collected from 200 farm households in Sherman County. In 1959 these sample farmers had an average cash income (after allowing for farm operating expenses) of $1,820. More than half of these households had little income for living expenses (Table 80); some received less in net cash income than they spent on farm production.

Actual returns to labor and management were, of course, considerably less than indicated above since depreciation and interest on investment were not taken into account.

When these 200 sample households were classified by consumer requirements, nearly half of them clearly had inadequate incomes, even when allowance was made for home-consumption of farm-produced food and for the use value of the farm dwelling (Table 81).

Although the flexibility in living requirements associated with frontier days no longer characterizes the modern farm community, sharp changes in income affect certain family living expenses. Of the 200 sample farmers in Sherman County, 70 percent said they postponed buying household equipment and furnishings in years of drought and low prices, such as 1956, when their expenditures on these items were

TABLE 79. Average Value of Products Sold, Sherman Co., Nebraska, Compared with State for Specified Years

| | Average Value of Products Sold | | Sherman County Value as Percentage of Nebraska Value |
| --- | --- | --- | --- |
| | Sherman County | Nebraska | |
| 1959 . . . . . . . . . . | $8,026 | $13,272 | 60 |
| 1954 . . . . . . . . . . | 4,752 | 8,748 | 54 |
| 1949 . . . . . . . . . . | 4,294 | 7,273 | 59 |
| 1939 . . . . . . . . . . | 649 | 1,587 | 41 |
| 1929 . . . . . . . . . . | 2,354 | 3,467 | 68 |

Source: *U.S. Census of Agriculture.*

TABLE 80.  AVERAGE NET CASH INCOME PER FARM BY INCOME QUARTILES,
200 SAMPLE FARMS, SHERMAN CO., NEBRASKA, 1955

| Income Quartiles | Net Cash Income per Farm |
|---|---|
| Lowest 50 farms. . . . . . . | $ 673 |
| Second 50 farms  . . . . . . | 882 |
| Third 50 farms . . . . . . . | 1,956 |
| Highest 50 farms  . . . . . . | 4,731 |

Source: Nebr. Agr. Exp. Sta. data.

only about 64 percent of what they were in 1952. Most families postponed clothing
purchases, and some effected economies in recreation. On the other hand, many
family expenses, such as those for food and utilities, are not easily deferred. Many
factors obviously play a part in the practical adjustment of living requirements to
the cash available in low-income years, but at least moderate austerity is the lot of
many families.

A more detailed view of the level of living attained by these farm families in the
Sherman County sample is provided in Table 82. The table consists of fourteen items
used in W. H. Sewell's standardized scale,[4] and five additional items representing
modern goods and conveniences. It is clear from this table that tenure status has
some effect on family living. For example, dwellings of tenants are less likely to be
excellent or good, compared with those of owner-operators. They are less likely to
have running hot water or telephones.

Living standards are more elusive than levels of living, but an attempt was made
to compare the two levels for twenty-four young beginning farmers in the Sherman
County sample. The average age of these household heads was twenty-five. The

TABLE 81.  PERCENTAGE DISTRIBUTION OF FARM HOUSEHOLDS BY CONSUMER REQUIREMENTS, NET
CASH INCOME, AND TOTAL INCOME PER FARM, AND PERCENTAGE WITH INADEQUATE INCOMES, 200
SAMPLE FARMS, SHERMAN CO., NEBRASKA, 1955

| Consumer Requirements* | Farm Households | Net Cash Income per Farm | Total Income per Farm† | Farm Households with Inadequate Incomes‡ |
|---|---|---|---|---|
| Total . . . . . . . . . . . | 100% | $1,699 | $2,748 | 48% |
| Less than $2,000  . . . . . . | 27 | 1,553 | 2,603 | 34 |
| 2,000–2,999  . . . . . . . | 29 | 1,107 | 2,156 | 48 |
| 3,000–3,999  . . . . . . . | 33 | 2,247 | 3,297 | 56 |
| 4,000 or more . . . . . . . | 11 | 1,972 | 3,022 | 55 |

Source: James D. Tarver, "Cost of Rearing and Educating Farm Children," *Journal of Farm Economics*, XXXVIII,
No. 1 (February, 1956), 144–153. Requirements were then calculated on the basis of the actual age composition of the
sample families in Sherman County.
 * Estimates based upon an Oklahoma study of the average annual cost of rearing farm children, age 1–9, in several
hundred farm families, 1954.
 † Net cash income, plus value of home-consumption of farm-produced food, plus use value of farm dwelling.
 ‡ Inadequate incomes are defined as those exceeded by consumer requirements.

[4] William H. Sewell, *Construction and Standardization of a Scale for Measurement of the Socio-Economic
Status of Farm Families*, Oklahoma Agricultural Experiment Station Technical Bulletin No. 9 (April,
1940), p. 42.

TABLE 82.  PERCENTAGE OF FARM HOUSEHOLDS REPORTING SPECIFIED LEVEL OF LIVING ITEMS, BY TENURE STATUS OF HOUSEHOLD HEAD, 200 SAMPLE FARMS, SHERMAN CO., NEBRASKA, 1955

| Level of Living Item | Tenure Status of Household Head | | | |
| --- | --- | --- | --- | --- |
| | Total | Owners | Part-owners | Tenants |
| Brick, stucco, or painted frame house . . . | 95% | 96% | 98% | 91% |
| Room–person ratio: | | | | |
| Less than 1 . . . . . . . . . . . . . . . | 9.4 | 6.6 | 9.4 | 12.5 |
| 2 or more . . . . . | 48 | 51 | 55 | 39 |
| Electricity in dwelling . . . . . . . . . | 96 | 93 | 98 | 97 |
| Piped water in dwelling . . . . . . . . | 76 | 77 | 81 | 72 |
| Running hot water . . . . . . . . . | 48 | 51 | 60 | 35 |
| Bathroom . . . . . . . . . . . . . | 46 | 46 | 58 | 38 |
| Power washer . . . . . . . . . . . . | 96 | 94 | 96 | 97 |
| Electric or gas refrigerator . . . . . . . | 95 | 94 | 96 | 96 |
| Radio . . . . . . . . . . . . . . . | 99 | 100 | 98 | 98 |
| Telephone . . . . . . . . . . . . . | 46 | 51 | 51 | 36 |
| Auto (other than truck) . . . . . . . . | 92 | 96 | 91 | 90 |
| Takes daily paper . . . . . . . . . . | 70 | 71 | 74 | 66 |
| Male head attends church (1/4+) . . . . . | 71 | 75 | 68 | 68 |
| Wife attends church (1/4+) . . . . . . . | 70 | 70 | 70 | 69 |
| Male head HS graduate . . . . . . . . | 28 | 14 | 36 | 38 |
| Wife HS graduate . . . . . . . . . . . | 42 | 30 | 51 | 50 |
| Furnace . . . . . . . . . . . . . . | 36 | 32 | 47 | 33 |
| Television . . . . . . . . . . . . . | 47 | 39 | 60 | 46 |
| Home freezer . . . . . . . . . . . . | 32 | 30 | 34 | 33 |
| Locker space rented . . . . . . . . . . | 60 | 59 | 70 | 61 |
| Dwelling, excellent or good . . . . . . . | 48 | 48 | 62 | 36 |

Source: Nebr. Agr. Exp. Sta. data.

extent to which living items were considered essential—and, in some instances, already possessed—is shown in Table 83. The average net income of these farmers in 1955 was one-third lower than the Sherman County sample average, and far below the level they considered reasonable (Table 84). Distant goals of these young families, such as anticipated costs of educating children, are probably reflected in their estimates of reasonable income levels.

One reason these people find it difficult to bring their living levels up to their standards is because the cost of living is higher in areas of widely dispersed population, even if the community facilities and conveniences are comparable. Other things being equal, distance from the city is a significant factor in living resources of the modern farm family.

A Bureau of Agricultural Economics study (1949) explored several of the basic services in rural and urban areas of the United States. The 3,071 counties were classified by the percentage of their people living on farms. In the most rural counties (those with 80 percent of their population on farms), 28 percent of births were in hospitals in 1946, in the most urban counties (those with 20 percent of their population on farms), it was 93 percent. The most rural counties had 45 hospital beds per 100,000 population, and the most urban counties had 432 beds. The former had 31 physicians per 100,000; the latter 112. Of the farm dwellings in the most rural

TABLE 83. Households Reporting Specified Level of Living Items Already Possessed and/or Considered Essential, 24 Sample Farm Households, Sherman Co., Nebraska, 1955

| Level of Living Item | Already Possessed | Considered Essential |
|---|---|---|
| Electricity . . . . . . . . . . | 24 | 24 |
| Gas for cooking . . . . . . . . | 11 | 12 |
| Gas for heating . . . . . . . . | 10 | 13 |
| Plumbing . . . . . . . . . . | 13 | 23 |
| Automatic washer . . . . . . . | 0 | 4 |
| Washing machine . . . . . . . | 21 | 22 |
| Automatic dryer. . . . . . . . | 2 | 5 |
| Deep freezer . . . . . . . . . | 7 | 12 |
| Refrigerator . . . . . . . . . | 20 | 24 |
| Radio . . . . . . . . . . . | 23 | 23 |
| Television . . . . . . . . . . | 6 | 11 |
| New car every 4 years . . . . . | 2 | 11 |
| Telephone . . . . . . . . . . | 9 | 16 |
| H.S. education (children) . . . . | | 22 |
| College education (children) . . . | | 17 |
| Vacation . . . . . . . . . . . | 3 | 14 |
| Hobbies, hunting, etc. . . . . . . | 12 | 16 |
| Clubs, lodges, etc. . . . . . . . | 5 | 11 |
| Church support . . . . . . . . | | 22 |

Source: Nebr. Agr. Exp. Sta. data.

counties, 19 percent had electricity, compared with 68 percent in the most urban (1945). Seven percent of the former had running water, and 47 percent of the latter. Ten percent of the adults had completed high school in the most rural counties; 27 percent in the most urban. Four additional items included in the study show similar differences. While these do not vary precisely with distance from an urban center, they are closely associated with the degree of rurality in the region.

The Northern Plains states have a high proportion of sparsely populated counties; distances are great and cities are few. Larger population aggregates in a given physical area provide better support for specialized services. Thus a large rural area is likely to be at a disadvantage because of its distance from population centers. For example, more than 20 percent of all counties in the four Northern Plains states reported no hospital beds in 1954; and twenty of the rural counties had no resident physician. Indeed, several sparsely populated counties had no resident barber in

TABLE 84. Gross and Net Income per Farm, Actual and Reasonable, 24 Sample Farm Households, Sherman Co., Nebraska, 1955

| Income | Actual (1955) | Considered Reasonable |
|---|---|---|
| Net . . . . . . . . | $1,216 | $ 5,558 |
| Gross . . . . . . . | 5,577 | 10,630 |

Source: Nebr. Agr. Exp. Sta. data.

1959. Such illustrations of community differences between urban and rural counties could be multiplied.

As living standards of farm families in the Northern Plains have risen, the resource base of the rural community, as well as of the family, has proven inadequate. Adjustment is both complex and costly. Enlargement of farms to support higher standards implies a reduction in numbers of families. Similarly, raising the level of services in the rural town presumably will require fewer rural centers. Community life in the Northern Plains must be adapted to its unique environment. Distances will be greater here than in more humid areas, but communities can be organized to compensate, at least in part, for the more dispersed population.

# CHAPTER 14

# Public Services in
# the Farm Community

## LOCAL GOVERNMENT

THE DEMANDS upon the machinery of local government reflect the environment in which it operates. A given socio-economic environment provides the resource base; and its institutions must be adapted to this environment. The development of the Plains was attended by many problems of local government, and new ones have arisen in recent times. Yet the rapid economic adjustments in farming have not been paralleled by a corresponding adaptation of institutions to the unique conditions of Plains living.

The Northern Plains have a population density of about fifteen persons per square mile, but over wide areas this reduces to fewer than two persons (Figure 51). Government units are therefore small in terms of population, or, alternatively, very numerous as compared with other parts of the country. Only ten states outside the Plains have as many government units as Nebraska's 1,715, and each of those states has far more than twice Nebraska's population. While all counties in the United States have an average of 38 governmental units, counties in the four Northern Plains states range from an average of 66 government units per county in Kansas to 86 in Nebraska. In 1952, one-fourth of the 319 counties in the region contained more than 100 units of local government. As one might expect with so many units, the average population per unit is quite low. For the nation as a whole, there are 1,280 persons per governmental unit, while for the Plains states the corresponding averages are Kansas, 275; Nebraska, 166; North Dakota, 156; and South Dakota, 133.

Counties in these states differ greatly in the number of persons per governmental unit. Nebraska counties range from about 4,000 to less than 30 persons per unit. The following summary of the most and least populous counties in the state reveals the great variation in patterns:

Counties representing more than 25,000 persons (8 counties):
Range in total government units . . . . . . . . .   71 to 178
Range in persons per unit . . . . . . . . . . . .   158 to 3,958

Counties representing less than 2,500 persons (12 counties):
Range in total government units . . . . . . . . .   4 to  88
Range in persons per unit . . . . . . . . . . . .   27 to 245

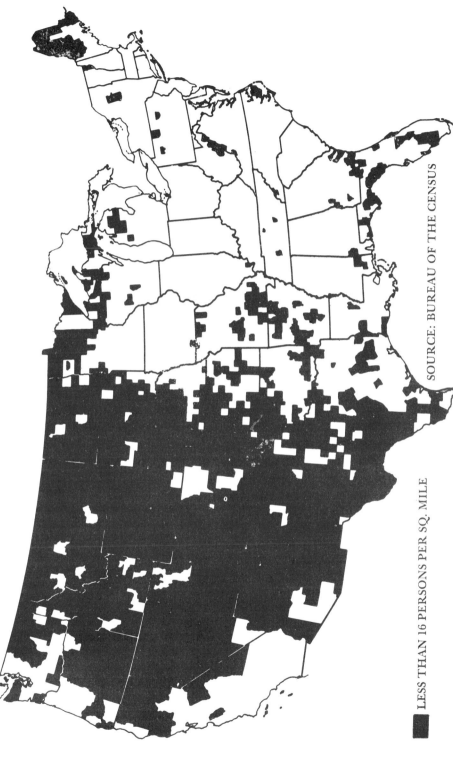

■ LESS THAN 16 PERSONS PER SQ. MILE

SOURCE: BUREAU OF THE CENSUS

Fig. 51. Sparsely Populated Counties in the U.S., 1960

241

Yet total population of counties is only one factor influencing the number of persons per government unit, as is shown by the following list of the ten counties most successful in this respect.

| County | Population per Govt. Unit | Total Govt. Units | Total Population |
|---|---|---|---|
| Douglas . . . . . . . . | 3,958 | 71 | 281,020 |
| Lancaster . . . . . . | 820 | 146 | 119,722 |
| Scotts Bluff . . . . . . | 406 | 81 | 33,939 |
| Sarpy . . . . . . . . . | 307 | 51 | 15,693 |
| Hall . . . . . . . . . . | 304 | 106 | 32,168 |
| Adams . . . . . . . | 286 | 101 | 28,885 |
| Madison . . . . . . . | 270 | 70 | 24,338 |
| Hooker . . . . . . . | 245 | 4 | 1,061 |
| Dodge . . . . . . . . | 217 | 121 | 26,265 |
| Cheyenne . . . . . . | 216 | 56 | 12,081 |

It seems from this that high population density gives a high population per government unit, but this is not necessarily the case—as is suggested by Hooker County. Proper organization can triumph over the handicap of sparse population. However, most Nebraska counties are liberally endowed with governmental units in relation to population. The five Nebraska counties lowest in terms of persons per government unit also tend to be low in total population.

| County | Population per Govt. Unit | Total Govt. Units | School Units | Total Population |
|---|---|---|---|---|
| McPherson . . . . | 27 | 31 | 30 | 825 |
| Arthur . . . . . | 35 | 23 | 21 | 803 |
| Wheeler . . . . . | 42 | 36 | 33 | 1,526 |
| Keya Paha . . . . | 47 | 46 | 43 | 2,160 |
| Gosper . . . . . | 47 | 58 | 53 | 2,734 |

Thus these counties would have had an average of only ten families per government unit in 1952. It should be noted that 180 of the 194 government units in these counties are school districts, and that none of these rural counties had township units. The following distribution of Nebraska counties illustrates the general relationship between population density and persons per unit.

*Number of People per Govt. Unit:*

| County Population per Sq. Mi. | Total Counties | Less than 60 | 60–79 | 80–99 | 100–139 | 140–199 | 200 or more |
|---|---|---|---|---|---|---|---|
| Total counties . . . | 93 | 13 | 14 | 22 | 15 | 19 | 10 |
| Less than 2 . . . . | 9 | 6 | 1 | 1 | – | – | 1 |
| 2– 4 . . . . | 11 | 4 | 3 | 4 | – | – | – |
| 5– 9 . . . . | 14 | 3 | 2 | 4 | 3 | 2 | – |
| 10–14 . . . . | 20 | | 7 | 5 | 5 | 2 | 1 |
| 15–19 . . . . | 19 | | 1 | 8 | 7 | 3 | |
| 20–29 . . . . | 9 | | | | | 9 | |
| 30–49 . . . . | 6 | | | | | 3 | 3 |
| 50 or more . . . . | 5 | | | | | | 5 |

It will be noted that one-fifth of these 93 countries have less than five persons per square mile and that more than two-thirds of these have less than eighty persons per government unit (about 23 families). One-fifth of the counties have twenty or more persons per square mile, and none of these has less than 140 persons per unit. Thus sparse population is a necessary condition for low densities per unit, but it is not sufficient. Poor organization must go along with it.

Population density affects the cost of local government. Since the total cost of such services often is constant, or at least slowly rising, over a broad range of population bases, it follows that densely populated areas tend to enjoy lower unit costs than areas with relatively few people (Figure 52). Thus rural areas are at a disadvantage

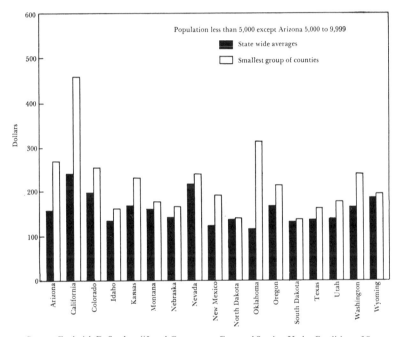

Source: Frederick D. Stocker, "Local Government Costs and Services Under Conditions of Sparse Population," *Proceedings of the Western Farm Economics Association*, Laramie, Wyo. (July 25, 1963).

Fig. 52.    Per Capita General Expenditure of Local Governments on all Functions in 17 Western States, 1957

in this respect, and nowhere more so than in the Plains—whose vast distances and scattered, sparse population aggravate the already knotty problem of organizing to provide services efficiently.

Farm people have traditionally adopted smaller-scale services, such as fewer pupils per school, fewer beds per hospital, fewer members per church, and fewer citizens per county officer, than urban people. With other things remaining equal, this solution ordinarily involves higher unit costs for similar services. To cut these costs, they have in the past settled for inferior services, such as mediocre teachers, poorer roads, more limited recreational facilities, and less church service. But today, as we have seen, rural standards are rising; farm people increasingly expect the same quality in their services that city people enjoy.

Time alone will not take care of the problems of local governments in the Northern Plains. Current developments in transportation, as well as population dynamics, point to an intensification of the maladjustments in the future. However, many people in the region are aware of the difficulty of the problem. The editor of a North Dakota daily, in a conversation about postwar community reorganization at mid-century, remarked that "this will be almost like rebuilding London." True; and yet we must keep in mind that Londoners set about their difficult task, and eventually London was rebuilt. Plains people will have to be particularly ingenious in organizing to provide public services if they are to have them on a sufficiently large scale to guarantee the requisite quality with reasonable efficiency.

## PUBLIC SERVICES

### Roads

The Northern Plains region, with relatively few large cities, is a vast mosaic of small farm communities. At least 2,000 such communities dot the 300,000-square-mile area of the four Northern Plains states. This implies an average community area of 150 square miles with a 6-mile radius (on north–south and east–west roads). More than half of the 319 counties are entirely rural, with no town of 2,500 or more persons. Such counties often occur in blocks, some extending over 25,000 square miles, with large areas having only small villages. Towns are relatively few and far between in the western part of the region, where farms and ranches are large.

Across the four Northern Plains states, towns of 1,000–2,000 population, serving from 3,000 to 6,000 people, may represent community radii ranging from 7 to 24 miles. In the one case, the population is concentrated in 200 square miles; in the other, it is scattered over 2,500 square miles. Towns of from 2,000 to 3,000 population, serving 8,000 to 12,000 people, similarly range in service area from 200 square miles to 7,500 square miles (with radii of 7 and 44 miles, respectively). Obviously, road systems cannot be identical in such sharply differing environments. Because of greater distances in the sparsely populated zone, a given size of town may maintain its service radius more easily in the face of changing population patterns than where families and towns are closer together.

According to the Department of Roads and Irrigation, Nebraska had nearly 90,000 miles of county and township roads in 1956. This represents a state average of one mile of road per commercial farm. More than half of this was earth road. About 700 miles were bituminous or paved, and about 37,000 are gravel or crushed stone. State roads (9,260 miles) are largely surfaced, with 58 percent bituminous or paved and the rest gravel or crushed stone.

The magnitude of the state's difficulty in maintaining good roads is indicated by these facts. In 1959, Nebraska ranked 12th in the nation in total mileage of roads, while it ranked only 34th in population. In terms of the share of the state's resources that go to road maintenance, Nebraska makes a reasonable showing. Of all expenditures of state and local government in 1959, the proportion going to highways was 27.1 percent in Nebraska, as compared with 19.6 percent in the nation as a whole. Nebraska thus ranked 12th, the same as it did in total road mileage. However, with respect to per capita expenditures on roads, perhaps a better measure of a people's effort, Nebraska ranks only 21st among the states. Nebraska's citizens spent an average of $64.84 per person on roads in 1959; the U.S. average was $54.39 per capita.

One way to increase the state's efficiency in its road maintenance program would be to lower its total road mileage. Roads are, of course, especially important in sparsely settled regions such as the Plains. They condition the activities of isolated families in many ways; they affect the functioning of all institutions in farm communities. The cost of maintaining good all-weather roads is at present prohibitive in some areas, so some farmers and ranchers are not fully enjoying the advantages of modern transportation., Since surfaced roads are generally the strategic lines of communication to central points, relocation of farm headquarters along these roads would be highly desirable. Because of capital investment in improved roads, structures, business enterprises, etc., such adjustments are often costly. They are also especially risky when accomplished by individual decisions and actions. Yet they are even now being made. Town-farming and line-residence patterns are gradually developing in the Western Plains; they offer possibilities for other sparsley populated areas.

Investment in farm buildings inhibits systematic change to fewer miles of better roads. But this situation could be much improved by the development of long-range highway-improvement planning which would include the gradual closing of rarely used roads. Such a move would significantly lower the risk taken by individuals, who might otherwise relocate on a haphazard basis.

*Education*

Few institutions in our society are as dear to people as their children's schools. Plains people are no exception. It is natural for them to want their children to live at home and attend a school nearby, for this desire for convenience is almost universal. They also want their children to obtain a good education; that is, they want the schools to be of a high quality. But in sparsely settled areas, convenience and quality may be difficult to attain together. One can be obtained only at the expense of the other. There is a certain critical size which any social institution must attain in order to provide quality service in an efficient way, and schools are just as subject to this law as any other organization. In many parts of the Northern Plains there is little doubt that convenience is being purchased at a high price, in terms of the lowered quality of education the children are receiving.

In general, Plains states are not niggardly in their school support, as this is measured by the proportion of their expenditures earmarked for education in this respect. In Nebraska, for example, 37.8 percent of state and local government expenditures are used for schools, compared with 35.4 percent in the nation as a whole. Nebraska ranks 15th among the states in this respect. But because its tax burden is rather light, Nebraska ranks lower in the amount of money spent for education.

It ranks 30th, for example, in per capital expenditures on education, with $90.45, while $98.00 per person is the national average. On a per pupil basis, expenditures are even lower, relatively speaking. Nebraska ranks 35th among the states on expenditures per pupil (in public schools), with $308.92 supporting each Nebraska pupil compared with a national average of $341.05. Yet Nebraska ranks 25th in per capita income, the usual measure of ability to pay. Part of the explanation probably lies in its tax structure. The state ranks 38th in taxes per person; only twelve other states have lower taxes.

Yet it is possible to draw exaggerated meanings from these differences in rankings. In other respects, Nebraska—as well as the other Northern Plains states—makes a reasonable showing in its support of its schools. Its rankings in population, in pupils enrolled, in expenditures for education, and in expenditures per pupil are all very close (34th or 35th).

The problems of school organization in these states have been pointed out by many people. As one writer puts it:

> The seven states of Kansas, Nebraska, North Dakota, South Dakota, Minnesota, Missouri, and Iowa have similar problems in school district organization. These states comprise about one-seventh of the states in the United States, and have less than 7 percent of the public school children of the nation. In 1958 they accounted for over 44 percent of the public school districts in the country. In that year, these states had over 80 percent of the non-operating school districts, more than 50 percent of the one-room rural schools, and 55 percent of the districts with nine or fewer teachers. On the other hand, these seven states accounted for only 7 percent of the districts with forty or more teachers.[1]

Nebraska has the dubious distinction of being in the forefront of this melancholy parade of statistics. It has more school districts and more one-teacher schools than any other state. Yet there has been considerable improvement since 1949, when the state legislature passed the School District Reorganization Act that provided for a state school district reorganization committee and for a county committee in each of the ninety-three counties. At that time, Nebraska had 6,734 school districts, a figure which has now been reduced by 54 percent.

In 1955 the Nebraska legislature directed the county committees to submit comprehensive plans for the organization of school districts in each county. These plans were to be submitted for the approval or disapproval of the state committee within two years after 1955. Yet only three counties have put into action their approved plans. Thirty more counties have had their plans approved, but this leaves sixty of the state's ninety-three counties with much work left to be done on their plans for school district reorganization.

Obviously, many people are dragging their feet on reorganization because they fear the loss of local control; others fear increased taxes. Local control of a school system can confer many benefits, such as flexibility and ability to adapt to local conditions; but, carried to an extreme, it can lead to unevenness in the quality of education, and it frequently results in schools so small that quality is low while costs are relatively high. Control can be exerted over a reasonably large area as well as a small one, as the experience of many other states has demonstrated. Nevada, for example, with a much larger area and a smaller population than Nebraska, has only 17 school districts, as compared with Nebraska's 3,077.

In the study area of central Nebraska, as in any rural area, the school problem is especially acute. In Sherman County, for example, enrollment in rural schools has decreased by 60 percent in the past twenty-five years. The number of rural schools

[1] J. S. Knezevich, "The Changing Structure of Public Education in Iowa and Its Relation to the Educational Needs of Rural and Urban Areas," *Urban Responses to Agricultural Change*, Clyde F. Kohn (ed.) (Iowa City: State University of Iowa, 1961), p. 179.

declined by 45 percent, and average enrollment per school dropped from more than sixteen to about ten pupils. These developments are obviously associated with the sharp decline in farm population. Some school consolidation has taken place, but it has not nearly kept pace with the population changes.

A survey of some 250 cooperating teachers in central Nebraska in 1956 revealed some discomfiting features of the schools in this area. Of the teachers in rural schools, more than half were teaching in schools with a total enrollment of fewer than ten pupils. Of the rural schools represented in the survey, 19 percent had no electricity, 81 percent did not have running water in the school buildings, and only 10 percent had indoor toilet facilities. Thirty-eight percent had all-weather roads to their schools, while 42 percent had medium-to-good roads.

Many of the high schools in the transition area have very low enrollments. Of the secondary school teachers cooperating in the survey, one out of five served in a school with fewer than fifty students, and 60 percent taught in high schools having fewer than one hundred students.

In the centralized elementary schools (usually associated with secondary schools), enrollments ranged from fewer than twenty-five pupils to more than two hundred. One teacher in five reported less than fifty pupils in the elementary school; 23 per cent reported from fifty to ninety-nine pupils. With fifty kindergarten to eighth-grade students, each grade would average only about five pupils. Some of these schools show the trend toward centralization of rural education with adjoining one-room school districts combining with a village school district. Since the system of highways and country roads is generally related to the incorporated places, further reorganization along these lines could result in considerable economy in future bus routes.

### Libraries

The Northern Plains states have provided for the education of all children through statewide systems of public schools; they rank high in the proportion of people who can read and write. But education cannot stop with formal elementary schooling; self-education, through reading and group discussions, must supplement it. Rural library service presents many of the same difficulties already discussed. The disparity between rural and urban areas is frequently substantial. Here again, consolidation of facilities and centralized direction of operations could lead to the provision of more specialized services at reasonable cost. In the most sparsely settled areas, newer methods—such as mobile libraries—might be a more feasible solution.

### Health

Sparse population, low incomes, and dependence upon small service centers call for unusual adjustment in this highly specialized service. Nebraska and Kansas have, respectively, 105 and 106 physicians per 100,000 persons (1959 data). Though this is substantially below the national average of 133, it is still within the range of a desirable balance. But the other Northern Plains states, North and South Dakota, have only 78 and 71 physicians, respectively, per 100,000 population.

Even in the more fortunate states there is often a wide gap between the health facilities available to urban people and those in rural areas. Most small places have no local doctor. Indeed, many counties in the region have no resident physician and no hospital facilities. For example, eleven Nebraska counties were without a physician in 1953, three had 5,000 persons per physician, and ten had from 3,000 to 5,000. Thus twenty-four of the state's ninety-three counties could be considered inadequately served, with less than half the desirable number of doctors.

### CONCLUSION

With discovery and exploitation of material resources as major goals in modern life, the importance of social goals is sometimes obscured. The shocks of technological change have often produced institutional stress, and adjustment tends to lag in all areas of organized community life. The farm community of the Plains faces all of these, plus the difficult problem of adapting its institutions to a sparse and declining population.

The gradual adjustment of population to land resources is putting increasingly greater distance between a farmer and his neighbor; it has necessitated maintenance of more miles of highway per family. It has reduced school population in rural areas and has reduced the number of country schools and churches.

To collect all the benefits from a new man-land adjustment, two things are indicated: (1) gradual but systematic relocation of isolated farm residences to the most advantageous all-weather road, or to a village or town; (2) basic adaptation of community institutions and services, such as reorganization of school districts, of local government, and of other public services.

# CHAPTER 15

# The Small Town
# at the Crossroads

## CHANGES IN TRADE STRUCTURE

WE have already noted how the smaller towns in the Northern Plains have been losing population. Since this migration is expected to continue, it leads to speculation about their economic future. Some observers believe the rural small town is on its way out. A recent article by the Federal Reserve Bank of Chicago puts it:

> The small town is in the position of finding its highly important rural trading area slowly eroding. The advent of rapid and easy automobile transportation has made the larger communities with their wider range of goods, services, and recreational activities seem relatively "close by." Like a two-edged sword, the loss of trading areas forces a reduction in goods and services which can be offered profitably, and, in turn, the reduction in shopping alternatives makes the larger communities seem even more attractive.[1]

If this were true, we could expect to find evidence of it in the business statistics of Nebraska communities, since, of the state's 538 municipalities, 495—92 percent—of them can be classed as small, having populations of less than 2,500. Fortunately, data for testing the hypothesis are available in the Census of Business for 1948, 1954, and 1958. These data show a substantial increase in the total retail sales of cities with 2,500 or more population; they also show a lesser, but still substantial, increase in the retail business of the smaller towns (Table 85). The economic life of these towns seems much more vigorous than their population losses would lead us to assume. Since sales of consumer goods follow population changes rather closely, the explanation of these smaller towns' viability may lie in their role as suppliers of production goods.

As we saw earlier, farmers are rapidly increasing their use of purchased inputs, such as machinery, seed, feed, fertilizer, and pesticides. Even though some farmers may move out of an area, as long as the land there remains in farming the quantities of many of these inputs that are demanded may not change much; the demand for some may even increase. The Census of Business does not isolate farm inputs as a group, but its category, "Lumber, Building Material, Hardware, Farm Equipment," clearly includes farm machinery dealers; and its "Other Retail Sales" category

[1] The Federal Reserve Bank of Chicago, "The Declining Small Town?" *Business Conditions* (May, 1959), p. 11.

249

TABLE 85. Nebraska Retail Sales and Number of Stores, by Size of Town, 1948, 1954, 1958*

| Item & Size of Town | 1948 | 1954 | Change, 1948–54 | 1954 | 1958 | Change, 1954–58 | 1948 | 1958 | Change, 1948–58 |
|---|---|---|---|---|---|---|---|---|---|
| | | | SALES (IN THOUSAND DOLLARS) | | | | | | |
| Total retail sales: | | | | | | | | | |
| All towns . . . . | $1,304,357 | $1,574,441 | +20.7% | $1,587,649 | $1,730,134 | +9.0% | $1,304,637 | $1,715,592 | +31.5% |
| Under 2,500 . . | 440,795 | 514,277 | +16.7 | 521,479 | 560,667 | +7.5 | 441,075 | 552,343 | +25.2 |
| 2,500 or more . . | 863,562 | 1,060,164 | +22.8 | 1,066,170 | 1,169,467 | +9.7 | 863,562 | 1,163,249 | +34.7 |
| Sales of "Lumber, etc.": | | | | | | | | | |
| All towns . . . . | $224,819 | $227,625 | +1.2% | $227,649 | $253,318 | +11.3% | $222,034 | $251,499 | +13.3% |
| Under 2,500 . . | 118,709 | 123,260 | +3.8 | 123,542 | 137,936 | +11.7 | 116,884 | 136,780 | +17.0 |
| 2,500 or more . . | 106,110 | 104,365 | −1.6 | 104,107 | 115,382 | +10.8 | 105,150 | 114,719 | +9.1 |
| Sales of "Other Retail, etc.": | | | | | | | | | |
| All towns . . . . | $37,490 | $53,852 | +43.6% | $57,294 | $53,890 | −5.9% | $35,368 | $58,052 | +64.1% |
| Under 2,500 . . | 15,291 | 22,988 | +50.3 | 27,869 | 29,632 | +6.3 | 17,108 | 32,550 | +90.3 |
| 2,500 or more . . | 22,199 | 30,864 | +39.0 | 29,425 | 24,258 | −17.6 | 18,260 | 25,502 | +39.7 |
| | | | NUMBER OF STORES | | | | | | |
| Total retail sales: | | | | | | | | | |
| All towns . . . . | 16,632 | 16,824 | +1.2% | 17,027 | 16,808 | −1.3% | 16,641 | 16,602 | −0.2% |
| Under 2,500 . . | 8,767 | 8,163 | −6.9 | 8,286 | 8,428 | +1.7 | 8,776 | 8,295 | −5.5 |
| 2,500 or more . . | 7,865 | 8,661 | +10.1 | 8,741 | 8,380 | −4.1 | 7,865 | 8,307 | +5.6 |
| Sales of "Lumber, etc.": | | | | | | | | | |
| All towns . . . . | 2,192 | 2,087 | −4.8% | 2,083 | 1,989 | −4.4% | 2,168 | 1,966 | −9.3% |
| Under 2,500 . . | 1,503 | 1,409 | −6.3 | 1,405 | 1,307 | −7.0 | 1,487 | 1,292 | −13.1 |
| 2,500 or more . . | 689 | 678 | −1.6 | 678 | 682 | +0.6 | 681 | 674 | −1.0 |
| Sales of "Other Retail, etc.": | | | | | | | | | |
| All towns . . . . | 662 | 750 | +13.3% | 755 | 820 | +8.6% | 706 | 980 | +38.8% |
| Under 2,500 . . | 290 | 347 | +19.7 | 386 | 476 | +23.3 | 348 | 557 | +60.1 |
| 2,500 or more . . | 372 | 403 | +8.3 | 369 | 344 | −6.8 | 358 | 423 | +18.2 |

Source: U.S. Bureau of the Census: 1948, 1954, and 1958 *Census of Business*, Vol. II (Vol. III in 1948), Retail Trade, Area Statistics, Part 2, Nebraska Table 102 (Table 103 in 1948).

* Comparisons between any two years were made only for those towns for which data were available in both years. Thus data for 1948 in column 1 do not agree with data for 1948 in column 7. The omissions were not numerous for total retail sales or for the "lumber, etc.," but there were many omissions in "other retail, etc.," which make the comparisons for that group less reliable.

includes feed dealers—so these two categories can be used as rough indicators of farm input sales. As Table 85 shows, sales of these two kinds of stores rose much more rapidly in the smaller towns than in the larger ones. For the "lumber, etc." group, this was accomplished by a sharp rise in average sales per store, since the number of stores was decreasing more rapidly in the smaller than in the larger towns, while small-town sales were increasing faster. In the "other" group, the number of stores, as well as sales, were increasing faster in the smaller towns.

It seems, then, that the smaller towns are not so much dying as changing their role. They are becoming more specialized as agricultural supply centers and therefore less likely to have balanced retail business structures. The one exception to these conclusions is the very smallest towns, those with fewer than 500 people. Although the Census of Business does not provide any detailed data for towns of this size, we were able to make some rough estimates of the degree to which their sales were changing by making some simplifying assumptions. We found that, for these very small towns, total retail sales were increasing at a slower rate than those of any other size of town, and that both number of stores and sales of the two farm input categories were decreasing—even in those instances where they were increasing for towns of all other sizes. These smallest towns seem to be dying. It is quite possible, and even likely, that some of the towns in the 500–2,500 population class are also moribund, but the group as a whole is not.

This does not imply that these larger small towns are economically viable in the same sense that the bigger places are. They are becoming more exclusively farm-supply centers and therefore are losing some of their consumer-supply functions to the larger places. But all towns are becoming more specialized and interdependent, and rural consumers no longer identify completely with one nearby center but tend to go to different ones for different needs.

The traveler crossing the Northern Plains by car might pass through, in his day's drive, forty or fifty towns. These would range from a "wide place in the road" to a modern city. The former would have a business district, consisting of two or three stores, a gas station, and a grain elevator, surrounded by a few dwellings. Everywhere across the region, the feedlot, the loading chute, the farm machinery lot, and the grain elevator bespeak the predominance of the agricultural economy.

If the traveler should stop in the smaller village, he could not be sure of finding any given type of store or service. The highest odds would be in favor of a feedstore; he would have only a 50–50 chance of finding a general store, a grocery, a gas station, or a cafe. In a town of 500–1,000 people he could count on finding all of these, as well as a drugstore, and, very probably, a hotel or motel.[2] To find at least one clothing or household equipment store, he would have to look in towns of 1,000 or more people.

Of course, this merely reflects the fact that many types of businesses cannot be operated efficiently with the patronage offered in the smallest towns. They require a higher "threshold" of population before they can even begin to be profitable. Thus the number of business establishments and their variety generally tend to increase with the size of the town. Yet this relationship is not linear. The smallest towns in Nebraska—say, all population classes below 2,500—have many more business

---

[2] Edgar Z. Palmer and C. H. Lee, *Estimating the Number of Business Establishments in Nebraska*, Business Research Bulletin No. 68, University of Nebraska (1963), pp. 30–36.

establishments related to their trading-area population than the general average for the state. On the other hand, the largest cities—those with 16,000 or more people—have far fewer businesses relative to their trading-area populations.

This does not mean that the smallest towns offer more service, however, nor that they do more business. Their establishments tend to be small, so that three or four of them together still wouldn't offer the variety available in one larger store in a big city. This is particularly true of retail stores whose number per 10,000 population declines from 215 in the smallest Nebraska towns to well under 100 in Lincoln and Omaha.[3] Yet no one would deny that the latter cities provide far more quality, variety, and services than the former.

Table 86 shows the distribution of Nebraska's people and business establishments by broad classes. Almost two-thirds of the state's places have fewer than 500 people; and 209 such places, or more than three-fifths of them, have fewer than 250—with

TABLE 86. DISTRIBUTION OF PLACES, POPULATION, AND BUSINESS ESTABLISHMENTS, BY SIZE OF PLACE, NEBRASKA, 1960–61

| Size of Place | Number of Places, 1960 | Total Population, 1960 | Average Population per Place, 1960 | Total Number Establish- ments, 1961 | Average No. of Business Establish- ments per Place, 1961 |
|---|---|---|---|---|---|
| Total . . . . . . . . | 538 | 972,687 | 1,808.0 | 46,313 | 86.1 |
| Under 500 . . . . . . | 338 | 73,742 | 218.2 | 5,479 | 16.2 |
| 500–2,499 . . . . . . | 157 | 165,350 | 1,053.2 | 11,641 | 74.1 |
| 2,500–16,000 . . . . . | 37 | 219,440 | 5,930.8 | 12,171 | 328.9 |
| 16,000 or more . . . . | 6 | 514,155 | 85,692.5 | 17,022 | 2,837.0 |

Source: Columns 1–2: U.S. Bureau of the Census, *U.S. Census of Population, 1960*, Nebraska, Number of Inhabitants, PC(1), 29A (1960); column 4: E. Z. Palmer and C. H. Lee, *Estimating the Number of Business Establishments in Nebraska*, Business Research Bulletin No. 68, University of Nebraska (1963), pp. 30–36, and tables 2 and 3, pp. 27–29 (since these tables do not use the same class divisions as this one, one class had to be assigned to another on the basis of an estimate); columns 3 and 5 derived from columns 1, 2, and 4.

an average of only 11 business establishments. Clearly, these are essentially neighborhood centers, patronized chiefly for convenience goods. The true community center would be the 157 places with 500–2,500 people and an average of 74 businesses. The average county would have one, or perhaps two, of these centers, typified by the county seat towns. The 43 urban places, with more than 2,500 people, tend to serve as central shopping points for surrounding rural and smalltown communities. Their patronage extends over two or three counties, and the six very largest urban places embrace a trade area of a dozen or more counties. This Nebraska pattern is characteristic of the Northern Plains, as other studies have verified.

## WHERE DO FARMERS TRADE?

The attachment of rural people in the Northern Plains to a number of different centers was borne out by the Sherman County sample families, whose association patterns are shown in Table 87 and Figures 53–60. Other studies have shown that

[3] *Ibid.*, p. 30.

TABLE 87.   PERCENTAGE DISTRIBUTION OF SPECIFIED PURCHASES OF SAMPLE FAMILIES BY SIZE OF TOWN
WHERE PURCHASED, SHERMAN CO., NEBRASKA, 1956

| Size of Town | Groceries | Clothing | Feed | Machinery | Recreation |
|---|---|---|---|---|---|
| Total . . . . . . . | 100% | 100% | 100% | 100% | 100% |
| Under 1,000 . . . . | 26 | 7 | 10 | 24 | 20 |
| 1,000–5,000 . . . . | 74 | 57 | 90 | 70 | 80 |
| 5,000 or more . . . | 0 | 36 | 0 | 6 | 0 |

Source: Sherman County survey data, 1956.

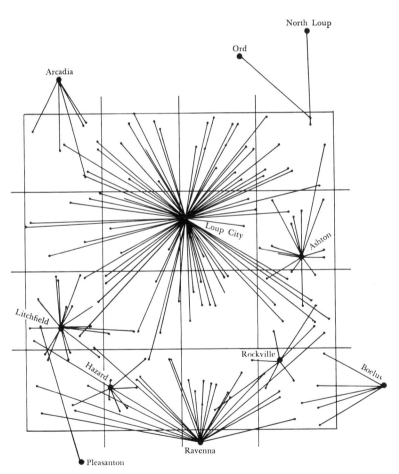

Source: Nebr. Agr. Exp. Sta. data.

FIG. 53.   TOWN VISITED MOST BY SAMPLE FARM FAMILIES, SHERMAN COUNTY,
NEBRASKA, 1957

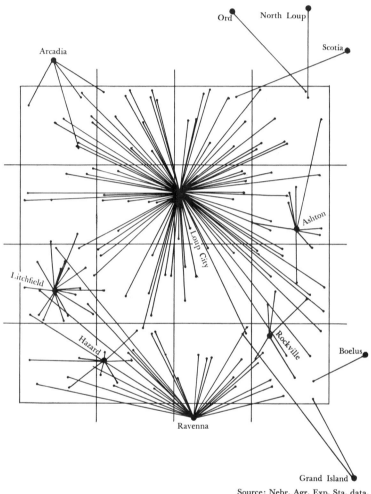

FIG. 54. PRINCIPAL TOWN AT WHICH GROCERIES WERE PURCHASED BY
FARM FAMILIES, SHERMAN COUNTY, NEBRASKA, 1957

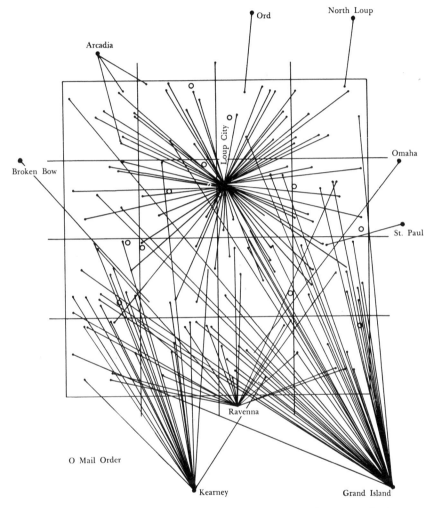

Source: Nebr. Agr. Exp. Sta. data.

FIG. 55.  PRINCIPAL TOWNS AT WHICH FARMERS PURCHASED GOOD CLOTHES,
SHERMAN COUNTY, NEBRASKA, 1957

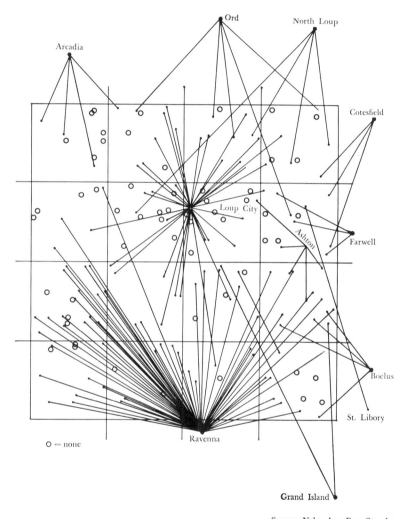

Arcadia

Ord

North Loup

Cotesfield

Loup City

Ashton

Farwell

Boelus

St. Libory

O = none

Ravenna

Grand Island

Source: Nebr. Agr. Exp. Sta. data.

Fig. 56. Principal Grain–Marketing Towns for Farm Families in Sherman County, Nebraska, 1957

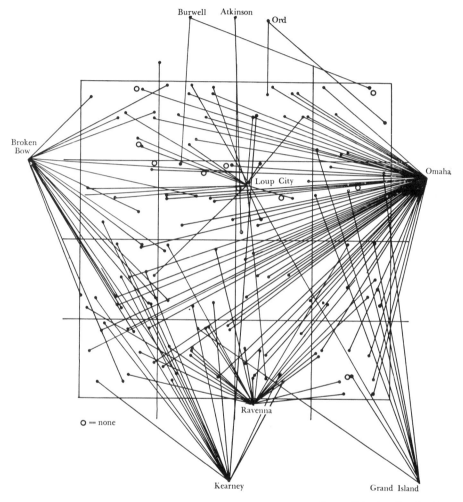

Burwell   Atkinson   Ord

Broken
Bow

Omaha

Loup City

O = none

Ravenna

Kearney                    Grand Island

Source: Nebr. Agr. Exp. Sta. data.

Fig. 57.   Principal Towns at which Farmers Marketed Beef Cattle, Sherman
County, Nebraska, 1957

257

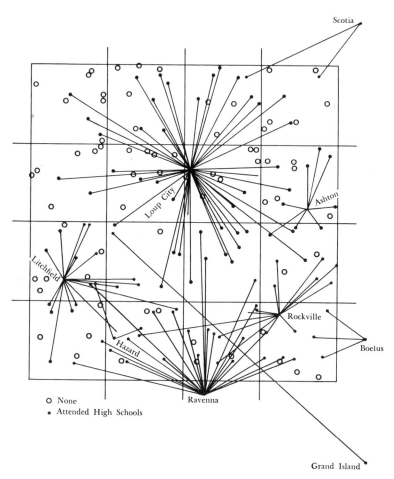

Source: Nebr. Agr. Exp. Sta. data.

FIG. 58.  HIGH SCHOOLS ATTENDED BY CHILDREN IN SAMPLE FARM FAMILIES,
SHERMAN COUNTY, NEBRASKA, 1957

Nebraska farmers tend to buy convenience goods in nearby towns and villages but go to the larger centers for shopping goods. For example, 14 per cent of the purchased food is obtained in cities of 5,000 or more people, while 43 per cent is bought in villages of less than 1,000. On the other hand, 55 percent of the clothing is purchased in cities with populations of 5,000 or more, and only 9 per cent is obtained in places of less than 1,000 population. Farm families generally seem to depend most on the small local center for food, fuel, building materials, feed, and fertilizer. They depend more on the larger cities for clothing, furniture, and appliances.

With improved highways for modern cars and trucks, these small rural towns may be assuming a role comparable to the suburban service areas of the modern large city. People served by these villages may increasingly show a suburban relationship to the farm city. The rural urban areas here visualized—a farm city in a constellation of associated centers—is not identical to the metropolitan city with its suburbs, but it may be its rural counterpart. Most of the modern services demanded can best be supported by the broader resource base. On the other hand, many of the rural towns of 500–2,500 population have an important part to play as community centers, especially in a sparsely settled region.

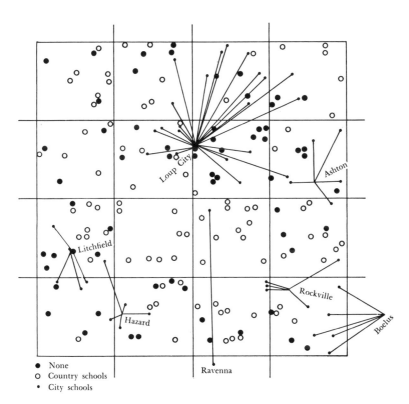

Source: Nebr. Agr. Exp. Sta. data.

FIG. 59.  LOCATION OF ELEMENTARY SCHOOLS ATTENDED BY CHILDREN IN SAMPLE FARM FAMILIES, SHERMAN COUNTY, NEBRASKA, 1957

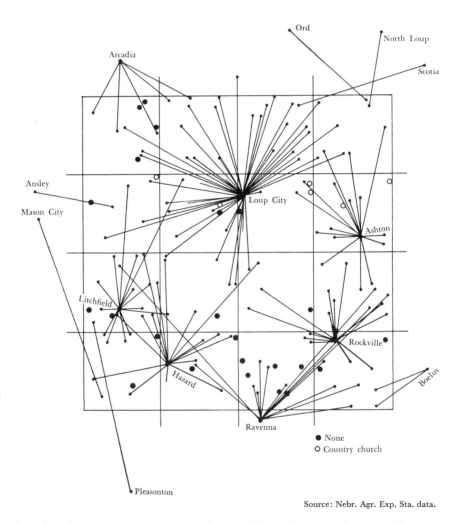

Ord

North Loup

Arcadia

Scotia

Ansley

Mason City

Loup City

Ashton

Litchfield

Rockville

Hazard

Boelus

Ravenna

● None
○ Country church

Pleasonton

Source: Nebr. Agr. Exp. Sta. data.

FIG. 60. CHURCHES ATTENDED BY SAMPLE FARM FAMILIES, SHERMAN COUNTY, NEBRASKA, 1957

If this notion—that a farm city with its satellite centers and surrounding rural area represents a large metropolis spatially extended into the countryside—has any validity, it would follow that social and economic planning should take this into account. Especially in such work as rural-area development, the units frequently used at the present time—a small town, a county, or even two or three counties—are often too small.

What can we say about area economies? Further consideration of this question will be deferred until Chapter 21.

# Part III

## FEASIBLE ADJUSTMENTS IN THE TRANSITION AREA

# CHAPTER 16

# Philosophy, Framework, and Criteria—A Near and a Far Look

J. Lewis Fowell has compressed the 50,000 years of mankind's recorded history into 50 years, and on this basis has developed the following chronology: (1) Ten years ago man left his cave for some other kind of dwelling; (2) Five years ago writing was invented; (3) Two years ago Christianity appeared; (4) Fifteen months ago Gutenberg developed the printing press; (5) Ten days ago electricity was discovered; (6) Yesterday morning the airplane was invented; (7) Last night, radio; (8) This morning, television; (9) The jet airplane was invented less than a minute ago.[1]

In the two preceding sections of this book we explored the social and economic development of the Northern Plains and its eastern transition area. Early in the region's history we found men using the gifts of nature: buffalo, deer, grass, furs. Social organization, and life itself, was elemental. We traced the course of settlement and the development of communities. New technologies were used to subdue or exploit nature, bringing new problems in their wake.

Then came trial and adversity. Men—or, more specifically, their institutions— were tried and found wanting. Unfriendly weather pushed settlement eastward, and pioneers stubbornly inched it westward again. The frontier advanced and retreated like a battleline of infantry. More recent economic upheavals, such as those of the 1920's and 1930's, led to further great adjustments, though this time they did not pass unnoticed on the national scene. The cumulative result has been an economic reorganization, illustrated by the extensification of farming, but the social reorganization of Plains institutions has lagged far behind.

Within the framework of these general trends we have noted how the transition area has adapted, or failed to adapt, to its changing conditions. And the area's problems have been many and varied: low farm prices, dry weather, tenure arrangements, taxes, land prices. It is easy to become swamped in such a sea of troubles, each of which demands solution. In a sense, we are always trying to devise solutions to yesterday's problems, or, at best, to apparent immediate ones. The Plains doesn't provide much time for broad contemplation; since the first settler directed his breaking plow into its sod, it has confronted its people with a series of emergencies.

---

[1] Bernard Karsh, "White-Collar Labor," *The Nation*, 188, No. 5 (January 31, 1959), 93–94.

We must not lose sight of the forest of the future for the trees of the present. As compelling as current problems are, let us turn from them to a broader vista, the perspective of the future in the Northern Plains.

The face of nature may be forever the same but human institutions are not. Man cannot fight the Plains environment and win; rather, he must fit himself and his society to it. There is no reason why the transition area, and the Northern Plains in general, cannot be just as economically viable and socially satisfying as any other part of the country. The fundamental questions concern the balance between resources and people, the institutional arrangements that tie them together, and the possibilities afforded by technology to give Plains people greater control over their resources.

### IMPLICATIONS OF TODAY'S SOCIETY

In this excursion into the future we must recognize the realities of the society in which we live. Ours is a relatively free society, where a large measure of decision-making rests with individuals. We are apt to be inconsistent in the use of the term, like the politician who lauds free enterprise and denounces government intervention at the Fourth of July celebration, but who plumps with equal vigor for a new federal reclamation project for his district in the next session of Congress. Or, in another context, we frequently view trends—whether of population growth, land prices, or the supply of hogs—as impersonal, inevitable facts of nature rather than as phenomena that result from decisions made by people, individually or collectively.

There is a difference between a relatively free society and an institutional vacuum. Most of the far-reaching changes that have occurred in the Plains have been influenced by the social environment. And this environment itself is subject to gradual change over time. These developments sometimes require some restriction on individual freedom of action, but this does not mean that civilization, as we know it, will perish. Our relatively free society will survive though some of its features may be altered. Certainly the changes facing the Plains during the next few decades will occur because of planning and deliberate action taken by groups of people, whether corporate, community, or governmental.

The Northern Plains inevitably will be tied more closely together as a unit, and more tightly integrated into the general economy, as time goes on. The stockman and the wheat farmer have become "urbanized," thanks to modern communications. The state capital is no farther from its citizens in terms of travel time than the county seat of sixty years ago. What goes on in the state legislature, in the nation's capital, and even in the United Nations becomes known to the farmer in central South Dakota in infinitely less time than the actions of the county board of that earlier era —or even of today's, for that matter.

People's knowledge, aspirations, and values today are much more uniform, and more subject to the actions of the national community, than they used to be. Also, because of communications, they expect change faster, and are more impatient of delays. They demand public action when threatened with emergencies, and they travel to Washington to get it. They do not tolerate adversity as long as they used to; witness the population movements during the drought of the fifties. The romanticized self-reliance and independence of the frontier is gone, and Plains people are ever more a part of the national economy and dependent on its fortunes. Yet there is still room for ingenuity, and the last section of this book is primarily an appeal to Plains people to be inventive and ingenious.

## MEASURING STICKS FOR ADJUSTMENT

Criteria for measuring economic development were suggested in Chapter 8. We noted that, for an area to be economically viable in the long run, the earnings of the major resource categories—land, labor, and capital—must at least equal those they might earn elsewhere in the economy. Their contributions to the national economic product should be as large as they would be if these resources were used somewhere else. If additional quantities of a resource, such as capital, are to be shifted to the Plains area from some other part of the economy, their economic contribution must be higher when they are used in the Plains.

Choices can still be made within this framework. Farming can be intensive or extensive; that is, varying amounts of labor and capital may be combined with land. If earnings of capital are low, a shift toward more extensive farming is warranted. This would entail an increase in size of farm, which ordinarily implies the use of less labor with a given amount of land. The net income to the resources used by a farmer thus is a result of the way he combines them in farming and in the size of his operation —that is, the total amount of resources used. If the amount and combination of resources are efficient, income will be maximized. Its level will, of course, be influenced by input costs and output sales price.

The level-of-income criterion is really an outgrowth of the efficiency norm outlined above, but it has some distinctive aspects. We recognize standards for levels of income; most people have a notion of a "fair day's pay for a fair day's work." This usually amounts to requiring income for an "adequate" level of living—as well as income to cover depreciation (replacement of physical items used in production) and income for capital accumulation or saving—as necessary components of a minimum income.

Stability is a second income criterion against which to measure the effectiveness of adjustments. Everything else being equal, people usually prefer stable to unstable incomes, although they will trade some stability for a chance to make occasional large gains. Individual farmers can take measures to stabilize their own incomes by using reserves, by certain kinds of diversification, or by selecting enterprises with more stable yields or prices. Society can reduce income variability by price policy, storage programs, or tax policy. As time goes on, Plains people will probably be less tolerant of extremely variable incomes, partly because income stability has become traditional in our culture, and partly because of their increased cash commitments both in production and consumption.

The economic criteria we have suggested hold for farm and nonfarm people alike, but they are usually taken to apply to private activities rather than public or governmental ones. Yet efficient organization should characterize public activities as well. For example, we expect local government to provide roads, schools, police protection, etc., in quantities to meet our minimum needs or standards, and to do this efficiently. Similar considerations attach to power, communications, and other utilities.

A local government can be effective or ineffective in the extent to which it gives us services we want; and it can be efficient or inefficient in terms of the unit costs of these services. People typically have been surprisingly "tolerant" about the ineffectiveness and especially the inefficiency of local services, but they have turned, instead, to state and even more to federal agencies, while waxing increasingly critical of the costs of these services. In the future, people probably will expect more, rather than less service from their local and state governments, and they will grow more concerned with their efficiency.

In a sense, this will be forced by the decreasing beneficence of the federal government toward regional areas like the Plains—in view of its commitments to national and international problems, such as defense, social security, minimum wages, and foreign aid. We probably can expect fewer massive federal programs of a distinctively Plains nature in the future since Plains agriculture will bulk less large in the country's economy as our nonfarm population continues to grow and to become more concentrated in urban areas. Plains people, consequently, will be thrown more on their own in solving problems of a strictly regional nature. If this is true, one can expect them to seek the streamlining of their government and community organizations to provide them with the new things they will want and to improve the quality of present services: employment, education, medicine, roads, power, recreation, religion, and the arts.

Kraenzel has outlined some additional "keys for survival" for the Plains. He suggests that the institutional forms imported from the humid region must acquire one or more of these three traits—*reserves*, *flexibility*, and *mobility*—if they are to function effectively in the region.[2] These are useful operating principles—to be applied in connection with measuring sticks—for the long-run viability of the Plains transition area.

## SOME DISCERNIBLE SHAPES

What are some of these shapes to be dimly seen down the corridors of the future in the Plains transition area? We shall note them here briefly, and elaborate on them in the sections to follow.

A simple continuation of past trends would point to transition-area farms larger and more extensively operated by 1980 than they are today. For example, we would project an average size of 700 acres in central Nebraska by 1980, as compared with 500 acres in 1959. These farms will devote fewer acres to grain and more to grass than they do now. Much less corn will be raised, except where land is irrigated. Wheat will be produced for cash sale and for feed, but it will be partially replaced by hybrid sorghum. Some of the farms will become ranches, for all practical purposes, specializing in the production of feeder cattle. Specialized feedlot operations will also be seen. These shifts will be encouraged by the federal programs of the 1960's, which involve expanded acreages in conservation reserve or, more likely, some program that permits grass but not grain production on less productive, more erodible land.

With an increase in size of farm, the number of farms will be reduced by 22 percent, compared with 1959, or 52 percent compared with 1930. Opportunities for youths to

[2] C. F. Kraenzel, *Great Plains in Transition* (Norman: University of Oklahoma Press, 1955), p. 324.

enter farming will have shrunk accordingly. In fact, no more than a third of the boys attaining adulthood every year will find jobs in farming, but the proportion of college graduates who farm will be higher.

With an increase in size of farm, the capital used per man in farming will also rise. Continually developing new farm technologies will enable a man to cover more ground. These technologies also mean more capital per man as power and machinery continue to replace labor. Increased capital requirements will intensify the problems of getting started in farming and of financing farm businesses.

Steeper financial requirements will lead to a greater reliance by agriculture on borrowed capital; and we are likely to see more financial planning between borrowers and their credit agencies, whether commercial bank, cooperative agency, or federal agency. The FHA has shown the way here. Credit agencies will have to employ farm-management specialists who can understand the intricacies of their clients' businesses and can tailor credit to their needs on a continuing, long-run basis. They will be better able to do this, of course, because they will be dealing with fewer and larger farms.

New tenure arrangements, and variations in old ones, will be introduced. The problems of a young farmer getting established in farming with insufficient capital will give them their impetus. Without such innovations, the time is imminent when the only young men who can start in farming as owner-operators will be those with very substantial family backing. Ways could be devised to make the process of establishment in farming by those with limited capital more orderly and systematic.

Obviously, there will not be farms available for all the farm boys raised in a community; on the other hand, it would seem to be in the community interest for some boys with limited capital to get a toehold in farming. Perhaps the solution lies in cooperative activity between credit agencies who are willing to place their chips on a limited number of otherwise qualified boys. Or new tenure forms may appear; farming companies may employ qualified men on a wage-plus-share-of-the-earnings basis on each of a chain of farms.

Such companies may introduce more risk capital and management into farming. The increasing competition among landlords for tenants could also lead to a similar wage-plus system with little or no capital investment necessary on the tenant's part. We shall also see more family corporations that will facilitate the orderly transfer of farm businesses from one generation to the next. These corporations may hire employees as laborers or manager-operators, and provide another means of introducing risk capital into agriculture.

Accompanying the increase in farm size will be a proportionate reduction in the rural population. This will have important effects on the community. Gross farm income in a given area, such as a county, will decrease with more extensive farming. Possible exceptions may be a few localities where large-scale, specialized feedlots or other input-increasing activities have been established. Lower gross income will have its greatest impact on the merchants who supply the items used in farm production —gas, seed, fertilizer, and sprays—since extensification will mean less resources used per acre. Eventually, fewer of these merchants will be needed.

On the other hand, net income to agriculture is more conjectural; it may increase, decrease, or remain the same. Suppliers of consumer goods and services in the area will also be affected in mixed fashion. Consumption of food and other staple items will decrease. On the other hand, the consumption of luxury items, such as dress clothing, automobiles, and recreation, may increase.

The nonfarm population will also decline, but probably at a lower rate than the farm population. Some small towns, now struggling for existence, will disappear; yet some of the larger towns will grow. They will absorb certain economic activities given up by small towns as farmers shift their emotional orientation and their trade to these larger "farm cities."

Farmers will be traveling farther, on better roads, for shopping, recreation, religion, and other services. Some small towns will in effect be rural suburbs of these farm cities, related to them as suburban shopping centers are to metropolitan areas. Increasing numbers of farmers will find part-time work in these farm cities, although the possibilities in the Plains transition area will be much more limited than in other regions where there are large cities.

Rural housing will be improved substantially, perhaps with federal assistance. Many farmsteads will be moved to all-weather roads, which then will touch nearly all of the enlarged farms. Some farmers will relocate completely away from their land, in nearby towns.

A marked contraction and consolidation is in store for rural services: roads, schools, telephone, and power. Surely there will be fewer roads, but all will be surfaced. Telephone service should be universal in sparsely populated areas. The level of education in the consolidated schools will improve, partly through the use of traveling teachers. Vocational education of all kinds will be expanded, and its agricultural branch will be reoriented toward a broad complex of agricultural industries —in place of its former emphasis on training for farming alone.

A greatly increased demand is anticipated for all forms of recreation: public golf courses, tennis courts, parks, picnic areas, and hunting, fishing, and boating facilities. People will lose patience with inadequate medical and hospital facilities, and will engage in more planning and action to consolidate redundant services and expand needed ones.

Most surprising of all will be the pressure toward consolidation of county governments. Perhaps the day will come when the Northern Plains states will get along with one-fourth as many county governments as they now have, with a resulting increase in efficiency and effectiveness. Similarly, the consolidation of churches will continue; the independent country church of less than two hundred members will be an anachronism by 1980. In the areas of sparsest population, smaller church groups can still exist as satellites of enlarged rural churches.

Other developments will take place with the support of the state and national community. Federal crop insurance may well be universal on farms; in fact, participation may be a prerequisite for assistance from other federal programs. Federally subsidized hospital care for the aged is now in effect, and a medical care program is on the way. This will particularly benefit small communities with a heavy concentration of older people. Income tax laws may be changed so as to be better adapted to the variabilities of Plains farming. The Federal Employment Service will become a much more active force in the rural community, offering reemployment assistance to farm people.

These are some of the future prospects for the Northern Plains and its eastern transition area after the 1960's. Will they materialize? Only the future holds the answer. If many of these predictions come to pass it will be because rural communities recognize the possibilities, analyze their situations, consider the alternatives, and then decide to capitalize on the reasonable alternatives they face. Again, our underlying philosophy bears repeating: There is no fundamental reason why the Northern Plains transition area cannot be as efficient, prosperous, healthy, and satisfying a place to work and live as other areas. It is a question of man, and his resources, and how they are organized. The next chapters will unfold some additional thinking on these things.

# CHAPTER 17

# Farms of the Future
# in the Transition Area

In fifteen, twenty-five, or thirty-five years, what will the farms in the Northern Plains transition area be like? Farm technology undoubtedly will continue to improve. We can expect higher yields of corn, sorghum, and small grain. Larger, faster, and more efficient machinery will be available; and with it farmers will apply better tillage practices and will practice soil and water conservation more effectively. They will use more fertilizer and will time its application after consulting long-range weather forecasts. In the livestock enterprise, farmers will use improved rations; feed additives will increase the speed and efficiency of gains. Livestock production will be more efficient because of better breeding, and new methods and new equipment will be devised for their feeding and care. These technologies will allow a given number of men to care for a larger number of animals.

The provision of money capital should also continue to improve. Farms are financed on a much more specialized, adequate, and stable basis today than in the hectic days of the 1920's or the 1930's. The commercial banks have learned how to lend short-term money to farmers. The Production Credit and the National Land Bank associations have shown their staying power through the latest crises during the drought of the 1950's. The Farmers Home Administration has focused its lending program more and more on beginning farmers who do not have enough family capital. We can expect this agency to continue developing this role. Insurance companies, also, are showing renewed interest in the farm-loan field.

The field of farm credit will be increasingly characterized by specialization and larger long-term loans. In addition to the cooperative and federal agencies, banks will specialize by organizing specific departments to handle farm loans; they will employ people with specialized training in agriculture and business. Credit programs will be tailored to the total needs of going farm businesses—instead of to the security offered or to the farmer's friendship with the local banker. There will be less distinction between short-term and intermediate credit, and a greater use of lines of credit for a year's operation, designed in advance for each successive year—and perhaps never being paid off in the absolute sense. Long-term loans for the purchase of land will be of much greater duration, and loan limits will increase in relation to security offered.

Competition for land will slacken as size of farm increases and as the number of young people competing for farm land declines. It is easier for young people to leave farming today than in the past because of their better training, their greater knowledge of off-farm opportunities, and their relative sophistication and mobility. As the pressure for farmland eases, we can expect the price of land to stabilize, perhaps increasing no more rapidly than the rate of inflation. It may even soften in real terms, that is, in constant dollars, resulting in somewhat smaller claims by land on net farm income.

With the continued out-migration of farm people, wage rates will increase and it will be more difficult to hire farm labor.

Government programs are likely to affect farm-management decisions for a long time to come. Those related to price support and production control will be voluntary. They will be a variation of the conservation reserve or feed grain program. These programs will inevitably encourage further seeding of the marginal lands of the transition area to grass. They will thus complement the economic incentives toward more extensive farming and will provide an additional incentive to increase farm size.

## FUTURE TRENDS IN FARM SIZE

No topic, with the possible exception of price policy, arouses more thought and discussion among farm people than farm size. They have been asking themselves for decades whether average farm size has not reached a plateau and is not now likely to stabilize. However, size of farm has increased steadily year by year. What will be its future course in the transition area?

One way to make a guess is simply to project past trends. This has been done in Figure 61, where average size of farm is plotted by five-year intervals for the period 1930 to 1959 for the five-county central-Nebraska transition area. Note how steady the rate of increase has been; it is practically a straight line trend. Average size of farm in this area rose from around 320 acres in 1930 to about 520 acres in 1959, an average increase of about 8 acres per year. A simple projection of the trend line, as shown in Figure 61, suggests that by 1980 the average farm will consist of 700 acres, and by 2000 of about 860 acres.

Another way to reach an estimate of future farm size is to study the long-run trend in number of farms. Obviously, since the supply of arable land is relatively fixed, average farm size is a function of the number of farms. As Figure 62 shows, between 1930 and 1959 the number of farms in the five-county area dropped by more than 3,500, or 38 percent; in other words 120 farms were eliminated annually. Again by simple projection, we might estimate that by 1980 there will be only 4,430 farms in the area, compared with about 5,700 in 1959; by 2000 there will be 3,500 farms.

Of course, projections are not predictions; they are simply one way of guessing. As another approach, we might try to estimate how many farms there would be in the transition area if some particular income criterion were met. We can do this by using the economic classes of farms defined in the 1959 Census of Agriculture for these five counties.

In Chapter 11 we suggested that a farm family needs a minimum of $3,500 annually for family living. In the long run, of course, it also has to save for

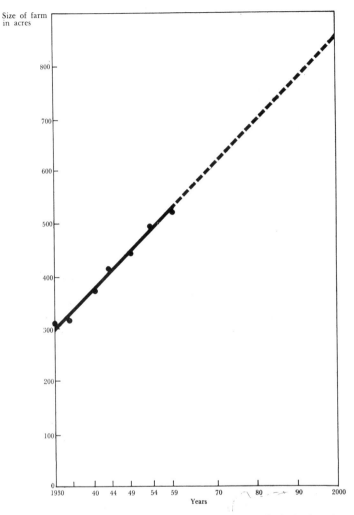

Source: U.S. Census data; projection by the authors.

FIG. 61. AVERAGE SIZE OF FARM IN THE CENTRAL NEBRASKA TRAN-
SITION AREA, BY CENSUS YEARS, WITH PROJECTION TO 2000

replacement of household goods and machinery, for insurance, for principal payments on the farm, and for education of the children. We might estimate its required
savings at $1,500 per year. Thus $5,000 per year might be considered a long-run
minimum net income level.

The economic classification of farms in the agricultural census is in terms of gross
income. Conservatively, at least two-thirds of this goes for expenses, leaving one-third
as net farm income. On this basis it would take about $15,000 of gross income to
yield the $5,000 minimum income level. Only 1,100 farms in the Nebraska transition
area met the criterion of $15,000 gross income level in 1959; the remaining 4,600
farms had lower incomes. It is clear that a "size of farm problem" still remains in

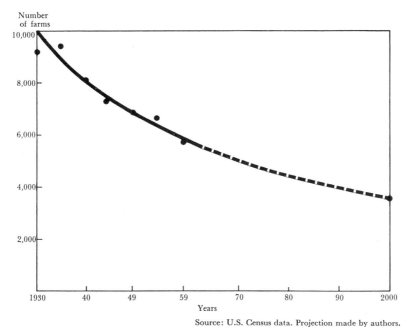

Source: U.S. Census data. Projection made by authors.

FIG. 62. NUMBER OF FARMS IN CENTRAL NEBRASKA TRANSITION AREA, BY
CENSUS YEARS, WITH PROJECTION TO 2000

this area, but it pertains to small rather than to large farms. This problem is enhanced during drought periods, when income levels decline.

How many farms would we have in the five-county area if all of them were to reach the $15,000 gross income minimum? If we divide the $56 million of 1959 gross farm income in the area by $15,000, we obtain about 3,700 farms of equal size that could theoretically meet this income criterion. But this is unrealistic; we know the larger farms are not going to decrease in size simply to accommodate us. We could get a better estimate by simply increasing the size of the farms now earning less than $15,000 gross income until they attain the $15,000 level, letting the larger farms remain as they are.

In doing this, we might just as well leave the noncommercial farms, of which there were 565 in 1959, as they are. These noncommercial farms are either part-time farms, operated by people who are working off the farm for a living, or part-time retirement farms that are operated by retiring farmers. The average gross income on these noncommercial farms is very low, perhaps $1,000 to $1,100 per year, thus they do not account for much of the gross income accruing to the farmers of the area. There are also five "abnormal" farms—as classified by the census—in the area, probably operated by institutions. These we can also safely ignore.

Thus, if we let the approximately 1,090 "adequate" farms and the 570 noncommercial and abnormal farms remain, allocating to them their present income, and if we divide the remaining gross income among the number of smaller commercial farms that will yield an average gross income of $15,000, we are left with a total of

2,277 "enlarged" commercial farms. The total number of farms in the area would then be 3,937.

In Figure 62 we reach this number by simple extrapolation of the present trend about 1995. Referring to Figure 61, we can see that the average size of farm in the area would be slightly over 800 acres at that time.

As a matter of fact, on the basis of the census data for 1959, and under the methods of farming used by farmers in the Nebraska transition area in that year, about 800 acres of land were required to produce the minimum gross income of $15,000. The year 1959 was fairly representative of the economic conditions of the fifties.

Thus it is not impractical to look ahead to a time when the size structure of farms in the transition area will be such that minimum income standards will be met on all commercial farms. At that time the number of farms—and consequently the number of farm families—and the rural population will be 30 percent less than it is today. It is possible that the future rate of increase in farm size will be higher than in the past; if so, commercial farms would meet the average income standard before 1990–1995. The past trends do not suggest any acceleration in the rate of farm consolidation, however.

One qualification is necessary in interpreting these data; our analysis was made on the basis of owner-operator farms in the area. It is not realistic, of course, to assume that all farms are going to shift to an owner-operator basis. The more rented farms or part-owner farms assumed for the future, the larger the average size of farm will have to be to meet the minimum income standard for its operator; and the fewer farms there would be.

### Economic Basis for Adjustments in Farm Size

Although prospective changes in farm size seem substantial, based on projections and income criteria, farmers in the area seem quite unaware of the dynamics of farm-size adjustment. They fail to visualize an increase in farm size as a tangible way to raise their income. At any rate, 52 percent of the 145 dry-land farmers surveyed in Sherman County suggested that the desirable size of farm was about 320 acres. Three-fourths of the farmers operating 320-acre farms thought this size was about right. A few felt that less than 300 acres was large enough; and a few more suggested sizes larger than 320 as desirable, with 480-acre and 640-acre sizes most frequently mentioned. Only two respondents out of 145 suggested farms larger than 640 acres.

The actual increase in farm size is occurring as a phenomenon external to the farmers themselves. Increasing size apparently is not an aggressive goal of most farmers; in fact, of those who suggested a desirable size different from what they were operating, almost as many suggested smaller farms as suggested larger ones.[1]

Intensive study was given to the potentials of 320- and 480-acre farms to produce income and support a family under more intensive farming systems than now used. These analyses utilized budgeting procedures, including linear programming. By these analyses we were able to take into account such things as superior soils, superior management, and other special opportunities.

[1] Joseph F. Havelka, "Present and Potential Adequacy of 320-Acre Farms in the Transition Area of Nebraska to Support Minimum Family Living Standards" (M.S. thesis, University of Nebraska, 1960), p. 51.

## The 320-acre Farm on Above-average Soils

A case study was made of a 320-acre farm, representative of farms of that size in the Nebraska transition area except that its soil resources were above average. Located in the northeast part of Buffalo County, this farm had 48 acres of permanent pasture and 267 acres of tilled land. Its principal crops have been corn, wheat, and temporary hay and pasture, with smaller acreages of sorghum, oats, and fallow (Table 88). Its livestock, when surveyed in 1956, included beef cows and fattened calves and steers, with smaller enterprises of milk cows, hens, and hogs. Under long-run projected prices and yields, this farm would have grossed $8,558 in 1965. Its net income, including a charge on capital of about $1,400, would have been $3,630. Thus it would not meet the family income requirement suggested earlier.

The possibility of increasing the volume of business and net income of this farm under various combinations of crop and livestock enterprises was analyzed by budgeting analysis. The results are given in Table 88. At the bottom of the chart, purchased feed and cattle have been subtracted from the gross returns to give a net volume of business, which we have called gross income; this is a measure of the business services being produced by the farm itself. The net income is a measure of the returns to the operator's capital investment, his labor, and that of his family. All these analyses are on an owner-operator basis; if they were being considered as rented farms, about $800 more net income would be necessary to give the landlord a return of 5 percent on his investment; or, to put it the other way, $800 would be deducted from the net income on rented farms in figuring the net income to the tenant.

Under the present cropping system, soil was eroding—particularly on class IV and VI soils. Systems A-1, C-1, A-2, and A-3 would involve the seeding of these soils into native pasture, leaving the farm with almost half its acreage in permanent pasture. Soil erosion would thus be controlled, and class I, II, and III land would be used for crop production, chiefly corn and wheat, with some forage sorghums being included as a source of roughage for the livestock programs in plans C-1, A-2, and A-3. Land classes II and III were assumed to be farmed on the contour, terraced, and stubble-mulched in all alternative plans.

The crop yields, livestock coefficients, and production practices used in all the organizations tested were not the levels currently found in the Nebraska transition area, but were projected to represent what might be expected in the near future— say, during the next ten years. Prices and costs also were projected to what we might expect in the near future, based on anticipated supply-demand conditions in agriculture. We should note that the present organization shown in Table 88 is not that of the actual farm as it was operated at the time of the study, but is based on the crop and livestock combination found at that time, adjusted for changes in practices, yields, prices, and costs in the projection period.

The first four alternative systems represent widely varying livestock organizations. Thus A-1 includes beef cows and hogs, while C-1 is based on hogs and steer calves wintered, grazed, and sold as feeder cattle. A-2 involves a larger hog enterprise than C-1, while A-3 is a specialized deferred feeding system for steers. The amount of feed to be purchased under these alternative plans is little different from the present; on the other hand, the amount of livestock purchased per year would be larger under

TABLE 88. Present and Alternative Farming Systems Budgeted for 320-acre Transition-area Case Farm on Above-average Soils, under Projected Prices and Yields

| | Present | A-1 | C-1 | A-2 | A-3 | C-2 | C-3 | B-1 | B-2 | C-4 |
|---|---|---|---|---|---|---|---|---|---|---|
| **Tilled Acres** | | | | | | | | | | |
| Corn | 90 | 54 | | 72 | 68 | | | 79 | 68 | |
| Fallow | 31 | 54 | 54 | 41 | 41 | 70 | 70 | 91 | 68 | 70 |
| Winter wheat | 47 | 54 | 54 | 41 | 41 | 45 | 45 | 45 | 34 | 45 |
| Winter barley | | | | | | 25 | 25 | 46 | 34 | 25 |
| Oats | 20 | | | | | 5 | | | | |
| Rye | | | | | | 10 | 31 | | | 31 |
| Grain sorghum | | | 36 | | | 84 | 40 | | 34 | 40 |
| Forage sorghum | | | 18 | 8 | 12 | | 30 | 12 | 34 | 30 |
| Tilled hay and pasture | 80 | | | | | 34 | 32 | | | 32 |
| Total tilled acres | 268 | 162 | 162 | 162 | 162 | 273 | 273 | 273 | 273 | 273 |
| Native pasture | 45 | 151 | 151 | 151 | 151 | 35 | 35 | 35 | 35 | 35 |
| Farmstead & waterways | 7 | 7 | 7 | 7 | 7 | 12 | 12 | 12 | 12 | 12 |
| Total acres | 320 | 320 | 320 | 320 | 320 | 320 | 320 | 320 | 320 | 320 |
| **Livestock numbers** | | | | | | | | | | |
| Milk cows | 4 | | 2 | | | 2 | | | | |
| Beef cows | 16 | 14 | | | | | | | | |
| Replacement stock & bull | 4 | 3 | | | | | | | | |
| Hogs | 28 | 49 | 62 | 84 | | 179 | | 56 | | |
| Drylot fattened calves | 17 | | | | | | | | | |
| Steer calves, wintered & grazed | | | 22 | 24 | | | | | | 54 |
| Steer calves, deferred-fed | | | | | | 10 | 35 | | | |
| Yearling steers, deferred-fed | | | | | 38 | | | | | 36 |
| Yearling steers, wintered & fed | | | | | | | | 30 | 59 | |
| Laying hens | 500 | 500 | 225 | | | 225 | 225 | | | |

| | Present | A-1 | C-1 | A-2 | A-3 | C-2 | C-3 | B-1 | B-2 | C-4 |
|---|---|---|---|---|---|---|---|---|---|---|
| | | | | | | DOLLARS | | | | |
| Gross returns | 8,558 | 7,084 | 7,388 | 9,568 | 11,105 | 10,458 | 10,090 | 13,407 | 19,044 | 25,423 |
| *Less:* | | | | | | | | | | |
|   Feed purchased | 734 | 875 | 556 | 650 | 282 | 1,060 | 601 | 687 | 730 | 5,941 |
|   Cattle purchased | 325 | 325 | 2,627 | 2,225 | 3,875 | 2,848 | 3,241 | 4,667 | 8690 | 8,618 |
| Gross income | 7,497 | 5,884 | 4,205 | 6,693 | 6,948 | 6,550 | 6,348 | 8,053 | 10,624 | 10,864 |
| Net income | 3,630 | 2,388 | 1,102 | 3,123 | 3,522 | 2,944 | 2,321 | 4,361 | 5,344 | 5,296 |
| Return to labor & management† | 2,260 | 1,081 | (51) | 1,830 | 2,182 | 1,765 | 1,075 | 3,030 | 3,567 | 3,502 |
| Capital investment | 28,132 | 27,123 | 24,547 | 26,884 | 27,674 | 24,986 | 26,111 | 29,087 | 34,959 | 35,248 |

Sources: Joseph F. Havelka, "Present and Potential Adequacy of 320-acre Farms in the Transition Area of Nebraska to Support Minimum Family Living Standards" (University of Nebraska, M.S. thesis, 1960); and A. Dale Thompson, "Budgeted Incomes on 320-acre Farms in the Transition Area Using Recommended Crop Combinations" (University of Nebraska, M.S. thesis, 1959).

\* The original letter-number designation for systems under which they were programmed were retained for convenience.
† Based on gross income less 4 percent interest charge on land and buildings, and 6 percent on other capital.

plans C–1, A–2, and A–3 than under A–1 and the present plan. The amount of investment required for these organizations would be pretty close to the present sum, ranging between $25,000 and $28,000.

Only in plan A–3 does net income approach that of the present organization. However, a fundamental difference between plan A–3 and the present organization is that under the former the farm would achieve a satisfactory level of soil conservation. Even so, it falls short of our $5,000 net income criterion by $1,500. It would provide a minimum level of living for the farm family, but would not leave any residual income for savings or the payment of principal on loans. We should note that family living derived from the farm, including food raised for home consumption and the rental value of the house, totaling about $1,000 per year, is not included in any of these comparisons. Our $5,000 minimum also excluded this item, so our comparisons are not biased from this standpoint.

In the last five plans—C–2, C–3, B–1, B–3, and C–4—we have included all the class IV land in the cultivated cropping system. This would necessitate the use of 5 acres of grassed waterways, contouring and terraces, and stubble-mulch farming on the class IV land, as well as on class II and III land. The crop combination used on class IV land would, along with the other erosion control practices, reduce soil erosion to an acceptable level, according to Soil Conservation Service technicians.

Even under the more intensive farming in plans C–2, C–3, and B–1, net income levels do not reach the minimum. However, plan B–1, involving a larger investment in livestock annually than the other plans, does show higher gross and net income than any of the other plans tested, including the present organization. Plan B–2 involves much larger amounts of money invested in feeding cattle, almost $9,000 per year. Its gross income exceeds $10,000, and the net income is over $5,000. Plan C–4, which includes larger amounts of feed purchased and about two months of hired labor, shows a similar net income. Both of these plans involve larger amounts of farm capital—$7,000 more than the present organization.

It is apparent that only under very intensive feeding systems, involving above-average management, can erosion-controlling plans achieve net incomes higher than under the present plan without much additional capital. None of them achieves the minimum income of $5,000. Under systems requiring less management, the income levels associated with conservation systems are less than would be achieved under the present organization on this case farm. Substantial amounts of additional capital, used for specialized livestock feeding, would be necessary to achieve minimum income.

Had we deducted $800 from the net income levels shown in Table 88 to convert these comparisons to a rented-farm basis, the 320-acre farm would in no case generate enough income to support a tenant farmer at the minimum income level.

The returns to labor and management shown in Table 88 indicate the earnings of the operator and his family as workers. They were computed by subtracting 4 percent of land investment and 6 percent of other capital from net income. The operator and his family represented about 1.2 man-years of labor.

We should recall again that the 320-acre farm analyzed here had land of above-average productivity. Obviously, similar analyses of farms on average land would have shown inferior incomes. Our general conclusion, suggested earlier, still holds;

namely, that the 320-acre farm in the transition area is too small to generate an adequate income for its operator.

## The 480-acre Farm on Above-average Soils

The possibilities on a 480-acre farm in the Nebraska transition area, on soils of above-average productivity, were analyzed by linear programming techniques. The hypothetical farm was assumed to include 169 acres of class II and III land, 108 acres of class IV land, and about 200 acres of permanent pasture. The results are summarized in Table 89. In both plans shown, cropping would be on the contour, and terraces and grass waterways would be applied as necessary. Stubble-mulch farming would be carried on, and other practices—such as fertilization—would be used up to profitable limits. Again, projected prices and costs were assumed, as well as projected yields and livestock production coefficients.

In plan 1 the owner-operated farm, with 1.3 man-years of family labor available, was limited to home-raised feeds—grain, hay, and pasture—in the production of livestock.

The most profitable crop system in plan 1 included continuous grain on class II and III land, and a long-run alfalfa-grain-sorghum-oats rotation on class IV land. The livestock enterprise was based on feeding steers and heifers. The net income from this organization amounted to almost $8,600. The capital investment in this farm business would include $37,000 in fixed assets and machinery, and about $16,000 in working capital. It was assumed that the operator could borrow as much working capital as he needed. Obviously, this farm would meet the minimum income criterion of $5,000.

TABLE 89.  High-return Farming Systems as Programmed for 480-acre Case Farm on Above-average Soils, Nebraska Transition Area

|  | Plan 1 | Plan 2 |
|---|---|---|
| Tilled Acres | | |
| Land Class II & III . . . . . . . . . . . . . . | 169 grain | 169 grain |
| Land Class IV . . . . . . . . . . . . . . . | 108 Gs-O-AAAA* | 19 sudan pasture |
|  |  | 76 Gs-O-AAAA* |
|  |  | 13 F-W-Gs |
| Acres | | |
| Permanent pasture, roads, & farmstead . . . . . | 203 | 203 |
| Livestock (Head) | | |
| Pasture-fed steers . . . . . . . . . . . . . | 88 | 224 |
| Short-fed heifers . . . . . . . . . . . . . | 25 | 20 |
| Common steers . . . . . . . . . . . . . . . |  | 20 |
| Grain bought (tons) . . . . . . . . . . . . . . | 0 | 208 |
| Hay bought (tons) . . . . . . . . . . . . . | 0 | 223 |
| Net income† . . . . . . . . . . . . . . . . | $8,578 | $13,774 |
| Return to labor & mgmt.‡ . . . . . . . . . . | $6,038 | $9,510 |
| Capital investment. . . . . . . . . . . . . . | $52,000 | $81,400 |

Source: Unpublished data, Department of Agricultural Economics, University of Nebraska.

* Gs = grain sorghum, O = oats, A = alfalfa, F = fallow, W = wheat. Each initial represents one year of the cropsequence.
† After deducting operating expenses, real estate taxes, personal property taxes, and depreciation.
‡ Net income less 4 percent on land investment and 6 percent on all other capital.

In plan 2 we removed the limitation on the buying of hay and feed, and again allowed the farmer to borrow all the working capital he needed. In this case large quantities of feed were purchased and a rather sizable feeding enterprise, based on over 200 head of pasture-fed steers, resulted. The operator would use $44,400 of working capital, excluding machinery; his net income would be $13,774 per year. If he borrowed all working capital at 6 percent, his net income would be over $11,000.

In these plans the, assumption that the operator could borrow all the capital he needed is a crucial one. Without access to ample credit, the operator could not generate the volume of business necessary to produce these net incomes. This assumption enabled us to push the 480-acre farm to its limit in testing its income-producing ability.

What of other crops and livestock on this 480-acre farm? Although reported only briefly, the data in Table 89 result from a very complex analysis. All the different crops grown in the area were available in the linear programming, as well as sixteen different livestock enterprises. Those shown in Table 89 give the highest returns under the assumptions made. Under different conditions of prices, costs, yields, or resource availability, the enterprises chosen by the programming might have been somewhat different.

Our conclusion is that the 480-acre farm with above-average soils meets the minimum income test if it is operated intensively and with above-average management.

*Three Sizes of Farm on Average Soils*

As another check on the income-producing ability of farms in the transition area, linear programming was applied to three hypothetical farms on soils of average productivity. The locale assumed was Sherman County; the farms were 480 acres, 960 acres, and 1,600 acres in size. The results of this analysis are outlined in Table 90.

In this analysis, 1.4 man-years of family labor were assumed available on each farm. Except for small amounts of hired seasonal labor, no other labor was used. No feed was purchased; the farming system was based entirely on the home-raised feed supply. The same proportions of various types of soils were assumed for each size of farm.

As in the previous programming analyses, the crops raised were restricted to combinations which would control soil erosion on all soils. Under this restriction, all land of class IV and VI would be in permanent pasture. All crops that can be grown in the area were available to the programming process; they were assumed to be raised under tillage practices recommended by agronomists. Sixteen different livestock enterprises were also available, all presently used in the area. Projected prices and costs were assumed.

Table 90 indicates that the cropping systems followed on the three farm sizes were similar, with sorghum and wheat being particularly important. The livestock systems involved some type of cattle wintering, pasturing, and feeding in all three cases.

Of the total investments indicated in Table 90, over $14,000 of operating capital would be necessary on the 480-acre farm, in addition to land, buildings, and machinery. Over $20,000 was used on the 960-acre farm, while the operating capital used on the 1,600-acre farm was about $48,000.

Obviously, the data have to be interpreted as reflecting a high degree of managerial

TABLE 90. HIGH-RETURN FARMING SYSTEMS AS PROGRAMMED FOR 480-, 960-, AND 1,600-ACRE FARMS ON AVERAGE SOILS IN THE CENTRAL NEBRASKA TRANSITION AREA, UNDER PROJECTED YIELDS, PRACTICES, COSTS, AND PRICES

| | Size in Acres | | |
|---|---|---|---|
| | 480 | 960 | 1,600 |
| Crops (Acres) | | | |
| Wheat . . . . . . . . . . . . . | 23 | 46 | 76 |
| Fallow . . . . . . . . . . . . . | 51 | 74 | 119 |
| Rye . . . . . . . . . . . . . | 36 | 65 | 95 |
| Corn . . . . . . . . . . . | 0 | 0 | 75 |
| Grain sorghum . . . . . . . | 74 | 104 | 159 |
| Oats . . . . . . . . . . . . . | 0 | 15 | 0 |
| Total Cultivated Crops . . . . | 184 | 304 | 524 |
| Alfalfa . . . . . . . . . . . . | 45 | 155 | 240 |
| Total Tilled Land . . . . . . | 229 | 459 | 764 |
| Permanent pasture, roads & buildings . . . . . . . . . | 251 | 501 | 836 |
| Total acreage . . . . . . | 480 | 960 | 1,600 |
| Livestock (Head) | | | |
| Long-deferred-fed steers . . . . | 34 | 109 | 192 |
| Steers wintered & grazed . . . . | 0 | 0 | 137 |
| Summer-pastured steers . . . . | 27 | 0 | 53 |
| Hogs . . . . . . . . . . . | 61 | 0 | 0 |
| Feed purchased (net) . . . . . . | none | none | none |
| Net income* . . . . . . . . . . | $4,662 | $10,208 | $14,592 |
| Return to operator's labor & mgmt. | $2,198 | $6,062 | $7,785 |
| Investment . . . . . . . . . . . | $51,400 | $88,440 | $165,000 |

Source: Howard E. Hanson, "The Minimum Size of Farm in Sherman County" (University of Nebraska, M.S. thesis, 1963).

* After deducting interest charges of 6 percent on working capital and 4 percent on land and buildings.

skill, careful planning of operations, and the availability of large amounts of working capital from either family or credit sources. We should note that net incomes would be reduced by interest payments on borrowed funds. Interest charges on working capital have been deducted in figuring the returns to operator labor and management, but they are included in the net income shown in the table.

Our general conclusion is that the 480-acre farm on average soils does not meet the minimum long-run income criterion, even when operated with the highest degree of efficiency. It does not fall far short, however. A slightly larger size would have exceeded the $5,000 level. Or, if it were operated more intensively—for example, by hiring a man—it is possible that the minimum requirement could be met. On the other hand, the 960-acre farm exceeds the criterion by a comfortable margin, as does the 1,600-acre farm.

OTHER DEVELOPMENTS IN TRANSITION-AREA FARMING

With increasing farm size and advancing capital requirements, will corporation farming take over, replacing family farms? This is the subject of numerous newspaper editorials and heated discussions among farm people. One variable that throws some light on this question is the amount of labor hired. Assuming that family farms may be defined as those hiring less than 1.5 man-years of labor, there is no evidence to support the hypothesis that other kinds of farms are replacing family farms.

In the Northern Plains, 96 percent of the farms hired less than 1.5 man-years of labor in 1944, and only 4 percent of them hired more than this. In 1954 the proportion of farms hiring less than 1.5 man-years had increased to 98 percent; and this means that the percentage hiring more than 1.5 man-years had been halved in that time. During the same period, the number of farms hiring less than 1.5 man-years had declined by 9.9 percent; however, the number of farms hiring more than that had dropped by 53.9 percent.[2] In the Nebraska transition area, the farms reporting hired labor represented only 5.8 percent of the total number in 1959, a slightly larger percentage than in 1954. On the average, hired labor on all farms amounted to only .07 man-years in 1959, or about one month per farm.

We may very well see some development of corporate arrangements in special cases of large, factory-type enterprises, like cattle feeding and hog feeding, which lend themselves to large-scale operation, professional specialized management, and corporate types of financing. Some farm families will also incorporate to facilitate the transfer of farms from one generation to another. Heirs who have moved to the city can own shares of stock in the farm, leaving the management to the member on the farm.

The feature of limited liability is of course the main advantage of the corporate farm. However, general farms do not lend themselves to incorporation because of the difficulty of standardizing their paper and because of the risks involved. Other disadvantages of incorporation are the required directors' and stockholders' meetings, the costs of incorporating, and the possibility of being "locked" in a small corporation with stock having no ready market. Also, incorporation involves the possibility of double taxation. This disadvantage can be met by qualifying as a small-business corporation and electing to be taxed like a partnership.

Another possibility is an increase in the number of two-man farms. These might operate under a father-son arrangement, or under a partnership agreement between two families, whether related or not. Because of unlimited liability in a partnership, the choice of partners becomes a serious problem. This complication can be avoided if the relationship between the two parties is one of employer-employee. As size of farm continues to grow, the technical requirements in farming will increase in complexity, and the qualifications required by farm employers of full-time hired men will surely increase. They will pay higher wages, perhaps with a share of the net returns. Two-man farms give the workers involved a chance for specialization in farm tasks, which enhances efficiency.

The livestock share lease offers another way for two people to participate in the management, capital investment, and operation of the farm without setting up a formal partnership. This arrangement has distinct advantages to the young man who is beginning to farm. He can accumulate capital faster than if he farmed for himself on a smaller farm as an owner-operator. The livestock share lease is flexible and can

---

[2] Radoje Nikolitch, *Family and Larger than Family Farms*, Agricultural Economics Report No. 4, USDA Farm Economics Division (1962).

accommodate any amount of capital the beginner may have. We may see this arrangement used more frequently in the future.

Buying land under contract has been used by young men who are starting with only small amounts of capital. However, this arrangement carries considerable risk in the transition area, unless the payments are small enough to be regarded as little more than rent. Land contracts, on the other hand, may be increasingly useful for operators who are expanding their acreages from an existing base.

### Reducing Uncertainty in Leases

The transition area, because of greater variability of crop yields, merits special attention in the matter of risk in leasing arrangements. Crop-share leases, of course, involve the direct sharing of yield uncertainty with landlords. However, there are certain disadvantages in crop-share leases because landlords and tenants do not commonly share most operating expenses. These disadvantages are not found in the cash lease, but cash leases involve greatest uncertainty for the tenant. The flexible cash lease, which has not yet been used very much, has the advantage of keeping the respective returns to the landlord and tenant associated directly with their expenses; at the same time, it permits some sharing of yield and price uncertainties. In this arrangement, the cash rental is "flexed" from one year to another by an index of crop yields or prices in the area.

The flexible cash lease should come into wider use in the future as a permanent arrangement under which some operators will be content to specialize in farming per se, rather than in land ownership.

### Farming Strategies

Transition area farmers have always had to adjust their farming to the unexpected —to the vagaries of weather and economic conditions. We can expect them to pay more attention in the future to ways of keeping flexible, to management strategies by which the adverse effects of unexpected events can be avoided or minimized. It has often been said that it takes more management to farm in the Plains. This is true in the sense that the Plains farmer must continually reexamine his management policies and make changes in his resource inputs or farming enterprises, as compared with his counterpart in more stable areas.

### The Importance of Size of Farm

Everything else being equal, the larger the farm, the greater the opportunity to employ stratagems. The amount of resources committed to stratagem, and the seriousness of an error, will depend on the amount of capital surpluses present. In other words, a farm has to be big enough to accumulate capital surpluses before there will be much room for the use of long-chance strategy, for example, feed reserves. Of course other measures, like insurance, are open to anyone.

The stratagems available to Plains farmers, including financial management, financial reserves, feed reserves, and diversification, are discussed in Chapter 20.

### Contract Farming

There is no evidence that contract farming is going to "take over" in the near future. However, certain opportunities will be available to transition-area farmers to enter into production contracts with cooperative or private processing firms as a means of reducing price risk, to get management assistance, or to get credit. The opportunities for contracting may be found particularly in such livestock products as cattle, hogs, or poultry.

*Specialization in Farming*

With an increase in farm size, we can expect to see much more specialization among farmers in the products produced. Some will tend to be cash-crop farmers, utilizing native pastures and other roughage through beef cows. Others will specialize in intensive cattle feeding operations, perhaps buying most of their feed from their neighbors on a contract basis. Some farmers will make a major enterprise of feeder pig production; others will specialize in the raising of market hogs, depending upon their neighbors for both their pigs and much of their feed. Some farmers may specialize in providing custom services, such as tillage, harvesting, and planting.

Specialization makes possible the mastery of the intricate technologies of producing farm products; it cuts overhead costs since buildings and equipment can be used more efficiently. It increases labor efficiency because workers are required to perform fewer jobs more often.

In such specialization we may see a tendency for the development of livestock "factories" near transportation points, and the consequent tendency for the general farm to become a cash-crop operation. These livestock factories will lend themselves to specializing in financing, corporate organization, contract buying of raw materials (cattle and feed), and contract selling of products (finished livestock products). This development is indeed a long way in the future, but who can say that this is not the direction in which agriculture will tend steadily during the next half century?

*Irrigation*

Because of our focus on dry-land farming, we have not discussed the role of irrigation in future transition-area farming. We can expect to see some further development of pump and ditch irrigation, although at a slower rate, with the diminishing of water supplies. The economically desirable irrigation possibilities already have been exploited.

While it does not eliminate variation in crop yields, irrigation yields are higher on the average, and the variability occurs around these higher levels. Thus, irrigation reduces the relative variation in livestock numbers if adjusted to feed supply, or the feed reserves necessary to maintain a basic livestock enterprise. Combination of irrigation and dry-land acreage is desirable from the standpoint of economic stability.

Irrigation also increases the income-producing ability of land per acre, necessitating fewer acres per farm to meet the minimum income criterion, and making possible greater density of population in the farming area. For example, in the Middle Loup area of the central-Nebraska transition area, the 160-acre farm, with 112 acres irrigated, meets the $5,000 net income standard assumed earlier.[3] Of course, an irrigated farm involves much higher capital investment per acre than a dry-land farm. The capital requirements on a 160-acre irrigated farm are quite similar to those of an intensively operated 320-acre dry-land farm or a 480-acre farm meeting the minimum income criterion.

[3] Karl Gertel, J. W. Thomas, T. S. Thorfinnson, and H. W. Ottoson, *Adjusting to Irrigation in the Loup River Area in Nebraska*, Nebraska Agricultural Experiment Station Bulletin 434 (1956).

# CHAPTER 18

# Adjustments in Farm Finance

THE DROUGHT of the fifties aroused some concern, but it did not last long enough to provide a real test of the farm-credit system in the Northern Plains. Though there was some evidence of stress, transition-area farmers generally remained in good financial shape, as compared with the thirties. They expressed little awareness of external capital rationing—of being restricted by credit agencies in their use of borrowed funds. In fact, at a time when their interest in credit should have been highest, in 1955, farmers still knew amazingly little about the various sources of credit available to them. Before they were forced to acquire more knowledge, rain and improved cattle prices eliminated the need.

Yet basic problems of farm finance still exist. They are interwoven with land use and farm size, which are subject to farmers' control, and with price-cost conditions in agriculture as a whole, which individual farmers cannot change. These latter forces are inexorable; there is a limit to which farmers can offset them by their own adjustments.

The basic problems of agricultural supply and demand cannot be solved through farm finance; in fact, the reverse would be closer to the truth. What other industry, for example, is called on to cope with the degree of price fluctuation that farmers face? If this were corrected, one of the bugaboos of farm real estate financing would be eliminated. Greater price stability would not stabilize incomes completely; production variability would still remain to cause income fluctuations. But the impacts of general agricultural policy are external to our main concern here. We can only assume that agriculture's house will be righted in time, and that at least a tolerable economic climate will continue to prevail meanwhile.

A more immediate policy dilemma is posed by the problem of farm finance: How can we supply agriculture with the increasing capital needed in farming without disturbing the out-movement of excess labor resources—labor released by the same technological changes that necessitate the increased capital? We have assumed that this process is automatic, that if we cudgel farmers with sufficient vigor, enough of them, and the right ones, will decide to leave the industry and eventually find their proper niche elsewhere. Should we rely on the "unseen hand" of economic determinants to achieve this result? As we have seen, farmers move out, and in large numbers, but is the process orderly? Are we requiring too large a sacrifice by farmers who are caught in a trap, one jaw of which represents our past mistakes in land policy and the other our technological progress?

The specific capital problems of transition-area agriculture at the moment are related to these general adjustments. Mechanization proceeds; equipment replaces labor in farm operation as new ways are devised to cover land faster with less work. Besides increasing capital outlays, this new equipment entails additional recurring cash commitments for taxes, insurance, and repairs. Outlays for working capital, such as fuel, oil, power, fertilizer, hybrid seed, commercial feeds, and chemical sprays, have replaced noncash items, such as oats for the horses, barnyard manure, and hand labor in weeding corn.

The increased farm size now regarded as essential increases the amount of capital that must be invested in land in establishing a farm. These problems of increased capital needs are particularly crucial for beginning farmers. There is more truth than poetry in the old adage that the easiest way to get a farm is to inherit or marry one. Are these the proper criteria to use in determining who will do our farming? Or should we create other avenues into farming for those who cannot enter through marriage or inheritance, even while recognizing that opportunities in farming are exceeded by the number of would-be entrants? What kind of rationing process should be used?

Another financial problem is bound up with income variability, which results from the interaction of variable prices and yields with the more stable cost commitments. This calls for strategic measures by the individual farmer as he seeks to make financial progress over time—without losing his shirt or his farm through costly mistakes. It also calls for an understanding and flexible attitude by the credit institutions that lend to farmers.

This chapter suggests some measures that might improve the situation in the future. We shall be concerned both with everyday financial problems and with those arising from extraordinary economic conditions which call for special measures.

## FARM FINANCIAL MANAGEMENT

Financial management may be defined as the management of income, savings, and credit. Rules of thumb in these matters often do not apply neatly to farmers, especially those of the transition area. It is not enough to tell a farmer that he ought to save money, have a farm plan, try to run a larger business, or keep better books. Yet these rules frequently represent the limits of the wisdom we have to impart. Unquestionably, more research is needed on the cause-effect relations of different financial practices.[1] We can suggest a few things here as a result of our own study in the Nebraska transition area.

### Allocation of Resources

Our data have indicated the relatively higher productivity of capital invested in additional land compared with other uses. These data foreshadow further pressure

---

[1] Work conducted by the Great Plains regional committee, GP–2, under the title "Farm Organization Strategies in the Plains," and by North Central Research Committee NC-32 on "Farm-Family Financial Management," are two pioneering efforts on the subject.

toward increased farm size in future years. The most important financial decisions made by transition-area farmers may well be those pertaining to acreage enlargement. They must decide how to invest any given amount of money, whether it is obtained from savings or from lenders. Should it go toward a new self-propelled combine, or sixty additional acres?

According to our survey, while farmers recognize land as a profitable investment for the long run, their immediate inclination is to buy more machinery. Of course, a minimum set of machinery is one of the requirements for farming, but adding to this set is not the only path to increased income. Land can be substituted for labor and machinery; a man can cover more acres less intensively if he plans his operations that way. This does not mean that a farmer with plenty of capital should not equip himself with machinery in any way he chooses. It means that farmers with limited capital need to weigh carefully the choice between land and machinery.

There is an analogous choice between buildings and livestock. Farmers in this area, where cash sales of crops are sizable, recognize the profit possibilities in more livestock. Yet their immediate plans emphasize the "need" for building investments more than for livestock. This is true even in areas which, in general, have been overbuilt.

Livestock represents a direct addition to business volume. The services of farm buildings are sold only indirectly, and the returns depend on the quantity of livestock put through the buildings. The ever-present question is: Are there cheaper ways of getting the same service? It is apparent that both buildings and machinery have been status symbols in the past. We are not questioning their value for this purpose, but capital-short farmers should carefully count their cost.

*Reserves*

Farmers in the Plains are aware of the use of reserves to alleviate the effects of drought on their farm organization and income. Most of the survey farmers kept reserves of feed or convertible assets—stocks, bonds, savings accounts, and cash— although the amounts were not large in 1957. As noted earlier, inventories of feed on hand on January 1 of that year were only about $1,000 on the 480-acre farms. The average investment in nonfarm assets for all survey farms was about $2,700, of which about $700 was in real estate.

Feed reserves can be used to alleviate the effects of one or two years of extreme drought. Barber, in work based on crop yields at Colby, in western Kansas, found that 5,000 bushels of wheat in farm storage on a 605-acre farm with 231 acres of wheat, producing an average of 2,500 bushels per year, would maintain net income for two years of extreme drought. Droughts of longer periods than this could not be met with even this substantial reserve. Of course, Colby is located in the specialized wheat area and has a yield variability of over 70 percent of the average, compared with the Nebraska transition area which has about 50 percent variability for wheat.[2] In central North Dakota, with an average variability of 58 percent, and more

[2] E. Lloyd Barber, *Meeting Weather Risks in Kansas Wheat Farming*, Kansas Agricultural Economics Report No. 44 (September, 1950), p. 6.

typical of the transition area, a grain reserve was more effective in stabilizing income, mainly because the droughts were not so long-lasting nor so severe.[3]

Grain reserves involve an annual cost for the storage facilities; this cost represents a small loss taken every year to avoid larger losses that might occur rarely. The deterioration of the stocks represents another cost. Finally, the reserve necessitates some initial years of above-average yields to build it up to an operational stage. On the plus side, there is an income tax benefit from postponing the sale of part of the crop during a high-income year. (What we have said for wheat would also hold true for corn, except that corn variability is somewhat higher.) A farmer considering grain reserves should not incur greater annual costs for the stocks than the cost of alternative sources of grain available to him. These would include stocks held in government storage or the grain carryover held in commercial facilities. On these he would allow for transportation costs, of course.

We do not know enough about the role of forage reserves in stabilizing income. Research work indicates that silage can be held for periods of several years without substantial deterioration. Ranchers customarily hold enough hay reserves to feed their cattle for one month to a year. Forage costs more to transport than grain; consequently its local price varies much more than that of grain in response to surplus or deficit conditions. Forage reserves may be more economic than grain reserves. However, in a budgeting analysis based on a 38-year period on a Sherman County, Nebraska, 480-acre beef farm, an operator choosing a system where the beef cow enterprise was kept stable by use of hay reserves gave up net income equivalent to 21 percent as compared with the operator who kept no reserve and flexed his livestock system along with feed supplies.[4] This illustrates the cost of stability.

Beginning operators who are in debt are not very interested in nonfarm investments as a form of reserve. They probably are most concerned with investing their accumulated capital in such things as fertilizer, livestock, machinery, and debt repayment. However, farmers accumulate capital at a rather impressive rate under favorable conditions. An alternative to physical reserves on the farm is the investing of some funds in savings accounts, bonds, insurance, stocks, and nonfarm real estate as a way to spread risk through diversification.

Insurance provides not only an estate that would be available in case of death, but also cash reserves to be used in emergencies, or left to accumulate. As noted earlier, farmers' insurance programs are typically inadequate. Savings accounts, bonds, and checking accounts are readily convertible for use at strategic times. Investments in stock or nonfarm real estate are less convertible, but have the advantage of hedging against inflation and maintaining the purchasing power of the funds invested. The survey data indicate the rather large proportion of nonfarm assets held as cash (over one-third) as compared with bonds and other interest-bearing types.

[3] Philip J. Thair, *Stabilizing Farm Income against Crop Yield Fluctuations*, North Dakota Agricultural Experiment Station Bulletin 362 (1950), p. 8.

[4] Leon E. Langemeier and Robert M. Finley, "The Use of Hay Reserves as a Method of Stabilizing Farm Income," *Management Strategies in Great Plains Farming*, Great Plains Agricultural Council Publication No. 19 and Nebraska Agricultural Experiment Station Miscellaneous Publication No. 7 (1961), pp. 69, 70.

*Diversification*

This is a byword in the Northern Plains. Since the country was first settled, farmers have been urged to get their "eggs into more than one basket" to reduce risk. However, this naive concept has been generally outmoded and rejected by Northern Plains farmers. Too many enterprises cause inefficiency in the use of labor and machinery. Moreover, bad weather in the Plains is often equally deleterious to different enterprises. Farmers are learning the importance of building up a volume of business, which means getting a large output per hour of labor. A few milk cows, a few hens, a sow, and a garden as sources of home-raised products are still advocated by some nonfarmers, but they provide small returns per hour and thus contribute little to volume.

New concepts of diversification offer some hope. One of these is area diversification, the locating of tracts of land in several places in an area to reduce the effects of hail, local droughts, and other sources of risk, as well as to reduce variability by taking advantage of localized rain clouds—which may be limited to a few miles. Of course, this practice involves costs (such as time and expense in moving machinery), which have to be balanced against the gains in terms of stability. Area diversification has come into use in the Western Plains wheat area, and it would seem to offer possibilities in the transition areas as well.

The trouble with diversification in the orthodox sense is that it violates the objective of specialization. In the Plains area the economic alternatives are limited: grass, wheat, sorghum, beef cattle, and corn in the eastern area. The problem is how to take advantage of specialization without losing one's shirt. A modern type of diversification that permits this is flexible farming. Flexible farming is organizing in such a way that one's resources are never irrevocably committed, so an avenue of retreat is always open. A crop farmer does not have to commit himself to a regular crop rotation, which might, in the western transition area, include a regular sequence of wheat and fallow. Instead, he may plant wheat only if enough soil moisture is available. This means that wheat may follow wheat, or fallow may follow fallow, from one year to the next. Farther east he may defer corn planting, or he can substitute sorghum for corn; he can utilize summer emergency crops, like millet, should the spring be dry but the rains come later. In other words, he waits to commit his cash crop inputs to the ground until the last minute, and then only if he can reasonably expect results.

Livestock offers another possibility of flexibility in the organization, besides providing some orthodox diversification. A basic cow herd can be geared to the native pasture available. The enterprise can be expanded rapidly by keeping the calves and feeding them out from grain reserves, or purchased grain, in years when the crop output shrinks owing to drought. It can also be expanded in the same way in years of unusually large feed supply. Similarly, hogs, laying hens, or turkeys can be rapidly expanded to utilize increased supplies of grain, or sharply contracted when crops are short.

*Crop Insurance*

Federal crop insurance has been available on wheat since 1939 in specialized wheat counties. However, the multiple type of crop insurance, of more appeal in the transition area, has been available only since 1948. Losses are paid under this arrangement when the total production from all crops in the farm business goes below the amount covered by insurance. Since the risks are somewhat lower, the premiums are also lower. Multiple crop insurance is more effective than grain reserves in providing some income in times when the droughts last more than two years, as in Kansas, according to the research work mentioned previously. In North Dakota, with shorter drought periods, feed reserves give more stable incomes. For farmers in debt or with limited capital, the crop insurance arrangement offers particular advantages as an income stabilizer. Also, it can be used as collateral for loans for crop expenses.

A specialized form of crop insurance is hail insurance. It is offered by commercial companies under rates related to the risk structure of each county. These rates vary from $4.00 per acre in the Eastern Plains to $12.00 or more in the Western Plains. Again, hail insurance provides a means of taking a predictable small loss every year instead of an unpredictable large one. It appeals most to the farmer with limited capital who cannot carry such risks by himself.

### Use of Credit

We noted in Chapter 12 that many farmers know little about the use of credit or about credit agencies. This deficiency would seem to be easily remedied by educational efforts by credit agencies and agricultural extension workers. However, simply providing more descriptive material may not be enough. Farmers need to develop a concept of financial planning and programming which includes a consideration of the role of credit in their operations. New teaching materials and methods apparently are called for.

### Reducing Cash Expenses

The time is past when farmers can be counseled to reduce cash expenditures for farming and living as a means of surviving periods of economic adversity. Their flexibility has been reduced by both changing values and standards, and by technology. Consider, for example, the cob-burning cook stove. How many younger farmers could persuade their wives to replace their gas ranges with the old cob burner? And if they did, where could they buy cob burners? Most basic consumption items, and a large part of the inputs used in production, are fixed-cash commitments which cannot be reduced by substituting home-produced materials as was true in times past.

### THE FARM CREDIT SYSTEM

The farm credit system has been criticized as a major source of agriculture's ills. Perhaps one reason for this is that farm credit people are conservative by nature and vocation. They have not always been noted for suggesting innovations in credit arrangements. Perhaps we expect too much of farm credit; it cannot solve the income problems of farming, but neither should it impede apparent solutions.

Much progress has been made over the last forty years in farm credit institutions and practices. We have seen the reorganization and strengthening of the commercial bank system. Cooperative farm credit has grown into a national system whose agencies are found in every community. We have also provided a federal agency to lend to those unable to borrow from commercial sources. The new agencies have issued long-term loans at low interest rates, loans to farm cooperatives, and short-term and intermediate credit fitted to individual farm enterprises, and have supervised loans for families getting started, and emergency loans. Somewhat against its will, the commercial system has followed this lead. It has often competed "toe to toe" with the cooperative FCA system, meanwhile finding common ground with the supervised FHA system. The general progress has been rather impressive.

In spite of the improvements, certain practices of these agencies remain poorly suited to transition-area farming. Some of these problems will be noted here, with suggested modifications.

*The Cooperative Farm Credit System*

The cooperative system emanates from the Farm Credit Administration, which is an independent agency administered by the Farm Credit Board. The board supervises and coordinates the activities of the various agencies in the system, including the federal Intermediate Credit banks, the federal Land Banks, and the Banks for Cooperatives—all of which operate in each of the twelve districts. It also includes the Production Credit associations and the federal Land Bank associations (formerly known as the National Farm Loan associations) which operate on a local basis. The district and local agencies are farmer-owned and -controlled, although government capital remains in the federal Intermediate Credit Banks, a few PCA's, and the Banks for Cooperatives. All the government capital in these agencies will be retired in time, on a definite schedule. (Since the Banks for Cooperatives lend only to farmers' cooperatives, they are tangential to our interest and will not be considered further.)

The cooperative credit system is not just another commercial system; it is unique in the direct channel it provides between investment centers and the farm through its use of land-bank bonds and the debentures of the FICB's. Because it is sponsored by the federal government, it also provides a mechanism through which credit could be expanded by government action in times of agricultural emergency. The Production Credit associations were roundly criticized in the early fifties because their loans to farmers were written on a one-year basis,[5] subject, of course, to renewal. Other complaints were that the PCA's were operating too conservatively, even more so than the commercial banks, and that they dealt only with the largest farmers. For a time, the PCA's were on the defensive, rationalizing existing practices rather than trying to make improvements.

More recently, however, these criticisms have had some effect. Under the Farm Credit Act of 1956, the system was streamlined by the consolidation of the production credit and intermediate credit system, and by the elimination of the Production Credit Corporation. The PCA's could then purchase stock in the Intermediate Credit banks, replacing the government capital of the latter. Finally, the FICB's were permitted

---

[5] See, for example, Committee on Tenure, Credit, and Land Values of the Great Plains Agricultural Council, "Proceedings—Conference on Intermediate Credit for Agriculture," Great Plains Agricultural Council Publication No. 12 (1954), Mimeographed.

to discount loans for up to five years for the PCA's rather than for three years, the former limit, and intermediate credit became officially recognized as legitimate. Loans for the purchase of breeding stock, machinery, or improvements in land and buildings are now written for up to five years, with annual payments adapted to the income stream from the investment for which the loan is used. "Barnyard loans," credit for general operating purposes, are becoming more common. A new aggressive spirit is evident in the whole organization.

Commercial banks have traditionally resented the PCA's as unwanted and unnecessary intrusions of the federal government into private enterprise. The extent of the competition offered by the PCA's has probably been exaggerated; what little there is has had some desirable effects. It has forced commercial banks to be more imaginative in their short-term and intermediate credit operations. It has introduced interest-rate competition in areas where single banks would have otherwise had monopolies. The volume of credit extended by each system does not indicate that the PCA's are driving the commercial banks out of business. The force of the banks' criticism has also been weakened by the reduction of government capital in the PCA system, as well as by the increased measure of farmer control.

### Federal Land Bank Associations

The cooperative local agencies of the federal land banks, formerly known as National Farm Loan associations, extend loans of from five to forty years duration for the purchase of land or for improvements. The amount of these loans is limited to 65 percent of the appraised "normal value of applicants' farms." An important feature of the 1959 act was the transfer, from the Farm Credit Administration to the land banks, of the responsibility for making appraisals of farm property offered as security for loans.

The federal land banks have been criticized for these appraisals. As recently as 1950, the "normal values" in the land bank appraisals were based on prices received during the 1931–40 period.[6] This meant that 65 percent of the appraised value of many farms turned out to be only a fraction of the sale price of these farms. Of course, lending agencies, particularly long-term lending agencies in agriculture, must be aware of the peculiarly changing fortunes of agriculture. On the other hand, this degree of conservatism implied that the general economic changes taking place since that time were only temporary, a questionable assumption.

The result of these policies was that those who borrowed from the land banks during the early fifties had to put up most of the cash involved in any land purchase. Since that time, however, the price levels used in appraisal have been changed. In a single year, from 1958 to 1959, the number of borrowers rose 36.8 percent and the amount of loans 67.1 percent, chiefly owing to these higher appraisal levels.

### Commercial Banks

A reliance on demand deposits characterizes the financial operations of commercial banks. This limits their activity in the farm-mortgage field, except for a few highly select, short-term loans. Yet they are the major source of short and intermediate

[6] John L. Smith, "The Federal Land Bank Dilemma," *Farm Policy Forum*, Iowa State College Press (March, 1950), p. 11.

credit to farmers. There are several reasons for this; they can be flexible about loan procedures; they can extend credit quickly, using little time for preliminary checking; and, on small loans, they can eliminate some of the closing costs associated with federal or cooperative credit loans.

Banks have traditionally lent funds for periods of a few months. In a survey of bankers in the Tenth Federal Reserve District, it was found that 68 percent of the total volume of commercial bank loans to farmers was for terms of $7\frac{1}{2}$ months or less.[7] Recently, they have been increasing their intermediate credit, as for breeding stock, machinery, and the like. Yet, in the survey cited above, 65 percent of the credit issued on intermediate investments was written for $7\frac{1}{2}$ months or less, with the bulk of these notes being for six months.

How do banks lend money for intermediate purposes with short-term notes? The answer is "planned renewal," under an understanding with the borrower. While there are certain advantages in this course, such as the necessity for frequent reviews, the disadvantages would seem to outweigh them. Intermediate-term notes for intermediate-term loans would make for better planning by both bank and borrower, would be more efficient, and would lessen the borrower's uncertainty. In time, the banks will undoubtedly follow the lead of the PCA's and shift to notes of longer term than one year for this type of credit.

Banking laws have frequently been cited as an obstacle to the banks' issuance of intermediate-term farm credit. There are no federal laws that prevent the extension of such credit by commercial banks.[8] Apparently, such restrictions as may exist originate in state laws or the practices of state bank examiners.

## Life Insurance Companies

Insurance companies issue farm credit only in areas they select. They make only long-term mortgage loans. The volume of their farm loans was somewhat larger than those of the land banks in 1959. Many commercial banks serve as middlemen for the insurance companies in negotiating their loans. The insurance companies have improved their practices in several ways since the 1930's; and one of the most beneficial changes has been lengthening the term of their loans.

## Farmers Home Administration

This agency is the only bona fide federal agency operating in the farm credit field. It lends only to farmers who cannot obtain credit through commercial sources. As such, it came to be kindly regarded by commercial banks in the Plains during the drought of the fifties. It combines credit with managerial assistance to its farmer customers, exercising a rather close supervision over their financial affairs. A county committee assists the county FHA supervisor, and no loan can be made without its approval.

Several types of loans are available through the FHA. Its operating loans of up to seven years' term, with a maximum limit of $10,000, represented for a time the only

---

[7] "Financing Intermediate-Term Farm Investments," *Monthly Review*, Federal Reserve Bank of Kansas City (February, 1957), p. 12.

[8] *Intermediate-Term Bank Credit for Farmers*, Agricultural Commission of American Bankers Association (1957), p. 3.

"official" intermediate credit in agriculture. They are issued for part or all of the value of livestock and machinery purchased, or for necessary operating funds. Farm-ownership loans are used for the purchase of farmland; they can range up to forty years in term, and up to 100 percent of the "fair" value of the farm. They are limited in amount to the "county average value of efficient family-type farms," a restriction which has unduly limited the size of farms in some areas where small farm size is a problem. Soil and water conservation loans are granted for the development of irrigation and farmstead water systems, soil conservation measures, and drainage installations. The loan limit is $25,000, and the maximum term is twenty years. Farm housing loans for building and repairing farm houses, barns, and other buildings are also issued at a 4 percent interest rate. In officially designated emergency areas, the FHA can make emergency loans to farmers from a special revolving fund established by Congress in 1949.

Another program of FHA is loan insurance. Insured loans are made from funds provided by private lenders but guaranteed by FHA. The interest rate on these loans is 5 percent, of which the lender gets four-fifths and FHA gets one-fifth. The latter covers administrative costs and insurance.

Since 1938, the loss rate on FHA loans has been extremely small, .3 percent on farm-ownership loans and .8 percent on operating loans. Yet the organization's loan volume is limited by its dependence on annual congressional appropriations for its loanable funds. After this long a history, it would seem that FHA is here to stay. It might well be put on a completely revolving-fund basis.

Despite its relatively small scale, the FHA has played an important role, particularly for beginning farmers and for those in emergency areas. It has shown its value as a standby mechanism that can be quickly expanded in emergencies.

*Individuals and Dealers*

Individuals still provide over 40 percent of the long-term credit in agriculture. This shows the heavy reliance placed on relatives and nonrelated sellers for funds with which to buy land. Dealers provide almost as much short-term credit as commercial banks.

Unsolved Problems

All three of the major components of our farm credit system—banks, cooperative agencies, and FHA—are here to stay because each performs a somewhat distinctive role. Banks can operate quickly and flexibly in providing short-term and intermediate credit. The cooperative system operates from a broader financial base and taps a different source of funds. Because of its government sponsorship, it should be able to tolerate periods of stress with a minimum of adjustment. The FHA system can lend to people who cannot be reached by ordinary credit; it also stands ready to help during emergencies.

What are the major remaining problems of farm credit in the Plains? A discussion of these follows.

*Farm Planning and Management for the Use of Credit*

The technological advances of agriculture are throwing an increasingly heavy burden on management, including finance and credit management. This burden is complicated by the fact that farmers have available to them a number of credit agencies. Except for FHA, these credit agencies in agriculture have not given much help to their former clients in financial planning. There are several reasons for this. First, these agencies have been dealing with a large number of comparatively small loans, a condition that makes planning costly. Second, creditors have not always known as much as they should about farming. Third, farmers do not recognize the importance of financial planning.

However, with increasing farm size and more advanced technology, financial planning will become more important. With fewer but larger loans, credit agencies will be more inclined to help their customers work out complete financial plans and gear their credit programs to them. Ideally, there should be one credit program for each farm, with all borrowings and repayments integrated into it.

The FHA engages in financial planning with its limited clientele at the present time. This is made easier because the borrower deals with only one agency; but the other agencies should play their parts, too. Even though a farmer borrows from a bank and a land bank association, or from an insurance company and a PCA, there should still be one financial plan. More communication is needed between the local credit agencies. Recognizing that they are competitors for the farmers' business, they still need to take a clinical approach to farmers' credit problems. Of course, a farmer should shop around, but after he has decided on the sources of his long-term and short-term credit, the agencies and the farmer should plan together for his needs.

In the future, commercial banks will have to offer more specialized service for farm loans. They can accomplish this through the use of professionally trained agricultural representatives and specialized farm-loan departments. They can thus become more intimately acquainted with the businesses of farmer customers, can provide credit tailored to their particular needs, and can engage to a greater extent in planning—and even in assistance with managerial decisions.

The cooperative agencies must look more carefully than they have in the past into the qualifications of their professional field personnel—the secretary-treasurer of federal Land Bank and Production Credit associations. Certainly there should be more coordination between FLBA's and PCA's. Location of these agencies is a limiting factor, but it should ultimately be possible to bring more PCA's and FLBA's together under the same roof. A further step would be for them to have the same boards of directors, and perhaps even the same secretary-treasurer.

There is an even broader context for farm planning. Credit agencies are not the only organizations that have an interest in farm plans. The Soil Conservation Service draws up conservation plans which provide a physical base for farm planning. Farmers have to do a certain amount of planning in connection with the ACP programs. FHA loans are based on comprehensive farm plans. Extension service personnel help farmers make farm plans in connection with the Farm and Home Development program.

In view of these various and possibly conflicting interests, these farm plans should be coordinated into one comprehensive plan for each farm. An advantage of such a coordinated plan would be that credit, conservation payments, and farming practices could all fit together. Credit agencies would be helped by other agencies' analyses of the income-producing ability of the farm business. In all cases, the planning needs to be carried to the point where the estimated borrowings and repayments can be budgeted and the desirability of loans judged from such information.

### Variable Payments

This device has been repeatedly proposed to reduce the risk introduced into farming by the combination of variable prices and production with fixed debt repayments. Variable payments have been used by the FHA in connection with its farm-ownership loans since 1946. Under this arrangement a borrower may prepay in years of above-normal income and may defer payments in poor years. Land bank borrowers may approximate the same thing by prepaying on their loans into a future-payments fund and drawing interest. The assumption implicit in both these arrangements is that the borrower will experience above-average years before he has below-average years. Other borrowers unofficially defer payments during short periods of adverse conditions.

A true variable payments arrangement, where the principal payments, and even the interest payments, might vary from one year to the next with changing income conditions, would recognize the unique environment in which farmers operate. The problem is to find a good basis for flexing the payment. One possibility is to gear it to farm prices, or to crop yields. The rental-share arrangement, where the creditor would receive a specified share of the crops, combines both yield and price variation and is attractively simple. The most sophisticated arrangement would be the use of flexing geared to net income. It would require reliable bookkeeping, more intimate contact between lender and borrower, and more supervision by the lender.

The variable payments arrangement does not involve any subsidy by the lender or any change in the total principal payment. Its only objective is to shift from a constant payment schedule to a changing one. If set up for a long period of years, it should involve no change in the term of the loan.

This plan is sometimes thought to place more risk on the creditor, making him more dependent on the management ability of the borrower, but there is little logical basis for such a belief. Whether the payment schedule is variable or fixed, the long-run success of the loan, as far as the creditor is concerned, is just as dependent on the management ability of the farmer. Loans in the transition area, with its extreme ups and downs, should be planned in long-run terms. Variable payments may add to a creditor's costs, but these could be handled by extra charges, such as slightly higher interest rate. The device should probably be used on an optional basis, with the lender having the choice of a fixed or a variable schedule.

### Loan Insurance

One means of spreading the risk associated with farm-mortgage lending is loan insurance. Although discussed at great length, it is used only in FHA- and GI-insured loans. The FHA charges an additional one-half of 1 percent to go into an insurance reserve. Loan insurance is also used in connection with urban residence loans.

The major difficulty with loan insurance applied on a wide scale is that of separating risk due to general economic variation from that due to individual management. Even though the objective of the program may be to insure against managerial risk, the task of developing actuarial data on this type of risk is formidable. The second difficulty is that farmers with superior management ability would not be willing to pay the rates necessary to cover managerial losses suffered by others. Loan insurance would be manageable if it were directed at a specific variable capable of actuarial treatment, such as the probability that an operator will abscond, but it rarely is so clear-cut. The combination of variable payments with crop insurance probably offers a simpler way to eliminate one risk and spread another than does loan insurance.

## The Beginning Farmer

Young men who want to become farmers form two distinct classes, which, in simple terms, can be called the "haves" and the "have-nots." Those with sufficient family backing to enter farming without heavy reliance on credit are a fortunate group; even if they need to borrow funds, thay can do so on their inherited security or over their father's signature. It is the second group that has the problems, for these young men have little or no family backing with which to acquire a farm of adequate size. The availability of credit to this latter group is probably the most important determinant of whether they become satisfactorily established in farming. "Satisfactorily established" implies operation of a farm large enough to provide income for adequate family living, and with sufficient capital for repayment of loans, replacement of depreciating assets (like buildings and equipment), and for such improvements as erosion control, regrassing, or better breeding stock.

One possibility is to let capital alone ration farming opportunities. In the transition area, this could well mean that farming might be restricted to those with substantial family backing. The fundamental question here, from the standpoint of the efficiency and effectiveness of farming in the area, is whether this is a suitable rationing mechanism. Even if it were, it might not work perfectly, since not all children with adequate family backing want to farm, and not all of them have the ability to operate and manage a modern farm.

An opposite extreme would be to remove capital as the rationing mechanism and to make capital available, through credit, in such quantities that anyone who wanted to start would find capital no limiting factor. This would lead to heavy competition for land, increased land values, and a dampening of the expansion in farm size in areas where this is still economically desirable.

The third possibility is to continue our present system, which opens the field to those with family backing, to those who have sufficient equipment to persuade landlords to rent land to them, and to those who can qualify for FHA farm-ownership loans. Some young men may leave the area, work in other industries, save some money, and then return to become renters or encumbered owner-operators. Others leave permanently for other occupations.

Most people would not willingly accept the first or the second alternative. The challenge, then, is to improve on our present system. It seems wasteful of human energies to encourage some young men to start farming simply because they have family backing. It is also wasteful for young men to start with inadequate capital on small rented or encumbered farms, work hard for several years, and then "adjust out" because they cannot accumulate capital—not necessarily through any fault of their own.

The real rationing criterion in which we are interested is probably personal ability.

For the future of the industry, we would like to see that young people entering farming represent the best possible resources in terms of managerial ability, interest, and other personal qualities related to success in farming. Agriculture in the future will require and reward personal abilities to a greater degree than in the past. The important question, then, is whether we can improve the system by which people are selected for farming. There are several possibilities.

A first requirement is education. To make an effective decision on a vocation, young people should have as much knowledge as possible about alternatives. These include not only nonfarm occupations but the multitude of jobs in agricultural businesses of various kinds: feed mills, machinery agencies, large specialized farm enterprises (like feed lots), and others. In the new agriculture, many young people might better work at specialized activities under someone else's direction than take responsibility for the management and operation of a modern farm. These decisions require knowledge and guidance, responsibility for which falls largely to the high school.

Awareness of the number of farming opportunities available is also important. In any farming area where all farms have reached at least minimum size (from the long-run income standpoint), there is an "ideal" number of replacement families moving into farming to replace those retiring. A larger number than this ideal will result in a decrease in average farm size; a smaller number will increase average farm size.

In an area where farms are too small, the ideal replacement rate would be on the low side. The community interest would be served, then, if there were moving into farming each year as near to the ideal number of selected young families as possible, and certainly no more than this number. Among those with adequate family backing, knowledge and guidance will be the "rationing" factors; among the others, credit will be crucial. Yet, a certain number of families with inadequate family backing *should* move into farming. How can this best be achieved?

Credit for beginning farmers should be treated as a specialized problem by all credit agencies. One possibility would be the creation of specialized county or area credit committees composed of representatives of all credit sources in the county: commercial banks, cooperative agencies, FHA, dealers, and insurance companies, as well as farmer representatives. This committee might be a subcommittee of the Rural Development committee. It would have as its primary interest the credit problems of beginning farmers, although it might naturally involve itself in other credit problems relating to farming in the community, such as credit for livestock or conservation practices.

The first function of the committee would be the exchange of information and ideas by the various credit agencies of the community. It would have to appraise general economic conditions impinging on farming in the area. It should consider ideal farm size, desirable farm-enterprise organization, and land values. It should appraise the farm-size structure of the area, and should acquaint itself with population trends, the future needs for beginning farmers to replace those who retire, and the "supply" of young farmers available to take up these opportunities, as well as the personal requirements in farming. This educational process would inevitably create an awareness of farm placement as a community problem, transcending the individual interests of the agencies.

The second function of the committee would be to take action. It could evaluate individual cases of promising young farmers who have lined up specific rental or purchase opportunities but who are short of capital. The committee could then recommend which individuals should be endorsed or discouraged. If a candidate is endorsed, the committee would help him explore the credit facilities available to him in the county and would support his case with the agencies selected.

This sort of thing is done now by the county FHA committee. Certain bankers have also taken a particular interest in financing young beginning farmers and have been successful at it. This proposal would generalize these activities to an area basis. The committee would follow through with the young man during the process of establishment. Its interest in him might cease when he has become established; that is, when he achieved a net worth that would qualify him for the commercial credit facilities available.

If they were buying land, many of the candidates would have FHA loans. However, commercial banks and Land Bank associations would undoubtedly lend beyond their usual limit to a select few for the purchase of land. For working capital loans, the FHA, banks, and PCA's would each work with certain candidates to provide them with adequate amounts of capital for breeding stock, machinery, and other items. For young men starting via the rental route, working capital might be the chief problem. Many would start out with both rented and purchased land.

Some landlords might look to this committee for outstanding candidates for tenants, and perhaps also work out arrangements for providing working capital to these tenants as part of the rental arrangement. There might be periods and areas when such a committee would strictly ration its support of candidates since its primary purpose would be to ensure that they become established on units of adequate size, while avoiding severe capital restrictions.

In addition to its work with beginning farmers, the county credit committee might concern itself with farmers in the area who were having special credit difficulties. In periods of general distress, it could provide for exchange of information between credit agencies. It might make policy recommendations. It could engage in conciliation activities between debtors and creditors to prevent foreclosures and pave the way for voluntary debt adjustment. To be effective in this, it should have a membership broad enough to include the various interests of the community—agriculture, credit, business, and education.

## Term of Mortgage Credit

Farmers who buy their land on credit usually repay the loan in from twenty to forty years. A commitment such as this implies that a farmer can and should accumulate the capital needed for the farm business within his operating lifetime, but the rapidly increasing capital requirements in Northern Plains farming make this assumption ever less tenable. Credit agencies are moneylenders; after all, they are primarily concerned with the interest earned by their loans rather than in the repayment of principal.

Thus there seems to be a place for loans of very long terms, for example, 50–100 years, which farm families would not be expected to repay in full during a single operator's life span. Instead, they would make interest payments on the capital while they use it, repay part of the principal, and then bequeath their equity to an heir or sell it to an interested buyer when they retire. This might necessitate a provision in the loan agreement giving the creditor a voice in the selection of a buyer, such as a veto power. The loan also might have to be renegotiated at the time of sale, perhaps adjusting its terms for changes in the value of the dollar. But there is no reason why such modifications of current practices cannot be introduced; they merely recognize the creditor as a permanent source of capital in farming rather than as a strictly temporary moneylender. Agriculture's voracious appetite for capital, likely to continue in the Northern Plains for a long time to come, demands that it look beyond the farm family itself for the funds required.

*Emergency Credit*

During the drought of the 1950's, especially in the Southern Plains, the FHA extended loans—primarily for the purchase of feed, seed, livestock, and other drought-affected items—to hard-pressed farmers in counties designated as emergency areas. In Cimarron and Texas counties in Oklahoma, more than three hundred farmers (15 percent of all farmers) received these FHA emergency loans between 1951 and 1954, compared with fifty who received regular production and subsistence loans.[9] This took the pressure off the commercial banks and the PCA's, relieving them from making less desirable loans.

Droughts are not uncommon in the Plains. They can be expected to affect some part of the region every year. A standby mechanism, like the FHA emergency loan, seems a most desirable safety valve to use whenever private and cooperative credit sources are unduly strained. Nor does it have to subsidize an area in the long run; it can be self-liquidating. It must, however, be sensitive to changing conditions, and a sufficiently large revolving fund must be provided so it can cope with situations even graver than those of the fifties.

A similar provision for long-term emergency credit would also be desirable. The Federal Farm Mortgage Corporation, established in 1934, was of this type. The FFMC was empowered to issue government bonds, the proceeds of which were used to lend money to farmers—under second mortgages—through the Land Bank mechanism. An agency like this should be available to long-term lenders, such as banks and insurance companies, as well as land banks. Admittedly, the long-run credit system is subject to fewer and slighter economic shocks than the short-term credit system, but even one debacle is more than we need. The proper time to design the pill is before the disease strikes.

*Crop Insurance*

Although its coverage has been expanded in recent years, it is not available in all transition-area counties (Figure 63). As a device for spreading weather risk and stabilizing income, crop insurance is a workable and logical arrangement. To be successful, it must have a sound actuarial basis, rates that make it self-liquidating in the long-run, and sufficiently wide adoption by farmers in an area to make it economical to administer. Research in North Dakota found that crop insurance can more effectively reduce risk than feed, livestock, and cash reserves. In counties where the

[9] Marlowe M. Taylor, *Farm Credit in a Southern Great Plains Drought Area*, USDA, ARS, 43–12 (June, 1955), p. 70.

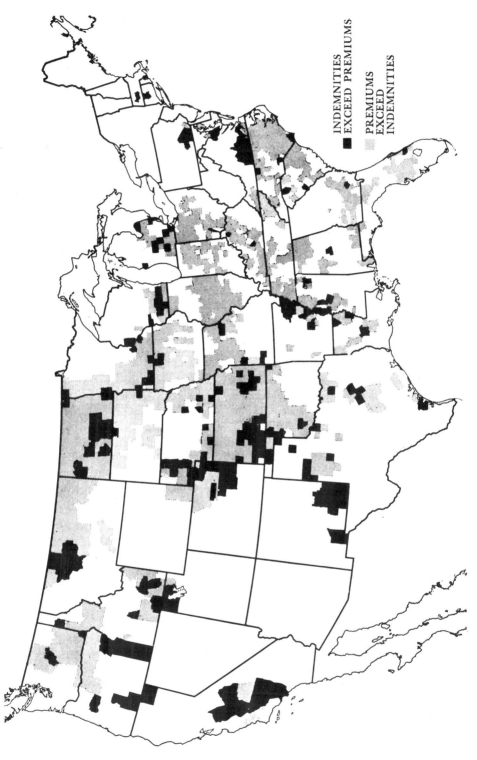

INDEMNITIES
EXCEED PREMIUMS

PREMIUMS
EXCEED
INDEMNITIES

Fig. 63. Counties Covered by Multiple Crop Insurance, 1963

Source: Federal Crop Insurance Corporation.

302

multiple contract was offered, participation in crop insurance was higher, and rates consequently lower, than in counties with insurance only on single crops.[10]

All transition-area counties should be covered by multiple crop insurance. Of course, the need for a sound actuarial base is recognized. The new "guaranteed production" plan offered in 1960, under which a farmer can select low, medium, or high coverage, should give the insurance wider appeal and help to reduce the danger of unfavorable selectivity of risks which exists with low sign-up. Another feature that would reduce selectivity is a contract for more than one year—say, for five years—which would prevent people from going in and out of the program. Crop insurance is neglected in extension and other educational activity; but more intensive education should result in increased participation.

Crop insurance might well be made compulsory for all farmers in an area before the area is designated eligible for emergency and other types of assistance. It could be made a prerequisite to participation in other federal programs, including price support. The contribution that crop insurance can make to a community's economic stability has been overlooked in the Plains.

### Income Tax Changes

There has been much discussion but little action on a particular tax problem faced by Plains farmers. Under present law, operating losses can be carried forward or backward for two years. However, this is of limited benefit in the face of income variability in the Plains area. Variability affects farmers' income taxes in two ways.

1. The total tax paid over a period of.years is higher with variable than with constant income since the rates are higher on higher income brackets in any one year.
2. Part of the income in a year of unusually high income should really serve as a reserve against a year of low income.

One device suggested to alleviate the effects of income variation is the tax saving certificate.[11] Under this method a farmer could buy tax saving certificates, up to a certain proportion of his current taxable income; say, one-third. These certificates would be tax-free until they were cashed during years in which his income was low. Thus the taxable income would be stabilized and the certificates would represent cash reserves. Work in Kansas and North Dakota has demonstrated that the combination of such a variable tax payment with crop insurance is the most effective arrangement yet proposed for offsetting the economic effects of yield fluctuations in the Plains area.

### Alternatives in Gaining Control of Land

Establishment in farming is all too often thought to involve a choice between two distinct alternatives: renting or purchasing land. If a man is short of capital, he rents; if he has sufficient funds for a down-payment (which may be sizable), he buys. The step between one form of land control and the other may be a difficult one. There are, however, intermediate alternatives which should be of interest to both

[10] Thair, *op. cit.*, p. 18.

[11] E. Lloyd Barber, "Modifying the Federal Income Tax to Promote Greater Stability of Farm Income," *Journal of Farm Economics*, XXX, No. 2 (May, 1958), 337.

beginning operators and land sellers; and these include various forms of land contract.

Basically, a land or purchase contract is a means of acquiring more control over land than a lease provides, without requiring much additional capital. The buyer under a contract typically makes a small down-payment without getting title to the land. The title does not pass until he has accumulated some specified equity in the property. Should a buyer default, he may forfeit his down-payment and subsequent payments. Thus there is a considerable element of risk introduced for a buyer who is committed to a series of constant payments to be met from a variable income. Of course, the possibility of default represents some risk to the seller as well, since he cannot consider the property completely sold.

There are variations in the land contract that may reduce the buyer's risk. One device is the rent-plus arrangement, where the seller receives a rental sufficiently larger than normal so that the difference—which is credited to the buyer's account—and the interest earned on it will eventually pay off the farm.[12] After the buyer has built up sufficient credit, for example, equivalent to half the purchase price of the farm, he receives title and gives a mortgage for the balance.

Another arrangement, the product-payment plan, reduces the buyer's risk still further. Here the buyer may deliver to the seller a share of the product at least equivalent to the normal rent every year until a fixed total amount has been delivered. The number of years is not specified, since production is variable. A variation requires the buyer to deliver to the seller a fixed proportion of the products raised each year for a fixed number of years.

## POSSIBLE DEVELOPMENTS

The "farm city" has important implications to country banking. The traditional picture of the small country bank is as outmoded as the 160-acre farm. In the future we shall find fewer, but larger, country banks, centered primarily in the farm city. While lending to both farm and nonfarm customers, they will provide specialized farm service. These banks will employ both crop and livestock specialists to handle their farm-loan operations. They will have fewer but larger farm customers, and most of the credit will be extended in terms of complete lines rather than in small amounts for specific uses. Much more attention will be given by the banks to managerial decisions on the farm than is presently given.

The cooperative agencies will still be in the picture, although they too will probably operate on a larger scale and with more specialized service. Instead of a secretary-treasurer handling all the business affairs of the agency, there will be several professional employees. In the meantime, the business of the FHA will become centered almost exclusively on beginning operators. This agency will experience continued pressure to expand loan limits, which will probably double in the next twenty years.

Will these arrangements succeed in attracting all the risk capital that will be needed in agriculture after 1980? Will we have the formation of farm corporations capitalized through sales of common stock, like other industries? The answer to both

---

[12] Charles L. Stewart and Fred E. Justus, Jr., *Paying for Farms on Rent-Plus and Product-Payment Plans*, University of Illinois, Department of Agricultural Economics Research Report 13 (1955), p. 1.

these questions is "probably not." However, we probably will find risk capital coming into agriculture from outside sources in greater amounts through less dramatic means.

The key organization to be watched is the farm-management company. These companies, large and small, already have imbedded in them the potential for a variety of different functions which go far beyond the scope of their present operations. First, they may provide a home for the investment capital of absentee landlords (who may be converted to stockholders) in incorporated farm chains, horizontally integrated. The important management decisions for such groups of farms—buying production materials and marketing products—will be made by the salaried management of the company. Many of the production decisions, such as time of planting, tillage, etc., would be left with the tenants. Production materials will be purchased in carload lots on a wholesale basis. Products will be sold on a graded basis in carload or truckload lots. Much of the marketing will be under contract. These chains will deal with banks on a large-scale basis for working capital.

As time goes on, qualified tenants for the chain farms would be harder to find, and farm chains will compete for their services. This will provide the incentive for a minimum cash wage plus a share of the earnings. Since the managerial resources of the chains may be under considerable strain, particularly well-qualified tenants may be advanced to more managerial responsibility as they gain experience. They may specialize in certain types of managerial activity for the whole chain.

The augmented family farms also will probably engage the specialized service of management companies as some of their managerial problems become highly complex. Such services might include income tax reporting, accounting, credit buying and selling of livestock, buying of land, and contractual negotiations with an agricultural industry. The management companies might act as middlemen for contractual arrangements of all kinds.

Certain basic premises underly the changes suggested above, primarily the assumption that the agricultural products industry will become even more specialized and demanding about the quantities, timing, and quality of the products moving into trade. With increasing size of farm, managerial problems will become more complicated. The increased need for outside capital in farming will be met only if devices are adopted by which this capital can be associated with more management.

### Adjusting Out

A discussion of credit and finance in transition-area agriculture is not complete without reference to another problem that is given little attention by people interested in the credit problems of agriculture. This concerns the financial problems of people who are adjusting *out* of farming. Further reference will be made to this matter in the next chapter.

# CHAPTER 19

# Population Adjustments in the Transition Area

In the transition area, as in the Northern Plains as a whole, the subject on everyone's lips is the large number of people moving away. This population loss is almost universally deplored; it is viewed as evidence of the area's failure and as a harbinger of decline for its economy. The resentment is keenest in rural areas, where an entrenched tradition is being shattered: that farm boys should farm like their fathers before them.

This painful subject is impossible to ignore; abandoned farmsteads are ever-present reminders of those who have gone. To farmers, they suggest the loss of neighbors and a disruption of social life; to local businessmen, a dwindling clientele; and to public-spirited citizens, a shrinking tax base and heavier tax burdens for the people who remain.

Farm sales during droughts show that the process is not yet complete. Another evidence of its continuity is the steady stream of high school graduates who leave the area each year. This loss of its youth, for an area as for an individual, is the bitterest pill to swallow.

Yet population changes occur not spontaneously but in response to economic imperatives. The emigration of people from the transition area is merely the visible symptom of an underlying economic development; an increase in the ratio of land to people. This is clearly manifested not only in increased farm size but also in the reduced number of people in country towns, most of whom depend on the land for their livelihood, albeit indirectly.

It is highly unlikely that this trend can be reversed, or even arrested, in the transition area. We live in an age of mobility. People now move from one part of the country to another, often with positive relish in place of their former reluctance. They shift to different jobs, many of them new occupations unheard of even two decades ago. Children are no longer tied to their parents' way of life; they frequently follow quite a divergent pattern. This fluidity was spawned by communications and education; it was facilitated by new technologies and by the general improvement in real incomes.

Nothing on the horizon shows any promise of altering these developments. Consequently, Northern Plains communities must learn to adjust to these forces, which will not be gainsaid. Farm-population losses in the transition area probably cannot be slowed appreciably. Nor would this be desirable, even if it were possible, until the economic base (primarily land) per person in agriculture reaches the point where satisfactory average incomes are attained.

The people of the Northern Plains must recognize the economic force acting upon them and adapt themselves to it. Their challenge is to plan for satisfactory new communities in the face of reduced population density. This is admittedly a difficult task, but surely it is more satisfying than the frustration they now feel trying to keep the boys "down on the farm," an exercise in futility.

### FUTURE POPULATION OF THE NEBRASKA TRANSITION AREA

To illustrate the future population base, we estimated the population of the Nebraska transition area in 1980. To do this, we took account of past trends in population and in farm size. We assumed that farms will continue to expand until satisfactory income levels are achieved. At this point—hopefully attained before the end of the century—the farm population may be closer to an equilibrium level. Added to this agricultural population base will be the nonfarm workers required to sustain it.

*Estimate from Past Trends*

Extrapolating a trend is like climbing out on a limb; the farther you get from the base, the more precarious your position becomes. Yet, extrapolation serves as a rough indicator of probable developments, provided that underlying conditions in the future remain what they were in the past.

By projecting trend lines based on data for the years 1940–60, we found that total population in the five counties of the central-Nebraska transition area would approximate 30,000 in 1980, a decrease of almost one-fourth from the 1960 level of 39,625. This would comprise a farm population of almost 15,000, down 23 percent from 1960's 19,354, and a nonfarm population of around 15,000, down 26 percent from 1960's 20,271. These projections reflect the rural nature of the area, as contrasted with agriculture's position in the national economy. In 1960 there were 15.6 million people in farming—or 8.7 percent of the total population of 179.3 million. National projections point to 9 million farm people by 1980, representing only 4 percent of the population.[1]

*Estimate from Agricultural Resource Base*

In Chapter 17 we discussed how farm size might change in the transition area during the next twenty years. If all farms now earning less than minimum acceptable incomes were consolidated into larger units, each earning at least this standard return, this process would result in a total of 3,937 farms, compared with 5,600 in 1960.

By assuming this agricultural base, we can gradually build up a population estimate, first determining the required agricultural labor force and then the derivative nonfarm employment. The agricultural labor force in the transition area numbered 7,538 in 1960, or 1.35 workers per farm. Since new labor-saving technology may well offset the increased need for workers that would accompany the expansion in farm

[1] U.S. estimates from Earl O. Heady and Luther G. Tweeten, *Resource Demand and Structure of the Agricultural Industry* (Ames: Iowa State University Press, 1963), p. 491.

size, it seems realistic to assume the same labor force per farm in the future. Thus, under adjusted conditions, the number of farm workers would be 5,315, about 30 percent lower than in 1960. Before proceeding to an estimate of nonfarm employment, we should examine the concept of the community multiplier.

*The Community Multiplier.* The notion of the multiplier assumes a logical relationship between the basic or "export" activities in a community and the service, or derivative, activities.[2] The basic activities produce goods and services for export beyond the community borders, such as food, other raw materials, or manufactured products. The service activities are those whose output is not exported but consumed internally; and these include banking, trucking, exchange, and government, as well as that portion of the basic production used to support the local population. If we use employment as an indicator of economic activity, we can compute a ratio of the total employment in area to the employment in basic activities. This ratio is the community multiplier. Another expression of the same concept is the derivative ratio; that is, the employment in service activities divided by basic employment.

Few of these data are available for farm communities in the Northern Plains, yet their situation can be deduced from that of selected Plains counties whose boundaries coincide with the trade areas of small farm cities (Table 91). In these six counties, 85 percent or more of the basic activity is agricultural; thus they are fairly "pure" examples. They indicate what may be expected in rural communities. Thus, in Tripp County, North Dakota, about 1.3 persons were employed in derivative activity for each person in basic production activity, 90 percent of which was farming.

Agriculture is not a wholly basic or export activity; some if its production is consumed locally, and this part represents a service or derivative activity from the standpoint of the multiplier. Among the six counties shown in Table 91, about one-fourth of the farm labor force was considered chargeable to services, leaving three-quarters employed in strictly basic activity.

TABLE 91.  TOTAL, BASIC, AND DERIVATIVE EMPLOYMENT AND RATIOS FOR SELECTED GREAT PLAINS FARM CITIES, 1950

| City, County, & State | Employment | | | Derivative Ratio | Multiplier |
| | Total | Basic | Derivative | | |
|---|---|---|---|---|---|
| | (1) | (2) | (3) | (3) ÷ (2) | (1) ÷ (2) |
| Rugby (Pierce), N.D. . | 2,819 | 1,434 | 1,385 | .966 | 1.966 |
| Winner (Tripp), S.D. . | 3,409 | 1,464 | 1,945 | 1.328 | 2.328 |
| Norton (Norton), Kan.. | 3,509 | 1,295 | 2,214 | 1.709 | 2.709 |
| Clay Center (Clay), Kan. | 4,512 | 1,616 | 2,896 | 1.792 | 2.792 |
| Hollis (Harmon), Okla.. | 2,578 | 1,183 | 1,395 | 1.179 | 2.179 |
| Clayton (Union), N.M.. | 2,449 | 914 | 1,535 | 1.679 | 2.679 |

Source: Edgar Z. Palmer (ed.), Gerald E. Thompson, Moon H. Kang, and William H. Strawn, *The Community Base and Multiplier*, University of Nebraska Business Research Bulletin 63 (1958).

[2] Edgar Z. Palmer (ed.), Gerald E. Thompson, Moon H. Kang, and William H. Strawn, *The Community Economic Base and Multiplier*, University of Nebraska Business Research Bulletin 63 (1958), p. 32. Also, Walter Isard, *Methods of Regional Analysis: An Introduction to Regional Science* (New York: Wiley, 1960), p. 183.

In a predominantly farming community, most nonfarm workers perform tasks related directly or indirectly to agriculture. Farming is the "factory"; the entire community is organized around its needs. A great variety of occupations is represented in this agglomeration. Supplying agriculture with its purchased inputs are all who work for building materials, fuel, feed, seed, fertilizer, and machinery dealers. Some people perform processing activities, such as milk pasteurization and bottling, grain grading and storage, vegetable canning, cattle slaughtering, and meat packing. Others market these products, transporting most of them—as well as unprocessed farm products—out of the community. Still more workers are required to provide purchased food, clothing, and other consumption items used by farmers. Another part of the population supplies professional services, such as medical and legal counsel, banking, and insurance. Added to this private sector is a public or quasi-public sector that provides education, police and fire protection, communications, utilities, road construction and maintenance, and town and county government. When all the various tasks performed in a community are listed like this, a multiplying effect becomes apparent. For example, grocery stores sell not only to farm families but to those of bankers and even to grocery clerks themselves.

The multiplier and derivative ratio can differ between two communities, even though the basic activity is the same in both places. Thus, fat cattle can be packed locally, or exported to some other processing center. Feedlots may rely entirely on locally grown feed, or import it from other producing areas. Grain can be exported, or ground and fed within the region. Agricultural communities can thus have different economic structures and population patterns even when their basic resources are similar.

Agriculture is not, of course, the only basic activity, though its overwhelming importance in the transition area makes it seem so. In many parts of the country, the basic employment is primarily nonagricultural. It might be found in the extractive industries, such as oil production or coal mining. It could be in a factory manufacturing some product for export from the region, such as textiles or jewelry. Or it might be in the provision of some special service patronized by nonresidents, like recreation. Associated with these basic activities is a supporting derivative segment, corresponding to the one described above for agriculture.

The 1960 labor force in the central-Nebraska transition area was divided between basic and derivative employment, approximately as follows:

| *Type of Employment* | *Number Employed* |
|---|---|
| Total . . . . . . . . . . . | 14,963 |
| Basic . . . . . . . . . . | 6,329 |
| Agriculture . . . . . . . | 5,653 |
| Other . . . . . . . . | 676 |
| Derivative . . . . . . . | 8,634 |

(Derivative ratio: 1.36; multiplier: 2.36)

The importance of farming is clearly illustrated. If the derivative ratio is assumed to be the same for farming as for other basic employment, then agriculture, broadly defined, accounted for more than 13,300 workers—or for almost 90 percent of the total labor force.

With the above information on employment in the Nebraska transition area, we can now hazard a guess as to the labor force that might accompany an adjusted farm size structure. The estimates are as follows.

| Type of Employment | Number Employed |
|---|---|
| Total . . . . . . . . . . . | 11,002 |
| Basic . . . . . . . . . | 4,662 |
| Agriculture . . . . . . . | 3,986 |
| Other . . . . . . . . . | 676 |
| Derivative . . . . . . . | 6,340 |

It is assumed here that nonfarm basic employment will remain at its 1960 level and that the 1960 derivative ratio of 1.36 also will continue to hold. Any future increase in the area's level of industrialization would render at least the first assumption, and probably both of them, untenable. In this event, the estimates given above would understate the true level of employment in the area. Also, the ratio will not necessarily remain static. In the light of past experience, however, these assumptions seem quite realistic.

The estimate of the future labor force can be expanded to an estimate of the entire population by using the relationship between the actual labor force and the total population of the area in 1960. This procedure results in an estimated future population of the Nebraska transition area, after farm-size adjustments, of 29,155—a decrease of 26 percent from the 1960 level of 39,625.

It would be presumptuous to consider these data as anything more than educated guesses. They are rough guidelines rather than firm predictions; consequently, it is impossible to state precisely when they might become a reality. We suggested in Chapter 17 that, at past rates of farm size changes, farms might meet minimum income standards around 1990–95. It will probably take at least that long for the concomitant population adjustments to occur.

## THE PROCESS OF POPULATION SHIFTS

In the meantime, a continued emigration from the central-Nebraska transition area is clearly heralded. Much of this population outflow will originate in agriculture. A small number of active farm families will sell out, either to move to another farming area or to leave farming for another job. A variant of this group is the farmer who takes a nonfarm job in the winter, commuting to a nearby town and thus becoming a part-time farmer. He may decide to operate this way permanently or he may switch to a full-time nonfarm job, either operating his farm very extensively or renting or selling part of it. Whatever course he chooses, he represents a kind of migration; he and his family are no longer fully chargeable to the agricultural labor force. Once established in a nonfarm job, he is more likely to leave the area entirely. This type of operator has become common in industrial states like Indiana and Ohio, as well as in the vicinity of urban centers, as in the Northern Plains. The number will increase in the transition area, too, if industrial development takes place.

A second group that will leave agriculture is the retired. The average age level is high among transition-area farmers, much higher than in the general population. This foreshadows relatively heavy retirement rates during the next twenty years. These people will increasingly tend to leave the area rather than retire to a local community. Retired people now constitute an important part of the nonfarm population in the transition area. This component thus may shrink in the future.

Young people over eighteen are the third group that will be leaving. Between 1965 and 1975, 4,156 farm boys in the Nebraska transition area will reach the age of twenty-four; if they are going to farm, they should become operators at that age or soon afterward. During the same twenty-year period, 2,643 farm operators will reach age seventy; most farmers have relinquished active operatorship by that time. Thus an average of one farm situation would presumably be available for each 1.6 farm boys reaching an eligible age, if the number of farms remained constant.

But we know the number of farms is not constant but declining. The number of farms will probably decrease by at least 1,200 because of farm consolidations. This represents a drop in the number of farming opportunities available to beginning operators. On a net basis, only 1,443 opportunities will be available, or one for each 2.9 eligible young men. Of the 4,156 boys, 2,713 will have to find opportunities outside of farming. An equal number of girls will also be so affected. These young people will be forced out of agriculture, into nonfarm jobs, and, since nonfarm work is quite limited in the area, most of them will eventually leave the community.

Thus, emigration from transition-area agriculture will be largely by the old and the young. The former, as they retire, will make their land available to other farm operators. Many of the farm boys will not compete seriously for farmland, being pulled away by other vocational opportunities. Additional land will be made available for consolidation by the smaller numbers of operating farmers who leave.

The process of migration will be similar in the nonfarm sector and will be associated with the same sort of enterprise consolidation. As operators of small enterprise (grocery stores, drugstores, cafes) retire, some of them will not be replaced by young operators, especially since prospects of success will be dim in view of the general decline in population. Many of the young people of the nonfarm sector will leave the area for jobs or for higher education. Employed people—clerks, mechanics, and other technicians—are more mobile than farmers; they react to relatively low wages by moving to another town. They may first commute to another community and then eventually move their families.

### IMPLICATIONS FOR EDUCATION

These population adjustments offer some special challenges to the educational system. They both affect, and are affected by, education. Let us now look at some of the ways education relates to these adjustments.

### Vocational Guidance

In view of the great variety of new jobs continually being created in our society and the export of young people from farming areas, vocational guidance and testing assume new importance. This is not to say that young people can or should be trained for specific jobs—too narrow a focus can actually jeopardize their chances—but they need to decide, to gear their training toward broad areas like farming, skilled labor, business, science, or the other professions. Adequate guidance programs are more crucial to rural than to urban youth since most of the former will be moving into a wholly new environment.

*Training for Farming*

Farming is becoming an increasingly complex business. Its personnel requirements demand a new orientation of 4–H and vocational agricultural programs, as well as general high school education. Management of a farm is growing more specialized and demanding. The farmer of the future will have to be a skilled technician and a competent business manager. The task of merely *finding* technical information, much less mastering it, will be burdensome. In the distant future, of course, even this management function will be divided and specialized; some will work as entrepreneurs, and others as skilled technicians in crop or livestock production.

Whether they manage family farms, specialized feeding operations, or hog or egg "factories," many farm managers will eventually need agricultural college training. In addition to the usual physical and biological science courses, traditional in agricultural colleges, they will have to study law, finance, farm management, marketing, personnel management, and insurance.

Technical workers in farming—those with abilities along manual lines—will also need more specialized training in high school, or shortly thereafter. Those who work as hired crop technicians on cash-crop farms will have to study power and machinery maintenance and operation, and such agronomic operations as spraying, fertilizing, and irrigating. Those hired by specialized livestock plants will require similar training in the feeding and care of cows, hogs, cattle, or poultry. As specialization develops in farming, coupled with an increase in farm size, we can expect to see a tendency toward the production of livestock products in factory-type enterprises, with family farms tending toward cash-crop production.

*Training for Agri-business*

Agri-business refers to the fringe industries surrounding agriculture; that is, those that supply its inputs and those that process and market its output. Twice as many people were employed in agri-business as in farming in 1954.[3]

In 1954 the farm-supply industries employed an estimated 6 million people, and another 10 million were engaged in processing and distributing agricultural products —while only 8 million were employed in farming. Since 1954, the farm labor force has dwindled even further. Perhaps one-fourth of the people engaged in the total agricultural complex are in farming itself, and this fraction is steadily shrinking.

Opportunities for college graduates specializing in agricultural chemistry, nutrition, crop and livestock breeding, and agricultural engineering will continue to multiply. Agricultural business management is another expanding field, requiring college men for farm credit, the management of supply and marketing firms, and professional farm management. Technological innovations will continue to depress the demand for unskilled or semiskilled workers, while more skilled workers will be needed in marketing firms of all kinds. Neither the skills used in agri-business nor the training required to develop them have been systematically identified.

*Training for Other Occupations*

Young people who will go into nonfarm jobs pose the knottiest educational problem. In the past, this group has included the majority of high school rural

[3] John H. Davis and Ray A. Goldberg, *A Concept of Agribusiness* (Boston: Alpine Press, 1957), p. 14.

youth, though the proportion will probably decrease as farm population declines further. These young people should not be enrolled in high school vocational agriculture; they should be taking college preparatory or vocational curricula. The training of potential college students has improved during the past decade, but students who will enter the trades are being largely ignored. They receive scant vocational training in country high schools; and what little is given is often ill suited to the demands of modern industry. This problem needs much more attention from rural high school boards and administrators.

What is the proper role of 4–H and vocational agriculture programs? Obviously, they can no longer function merely as recruiters for family farming. In view of the limited number of farming opportunities available, we should be wary of attracting too many young men into farming. The old idea that farm boys—even those going on to agricultural colleges—should take three or four years of vocational agriculture in high school is outmoded; but Vo-Ag instructors (and extension agents) can play a unique role in guiding young people from rural areas. Their emphasis should be directed at the entire agri-business complex, and even at future nonfarm careers for farm youth.

Agriculture and other vocational instructors should integrate the training programs available to students, rather than compete between themselves for students. Apprenticeship training should be arranged, perhaps providing for a combination of part-time employment and classwork. All these things should be done, not only in the future, but today. We are already out of date in serving the educational needs of farm young people.

### IMPLICATIONS FOR AGRICULTURAL POLICY

The arduous debates on farm policy, which have occurred almost as regularly as the spring thaw, have centered primarily on alternative price and income policies for agriculture during the past decade. While many different positions have been taken, two basically opposite philosophies stand out in the discussions. On one side are those who urge free market prices for agriculture as a means of equating supply and demand, and of giving farmers economic incentives to adjust. In general opposition are those concerned with low prices and incomes in agriculture—the result of excess production capacity coupled with inelastic demand. The latter believe that farmers are already adjusting as fast as we can reasonably expect, and that price supports, usually with production controls, are necessary as a welfare measure.

Although not completely ignored in the debates, the effects of these policies on farm population adjustments have been largely overlooked. The free-marketers seem to think that resource adjustments in agriculture (in other words, the out-movement of farm people) will occur at a faster rate under free (and lower) prices. They want to induce an emigration so large and so rapid that farm production actually will fall or at least be held in check. Yet they do not specify how this movement would take place, nor where the increasing number of migrants would go. National unemployment rates have shown a stubborn tendency to remain excessively high. Our economy shows little promise of bring able to absorb large numbers of displaced farmers. There are ample job opportunities for highly trained people even when unemployment rates are high, but farm operators are not apt to possess the skills that are in short supply. They are more likely to join the ranks of those already technologically unemployed in industrial areas.

On the other hand, the price support and production control advocates have hardly noticed the effect of their agricultural programs on farm population adjustments. Congress has been reluctant to support such proposals as the whole-farm Conservation Reserve, which would encourage the out-migration of rural people. Legislators have responded to the outcry from rural towns, which have seen in these proposals their own eventual economic attrition. Programs aimed at shifting marginal land toward more extensive uses encourage movements of farm people out of agriculture if they are on a whole-farm basis, or at least if acreage limitations are not imposed on each farm. However, diversion programs tend to inhibit population movements if they are applied to all farms on a proportionate basis. This distinction is often overlooked.

The population problem should be made more explicit in farm policy discussions. This would discomfit the many people who are upset by the farm population decline, and who want to stop it. They seem to think that, if we don't mention it, maybe it will go away. However, almost no one who traces the historic shift of farm people to the city, who considers the technological base on which it feeds, or who sees the implications of this shift to economic growth can resist the logic very long. The problem is not one of keeping farm people from leaving, or even of slowing down their migration, it is whether the movement can be facilitated by various policies available to us.

The Employment Act of 1946 commits the country to full employment as a matter of national policy. Supposedly, then, any farm person who is disemployed by advancing technology is assured of the availability of other employment opportunities. When we speak of the need for further resource adjustments in agriculture, we have to assume that these opportunities are available. Even if they are, does the adjustment process function automatically? Is it enough to have the federal Employment Service provide the necessary information to anyone ignorant of job opportunities? The population adjustment problem involves more than the mere availability of job information, which is clearly beyond the power of the local community or even the state to handle. It is a national problem, since issues of employment opportunities and unemployed people involve the national job market.

One issue concerns the number of job opportunities. Where are future job opportunities to be created? Where is future economic growth going to take place? There has been much wishful thinking in rural communities about the possibilities of attracting new industry. Uneconomic ventures have been subsidized heavily by communities for long periods of time only to prove incapable of survival. The development of industry in rural areas involves a cost, but so does the out-movement of people. Are there places where new economic activity can be generated in a rural area at a lower social cost than that in moving farm people to already heavily industrialized areas, and setting up the educational and other facilities to service them? We have never examined this question systematically at the national level. States and cities compete for new plants; corporations decide on the location of new plants; military agencies choose the location of defense installations, which represent a good part of the national defense budget of over $50 billion. In this process we have created a few extremely populous areas—super cities—while depopulating other regions. Between 1950 and 1960, some 300 metropolitan counties accounted for 85 percent of the nation's population growth; and more than half of this occurred in 50 metropolitan counties. Yet no planning for this growth occurred at the national level, and no national policy on the location of future industrial growth has been promulgated.

It is true that the Area Redevelopment Act of 1961, administered by the Department of Commerce, was aimed at stimulating economic activity in certain eligible areas. Also, the Rural Areas Development program of the USDA is designed to help local groups with their economic development projects in rural areas. But much more attention should be given to the locational aspects of industrial development than in the past, particularly at the national level. Except in times of emergency, industrial development has gone its own way, with society following along, making such adjustments and additional investments to support it as are forced upon it.

A second important issue is the kind of help and encouragement that might be given to those willing to move from rural areas to new nonfarm jobs. "Homesteads in reverse" proposals offer possibilities.[4] Important progress has been made recently under the Manpower Development and Training Act of 1962 and the Vocational Education Act of 1963. These programs include many of the measures which have been suggested in time past, such as broadened concepts of vocational training, new vocational programs—such as agri-business—and part-time employment for needy students while taking training. They include counseling, and more aggressive efforts in job placement.

These efforts should not be regarded as emergency—and thus temporary—measures. They have been needed for a long time; they are but a start in getting at the roots of the problem of effective use of human resources.[5] For example, should we supply long-term credit to young people from designated areas of surplus population who are willing to leave the area to find jobs? Could we issue special funds to families that have tried and failed at farming to help them become established in some other vocation? Such subsidies might include moving allowances and relocational rental allowances for specified periods, as well as the costs of specialized training.

[4] Theodore W. Schultz, "An Alternative Diagnosis of the Farm Problem," *Journal of Farm Economics*, 38 (December, 1956), 1137–52.

[5] See Howard W. Ottoson, "Lessening Impacts of Land Withdrawals on Nonfarm Resources and on Rural Communities," ch. 19 in *Dynamics of Land Use—Needed Adjustment* (Ames: Iowa State University Press, 1961), pp. 298–316.

# CHAPTER 20

# Adjusting Community Services in the Northern Plains

WHAT is a community? One may think of the term as either a social or economic concept. From the social standpoint, a community must contain elements that make it interesting and satisfying to its residents. From the economic point of view, it must be large enough to provide, in an efficient way, the various services desired by its residents. Compromise is required to reconcile these two viewpoints; thus people do not want to spend too much in order to provide a satisfactory local environment. When this happens they will either move to a community where services are cheaper, or change the organization by which the services are provided.

People are actually related to several communities at once. They may live in one community, in a certain geographical area, but they may also identify themselves with other centers from which they obtain consumption items; education for their children, medical service, or other services. Each type of social or economic service has its own unique service area, differing from others in size and shape, and over-lapping or encompassing others in varying degrees. Thus the concept of community involves a complex of social and economic interests and public administration.

Our concern in this chapter is with how the various services desired by Northern Plains people can be provided efficiently, particularly in view of the large spatial areas involved. We shall deal here with the public and quasi-public part of the community; in Chapter 21 we shall focus on the farm city and its economic importance.

In our concern about the spatial aspect of Northern Plains communities, we should not overlook the implications of transporatation technologies. They force us to broaden our concept of space, to view it in the context of time as well as distance. In terms of transportation time, today's Northern Plains communities have much broader physical limits, a fact which offsets the effects of population loss in some ways. Thus in 1910, one could travel about 6 miles in the Northern Plains country in an hour. In the same time today, one can travel at least 40 miles. With the north–south and east–west grid system of roads, typical of the Northern Plains country, a town's area of influence might have covered 72 square miles in 1910 (Figure 64).

With a population density of 12.8 persons per square mile (which actually obtained in the five-county central-Nebraska study area in 1910), the area would have in-cluded 922 people. Viewing space in the time-distance context, and with a decline to the present density of 8.2 persons per square mile, a similar town's influence

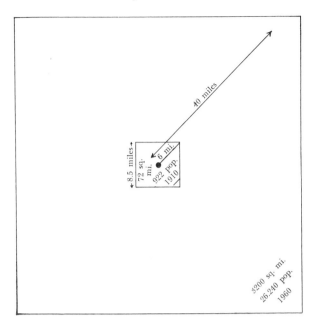

FIG. 64. THE EXPANDING PLAINS COMMUNITY, 1910 TO 1960

today would extend over a 3,200-square-mile area with a population of 26,240. Thus, even though some communities have been losing population, the shrinkage of distance, in term of time, has had a compensatory effect. It provides some of these communities with the opportunity to enlarge their population and resource base through reorganization and consolidation. Modern transportation allows the town to reach farther out toward its rural clientele, and it gives the farmer a wider choice of communities to satisfy his economic and social needs. Shrinking population per square mile accents the need for community reorganization in the Northern Plains. The revolution in transportation provides its opportunity.

## LOCAL GOVERNMENT

What kinds of local government shall we have in the Northern Plains transition area in 2000 A.D.? The general trend should be toward streamlined functions and fewer units. Let us now examine each type of government as to its functions and probable future.

### The Township

With all due respect to the place they once served in rural government, townships in Nebraska and other Plains states seem to be completely outmoded. Their mortality has not been high during the past twenty-five years in Nebraska—their number declined only from 506 to 478—but their eventual demise appears inevitable.

Most citizens take little interest in their township government. It is inefficient; the costs of township-county government in supervisor counties in Nebraska is substantially higher than the costs of county government in commissioner counties with comparable services.[1] The traditional functions of townships have gradually been transferred to other units of government, leaving them largely with the provision and maintenance of rural roads. However, they are too small to make effective use of modern machinery or to employ other than part-time labor in road maintenance. The counties and the state provide the more important rural roads. Townships are also too small for efficient and effective tax assessment.

### The County

Although county consolidation has been discussed in the Plains for decades, no action has ever resulted. Indeed, between 1942 and 1957, the number of counties in the entire nation declined by only three.[2] Since that time, Connecticut has abolished all of its eight counties, but Wisconsin has added one (formerly an Indian reservation). Despite the lack of progress, interest in the matter continues.

Several standards can be applied to counties to determine their economic efficiency. In the first place, the county seat should be accessible to the population. A Kansas survey found that citizens visited their courthouse an average of 2.4 times per year; and therefore it should be possible to drive to the county seat and return in one day. This means that, in terms of today's driving, the county seat should probably be within 100 miles of any point in the county. A second criterion is based on the county's area. Some competent authorities have concluded that " the maximum area of a county may vary from 900 to 6,400 square miles, the figure taken depending upon the location of the county seat, the distribution of the population to be served and the rate of driving speed."[3] By this standard, a square county would not exceed 80 miles on a side.

A third criterion is population. A common rule of thumb in the past has been a minimum of 30,000 people, though further savings are possible up to a population of 50,000.[4] Perhaps the most important criterion is the quantity of resources represented by the area; and the value of taxable property is a useful measure here. An efficient level of resources was found to be around $20 million in the 1930's.

In applying these four standards to Nebraska counties, we must first upgrade the assessed valuation figure to reflect the changed price level today. Thus in current dollars, a workable minimum might be $40 million. We must keep in mind, too, that advances in transportation have shrunk distances since the 1930's. Also, a "maximum" area in another part of the country tends to be more nearly an ideal—or even a minimum—in the Northern Plains, where distances are so vast. Thus a 6,400-square-mile area, which indeed might represent a maximum in the more densely populated states of the east, might be a reasonable goal for Nebraska. When we apply the minima of 30,000 people and $40 million assessed valuation to Nebraska's 93 counties, we find that only six counties meet both criteria. Fifteen counties meet one but not both standards, and seventy-two are deficient on both counts. In addition,

[1] *Survey of the Financial Administration of Nebraska Counties*, Works Progress Administration (June, 1938), p. 142.

[2] Clarence J. Hein, "Local Government in Sparsely Populated Areas," *Journal of Farm Economics*, XLII, No. 4 (November, 1960), 835.

[3] *Survey of the Financial Administration of Nebraska Counties*, p. 20.

[4] *Ibid.*, p. 154.

seventy-three Nebraska counties have areas of less than 900 square miles. More than two out of three counties in the state cannot satisfy any of the three criteria; area, population, or assessed valuation.

Since each of these deficiencies contributes to higher costs of services, one would conclude that the present system of counties in Nebraska is inefficient. Almost any move in the direction of county consolidation would be an improvement.

As an example of the possibilities, consider four rural counties in the Nebraska transition area, each of which has a population of 1,500–2,000 families and per capita tangible wealth of less than $2,500. With a tax base between $10 million and $17 million per county, one would expect county services to be handicapped. On the other hand, if these four counties were to be combined into a single unit, with an area of 2,300 square miles and a population of more than 23,000, county institutions could be supported by $56,530,000 of tangible property, providing a larger base for the support of services and the possibility of efficiency in providing them.

It would be possible to administer these counties with a staff not much larger than that of each of them today. This is not to imply that costs could be reduced by three-fourths or more, but, with the spreading of fixed costs of staff, buildings, and equipment over a much larger base, substantial savings should be attainable. And this improvement would not be at the expense of travel convenience since everyone in such an enlarged county would still be within an easy hour's drive (less than 45 miles) from an administrative center.

To illustrate the possibilities, we attempted to redraw the map of Nebraska by outlining groups of counties which might be candidates for consolidation, keeping in mind the criteria listed above. As a starting point, we used the Economic Areas of the Census Bureau, which are shown in Figure 65. These areas are formed by combining counties with similar characteristics; thus the way of life of the people, the type of farming carried on, etc., are fairly homogeneous in each area. The largest cities, with their counties, are distinguished as Metropolitan State Economic Areas. As Figure 65 shows, some of these areas, such as area 1, the Sandhills, are much too large for effective local administration, and would have to be subdivided for our purposes. There are also instances where one county, such as Boyd or Box Butte, must be taken from its Economic Area and included with a different one to make the grouping more nearly square for travel efficiency. With these exceptions, then, the groups of counties, based broadly on Economic Areas, is shown in Figure 66.

As Table 92 indicates, all of the grouped counties meet the assessed valuation criterion and only two fail to meet the 20,000 population minimum. It should be noted that the latter are in the Sandhills, an area so sparsely settled that normal rules of thumb on population cannot be applied. The areas of these supercounties appear at first sight to be enormous, but this is largely owing to the unrealistically small size of our present-day counties. The largest, with about 8,000 square miles, would still be only about 90 miles square. Thus the person living farthest away from a centrally located county seat would be about a 90-mile drive away from it on rectangular roads (N–S and E–W). Such a trip would be well within the one-day limit we have set. If a radial road system were eventually developed, he would be much closer. And this, it should be remembered, is the person worst situated; the bulk of the population would be much nearer to the center of administration.

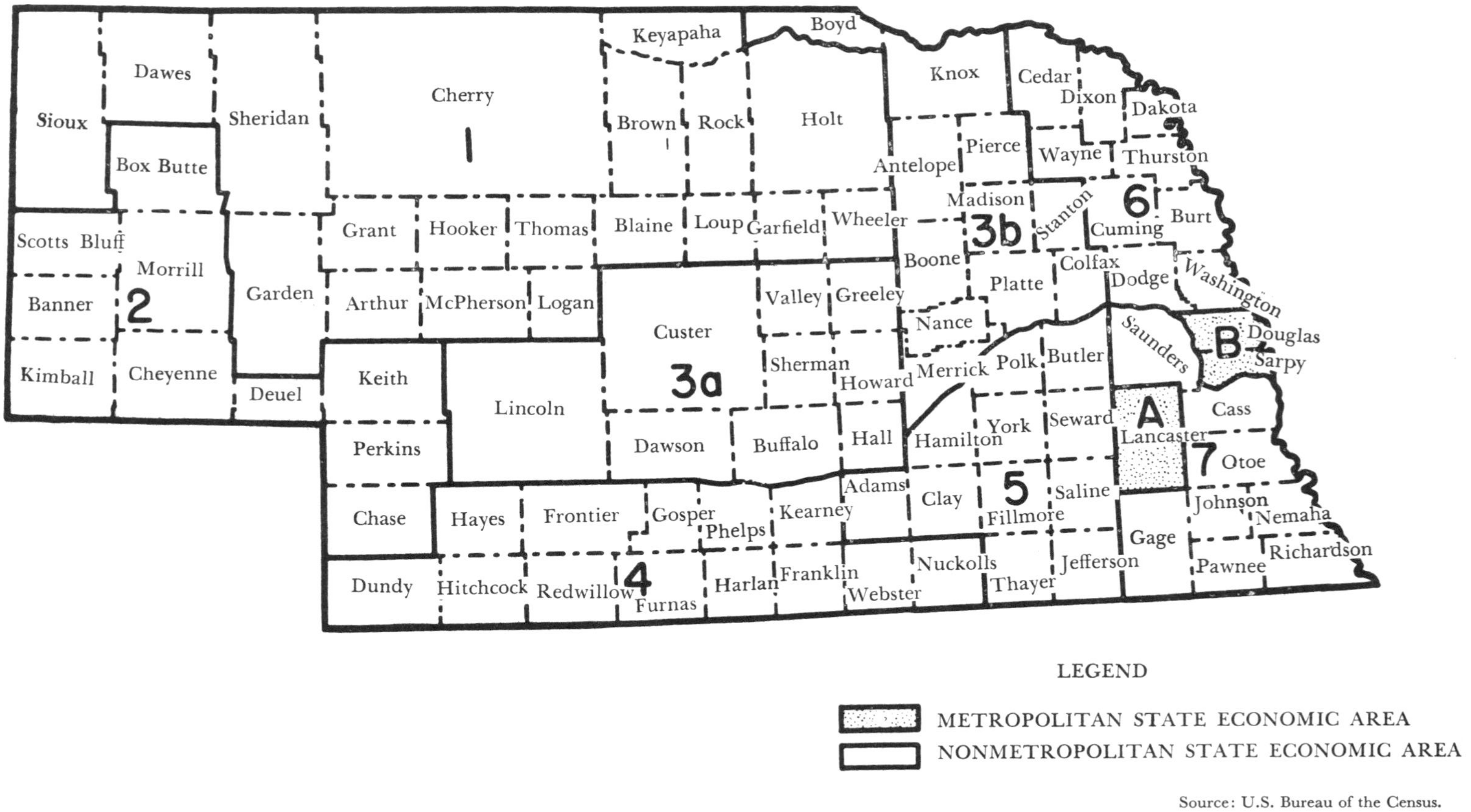

Source: U.S. Bureau of the Census.

LEGEND

METROPOLITAN STATE ECONOMIC AREA

NONMETROPOLITAN STATE ECONOMIC AREA

FIG. 65. NEBRASKA STATE ECONOMIC AREAS

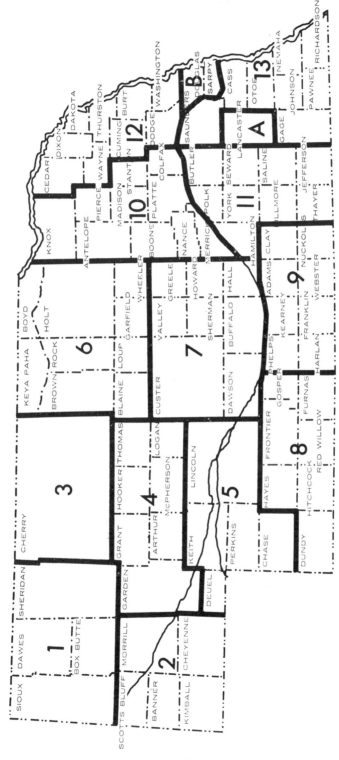

FIG. 66. ENLARGED COUNTIES IN NEBRASKA, A FIRST APPROXIMATION

TABLE 92.   AREA, POPULATION, AND ASSESSED VALUATION (IN THOUSAND DOLLARS) FOR COUNTY GROUPS SHOWN IN FIGURE 66 (NEBRASKA)

| County Group | Number of Counties Included | Area (Sq. Mi.) | Population | Assessed Valuation |
|---|---|---|---|---|
| 1. . . . . . . | 4 | 6,984 | 32,848 | 87,814 |
| 2. . . . . . . | 5 | 5,006 | 64,938 | 194,008 |
| 3. . . . . . . | 1 | 5,982 | 8,218 | 41,647 |
| 4. . . . . . . | 7 | 6,016 | 9,212 | 46,022 |
| 5. . . . . . . | 5 | 5,806 | 48,080 | 143,275 |
| 6. . . . . . . | 9 | 8,376 | 33,006 | 97,309 |
| 7. . . . . . . | 8 | 7,309 | 121,023 | 289,643 |
| 8. . . . . . . | 7 | 5,212 | 37,769 | 104,292 |
| 9. . . . . . . | 8 | 4,475 | 79,012 | 202,353 |
| 10. . . . . . . | 10 | 6,199 | 119,845 | 295,230 |
| 11. . . . . . . | 9 | 5,011 | 96,246 | 282,944 |
| 12. . . . . . . | 9 | 4,280 | 118,039 | 305,755 |
| 13. . . . . . . | 8 | 4,542 | 113,051 | 278,639 |
| A. . . . . . . | 1 | 845 | 155,272 | 231,163 |
| B. . . . . . . | 2 | 569 | 374,771 | 677,900 |

Sources: Data on area and population from U.S. Bureau of the Census, *U.S. Census of Population, 1960,* Nebraska, Number of Inhabitants, PC(1), 29A, table 6. Data on assessed valuation from Nebraska State Tax Commissioner and the State Board of Equalization and Assessment, *Annual Report,* 1961, p. 95. Data refer to assessed valuation of all tangible property in each county.

In terms of today's driving conditions, a grouping like the one shown seems such reasonable way to organize for public administration in Nebraska that it should l well-nigh irresistible. The political realities are such, however, that any move towa combination is doomed to defeat. Nevertheless, the grouping shown may give pr gressive county administrations some hints as to where to look for natural ways consolidate functions among counties, even when the legal units are to rema separate.

The county groups in Figure 66 are not by any means the best that could devised. They are, in fact, only a first approximation. For example, if present coun boundaries were ignored, new boundaries could be based on natural topographic divisions, which would be more logical. The supercounties shown are present partly for their shock value: they seem so huge that the initial reaction is to thi "This is going too far." Yet with modern transportation and with the populati changes in the Plains, which give every indication of continuing, these combinatio may not go far enough for a permanent long-run solution.

Particularly when the most efficient operation is associated with populations more than 50,000, it is difficult to see how these groupings could be made mu smaller without diluting the possible economies. All this is not to imply that coun consolidation is just around the corner. It is not going to come easily, or it wou have started before this in the Plains. Yet some move in this direction seems eminen logical, and pressure for it will increase as costs of local government keep rising.

In the meantime, other changes have been suggested to improve the effectiven and to reduce the cost of county government. Some of these, but not all, a substitutes for consolidation.

*Administrative Reorganization*

A simple way to economize where the workload of county officers is low is to reduce the number of elected officials by combining some offices. Thus the county clerk, the registrar of deeds, and the county treasurer might be combined into one office. Most Nebraska counties have combined some elected offices.

A more complicated set of suggestions involves the relations between the county board and other county officials. Counties often suffer from ineffective administration. The chief governing body of the county, the board, performs both legislative and executive functions. However, it has no control over the independently elected county officers: the treasurer, the sheriff, the county superintendent of schools, and the others. No single person has responsibility for the government of the county or can view the county as a whole—in the same way as the mayor of a city or a state governor. No one has the authority to plan improvements, nor the responsibility for carrying them out. This situation hardly makes for progress.

The improvements of county government would involve a separation of the legislative from the executive function and the organization of the executive branch to provide a central office with clear responsibility for administration. The county board could be given all legislative responsibility. Representing the voters, the board would make policy for the county in the same way as a city council or a state legislature. The executive branch could be headed by a county president, who might be elected, or by a county manager appointed by the board.

The executive officers of the county—the registrar of deeds, the sheriff, and the rest—could be appointed by the president or manager, and be responsible to him. He would have the power to fire as well as to hire, and of course his actions would always be answerable to the board. The county judge would be elected independently, constituting the judicial branch of government. There may be some argument in favor of keeping the county superintendent as an independently elected official.

It must be noted that improvement in county government is basically in the hands of the state, since the county is a creature of the state and is legally an extension of state government. In Nebraska, for example, a county manager system is unconstitutional because all county officers must be elected. Any discussion of county government improvement must consider the relations between county and state government. Specialists in government suggest the need for "functional reallocation," a redistribution of functions between county and state government in accordance with logical principles. In considering the total task of state and county government, it is apparent that the following functions have passed largely in fact, if not in theory, from the jurisdiction of the county to that of the state: law enforcement, highway construction and maintenance, health work, relief and welfare work, education, and assessment of property for taxation.

What will be the responsibilities of the county of the future? Perhaps we have not yet been imaginative enough in considering the problems with which the county will have to deal, and perhaps this may help explain our failure to improve county government. Contrary to the opinion of some people, the county is not on the way out. The focus of county governmental activity is going to change, and, as it does, there will be a demand for improvement of its processes. Thus, in the future, counties are going to be more concerned with the development of local recreational facilities, including such activities as hunting, camping, boating, and other things particularly involving local residents. County hospitals, libraries, museums, and airports may become more common. Local roads will continue to be a county responsibility, and will remain a problem in the face of farm enlargement and declining rural population.

Land-use zoning is a natural for counties, although few of them have as yet become involved in zoning activities. With increasing competition for land and water, citizens will become more concerned about uses of land that may be contrary to the public interest. Counties will become involved with the location of industrial enterprises, particularly outside the boundaries of cities. They will also become more active in the licensing and supervision of rural entertainment facilities—night clubs, taverns, and rural lodging and eating places. They may also regulate the construction or alteration of buildings, including even farm buildings.

Counties will become increasingly concerned with issues of economic development. It is more logical for counties—especially enlarged ones, whose boundaries roughly coincide with the emerging rural trade areas—to be involved in the inventory of local resources, analysis of development alternatives, and planning for action to encourage economic development than it is for several small towns to individually undertake these same activities with duplication of effort and frustration because of limited possibilities. Viable counties could have permanent planning boards that study all types of changes involving public support in the county area.

The above discussion implies that counties will become more and more like cities in the way that they are organized and operated. They will be more responsive to public demands for change, more aggressive in pursuing interesting possibilities for change, and more responsible in carrying out local policies. If they are to achieve these, they will not only have to be reorganized but they will also have to be given sufficient legislative power to act—and certainly as much power as is now enjoyed by incorporated cities. The alternative to "home rule" may well be "home ruin."

### Intercounty Districts

An alternative to county consolidation is the creation of special-purpose districts, composed of two or more counties to carry out some special task. Thus, in the Northern Plains, we are beginning to see the formation of extension districts through which agricultural extension programs in several counties with fairly homogeneous agriculture can be coordinated to take advantage of resident specialists. These specialists may replace most of the "generalist" county agricultural agents, in time. Similar district arrangements might be used for the administration of education: thus, a district superintendent of schools instead of a county superintendent.

Property assessment for taxation could be handled by district assessors. Health districts might include several counties so as to provide for adequate staffing in sparsely populated areas. Similarly, several counties could establish county road districts that are large enough to justify full-time trained engineers and proper equipment. A number of counties might cooperate for economic development—with a permanent district planning board whose recommendations would, of course, be referred to the individual counties for action.

## OTHER SERVICES

*The Schools*

In viewing the future of education in the Northern Plains transition area, it is apparent that consolidation will continue for a long time. The rural one-room school, despite the remaining numbers, is dying rapidly. We shall continue to see rural one-room school districts consolidate with larger districts, and even the latter will be further combined into larger units.

In planning for education in the transition area, the distinction between country and town in the minds of the people must be eliminated. School reorganization will eventually involve districts that encompass all the countryside, as well as the towns. The high school is the logical starting point in planning the reorganized school district. A four-year high school, with two hundred students, is regarded as an absolute minimum from the standpoint of efficient operation, as well as breadth of program.[5] Dr. James B. Conant, in his study of the American high school, recommended a size large enough to have one hundred in the graduating class. This would mean a four-year high school of more than four hundred, the actual number depending upon dropouts. In the central-Nebraska transition area, meeting even the 200-student minimum would entail a reduction in the number of high schools—from the present twenty-five to fourteen.

The high school should preferably be located in a farm city, both from the educational standpoint and because the network of rural roads will converge on the farm city. It should be near the center of the high school district.

To produce a secondary enrollment of three hundred, which we might pose as a compromise target, the minimum number of children in kindergarten through eighth grade in the reorganized district would have to reach 675. This means that the total number of young people in kindergarten through the twelfth grade would number 975. Yet this is a bare minimum; the smallest defensible total enrollment in a modern school district is generally considered to be 1,200.[6] One might, on this basis, reduce school districts in the five-county Nebraska transition area from the current 242 to 8, in districts of about 1,200 students each, with today's population levels. Admittedly, with further loss of population these numbers will shrink. It would be best to plan in terms of numbers larger than the minimum of 1,200 to allow for this decline, say a minimum of 1,500 students.

Jealousy between communities and local pride are continuing obstacles to the consolidation of schools in rural areas. Small towns face a difficult choice between closing up the antiquated local school and sending their students to a neighboring town, on the one hand, and having their children continue their education in inadequate facilities, or incurring excessively high costs in improving small-scale plants, on the other. Having their students go elsewhere to school becomes a symbol of decline; but consolidation, by definition, means that a certain part of the existing school facilities will be closed. However, it does not mean that all the schools have to be located in one town.

---

[5] S. J. Knezevich, "The Changing Structure of Public Education," *Urban Responses to Agricultural Change,* Clyde F. Kohn (ed.) (Iowa City: State University of Iowa Press, 1961), p. 181.

[6] *Ibid.,* p. 181.

Elementary schools need to be large enough to operate with one teacher per grade. With a minimum of 20 pupils per grade, this means that an elementary school (K–8) needs a minimum of 180 pupils. In other words, in a district with 1,200 students in grades kindergarten through 12, five elementary schools could operate economically. There is no reason why the towns of the new consolidated district could not work together, deciding mutually on the location of elementary schools in the district. The high school could then be located in the largest central town, along with the necessary elementary facilities, also servicing the students living in that town. Adoption of such a plan would provide substantial economies.

School consolidation has other implications for sparsely populated areas. First, it is obvious that consolidation of schools depends on the presence of all-weather roads by which students can be transported to schools. The tendency of some farmers to move to town or to maintain two residences—one in town and the other on the farm —will be encouraged by consolidation, as will the location of new farmsteads on all-weather roads. The costs of transporting children to school would be materially reduced if rural farmsteads were concentrated along a few good roads rather than dispersed over the countryside. With the integration of town and farm people in large school districts, the latter will have more to say about the educational programs in the high school of the central city. On the other hand, city people are going to have an interest in the factors affecting the cost of educating farm children, such as the location of farmsteads.

Other changes are possible. What about hiring traveling teachers for specialized subjects, such as music and languages at the elementary level, who might commute between elementary schools in a district on a regular basis? Television may also offer new possibilities for reaching larger classes in specialized subjects, such as advanced high school mathematics. The larger high schools will permit greater specialization in curricula, such as college preparatory, vocational agriculture, and other vocational and business subjects. A small number of specialized vocational high schools, supported by several districts or directly by the state, would fulfill an educational function now poorly served in the Northern Plains area. The larger district high schools could also provide a variety of adult evening classes and short courses that are currently unavailable in small high schools because of lack of diversity and specialization in teaching staff.

The ideas on education outlined here are unenthusiastically received by many people in the Northern Plains. However, our objective is to strengthen rural areas by raising their elementary and secondary training to a level more comparable with that of larger urban centers.

*State Aid and School Consolidation.*   The connection between state aid and the consolidation of schools in rural areas has been missed in the discussions of the pros and cons of state aid. Actually, state aid is a means of equalizing the educational opportunities of children in rural districts with those in urban areas. It is also a "carrot" that the state can use to encourage backward regions to improve the quality of facilities and instruction. It will be the means by which the consolidation of rural schools eventually becomes complete. The contribution of states to local education is going to increase; in fact, we shall probably see the time when the bulk of the costs of local education will be borne by the states.

## Roads

The dual problem in the transition area with respect to roads is how to improve service, on the one hand, and consolidate facilities, on the other. Intercounty co-operation in trained personnel and equipment has already been suggested. Future road systems can be planned for much greater economies and better quality if a sufficiently long perspective is employed. The ideal road system would provide an all-weather road to every farm. Such roads are costly to build and to maintain, especially if they are to be kept free of snow in winter.

How can the cost be minimized? Part of the answer lies in long-range planning of the location of rural residences, and schematic analysis is illustrative here. Figure 67a shows a hypothetical residence pattern in a Nebraska township. There are 72 miles of roads in the township, originally serving 144 farmsteads, with an average farm size of 160 acres. With farm consolidation and the vacating of half of the farmsteads, the same road system would serve 72 farmsteads, or one mile per farmstead. If farm size were eventually to average 720 acres, there would be two miles of road per farmstead.

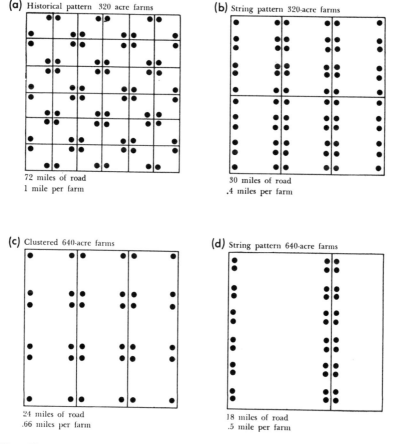

(a) Historical pattern 320 acre farms

72 miles of road
1 mile per farm

(b) String pattern 320-acre farms

30 miles of road
.4 miles per farm

(c) Clustered 640-acre farms

24 miles of road
.66 miles per farm

(d) String pattern 640-acre farms

18 miles of road
.5 mile per farm

FIG. 67. ALTERNATIVE RESIDENCE PATTERNS IN A RURAL TOWNSHIP, WITH
RESULTING ROAD SYSTEMS

Of course, as farms have been consolidated, certain rural roads have been closed (where possible).

However, let us assume that, over time, certain selected roads were closed deliberately to give the road pattern shown in Figure 67*b*. The total mileage would shrink to 30 miles, or .4 mile per 320-acre farm. The neighborhood aspects of the road would be maintained in the process. With a further consolidation of farms to an average of 640 acres, and the closing of an additional 6 miles of roads, the pattern might result as shown in Figure 67*c*. It would take an average of .67 miles of road to service the farmers under this plan. It would be possible to eliminate another 6 miles of road, as in Figure 67*d* if the 640-acre farms were a half-mile wide and two miles long, instead of a mile square. This would cut the road mileage per farm to .5.

Nor does this exhaust the possibilities. The federal government has subsidized the construction of several hundred thousand miles of secondary roads in the country. Should this program continue or be expanded, there might well be economies in subsidizing the relocation of rural residences, as an alternative to road construction, in some sparsely populated areas.

Every county should have a long-run road plan that is geared to estimated future population levels and farm size—as well as to the long-run goals of the people regarding school reorganization, economic development, and other changes they might wish to make.

## Churches

Rural churches will continue to be affected by the combination of population decline and the revolution in transportation, in the same way as the schools and other institutions. Their basic economic problem is also the same: how to achieve a "volume of business" large enough to be efficient in providing the values desired by the members.

We distinguish between the sect-type of religious organization, referred to as fundamentalist, and the church-type, which includes the organized denominations. Commonly, the first type operates with small congregations, meager budgets, and poorly trained leadership; it is typically found among economically disadvantaged groups, both rural and urban. This discussion, however, relates to the denominational churches.

The future of the rural church can be seen in projections of current trends in rural communities. The congregations have been shrinking; and they will have to be reorganized, very much as the schools will be, if they are to grow to an "efficient" size. It is useful to have a minimum standard for the size of rural congregations (and more research is needed on the subject), but some experts suggest 300 to 400 members as a minimum. One organized church per 1,000 population has also been suggested as a maximum density.[7]

At any rate, a congregation should be large enough to provide a budget which supports a full-time minister with adequate training, together with the facilities and equipment to carry on a challenging program. At the rate of 300 members per

[7] O. F. Larson and E. A. Lutz, "Community Facilities," ch. 11 in *Adjustments in Agriculture—A National Basebook* (Iowa City: State University of Iowa Press, 1961), p. 308.

congregation, in the five central-Nebraska transition-area counties this would mean a maximum of 45 congregations, compared with the present 106.[8] Several steps have been taken to remedy this "overchurched" condition, and no doubt more of them will be taken in the future.

In the first place, it is clear that the rural church will continue to "move to town." Both the farm-city and the satellite towns are logical centers for church activity. They provide nuclei of populations around which to build congregations. With the urbanization of farmers, they will attract farm people to them. The rural church of the future is going to have farm and town members working together.

The rural church that is large enough to function efficiently will have several advantages in attracting all age groups. Properly trained ministers will be better equipped to deal with the human problems of their parishes, and expanded educational programs will become feasible. These churches will offer greater social opportunities for young people. Specialization among church staff-members will be possible where the congregations are large enough to support more than one staff person.

It seems obvious that more planning will be required than has been given in the past to both the demise of dying churches and the creation of new ones. The "larger parish" plan provides denominations with a means of serving widely scattered congregations of the same denominations with several staff-members working together and using existing buildings in outlying areas. It is also a convenient way to move toward eventual consolidation of facilities, as when a new church building is constructed.

Cooperation between Protestant denominations, through the Council of Churches, can result in comity arrangements in rural areas, and one denomination can be assigned primary responsibility for recruitment in an area that has been judged capable of supporting a community church. This approach will probably be more widely used in the future than the federated type of church.

## Recreation

The evidence at hand points to an increasing demand for recreation by people in the Northern Plains transition area. Organizing for recreation presents some difficult problems for people in the Northern Plains. They are conscious of the spectacular scenery of the mountains to the west—and also of the traditional characterization of of the Plains as "mere space" separating the more populous regions to the east from the western attractions. Yet Plains people are going to be willing to spend more money for recreation of all kinds in the future. If the Plains are to offer a satisfying environment for living, deliberate planning for recreation will be necessary.

Larger high schools offer an opportunity for encouraging various types of cultural recreation: painting, music, drama, folk dancing, pageants, and writing; the opportunities are unlimited. The churches also have a contribution to make here. Expanding towns will need to plan for recreational facilities, such as swimming pools, tennis courts, and community centers, to serve not only the resident population but also the surrounding farm areas.

---

[8] Based on data in *Churches and Church Membership in the United States*, National Council of Churches, Bureau of Research and Survey, Series C, No. 28, table 64, part II. Data on church membership as of 1953.

Plains communities have been particularly lax in developing outdoor recreational facilities for local use. The states, however, have been doing a more effective job in this respect, and it is to be expected that they will continue to take the lead in the development of camping and picnic facilities. However, counties should have a special place in the development of picnic areas, county campgrounds, swimming facilities, fishing facilities in connection with reservoir development, and hunting areas. Such facilities might be designed for local residents or for tourists.

Under the Food and Agriculture Act of 1962, nonprofit organizations, such as soil conservation districts, local governments, or sportsmen's associations, can obtain loans from the Farmers Home Administration for many of these purposes. Farmers and ranchers can also borrow FHA funds for the development of recreational facilities for income purposes on their lands.

It would seem that in many areas the opportunities for developing small-game hunting have been unexploited. The number of small-game hunters is going to rise steadily; on the other hand, there is an increasing tendency to post rural lands to prevent hunting. We need to find ways to bring this supply and demand together; and many different arrangements are possible.

There should also be opportunities for farmers to provide farm experiences to city people—riding, farm work, or viewing Plains sunsets. The dude ranches of the west indicate what can be done along these lines.

# CHAPTER 21

# The Farm City as an Emerging Economic Center

CHANGE has characterized Northern Plains towns since settlement days.[1] People first settled in neighborhoods centered around schools, churches, blacksmith shops, general stores, or taverns. Villages and towns sprang up at crossroads or at other strategic transportation centers. In the west, they sometimes preceded the settlement of the land, being created by the railroads or the speculators who anticipated or followed the route of a new line. Other towns or villages were created to satisfy the settlers' demands for goods and services.

The "team-haul" distance determined their density. Most of them incorporated as municipalities and cut themselves off governmentally from the township into which the rural areas organized. A few fortunate sites became county seats of the newly organized counties. Later, there emerged the interdependent community in which farmers became more closely identified with the town in whose trade area they lived, while townspeople began to appreciate the extent to which their fortunes were tied to those of nearby farm people.

More recently, we have come to recognize the interdependence between various communities. In such a closely meshed network, there is little basis for exploitation or competition between farm and town people in the Northern Plains. Their future economic progress depends on recognition of their mutual interests.

*Effects of Emigration*

Population dynamics in the Northern Plains have been discussed already, and future levels of out-migration have been estimated. These declines will affect the economic life of the towns chiefly through their influence on farm incomes.

In the transition area, as large numbers of people leave agriculture, gross farm income may not be greatly changed. If farming should become more intensive, for example through the use of more fertilizer or irrigation, gross income in the area might even rise. If, as farm size expands, farming becomes less intensive(which seems more likely in the transition area), total farm marketings—and therefore gross income

[1] See Olaf F. Larson and E. A. Lutz. "Adjustments in Community Facilities, Taking Place and Needed," ch. 11 in *Adjustments in Agriculture—A National Basebook* (Iowa City: Iowa State University Press, 1961). Also John H. Kolb. *Emerging Rural Communities* (Madison: University of Wisconsin Press, 1959), ch. 1.

—would probably fall. Yet it would not tend to fall as fast as the number of farmers, so that income per farmer is likely to rise as size of farm grows. This occurs as farmers take advantage of cost economies in the use of fixed inputs, such as machinery.

The towns will feel the effect of these changes through the altered spending patterns of farmers. Consumption expenditures will probably rise for items whose income elasticity is high, for example, education, recreation, and other "luxuries." Spending for staple items with low elasticities—food, work clothing, small household appliances—will probably decline. Purchases of production factors, such as machinery, fertilizer, fuel, and building material, may drop slightly—although it is dangerous to generalize here. Thus when farms grow larger, the total number of tractors needed may lessen, but the average size of each—or the total investment in tractor power—in the community may well rise. Similarly, fewer farm houses may be used, but new, more expensive ones may be built. If fertilizer has not been used up to its economic potential, its total consumption might increase on the fewer but larger farms, especially as decision-making becomes more sophisticated.

Earlier we noted the tendency for large communities in the transition area to expand in population, those of medium size to remain stable, and smaller ones to contract during the past decades (Chapter 15). There is no reason to suppose these trends will not continue for some time; in fact, if consumption patterns change as we have indicated above, these trends will be reinforced. Let us now consider some approaches these towns may take in adjusting to change.

*Declining towns.*   One strategy a declining town might pursue is to maintain the present level of public facilities and services. Even in the face of shrinking high school enrollments, the school board may decide to maintain the same teaching program, and even to make the additional investments necessary to meet rising standards. It may choose to maintain, and even upgrade, recreational facilities. Such a course of action will cost more money and take more effort per person in the declining community than in a town of larger size. However, in many declining communities, with the out-migration of younger people, a vicious circle comes into play. The leadership comes to rest in the hands of older, more conservative people whose reluctance to commit energy and funds to improvements simply speeds the demise of the community.

An alternative course of action the small town can take is to "roll with the punch." Admittedly, small communities of the size that is now declining face heavy odds against their independent survival. Perhaps the better strategy may be to try to determine their most likely role in the future and to capitalize on their best possibilities. Perhaps the fortunes of Jonesville, a town of 500, are tied more closely than its citizens realize to those of Smithburg, 10 miles away, with 2,500 people. Transportation has made them a part of the same larger community.

The long-run future of Jonesville may be that of a suburban center in relation to Smithburg. It probably makes no sense for Jonesville to try to keep its high school going; on the other hand, it can concentrate on having an up-to-date grade school to service its residents, as well as the farmers in its surrounding area. There should be an understanding with Smithburg on this matter.

Joint analysis and planning with Smithburg may also reveal that there is a place in Jonesville for a shopping center providing groceries, drugs, and other convenience items, medical service, a filling station, and a garage. On the other hand, the residents of Jonesville will look to Smithburg as a recreational and cultural center. Perhaps Jonesville might capitalize on some phase of outdoor recreation that might attract people from the whole economic area.

The point here is that Jonesville will survive only by specializing, by willingly giving up some of the features of a balanced town and by planning its future in cooperation with the other towns of the larger economic and social area of which it is a part.

*Stable and Expanding Towns.* In order to hold its own, or to expand, a town must first be large enough to take advantage of economies of scale in providing various social services—education, recreation, hospitals, and others. Second, it must get about the business of providing these services. People in Northern Plains communities are no longer satisfied with minimum levels of services. With modern-day communication, urban standards prevail among both farm people and residents of small towns. The problem of municipal government is to upgrade the level of existing services, as well as to provide the additional ones that will be requested by the citizens. Our culture is urban; in competing for people, and for growth activities, Northern Plains towns will have to be as attractive and satisfying places in which to live and work as are the larger cities. And thinking of them as places to work suggests the possibility of industrialization, often regarded as a panacea for the economic ills of Plains communities.

Rural communities are fighting an uphill battle in their attempts to attract new industry. Recent data on industrial expansion in this country show that new industry is developing in those areas that are already highly industrialized.[2] This does not mean that *no* industry is coming to rural areas, but it is a fact that this is contrary to the main trend. Thus rural areas will have to be particularly ingenious in capitalizing on their advantages if they are to be successful.

What are the general characteristics of industries likely to settle in rural areas? Rural communities have an advantage in attracting plants that (1) employ less than fifty workers, (2) do not require a highly skilled labor force, (3) are attracted to local raw materials, (4) do not require another local industry to service them, (5) have similar industries nearby, to contribute to a pool of trained workers, and (6) have managements that like a rural atmosphere.[3] Access to adequate rail and road transportation facilities also is essential.

Other factors that are considered by management when establishing a new plant area are:

| | |
|---|---|
| 1. Recreational facilities | 6. Fuel supply |
| 2. Educational facilities | 7. Tax structure |
| 3. Available housing | 8. Finances |
| 4. Water supplies | 9. Community facilities |
| 5. Sewage facilities | |

[2] L. T. Wallace and V. W. Ruttan, "Area Development and Industrial Decentralization," *Proceedings of a Conference on Area Development* (Athens: University of Georgia Press, 1962), p. 194.

[3] L. T. Wallace, "Your Community and Industrialization," Purdue University Extension Service Mimeograph EC–231.

For Northern Plains communities, most of the opportunities for industrial development seem to be associated with their large source of raw materials: agriculture. Communities have frequently overlooked this in seeking out more glamorous types of activities. Manufacturing based on agricultural raw products which should have promise in the future include (1) specialized feedlot operations, particularly in areas now exporting an important part of their feed production; (2) meat products, particularly pork; (3) vegetable and animal oils, such as soybean; (4) corn products; (5) cereal products; (6) liquid, frozen, and dried eggs; and (7) feed mixing.

A second type of industry adapted to the Northern Plains is aimed at serving local production needs by providing inputs for farming. Examples include (1) fertilizers, (2) herbicides and insecticides, (3) irrigation equipment, (4) hand tools and other farm equipment, (5) hay and grain dryers, and (6) building materials, such as bricks.

A third kind of industry that might do well in the Plains is one that produces for local consumption, using resources produced mainly or wholly within the area. Examples are fluid and dried milk, ice cream, bakery products, soft drinks, newspapers and books, and meat products.

A fourth prospect for Plains towns to consider is an industry that sells in a national or regional market—one whose raw material, though imported, represents only a minor part of the product's total cost; whose labor is an important cost component; and whose finished products are light and valuable. Examples include electrical equipment, machine tools, textiles, valves and fittings, and scientific instruments.

The prospects for products of these four types of industries vary. The demand for agricultural products, *in toto*, is directly related to the rate of population growth, though it may vary considerably from one product to another. Thus the demand for bread decreases as incomes rise; on the other hand, the quantity of meat consumed per person increases with gains in real income. As far as exports of farm products to other regions of the country are concerned, the brightest prospects for the Northern Plains seem to be in the growing Pacific Coast area and its increasing demand for meat products. The Northern Plains should have a transportation advantage over meat-producing areas to the east. Apart from this, the region should be able to maintain its share of the national market for farm products.

Industrial production of agricultural inputs can be expected to expand in the Northern Plains. Farmers will continue to increase their use of fertilizer, although at a slower rate. With more specialization in the farming industry, the market for mixed feeds, feed-handling equipment, and livestock equipment will be enhanced. Farmers will also continue to expand their use of insecticides, herbicides, and other specialized inputs.

The local market for consumption goods is directly related to population growth. Since this will be slower in the Northern Plains than in the country as a whole, growth in this market will be relatively modest.

Expansion in light, nonagricultural industry will come harder. Cities that already have such industries will find it easier to attract still more. As larger cities—Omaha, Kansas City, and Denver—continue to develop large industries, satellite plants can be established in smaller towns to take advantage of the labor market, or cheaper land. Plants based on female labor or winter farm labor would be particularly eligible. The latter are usually in marginal industries, however; rising labor productivity and rising wages associated with more efficient production tend to squeeze them out of prosperous areas.

In general, the Northern Plains is still at a disadvantage in the location of light, nonagricultural industry; it probably will not experience expansion at the national average rate for some time to come. Yet, as competition for space increases, and as educational, recreational, and other facilities are improved in the region, its competitive position may improve in the long run.

### The Emerging Farm City and Its Implications

This discussion of the prospects for industrial development brings to the fore a misconception widely prevalent in the Plains: economic development is viewed as the inherent "right" of every town, and any Chamber of Commerce worth its salt should be able to bring in a new plant. Also, the economic unit visualized is the individual town; if it is a county-seat town, the county may also be included, since its influence on the welfare of the county seat is recognized.

This tendency to view economic development in the context of the small town is reinforced by the sentimental attachment most people have toward their hometown and by the power local governments have to act on matters that affect industry, such as water and sewage facilities. Yet neither of these factors can supersede economic principles, which point to the need for planning and action in terms of much broader areas.

The notion of a "hierarchy of central places" is useful in showing the relations between towns and in locating the logical center for economic development.[4] A geographer, Alan Philbrick, classified all populated places in seven categories, based on their function. The first-order place is the household—the consuming unit (and, coincidentally, the farm business). The second-order place is a cluster of commercial and residential establishments plus the surrounding economic area, that is, the village or small town, whose principal function is retailing.

The next type, the third-order place, includes wholesaling as well as retailing; and its supporting area includes a number of second-order places (a typical example is a county-seat town). The fourth-order place includes the above functions, as well as transportation by rail and truck; again, it subsumes several third-order places and their supporting areas (Lincoln, Nebraska, is an example of a fourth-order city). Fifth-order places, such as Kansas City or Minneapolis, also serve exchange functions. Sixth-order places, like Chicago, exercise economic control; while New York City, a seventh-order place, in addition to all these other services provides leadership.

Which of these places can serve as a center for regional economic development? It should be large enough to support the commercial facilities and public services expected in a balanced, self-contained community. It should be so located as to make these services conveniently available to all residents of the area. The area must be large enough to embrace a labor force with some diversity in skills, but small enough to permit commuting between various points in the region. The area must have efficient and effective communication with the economy beyond its borders.

[4] See Karl A. Fox. "The Study of Interactions between Agriculture and the Nonfarm Economy: Local, Regional and National," *Journal of Farm Economics*, XLIV, No. 1 (February, 1962), 1–34, and Alan K. Philbrick, "Principles of Area Functional Organization in Regional Human Geography," *Economic Geography*, 33 (October, 1957), 299–336.

To decide such matters, we need to know something about the economies of size of various businesses.[5] For every kind of commercial establishment or public service, there is a minimum size that results in lowest unit costs. This occurs when fixed costs are spread over a sufficiently large number of units or volume of patronage. As one increases the size of business from small plants to larger and larger ones, unit costs fall rapidly. However, beyond a certain point, they cease falling, and we say that an efficient size has been reached.

A few clues concerning economies of size can be suggested. Thus about 2,000 families—or 6,000 people—are necessary to support one grocery supermarket of efficient size, while 15,000 to 20,000 residents are required to justify a radio station. A small grocery store needs a population of 1,540, a men's clothing store needs 2,680, and a hardware store needs 6,720—according to a Kansas study.[6] On the public service side, a good library needs 5,000 residents to be efficient. We have already suggested an enrollment of 1,200 students in a modern school district; and this implies a population of about 5,000.

These measures suggest that a self-contained area would include a minimum of 50,000 people, some of whom would live in the central city, some in smaller towns, and some in the country.

How large will our economic area be? It will probably be bounded by the maximum distance people are willing to travel to and from the central city for work or trade. Many people will drive for as much as an hour to a good job, which is equivalent to 40 or 50 miles, depending on the roads. They would prefer to drive no further for hospital care, to visit a medical clinic, or to obtain legal counsel.

Yet these "normal" distances are lengthening because of advances in transportation. A recent study reported that—

> Residents of a county in the Great Plains region—Kit Carson County in Colorado—used more than 200 different physicians in 1958. Seven physicians practiced in the county at the time. Most of the out-of-county physicians consulted were specialists, nearly one-half of whom practiced in Denver, more than 150 miles from Burlington, the county seat.[7]

The shape of an area and the road design affect its size when it is tailored to a maximum driving distance from the central city. Let us assume, for the moment, a 50-mile limit as the maximum. A square area meeting this limit, with a rectangular road system, would be 50 miles on a side, including 2,500 square miles. No resident would have more than 50 miles to travel to the center (Figure 68). Such an area would be equivalent to 4.3 "standard" counties, 24 miles square. In contrast, if the square were tipped 45 degrees, given the same road system, the 50-mile limit would give a diamond-like area of 5,000 square miles, equivalent to eight standard counties.

With a radial road system, even more area can be enclosed by a circle, no point

[5] This section has drawn substantially on Karl A. Fox, "Delineating the Area," *Proceedings of a Conference on Area Development* (Agricultural Policy Institute) (Raleigh: North Carolina State College Press, 1962), pp. 129–153.

[6] See Dwight A. Nesmith, "The Small Rural Town," (in the *Yearbook of Agriculture, 1963*), *A Place to Live* (U.S. Government Printing Office, 1963), p. 181.

[7] Helen L. Johnston, "Health Trends in Rural America" (in the *Yearbook of Agriculture, 1963*), *A Place to Live* (U.S. Government Printing Office, 1963), p. 194.

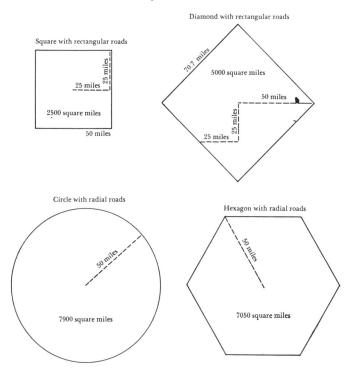

FIG. 68.　SHAPES AND ROAD PATTERNS FOR A MAXIMUM ECONOMIC
AREA

of which is more than 50 miles from the center. More practically, a hexagon meeting this limitation would include 7,050 square miles, with radial roads.

Probably 50 miles is a more realistic maximum in other more densely populated parts of the country. But certain parts of the Northern Plains have so few cities of large size that their people are accustomed to traveling much farther. A comparable maximum for the Northern Plains, then, would probably range between 50 and 100 miles.

If we were to use 70 miles as a maximum distance to the central place in an integrated economic area of the Plains, we might first visualize a square area 70 miles on a side. With a rectangular road system, no one in this area would be more than 70 miles from the center. It would include 4,900 square miles. However, a diamond area, with the worst-situated person 70 miles from the center, would be 99 miles on a side and would contain about 9,800 square miles. It would be equivalent to seventeen "standard" counties, 24 miles square.

It would be convenient if the maximum area, from the standpoint of transportation, also included the minimum number of people to support the facilities required in the central place. In some sparsely populated areas this arrangement may not be possible. The costs of living in areas like this are usually higher owing to the greater distances traveled and the higher per capita costs of public and private facilities.

*The Farm City and Its Satellites.* The concept of the farm city, then, includes a central place surrounded by a natural economic area large enough to support the facilities found there. The area normally includes several "satellite" towns.

Can we identify these farm city areas? The fourth-order places and their supporting areas certainly seem to qualify. There are relatively few of these in the Plains. However, a few third-order places are emerging into positions of dominance, as compared with their neighbors. They appear to qualify as economic centers or farm cities. These centers can be identified in several ways. They have populations of at least 12,000. They are served by railroads, airlines, and major highways. The country road systems tend to gravitate toward them, a tendency that will be more marked in the future. Such a city will have a senior high school of adequate size, and, in some cases, a junior college. Specialized vocational training is available in the school system. A civic auditorium provides facilities for public meetings for the whole area. It has good movie theaters, and it also supports such home-talent activities as plays, civic bands, orchestras, or vocal groups.

The farm city tends to become a finance center for its area, with one or more banks, a Production Credit association, and a Land Bank association. It has agricultural-product processing plants, such as meat packing, machine shops, construction companies, department stores, a radio station, a television station, wholesale agencies of various kinds, a strong newspaper, a general hospital, and one or more medical clinics. In other words, the central farm city is large enough to provide almost any type of goods or services that people expect in the course of daily living.

In our natural economic area, the other towns occupy a subsidiary position relative to the central farm city. They serve as residence areas for retired people, for many farmers, and for workers who prefer to live in a small town and commute to a job in the central city. They contain primary schools, drugstores, service stations, and grocery stores.

These smaller towns may be assuming a role comparable to the suburban service areas of the modern large city. People served by these villages may increasingly show a suburban relationship to the farm city. The rural-urban area here visualized—a farm city in a constellation of associated centers—is not identical to the metropolitan city with its suburbs, but it may be its rural counterpart. Most of the modern services demanded can best be supported by the broader resource base. On the other hand, many of the rural towns of 500–2,500 population have an important part to play as community centers, especially in a sparsely settled region.

If this notion—that a farm city with its satellite centers and surrounding rural area represents a large metropolis spatially extended into the countryside—has any validity, it would follow that social and economic planning should take this into account. But this brings us back to the problem of identifying these area economies so that planners can use them.

A great deal of research is currently being devoted to this question.[8] Unfortunately, what is available pertains to areas other than the Plains, and what is concerned with the Plains is not yet available. Nevertheless, on the assumption that a guess is better

[8] See, especially, Karl A. Fox, "Economic Models for Area Development Research," in *Regional Development Analysis*, Proceedings of a workshop sponsored by the Agricultural Policy Institute, North Carolina State University and the Great Plains Resources Economics Committee, May, 1963.

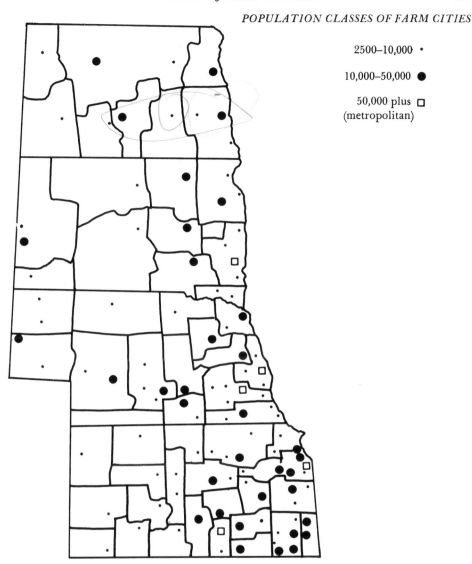

POPULATION CLASSES OF FARM CITIES

2500–10,000 ·

10,000–50,000 ●

50,000 plus □
(metropolitan)

FIG. 69. A FIRST APPROXIMATION TO AREA ECONOMIES IN THE NORTHERN PLAINS (1960)

than nothing, Figure 69 shows a first approximation to area economies in the four Northern Plains states. These have been based on city populations and distance, and virtually nothing else; their boundaries would undoubtedly be changed by the results of specific local studies. Yet, even as they stand, they have the merit of revealing that the 315 counties in these states could be replaced, for planning purposes, by a mere 58 units.

For Nebraska, central to the region and reasonably typical of the other three states, we were able to improve on this estimate of area economies. As Figure 70

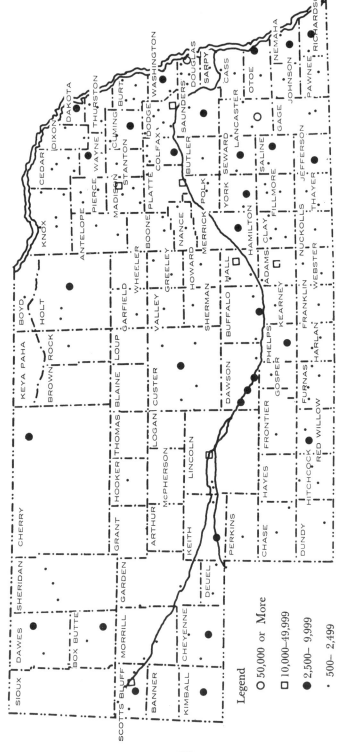

Fig. 70. Incorporated Places with Populations of 500 and More, Nebraska, 1960

Legend

○ 50,000 or More

□ 10,000–49,999

● 2,500– 9,999

· 500– 2,499

indicates, any subdividion of Nebraska into area economies must take into account its lopsided distribution of people and places. Although settlements tend to follow the Platte River, the state's major east–west artery, the bulk of the population and the major cities are in the eastern third of the state. There is a considerable thinning out in the center, including the transition area, then a slight increase in density in the western third. To what extent do the surrounding areas depend on these cities, that are chiefly strung out along the Platte?

This is not an easy question to answer, especially in view of the sketchy data available. In the corn-belt, one researcher found that the proportion of the labor force in each county that worked in another county was a good indicator of economic dependence.[9] However, the application of this standard to Nebraska counties results in little meaningful choice between counties. While it is true that the counties contiguous to those containing Lincoln and Omaha have a high percentage of their labor force commuting to jobs outside them, the data for the remaining counties do not provide a systematic basis for deciding on the extent of other cities' spheres of influence.

The relation of Nebraska's rural people to their cities is undoubtedly much stronger on the consumer-purchases side than on the labor-supply side. Unfortunately, detailed studies of consumer shopping patterns for the entire state have not been made. As far as labor supply is concerned, if one considers the workers as already having moved to the central city—rather than as commuters—it is possible to get some notion of probable area economies. For this purpose, we use the ratio of persons who "always lived in this house" to the total number of persons in each county, as provided by the 1960 Census of Population.

This measure worked very well, and largely confirmed the intuitive approach to the problem—which involved considerations of population, distance, and homogeneity of way of life, such as type of farming and the highway system. Figure 71 shows the area economies in Nebraska that resulted. In almost every instance, the stable portion of the population (that is, those who have always lived in this house) is lowest in the county containing the central city, and becomes progressively larger as one moves toward the counties on the borders of the area.

Although the areas were determined by the above process, they meet our other criteria reasonably well. In almost all instances, the central city has a population of 12,000 or more, the area has a population of 50,000 or more, and the area does not exceed 10,000 square miles in size (Table 93). Area 5, whose central city is McCook, is a little short of people, both in the city and the area, but it is close enough to the norms we set to be acceptable. Area 3, centered upon Ogallala, is also rather deficient in population. Future studies may show that this area is part of areas 1 and 4, with Ogallala in a satellite role to Scottsbluff and North Platte. On the other hand, with Lake McConaughy just outside Ogallala, that city's growth potential as the center of a major recreational area is substantial, so we decided to let it remain a separate area in its own right.

The only other area that deserves a special comment is area 2, centered on Valentine. This city is far too small to qualify as a true central city, and area 2 is probably twice the size it should be for travel efficiency. In fact, area 2, as shown here, is not an area in the sense in which we have been using that term. This is the Sandhills region

[9] *Ibid.*

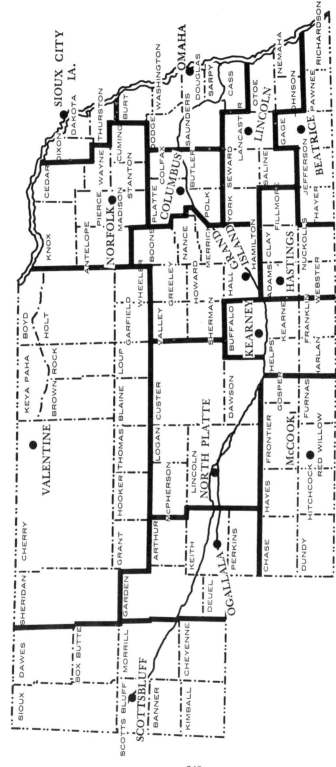

Fig. 71. Estimated Area Economies of Nebraska, with Their Central Cities, 1960

342

TABLE 93. SELECTED DATA ON ESTIMATED ECONOMIC AREAS OF NEBRASKA, AS SHOWN IN FIGURE 71, 1960

| Area | Central City | Central City Population, 1960 | Number of Counties in Area | Area's Population, 1960 | Area's Size (Sq. Mi.) |
|---|---|---|---|---|---|
| 1 . . . . . . . . | Scottsbluff | 13,377 | 8 | 88,737 | 9,524 |
| 2 . . . . . . . . | Valentine | 2,875 | 14 | 53,490 | 19,024 |
| 3 . . . . . . . . | Ogallala | 4,250 | 5 | 19,424 | 4,783 |
| 4 . . . . . . . . | North Platte | 17,184 | 5 | 66,256 | 7,489 |
| 5 . . . . . . . . | McCook | 8,301 | 8 | 42,086 | 6,103 |
| 6 . . . . . . . . | Kearney | 14,210 | 5 | 53,146 | 3,141 |
| 7 . . . . . . . . | Hastings | 21,412 | 5 | 61,527 | 2,863 |
| 8 . . . . . . . . | Grand Island | 25,742 | 9 | 90,711 | 4,945 |
| 9 . . . . . . | Norfolk | 13,111 | 8 | 98,888 | 5,291 |
| 10 . . . . . . | Sioux City, Ia.* | 89,159 | 3 | 27,511 | 1,123 |
| 11 . . . . . . | Columbus | 12,476 | 4 | 51,109 | 2,092 |
| 12 . . . . . . | Omaha | 301,598 | 7 | 464,628 | 3,279 |
| 13 . . . . . . | Lincoln | 128,521 | 7 | 227,002 | 3,962 |
| 14 . . . . . . | Beatrice | 12,132 | 5 | 66,815 | 2,993 |

Source: U.S. Bureau of the Census, *U.S. Census of Population, 1960.*

* These data refer only to the part of the area within Nebraska. If Woodbury County, Iowa (containing the central city, Sioux City), is added, this would result in four counties with a population of 135,360 and an area of 1,994 square miles. The true area is undoubtedly larger than this because Sioux City probably draws people from adjoining Iowa counties as well.

of Nebraska, where the population density is less than two persons per square mile, over a vast expanse of land. There is no city with as many as 3,500 people in the entire region. Thus all normal rules of the thumb must be abandoned here. The "area," as shown in Figure 71 and Table 93, is intended only to set apart the Sandhills region from the remainder of the state, not to imply that it is truly an economic area. Special studies will be required to subdivide this into actual economic areas.

### Economic Areas and Planning

If we were starting fresh, with a blank map of the Plains, we might devise a system of economic areas quite different from the one shown. We would not be restricted by present legal boundaries, such as county lines, but would establish enlarged counties to coincide as closely as possible with the natural farm city areas. The central farm city would then become the county seat, the municipal government of the central city and the county government would be in the same building, and some of their functions would be consolidated. The road system would tend to radiate into the central city.

The central city would be the logical place for various kinds of federal offices, which could be housed in a federal building. The economic area would be their logical service area. Similarly, state activities, such as highway departments—and others that use regional offices—could be headquartered in the central city, perhaps in the federal building—which might be a federal-state building.

Industry will consider the resources of the economic area in making its decisions about expansion, and the central city will be the likely site of a new plant. If past trends continue, both population growth and business expansion will be largely focused on the central city. It is the logical center for promotional activity; and the whole area will make progress if all the towns in it "pull together" rather than compete between themselves for new industry. Critical competition should take place between areas rather than between towns within an area. Similarly, the Chamber of Commerce of the central city should represent the interests of the entire area and should promote its economic progress—rather than that of the central city alone.

We recognize that economic areas, composed of several counties, do not have the legal status of towns or counties, with the power to tax and spend. But states can pass legislation enabling areas to organize on an intercounty basis, perhaps with tax-supported economic development commissions. These might be supported jointly by several towns and counties. At the same time, state and federal aids to economic development should be directed as much as possible toward such economic areas rather than to planning units of smaller size.

If we are serious about wanting economic development, some of these changes must eventually occur. We foresee, in the very distant future, the final emergence of economic areas as the primary governmental, political, and economic units below the state level. These areas will have enough people and resources to be vital, to get things done, and to be responsive to the changing needs of their citizens.

# CHAPTER 22

# Public Policy with Respect to Resource Use in the Northern Plains

THE PLAINS has not lacked for attention from government agencies during the past three decades, as we have seen. The keynote was sounded in the 1936 report of the President's Great Plains Committee, entitled "The Future of the Great Plains."[1] The committee recommended both federal and state involvement in Great Plains problems.

For federal agencies, it suggested additional research and surveys, federal acquisition of land in range areas, measures to increase size of farms, resettlement of disadvantaged Plains families, and the development of water and other resources. The states were urged to revise state laws on land and water conservation, to zone Plains land for its best use, to establish grazing associations and erosion control districts, to change community and financial arrangements, to modernize tax assessment of rural property, to develop water resources, and to improve tenancy.

The committee specifically recommended agricultural shifts in crops grown, feed and seed reserves, supplemental irrigation, soil and water conservation, flexible cropping systems, and development of additional water supplies and farm windbreaks. The report also listed twenty-five federal departments, administrations, boards, commissions, and other agencies with roles to play in the readjustment of the Plains economy. The committee recommended that an agency be established to coordinate and integrate the various federal, state, and local programs for economic reorganization in the Plains; to encourage research; to promote education on conservation; and to recommend policy changes. This agency was not to displace existing ones nor to assume any administrative control.

After this flurry of interest in the thirties, the nation's attention was diverted from economic development of the Great Plains by World War II. Land use planning and resettlement were soon forgotten, yet the conservation programs under SCS and ASCS became an accepted part of the established order. Good weather and high prices led to a carefree attitude, although a few thoughtful people were still concerned about the plow-up of wheatlands.

The drought of the fifties ushered in a period of renewed activity. A conference held in Denver in 1955 recommended a long-range program for the Plains. The

---

[1] *The Future of the Great Plains*, Report of the Great Plains Committee (U.S. Govt. Printing Office, 1936).

topics covered were quite reminiscent of those in the 1936 report. Again, the responsibilities of federal and state governments were suggested, as well as those of local governments and individuals. The report recommended expanded soil surveys and land classification, improved irrigation planning, research on climate and crop production, expanded educational programs for farm people, accelerated conservation programs, improved credit arrangements, a strengthened crop insurance program, adaptation of support programs to Plains conditions, and aids for adjusting severe area problems.[2]

The following year, President Eisenhower submitted a message to Congress on this subject. In July, 1956, Congress passed PL 1021, the Great Plains Conservation Program. President Eisenhower and his Secretary of Agriculture visited some of the drought areas early in 1957, and held a meeting at Wichita, Kansas, to discuss the progress made in coping with the drought. Most of the recommendations made at the 1955 Denver meeting were repeated here, with occasional shifts in emphasis.

Land use adjustments, water, and total resource development were treated at length.[3] The Small Business Administration was mentioned several times, especially in connection with its drought loan program. As at the Denver meeting, considerable attention was given to the division of responsibility between federal, state, and local government agencies. A regional organization, concerned with development of the region's economic base, was recommended. Federal and state participation in research on economic development was mentioned. Vocational training for commerce and industry, as well as for agriculture, was suggested.

After the Wichita meeting, the President again addressed a letter to Congress on the drought and transmitted a list of proposals from the Secretary of Agriculture.[4] Both officials urged state and local governments to assume a larger share in relief and disaster programs; and the Secretary commented on the small state contributions up to that time.

Thus the Great Plains was once again the spotlight. A major step had been taken in designating the region a special-program area. To a greater extent than ever before, there was at least informal coordination among the various agencies. The Great Plains Agricultural Council had played an important role in recommending policies adopted by action agencies, and in serving as an informal coordinating mechanism.

PROGRESS TOWARD ECONOMIC ADJUSTMENT OF PLAINS AGRICULTURE

The recommendations of the Denver and Wichita conferences might, at first glance, hint at a lack of progress in Plains agriculture since the drought of the thirties. Major economic adjustments come slowly, although important changes have been occurring all along, but others are still desirable. Although not an overt objective of any program, size of farm has continued to expand in the Plains. In time, this

---

[2] "Proceedings of the Great Plains Agricultural Council" (Denver, May 21–June 2, 1955), mimeo.

[3] *Report on Drouth and Other Natural Disasters*, USDA Office of Information, Washington (1957), Document 110, 85th Congr., 1st sess.

[4] President Eisenhower's Message to Congress on the drought program, March 5, 1957. Also a letter from Secretary Benson to the President, dated February 28, 1957, Document 110, 85th Congr., 1st sess.

process will correct the old error of inadequately sized units. Soil-blowing and erosion are other major problem areas, and several agencies, through educational assistance and payments, have encouraged farmers to control them. Improved tillage practices helped Plains farmers weather the droughts of the fifties and the early sixties much more successfully than that of the thirties. Other progress has been made. In soil-mapping, retirement of low-grade cropland, and water management, the Northern Plains has continued to move ahead. But much remains to be done.

### Organization for Great Plains Development

The casual critic of "big government" may look askance at the array of government agencies that influence the development of agricultural areas in the Plains, as well as in other regions; and some less casual and more vocal critics have suggested that many might be discontinued. Yet each was created in response to an expressed need, and most of them can cite specific accomplishments to justify their continued existence. The following agencies are active in the Northern Plains:

*National Agencies*

Department of Agriculture
  Agricultural Marketing Service
  Agricultural Research Service
  Cooperative State Research Service
  Extension Service
  Economic Research Service
  Soil Conservation Service
  Agricultural Stabilization and
    Conservation Service
  Statistical Reporting Service
  Farmers Home Administration
  U.S. Forest Service
  Federal Crop Insurance Corporation
  Rural Electrification Administration

Department of Interior
  Bureau of Land Management
  Bureau of Reclamation
  Bureau of Outdoor Recreation
  National Park Service
  Bureau of Indian Affairs
  U.S. Geological Survey

Department of Labor

Department of Commerce
  U.S. Weather Bureau
  Federal Employment Service
  Office of Area Development

Department of Health, Education, and
    Welfare
  U.S. Public Health Service

Farm Credit Administration

U.S. Army Corps of Engineers

Veterans Administration

Small Business Administration

Council of Economic Advisors

*State Agencies*

Land-Grant Colleges
Highway Departments
Education Departments
Conservation Departments
Agriculture Departments
Forestry Departments
Game and Fish Departments
Health Departments
Resource Development Agencies

*Regional Organizations*
Great Plains Agricultural Council
Missouri Basin Inter-Agency
  Commission

*District Organizations*
Soil Conservation Districts
Irrigation Districts
Grazing Districts
School Districts
Weed-Control Districts
Water Districts
Drainage Districts

In such a collection of agencies, the usual organizational defects—duplication of services, jealousy, and empire-building—can be found. On the other hand, their redeeming qualities—dedication, efficiency, and a voluminous record of accomplishments—can as easily be identified.

The relative importance of these government agencies may well change in the future. The political and economic influence of the Plains will probably decline. For example, in the redistricting of 1961 the four Northern Plains states lost two seats in Congress, an indication of their shrinking political power.

With the increased involvement of the federal government in national and international problems, it is not apt to be as sensitive to the problems of the Northern Plains as in the past, nor to respond with its former alacrity to a "delegation to Congress." Of course, influential groups—such as those that support the Bureau of Reclamation or the Soil Conservation Service—will continue to pressure Congress for their programs, and the Corps of Engineers will effectively enlist congressional support for its flood-control and navigation projects. But even these agencies may be subjected to more strenuous scrutiny as alternative demands for federal funds compete for the attention of overworked lawmakers. In the future, economic problems presented to Congress will need overall regional identification, as in the Great Plains Program, or orientation toward a problem of national scope, as in the Rural Areas Development or the Economic Opportunities program.

What does this mean to the Northern Plains? Federal activities in the region have in the past relied primarily on the spending powers of government and voluntary participation—without public acquisition of permanent rights (the ten-year contracts of the Conservation Reserve, for example) or without the assurance of permanent adjustment, as in the plow-up of grasslands during wartime. A less generous federal purse will require greater reliance on other powers of government, especially those at state and local levels, such as zoning and land use regulation, if certain policies are to be pursued. The states have a challenge here that they have never really accepted. This challenge calls for the marshaling of knowledge, the application of imagination, the definition of goals for achievement, and planning towards these goals to a greater extent than most Plains states have ever done. If they are to meet this challenge, the states will have to do their share of leading, rather than being led, evidencing their leadership in terms of men to carry out their plans and money to finance them.

Another implication of the new environment is that greater coordination will be required at all levels—regional, state, and local—both in setting goals and in working toward them. The purpose is to make more efficient use of the administrative resources represented in the various government agencies in solving economic problems. The states, especially, must take on a more influential and decisive role. They must carefully appraise their problems, consider alternative solutions already available to them, and rigorously direct policy execution by their agencies. Leadership of this kind cannot develop without responsible state legislatures who employ criteria beyond "cutting expenditures" in weighing the merits of proposals.

### DIRECTIONS OF FUTURE RESOURCE POLICY

#### Land Use

In spite of the attention given to land use in the Northern Plains since the 1930's, several unsolved problems remain. The subject is complicated by the variety of soil types and climatic conditions found in the region and by the division of responsibility for land use policy among several agencies.

Although measures have been introduced to protect against it, wind erosion damaged 2.3 million acres of land in the 1961 season,[5] most of it in the Northern Plains; and an additional 6.1 million acres is in condition to blow. This was much less, of course, than the 16 million acres damaged in 1955 and the 10 million acres in 1957 (Figure 72). Land use specialists were chagrined, however, to find that the damage during the worst part of the drought in the fifties exceeded that of the 1930's. (Part of this difference can be ascribed to possible deficiences in reporting during the earlier period.)

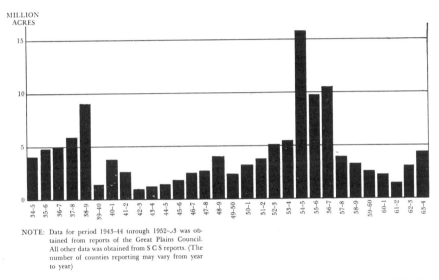

NOTE: Data for period 1943–44 through 1952–53 was obtained from reports of the Great Plains Council. All other data was obtained from S C S reports. (The number of counties reporting may vary from year to year)

FIG. 72. ACRES OF LAND DAMAGED ANNUALLY IN THE GREAT PLAINS, 1934–64

Blowing can be reduced by proper vegetation cover before the soil becomes vulnerable; after that, it must be combatted by mechanical means. Five states in the Plains have various laws authorizing county boards to administer blowland regulations: Texas, Kansas, Oklahoma, New Mexico, and Colorado. In some states these laws have been frequently invoked; however, five Plains states have no such regulations.[6]

All Plains states, except Kansas, authorize Soil Conservation districts to regulate land use; for example, in prohibiting plowing of certain types of land, or in regulating grazing. Only five Colorado districts, and only one in North Dakota, have land use regulations in effect. Three of the Colorado districts have sodland regulations in force; and the North Dakota district has regulations on grazing intensity. In Colorado, these regulations apparently have prevented land-breaking in one district, and have

[5] *Proceedings of the Great Plains Agricultural Council* (Bozeman, Mont., July 26–27, 1961), p. 8.

[6] Harry A. Steele, Erling Solberg, and Howard L. Hill, "Measures to Facilitate Land Use Adjustments in the Great Plains," *Proceedings of the Great Plains Agricultural Council* (Bozeman, Mont., July 29–31, 1958), pp. 46–48.

slowed it down in two others; they have also guided breaking to the least hazardous land.[7]

There is no evidence available on the success of the grazing regulations in the Cedar Soil Conservation District in North Dakota. The Colorado experience has shown that successful land use regulation at the local level depends upon legal correctness of the regulations, support of the local people, and enthusiasm, fairness, and technical competence on the part of the local administrators. The general-public concern with land use in the Plains has not been translated into local action, except in these few isolated instances.

Another tool for regulating land use is zoning. It would not be used to encourage grass-seeding but rather to keep land already established in grass. The Plains states, except for Texas and New Mexico, permit zoning by rural governments; yet only South Dakota specifically authorizes counties to regulate the way agricultural land is used. There is no evidence that any Plains county has actually such powers for this purpose.

The steady increase in wheat production in the Plains, despite acreage allotments, has frustrated both wheat farmers and legislators. With shrinking allotments, farmers have increased yields on their remaining acres while substituting other crops on those kept out of wheat (except fallowed ground, of course). Price-support payments have been capitalized into land values, which then become a permanent feature of the economic landscape, serving as a base for tax assessment and representing a higher admittance fee for the beginning farmer. In many areas, wheat is clearly the most profitable farm crop, by a wide margin. If its production is to be reduced in these areas, control will have to be exerted, not indirectly through acreage allotments, but directly through bushels produced. In other areas of poorer soil and lower rainfall, yields are profitable in good years, but wheat leaves the soil vulnerable to wind erosion in dry years. These acres should be seeded to grass.

One drawback to effective land use in the Plains is the retarded state of land classification. Modern soil surveys have been made for only a fraction of Great Plains soils, despite the accelerated work under the Great Plains Program. Yet detailed information on soil productivity is absolutely necessary for the effective administration of any land use program. This penchant for getting results without doing the necessary preliminary spadework is typical of many of our policy approaches, which might be summed up as "millions for action, but not one cent for information." Work on the economic classification of soils is at an even more rudimentary level than that on the physical aspects.

The Conservation Reserve was a logical shift away from acreage allotments. It was a way to control production as well as to encourage resource shifts. The program, whose authority to write contracts expired in 1960, has contributed at least in a small way to the movement of people out of farming. The program was attractive to cash-crop farmers, and lands of lower productivity were retired. Some of this will very likely remain in grass after contracts expire.

On the minus side, the Conservation Reserve seemed, at the outset, to be on a

---

[7] Stanley W. Voelker, *Land Use Ordinances of Soil Conservaton Districts in Colorado*, Great Plains Agricultural Council Publication No. 5, Colorado Agricultural Experiment Station Technical Bulletin No. 45 (1952), pp. 52–53.

hand-to-mouth basis from one year to the next. There was little chance for long-run planning by farmers. A most serious criticism from the long-run standpoint was the lack of any assurance that diverted land would not be plowed up and put back into cultivation with the expiration of the contracts between 1961 and 1969. In fact, plow-up was practically assured by the loss of acreage allotment if the land was left uncultivated. This situation was partially remedied by a 1960 law that protected the acreage allotment for as many years after expiration as the length of the original contract if the land was left uncultivated. The effects of this change remain to be seen. Perhaps a better plan would have been to raise the total rental payment to farmers enough to attract the reserve land for a much longer period—say twenty or thirty years—rather than the five to ten years originally envisioned.

The Great Plains Conservation Program has not been without its problems. In the first place, there was a lack of coordination between the SCS and the ASCS. An example of such a problem, and the complications involved in remedying it, was cost-sharing on seeding of cropland to native grass. Both agencies are authorized to share the cost of seeding with farmers, each under its own program—but not, of course, on the same land. Competition crept in because of differences in rates paid.

In 1958, after one year's operation of PL 1021, reports presented to the Great Plains Agricultural Council showed that the average cost-share for this practice was $5.15 per acre for the ASCS, compared with $9.02 for the Soil Conservation Service.[8] The council expressed its concern to the U.S. Department of Agriculture, the home office for both agencies. Some effort was made to remedy the situation, but it was not completely successful, and continued concern was expressed at the 1959, 1960, and 1961 meetings of the council.[9] The problem was also taken up with the Assistant Secretary of Agriculture and with the USDA Liaison Committee on the Great Plains, a group of USDA agencies which belong to the Great Plains Agricultural Council.

Another difficulty with the Great Plains Conservation Program was the allocation of cost-sharing funds for various purposes. Testifying before Congress in support of the program in 1956, Assistant Secretary of Agriculture Peterson suggested as a goal that 10 million acres of cropland in the Plains should be seeded to grass, and that 6 million acres of rangeland should be reseeded. (Irrigation system reorganization was not mentioned as a primary goal.) He suggested that conversion itself would cost about $132 million, while "associated" conservation measures would require $8 million. PL 1021, which provided for the Great Plains Conservation Program, authorized the USDA secretary to enter into contracts with farmers and ranchers

> designed to assist . . . (them) . . . to make . . . changes in their cropping systems and land uses which are needed to conserve the soil and water resources on their farms and ranches and to install the soil and water conservation measures needed under such changed systems and uses.[10]

[8] *Proceedings of the Great Plains Agricultural Council* (Bozeman, Mont., July 29–31, 1958), pp. 26, 39, 148.

[9] See *Proceedings* of issues of the Great Plains Agricultural Council as follows: 1959, pp. 149–52; 1960, p. 294; 1961, p. 178.

[10] Public Law 1021, 84th Congr., ch. 1030, 2d sess. HR 11833, August 7, 1956.

By June 30, 1963, a total of $27.5 million had been spent for cost-sharing under this program. Of this, $6.1 million had been spent for establishment of permanent cover on 461,674 acres of cropland and for reseeding 429,066 acres of rangeland.[11] At this rate it will take a long time to reach the goals set by Assistant Secretary Peterson, either in terms of funds expended or acres seeded. During the same period, $2.4 million had been spent for 15,333 miles of terraces, $1.3 million for 8,125 erosion control dams, and smaller amounts for other types of soil erosion control practices. More surprising, perhaps, was the nearly $4 million spent for reorganizing irrigation systems, land leveling, and other practices associated with irrigation development. Irrigation was not mentioned, at least by name, in PL 1021, which was addressed to the mitigation of wind and water erosion. Surprisingly, the Great Plains Agricultural Council has not addressed itself to this matter.

Another deficiency in the Great Plains Conservation Program is that participating farmers are required to maintain the practices for which they receive federal cost-shares only for the length of the contract period applying to the specific practice. This is in contrast to the procedure under ASCS where practices are to be maintained for their normal life span. Under the Great Plains Conservation Program, reseeded grass can be plowed up at the end of the contract period. The Great Plains Agricultural Council also has addressed itself to this question; in 1961 the USDA adopted a policy requiring both ASCS and SCS to spotcheck fields for the maintenance of practices that were cost-shared.

*Future Policy Alternatives.*    Prospects for encouraging land use shifts in the Great Plains have not by any means been exhausted. Several suggestions have been made, from the standpoint of both the permanency of the shift and economy to the government. For example, a compulsory form of the conservation reserve would cost less money than a voluntary program that depends on monetary incentives. A difficulty with the compulsory arrangement is that each farm inevitably would have to be treated proportionately from the acreage standpoint, whereas, from the economic standpoint, the lands of lowest productivity should go into the reserve first. In the present program, it would be more logical to lease the land under indefinite contract rather than for a specific term. The federal government could decide when the land would be released for cropping. Or the federal government could stand ready to purchase land already under Conservation Reserve contract, bring it to acceptable levels of grass cover, and then resell it—with restrictions in the deed against future tillage. In areas with substantial amounts of marginal land, the tracts could be combined into large areas, following major soil boundaries, and could be grazed by districts of the Taylor-type or leased to cooperative grazing associations.

There are satisfactory precedents for this last approach. The Forest Service presently administers 7.3 million acres of land, purchased in the 1930's under the Bankhead-Jones Act, in what are known as "land utilization projects"; and most of this land is used for grazing. Local people participate in the management of these lands through soil conservation districts, state grazing districts, and state grazing associations. The

---

[11] Great Plains Conservation Program Cost-Share Report, USDA Soil Conservation Service. Fiscal year 1963, and cumulative as of June 30, 1963.

Bureau of Land Management administers more than 9 million acres in the Plains, largely in Taylor Grazing Districts.

Another possibility is the easement device, under which the federal government would purchase from landowners, in perpetuity, the right to raise specified crops at a rate that could be determined by bargaining. The market price of the land presumably would be deflated by a comparable amount if the easement represented a change to a lower use.[12] The land could be bought and sold by private owners, as before, but it would remain subject to the restrictions of the easement. The government could subsidize the cost of reseeding the land to grass. The cash payments would assist operators of small farms on poor lands to leave farming, or to buy additional land and make larger units. Such an easement program could be administered locally by districts or by county committees. These, or more drastic approaches will undoubtedly be used in the future because people are losing patience with constantly mounting surpluses.

*Water*

Projections have been made for total water use and supply in the Plains for 1980 and 2000.[13] They indicate for the upper Missouri basin—which approximates the area of the Northern Plains—that, assuming a medium rate of population increase (approximately our present rate), the water requirements for all uses will have exceeded the available supplies (without tapping underground water) by 1980. By the year 2000, the projected requirements exceed the long-run supply by 14 percent. The situation in the Southern Plains is less critical, but their projected requirements should equal supplies by the year 2000.

Future deficits might be offset by mining ground water, using water more efficiently, or diverting water from one use to another. Agricultural uses now account for the major share of water depletion, about 40 percent in the Northern Plains. With the development of pump irrigation, there has been a serious depletion of underground water in the high plains of Texas and New Mexico, where the rate of withdrawal, in some instances, is as high as 25 times the recharge rate. Some depletion of groundwater supplies has also occurred in other parts of the Plains.

As the above figures indicate, the water situation is already serious. Yet the problem does not lend itself to a simple or direct attack because of these complicating factors: (1) the present inadequate state of knowledge on water supplies, especially groundwater supplies; (2) a division of responsibility for water policy in the Plains

[12] A step in this direction was the Pilot Cropland Conversion Program of 1963, which applied, in the Plains, to two counties in North Dakota and three in Kansas. It provided for federal payments, on a per acre basis, to participants who shifted cropland to other uses: grass, trees, wild life, and recreation. The participants agreed to leave the land in the program for five years. The payments to the farmers were of two types: a lump-sum adjustment payment at the start of the agreement, and a cost-sharing payment for practices needed on the designated acreage. The total cost per acre for this program appears to be less, on an annual basis, than that of the Conservation Reserve. (Of course, the latter involved a shift to non-use.) See James Vermeer and Ronald O. Aines, *The Pilot Cropland Conversion Program*, USDA Agricultural Economics Report No. 64, November, 1964.

[13] Harry A. Steele and Karl Gertel, "Water for Agriculture and Competing Uses in the Great Plains," *Proceedings of the Great Plains Agricultural Council* (1960), p. 60.

between the states, the Corps of Engineers, and the departments of Agriculture, Interior, and Commerce; and (3) the confused state of surface-water law, which in many Plains states is a mixture of riparian and appropriation doctrines. There is still time to revise and simplify the legal framework before the pressure of lawsuits becomes intense—as it assuredly will when competition for water supplies becomes severe.

Most water problems cut across state lines. Supplies that originate in one state may flow to another before they are used. And a use in one state competes with a different use in another. Watersheds do not respect state boundaries. In such a situation, it is understandably difficult to agree on the proper kind of organization to develop regional water policy. The Missouri Basin Survey Commission, in its report of 1952, recommended a Missouri River Commission as a compromise between a proposed Missouri Valley Authority and a federal-state compact.

This commission was to direct and coordinate all federal activities concerned with resource development in the basin, and to remedy the duplication of effort existing among agencies operating in the basin. The Presidential Advisory Committee on Water Resources Policy stated that "the greatest single weakness in the Federal Government activities in the field of water resources development is the lack of cooperation and coordination of the Federal agencies with each other and with the States and local interests. . ."[14]

The recommendation of the Survey Commission has never been adopted, although the President submitted a bill to Congress in 1961 calling for the establishment of a national Water Resources Council and for river basin resource commissions with duties and authority more limited than those recommended by the commission. The general agency now operating in the Missouri Basin is the Missouri Basin Interagency Committee, a voluntary organization which functions chiefly as a forum where information is exchanged. Conflicts, such as those between the Corps of Engineers and the Bureau of Reclamation in the Missouri Basin, have demonstrated the need for a commission with real coordinating power. Growing competition for scarce natural resources may well force the creation of such an agency in the future.

### Agricultural Research

Progress in agricultural research by state experiment stations and federal agencies has been noteworthy, and the record of accomplishments is impressive. However, the Plains has in a sense been an orphan area since it is split among three regions—the western, the southern, and the north-central regions. To provide a regional basis for Plains research, the Great Plains Agricultural Council in 1957 established a Plains Research Committee, to be made up of the directors of experiment stations in the ten Plains states and representatives from the USDA. Under this administrative committee, technical committees composed of representatives from the stations and federal agricultural research agencies were to be appointed to study problems of regional significance. The research committee would approve regional projects, channel funds for regional research, and focus attention on regional topics. Since the establishment of this committee, several Great Plains projects have been initiated on

---

[14] Quoted from *Drouth.* Prepared under the direction of the special assistant to the President for Public Works Planning (Government Printing Office, October, 1958), p. 30.

topics in the physical sciences and economics. This new committee is an important organizational innovation in the region.

The productivity of additional research funds devoted to Great Plains problems could be quite high. Neither the states nor the federal government has ever financed an adequate continuing research program in the area; research has been on a hit-or-miss basis, often associated with periods of emergency, or financed by special appropriations. Yet subjects for long-run study are not in short supply, as the following list shows.

Weather prediction (including probabilities), and control
Technologies related to grass seeding
Grass breeding
Technology and economics of feed reserves
Tillage practices for moisture conservation
Measurement of grass productivity
Water-storage technologies, including reduction of evaporation
Recharge of ground water
Water law
Economics of groundwater
Soil inventory
Fertilizer in semiarid regions
Nature of economic development
Crop-breeding for moisture conservation
Soil management of moisture conservation
Water inventory
Water productivity in alternative uses
Crop insurance
Farm and family finance
Strategies in farm management
Rural government organization and services
Group arrangements for local resource-control

The research committee recently proposed soil-moisture conservation and plant-environment research laboratories, each to be located in the Plains.

### The Need for Coordination

We noted the need for more coordination between various government agencies. For specific policy tasks, particularly those involving large integrated systems of physical facilities—and cutting across several agencies—regional commissions such as the proposed Missouri River commission might be the best choice. To be effective, these agencies need broad power and authority. Such commissions might be used not only for river basins but also for industrial development and transportation.[15] Yet they are not a universal panacea; in solving some problems, a regional authority could do little more than existing state and federal agencies.

For example, some policies can be executed only by reliance on local authority over private property; and examples of this are zoning and land use regulation. States can authorize districts to use such power, whereas a regional authority could

[15] For more detailed discussion of the alternatives along this line, see Kraenzel, *The Great Plains in Transition*, chs. 25, 26.

use only the power of persuasion and the purse now exercised by federal agencies. The diverse collection of Plains problems calls for a collection of programs, each with individual adaptations, some of which—but not all—are available through a regional commission. But this is not to gainsay the need for coordination and an integrated approach.

The Great Plains Agricultural Council, a unique innovation of the Plains, is in a position to supply the needed coordination. The council's purpose, as outlined in the Memorandum of Understanding, signed in 1961 between the USDA and the Plains experiment stations and extension service, is to "provide an organization for effective cooperation on emerging Great Plains problems." The specific functions listed in the memorandum include the following:

*a*) To delineate and analyze the problems of Plains agriculture
*b*) To suggest priorities in the attack on problems
*c*) To appraise the adequacy of existing research, education, and action programs in the Plains
*d*) To encourage the development of needed programs of research, education, and adjustment
*e*) To promote the adaptation of agricultural programs and policies of Plains conditions
*f*) To promote cooperation in a coordinated attack on agricultural problems
*g*) To develop possible solutions to selected problems
*h*) To provide for the exchange of ideas between Washington and the field for solution of Plains problems
*i*) To stimulate state and local participation in the study of agricultural problems and in the development of programs for solution

The council is a neutral meeting ground, a forum where ideas are exchanged and suggestions offered. The committees of the council illustrate its wide range of interest; they included, in 1963, the Plains Research Committee, the Insect Control Committee, the Health Committee, the Plains Extension Committee, the Forestry Committee, the Program and Evaluation Committee, the Resources Economics Committee, and the Information Committee. In addition, the following technical committees were operating under administrative direction from the Plains Research Committee.

GP–1 Patterning of Critical Weather Factors and Characteristics of the Weather Pattern
GP–2 Adapting Farm Organization Structure to Climatic and Changing Economic Conditions in the Plains
GP–3 Supplying and Financing State and Local Governmental Services in the Great Plains
GP–4 Factors Influencing the Distribution and Abundance of Grasshoppers in the Great Plains
GP–5 Appraisal of Alternative Economic Programs for Agriculture with Special Reference to Wheat in the Great Plains
GP–6 Seeding Establishment of Range Plants in the Great Plains
GP–7 Weed Control in Cultivated Crops in the Great Plains
GP–8 Crop Insurance in the Great Plains

The record of the council is imposing, particularly as one studies its effects over a span of years. It is particularly effective in isolating problems and clarifying objectives. It has made important policy recommendations that were considered seriously by administrative agencies. Beyond its research program, the council itself, of course, carries no administrative responsibility.

To make sure all interested parties are represented, the membership of the council should probably be broadened. The most obvious missing agencies are the Department of Interior, with its bureaus of Land Management and Reclamation, and the U.S. Park Service, with its large programs involving Plains land and water. The Corps of Engineers should also participate as the council becomes more heavily involved in water problems. On economic development, it would be useful to hear from the Department of Commerce and the Small Business Administration.

In the Plains, the solutions to problems of coordination do not lie in the sandwiching in of another layer of government at the regional level. This would serve to lengthen, rather than shorten, the distance from Washington to the state capitals. It would not be advantageous to dilute the strength of the departments at the national level nor to weaken the political power of the states. The states can take as much action in resource development as they are willing to finance. However, with the agencies and policies we now have, the task of the future is to use them more wisely, reducing friction and developing cooperation between them.

# Index

labelled 'indoctrination', and one is indoctrinating when one is getting children to learn up geographical facts for rote reproduction, or when one is teaching algebra by 'chalk and talk'.

The above examples are enough to show that there is considerable room for clarification on what is meant when one talks of 'indoctrination'. The confusion surrounding the word is further increased by reports from Russia and China about indoctrination programmes based on 'brainwashing' techniques. Is not indoctrination, after all, some sort of tampering with and restructuring of the brain as Sargant presents it in 'Battle of the Mind'? If so, what is the connexion between brainwashing of this sort and the forms of so-called indoctrination which we have just examined? Are the other examples of indoctrination not examples at all, because they do not rely on brainwashing techniques? Or do they, in some subtle way, involve brainwashing? What, after all, is brainwashing?

## 2. THE AMBIGUITY OF 'INDOCTRINATION'

Questions about indoctrination tend to arise in the sorts of contexts which I have mentioned, but it is not clear that in every case when people talk about indoctrination, they mean the same thing. It will be helpful to distinguish here a number of different intentions which a parent or schoolteacher might have in getting children to learn things. We can distinguish the intentions that :

(i) the child should learn words or phrases that he is able to repeat by rote.

(ii) the child should believe that a proposition 'p' is true. This is different from (i) in that in (ii) the child must *understand* what 'p' means. The child in (i) may learn to repeat the words 'I ought not to steal' without understanding what stealing is. (This is not, of course, to deny that rote learning *excludes* understanding, but merely to affirm that it does not *require* it). But the child in (ii) cannot believe 'p' if he does not know what it means.

(iii) the child should believe that 'p' is true, in such a way that nothing will shake this belief.

(iv) the child should believe that 'p' is true, if and only if he has come to see that there are good grounds for believing it. This implies the intention that the child reject 'p' if he comes to see that there are no good grounds for believing it.

179

Both (ii) and (iv) are compatible with (ii); but they are incompatible with each other; for the teacher with intention (iii) intends so to fix 'p' in the child's mind that the later production of good grounds for rejecting 'p' will not lead the child to give up 'p'.

Some, but not all, of the controversies about indoctrination have arisen because all three intentions (i), (ii), and (iii) have been used as defining attributes of indoctrination—and some uses of the term cover (iv) as well.

(i) Those who claim that a teacher is indoctrinating because he is merely getting his pupils to learn things by rote, are defining 'indoctrination' in terms of intention (i).

(ii) Those who argue, like Green (above, p. 178), that early moral education must be indoctrination because the teacher is getting the child to believe that he ought to behave in such and such a way without giving reasons, define 'indoctrination' as a non-rational way of trying to achieve intention (ii).

(iii) Those who deny that early moral education is indoctrination as long as the teacher has no intention of getting the child to believe unshakably that he ought to behave in such and such a way, are not really at issue with those of Green's persuasion, because they define 'indoctrination' in terms of intention (iii).

(iv) For those child-centred theorists who hold that all attempts to get a child to learn anything (as distinct from letting him 'discover' things) are forms of indoctrination, the term is broad enough to cover all four intentions.

The word 'indoctrination' was often used in the past to refer to teaching generally : to indoctrinate a person was merely to get him to learn something. In this century the word has taken on more precise meanings. It now usually refers to particular *types* of teaching, distinguished by different intentions that some teachers have in mind, e.g. to get children to learn by rote, or without reasons, or in an unshakable way—intentions that were not clearly distinguished in the past when the word was used more widely. As different educationists tend for different reasons to disapprove of one or more of these intentions, the word has come to be used pejoratively in most cases. (But not in all : the American Army clearly approves of the Indoctrination Courses it arranges for its troops, although it is not clear in what sense 'indoctrination' is to be taken here.)

### 3. INTENTION, METHOD AND CONTENT
### AS CRITERIA OF INDOCTRINATION

Teachers who are worried about indoctrination in schools today are not on the whole worried because they are teaching children to learn by rote; neither do they mean by 'indoctrination' any sort of 'formal' teaching. Like myself, in my history teaching days, they have in mind, as paradigm cases of indoctrination, communist systems of 'political education' or, perhaps, the teaching of religion in Roman Catholic schools. I want to argue that 'indoctrination' in this sense is definable solely in terms of intention (iii). Indoctrinating someone is trying to get him to believe that a proposition 'p' is true, in such a way that nothing will shake that belief.[5] Definitions in terms of the sort of proposition which is taught (content) or in terms of the methods of teaching 'p', will not do. To show this, I would like now to consider in detail some attempts which have been made to define 'indoctrination' otherwise than in terms of intention (iii) alone.

(a) John Wilson[6] implicitly denies that the indoctrinator need have *any* intention of getting a person to believe anything. (For him indoctrination is distinguished by the *content* of what the pupil comes to believe : the beliefs are uncertain, not in the sense that they cannot be 100 per cent proved, but in the sense that there is no publicly acceptable evidence for them. Religious, political and moral beliefs provide, for Wilson, paradigm cases of beliefs that can be indoctrinated.) He argues that if a child kicks up a row when there are adults in the room who want a quiet conversation and we don't make the child shut up, this 'is as much indoctrination as to stop it making a noise in its own playroom, because it presents the child with a false picture—a picture of lunatic adults who are willing to stop talking just because some kid is screaming'. Here, notice, we need not have the intention of presenting the child with a false belief —we may just intend to make it stop screaming. The false belief that the child gets may be an unintentional result of our behaviour.

But *is* this 'indoctrination'? If so, the term becomes so wide as to be meaningless. For if whenever a person comes to have a false belief 'y' as a result of my acting on intention 'x', I am indoctrinating him, then I may be indoctrinating someone whenever I act on *any* intention. Wilson's case is one of neglect, rather than of indoctrination. To say that it is one of neglect is to say that the adults responsible for the child *did not do* what they ought to have done (i.e. shut him up). At least a minimal necessary condition of something's being indoctrination is that it is an activity : the indoctrinator must be *doing* something. Now, we normally distinguish one activity from another in terms of the agent's intention.[7] We can say that a person raising his arm is engaged in one activity rather than another, say signalling rather than doing P.T., not from observing his bodily movements (which may be the same in both cases), or from looking at the results of what he is doing (in both cases a taxi may draw up), but only when we know what intention he has in mind. Since indoctrination is an activity, it can only be distinguished from other activities in terms of the particular intention the indoctrinator has in mind

(b) A second argument that intention (iii) is not a necessary condition runs as follows. *Some* indoctrinators may have the intention of fixing their pupils' beliefs so that they are unshakable, but not all. For many indoctrinators—e.g. of Marxism or of Roman Catholicism —have themselves been indoctrinated. They believe that the doctrines that they hold cannot but be true. Therefore many of them are fully prepared to accept rational discussion of these doctrines in their teaching, for they do not believe that such discussion could ever undermine them. If asked to describe what their intentions are in teaching, they say that they are trying to get their charges to think for themselves and deny that they are trying to rivet unquestionable beliefs into the mind. That is, they claim that they are motivated by intention (iv), not intention (iii). Yet however what they are doing might be described from within the religious or political system in which they are working, if viewed from outside the system, they would rightly be called indoctrinators. We would call them this not because they have intention (iii), but because of the particular subject matter which they are teaching : it is because they are teaching religious and political *doctrines*, that we call them 'indoctrinators'.

Not all arguments that the content of what is taught is important in deciding whether or not this is a case of indoctrination deny the importance of a particular intention as an additional criterion. We shall examine just such an argument in a moment. But what of arguments like the present one, which claim that the indoctrinator need not have any particular intention? One criticism of it, as it stands, is that it assumes that the teacher's avowed intention is necessarily his real intention. But is it conceivable, that his avowed intention is also his real intention? If so, then if any of his pupils questions a fundamental proposition of the doctrine, like 'There is a God' or 'The course of history is predetermined', he will not fob him off with specious argument or use non-rational techniques of persuasion to get him to believe the proposition, but will try to explore with the pupil whether there are any good grounds for it. But if he is as open-minded as this, would we, seeing him from outside the system, say that he is indoctrinating? If so, then there seems no reason why the philosopher of religion or of politics, who is also concerned to explore whether or not there are good grounds for the propositions mentioned, should not also be called an indoctrinator, a conclusion which the original proponent of argument (b) would surely wish to deny. If the teacher inside the system *is* an indoctrinator, it is therefore inconceivable that his avowed intention is also his real intention.

(c) Let us now look at the argument, that while intention (iii) to implant unshakable beliefs, is a necessary feature of indoctrination, it is not sufficient, for the beliefs to be thus implanted must be of a certain sort, i.e. doctrinal beliefs. What is meant by 'doctrinal beliefs' are beliefs in e.g. the two propositions discussed in the previous section, which form part of a religious, scientific or political system of beliefs, or ideology.

But what grounds are there for restricting the content of indoctrination to such beliefs as these? One might argue that the very word 'indoctrination' indicates that one is concerned with doctrines. But what turns on this? It is true that one meaning of 'doctrine' is 'a belief forming a part of a religious, scientific or political system'. But another meaning of the word, given in the O.E.D., is simply 'What is taught': and we have already seen that once all teaching could be referred to as 'indoctrination'. So appealing to linguistic usage is not helpful.

One problem with this analysis is that it does not seem to cover all cases of what people have in mind when they worry about indoctrination. What of those schools where in a hundred and one different ways some teachers try to get their pupils to see themselves as future hewers of wood and drawers of water? Such indoctrination may use an ideology, as Plato's guardians used the Myth of the Earthborn for a similar purpose; but this is not always present. What, too, of teachers who try to fix in some of their pupils' minds the ineradicable belief that they are of limited intelligence? I see no reason why this should not be called 'indoctrination'. One reply might be that in both these cases the teachers in question have themselves been indoctrinated into, say, political ideologies, of which the beliefs they are inculcating form a part. But it is equally likely that the teachers' beliefs rest on widespread untested assumptions about human nature which are not tied together into a close-knit system, like the religious and political beliefs we have been discussing.

I may, of course, be open to defeat on empirical grounds here, so I shall introduce what I hope is a stronger argument. It is not logically impossible to conceive of a teacher who tries to get a pupil to have an unshakable belief, which is not connected to a doctrine, in the 'system' sense. A teacher may want to get a child to believe that Melbourne is the capital of Australia. He may try to fix this belief unshakably by associating it with his charismatic influence on the boy: for the boy, whatever the teacher says *must* be right. The teacher may, further, try to prevent the boy from revising his belief in the face of contrary evidence by, for instance, not allowing any atlases in his school, getting the boy to believe that it is wrong to look up things in atlases at home, persuading him to enter a Trappist monastery on leaving school, etc. If a teacher did this, would it not be indoctrination? The fact that we *generally use* the word 'indoctrination' only in connexion with the teaching of ideological beliefs cannot be used to prove that the *concept* of indoctrination covers only such cases.

There are two ways at least in which one may attempt to deny that this is a case of indoctrination. First, one might argue that the example *is* inconceivable unless the teacher has some ulterior purpose in mind—for why else would he teach as he does? The only conceivable ulterior purpose is that he wants the belief to be held as a part of some wider ideology. One might object to this that the teacher might be crazy; but this objection could be blocked by the argument that there must be some reason why he is trying to get the boy to hold *this* belief, and that this is unintelligible unless one assumes that it forms part of some private, crazy ideology that the teacher has himself. But what of the teacher who is not crazy, but wants to get the boy to hold the belief unshakably, just to show that it can be done? He has no reason for selecting this belief rather than another, beyond the convenience of this one for his purposes; it would be harder, for instance, to get him to believe that Melton

Mowbray was the capital of England. In this case, the belief need not form part of an ideology.

The second argument is that in his attempts to prevent the boy from finding out the truth about the capital of Australia, the teacher has to get him to believe all sorts of other things, e.g. (in our own example) that it is wrong to look up things in atlases. If his intention is to be realized, he will also have to teach him that it is wrong to speak to Australians, to be interested in Test Matches, radio quiz games, etc. He may have to teach other beliefs to back up these demands if the child wants to know why listening to quiz programmes, for instance, is wrong. In this way a whole network of beliefs will be created, all clustering round and supporting the original belief. Together they form a self-contained ideology of their own. So, if this is to be called 'indoctrination', this is because of the way the belief is enmeshed in an ideological system, not only because of the teacher's intention.

There are two points to be made about this argument. First, if 'ideology' is to be taken to cover not only political and religious systems, as originally proposed, but to cover also such cases as these, then indoctrination has nothing to do with the *content* of beliefs, if one means by 'content' that they be political rather than religious, or scientific rather than metaphysical. If indoctrination has to do with content, then on the above argument, 'content' must refer to the fact that the beliefs to be indoctrinated must form part of an ideological system, in the broader sense. But, secondly, it is not necessary to indoctrination that the belief be associated with an ideology. This is only important when a pupil is likely to question a belief : he has to be taught that he should avoid certain people and certain books, etc. which might start him thinking. But a case could be imagined where the pupil is not likely to find counter evidence. Beliefs about what is happening on distant planets are less likely to be controverted than false beliefs about Australia. A teacher on a tiny, remote island might want to see if he can get a pupil to believe unshakably that Uranus has seven moons. The boy trusts him utterly : he has no access to books on astronomy; he is never going to leave the island; and no one ever visits the island. Given such conditions, the teacher would be indoctrinating, but without an ideology.

If this argument is correct, then the claim that all indoctrination is ideological throws no light on the concept of 'indoctrination' but only on one instance of it. It is, of course, always possible to make indoctrination require an ideology *by definition*, as this is how the term is generally used. One might deny that the imaginary case described above was really a case of indoctrination, for this reason. But in this case, there is nothing to argue about. The supporter of a 'content' criterion wins his case by making it trivially true. It may be true that we usually use the word 'indoctrination' only in ideological cases, but that is no reason to let the matter rest there. The problem is to find what concepts are necessarily connected to 'indoctrination' and what are only contingently so. The hypothetical example given above gives grounds for saying that while intention (iii) is necessarily connected, 'doctrine' or 'ideology' are not. If one asked the teacher on the island what he was doing, and he replied, 'I am indoctrinating the boy', why should we disbelieve him? The case is sufficiently like the more usual cases of ideological indoctrination to justify him in so calling it.

The contingency of 'ideology' is even more apparent if 'ideology' is used to refer not to the *content* of one's beliefs—e.g. a religious or political system—but to the various beliefs which might be taught in order to prevent a person questioning the particular belief or beliefs to be indoctrinated, like the beliefs used above to prevent the child from questioning whether or not Melbourne was the capital of Australia. For to say that in *this* sense indoctrination is connected with ideologies is to make a point, not as much about the content of what is taught, but about the *method* of teaching it. Ideological indoctrination in this sense of 'ideology' attempts to get certain beliefs drummed home, by enmeshing them in other beliefs, not only beliefs that one should not look at certain books, etc. but also, especially if the pupil is of an enquiring nature, beliefs which apparently provide grounds for the original beliefs (e.g. 'There must be an afterlife, because otherwise life would have no purpose'). Here ideologies are useful methods of indoctrinating people. But they are not the only method. Threats and torture might be effective in some cases. So may critical discussion, to a point. A skilful religious indoctrinator may get his class intelligently to discuss the validity of some religious argument. But the subject chosen may be such (e.g. Is God one person or three?) that merely to have agreed to enter into the discussion commits one to a belief in God, a belief which is reinforced by taking part in the discussion itself. (A discussion about whether the invention of the radio telescope will increase our astrological knowledge can only go on when the participants all accept that the stars influence our destinies.) The indoctrinator may encourage people, therefore, to air their views in such a discussion, because this commits them to accepting another (presupposed) belief. The only belief that cannot be subjected to critical examination is the belief presupposed.

The conclusion of this section is, therefore, that to say that indoctrination requires an ideology in this wider sense of 'ideology' is to confuse the concept of indoctrination with a particular method in which instances of indoctrination may be carried out. Threats, tortures, critical discussion are other methods, on a par with ideologies.

(d) This brings us to 'brainwashing'. It is sometimes said and often believed that indoctrination is a sort of process. It is a matter of breaking down established patterns of neural activity in a man's brain and building up fresh patterns, so that the man's beliefs become fixed in a new mould. What marks out the indoctrinator, therefore, is the *method* he uses to reach his end, i.e. the 'brainwashing' method.

This view is put forward in William Sargant's 'Battle for the Mind'. Religious and political conversions are said to be based on the same techniques which Pavlov used to produce 'experimental neuroses' in dogs; and these 'neuroses' are said to have involved the deliberate creation of structural changes in the brain. There are all sorts of difficulties in this thesis, and I cannot go into them all here. But what is clear is that while the structure of the brain *may* change when a person comes to hold a new belief, the indoctrinator does not do anything directly to the brain to bring about a change in belief. The term 'brainwashing', as Schein points out in his study of the Chinese Indoctrination Program for Prisoners of War in Korea (Maccoby, Newcomb and Hartley: *Readings in Social Psychology, Third Edition*), does not refer to a new and awe-inspiring process of social control, but to a whole battery of techniques, many used since antiquity, to enforce belief: punishment, reward, group discussion, lectures, social isolation, interrogations, forced confessions, self-criticisms. As he says, 'the only novelty in the Chinese methods was the attempt *to use a combination of all these techniques and to apply them simultaneously . . . .* ' (His italics). It is wrong, therefore, to identify indoctrination with a process; a polymorphous concept, like 'education' or 'gardening', the concept of 'indoctrination' may be used to describe all sorts of processes, as long as they are seen by the indoctrinator as effective ways of enforcing belief. But it is also wrong to identify indoctrination with brainwashing, taking this to mean the all-out assault on one's beliefs which has been described. This may be a particular form of indoctrination—and not apparently a very successful one— thought necessary in an age when, for one reason and another, *adults'* beliefs have sometimes to be remoulded; but this battering ram is not necessary for indoctrinating *children,* whose conceptual schemes are not yet formed, and therefore more susceptible to subtler methods. Once again, we might *choose* to define 'indoctrination' as brainwashing, but, as before, nothing turns on this.

#### 4. SOME EDUCATIONAL IMPLICATIONS OF THIS ANALYSIS

I would like to conclude by touching on the problems of indoctrination in particular areas—political history, religion and morality— which were adumbrated at the beginning of this paper.

(a) *Political history* The question I was here concerned with was : given that one has a free hand in choosing one's syllabus, how far can one teach recent political history without indoctrinating if one sympathizes with the views of a particular party? At first sight, it looks as if the answer depends on whether or not one intends to implant one's own political beliefs unshakably : if one is not doing this, one is not indoctrinating. But a difficulty arises. If several students of a particular political history teacher emerge with unshakable political beliefs similar to his own, we may well say, 'They have been indoctrinated.' Their teacher denies that he had any intention of indoctrinating. It is also clear that he is not deceiving us about this : independent observers report that he goes out of his way to show the many-sidedness of political issues and get the children to think critically about them. The difficulty is that even knowing all this, we might *still* want to say that students emerge from Mr. Jones' class indoctrinated with the belief that Tory freedom works. If it is legitimate to talk in this way, this would seem to imply that one can talk of unintentional indoctrination. Just as one can offend people without meaning to, so too, perhaps, one can indoctrinate them without meaning to. But it does seem rather odd to say this, for if indoctrinating is a matter of getting people to believe things unshakably, does it make sense to talk of *getting* someone to do something without meaning to? 'Indoctrinating' goes perhaps with 'marrying', 'sending for', 'signing' as a member of a whole class of activities that, as Anscombe points out,[8] can *only* be intentional or voluntary. If so, then do we merely mean, when we say the students have been indoctrinated, that they have come to hold unshakable beliefs? It cannot be *merely* this. For a man may come to believe unshakably that he had once seen a flying saucer, but we would not say he was indoctrinated. We would deny this, because no one was getting him to learn anything. It is because the students have come to hold fixed beliefs as a result of being in a learning situation, that we would call them—if indeed we would call them—'indoctrinated'. Whether or not we accept this extended use of the term does not affect the practical issue that a teacher of political history who is committed to a particular political viewpoint does run the risk that his pupils may adopt his attitudes unshakably if they identify with him in other respects. If the teacher's main aim is to get his pupils to think about current political issues, he might be better advised not to do this through history but more directly, by openly discussing them with his pupils.

(b) *Religion*   In religious education, as in history, there is also a danger that a pupil who identifies with a teacher who is himself a believer will be indoctrinated—or, if the term is inapplicable, will come to have fixed beliefs—even though the teacher is not intending to fix these. For taking part in a religious discussion, or in hymn-singing, or saying 'Amen' at the end of a prayer have no point unless the participants accept certain implicit propositions, e.g. that God exists, or that there is a life hereafter; and participating in these ways may reinforce acceptance of these propositions, so that they become entrenched in one's view of the world.

There is also reason to be concerned about the possibility of indoctrination in religion, not only in the sense described, but also in the full-blooded intentional sense. For many religious teachers openly avow that they want their pupils to have faith, to believe in God etc. This faith must moreover be held with intensity, with passion : the belief must be rock-like.

> 'Only believe and thou shalt see
> Thy joy and crown eternally.'

It looks as if such teachers are trying to get their pupils to hold unshakable beliefs. That this is indoctrination is only thinly disguised by the aura of mystery and positive emotion with which the notion of 'faith' is surrounded—an aura which effectively prevents one from analysing what it involves. The difficulty with religious education is that if the teacher denies having this intention, it is hard to see what other intention he might have which is compatible with there being such a subject as religious education. He might say that his intention is to get his pupils to think historically about the life of Jesus or the Prophets. But—apart from the difficulties about how far he could prevent his pupils getting fixed beliefs if he is a believer, which we examined just now—there is also the doubt whether, while he is certainly teaching history, he is still teaching religion. An alternative intention he might have might be to get his pupils to think for themselves about *all* religious questions, including the fundamental ones about the existence of God and immortality. But the only problem here would be—assuming that he can prevent his own beliefs from affecting his handling of the discussion—that he could never proceed beyond discussing the fundamental questions into more substantive issues unless everyone in the class was rationally convinced of the truth of the basic presuppositions. If rational conviction is here impossible, it is difficult to see how one could teach religion (*qua* religion) without indoctrinating.

(c) *Morality* Whether teaching moral rules without rational backing to a young child who is incapable of understanding such reasons is indoctrination depends on one's definition of indoctrination. If this merely means teaching without giving reasons, as it does for Green, (above, p. 178) then obviously early moral education involves indoctrination in this sense. What of Atkinson's claim (loc. cit.) that such teaching is only indoctrination if the moral rules which are taught cannot be known to be true? But this definition of indoctrination in terms of the content of what is believed will not do. For suppose moral rules were rationally justifiable and a parent tries to fix in his child's mind the unshakable beliefs that he ought not to lie, to steal etc.—is this man not an indoctrinator? The notion of indoctrination is independent of the notion of the justifiability or otherwise of the beliefs indoctrinated.

Hare's article (op. cit.) argues for a similar position. But it is important to notice that on the non-propositional account of moral judgments that Hare gives in 'The Language of Morals', his position could not be the *same* as this, because, on Hare's view to indoctrinate a child in the rule that he ought to do x cannot mean to get the child to *believe* unshakably that he ought to do x. If moral rules are not propositional, they are not the sort of thing that can be believed. Indeed, in his article on indoctrination, Hare never describes indoctrination in terms of belief. He says (p. 52), 'indoctrination only begins when we are trying to stop the growth in our children of the capacity to think for themselves about moral questions'. To decide whether Hare is justified in talking of indoctrination in terms of preventing thinking, but not in terms of getting people to believe things, would require an analysis of his non-propositional moral theory, which is here out of place. But it does seem, prima facie, odd to say that one could indoctrinate and not be interested in what one's pupils believed.

For the rest, the problems about indoctrination in morality concern the same issue as was raised when we discussed indoctrination in history. The moral educator has to be careful that his pupils do not grow up indoctrinated, in the sense that they have introjected his moral attitudes unshakably without his having intended this. The danger is more acute in moral education than in later learning, because here our attitudes are implanted so early and are so constantly reinforced in our behaviour that they may easily be held unreflectingly for the rest of our lives.


## NOTES

1. Green, T. F., 'The Topology of the Teaching Concept' in *Studies in Philosophy and Education*, Vol. III, No. 4 (Winter 1964–65), p. 312.

2. My bracket.

3. Atkinson, R.F., 'Instruction and Indoctrination' in *Philosophical Analysis and Education*, ed. Archambault, R. D.

4. Hare, R. M., 'Adolescents into Adults' in *Aims in Education*, ed. Hollins, T. H. B.

5. 'X indoctrinated Y' is ambiguous. X might have attempted to get Y to hold a belief unshakably, but not succeeded in doing so. In this case, we might say that 'X indoctrinated Y' is false because he did not succeed, or true because he attempted to do so. What we say depends on whether we take 'indoctrination' in the 'task' ('attempt' sense of the word, or in the 'achievement' ('success') sense. On the 'task-achievement' distinction as applied to education, see R. S. Peters' article in this volume.

6. Wilson, J., 'Education and Indoctrination' in Hollins, op. cit.

7. Not, of course, in the case of unintentional activities. But the criteria for identifying unintentional activities are parasitic on those for identifying intentional activities.

8. Anscombe, G. E. M., *Intention*, p. 84.

# 12

# ON TEACHING TO BE CRITICAL
## John Passmore

What is it to teach a child to be critical, and how can we tell whether we have been successful in doing so? Is it a matter of imparting facts, of inculcating habits, of training in skills, of developing capa cities, of forming the character, or something different from any of these?

Pretty clearly, it is not a matter of imparting facts. Of course a teacher can impart to his pupils a variety of facts about the practice of criticism—that it is vital to democracy, that it is essential to the development of science, and so on. He can tell them stories about Socrates or about Galileo. Perhaps, even, imparting facts about criticism, or telling stories about famous representatives of the critical spirit, is a useful method of encouraging children to be critical. But at least this much is clear : imparting facts of this sort to children is not *sufficient* to make them critical, any more than talking to them about the importance of honesty in commercial relations or telling them stories about honest men is sufficient to make them honest. Being critical is not only logically but empirically dissociated from being in possession of certain facts about criticism.

Then is being critical a habit? This question does not admit of so straightforward an answer. For the word 'habit' is sometimes used in a very broad sense to refer to any type of regular behaviour acquired in the course of experience, whether it takes the form of regularly scratching one's head in moments of stress, or using a tool intelligently, or making good decisions. Thus, for example, in his chapter on 'habit' in *The Principles of Psychology* William James seems to count even what he calls 'the power of judging' as a habit.[1]

James also says, however, that 'habit diminishes the conscious attention with which our acts are performed', and that 'in an habitual action, mere sensation is a sufficient guide'.[2] We can all cite examples of habits, thus defined. To take a simple instance of a habit learned at school, the child acquires the habit of translating 'merci' by 'thank you'. Although at first he has to think about what he is doing, eventually the appearance of the word 'merci' in a book—the 'mere sensation'—provokes the translation 'thank you'.

Consider now the case of the skilful translator, as distinct from the well-drilled schoolboy. The skilful translator will not automatically translate 'merci' by 'thank you'. Sometimes he will translate it by 'thanks' or by 'ta'. He retains a level of vigilance, of conscious attention, which is quite lacking in the person who acts merely out of habit. It is characteristic of a skilful person, a well-trained person, as distinct from somebody who has merely been drilled, that for him 'mere sensation' is *not* a sufficient guide to action.

Of course, there are habitual ingredients in any skill. The translator does not, for example, think about how to read : he responds automatically to 'merci' as a word, he does not pause to consider the possibility that it is simply a set of squiggles on paper. But what makes him a skilful translator is precisely that he does not respond automatically, without thought, to the 'mere sensation' of a French word. So acquiring a skill is not the same thing as acquiring a habit, although it is generally necessary first to acquire certain habits before we can acquire a skill.

James tells the story of an old soldier who was carrying his dinner home when a practical joker called out 'Attention!' The soldier at once stood to attention, at the cost of dropping his dinner. We can imagine someone who was so drilled that to any assertion he responded with 'I question that!', however inappropriate the response in relation to its association. Such a person might be said to have formed a habit of questioning, but he would certainly not have learnt to be critical. This case is, of course, an imaginary one, but there are real instances not so very dissimilar. A person can be drilled into uttering stock criticisms. He can be taught to say, whenever he sees a non-representational painting or hears jazz, 'That's decadent.' Or whenever he hears a certain type of philosophical view put forward: 'That's nineteenth-century materialism,' or 'That's old-fashioned rationalism.' Such a person has not been taught to be critical.

The process of drilling pupils in such stock-responses can properly be described as *indoctrination*. It is quite preposterous to say, although it has been said, that 'children are indoctrinated with the multiplication table',[3] for exactly the same reason that it would be preposterous to say of anyone that 'his *doctrine* is that $2 \times 2 = 4$'. The old soldier in James' example had not been indoctrinated. He had simply been drilled. Indoctrination is a special form of drilling in which the pupil is drilled—e.g. by way of a catechism—in doctrines and in stock replies to stock objections to doctrine. But if indoctrination is a special kind of drill, it is nevertheless a kind of drill.

By drill a child can be taught the multiplication table, irregular French verbs, a religious or political catechism, the order in which to test a motor-car for faults, the order in which to analyse the salts in a chemical solution. But a person cannot be drilled into appreciating a poem, making a good translation, detecting defects in a new type of car, or suggesting a modification in accepted chemical routines. Nor can he be drilled into being critical.

Should we say, then, that being critical is a skill to be taught, as skills are, by training as distinct from simple drill? There are certainly books which profess to teach critical thinking, just as there are books which profess to teach us how to drive.

But suppose an undergraduate has read and mastered, let us say, Max Black's *Critical Thinking*. Suppose, that is, he can work out all the problems Black sets for his readers, and can answer any questions we care to ask him about the content of Black's book. He never for a moment doubts, however, that everything Black says is correct; he is content to learn by heart what Black says and to follow in every detail Black's advice on doing exercises. His reverential attitude to whatever he reads, that is, remains unchanged; it never even occurs to him to apply the skills he has learned to anything except Black's exercises. Has such a person learnt to be critical? The answer, I should say, must clearly be in the negative.

It is, of course, obvious that a person could answer any question we cared to ask him about a book called *Better Driving*, without being, after reading it, a better driver than he was before. We should have no hesitation, under these circumstances, in denying that he had learnt to improve his driving. Skill in driving is quite different from skill in reading books about driving. Is the situation, then, simply this: that although my imaginary—or not so imaginary—student of Black's *Critical Thinking* has learned how to read Black and to do Black's exercises, what he still lacks is skill in critical thinking, just as the man who has learned how to answer the questions set as exercises in a book on *Better Driving* may still lack skill in driving?

The two examples, however, are not analogous. For in so far as critical thinking is a skill, it consists in being able to solve problems of the sort Black sets his readers, in a sense in which skill in driving does not consist in being able to ask the question about driving which the author of *Better Driving* might ask his readers. One can answer the question 'What should you do when you are about to descend a steep hill?' with the answer : 'Change to a lower gear' without being in the slightest degree a skilful driver. But one cannot be in a position to answer such questions as 'In what does the fallacy of the following argument consist?' without being in some measure skilled in criticism. If being critical simply consisted in possessing a skill, then it ought to be the case that to master Black's *Critical Thinking* would be to master, or gain some degree of mastery over, that skill. Our line of reasoning suggests, however, that one can master Black's book without having learnt to be critical, even in a slight degree.

'Being critical' is, indeed, more like the sort of thing we call a 'character-trait' than it is like a skill. To call a person 'critical' is to characterize him, to describe his nature, in a sense in which to describe him, simply, as 'capable of analysing certain kinds of fallacy' is not to describe his nature. It is a natural answer to the question 'What kind of person is he?' to reply 'Very critical', when it would not be a natural answer that the person in question is a skilful driver.

Skills, as Plato pointed out, are 'capabilities for opposites'. A driver can use his skill to put himself into, as well as to extricate himself from, dangerous positions. Similarly, an expert in the detection of fallacies can use his skill in order to conceal the fallacies in his own case, by drawing attention away from them, rather than in a disinterested attempt to arrive at the truth. It is one of Socrates' reasons for objecting to the Sophists that they taught their pupils precisely this sort of skill.

In contrast, the critical spirit, in the sense in which an educator is interested in encouraging it, cannot be misused. No doubt those who possess it may sometimes be led, as a result of their exercise of criticism, to abandon views which are actually correct, as a just man can make a wrong decision, in virtue of being just, in a case where he would have made the right decision had he allowed partiality to sway him. (There are examples of this in Mr. Allworthy's treatment of Tom Jones.) But this is quite different from the case where a judge uses the sort of skill he has acquired as a judge in order to pervert the course of justice. The skills of a judge, or the skills of a critic, can be used or misused; justice or the critical spirit can be neither used nor misused. And this is because neither being just nor being critical is a skill.

If it is true that to be critical is a character trait, we can easily understand why it is in practice difficult for teachers to teach their pupils to be critical. That sort of teaching which sets out to develop character-traits relies to a considerable degree upon example and upon what is often called 'the atmosphere of the school'. Admittedly, whatever the character of school and teacher, an exceptional student —exceptional in any respect, with no implication in this description of moral superiority—may react against it. But, for example, a school in which teachers never deviate from a fixed syllabus, in which masters and students alike frown on every deviation from the conventional norm, is unlikely to encourage originality in its pupils, although its products may be well-drilled and, within limits, highly skilled.

It is hard enough, the conditions of school-life being what they are, for a teacher to set an example to his pupils in respect to such qualities as courtesy, justice, consideration. But to set an example of the critical spirit is still more difficult. In this instance difficulties arise not only from personal defects of the teacher—out of his fear, for example, that he may be unable to cope with a class in which the critical spirit has been aroused—but even from the very conditions of his employment.

Of course, the teacher himself will, inevitably, in the everyday course of his work, be critical—critical of his pupils, of the answers they give to his questions, of the work they present for his attention, of their behaviour, of the principles by which they govern their conduct. If by a 'critical person' we mean nothing more than a person who regularly draws attention to defects in what confronts him, a teacher cannot help being critical. And no doubt many of his pupils will in some degree imitate him. They will take over his critical standards and apply them to their own behaviour and to the behaviour of their fellow pupils.

The teacher, however, is ordinarily content to draw attention to the deviations of his pupils from fixed norms : their failure to work out their sums by an approved method, to conform to the school rules, to say the right things about Shakespeare, to adopt the accepted techniques of folding a filter-paper. He may be in all these respects highly critical of his pupils, he may devote himself zealously, even fanatically, to criticizing them at every point at which they deviate from accepted norms and he may arouse a similar zeal, a similar fanaticism, in his pupils without being in the slightest degree a critical person, in that sense of the word which now concerns us. Authoritarian systems of education very commonly produce pupils who are extremely critical, but only of those who do not fully adhere to the accepted beliefs, the accepted rules, the accepted modes of action.

Critical ability of this sort is a skill : the sort of skill possessed by an expert tennis-coach as compared with an expert tennis-player. Every expert possesses in some degree, as part of his expertness, the capacity to criticize his own performance and the performances of others, but in teachers this capacity is raised to the level of a skill. When we call a person 'highly critical' we are not infrequently suggesting that he is the kind of person—his enemies may call him 'querulous' or 'arrogant' or 'pedantic' or 'priggish'—who demands of everybody around him that they conform to what he likes to call 'high standards'. To a considerable degree that, in every society, is the stereotype of the teacher—although ideas about what constitutes 'high standards' vary, of course, from society to society. Nor is the stereotype unjustified. The competent teacher will rightly demand from his pupils a high standard of performance in the skills he is teaching : he will be hostile to shoddiness, laziness, contented mediocrity. But in teaching his pupils skills at a high standard, or in encouraging them to examine critically their own performances and the performances of their fellow-pupils, the teacher is not, I have suggested, automatically engendering in them a critical spirit, as distinct from the capacity to be critical of certain types of specialized performance. For to exhibit a critical spirit one must be alert to the possibility that the established norms themselves ought to be rejected, that the rules ought to be changed, the criteria used in judging performances modified. Or perhaps even that the mode of performance ought not to take place at all.

Fagin, for example, taught his young thieves to be critical of their own performances and those of their fellow pickpockets; an authoritarian society may, through its teachers, teach its young to recognize and to be expert at criticizing heresy. But neither Fagin nor the authoritarian society is at all anxious to encourage in the young a critical attitude towards their own procedures—quite the contrary.

## On Teaching to be Critical

Teaching a child to be critical does, in contrast, involve encouraging him to look critically at the value of the performances in which he is taught to engage, as distinct from the level of achievement arrived at within such a performance. It is characteristic of societies in which criticism flourishes and develops that they abandon, under criticism, types of performance; they abandon, let us say, executions as distinct from seeking a higher level of skill in their executioners. A critical person, in this sense, must possess initiative, independence, courage, imagination, of a kind which may be completely absent in, let us say, the skilful critic of the performance of a laboratory technician.

To encourage the critical spirit, as distinct from professional competence as a critic of techniques, a teacher has to develop in his pupils an enthusiasm for the give-and-take of critical discussion. Sometimes he tries to do this by setting aside special occasions for formal debate. But debates are more likely to develop forensic skills than to encourage a genuinely critical spirit. A child will be encouraged to be critical only if he finds that both he and his teacher can be at any time called upon to defend what they say—to produce, in relation to it, the relevant kind of ground. This is very different from being called upon, on a set occasion, to produce a case in favour of one side in a debate.

The difficulty with encouraging critical discussion is that the teacher will almost certainly have many beliefs which he is not prepared to submit to criticism, and he will be enforcing many rules of which the same is true. These beliefs and these rules may be closely related to subjects which the pupils are particularly eager to discuss in critical terms—sex, for example, or religion and politics. If the teacher refuses to allow critical discussion on these questions, if he reacts to dissent with anger or shocked disapproval, he is unlikely to encourage a critical spirit in his pupils. If being critical consisted simply in the application of a skill then it could in principle be taught by teachers who never engaged in it except as a game or a defensive device, somewhat as a crack rifle shot who happened to be a pacifist might nevertheless be able to teach rifle-shooting to soldiers. But in fact being critical can be taught only by men who can themselves freely partake in critical discussion.

Secondly, even if the teacher is himself critical, there may be social pressure upon him not to admit that certain beliefs, certain practices, certain authorities, can properly be examined in a critical spirit. 'The values of rational critical inquiry', A. C. MacIntyre has suggested, 'stand in the sharpest contrast to the prevailing social values.'[4] The word 'prevailing' may conceal an exaggeration. In no society, certainly, is rational critical inquiry the dominant social force; in every society, it meets with opposition. But there are differences between societies: our own society not only pays a certain lip-service to critical inquiry but in some measure values it. So the teacher who tries to encourage the critical spirit is not wholly isolated. But he will certainly find life less troublesome if he permits criticism only of what is generally admitted to be a proper subject for criticism—astrology but not Christianity, promiscuity but not monogamy.

A third difficulty arises from the fact that the teacher's training is very often not of a kind to encourage in him a willingness to participate in critical discussion. In some cases this is quite obvious. A Roman Catholic critic of the *collèges* of Quebec has written of the teachers in them in the following terms: 'In the ecclesiastical world, statements concerning learning and dogma from a higher authority are unquestioningly accepted as the most potent of arguments. Priests are not really trained to discuss. . . . They try to make their pupils reflections of themselves. They find it difficult not to put a brake on independence or initiative.'[5]

In many systems of public instruction, indeed, it is a principal object of teacher-training to turn out teachers who will firmly discourage free critical discussion. For in all authoritarian schools, secular or ecclesiastical, the teacher counts himself successful when his pupils leave their school holding certain beliefs so powerful that no future experience could shake them; so committed to certain habits of behaviour that any modification of them will induce overwhelming feelings of guilt; so habitually deferential to authority that their unquestioning obedience can be counted upon. But even in democratic societies the emphasis in teacher-training may be such that the teacher is encouraged to think of his main tasks as consisting in the maintenance of silence in the classroom, 'getting through' the lesson laid down for the day, adherence to a syllabus, the preparation of his pupils for routinized examinations. The ideal teacher as turned out by such systems has been described thus:

'They concentrate their efforts on preparing their pupils for examinations . . . ; they teach precisely the subjects named in the curriculum, guiding themselves by the textbooks in use and attempting to

199

smooth the path for the children; they obey cheerfully the instructions issued by superintendent and principal, in so far as they can
understand them.'[6] Such teachers are unlikely to encourage critical
discussion amongst their pupils.

John Dewey's early educational writings were in large part
directed against this conception of the teacher's task. The 'progressive schools', designed to give institutional expression to Dewey's
educational ideas, took as their leading principle that neither teacher
nor subject should be allowed to dominate the pupil. But Dewey
himself was alarmed at the consequences : 'I am sure that you will
appreciate what is meant,' he wrote, 'when I say that many of the
newer schools tend to make little or nothing of organized subject-
matter of study; to proceed as if any form of direction and guidance
by adults were an invasion of individual freedom, and as if the idea
that education should be concerned with the present and future
meant that acquaintance with the past has little or no role to play in
education.'[7]

He went on to describe the effects of such an education thus :
'Energy is dissipated, and a person becomes scatter-brained. Each
[school] experience may be lively, vivid and "interesting" and yet
their disconnectedness may artificially generate dispersive, disinte-
grated, centrifugal habits.'[7] Other critics have drawn attention to the
fact that in such schools concealed manipulation by the teacher often
replaces direct authority; the children end up by thinking that they
always wanted to do what the teacher has got them to want to do—
the ideal of the demagogue.[8] Explicit instructions are open to criticism, even in the most authoritarian of societies, by the more bold
and adventurous spirits; secret manipulation is much harder to cope
with.

But there is not the slightest reason why, rebelling against authoritarian schools which are wholly devoted to formal instruction and
which inhibit the critical spirit, we should advocate the setting up
of schools in which instruction has no place. An educated man—as
distinct from a merely 'cultivated' man—must be, let us agree,
independent, critical, capable of facing problems. But these qualities,
while necessary, are not sufficient; many uneducated nineteenth-
century radical workmen possessed them in abundance. To be educated one must be able to participate in the great human traditions
of critico-creative thought: science, history, literature, philosophy,
technology, and to participate in these traditions one must first be

instructed, to learn a discipline. One has to be 'initiated', to use Richard Peters' language.[9]

I have introduced the phrase 'critico-creative' thinking, not through any fondness for it, but because 'critical thinking' may suggest nothing more than the capacity to think up objections. Critical thinking as it is exhibited in the great traditions conjoins imagination and criticism in a single form of thinking; in literature, science, history, philosophy, or technology the free flow of the imagination is controlled by criticism and criticisms are transformed into a new way of looking at things. Not that either the free exercise of the imagination or the raising of objections is in itself to be despised; the first can be suggestive of new ideas, the second can show the need for them. But certainly education tries to develop the two in combination.[10] The educator is interested in encouraging critical discussion, as distinct from the mere raising of objections; and discussion is an exercise of the imagination.

How does instruction come into the story? Consider a relatively simple instance of critico-creative thinking, playing a game of chess. In order to play we must first be taught how the pieces are placed on the board; what move each piece can make; under what circumstances our opponent's pieces can be moved from the board; that the king cannot be taken; that it is allowable to castle and so on. These rules we can be taught by an instructor or we can read them for ourselves in a book, but in either case they have simply to be learnt. No matter how clever we are we could never work them out for ourselves; presented with a chessboard and a set of pieces and told that they are used to play a game we could not possibly deduce how chess is played.

As well as rules, there are in any game useful routines, methods of coping with recurrent situations. Thus in chess there are certain routine ways of playing the end-game. At a certain point, a player who knows these routines cannot lose, provided only that he is not careless. To distinguish these routines from rules, let us call them 'dodges'. They are not arbitrary; we can demonstrate that a player is certain to lose if he disregards them, or certain to win if he pays attention to them.[11] But we can be trained, instructed, in their use; we can make ourselves as good as the best player in the world at coping with certain end-game situations, in a sense in which we cannot be trained to be as good as the best player in the world at the middle-game. At some time, indeed, these 'dodges' had to be worked out by the exercise of critico-creative thinking, but they have now been reduced to routines. It would be the height of foolishness not to learn and to adopt them.

The great traditions are not games. But they are like games in a number of respects; they contain ingredients which are arbitrary, and they have generated dodges. On the first point, they depend, for example, on a capacity to read and write. Now it is a wholly arbitrary rule that the spoken word 'cat' should be represented in English by a particular series of squiggles, and in Chinese by a quite different arrangement of squiggles. No one, however clever, could, on listening to spoken Chinese, work out for himself how it was written down. In order to read and write Chinese we have simply to learn these quite arbitrary connections between the spoken and the written language.[12] Languages differ : knowing how to spell a few Italian words we can work out how to spell any Italian word; knowing how to spell a few English words, we can work out how to spell a great many, but not all, other English words; in the case of Chinese there are very many ideograms which have to be separately learnt. But in every case the starting-point is arbitrary.

The student of chemistry, similarly, must learn a new language— what is signified by suffixes such as 'ic' and 'ous' and 'ate' in words like 'nitric' and 'nitrous' and 'nitrate'; how to read a symbol like '$H_2O$' or a molecular diagram. Furthermore, as a result of the enormous success of previous scientists, students are in a position to employ a great many dodges—dodges for collecting gases, for determining what substances a solution contains, for calculating in what percentages it contains these substances. A reasonably intelligent student can be trained to use these dodges as well as the greatest of scientists. Scientists, as well, have made a great many discoveries on a grander scale—laws. It would be wholly absurd not to take steps to ensure that students are acquainted, anyhow, with some of these laws and can apply them to particular cases.

Indeed, although science is the most striking example of critico-creative thinking, it is often taught in such a way as scarcely at all to exercise either the imaginative or the critical powers of the student. Depressingly enough, it might almost be regarded as an educational law that all subjects tend towards an instructional state. No subject, when introduced into a curriculum ever fulfils the hopes that were held out for it as an educational instrument. And this is not an unfortunate accident, nor the result of a conspiracy. It arises out of the large instructional ingredient inherent in developed subjects and the conditions of the schoolroom, which favour the use of instructional methods.

The problem which confronts us can be put thus : inevitably, instruction plays a large part in our school systems. In no other way can students be helped to participate in the great traditions. They have to learn to accommodate themselves to, and to work with, arbitrary rules. They have to learn a variety of dodges. They have to bring themselves abreast of the knowledge that has already been acquired. Only thus can they put themselves into a position fruitfully to criticize, usefully to suggest alternatives. To try to make of one's whole schooling a training in problem-solving, as the 'progressivists' hoped to do, is to produce students who will be quite unprepared to cope with the principal problems within the great traditions. At what point, then, is there room for teaching the child to be critical?

One possible answer is that there is room for it only at a late stage in the schooling process and for a select group of pupils. This, so far as he permitted criticism at all, was Plato's answer. The majority of the citizens in an ideal state are to be instructed, taught to understand how to conform to rules, to apply broad principles to routine cases, but are not to be allowed to realize, even, that there are possible alternatives to those rules, that they can be subjected to criticism and replaced by different rules. Only a small élite is to come to a rational understanding of the rules, an understanding which would proceed by way of a criticism of established principles. For Socrates, in contrast, if we are to believe Plato's *Apology,* the 'unexamined life in not worth living'; instruction should be left to the Sophists, the educator is by his very nature a disturber of the peace.[13]

Something like the Platonic assumption is not uncommonly accepted in our own communities. Only at universities, it is presumed, can students be taught to be critical. It is, indeed, by no means universally admitted that even at the University level students ought to be encouraged to think critically about the accepted beliefs and the accepted institutions of their communities; such critical reflections, it is sometimes suggested, should be restricted to 'mature minds'.[14] Furthermore, as the mass of instructible rules increases in volume, there is a growing tendency to postpone critical discussion, the confronting of genuine problems, to post-graduate levels. University teachers, especially in scientific and professional subjects, will sometimes tell you that they 'haven't time' to encourage independent thinking, or even independent reading, in their students.[15] But many people would, however reluctantly, admit that independent, critical thinking is permissible in universities; at lower levels, they would nevertheless argue, it has no place.

For one thing, it is sometimes suggested, the majority of people *cannot* be educated, cannot participate in the work of facing, and solving, problems. Whether this suggestion is correct there is no way of deciding *a priori*. Very likely, indeed, there is no way of deciding it at all. Most of us could mention some field of activity in which we have learnt more or less effective procedures, without ever having advanced beyond that point.[16] But whether, given better teaching, we could have done so is a matter in which we can speak with much less confidence.

In fact, our views on this matter tend to be determined by our social attitudes. Those who believe that it is right and proper for all but a small minority to accept uncritically the dictates of established authorities are very willing to believe that most human beings are incapable of doing anything else. The democrat is, in contrast, committed to believing that the majority of people are capable of participating at some level in discussions which lead to a change of rules, i.e. that they are capable of thinking critically about, as distinct from simply obeying, a rule. But he is not, of course, committed to believing that all men are equally capable of participating in every discussion which involves the criticism of existing rules or of accepted hypotheses.

This point is fundamental. It is related to the fact that critico-creative thinking is not a subject, in the sense in which chemistry or technical drawing or history are subjects. It can be fostered, or it can be discouraged, as part of the teaching of any subject—even if some subjects provide more opportunities for doing so, at least at an early stage, than others.[17] A student may exhibit it as a translator, but not as a mathematician; as a landscape gardener but not as a historian. There is always the possibility that in a new subject, or a new area of an old subject, a child will develop previously unsuspected critical capacities. It may be the case, too—although I do not know of any decisive evidence on this point—that an attitude of mind thus engendered toward, say, accepted techniques in carpentry will in some degree carry over to other modes of activity.

Plato certainly thought so; if men are allowed in any respect to innovate—in even so harmless-seeming an activity as music—the whole structure of the State, on Plato's view, is in danger. Totalitarian states, operating on this same principle, are rigidly conservative in art, pure science, moral habits; there is good reason to believe that the Soviet attempt to license technical, but no other, innovations has broken down. It would be absurd to suggest that a man must either think critically about everything or about nothing. But it is not absurd to suggest that the critical attitude, once aroused, may extend beyond the particular group of problems which first provoked it. The educator's problem is to break down the tendency to suppose that what is established by authority must be either accepted *in toto* or else merely evaded—a tendency to which, very probably, the child's early training will have inclined him. Once the teacher has done that, once he has aroused a critical attitude to *any* authority, he has made a major step forward.

In any case, even if the teacher wholly fails in his attempt to encourage this or that child to be critical, it is a fatal policy to restrict the attempt to do so to the university level. If from early childhood a child is taught to do whatever he is told to do, if he is discouraged from asking questions, except in order to elicit information or receive instruction, he will completely flounder when he is suddenly called upon to make up his own mind, to face a situation where 'authorities' disagree. Observations made in Australia confirm what we would have expected : children from schools where the emphasis is on formal instruction find it extremely difficult to adjust to the more 'open' university conditions.[18]

How then reconcile the two requirements : the need for building up a body of knowledge, a set of habits, from which criticism can take its departure, and the need for introducing children from an early stage to the practice of critical discussion? The contrast, thus expressed, sounds absolute. But in fact the teacher has failed even as an instructor if he has done no more than inculcate a rigid habit or instil a fixed body of beliefs : his main object—if he knows his business at all—is to help the child to acquire a skill. By means of sheer drill a driving instructor can teach a pupil to sit in a stationary car and change gear but this inculcation of mechanical habits is not itself instruction in driving; nor is it of the slightest use except as a preliminary stage in such instruction. Similarly, there is no point in a child's learning by heart the French equivalents of English names for parts of the body, or the eccentric behaviour of irregular verbs, except as part of the process of learning to speak, read or write the French language; no point in his learning the properties of the halogens unless this helps him to be, or—a more relevant consideration in the case of most children—to understand what it is like to be a scientist.

The exercise of a skill, unlike the capacity to recite a list of all the irregular verbs ending in '-oir', involves thinking—if not the criticism of rules, at least the application of them to circumstances which cannot be wholly predicted in advance. (This sort of thinking we might call 'intelligence' without too much disrespect to ordinary usage.) A French speaker never knows quite what French sentence he might be called upon to utter, whereas the child can know that the teacher will ask him to repeat words from a predetermined list. Furthermore, it is often in the course of exercising their skills that men discover the defects of accepted procedures. If the skill has been properly taught, in an atmosphere in which criticism is welcomed and the possibility of improving procedures emphasized, this discovery will not give rise to a sense of helplessness, or of anger against the teacher and a simple rejection of his authority; rather, it will stimulate the attempt to find an alternative procedure.

So far, then, as a school emphasizes, within the great traditions, the practice of skills rather than rote learning—the use of intelligence rather than the development of habits—it in some measure prepares the way for critico-creative thinking. A great deal depends on how a skill is taught. The crucial principle seems to be: wherever possible and as soon as possible, substitute problems for exercises. By a problem I mean a situation where the student cannot at once decide what rule to apply or how it applies, by an exercise a situation in which this is at once obvious. Thus, for example, a piece of English prose to translate into French is a set of problems involving that imaginative insight checked by facts characteristic of critico-creative thinking; a set of sentences for translation into French at the head of which the child is told that he is to use in each case the imperfect subjunctive—assuming the sentences otherwise contain no novelties—is an exercise. When a child has to ask himself whether a given set of relationships constitute a permutation or a combination, he is faced with a problem; when he is asked to determine the number of possible permutations of a given set, with an exercise. Whether for a particular child a question is an exercise or a problem may, of course, be dependent on what he has learnt.

## On Teaching to be Critical

Questions which look as if they present problems—e.g. 'Why does Hamlet attack Ophelia so fiercely?'—may turn out to be nothing more than an exercise designed to test whether the student can remember what he learnt in class; questions which would be exercises to the mathematics teacher, knowing what he knows, can be problems to the student.

Confronted by a problem, i.e. a situation in which we do not immediately see which way to turn, we can sometimes solve it by taking advice, by looking up a book. It would be absurd so to emphasize the independent tackling of problems as not to recognize this fact. Indeed, no other skill the pupil is called upon to master at school is of such permanent value to him as learning when, and where, and how, to look things up. But it certainly cannot be said of most schools that they concentrate their attention on this skill rather than on encouraging pupils to work problems out for themselves; on the contrary, very few students leave our schools, or even our universities, with any real skill in 'information retrieval'.[19]

However, important though this skill is, we cannot settle all our problems by looking up the answer in a book. Problems fall into two broad classes; those to which the answer is known to the teacher but not to the pupil, and those to which the answer is known neither to teacher nor pupil. (One should add that the very existence of the problem is not, normally, known to the student. One of the educator's tasks is to make his students puzzled.) Most of the time the teacher will be putting before his pupils a problem to which in fact the answer is already known. His pupils come to be practised in the regular methods of tackling this class of problem, in the intelligent application of accepted procedures. But the teacher should certainly place special emphasis, so far as he can, on problems to which the answer is not known, or is a matter of controversy—only in that way can he prepare his pupils for the future.

In practice, of course, a great many teachers deliberately avoid all controversial issues. This is partly because they feel that they are not teaching if they make their pupils puzzled and then do not resolve their puzzlement for them; partly because so many of them, as representatives of authority, think it bad for their pupils to be unsettled—greatly underestimating the degree to which their experiences outside the school are in any case unsettling them. It is certainly *safer* and more comfortable to all concerned not to raise controversial issues. (It is surprising what a range of such issues there are, in any ordinary classroom.) The fact remains that unless his pupils leave school puzzled his teachers have failed as educators, however successful they may have been as instructors.

But at the same time a teacher will not want his pupils to be *merely* bewildered although he will teach them that to be bewildered can be itself a virtue; he will hope to teach them in what way the questions which puzzle them ought to be discussed, what sort of evidence is relevant to their solution. Literature and history classes can be particularly valuable for the discussion of controversial issues. R. S. Peters has recently argued that 'disciplines like history and literature are debased and distorted if they are used consciously to inculcate 'critical thinking'.[20] What he has in mind, I think, is that the study of history and literature must not be thought of as a means to something else, e.g. to the acquisition of certain critical skills. But the fact remains that history and literature classes provide the teacher with opportunities for encouraging critical discussion of a wide variety of human activities, as well as of literature and history themselves. No one would wish to see all literature and history lessons turned into such discussions. But it is equally a mistake to divorce the study of history and literature from the understanding of human relationships.[21]

Quite ordinary children will be aware, for example, that the plays of Shakespeare are in certain respects imperfect. Hearing from all quarters, and most conspicuously from their teachers, that Shakespeare was an overwhelming genius, they are likely to conclude either that genius is not for them, or that education is merely a racket, or merely shrugging their shoulders, that this is one more thing to be learnt as a lesson and repeated in an examination.[22] But there is not the slightest reason why pupils should not be allowed, or indeed encouraged, to do their worst in criticizing Shakespeare, why they should not be allowed to defend the view that his plays are inferior to any well-made television play. Only through critical discussion of this sort can the pupil be brought to understand why Shakespeare is in fact a dramatic genius, as distinct from parroting the view that he is. If he ends up unconvinced, no harm has been done—he was not, anyhow, convinced in the beginning, he merely acquiesced—and he should have learnt a great deal on the way, not only about Shakespeare, but also about the critical discussion of literature in general. It can properly be demanded of him, of course, that at all points he supports his opinions with evidence from the plays.

But what about the earlier stages in schooling, the less intelligent child? From a very early stage he—or anyhow most children—can be taught what it is like to discuss a question critically. Most of us can recall two types of teachers : for the one any criticism of his own views, his own decisions, a school rule or a textbook principle was a moral misdemeanour, to be greeted with wrath and disciplinary measures; for the second teacher such criticisms, unless circumstances were unusually unfavourable, were made the occasion for a rational explanation, with the frank admission, whenever this was the case, that a particular rule was purely arbitrary, not defensible in itself, although perhaps defensible as a rule in the game.[23] (Compare : 'Why should I wear a tie?' with 'Why shouldn't I be allowed to come in late to class?') Any teacher has to instruct, has to teach rules which are arbitrary, at least in the context in which he teaches them. The fundamental difference between the educator and the indoctrinator is that the indoctrinator treats all rules as 'inherent in the nature of things'—as not even *conceivably* bad rules. What he takes to be fact, a principle, or presents as a person or work to be admired is deified as beyond the reach of rational criticism. The educator, on the contrary, welcomes criticisms, and is prepared to admit that he does not always know the answers to them.

Critical discussion, at this level, of accepted rules can begin at a very early stage in the child's life; what happens later, as he begins to enter into the great traditions is that the area of discussion widens and the difference between types of discussion more clearly emerges. Such critical discussion can be embarrassing to a teacher; he may himself not be convinced that a rule is a reasonable one or may never have asked himself how it can be justified. Anybody who sets out to teach his pupils to be critical must expect constantly to be embarrassed. He can also expect to be harassed, by his class, by his headmaster, by parents. If he gives up the idea of teaching his pupils to be critical and salves his conscience by training them in skills, this is not at all surprising. But he should at least be clear about what he is doing, and even more important, what he is *not* doing.

### NOTES

1. *The Principles of Psychology* (New York, 1890), Vol. 1, p. 127.
2. Ibid., pp. 114–15.
3. See the passage quoted in Atkinson, R. F., 'Instruction and Indoctri-

nation' in Archambault, R. D., *Philosophical Analysis and Education* (Routledge & Kegan Paul, London, 1965), p. 174, from Brubacher, J. S., *Eclectic Philosophy of Education* (Prentice Hall, New Jersey, 1951), p. 326 : 'Children are indoctrinated with the multiplication table; they are indoctrinated with love of country; they are indoctrinated with the principles of chemistry and physics and mathematics and biology.'

4. 'Against Utilitarianism' in *Aims in Education*, ed. Hollins, T. H. B., (Manchester, 1964), p. 21.

5. Duval, Roch, 'The Roman Catholic *Collèges* of Quebec' in *Year Book of Education* (London, 1957), p. 274.

6. Bereday, G. Z. F., and Lauwerys, J. A., 'Philosophy and Education' in *The Year Book of Education*, London, 1957. I should explain that in the text this is intended as a description of a conformist, not of an ideal, teacher. But in many quarters in Australia, at least, it would serve as a description of the ideal teacher.

7. *Experience and Education* (Ohio, 1938), quoted in Park, Joe, *Selected Readings in the Philosophy of Education* (Macmillan, London and New York, 1962), 2nd edition, pp. 138–9.

8. Kerlinger, Fred N., 'The Implications of the Permissiveness Doctrine in American Education' in *Educational Theory* (April 1960), pp. 120–7, reprinted in Burns, H. W. and Brauner, C. J., *Philosophy of Education* (New York, 1962), esp. pp. 384–5.

9. *Education as Initiation* (Evans Bros., London, 1963).

10. On the problems set for the educator by the attempt to train the child to be critical without killing his imagination see Getzels, J. W., 'Creative thinking, Problem-solving, and Instruction' in the *Sixty-third Yearbook of the National Society for the Study of Education* (Chicago, 1964), pp. 251–4. Does the Oxford tutorial system, for example, over-emphasize the need to be self-critical?

11. The chess-example was suggested to me by P. H. Nowell-Smith's 'Purpose and Intelligent Action' (*Proceedings of the Aristotelian Society*, Supplementary Volume XXXIV, pp. 103–4).

12. It is sometimes suggested that the resultant emphasis on rote learning in the early education of Chinese children helps to explain why China never developed a tradition of critical thinking.

13. See Anderson, John, 'Socrates as an Educator' in *Studies in Empirical Philosophy* (Sydney, Angus and Robertson, 1962).

14. See for example Wild, John, 'Education and Human Society : a Realistic View' in *Modern Philosophies and Education, Fiftyfourth Yearbook of the National Society for the Study of Education*, p. 44.

15. See Section 4.1, 'Teaching for Independence' in Cohen, S. W., Roe, E., Short, L. N., Passmore, J. A., *Teaching in the Australian Universities* (Melbourne University Press, 1965). To say that one 'hasn't time' for an activity implies that what one is now doing is more valuable than that activity. But what could be more valuable than to teach students to think for themselves? Professional men who leave the Universities 'abreast of the latest knowledge' but not knowing how to keep in touch with later developments are certainly not 'well-trained'.

16. For example, in mathematics. For a useful study of the problems confronting the educating of mathematicians see Beatley, Ralph, 'Reason and rule in arithmetic and algebra', *The Mathematics Teacher*, XLVII, No. 4 (1954), pp. 234–44, reprinted in Scheffler, *Philosophy and Education* (Boston, 1958).

17. This is an important consideration in constructing a curriculum. 'Although I will admit', writes R. M. Hutchins, 'that in the hands of Socrates any subject can be made important . . . because any subject can lead to important questions, there was only one Socrates, and I know of none in any educational system today. We have to frame the course of study of American schools, colleges, and universities in the light of the capacity of ordinary teachers.' (*The Conflict in Education in a Democratic Society* (Harper, New York, 1953), p. 13). This has as much application outside as inside America. We have to ask ourselves, too, what a subject is *actually like* at the level at which an ordinary student encounters it, as distinct from what it is like at the level of postgraduate research.

18. See for example Schonell, F. J., Roe, E., Meddleton, I. G., *Promise and Performance* (Brisbane and London, 1962), pp. 218–21.

19. See the Report on *Science, Government and Information,* by the President's Science Advisory Committee (Washington, D. C., 10th January 1963).

20. ' "Mental Health" as an Educational Aim' in *Aims in Education* (Manchester, 1964), p. 88.

21. 'It had never occurred to Sophia, nor to any of the other girls in the Latin class, to connect the words on the printed page with anything that ever really happened. Men marched, camps were struck, winter quarters were gone into; but to Sophia the Latin language did not concern men, camps, winter quarters and cavalry. It existed to provide Subjunctives and Past Participles and (Oh golly!) Gerunds.' (Quoted in Wilkinson, Rupert, *The Prefects* (Oxford, 1964), p. 66, from Lionel Hale, *A Fleece of Lambs*, p. 38).

22. On the child's reaction to the fraudulent picture of life around him commonly presented in courses on 'social studies' see *Design for Learning*, ed. N. Frye (University of Toronto Press, Toronto, 1962). Compare Locke, John, *The Conduct of the Understanding*, § 12.

23. Compare Hare, R. M., 'Adolescents into Adults' in *Aims in Education* (Manchester, 1964). The difference between the two types of teacher is obvious in practice, although not easy to describe in words.

# INDEX

ability, 37, 64, 65, 66, 70, 71, 109, 110,
112, 123, 163, 164, 165, 166, 167,
168
and novel response, 61
critical, 197
to feel and think, 175
to learn, 160
unlearnt, 63
*see also* skill(s)
abstract mental powers, 122
abstract
and concrete, 27, 32, 40, 41, 42
and general, 40, 41
abstraction, 147
process, 144, 145
abstractionism, 144–9, 150, 151, 154,
155n
abstractive teaching methods, 145
abstractness as criterion of difficulty,
30, 31, 32, 35, 40–1
accommodation, 38, 79
achievement, 9, 13, 21, 22, 124
and task, 1–3
aspects of education, 4, 6–9
human, 158, 159, 160, 161, 162, 163,
169, 170, 171, 172, 173, 176n
words, 141
acquisition
of knowledge, 38, 160
of linguistic tools, 34
action, 10, 66, 68, 69, 70, 168, 169
and rules, 92, 93, 94, 95, 97, 98, 99,
100, 101, 104n
causes of, 69
free, 67
on principle, 129, 130
reasons for, 97
'Action/Happening' argument, 67–71
activity, 80, 86, 92, 120, 156
children's, 76–77
intentional, 6
neural, 187
non-serious, 82, 87, 88
play, 83
routine, 76
serious, 81

spontaneous, 75, 142
adults, 79, 149, 181
beliefs of, 188
agent, rule-invoking, 97
aids to education, extrinsic, 10–11
aims, 68, 69
of education, 5, 22n
*see also* intention
analysis, logical, 47, 51, 60
Anscombe, G. E. M., 189
appreciation, 153
of general principles, 27
of instances, 40
*a priori*
concepts, 43n
truth, 30
Aristotle, 2, 17, 28, 38, 40, 75, 109, 110
articulation, verbal, 100, 101, 104n
assimilation, 38, 79, 100
assumptions, 18, 20, 184
unconscious, 148
Atkinson, R. F., 178, 190
attention, 10, 159, 104n
attitude(s), 128, 189
critical, 19, 205
social, 204
Augustine, 124, 125, 126, 127
paradox of, 125, 126
prompting theory of, 125, 126
authority, 95, 96, 127, 140, 164, 165,
205
of rules, 96

Bacon, F., 19
behaviour, 61, 70, 102
and conduct, 157
and rules, 98, 99, 100, 101, 102,
103n, 104n
goal-directed, 70
habits of, 199
interpretation of, 68
purposive, 70
behaviourism, 123
behaviourists, 133
'being critical', 195, 196
'being educated', 2, 6, 7, 8, 14, 19

# Index

# Index

# Index